The Illustrated Complete Guitar Handbook

[illegible] Polly Willis
Editorial Consultants: [illegible]in, Michael Leonard
Editor: Paul Robson
Picture Researcher: Melinda Revesz
Design: Tony Cohen, Lucy Robins and Jake
Production: Chris Herbert, Claire Walker
[illegible]otation by Ala[illegible] Brown [illegible]

[illegible] Goulding, Geoffrey Meadon, Sonya Newland,
Ross Plotkin, Sara Robson, [illegible]

FLAME TREE [illegible]
Crabtree Hall, Crabtree Lane
Fulham, London, SW6 6TY
United Kingdom
www.flametreepublishing.com

Music information site: www.musicfirebox.com

First Published 2005

05 07 09 10 08 06

1 3 5 7 9 10 8 6 4 2

Flame Tree is part of the Foundry Creative Media Company Limited

The CIP record for this book is available from the British Library.

ISBN 184451 204 5

Every effort has been made to contact copyright holders. We apologize in advance for any omissions and would be pleased to insert the appropriate acknowledgment in subsequent editions of this publication.

NOTE:

The Publisher of this book is the proud owner and user of a Fender 1975 American Standard Stratocaster, Rickenbacker 360 (6 string), Rickenbacker 1964 electric 12 string, Framus 1969 Atilla Zolla semi-acoustic, JJ special edition blues acoustic, Morris TF 50T acoustic, Almeria classical, Yamaha classical, Rodriquez Flamenco cutaway and Abrines (red) Flamenco, many of which are pictured throughout the book. Also, on the Mac OS X platform, software apps Cubase SX and Sibelius.

The Illustrated Complete Guitar Handbook

Rusty Cutchin, Cliff Douse, Adam Perlmutter,
Richard Riley, Michael Ross, Tony Skinner

General Editor: Michael Leonard

Forewords by Albert Lee & Juan Martín

FLAME TREE
PUBLISHING

CONTENTS

INTRODUCTION

If music is a universal language, there is no instrument more global than the guitar. It is easy to see why. It's a great do-it-yourself invention: like the piano, on a guitar it's relatively easy to play a melody and rhythm simultaneously but, unlike a piano, a guitar is portable. There is no other instrument that's musically as versatile either: 'guitar player' can mean African bushman, preening metal axe-god, classical virtuoso, rural bluesman and much more. The guitar itself has become an icon, too. In medieval times, it was a metaphor for spirituality and seductiveness. Picasso and other Cubist painters used guitars – albeit, strange, square-ish ones – to signify humankind. In more recent times, the electric guitar has become a potent phallic symbol – those 'cock rockers' derided by high-brow art commentators inevitably have 'geetars' in their hands. Depending on your world view, these might be good or bad things. However, this simply doesn't happen with trumpets...

It is this allure and power that keeps the guitar at the forefront of music. The guitar's key role in the birth of rock'n'roll is there for all to see (without the electric guitar, would Chuck Berry have been anything more than a flamboyant hairdresser?), and the guitar continues to defy predictions of its impending demise brought on by the innovations of synthesizer technology and computer-driven music. Every decade of every year, someone, somewhere, manages to play something new that wows another group of kids and makes them, in turn, pick up the guitar.

In the 1950s, Chuck Berry established the electric guitar as the ultimate new instrument for show-offs and bands who (suddenly) didn't need horns to play melodies. The 1960s saw Jimi Hendrix take that showmanship and skill to another level, yet he also rewrote the rules by making the electric guitar an eloquent yet wordless vehicle for political protest with his incendiary Woodstock version of 'The Star Spangled Banner'. The 1970s saw Eddie Van Halen blend technological advances (the Floyd Rose vibrato-arm) with unrivalled dexterity to herald a new era of hi-tech guitar virtuosity. Under fire from synthesiser music in the 1980s, the guitar simply adapted, yielding the effects-heavy, synth-esque lines of U2's The Edge and jazz player Pat Metheny. By the 1990s, anger was an energy for guitars once again, be it in the bald rage of Nirvana or the more intricate, sinister textures of Radiohead.

Complete Guitar Handbook

Here in 2005 – more than 50 years after rock'n'roll nominally began – the guitar is still providing numerous players with new sounds, new tones and avenues for expression. That's why the guitar is the most inspiring of instruments, ever. Not convinced? Well, you've heard the phrase 'guitar hero', right? Well, have you ever heard of a 'piano hero'? Ever encountered a 'sequencer hero'? What about a 'bassoon god' or a 'tuba don'? It doesn't happen. The guitar, simply, is out on its own...

But enough of the psycho-sociological banter. You've got *The Illustrated Complete Guitar Handbook* in your hands so you've grasped all this already. What you need to know is that this book will help you become a better guitar player. And with the rich heritage and history of the guitar – acoustic and electric – we've got plenty to cover. *The Guitar Handbook* aims to cover just about every aspect of playing you could wish for. There's plenty of technique – from basic tuning and simple chord sequences to string-bending, tapping and bottleneck tricks. We dissect guitar styles for you – from flamenco to metal, funk to country. We profile 28 legendary players, from Clapton and Jimi Hendrix, through Brian May and Keith Richards, up to Steve Vai and Jonny Greenwood. Add a gallery section on great guitars, plus advice sections on amps, recording, maintenance and more, and you have a lifelong companion for your life as a guitar player. Importantly, all your lessons and guides come from some of the most respected writers in the business, players who regularly teach and write in magazines such as *Guitar One, Guitarist, Guitar World* and *Total Guitar*.

Still, you'll want better inspiration than my mere testimonials. And what better than the call of one of the first ever electric guitar players, Charlie Christian, who back in 1939 declared: 'Guitar-men, wake up and pluck – wire for sound, let 'em hear you play!'

Or if you're feeling a little more 2005: 'Dudes. Time to crank it. Let's rock!'

Michael Leonard

2005

Complete Guitar Handbook

FOREWORD

by Albert Lee

My first memory of a guitar was when my father and I were visiting a friend's house in around 1950. This friend had a guitar on which Dad proceeded to pick out a melody using a cigarette lighter as a slide. I was intrigued, but didn't encounter a guitar again until a school friend produced one belonging to his brother. We both struggled with the horrible action, which of course we thought was how it was meant to be.

Lonnie Donegan was king in those days and many a young lad forsook his school work to follow the twang of his guitar. It wasn't long, of course, before we were exposed to a constant stream of rock'n'roll from the US. The sounds of the various players inspired, confounded and always

Complete Guitar Handbook

excited. Denny Wright, Franny Beecher, Cliff Gallup, James Burton, Scotty Moore, Buddy Holly, Les Paul, Duane Eddy and my all-time favourite, Jimmy Bryant, all were a wonderful source of inspiration. I learned what I could from the radio, which was woefully inadequate in the UK at that time, but worth listening if only to catch the latest gem from across the Atlantic!

My first playable guitar was a German Hofner, quickly followed by a strange-looking instrument which resembled the guitar played by Buddy Holly. This was a Grasioso which I later learned was made in Eastern Europe. It was quite expensive for the time, but I had to have it; George Harrison and Tony Sheridan also played them for a while. I soon discovered, however, that it wasn't the Fender Stratocaster I took it to be. Good American guitars were hard to find in the UK prior to 1960 but when the import embargo on luxury goods was lifted we were able to buy these works of art.

From the late 1950s, the guitar became the be-all and end-all of my life: it never left my side. Very soon I was earning my living with it, touring from the early 1960s until the present day. I've had the good fortune to work with many of my heroes over the years. I've been a Cricket, had a long relationship with the Everly Brothers, actually singing Phil's part on one or two tours. I have also had great fun working with contemporaries of mine, including Joe Cocker, Eric Clapton, Bill Wyman and Emmylou Harris.

After all these years perhaps I've taken it for granted: I've been lucky enough to do my practise on stage and not sweat over it for hours a day – I guess the practise came early on. I still get a thrill when I pick up a 1950s Fender or Gibson; the excitement will never diminish. Oh how I wish that there had been a book such as this to guide me through the world of guitar! At first it may appear daunting, but I promise you, there's a place for you in this wonderful world of the guitar.

Albert Lee,
Malibu, 2005

Complete Guitar Handbook

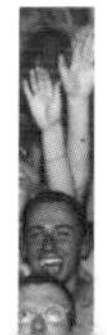

FOREWORD

by Juan Martín

The guitar, *la guitarra, la guitare, la chitarra*; what a wonderful and diverse instrument we are involved with. Yet an E chord is an E chord whether you play blues, rock, jazz, flamenco or any other style; there is a common musical language no matter how much the guitar or style we play differs. Very often it is what we do with our right hand that gives the clue to our musical genre. In my world the key to my particular musical style is the *rasgueado*, a right-hand roll or strum that is unique to flamenco; Django Reinhardt's attack is his signature sound, and through it one can identify with a precise geographical area.

Complete Guitar Handbook

The guitar is one of the few instruments where the fingertips of one's right hand or the pick one is holding come into direct contact with the vibrating medium, the strings. The guitar's body is held close to one's own, and becomes almost an extension of oneself. It is a very personal and intimate experience. If you consider that to produce a note on a piano you must first press the key that activates a hammer which then hits a string, or that with a violin the bow is what produces the sound, one realises just how special a guitar's sound is, and with what care we must make it.

The Illustrated Complete Guitar Handbook will suit those who wish to accompany songs through to those who are keen to get seriously involved with the instrument. The basics are covered for beginners, with tuning and simple chord sequences; if you wish to understand timing or music notation and scales, then these and many other topics are covered in the various sections of the book.

For the electric guitarist, there is a wealth of information from fuzz and distortion to ambient effects, to volume and wah-wah pedal. For those wanting to play lead guitar, there are scales and modes, as well as tips on better playing and performing. The various musical styles covered range from my own area of flamenco through myriad forms, including reggae, soul and funk, African, metal, blues and jazz to classical and folk. Chords and tunings, string-damping, slurs, slides, information on rhythm charts and strumming patterns are also covered.

If I'd come across this book when I first started playing I think I would have arrived where I am now a lot quicker! *The Guitar Handbook* will help you achieve true precision and knowledge and, if you love the instrument enough, may see you realise your dreams!

Juan Martín,
London, 2005

Complete Guitar Handbook

START HERE

There are a number of ways of uisng *The Illustrated Complete Guitar Handbook*: you can follow the contents page to find out where to start, work your way through each section or use this **Start Here** guide to identify your aims.

I WANT TO START PLAYING THE GUITAR RIGHT AWAY

- *Do you have a guitar and want to get to grips with how to get the most out of it, as quickly as you can?*
- **Go to page 16** to learn how to tune it – an essential skill to master.
- **Go to page 18** to learn how to hold it – you don't want to start any bad habits now that are hard to break.
- **Go to page 20** for some simple chords and you will soon be strumming away.

I JUST WANT TO LEARN A FEW SONGS

- *You know how to get a sound out of your instrument, and some basic chords, but want to take it one step further.*
- **Go to page 28** for easy-to-learn chords: the more you learn, the more songs you can play.
- **Go to page 30** to learn about keys and key signatures, and to understand more about major and minor keys.

I WANT TO PLAY CLASSICAL GUITAR

- *Rock'n'roll not for you?*
- **Go to page 26** to learn how to finger-pick – the foundation of the classical technique.
- **Go to page 152** to discover more about classical-guitar technique, and some of its greatest players.

I WANT TO PLAY FOLK GUITAR

- *Do you want to release your inner singer-songwriter?*
- **Go to page 100** to find out about plectrum technique, an essential skill to master.
- **Go to page 160** for more information on this most diverse of styles.

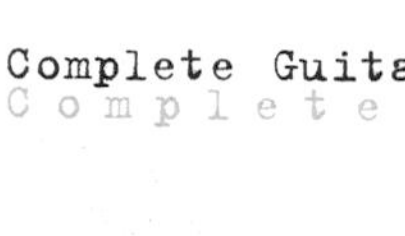

Complete Guitar Handbook

I WANT TO PLAY JAZZ

- *Fancy adding jazz to your repertoire?*
- **Go to page 40** to understand more about the basic chord progressions used by jazz players.
- **Go to page 192** to get the low-down on essential skills and the great masters.

I WANT TO PLAY ROCK GUITAR

- *There are many skills to master in order to become a good rock guitarist.*
- **Go to page 84** to learn about power chords – good for producing a strong sound.
- **Go to page 184** to discover more about the history of rock, some of its greatest exponents and some top tips on technique.

I WANT TO PLAY LEAD GUITAR

- *Want a chance to shine in front of the other band members?*
- **Go to page 48** to learn about how to improvise – lead guitarists do this to add flourish to their solos.
- **Go to page 52** to discover the secrets of scales: no self-respecting lead guitarist should go any further without this knowledge.

I WANT TO LEARN ABOUT RHYTHM-GUITAR PARTS

- *As a rhythm guitarist you will provide solid groove in your band.*
- **Go to page 32** to find out more about rhythm-guitar playing, the essential backbone of most songs.
- **Go to page 38** to discover the secrets of rhythm notation so that you get the most of song transcriptions.
- **Go to page 40** to learn how to follow a chord chart.

I WANT TO CHOOSE THE RIGHT EFFECTS FOR PLAYING ELECTRIC

- *Adding effects to your playing can enhance it no end, or detract from it, so choose wisely.*
- **Go to pages 120 to 143** for information on what different effects are available and how best to use them.

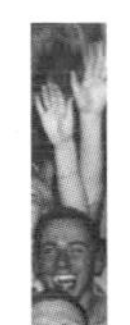

Complete Guitar Handbook

I WANT TO EXPLORE DIFFERENT STYLES OF MUSIC

- *Can't decide what style you want to adopt?*
- **Go to pages 144 to 207** for plenty of ideas.

WHAT ARE FINGER-PICKING AND FLAT-PICKING?

- *These are both essential techniques to master for different styles.*
- **Go to page 26** to learn how to finger-pick.
- **Go to page 162** for details about flat-picking techniques.

I WANT TO PLAY IN A BAND

- *Do you feel that it is time to put your new skills into action?*
- **Go to page 34** to learn about timing – essential if you are to play with other people.
- **Go to page 118** to discover more about stagecraft before you get your band on the road.

I WANT TO RECORD MY SONGS

- *Before you commit your masterpiece to vinyl (or hard-drive!), read some top tips.*
- **Go to page 324** to learn the essentials of good recording.
- **Go to page 332** to discover how to record from the comfort of your own home.

I WANT TO EXPLORE NEW SOUNDS OR CHANGE MY SOUND

- *Want a change from the old routine?*
- **Go to page 108** and discover how adding harmonics can add interest to your playing.
- **Go to pages 144 to 207** for inspiration and ideas.

Complete Guitar Handbook

I WANT TO LEARN SOME DIFFERENT CHORDS

- *The more chords you learn, the more you have to draw upon as a player.*
- **Go to page 74** to be shown how to play extended and altered chords.
- **Go to page 350** and take your pick from a huge variety of chords.

I WANT TO LEARN ABOUT SCALES AND MODES

- *Once mastered, these will form the foundation of playing and songwriting.*
- **Go to page 52** to discover more about scales.
- **Go to page 58** to find out all about modes.

I WANT TO LEARN ABOUT DIFFERENT GUITAR SOUNDS

- *What's the difference between a Fender Strat and a Gibson SG?*
- **Go to pages 240 to 271** to be inspired by how some of the all-time great guitars sound.
- **Go to page 322** to discover the set-ups used by great players.

I WANT TO LOOK AFTER MY GUITAR

- *It pays to invest some time in your instrument.*
- **Go to page 274** to learn about acoustic guitar anatomy
- **Go to page 276** to learn about electric guitar anatomy.
- **Go to page 290** for some tips on cleaning and storage.

I WANT TO TEACH MYSELF TO READ MUSIC

- *Not happy with playing by ear?*
- **Go to page 50** for the basics of notation.

I WANT TO PLAY LIVE

- *Once you feel ready to step on to a stage, your guitar will need to be heard by your adoring public.*
- **Go to page 308** for the low-down on amplification.
- **Go to page 320** for more information on set-ups and sounds.

I WANT TO LEARN ABOUT THE SOUNDS OF THE GREAT GUITARISTS

- *Learn from the great and the good.*
- **Go to pages 208 to 239** for further information on your favourite players.

Complete Guitar Handbook

TUNING

Tuning is the most essential skill any guitarist has to master: it doesn't matter how many hours you spend learning chords, scales or riffs – they won't sound any good if the guitar is out of tune! Although you can use an electronic tuner, the ability to tune by ear will always prove useful.

PITCH

A guitar can be tuned so that all the strings are 'in tune' with one another, and this can sound fine if you are just playing chords on your own. However, if you intend to play with other instruments or a CD then you'll need to make sure that your guitar is tuned to the correct pitch. Traditionally, guitarists use a 'tuning fork' so that they can hear the exact pitch that either the E or A string should be tuned to. If you have access to a keyboard, or a well-tuned piano, this could be used instead. The open strings of the guitar, from the lowest note (thickest string) to the highest (thinnest string) should be tuned as shown below.

TUNING AT THE FIFTH FRET

Once you have tuned the low string to the pitch of E you can use this as the starting point from which to tune all the other strings.

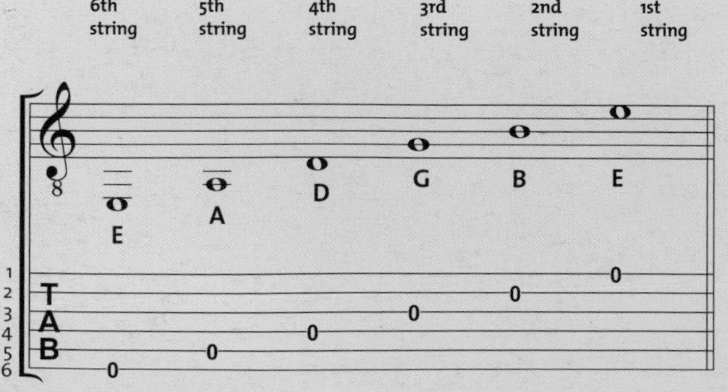

Tip

Unless you are fitting new strings, you will not need to make large turns on the machine heads. If you tune your guitar regularly, then a few small tuning adjustments should be all it normally needs.

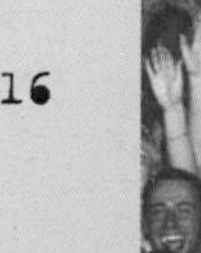

Complete Guitar Handbook

1. Begin by playing a note on the fifth fret of the low E string; this will produce the note A. You should then turn the fifth string machine head (tuning peg) until the pitch of this open string matches the fretted note on the lower string. If the open fifth string sounds higher than the fretted A note then you should rotate the machine head to slacken the string; if the open fifth string sounds too low then you should tighten the string.

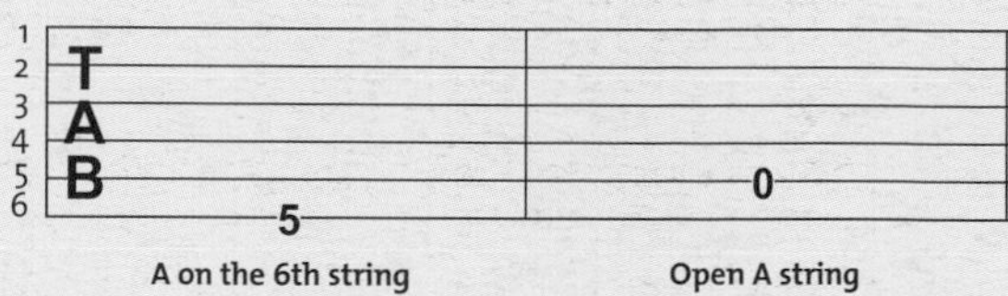

A on the 6th string — Open A string

2. Once you have tuned the A string, you can produce the note of D by playing at the fifth fret; this will provide you with the pitch to tune the open D string accurately. You can then use the same method for tuning the open G string, i.e. by adjusting it to match the note on the fifth fret of the D string.

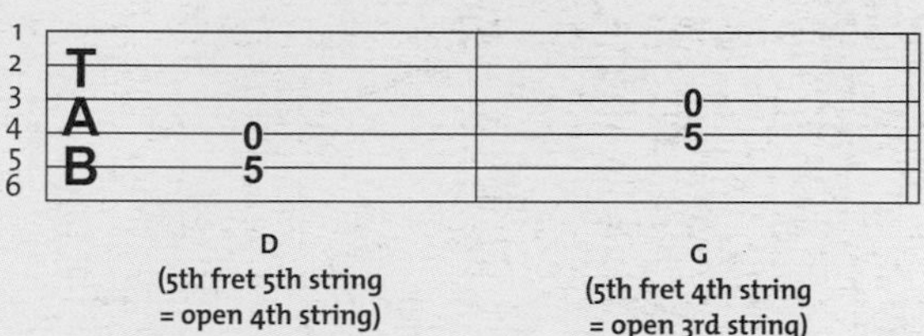

D (5th fret 5th string = open 4th string) — G (5th fret 4th string = open 3rd string)

3. The system alters slightly when you come to tune the B string. You need to tune this to the pitch of the note on the fourth fret of the G string. Once the B string is in tune, fretting it at the fifth fret will produce the note E; you should adjust the open first string to match this pitch.

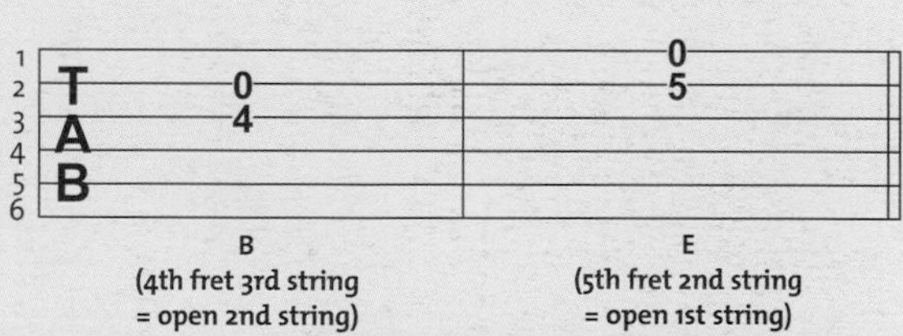

B (4th fret 3rd string = open 2nd string) — E (5th fret 2nd string = open 1st string)

Once this process is complete you should pick slowly through the notes of a chord that you are very familiar with and make any final tuning adjustments that may be needed.

► *You should now be able to have a go at tuning your guitar.*

Section One: The Basics

HAND POSITIONS

If you don't position your hands in the optimum way, learning to play guitar might prove to be an uphill struggle; playing with a good technique from the start, by positioning your hands correctly, will make learning new things relatively easy.

FRETTING HAND

▲ *The optimum position for your hand when you are fretting a note: fingers are close to the frets which minimizes any fret buzz.*

1. Regardless of whether you are playing chords or single notes, you should always press the fretting-hand fingers as close to the fretwire as possible. This technique minimizes the unpleasant 'fretbuzz' sounds that can otherwise occur. Pressing at the edge of the fret also greatly reduces the amount of pressure that is required, enabling you to play with a lighter and hence more fluent touch.
2. Try to keep all the fretting-hand fingers close to the fingerboard so that they are hovering just above the strings ready to jump into action when needed. This minimizes the amount of movement required when moving from one chord or note to another.
3. Unless you are playing more than one note with the same finger, you should always use the tips of your fingers to fret notes; this will produce the sound more directly and cleanly than using the fleshier pads of the fingers.

PICKING HAND

1. If using a plectrum (pick), grip it between the index (first) finger and the thumb. Position the plectrum so that its tip extends only just beyond the fingertip, by about 1/10 in (25 mm). Whilst this measurement doesn't have to be exact, make sure that the amount of plectrum that extends beyond the

Complete Guitar Handbook

▶ *Avoid holding the plectrum at right angles to your index finger, otherwise your wrist may lock.*

index finger is not excessive: this would result in a lack of pick control, making the plectrum liable to flap around when striking the strings – reducing both fluency and accuracy. Alternatively, if you find that when you try to pick a string you often miss it completely, the cause is most likely to be not enough plectrum extending beyond the fingertip.

2. Although you need to hold the plectrum with a small amount of pressure so that it doesn't get knocked out of your hand when you strike the strings, be very careful not to grip the plectrum too tightly. Excessive gripping pressure can lead to muscular tension in the hand and arm, with a subsequent loss of flexibility and movement.
3. The most efficient way to pick single notes is to alternate between downstrokes and upstrokes. Unless you want to achieve a particular staccato sound, this 'alternate picking' technique should be used for all melodies or lead guitar playing. (For information on fingerpicking, see pages 26–27.)

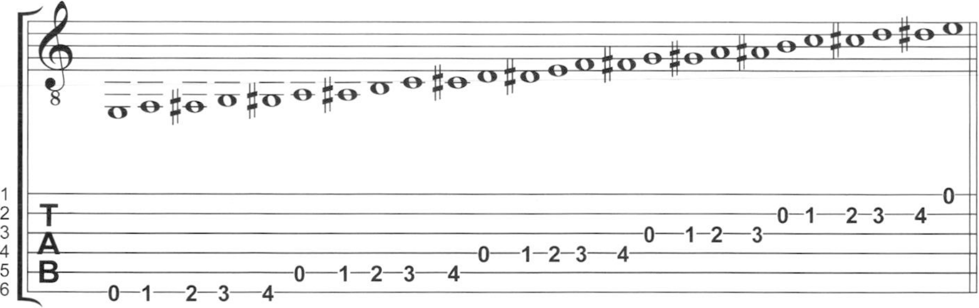

▲ *The E chromatic scale consists of a continual series of half steps, which means that every note in 'open position' is played. This makes the scale ideal for building technique as it uses all four fingers to fret notes. It should be played using alternate down and up plectrum strokes.*

Section One: The Basics

[...]RST CHORDS

Chords form the backbone of all music. As soon as you've mastered a few chord shapes you'll be well on the road to music-making. The really great thing about chords is that once you've learnt them they'll last you a lifetime: you'll still be using any chord you learn today 20 years from now.

CHORD SYMBOLS

There are two main types of chords that form the core of most popular music: 'major chords' and 'minor chords'.

1. The chord symbol that tells you when to play a major chord is simply the letter name of the chord written as a capital. For example, the chord symbol for the G major chord is 'G' and the chord symbol for the D major chord is 'D'. Major chords have a bright, strong sound.

FRETBOXES

Guitar chord fingerings are written in diagrams known as 'fretboxes'. These indicate which strings and frets to play on, and which fingers should be used for fretting the notes.

1. In this book, fretboxes are written with vertical lines representing the strings: the low E string is represented by the line on the far left and the high E string by the line on the far right.
2. The thick line at the top of the fretbox represents the nut of the guitar, and the remaining horizontal lines represent the frets.
3. The recommended fret-hand fingering is shown in numbers: 1 = the index finger and 4 = the little finger.
4. An o above a string line means this string should be played open (unfretted).
5. An X above a string line means this string should not be played.

2. Minor chord symbols consist of the capital letter of the chord name followed by a lowercase 'm'. For example, the chord symbol for the E minor chord is 'Em' and the chord symbol for the A minor chord is 'Am'. Minor chords have a mellow, sombre sound.

Chord Name	Chord Symbol
G major	G
D major	D
E minor	Em
A minor	Am

STARTING CHORDS

Begin with E minor, as this involves only two fretted notes and uses plenty of open strings. Place your fingers on the strings, pressing lightly yet securely with the fingertips, and then strum across all six strings. Once you're familiar with this chord, move your two fretting fingers from E minor on to the adjacent higher strings, and add the first finger on the first fret of the B string – this is A minor. Notice that the low E string should be omitted when you strum A minor.

Next try some major chords. If G major seems like too much of a stretch between the second and third fingers, allow your thumb to move down to the centre of the back of the guitar neck until the chord feels comfortable. Notice that only the top four strings should be strummed when playing D major.

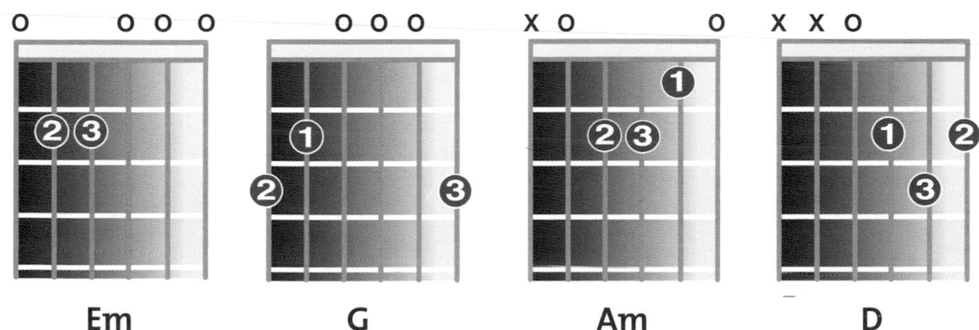

Section One: The Basics

SIMPLE CHORD SEQUENCES

Many songs consist of a short chord sequence that is repeated throughout. Once you have learnt a couple of basic chord shapes you can start playing a chord sequence by changing from one chord to another. It's then only a short step before you can play the chords to a complete song.

MINOR CHORDS

Begin by strumming downwards four times on an E minor chord, then without stopping change to A minor and play another four strums, keeping the same tempo. Without stopping or hesitating, move your fingers back to E minor and continuing strumming so that the whole sequence begins again.

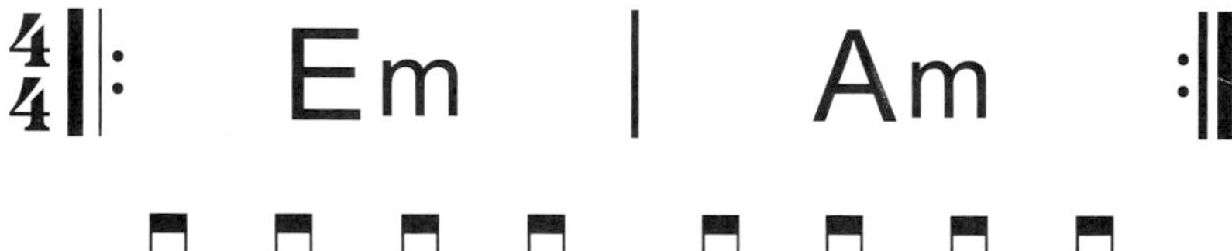

Notice the similarity of the E minor and A minor chord shapes: the second and third fingers are used at the second fret in both chords, the only difference being that they move from the A and D strings in E minor to the adjacent D and G strings in A minor. Try to keep this in mind when you change between these chords, so that you can minimize the amount of finger movement you make – this will make changing between the chords easier and quicker.

Complete Guitar Handbook

MAJOR CHORDS

Begin by playing four downstrums on a G major chord then, without stopping, move your fingers to D major and play another four strums. Repeat the sequence from the beginning by changing back to G major. Try to keep an even tempo throughout and practise slowly until you are able to change between the chords without pausing or hesitating.

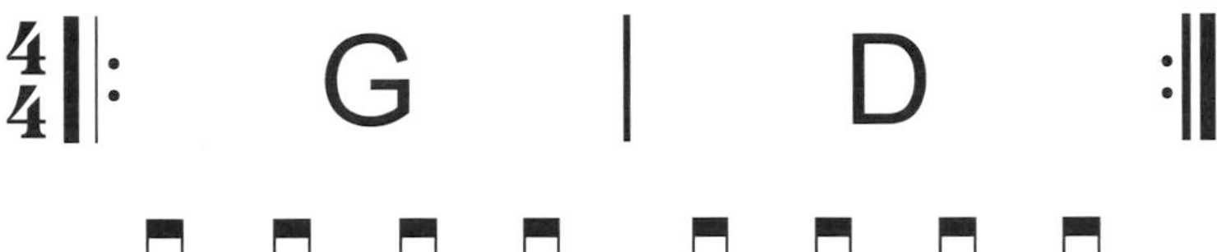

Notice how the third finger stays at the third fret for both G and D major. Use this as a pivot point to lead the chord change. Try to move all three fretting fingers as one shape when changing chord, rather than placing the fingers on one at a time; this will make the chord changes smoother.

COMBINING CHORDS

Once you feel fully familiar with the four chord shapes, try and combine them in this four-chord sequence, playing four downstrums for each chord.

1. Look for any links between the different chord fingerings so that you can minimize the amount of finger movement you need to make.
2. Remember to place the fingers for each complete chord shape on the fretboard together, rather than finger by finger.
3. Practise very slowly so that you don't develop a habit of slowing down or stopping between chord changes.

Section One: The Basics

STRUMMING

Strumming chords forms the foundation of any guitar player's range of techniques. Strumming can be used to accompany your own or some else's singing; it can also be used to provide a backing for lead-guitar playing. Being able to strum in a variety of styles will enable you to play rhythm guitar in a wide range of musical genres.

STRUM TECHNIQUE

For the music to flow smoothly it's essential to develop a relaxed strumming action. It will aid the fluency of rhythm playing if the strumming action comes from the wrist: a fluid and easy strumming action is best achieved this way, with the wrist loose and relaxed. If the wrist is stiff and not allowed to move freely then excessive arm movement will occur, as the strumming action will be forced to come from the elbow instead. As this can never move as fluently as the wrist, there will be a loss of smoothness and rhythmic potential.

STRUMMING EXERCISES

1. Begin by strumming an E minor chord using four downstrums per measure, and then experiment by inserting a quick upstrum between the second and third beats. The upstrum should be played by an upwards movement generated from the wrist, as though the strumming hand is almost effortlessly bouncing back into position ready for the next downstrum. Keep practising this technique until it feels natural, always making sure that the arm itself isn't moving up and down when you're strumming.

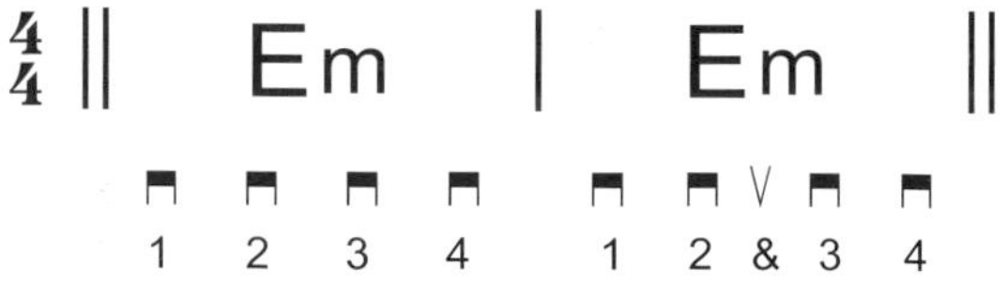

4/4 || Em | Em ||

1 2 3 4 | 1 2 & 3 4

Complete Guitar Handbook

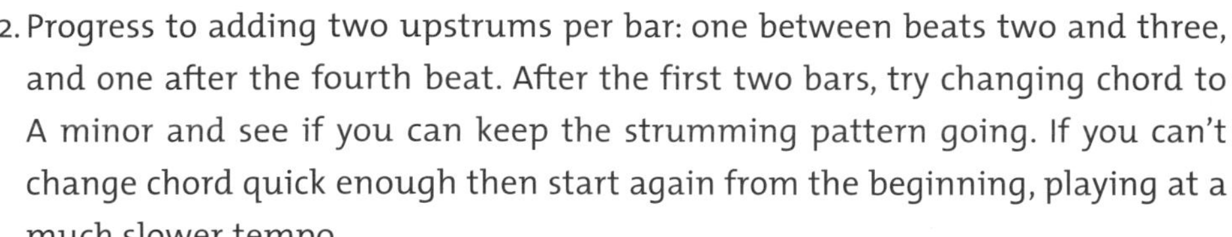

2. Progress to adding two upstrums per bar: one between beats two and three, and one after the fourth beat. After the first two bars, try changing chord to A minor and see if you can keep the strumming pattern going. If you can't change chord quick enough then start again from the beginning, playing at a much slower tempo.

3. To really get the strumming hand moving try adding an upstrum after every downstrum. Although this strumming style would be too busy for most songs, this exercise does provide practise in building a fluent strumming technique. Make sure that you have the plectrum positioned correctly, with its tip extending only just beyond the index fingertip, so that it does not drag on the strings as you strum.

Tip

You don't need to strum all the strings, particularly when playing upstrums. You'll often get a much clearer sound if you only strum the top three or four strings.

▲ *Strumming is an essential technique to master.*

Section One: The Basics

FINGER-PICKING

Finger-picking can provide a really interesting alternative to strumming. The technique is not just confined to classical or folk guitarists – many rock and pop players also use finger-picking as a method of bringing melodic interest to a chord progression and as a way of introducing musical subtleties to a song.

FINGERING

In music notation, each picking finger is identified by a letter: 'p' represents the thumb, 'i' the index finger, 'm' the middle finger and 'a' the third finger. (As it is much shorter than the others, the little finger is rarely used in finger-picking.)

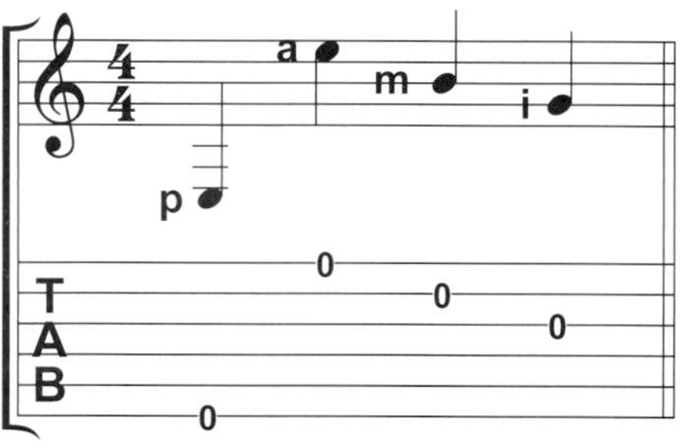

The thumb is mostly used for playing the bass strings (the lowest three strings), while the fingers are used for playing the treble strings. There are many different ways of finger-picking, but one of the easiest is to use the a finger for picking the first string, the m finger for the second string and the i finger for the third string.

PICKING PATTERNS

Many songs use a repetitive finger-picking pattern throughout to create a continuity of sound. Picking patterns nearly always begin by playing the root note of the chord (i.e. the note that gives the letter name to the chord) on the bass string using the thumb. For example, the low E string would be the first note of a pattern when fingerpicking on a chord of E minor, and the open A string would be the first note when fingerpicking on a chord of A minor.

Complete Guitar Handbook

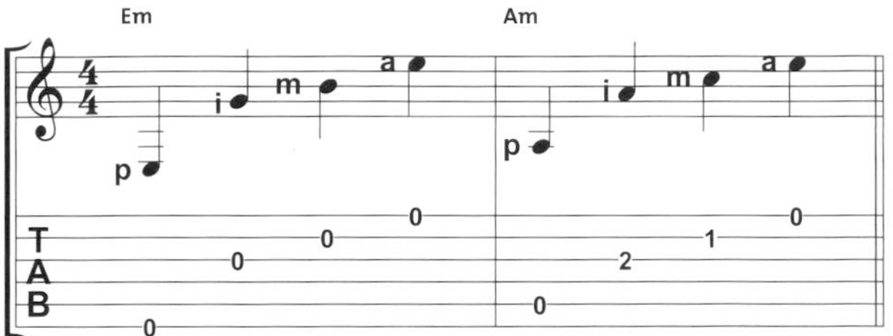

If the picking pattern on a chord is repeated then sometimes a different bass is used the second time. This will normally be another note from the chord, usually the adjacent bass string. This technique can completely transform a simple chord progression, making it sound quite complex because of the moving bass line. This style of finger-picking is known as 'alternating bass'.

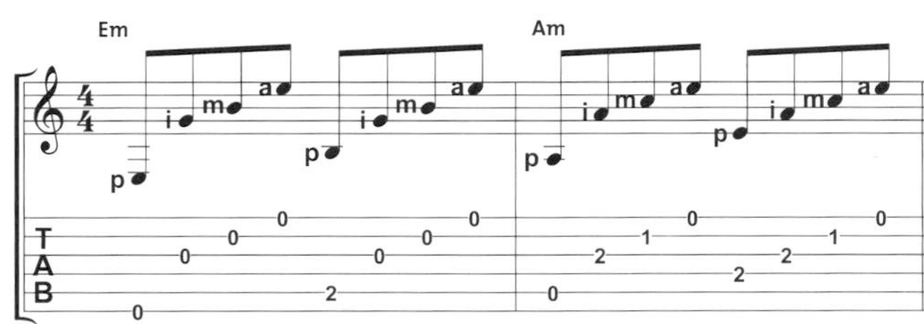

In some musical styles, more complex picking patterns might be used on the treble strings. It is best to practise these types of patterns on one chord until the picking pattern feels totally comfortable. Once you are familiar with a pattern it's relatively easy to apply it to a chord progression. You just need to take care about which bass note to pick on each chord, ensuring you use the root note as your starting point.

Tip

It's easier to finger-pick if you let your fingernails grow a little. Using nails to pick the strings will also give you a crisper, clearer and stronger sound.

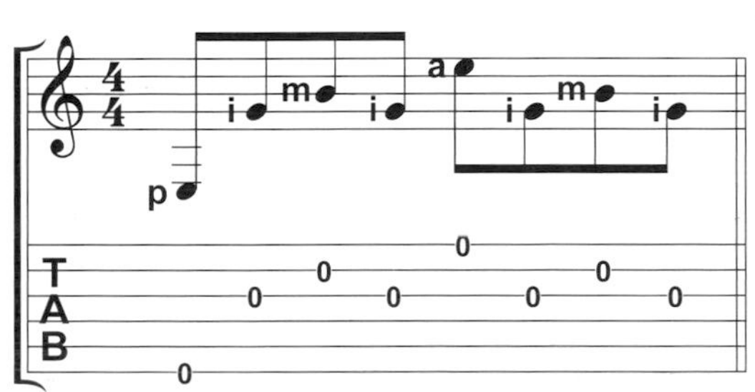

Section One: The Basics

MORE CHORDS

The more chords you learn, the more songs you'll be able to play. Developing knowledge of only the 10 most common chords will enable you to play literally thousands of songs, providing you practise them enough so that you can change fluently from chord to chord.

MAIN CHORD TYPES

Although there are dozens of different chord types, all of these can be considered as just variations of the two core types of chords: major chords and minor chords. For example, if you come across a chord chart that includes Am7, playing a simple A minor chord will work almost as well. Consequently, developing a good knowledge of the most popular major and minor chords will provide a firm foundation for all future chord playing.

MAJOR CHORDS

In addition to the G and D major chords that were covered on pages 20–21, some other important major chords to start with are A, C, E and F.

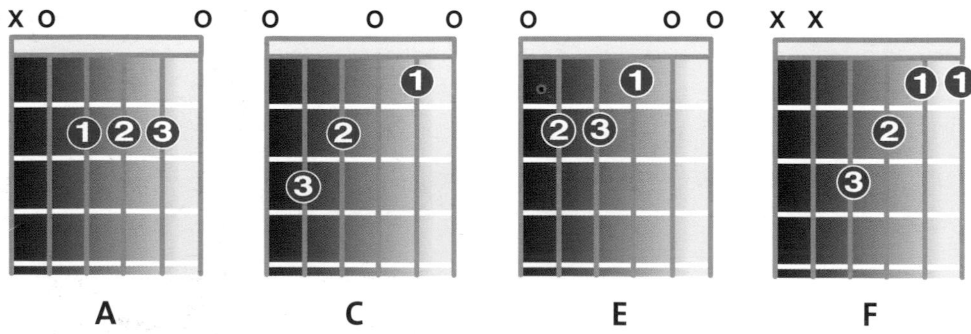

Complete Guitar Handbook

Notice that all the strings can be strummed on the E major chord, whereas the sixth string should be omitted when the A or C chords are strummed. The F major chord is different from the other chord fingerings in that the first finger needs to lie flat across both the first and second strings. You will find this easier if you ensure that your thumb is positioned quite low at the back of the guitar neck; this will help you keep your first finger flat while the second and third fingers press with the fingertips. Make sure that you only strum the top four strings when playing the F major chord.

MINOR CHORDS

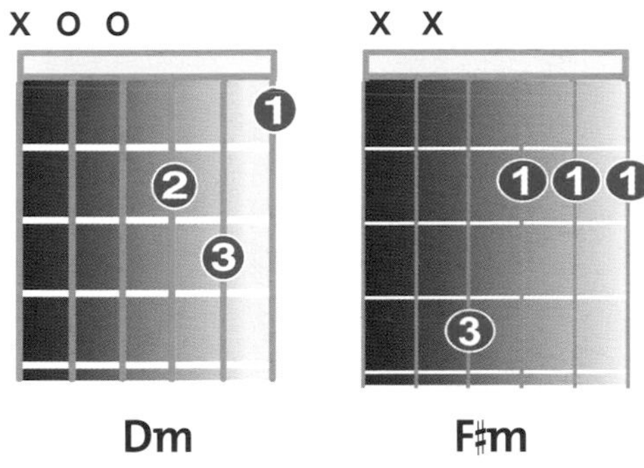

In addition to the Am and Em chords that were covered on pages 20–21, the other most important minor chords to learn at first are Dm and F♯m.

Both Dm and F♯m are four-string chords (i.e. the fifth and sixth strings should be omitted when playing these chords). The F♯m chord is a development of the technique that you gained when learning to play the F major chord, but this time the first finger needs to fret all the top three strings. If you find this tricky, you might like to try resting the second finger on top of the first finger; this will add extra weight and strength to help the first finger hold down all three strings. Positioning the fretting finger as close as possible to the fretwire will reduce the amount of finger pressure required.

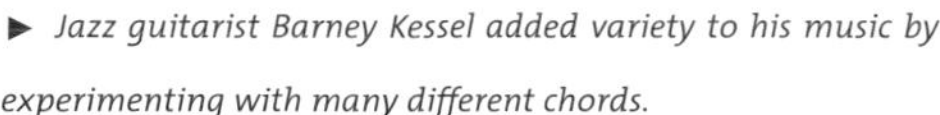

▶ *Jazz guitarist Barney Kessel added variety to his music by experimenting with many different chords.*

Section One: The Basics

KEYS

The 'key' of a song refers to its overall tonality, and dictates which scale will be used as the basis of the melody and which chords will occur. Understanding which chords go together in a key will help you work out the chord structure of songs, and will provide a framework to begin writing your own songs.

MAJOR KEYS

In each major key, three major chords occur – as shown below:

Key	Major Chords in the Key
C major	C F G
G major	G C D
D major	D G A
A major	A D E

A song or chord progression will normally begin with the tonic (keynote) chord. This is the chord that has the same name as the key. For example, in the key of C major, C is the tonic (keynote) chord.

Minor chords also occur in major keys. Some of the most commonly used minor chords in the keys of C and G major are shown below.

Key	Minor Chords in the Key
C major	Dm Em Am
G major	Am Bm Em

Although there are no fixed rules about which chords can be combined when you are composing a song or chord progression, if you select chords from the

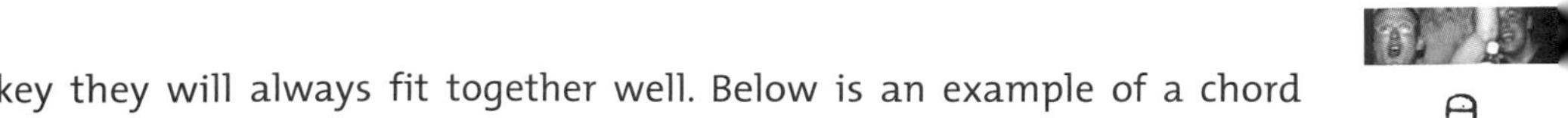

same key they will always fit together well. Below is an example of a chord progression using chords in the key of C major.

|| C | Dm | Em | F | Am | G | F | C ||

MINOR KEYS

In each minor key, three minor chords are closely related, and most commonly occur in popular songs. For example, in the key of A minor the chords of Am, Dm and Em are the most important. Three major chords also occur in each minor key. For example, in the key of A minor, C, F and G major chords occur. As all these chords are within the same key they can be combined in any order (after starting with the tonic/keynote chord) to make a pleasant-sounding chord sequence. An example is shown below, but you can experiment with rearranging the chords in a different order and then playing them through to hear the musical result.

Here are a few chord progressions demonstrating some of the most common chord sequences used in a few of the most popular major and minor keys.

|| Am | F | G | C | Am | Dm | Em | Am ||

▲ *Chord progression in the key of A minor.*

|| G | D | C | G | Em | Am | D | G ||

▲ *Chord progression in the key of G major.*

|| D | Em | F♯m | Em | G | A | G | D ||

▲ *Chord progression in the key of D major.*

|| A | E | F♯m | E | D | E | A | A ||

▲ *Chord progression in the key of A major.*

|| Em | D | C | D | Am | G | D | Em ||

▲ *Chord progression in the key of E minor.*

Section One: The Basics

INTRODUCTION

Knowing a number of chord shapes is useful, but it's only when you can put some of these chords together with an interesting strumming pattern, and change fluently between them, that you'll really start making music by playing rhythm guitar.

IMPORTANCE OF RHYTHM

Rhythm guitar playing is rarely given as much attention as lead playing, but it's important to remember that it's rhythm playing that forms the backbone of most songs. If you join a band, regardless of the musical style, you'll almost certainly spend more time playing rhythm guitar than lead guitar.

Notable rhythm guitar specialists are Bo Diddley (b. 1928), John Lennon (1940–80), Pete Townshend (b. 1945), Noel Gallagher (b. 1967), Paul Weller (b. 1958), Peter Buck (b. 1956) of REM, Fran Healy (b. 1973) of Travis and Badly Drawn Boy (b. Damon Gough, 1970).

GOOD RHYTHM

1. The first essential of becoming a good rhythm guitar player is the ability to keep in time: practising with a metronome, drum machine or backing tracks will provide the ideal preparation; always listen out for the drums and bass and try to stay in time

◀ One of the features of Damon Gough's unique sound is his rhythm guitar playing that underpins the majority of his tracks.

Complete Guitar Handbook

with them. Remember that as a rhythm guitar player you are part of the 'rhythm section' of any band, and you should try to interact closely with the other rhythm section musicians. (See pages 34–35.)

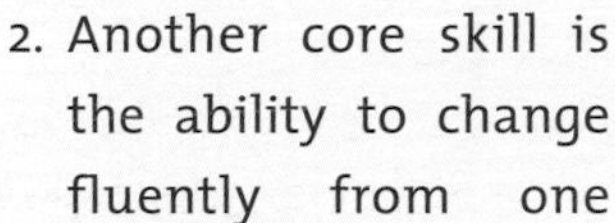

▲ *Pioneering guitarist Pete Townshend was a master of rhythm guitar.*

2. Another core skill is the ability to change fluently from one chord to another: always look for links, or common notes, between consecutive chords – so that you can minimize the amount of finger movement needed when changing chords; you may be able to keep some fingers on, or at least slide them along a string to the next chord. Leaving gaps between chords when strumming through a song or chord progression is a recipe for musical disaster – the performance will sound fragmented and if you're playing with a singer or other musicians it will prove impossible to keep in time. (See pages 82–83.)

3. Developing a reliable strumming technique is an essential part of becoming a good guitar player. Once you have mastered these basic rhythm-playing skills, then it's time to become inventive with your strumming patterns. It's the uniqueness and inventiveness of strumming that distinguishes great rhythm players from the rest. (See pages 46–47.)

4. Being able to understand and follow chord charts is another required skill for any rhythm guitar player. Depending on the style of music and who has prepared the chord chart, these could appear in a variety of formats, from a simple handwritten list of chords to a fully typeset chart with time signatures, notated rhythms and interpretation markings included. (See pages 40–45.)

Section One: The Basics

TIMING

The most important skill any rhythm guitar player needs is the ability to maintain an even tempo and keep in time with other band members. It's essential that your rhythm playing sits in the same groove as the other members of the rhythm section.

DEVELOPING TIMING SKILLS

Some people have a natural sense of rhythm and timing that just needs nurturing, while others have to concentrate on developing a secure sense of timing. A simple test to discover how well-developed your sense of timing is would be to try and clap along to a recording by one of your favourite bands. While listening to the recording, focus your attention on the drums and try to clap a regular beat that matches the main rhythmic pulses within the song. Listen carefully to your clapping and see if you can stay in time throughout the whole song – stamina is an important aspect of rhythm playing. Before you try to play through a song make sure that you have mastered any technical challenges, such as awkward chord changes, in advance. Otherwise, the temptation will be to slow down when approaching the difficult bits and perhaps speed up on the easy bits. You should try to avoid developing such poor timing habits from the start by always choosing a slow practice tempo at which you can master the whole song – difficult bits and all! Once you can play the song without any mistakes or hesitations, it's relatively easy to gradually increase the tempo each time you practise.

◄ *Nile Rodgers is known for the crisp timing of his rhythm chops.*

Tip

Record yourself playing along to a CD or a drum machine. Listen really carefully to hear if your playing is exactly in time.

Complete Guitar Handbook

TIMING AIDS

Ideally you should always try to practise your rhythm playing with a device that keeps regular time. The simplest method is to practise with a metronome. This is a small mechanical or electronic device that sounds a click on each beat. You can set it to click in increments from a very slow to a super-fast tempo. It's always best to practise anything new at a slow tempo, increasing the metronome setting by a couple of notches each time you've successfully played it the whole way through.

▲ *A metronome – a tried and tested way to keep in good time.*

If you have access to a drum machine this can be used in a similar way to a metronome. The advantage of the drum machine is that you can set it to play back interesting drum patterns to help inspire your strumming style. You can program the machine, or use preset patterns, so that it emulates different musical genres.

Playing along to records is also a good method of developing a secure sense of timing: the band on the recording won't wait around if you lose time or hesitate over a chord change. Because there will be a longer space between beats, playing along with songs at a slow tempo emphasizes any timing inconsistencies – so don't forget to practise a few ballads alongside the thrash metal!

◀ *A drum machine can help you play in time.*

Section One: The Basics

TIME SIGNATURES

The time signature is the most important element in setting the musical feel and mood of a piece of music. It provides the framework for the rhythmic structure of a song and plays a large part in establishing the character of the music.

RECOGNIZING TIME SIGNATURES

The symbol indicating the time signature is always written at the start of the music or chord chart. The time signature is normally written as two numbers, one above the other. The top number represents the number of beats per measure (bar), while the bottom number refers to the type of beats.

The most common time signature used in all styles of popular music is $\frac{4}{4}$ time. This indicates that there are four beats in a measure, and that these are quarter notes (crotchets). Sometimes the $\frac{4}{4}$ symbol is replaced with **C**, meaning 'common time'.

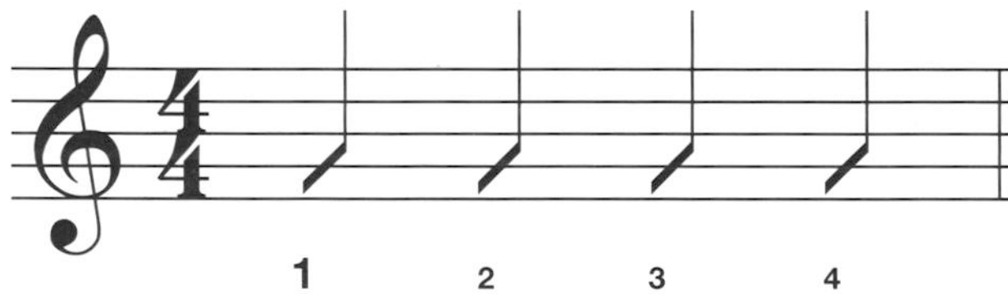

▲ *A bar in 4/4 time.*

Note that the time signature only tells you the number and type of 'beats' that will occur in a measure; this is not the same as the number of 'notes' you can play in the measure. For example, a measure of music in $\frac{4}{4}$ time will last for the equivalent duration of four quarter beats, but in this space you might play less longer-lasting notes or more shorter notes. In fact, you can play any combination of long, medium or short notes providing the duration per measure is equivalent to four quarter-note beats. (See pages 38–39 for more information on understanding notation.)

Complete Guitar Handbook

Other commonly used time signatures:

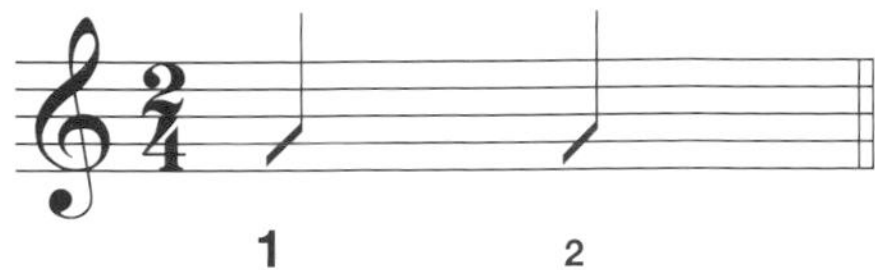

$\frac{2}{4}$: this has two quarter-note beats per measure. This time signature tends to give a march-like feel to the music.

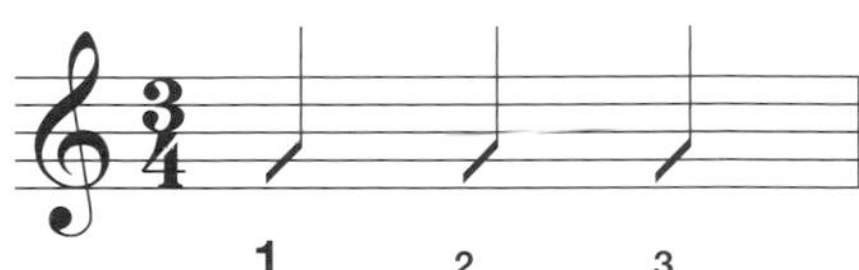

$\frac{3}{4}$: this has three quarter-note beats per measure. This time signature gives a waltz like character to the music and is often used in country and folk ballads.

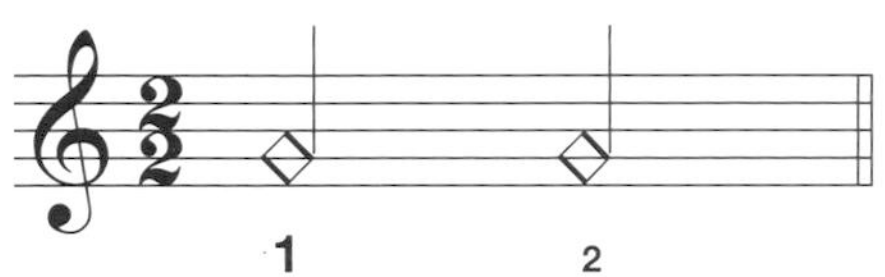

$\frac{2}{2}$: this has two half-note beats per measure. This is equivalent in length to $\frac{4}{4}$ time, but with two long beats per measure instead of four quarter-note beats.

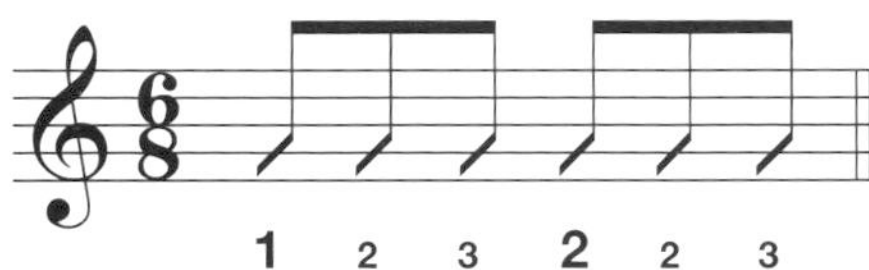

$\frac{6}{8}$: this has six eighth-note beats per measure. However, these are normally played as two groups of three.

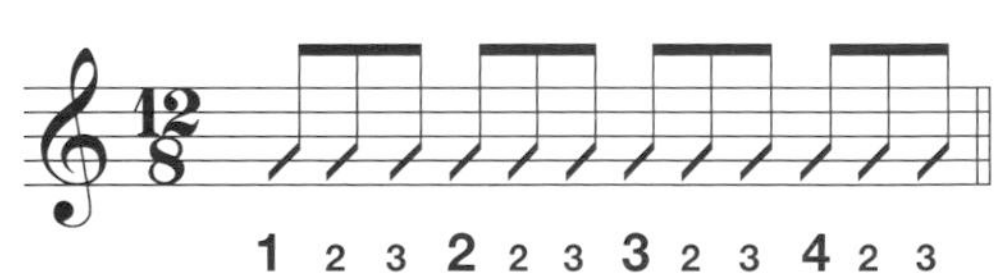

$\frac{12}{8}$: this has 12 eighth-note beats per measure. These are normally played as four groups of three. $\frac{12}{8}$ is commonly used in blues and jazz.

ESTABLISHING THE TIME SIGNATURE

If you were just to play a long series of chords all of equal strength it would be hard for the listener to recognize any rhythmic structure in the music – in other words, they wouldn't be able to 'feel the groove'. So normally the first beat of each measure is slightly accented, as this helps the sense of rhythm in a piece of music. In $\frac{6}{8}$ and $\frac{12}{8}$ time, an accent is normally played on the first of each group of three notes. (If you're playing in a band it might be the drums or other instruments that emphasize these accents.)

Section One: The Basics

RHYTHM NOTATION

Understanding how rhythms are written down will help you play through notated chord charts. The ability to notate your own rhythms is useful for passing the information to other players and as a memory aid. Even if you intend to rely mainly on tablature, a knowledge of rhythm notation will help you get the most out of the many song transcriptions that provide the full notation with the tab.

NOTE VALUES

Rhythm notation consists of pitchless notes and rests. The type of note used tells you how many beats a chord lasts; the type of rest used tells you how many beats a silence lasts. The diagram below shows the names of the most common types of notes, their symbols and how many of each type of note can occur in a single measure in $\frac{4}{4}$ time.

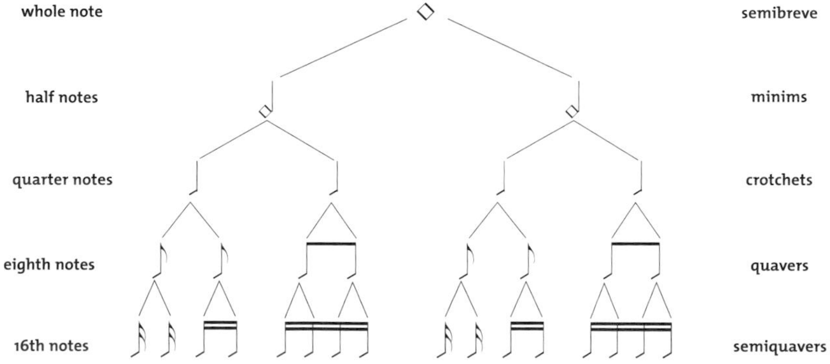

▲ *The terminology that is widely used in North America (and increasingly amongst pop, rock and jazz musicians in the UK and elsewhere) is different to that traditionally used by classical musicians in many parts of the world. In the diagram the modern names are shown on the left and the traditional names are shown on the right.*

Complete Guitar Handbook

RESTS

The table on the right shows the names of the most common types of rests, their symbols, their note equivalents, and the duration of each type of rest in $\frac{4}{4}$ time.

Name	Rest symbol	Note equivalent	Duration in $\frac{4}{4}$ time
semibreve rest (whole rest)	𝄻	𝅝	4 beats
minim rest (half rest)	𝄼	𝅗𝅥	2 beats
crotchet rest (quarter rest)	𝄽	𝅘𝅥	1 beat
quaver rest (eighth rest)	𝄾	𝅘𝅥𝅮	1/2 beat
semiquaver rest (16th rest)	𝄿	𝅘𝅥𝅯	1/4 beat

DOTTED NOTES

A dot after a note or rest means that the note or rest lasts for half as long again. This chart shows the values of dotted notes and dotted rests in $\frac{4}{4}$ time.

Name	Note	Rest	Duration in $\frac{4}{4}$ time
dotted minim (dotted half note)	𝅗𝅥.	𝄼.	3 beats
dotted crotchet (dotted quarter note)	𝅘𝅥.	𝄽.	1 1/2 beats
dotted quaver (dotted eighth note)	𝅘𝅥𝅮.	𝄾.	3/4 of a beat

TIES

A curved line known as a 'tie' is used to join together two notes of the same pitch in order to increase the duration of the note.

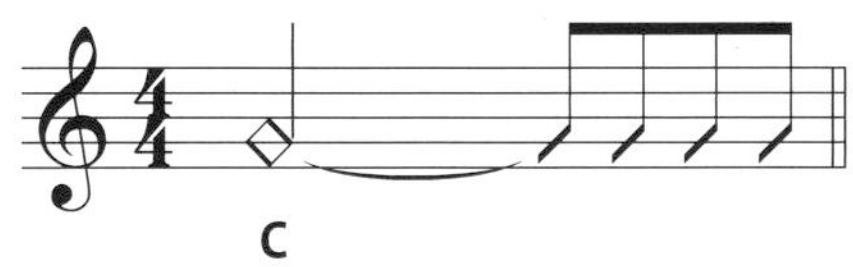

◀ *In this example, the first chord would be allowed to sustain for the equivalent of five eighth notes. It is not possible to use a dot after the initial chord as this would have increased the duration of the note to the equivalent of six eighth notes.*

Another common instance where ties are used is across bar lines as a method of sustaining a note beyond the end of a measure.

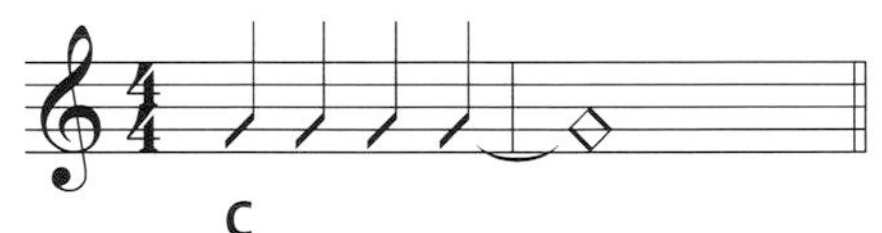

◀ *In this example, a tie is used so that the chord at the end of measure one can sustain into measure two.*

TRIPLETS

A triplet sign indicates where three notes should be played in the space of two notes of the same value.

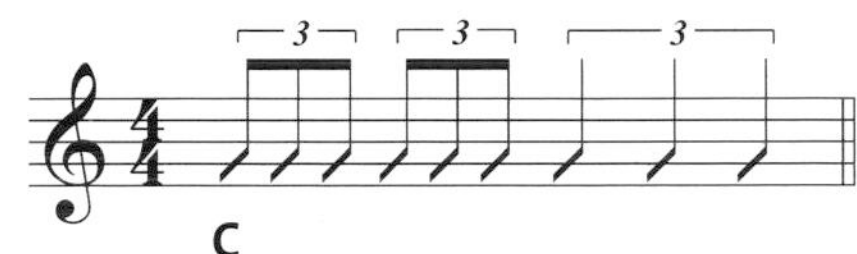

Section One: The Basics

CHORD CHARTS

Simple chord charts are the most commonly used way of notating the chord structure of a song or progression. If you audition for a pop or rock band, the music you'll be asked to play with will most likely be presented as a simple chord chart.

READING CHORD CHARTS

A chord chart normally has the time signature written at the very beginning. If there is no time signature then it's usually safe to assume that the music is in $\frac{4}{4}$ time.

Each measure is separated by a vertical line, with two vertical lines indicating the end of the piece. Chord symbols are used to show which chords should be played.

|| $\frac{4}{4}$ C | Am | Dm | G | F | Em | G | C ||

SPLIT MEASURES

When more than one chord appears in a single measure it can be assumed that the measure is to be evenly divided between the chords that appear within it. In a song in $\frac{3}{4}$ time, if three chords all appear in the same measure then you can assume that the measure is to be divided equally – with one beat per chord.

|| $\frac{3}{4}$ C | Am | Em F G | C ||

▲ *In the penultimate measure, each chord lasts for one beat.*

Complete Guitar Handbook

In many chord charts, in order to make the intention very clear and avoid any possible confusion, any division within a measure is shown by either a dot or a diagonal line after each chord: each dot or diagonal line indicates another beat.

|| 4/4 C / Am / | Dm / G / | F / Em / | G / C / ||

▲ *Each chord lasts for two beats: one beat indicated by the chord symbol and an additional beat indicated by the diagonal line.*

|| 4/4 C Em / / | F G / / | Am Em / / | G C / / ||

▲ *In this example, the first chord in each measure lasts for just one beat and the second chord lasts for three beats.*

|| 4/4 C . . Dm | Em . . F | Dm . . G | F . . C ||

▲ *In this example, instead of diagonal lines, dots are used to show the rhythmic divisions within each measure. The first chord in each measure lasts for three beats and the second chord lasts for one beat.*

INTERPRETING CHORD CHARTS

In standard chord charts, while the duration of each chord is clearly shown, the rhythm style that should be played is left to the discretion of the performer. In theory this means that you could interpret the chart in any way you wish in terms of the number of strums per beat, however you should make sure that your rhythm playing relates to the musical style and mood of the song.

◀ *Noel Gallagher's song-writing technique is based on a good understanding of chords.*

Section One: The Basics

FOLLOWING CHORD CHARTS

If every bar of a whole song was written out in a chord chart it would take up several pages and become cumbersome to read. Instead chord charts are normally abbreviated by using a number of 'repeat symbols'. In order to follow a chord chart accurately it is essential to understand what each repeat symbol means.

REPEAT SYMBOLS

𝄎 This symbol is used when one bar is to be repeated exactly.
𝄏 (2) This symbol is used when more than one bar is to be repeated. The number of bars to be repeated is written above the symbol.

Here is an example of these symbols in use.

|| 4/4 G | 𝄎 | C | D | 𝄏 (2) | Em | 𝄎 ||

should be played as

|| 4/4 G | G | C | D | C | D | Em | Em ||

SECTION REPEATS

A double bar-line followed by two dots indicates the start of a section, and two dots followed by a double bar-line indicates the end of the section to be repeated. If there are no dots at the start of the section, then repeat from the beginning of the piece. If the section is to be repeated more than once, the number of times it is to be played is written above the last repeat dots.

|| 4/4 Em | D |: G | C | Am | Em :| (x 4)

Complete Guitar Handbook

If two sections of music are identical, except for the last measure or measures, repeat dots are used in conjunction with first-time and second-time ending directions, as shown here.

|: 4/4 Am | G | F | [1.] Em :| [2.] Dm | Am ||

should be played as

|| 4/4 Am | G | F | Em | Am | G | F | Dm | Am ||

As well as repeat dots there are several other commonly used repeat signs:

- D.C. (an abbreviation of Da Capo) means play 'from the beginning'. For example, if the entire piece of music is to be repeated, D.C. can be written at the end to instruct you to play it again from the beginning.
- D.S. (an abbreviation of Dal Segno) means play 'from the sign': 𝄋. For example, if the verse and chorus of a song are to be repeated, but not the introduction, D.S. can be written at the end of the music with the D.S. sign written at the start of the verse. This instructs the performer to start again from the sign.
- Coda is the musical term for the end section of a piece of music. The start of the coda is marked by the sign 𝄌.
- Fine is the musical term for the end of a piece of music.

Some of the above repeat signs might be combined together in a chord chart.

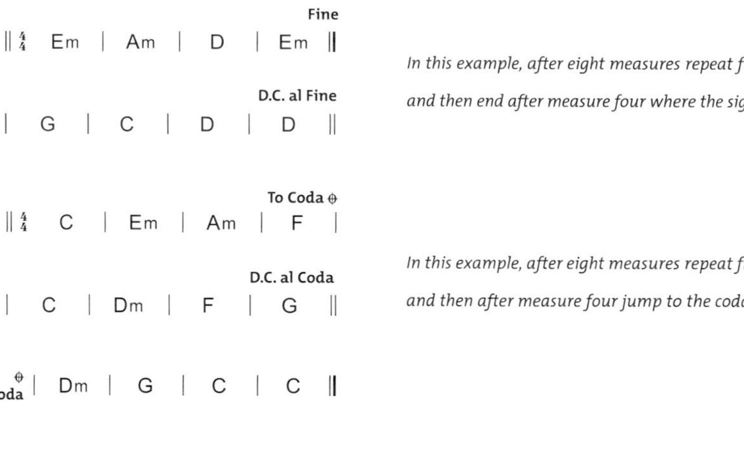

In this example, after eight measures repeat from the beginning and then end after measure four where the sign 'Fine' appears.

In this example, after eight measures repeat from the beginning and then after measure four jump to the coda section.

|| 4/4 G | Em | 𝄋 C | D | Am | C (To Coda 𝄌) | D | D (D.S. al Coda) ||

𝄌 Coda | Am | C | D | G ||

In this example, after eight measures repeat from the start of measure three to the end of measure six, then jump to the coda section.

Section One: The Basics

RHYTHM CHARTS

While standard chord charts are commonly used by pop and rock bands, more detailed and complex charts known as 'rhythm charts' are often presented to guitarists involved in recording sessions and those who play in theatre and function band settings. Learning to read rhythm charts will help expand your employability as a guitarist.

CHART STYLES

Some rhythm charts can be quite elaborate and may include a fully notated rhythm part, as well as detailed instructions about dynamics and tempo. Others may contain notated rhythms only at the beginning, in order to establish the feel of the song, with further rhythm notation only being used where specific rhythmic accents or features occur. The type of rhythm charts you might come across will depend on the context and the transcriber's personal preferences.

DYNAMIC MARKINGS

Symbols are often used in rhythm charts to indicate changes in volume – e.g. when you should play softly and when you should strum strongly. The symbols do not refer to any precise decibel volume level, instead their main function is to highlight changes in overall volume. The most common dynamic markings are shown to the right.

Symbol	Name	Meaning
pp	pianissimo	very soft
p	piano	soft
mp	mezzo-piano	medium soft
mf	mezzo-forte	medium loud
f	forte	loud
ff	fortissimo	very loud
<	crescendo	getting louder
>	diminuendo	getting softer

Complete Guitar Handbook

Accents, where certain individual beats are played stronger than others, are marked by this sign: >. The letters 'sfz' (*sforzando*) may be also used to indicate an accent.

TEMPO

Most rhythm charts will contain an indication of the speed at which the music should be played, and will usually be written at the start of the music. The tempo indication may appear in either traditional Italian musical terms or their English equivalents. Alternatively, a metronome marking may be shown to indicate the exact number of beats per minute (b.p.m.). The most common tempos are shown in the table on the right.

Italian Term	Meaning	Approximate speed
Largo	very slow	40–60 b.p.m.
Adagio	slow	50–75 b.p.m.
Andante	walking pace	75–100 b.p.m.
Moderato	noderate tempo	100–120 b.p.m.
Allegro	fast	120–160 b.p.m.
Presto	very quick	160–200 b.p.m.

Some music may contain changes in tempo. These are usually indicated through the use of Italian terms. The most widely used are:

- *Accel.* (an abbreviation of *accelerando*) means play gradually faster.
- *A tempo* indicates that you should resume the normal tempo after a derivation.
- *Meno mosso* (less movement) means that you should slow down at once.
- *Rall.* (an abbreviation of *rallentando*) means play gradually slower.
- *Rit.* (an abbreviation of *ritenuto*) means to hold back the tempo.

PLAYING RHYTHM CHARTS

Below you'll see a sample rhythm chart, incorporating some of the terms and symbols described above. Refer to pages 38–39 if you need to be reminded of the note values.

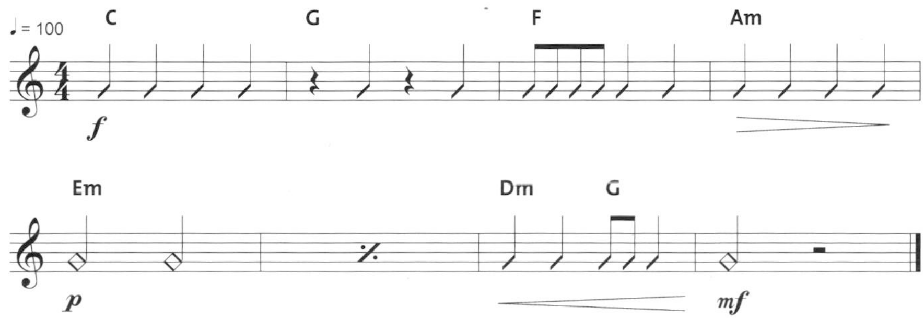

Section One: The Basics

STRUMMING PATTERNS

Building up a repertoire of useful strumming patterns is a good way of developing your rhythm guitar playing. Once you've mastered the core patterns used in rock and pop you can easily expand these by adding variations.

STRUM TECHNIQUE

Playing with a loose wrist action is an essential ingredient of developing a good strumming technique. Keeping the wrist tight and strumming by using the whole forearm will severely restrict the potential speed and fluency of your rhythm playing – so make sure that the strumming action comes from your wrist. It's a good idea to practise in front of a mirror, or film yourself playing guitar, so that you can see if you're using the right technique.

CHORD TECHNIQUE

Be careful not to over-grip with the fretting-hand thumb on the back of the neck as this will cause muscle fatigue and tend to limit freedom of the thumb to move. It is essential that the fretting-hand thumb is allowed to move freely when changing chords. If the thumb remains static this restricts the optimum positioning of the fingers for the next chord, which may result in unnecessary stretching and the involuntary dampening of certain strings (as the fingers are not positioned upright on their tips). Be aware that for the fingers to move freely the wrist, elbow and shoulder must be flexible and relaxed: try to ensure that this is not inhibited by your standing or sitting position.

STRUM PATTERNS

Opposite you'll find several examples of popular strumming patterns. It's a good idea to start by playing all the progressions using just four downstrums per measure – this way you'll become familiar with the chord changes before tackling the strum patterns.

Complete Guitar Handbook

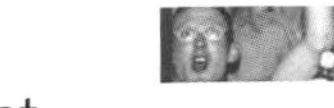

In nearly all styles of music, there is no need to strum all the strings on every beat – feel free to add variety, particularly by omitting some bass strings on upstrokes and some treble strings on downstrokes.

▲ *The second beat of the measure is accented to create dynamic variety. An upstroke is used after the third beat of the measure.*

▲ *This pattern uses a mixture of down and upstrokes, but notice how the fourth strum and the last strum are held longer than the others. This variety creates an effective rhythm.*

▲ *A simple down-up strum pattern, but the use of rests creates a very distinctive rhythmic effect.*

▲ *This 'Bo Diddley' type pattern is a good example of how to use rhythmic variations: notice that measure 1 and 3 are the same, while measures 2 and 4 are each variations on the first measure.*

▲ *This typical rock strumming pattern is essentially just one strum per measure. What makes it distinctive is the rapid down-up 'pre-strum' before the main beat. These 'pre-strums' do not need to be played across all the strings, and open strings can be used on the second of them to help get to the main chord quickly.*

Section One: The Basics

INTRODUCTION

Whether letting rip in an aggressive rock solo or playing a subtle blues, lead guitar playing is a great way to express your emotions through your instrument. However, underlying every great guitar solo is a foundation of scales and fingerboard knowledge that enables players to turn their musical ideas into reality.

▲ *The opening to 'Stairway to Heaven', as first played by Jimmy Page of Led Zeppelin is one of the most-copied intro riffs of all time.*

INFLUENTIAL PLAYERS

Some of the early pioneers of modern lead guitar styles are B. B. King (b. 1925), Buddy Guy (b. 1936), Eric Clapton (b. 1945), Jimmy Page (b. 1944), Jeff Beck (b. 1945), Ritchie Blackmore (b. 1945) and Carlos Santana (b. 1947). If you've never heard these players, try to check out some of their recordings.

Complete Guitar Handbook

▲ *Buddy Guy has inspired thousands over the years with his strong and inventive lead-guitar playing.*

IMPROVISATION

Later in this chapter all the essential scales that underpin lead guitar playing will be illustrated, but it's important to remember that playing scales up and down doesn't make a solo in itself.

Scales simply set the range of notes that will be in tune in any key. It's how well you improvise with a scale that dictates how good your solo will be. To get a feel for the song, it's always a good idea to play through the chord sequence before you play any lead guitar.

SIX STAGES TO IMPROVISING

1. When you first start playing lead guitar you could begin by simply playing the correct scale up and down over the chord progression. This way you can begin to hear the overall sound and tonality of the key, but always bear in mind that just playing scales up and down isn't enough to make a good solo.
2. As the first stage in learning to improvise, rather than playing the scale in straight time, experiment by playing some notes quickly while allowing others to ring on; you'll notice that this sounds more musical and inventive, even though you're still playing the same notes in the same order.
3. Next, try repeating series of notes, so that you begin to establish licks or phrases that will stick in the listener's ear. Once you have a phrase that you like, try to vary it slightly when you repeat it – that way it will sound fresh, while still giving the listener something recognizable to latch on to.
4. Leave some gaps between your phrases so that the music has space to breath. There's no need to fill every second with notes.
5. Try to make your lead playing fit with the musical style and mood of the song, so that it enhances what else is being played or sung.
6. The most important thing is to let your ears, rather than your fingers, guide you. Listen carefully to the musical effect of every note you play.

Section One: The Basics

BASICS OF NOTATION

There are three ways in which scales, licks and solos are written down: traditional notation, tablature and fretboxes. While you don't need to be a great sight-reader to play lead guitar, having a good understanding of each of the notation systems will help you learn lead guitar relatively easily.

TABLATURE

Tablature (TAB) uses six lines to represent the six strings of the guitar, with the top line representing the high E string and the bottom line representing the low E string. Numbers are written on the lines to indicate which fret to play at. A zero indicates that the string is played open. TAB is great for notating scales or chords and, although it doesn't usually include any rhythm notation, its simplicity means it's ideal for learning music that you have heard before.

▲ *This means play at the third fret on the second string.*

MUSIC NOTATION

Traditional music notation is written on a staff of five lines. Each line, and each space between them, represents a different note. For guitar music, a treble clef is written at the start of each line of music. Temporary extra lines (ledger lines) are used for any notes that are either too high or too low to fit on the staff.

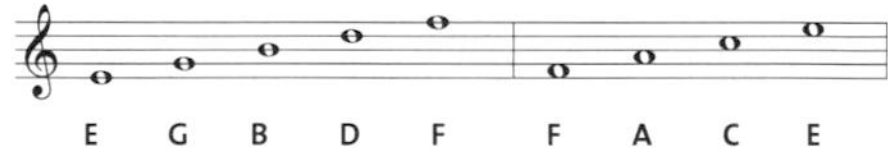

▲ *Notes on the lines and spaces in the treble clef.*

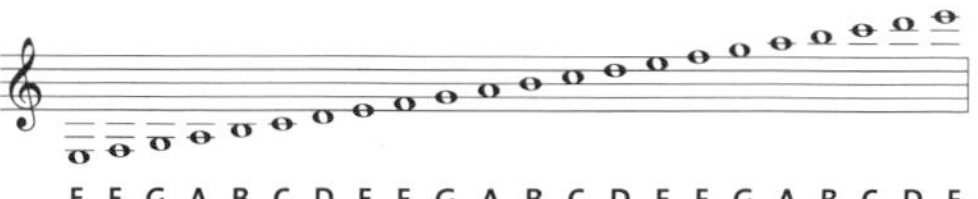

▶ *Using ledger lines, this diagram shows the notes from the open low E string to the E at the 12th fret on the first string.*

A sharp sign (♯) is written in front of a note, on the same line or space, to raise its pitch by a half step (semitone) i. e. equivalent to one fret higher.

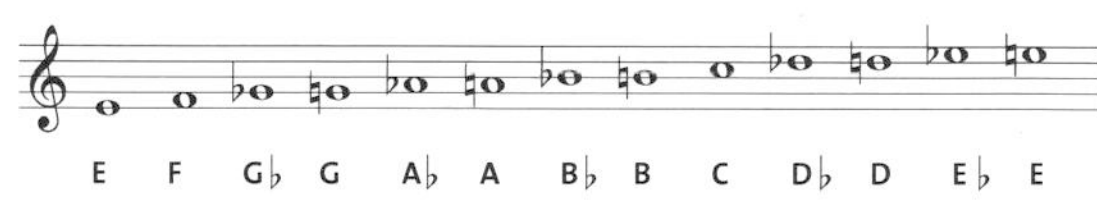

A flat sign (♭) is written in front of a note, on the same line or space, to lower its pitch by a half step (semitone). Any sharps or flats affect all the notes of the same pitch within the bar. A natural sign (♮) on the same line or space is used to cancel the previous sharp or flat.

KEY SIGNATURES

The key of a piece of music determines the main notes that will be included in it. In music notation a key signature is written at the beginning of every line of music to indicate the key. Key signatures make music easier to read because any sharps or flats in the key need only be written at the start of each line and will then apply to all those notes throughout the piece, rather than needing to write a sharp or flat sign every time such a note occurs. Each major key has a unique key signature, consisting of a collection of sharps or flats written in a set order; these sharps and flats match those that occur in the major scale for that key. The key of C major is unusual in that no sharps or flats occur in the keyscale, and therefore the key signature is blank.

Minor keys share key signatures with their relative major keys (i.e. major keys that have a keynote three half steps higher than the minor key).

Sharp key signatures

F major D minor | B♭ major D minor | E♭ major C minor | A♭ major F minor | D♭ major D minor | G♭ major E♭ minor

Flat key signatures

FRETBOXES

See page 20 for a description of fretboxes.

Section One: The Basics

MAJOR SCALES

By far the most important scale in music is the major scale. All other scales, and even all chords, can be considered as stemming from the major scale. The major scale is used as the basis for the majority of popular melodies. When used in lead playing it gives a bright and melodic sound.

SCALE CONSTRUCTION

The major scale is constructed by using a combination of whole steps/whole tones (W) and half steps/semitones (H). Regardless of the key, the pattern of tones and semitones is as follows: W W H W W W H.

For example, the C major scale, is constructed as follows:

- **C** plus a **whole** step = **D**
- **D** plus a **whole** step = **E**
- **E** plus a **half** step = **F**
- **F** plus a **whole** step = **G**
- **G** plus a **whole** step = **A**
- **A** plus a **whole** step = **B**
- **B** plus a **half** step = **C**

▲ *C major scale.*

TRANSPOSING SCALES

All the scales illustrated in this chapter are 'transpositional': they can be played in other keys simply by starting the finger pattern at a different fret. For example, to play the D major

▲ *D major scale.*

Complete Guitar Handbook

scale, use the exact fingering shown for C major but start two frets higher. For some keys, for example G major, you might prefer to start the scale pattern on the low E string in order to avoid high fingerboard positions.

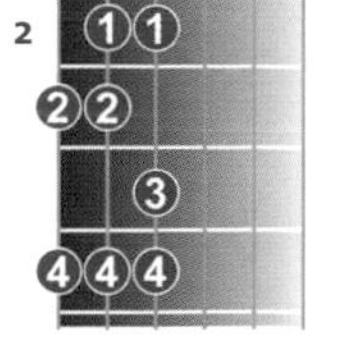

▲ G major scale.

PENTATONIC MAJOR SCALE

The term 'pentatonic' means 'five-note'; the pentatonic major scale is a five-note abbreviation of the standard major scale, with the fourth and seventh degrees of the major scale omitted. For example, the notes in the C major scale are C D E F G A B. To convert this into the C pentatonic major scale omit the notes F (the 4th) and B (the 7th), resulting in C D E G A.

The pentatonic major scale has none of the overtly sugary sound often associated with the standard major scale – instead it has a great combination of brightness with a cutting edge. It is a very useful scale for improvising in major keys; because it contains fewer notes than the standard major scale there is less chance of any of the notes clashing with the accompanying chords.

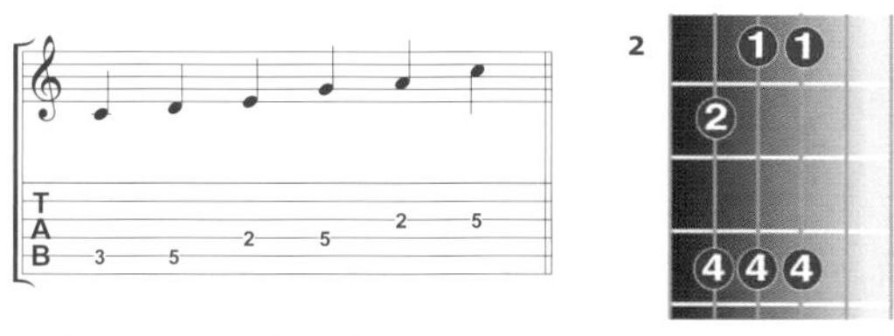

▲ C pentatonic major scale.

Traditionally, pentatonic major scales have been used in country music, but many rock bands – from the Rolling Stones and Free to Travis and Supergrass – have used them frequently on their recordings.

Brit Rock bands were great fans of the pentatonic major scale, particularly Noel Gallagher, who relied on them almost exclusively for his solos on the first few Oasis albums. Some of its greatest exponents were country rock players like Danny Gatton (1945–94) and Albert Lee (b. 1943).

Section One: The Basics

MINOR SCALES

There is a variety of minor scales to suit all musical styles, from the soulful natural minor scale to the exotic harmonic minor scale. But it is the rock-edged pentatonic minor scale that is by far the most widely used scale in lead guitar playing.

NATURAL MINOR SCALE

The natural minor scale is constructed using a combination of whole steps/tones (W) and half steps/semitones (H) in the following pattern: W H W W H W W. For example, C natural minor scale, is constructed as follows:

C plus a **whole** step = D
D plus a **half** step = E♭
E♭ plus a **whole** step = F
F plus a **whole** step = G
G plus a **half** step = A♭
A♭ plus a **whole** step = B♭
B♭ plus a **whole** step = C

▲ *C natural minor scale.*

The interval spelling for the natural minor scale is 1 2 ♭3 4 5 ♭6 ♭7 8, meaning that, in comparison to the major scale with the same keynote, the third, sixth and seventh notes are flattened by a half step. The natural minor scale is widely used in rock and blues based music. The scale has a soulful, yet melodic sound. Carlos Santana and Gary Moore (b. 1952) are two of its best-known exponents.

PENTATONIC MINOR SCALE

In all forms of rock music, the pentatonic minor scale is the most commonly used scale for lead guitar playing. The interval spelling is 1 ♭3 4 5 ♭7 8. It is a popular scale for improvising in minor keys because it contains fewer notes than the natural minor scale – this makes the scale easy to use and means that there is

Complete Guitar Handbook

little chance of any of the notes clashing with the accompanying chords.

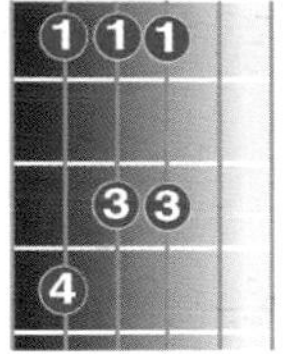

▲ *C pentatonic minor scale.*

HARMONIC MINOR SCALE

The harmonic minor scale is very similar to the natural minor scale. The only difference is that, in the harmonic minor scale, the note on the seventh degree is raised by a half step. This results in a large interval between the sixth and seventh degrees of the scale, giving the scale its distinctive, exotic sound. The interval spelling is 1 2 ♭3 4 5 ♭6 7 8. Ritchie Blackmore (b. 1945) was one of the first rock guitarists to exploit the melodic potential of this scale.

▲ *C harmonic minor scale.*

MELODIC MINOR SCALE

The step pattern of this scale alters depending on whether it is being played ascending or descending. When played descending it has the same notes as the natural minor scale; when played ascending the sixth and seventh degrees are each raised by a half step. The interval spelling is 1 2 ♭3 4 5 6 7 8 ascending and 1 2 ♭3 4 5 ♭6 ♭7 8 descending. The scale is mostly used in jazz-rock and fusion.

▲ *C melodic minor scale ascending.*

JAZZ MELODIC MINOR SCALE

The jazz melodic minor scale is the same as the ascending version of the standard melodic minor scale. The sixth and seventh degrees of the scale are raised by a half step in comparison to the natural minor scale, giving it a much brighter tonality that is well suited to some forms of jazz music. The interval spelling is 1 2 ♭3 4 5 6 7 8.

Section One: The Basics

FURTHER SCALES

Expanding your knowledge of scales beyond the common major and minor scales will broaden your musical vocabulary, enabling you to play lead guitar in a wide range of musical styles. A grasp of a broad collection of scales will also facilitate improvisation over complex chord progressions.

BLUES SCALE

The blues scale contains all the notes of the pentatonic minor scale, but with the addition of a ♭5 note. It is this note that gives the blues scale its distinctive blues flavour. All blues lead guitar playing uses the blues scale as its foundation. The interval spelling of the blues scale is 1 ♭3 4 ♭5 5 ♭7. C blues scale contains the notes C E♭ F G♭ G B♭.

▲ *C blues scale.*

3
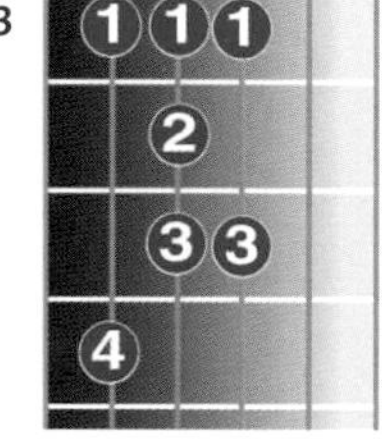

CHROMATIC SCALE

This scale contains every half step between the starting note and the octave. It is the only 12-note scale in music and does not relate to any particular key. Instead, when improvising, notes from the chromatic scale can be added to introduce notes that are not in the key of the backing. Including these 'outside' notes as chromatic passing notes within a lead guitar solo can help provide moments of harmonic tension.

▲ *C chromatic scale.*

Complete Guitar Handbook

COUNTRY SCALE

The country scale contains all the notes of the pentatonic major scale, but with the addition of a minor 3rd note. This gives it a slightly bluesy edge that suits 'new country' and 'country rock' guitar styles. The interval spelling is 1 2 ♭3 3 5 6 8.

▲ *C country scale.*

DIMINISHED SCALES

These are eight-note scales comprising alternating whole-step and half-step intervals. Diminished scales can start either with a whole step or a half step. Diminished scales that start with a whole step are described as whole/half diminished scales. These are generally used to improvise over diminished seventh chords. The interval spelling is 1 2 ♭3 4 ♭5 ♭6 ♭♭7 7 8. Diminished scales that start with a half step are described as half/whole diminished scales. These are widely used in jazz and fusion to create a sense of musical tension and colour when improvising over dominant seventh chords. The interval spelling is 1 ♭2 ♯2 3 ♯4 5 6 ♭7 8.

▲ *C whole/half diminished scale.*

▲ *C half/whole diminished scale.*

WHOLE-TONE SCALE

The whole-tone scale is constructed using only whole steps. Between any note and its octave there are six whole steps, therefore the whole-tone scale contains six different notes. Whole-tone scales are rarely used as key scales, but instead tend to be used for improvising over dominant altered chords (such as 7♯5). The interval spelling is 1 2 3 ♯4 ♯5 ♭7 8.

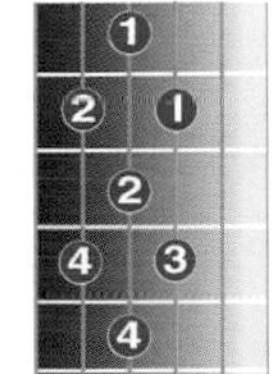

▲ *C whole tone scale.*

Section One: The Basics

MODES

Modes are scales that are formed by taking the notes of an existing scale but starting from a note other than the original keynote. This results in each mode having a unique tonality. The most common modes played on the guitar are those of the major scale, in particular the Dorian, Lydian and Mixolydian modes.

DORIAN MODAL SCALE

Taking the notes of the major scale starting from its second degree creates the Dorian modal scale. For example, the notes of the B♭b major scale are B♭ C D E♭ F G A B♭. The second note in the B♭ major scale is C, so the C Dorian modal scale contains the notes C D E♭ F G A B♭ C. The interval spelling is 1 2 ♭3 4 5 6 ♭7 8.

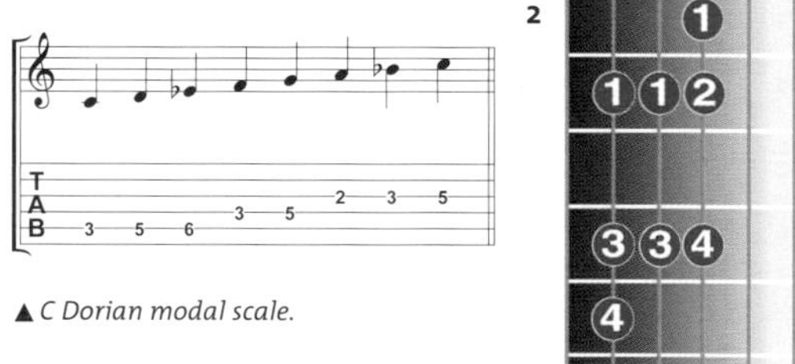

▲ *C Dorian modal scale.*

Even though the B♭ major scale and the C Dorian mode derived from it contain the same notes, they have a very different sound and character. For example, the major scale has a major third interval from the first to the third note and a major seventh interval from the first to the seventh note. In contrast, the Dorian modal scale contains minor third and minor seventh intervals – making it a type of 'minor' scale. Compared to the natural minor scale, the Dorian modal scale has a brighter, less melancholic, sound and is often used in funk, soul and jazz styles.

LYDIAN MODAL SCALE

The Lydian modal scale has a laid-back sound that is well-suited to jazz, fusion and soul music. The mode is formed by taking the notes of the major scale starting from its fourth degree. For example, the notes of the G major scale are

Complete Guitar Handbook

G A B C D E F♯ G. The fourth note in the G major scale is C, so the Lydian modal scale that is generated from the G major scale is the C Lydian modal scale – comprising the notes C D E F♯ G A B C. The interval spelling is 1 2 3 ♯4 5 6 7 8.

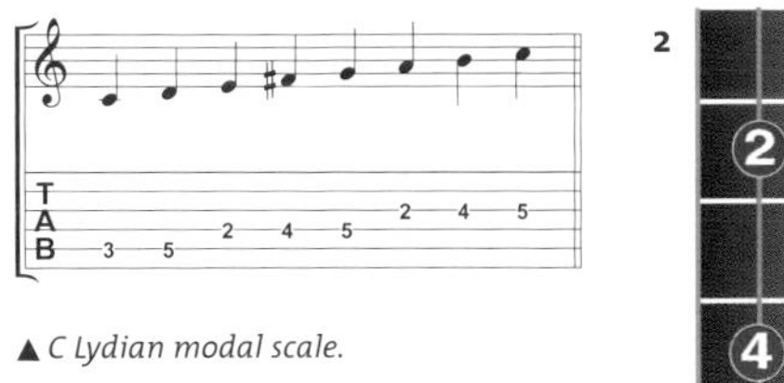

▲ C Lydian modal scale.

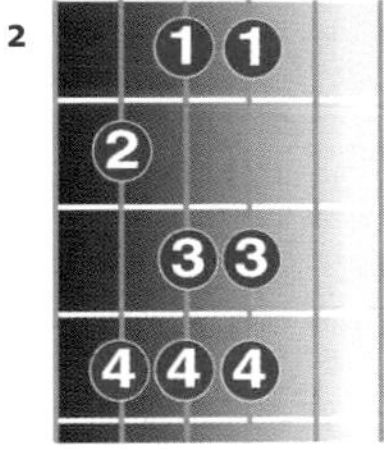

You might notice that when compared to the 'tonic major' (the major scale with the same starting note) the only difference is the inclusion of the ♯4 note in the Lydian modal scale.

MIXOLYDIAN MODAL SCALE

The Mixolydian modal scale is used in blues and rock music. It is formed by taking the notes of the major scale starting from its fifth degree. For example, the notes of the F major scale are F G A B♭ C D E F. The fifth note in the F major scale is C, so the Mixolydian modal scale that is generated from the F major scale is the C Mixolydian modal scale – comprising the notes C D E F G A B♭ C. The interval spelling is 1 2 3 4 5 6 ♭7 8.

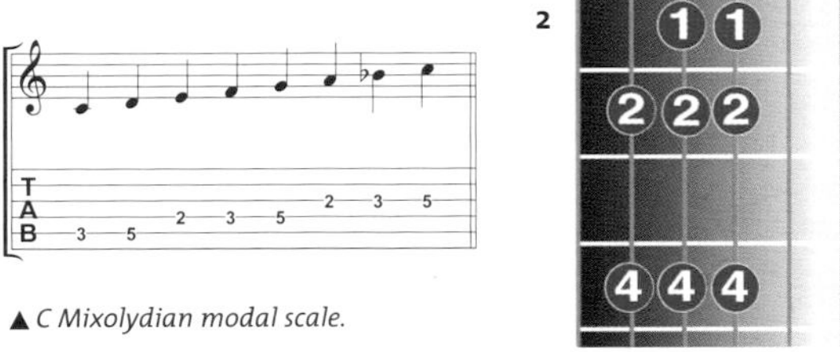

▲ C Mixolydian modal scale.

When compared to the 'tonic major' (the major scale with the same starting note) the only difference is the inclusion of the ♭7 note in the Mixolydian modal scale. This gives the scale a bluesy, yet melodic, sound.

Tip

The Ionian modal scale is an alternative name for the major scale, and the Aeolian modal scale is another name for the natural minor scale.

Section One: The Basics

FURTHER MODES

Learning some of the more esoteric modal scales can be a useful method of making your playing more individual. It can lead you to investigate musical styles and create sounds that you might otherwise leave unexplored; your playing might begin to include elements of Spanish flamenco or avant-garde jazz that you'd never even dreamed of.

PHRYGIAN MODAL SCALE

The Phrygian modal scale is quite unusual in that it starts with a half-step interval between the first two degrees. This gives it a typically Spanish flamenco sound. The scale is formed by taking the notes of the major scale starting from the third degree. For example, the notes of the A♭ major scale are A♭ B♭ C D♭ E♭ F G. The third note in the A♭ major scale is C, so the Phrygian modal scale that is generated from the A♭ major scale is the C Phrygian modal scale – comprising the notes C D♭ E♭ F G A♭ B♭ C. The interval spelling is 1 ♭2 ♭3 4 5 ♭6 ♭7 8.

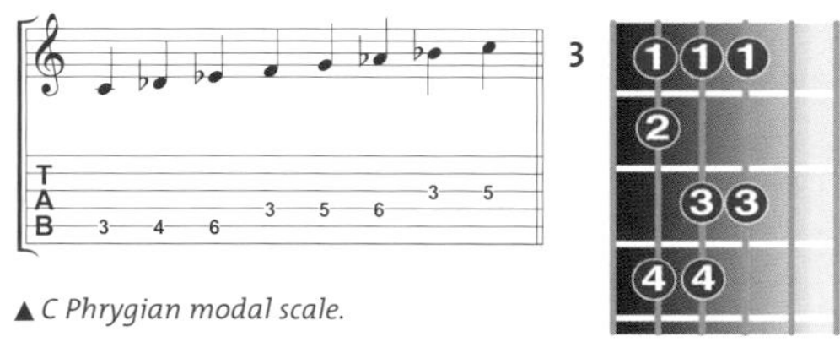

▲ *C Phrygian modal scale.*

PHRYGIAN MAJOR MODAL SCALE

The Phrygian major modal scale is actually the fifth mode of the harmonic minor scale, but it can be considered as a variation of the Phrygian modal scale: all the notes are the same except that

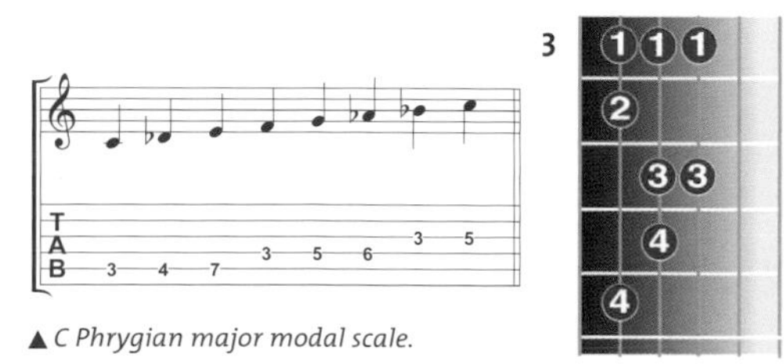

▲ *C Phrygian major modal scale.*

Complete Guitar Handbook

the Phrygian major modal scale contains a major (rather than flattened) third. The interval spelling is 1 ♭2 3 4 5 ♭6 ♭7 8.

As well as flamenco, it is commonly used in heavy metal guitar styles.

LOCRIAN MODAL SCALE

▲ *C Locrian modal scale.*

The Locrian modal scale is the mode that starts on the seventh degree of the major scale. For example, C is the 7th note in the scale of D♭ major, so the Locrian modal scale that is generated from the D♭ major scale is the C Locrian modal scale. The C note becomes the keynote of the Locrian modal scale and the remaining notes in the D♭ major scale make up the rest of the C Locrian modal scale. The interval spelling is 1 ♭2 ♭3 4 ♭5 ♭6 ♭7 8.

The Locrian modal scale is a minor scale with a diminished tonality, making it well suited for improvising over half-diminished chords.

LYDIAN DOMINANT MODAL SCALE

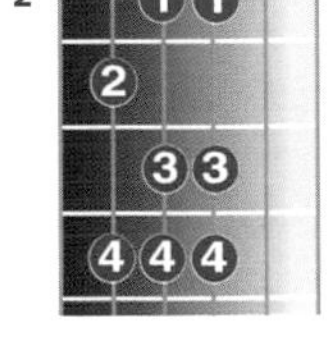

▲ *C Lydian dominant modal scale.*

The Lydian dominant modal scale is actually the fourth mode of the jazz melodic minor scale. However, the scale is often referred to as the Lydian ♭7 modal scale. This is because, apart from containing a ♭7 interval, it comprises the same notes as the Lydian modal scale. The interval spelling is 1 2 3 ♯4 5 6 ♭7 8.

The scale is mostly used in jazz and fusion styles.

Tip

Modes can be treated as key centres in their own right, with a group of chords to accompany each modal scale. Alternatively, modes can be used as chord scales – using a different mode over each chord.

Section One: The Basics

PITCH

In this chapter, scales have been shown with a starting note of C. You can alter the pitch of any scale easily by starting the same finger pattern at a different fret. However, you may need to change the fingering for each scale to play it in a higher or lower octave – or simply in a different fingerboard position.

FINGERBOARD POSITIONS

One of the interesting things about the guitar fingerboard is that the same note can be played at exactly the same pitch in several different places on the fingerboard.

If you play through the example to the right, you'll notice that each E note, although at exactly the same pitch, has a slightly different tonal quality. The same applies to scales and riffs – they will have a slightly different tone depending upon the chosen fingerboard position. You will also find that some riffs or licks might be easier to play in one fingerboard position compared to another.

TAB: 0 – 5 – 9 – 14 – 19

▲ *The note of E can be played at exactly the same pitch in five different fingerboard positions.*

If you're really serious about studying the guitar, you should make it a long-term aim to learn as many different fingerboard positions as possible for all your scales, because this will provide you with the maximum amount of flexibility in your playing.

Complete Guitar Handbook

To start you on your way, here are three positions of the C major scale – all at the same pitch.

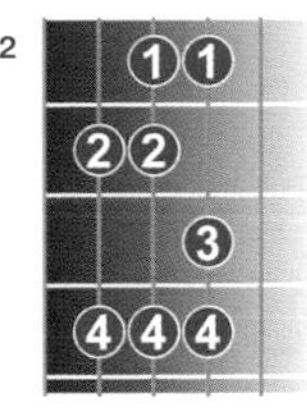

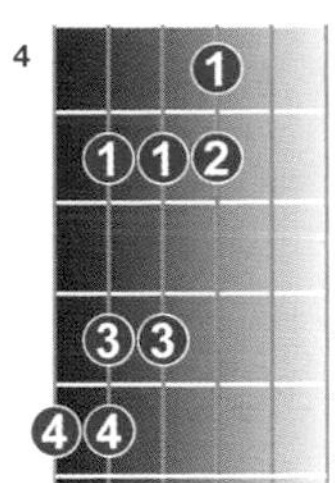

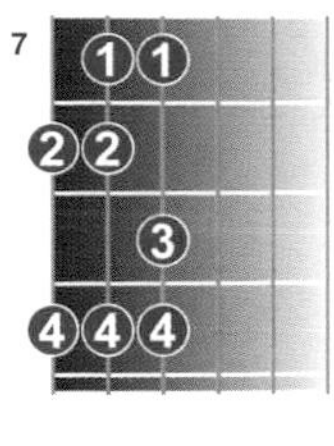

CHANGING OCTAVE

As well as learning scales of the same pitch in different fingerboard positions, you also need to be able to play them in different octaves. This will give you a wider sonic range to play across – from deep bassy riffs to high-pitched screaming solos. This fingerboard knowledge will help you play sympathetically with other elements in a song, for example, playing in a range that will merge well with the vocals or other instruments in some sections of the song, while moving to an octave that will make the guitar jump out of the mix in other sections.

Practising scales in a variety of fingerboard positions and octaves will help you develop a good knowledge of the location of notes on the fingerboard; this in turn will enable you to target notes to match with the chord structure when improvising.

Ideally you should aim to develop a practise regime that will enable you, over a period of time, to learn all the scales in this book in all keys and in all possible octaves and fingerboard positions.

As a starting point, the fretboard diagrams below show the same C major scale that is illustrated above, but this time in a higher octave and in five different fingerboard positions.

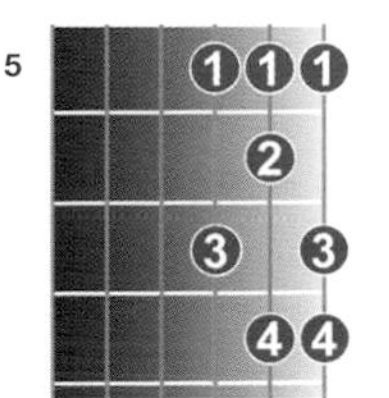

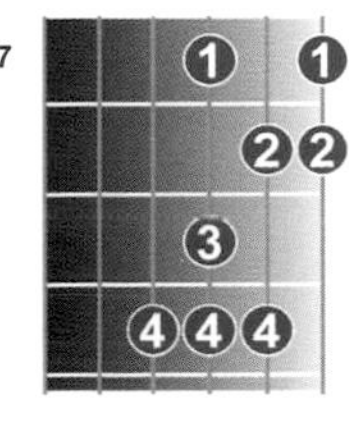

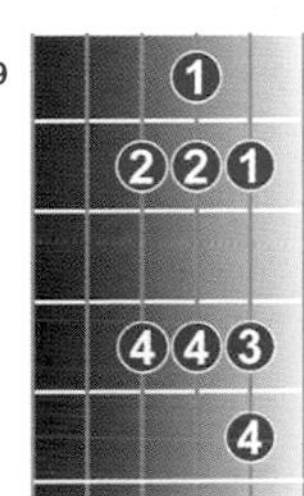

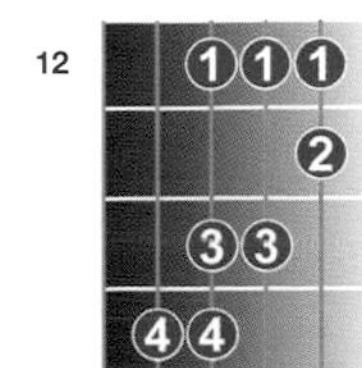

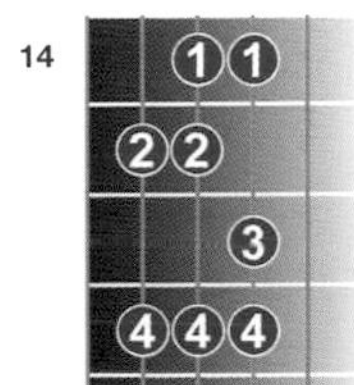

Section One: The Basics

CHORDS AND TUNINGS

INTRODUCTION

Knowledge of a wide range of chord types will enable you to play songs from almost any musical genre, and will provide a platform for writing your own songs. Understanding the music theory behind chord construction means that you'll be able to explore chord fingerings that suit your playing style, without reliance on a chord book.

EXPLORING CHORDS

While some players prefer the simplicity of sticking to common major and minor chords, others have made their music unique by exploring the range of chordal variations that can be played on the guitar. Some of the most experimental chord players include Barney Kessel (1923–2004), Pat Metheny (b. 1954), Peter Buck, Johnny Marr (b. 1963), Joe Pass (1929–94) and John McLaughlin (b. 1942).

◀ *Peter Buck provides the complex chordal structure that's integral to REM's sound.*

CHORD FINGERINGS

Because the guitar has a three to four octave range, and some notes can be played at exactly the same pitch in several fingerboard positions, the harmonic possibilities on the instrument are almost endless: even simple major or minor chords can be played in numerous fingerboard positions – each with a multitude of possible fingerings. It's important to remember this, because no instruction books will have space to illustrate all the possible fingering options available for every chord type. Therefore,

Complete Guitar Handbook

gaining an understanding of how chords are formed will allow you to devise your own chord fingerings – using shapes that suit your fingers and that work well with the other chord shapes you're playing in the song. Often you'll find that, rather than having to jump around the fingerboard to play the next chord in a song, you can devise an alternative fingering near to the previous chord.

BUILDING CHORDS

Although there are dozens of different chord types that exist in music, all of them stem from the basic major and minor triads (illustrated on pages 68–71). Once you have a good knowledge of the basic triads and an understanding of chord construction you'll realize that all other chords are merely extensions or variations of these foundation chord types.

TUNINGS

Using alternative tunings opens up a whole new world of harmonic possibilities on the guitar. You'll be able to discover chords that might be difficult or even impossible to play in standard tuning, yet which fall easily under the fingers in a new tuning. Of course, the main disadvantage is that none of the chord or scale shapes you've learnt in standard tuning will produce the same results when played in a different tuning. This means that a lot of effort will have to be put into exploring the possibilities of any new tuning – but, given the tremendous musical potential, you might just decide it's worth it (see pages 78–79).

▶ *Johnny Marr adds texture to his playing by making full use of a huge variety of chords.*

Section One: The Basics

INTERVALS

Intervals are the spaces between notes from the major scale, or other scales. Chords are constructed by combining various intervals. The name of a chord is often based upon the largest interval contained within that chord.

MAJOR SECOND

A major second is the interval from the first to the second note of the major scale (e.g. in the key of C, from C to D).

If you play the major second note an octave higher it forms a major ninth interval. This interval is included in all major, minor and dominant ninth chords.

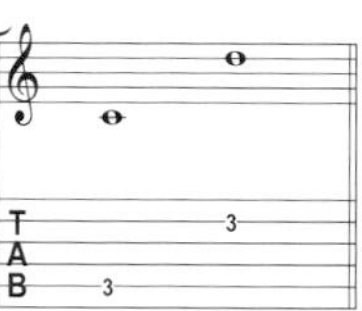

MAJOR THIRD

A major third is the interval from the first to the third note of the major scale (e.g. in the key of C, from C to E). This interval is important in that it defines the tonality of a chord; a chord that is constructed with a major third interval from its root note will always be a type of major chord.

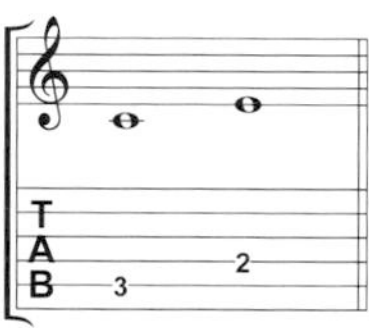

If you lower the major third interval by a half step it becomes a minor third. Just as the major third interval determines that a chord has a major tonality, the minor third interval determines that a chord is minor.

PERFECT FOURTH

A perfect fourth is the interval from the first to the fourth note of the major scale (e.g. in the key of C, from C to F).

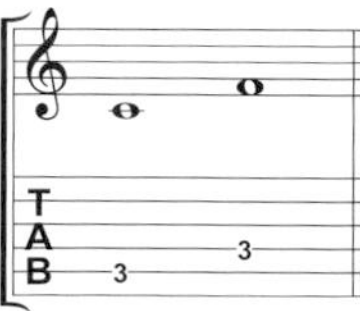

Complete Guitar Handbook

PERFECT FIFTH

A perfect fifth is the interval from the first to the fifth note of the major scale (e.g. in the key of C, from C to G). The perfect fifth occurs in nearly all chords, apart from diminished or augmented chords.

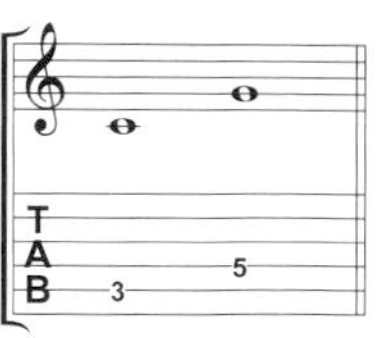

If you lower the perfect fifth interval by a half step it becomes a diminished (flattened) fifth. This interval occurs in diminished chords and any chords labeled with a flattened fifth note.

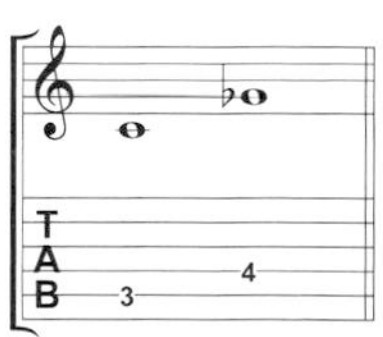

If you raise the perfect fifth interval by a half step it becomes an augmented (sharpened) fifth. This interval occurs in augmented chords and any chords labeled with a sharpened fifth note.

MAJOR SIXTH

A major sixth is the interval from the first to the sixth note of the major scale (e.g. in the key of C, from C to A). The major sixth occurs in both major and minor sixth chords.

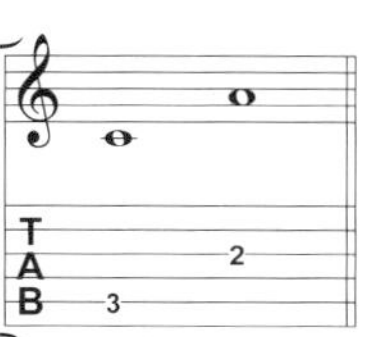

If you add an octave to a major sixth it becomes a major 13th interval. This interval is used in all 13th chords.

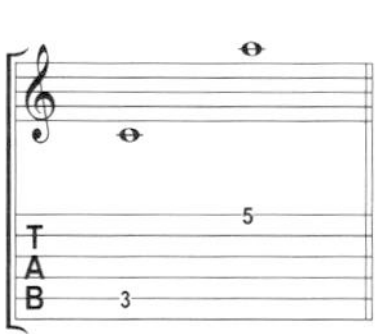

MAJOR SEVENTH

A major seventh is the interval from the first to the seventh note of the major scale (e.g. in the key of C, from C to B). The major seventh interval occurs in major seventh chords.

If you lower the major seventh interval by a half step it becomes a minor seventh. This interval occurs in both minor seventh and dominant seventh chords.

Section One: The Basics

MAJOR TRIADS

Chords that contain three different notes are known as 'triads'. All standard major chords are triads. All other chords, no matter how elaborate, can be considered simply as variations or extensions of these triads. Therefore, learning all the major triads will provide a firm foundation for learning any other chords.

	C Major Scale	C Major Triad
1	**C**	C
2	D	
3	**E**	E
4	F	
5	**G**	G
6	A	
7	B	
8	C	

The first, third and fifth notes of the major scale make up a major triad. For example, the C major triad is formed by taking the first, third and fifth notes of the C major scale.

You can work out which notes are in any major triad by selecting the first, third and fifth notes from the major scale with the same starting note as the chord. This would give the following results:

Major Triads	Notes in Triad
C	C E G
G	G B D
D	D F♯ A
A	A C♯ E
E	E G♯ B
B	B D♯ F♯

Major Triads	Notes in Triad
F♯	F♯ A♯ C♯
F	F A C
B♭	B♭ D F
E♭	E♭ G B♭
A♭	A♭ C E♭
D♭	D♭ F A♭

Although major triads only contain three different notes, strumming three-string chords could result in quite a thin sound, so quite often major chords are played with

Complete Guitar Handbook

some of the notes doubled so that five or six strings can be strummed. For example, in this open position G major chord, the G note is played three times (on the sixth, third and first strings), the B note is played twice (on the fifth and second strings) and the D note is played once.

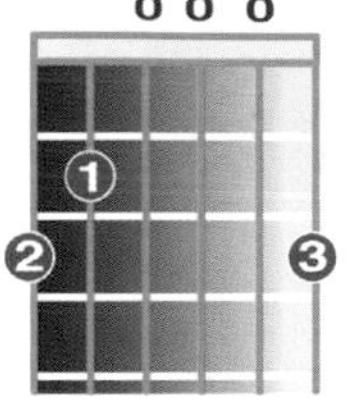

G G Major
1st (G), 3rd (B), 5th (D)

Now that you know the notes contained in each major triad you can devise as many different fingerings for each chord as you wish. To help you get started, there follows one fretbox example for each major triad. Other shapes are shown in the chord dictionary at the back of this book.

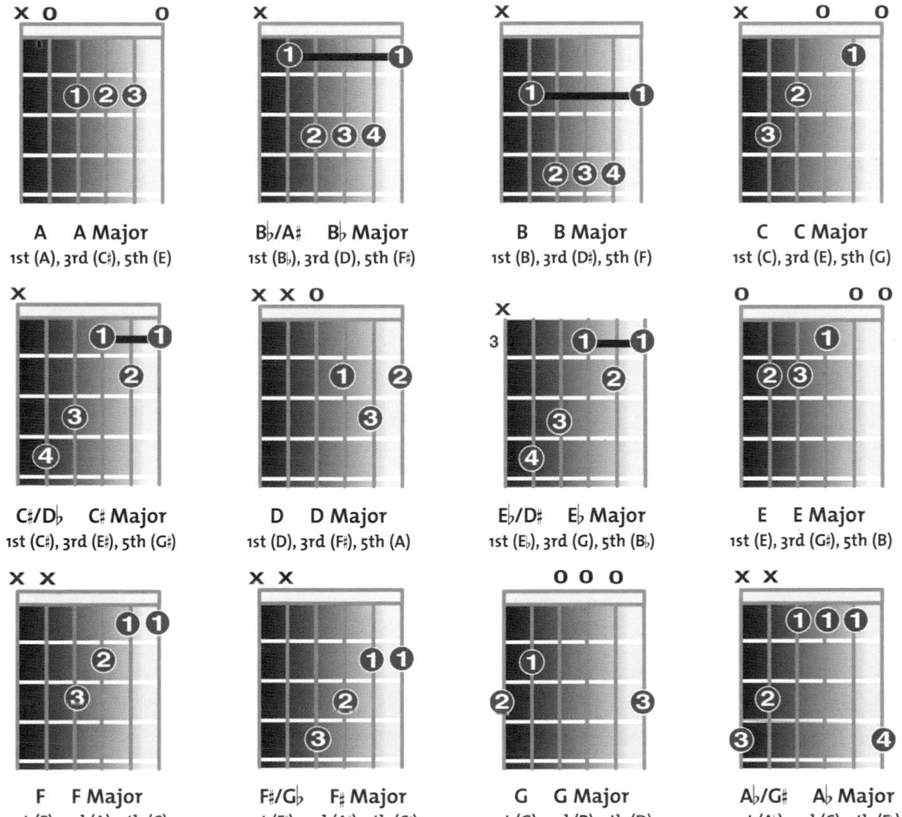

A A Major
1st (A), 3rd (C♯), 5th (E)

B♭/A♯ B♭ Major
1st (B♭), 3rd (D), 5th (F♯)

B B Major
1st (B), 3rd (D♯), 5th (F)

C C Major
1st (C), 3rd (E), 5th (G)

C♯/D♭ C♯ Major
1st (C♯), 3rd (E♯), 5th (G♯)

D D Major
1st (D), 3rd (F♯), 5th (A)

E♭/D♯ E♭ Major
1st (E♭), 3rd (G), 5th (B♭)

E E Major
1st (E), 3rd (G♯), 5th (B)

F F Major
1st (F), 3rd (A), 5th (C)

F♯/G♭ F♯ Major
1st (F♯), 3rd (A♯), 5th (C♯)

G G Major
1st (G), 3rd (B), 5th (D)

A♭/G♯ A♭ Major
1st (A♭), 3rd (C), 5th (E♭)

Section One: The Basics

MINOR TRIADS

Minor triads have a more mellow, mournful sound than major triads but, just like major triads, they also contain only three different notes. All other minor chords are built on the foundation of these minor triads, so learning at least the most common minor triads is essential for any rhythm guitar player.

	C Natural Minor Scale	C Minor Triad
1	**C**	**C**
2	D	
3	**E♭**	**E♭**
4	F	
5	**G**	**G**
6	A♭	
7	B♭	
8	C	

Minor triads contain the first, flattened third and fifth notes of the major scale. (The flattened third note can be found one fret lower than the major third note.) For example, the C minor triad contains the notes C E♭ and G. Taking the first, third and fifth notes from the natural minor scale will give the same results.

Major Triads	Notes in Triad
Am	A C E
Em	E G B
Bm	B D F♯
F♯m	F♯ A C♯
C♯m	C♯ E G♯
G♯m	G♯ B D♯

Major Triads	Notes in Triad
D♯m	D♯ F♯ A♯
Dm	D F A
Gm	G B♭ D
Cm	C E♭ G
Fm	F A♭ C
B♭m	B♭ D♭ F

You can work out which notes are in any minor triad by selecting the first, third and fifth notes from the natural minor scale with the same starting note as the chord.

Complete Guitar Handbook

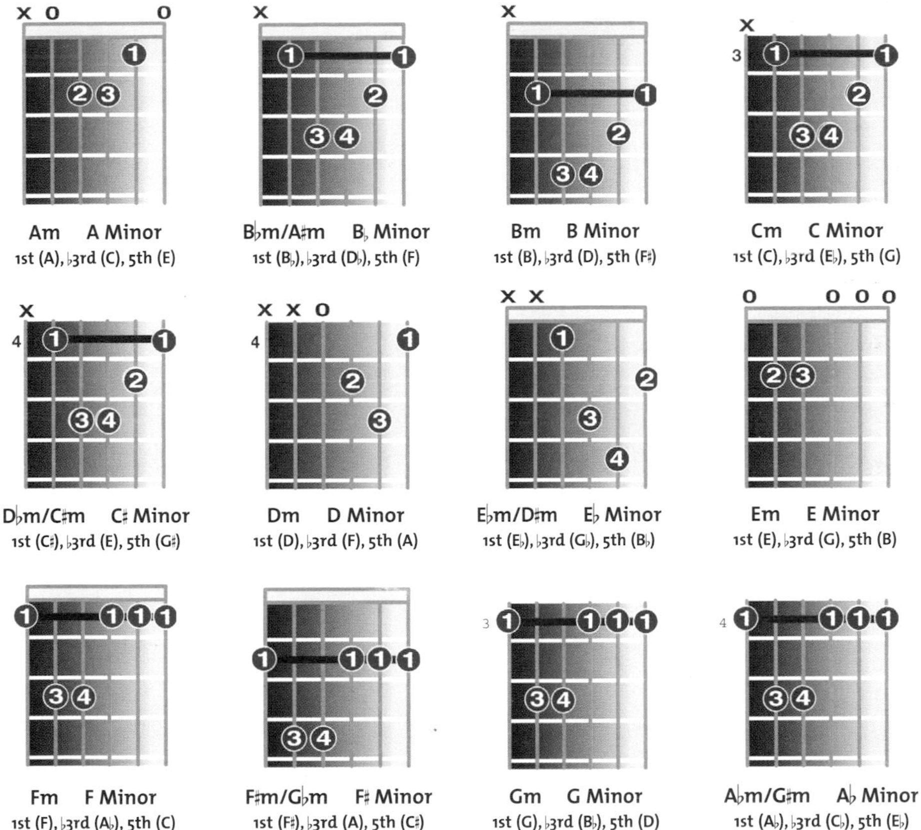

Am A Minor
1st (A), ♭3rd (C), 5th (E)

B♭m/A♯m B♭ Minor
1st (B♭), ♭3rd (D♭), 5th (F)

Bm B Minor
1st (B), ♭3rd (D), 5th (F♯)

Cm C Minor
1st (C), ♭3rd (E♭), 5th (G)

D♭m/C♯m C♯ Minor
1st (C♯), ♭3rd (E), 5th (G♯)

Dm D Minor
1st (D), ♭3rd (F), 5th (A)

E♭m/D♯m E♭ Minor
1st (E♭), ♭3rd (G♭), 5th (B♭)

Em E Minor
1st (E), ♭3rd (G), 5th (B)

Fm F Minor
1st (F), ♭3rd (A♭), 5th (C)

F♯m/G♭m F♯ Minor
1st (F♯), ♭3rd (A), 5th (C♯)

Gm G Minor
1st (G), ♭3rd (B♭), 5th (D)

A♭m/G♯m A♭ Minor
1st (A♭), ♭3rd (C♭), 5th (E♭)

Remember that although triads consist of only three different notes, you can repeat one of more of the notes when playing them as chords on the guitar.

OTHER TRIADS

As well as major and minor triads, there are other triads: diminished, augmented and suspended (see pages 72–75). There are also some chords, known as 'diads', that contain only two different notes (see 'Fifth Chords' page 73).

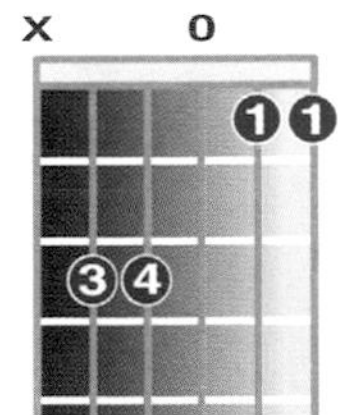

Csus4 C Suspended 4th
1st (C), 4th (F), 5th (G)

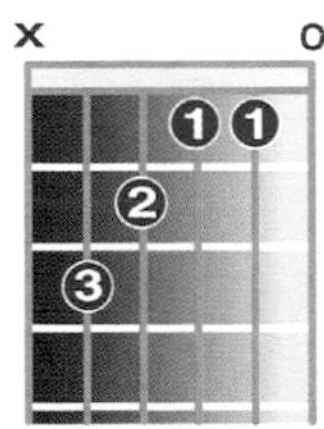

C+ C Augmented
1st (C), 3rd (E), ♯5th (G♯)

Section One: The Basics

CHORD CONSTRUCTION

Having studied the basic major and minor chords on the previous pages, the good news is that all other chords can be viewed as variations or extensions of these. To convert the basic triads into other chords, all that's normally required is to add to the triad a note from the major scale.

SIXTH CHORDS

To work out how to play any major sixth chord you just play through the major scale until you reach the sixth note in the scale. Find out the name of this note by counting up the fretboard and then add this note to the basic major triad – thereby converting it into a major sixth chord. For example, to play A major 6 (A6) you should add F♯ (the sixth note of the A major scale) to the A major chord. (You will find an F♯ note on the second fret of the first string.)

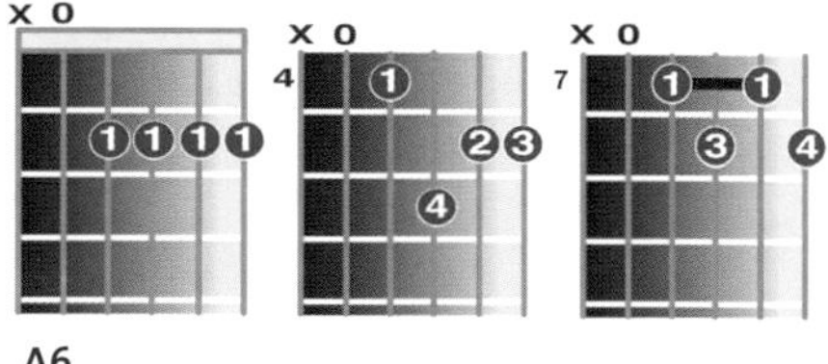

A6

Minor sixth chords are formed in the same way, by adding the sixth note of the major scale to the minor triad. Notice that you always use the major scale – even if the chord is minor!

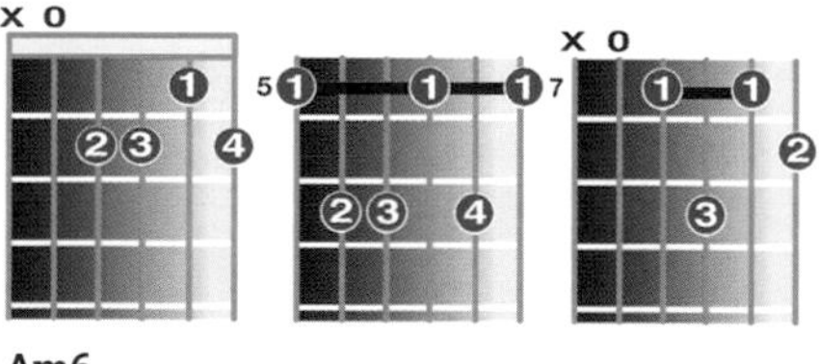

Am6

SEVENTH CHORDS

There are three main types of seventh chord: major seventh (maj7), dominant seventh (7) and minor seventh (m7). Only the major seventh chord uses the seventh note of the major scale; the other two types use the flattened seventh note of the scale.

Complete Guitar Handbook

The major seventh chord is formed by taking the basic major chord and adding the seventh note of the major scale to it. For example, Amaj7 comprises A C♯ E G♯.

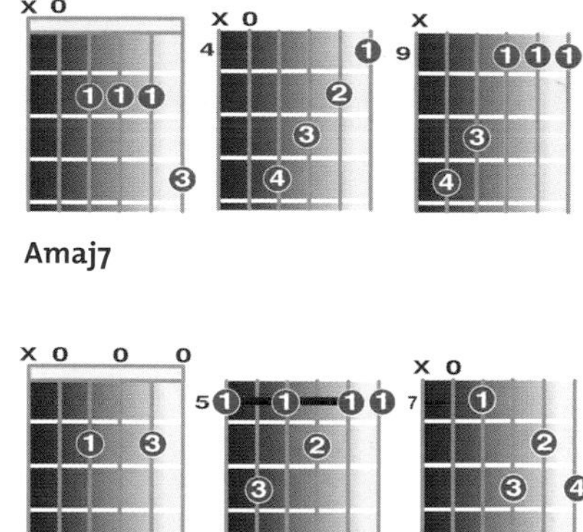

Amaj7

The dominant seventh chord is formed by taking the basic major chord and adding the flattened seventh note of the major scale to it. For example, A7 comprises A C♯ E G.

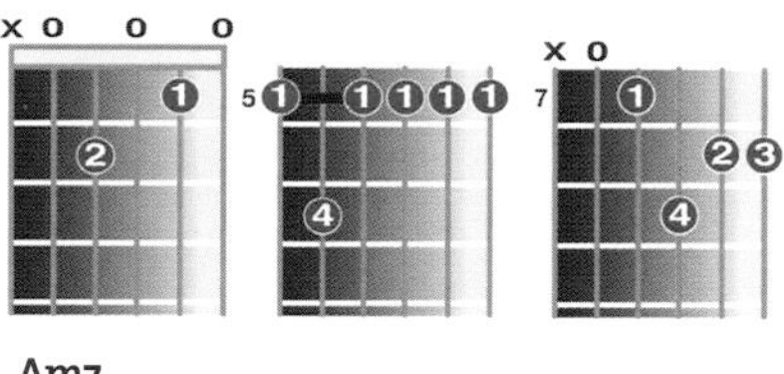

A7

The minor seventh chord is formed by taking the basic minor chord and adding the flattened seventh note of major scale to it. For example, Am7 comprises A C E G.

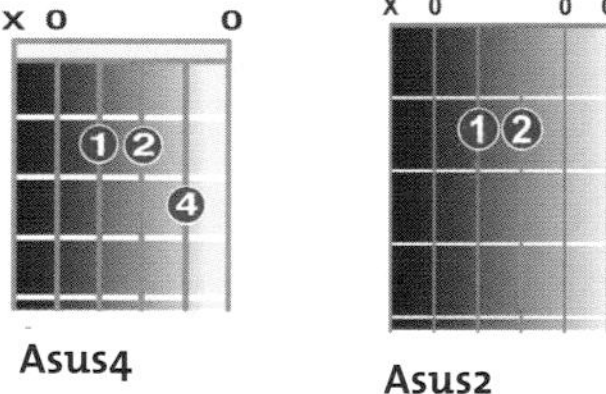

Am7

SUS CHORDS

Some chords are formed by replacing a note, rather than adding one. Sus chords are a good example of this, as the chord's third is replaced by the fourth note of the major scale in sus4 chords, and by the second note of the scale in sus2 chords. For example, Asus2 comprises A B E, and Asus4 comprises A D E.

Asus4

Asus2

Tip

When adding notes to chords, it's normally best if you can find the note on the first string before looking on the lower strings. Sometimes you might need to take a finger off a string to allow the new note to sound.

FIFTH CHORDS

Fifth chords, also known as 'power chords', are unusual in that they do not include a major or minor third. They consist only of the root note and the fifth. For example, A5 comprises A and E.

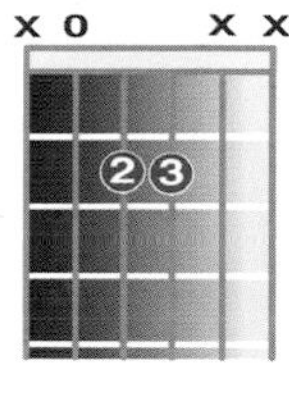

A5

Section One: The Basics

EXTENDED AND ALTERED CHORDS

Using extended chords, containing five or six notes, helps to create a rich sound and to extend your chordal vocabulary. Altered chords provide an ideal method of creating a sense of tension and adding harmonic dissonance to a chord progression.

EXTENDED CHORDS

Just as seventh chords are built by adding an extra note to a basic triad, extended chords are built by adding one or more extra notes to a seventh chord. The most common types of extended chords are ninths, 11ths and 13ths. Each can be played in either a major, minor or dominant form.

NINTH CHORDS

Major ninth chords are extensions of major seventh chords. They are formed by adding the ninth note of the major scale (with the same starting note) to a major seventh chord. The interval spelling is 1 3 5 7 9. For example, Cmaj9 contains the notes C E G B (the notes of Cmaj7) plus the note of D (the ninth note of the C major scale). Major ninth chords have a delicate sound that makes them highly suitable for use in ballads.

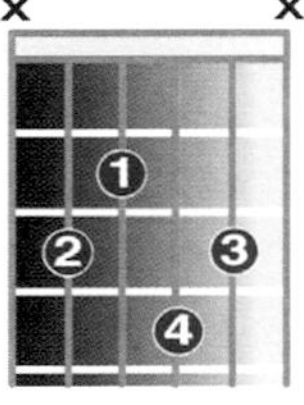

Cmaj9

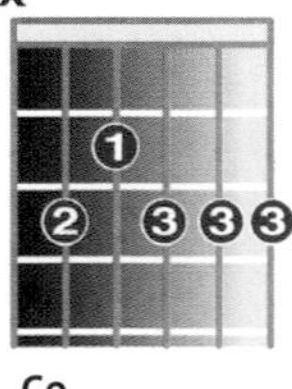

C9

Dominant ninth chords are formed by adding the ninth note of the major scale to a dominant seventh chord. For example, C9 contains the notes C E G B♭ (the notes of C7) plus D (the ninth note of the C major scale). The interval spelling is 1 3 5 ♭7 9. Dominant ninth chords have a rich, bluesy sound.

Complete Guitar Handbook

Minor ninth chords are extensions of minor seventh chords, formed by adding the ninth note of the major scale. For example, Cm9 contains C E♭ G B♭ (the notes of Cm7) plus D (the ninth note of the C major scale). The interval spelling is 1 ♭3 5 ♭7 9. Minor ninth chords have a suave, mellow sound and are often used in soul and funk music.

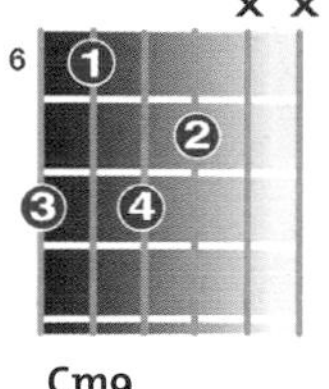

Cm9

ELEVENTH CHORDS

There are three main types of 11th chord as shown here. You'll notice that each incorporates some form of ninth chord, plus the 11th note of the major scale. In practise, the ninth note is normally omitted when playing 11th chords on the guitar.

Dominant 11th:	1 3 5 ♭7 9 11
Minor 11th:	1 ♭3 5 ♭7 9 11
Major 11th:	1 3 5 7 9 11

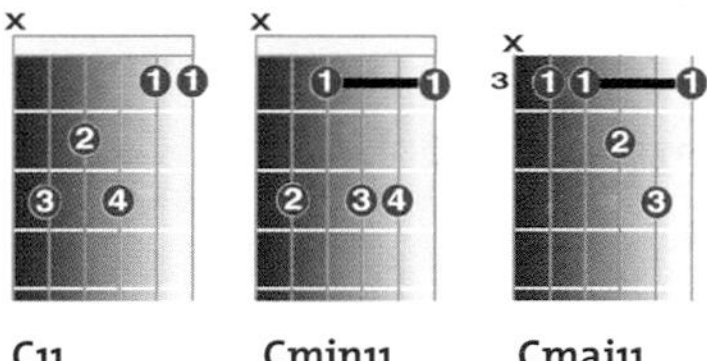

C11 Cmin11 Cmaj11

THIRTEENTH CHORDS

There are three main types of 13th chord, as shown in the table below. In practice, it is not possible to play all seven notes of a 13th chord on guitar, therefore some notes (normally the 9th, 11th and sometimes the 5th) are omitted.

Dominant 13th:	1 3 5 ♭7 9 11 13
Minor 13th:	1 ♭3 5 ♭7 9 11 13
Major 13th:	1 3 5 7 9 11 13

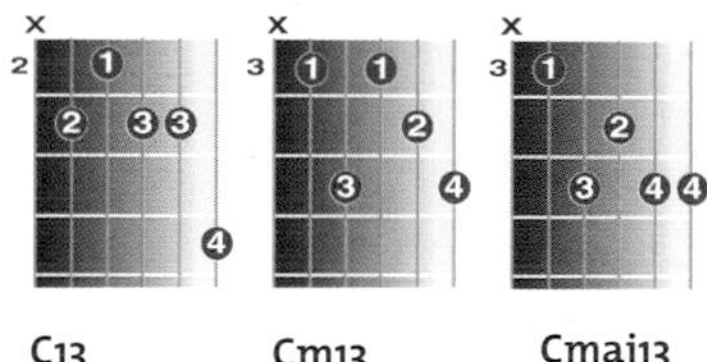

C13 Cm13 Cmaj13

ALTERED CHORDS

These are chords in which the fifth and/or ninth has been 'altered' – i.e. either raised or lowered by a half step. Altered chords are most commonly used in jazz. These are examples of commonly used altered chords. See the chord dictionary for sample chord fingerings.

Augmented triad: 1 3 ♯5	Dominant 7th ♭5: 1 3 ♭5 ♭7
Diminished triad: 1 ♭3 ♭5	Dominant 7th ♭9: 1 3 5 ♭7 ♭9
Diminished 7th chord: 1 ♭3 ♭5 ♭♭7	Dominant 7♯9: 1 3 5 ♭7 ♯9

Section One: The Basics

CHORD SUBSTITUTION

You can make your own interpretations of chords in a songbook by using chord inversions, embellishments and substitutions instead of the original chords. You can also use this approach when songwriting, by starting with a simple chord progression and turning it into something quite elaborate.

CHORD EMBELLISHMENT

Chord embellishment consists of varying a chord by substituting a note within it for a new note, or by adding an extra note. Whichever method is used, the new note should be taken from the 'key scale' of the chord: for example, you could add any note from the C major scale to the C major chord without changing the fundamental harmonic nature of the chord. By sticking to notes from the key scale, the new embellished chord can normally be used as a direct replacement for the simpler basic chord without causing any clashes with the melody of the song.

Chord embellishments are often easier to play than the basic major or minor chords. If you lift the finger off the first string when playing an open position D major chord shape, it will become a Dsus2 chord.

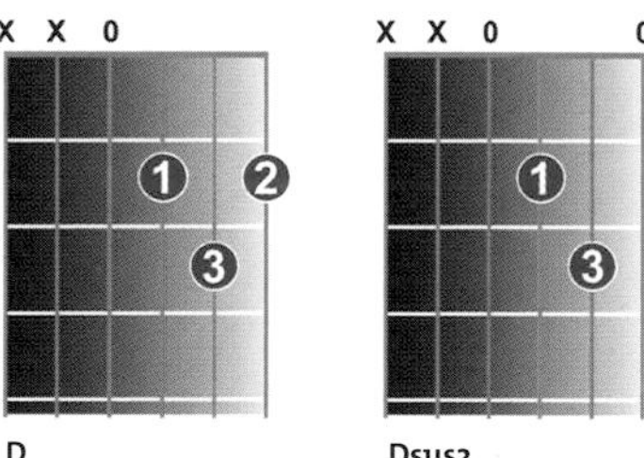

Adding an extra note to a chord is also an effective way of creating an embellishment. The ninth note of the major scale is often used, as this brings a certain warmth when added to a basic major chord.

The same approach can be taken with minor and dominant seventh chords. The table opposite gives examples of the most commonly used chord embellishments

Complete Guitar Handbook

– none of which will cause problems within an existing chord progression as the basic chord's harmonic nature will not be changed.

Basic Chord	Possible Embellishments
Major	major 6th, major 7th, major 9th add 9, sus2, sus4, major 6th add 9
Minor	minor 7th, minor 9th, sus2, sus4
Dominant 7th	dominant 9th, dominant 13th dominant 7th sus4

▲ *C major is extended to become Cadd9 by the addition of the ninth note, D.*

CHORD INVERSIONS

Rather than play every chord starting from its root note, you can play an 'inversion' by choosing another chord tone as the lowest note. There are three main types of inversion:

- First inversion: the third of the chord is played as the lowest note.
- Second inversion: the fifth of the chord is played as the lowest note.
- Third inversion: the extension of the chord is played as the lowest note.

Inversions are normally notated as 'slash chords': C/E is 'C major first inversion'.

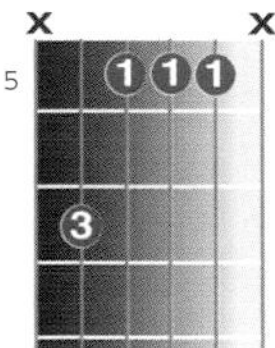

C/E (C major first inversion)

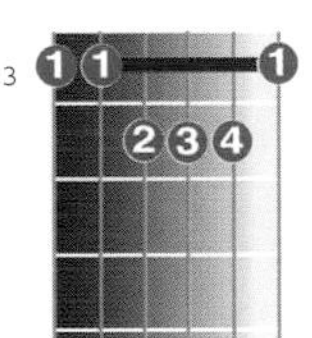

C/G (C major second inversion)

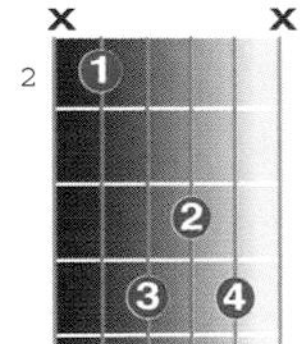

Cmaj7/B (C major seventh third inversion)

CHORD SUBSTITUTION

An interesting effect can be achieved by substituting one chord for another. Most commonly, a major chord can be replaced by its 'relative minor' (i.e. the minor chord with a root note three half steps lower). For example, A minor might be substituted in place of C major. Alternatively, a minor chord could be replaced by its 'relative major' (i.e. the major chord with a root note three half steps higher). For example, C major might be substituted in place of A minor.

Section One: The Basics

ALTERED TUNINGS

Discover a new range of beautiful chordal harmonies by simply tuning your guitar in a different way. If you sometimes start to feel restricted by sticking to the same chord shapes you've played before, then experimenting with alternative tunings is a great way of generating some fresh sounds and ideas.

DROPPED D TUNING

There are numerous ways in which a guitar can be retuned, but the simplest and most commonly used is 'dropped D tuning'. All you need to do is lower the pitch of the low E string by a whole step until it reaches the note of D (an octave lower than the open fourth string). You can check that you've retuned correctly by playing on the seventh fret of the sixth string and comparing the note to the open fifth string – they should produce exactly the same pitch.

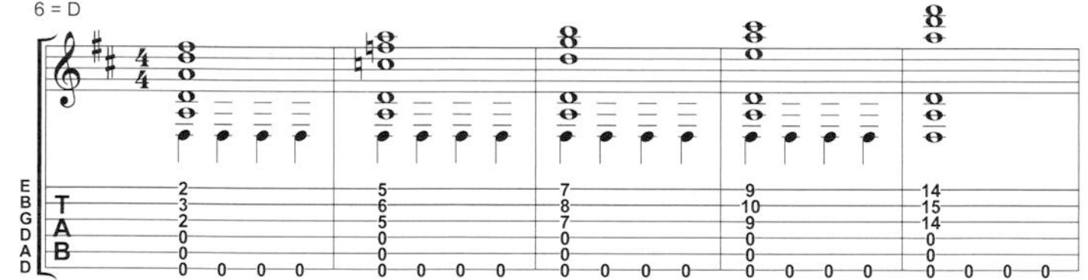

Dropped D tuning is perfect for playing songs in the keys of D major or D minor. Having the low D bass string is almost like having your own built-in bass player – it can add great solidity and power to your sound. To make the most of this bass effect many guitarists use the low D string as a 'drone' – i.e. they repeatedly play this low D note while moving chord shapes up and down the fingerboard. Moving a simple D major shape up the fingerboard while playing a low D drone gives a very effective sound.

D MODAL TUNING

Tuning the sixth, second and first strings down a whole step creates what is known as 'D modal tuning': D A D G A D. When you need to reach this tuning

Complete Guitar Handbook

unaided just remember that the A D and G strings are tuned as normal. Playing the open D string will give you the pitch for the lowered sixth string when it is played at the 12th fret. Playing the A string at the 12th fret will give you the pitch to tune the second string down to, and playing the D string at the 12th fret will give you the pitch to tune the first string down to. Once the guitar is correctly tuned it will give you a Dsus4 chord when the open strings are all strummed, thus creating instant ambiguity and a sense of interest. When first using this tuning, playing in the key of D will prove the easiest: by placing the first finger on the second fret of the G string you will make a nice deep-sounding D major (D5) chord. Traditional chord shapes will not work in the same way with any altered tuning, so it's really a case of experimenting to find chord sounds that you like. The secret is to be adventurous and see what ideas you can come up with when freed from the restrictions of conventional chord shapes.

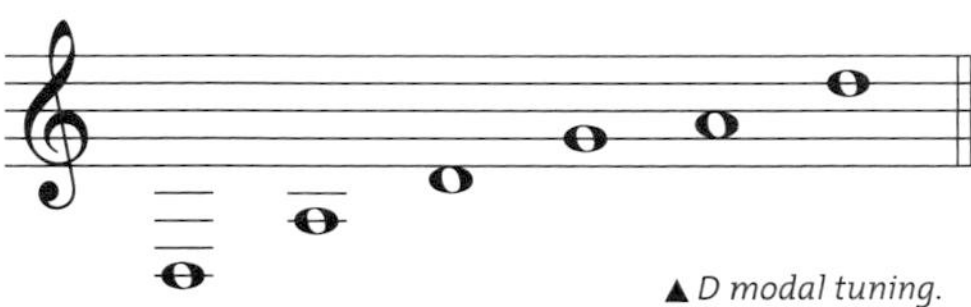

▲ *D modal tuning.*

OTHER TUNINGS

If the two altered tunings described above have given you the taste for experimentation, then here are a few other tunings you can try (all shown starting with the low sixth string).

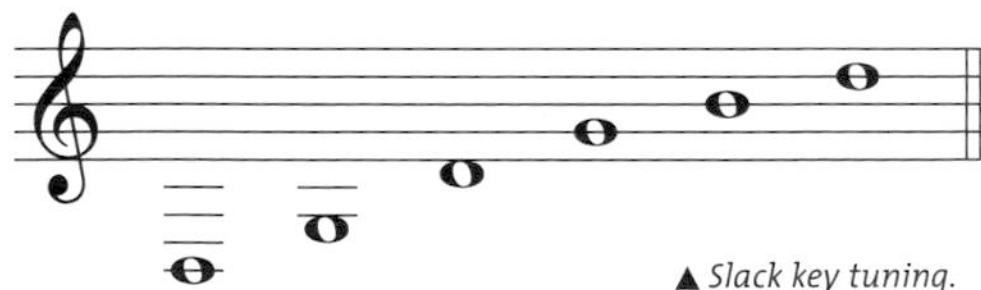

▲ *Slack key tuning.*

Slack key tuning – D G D G B D (the first, fifth and sixth strings are 'slackened' down a whole step to form a G major chord).

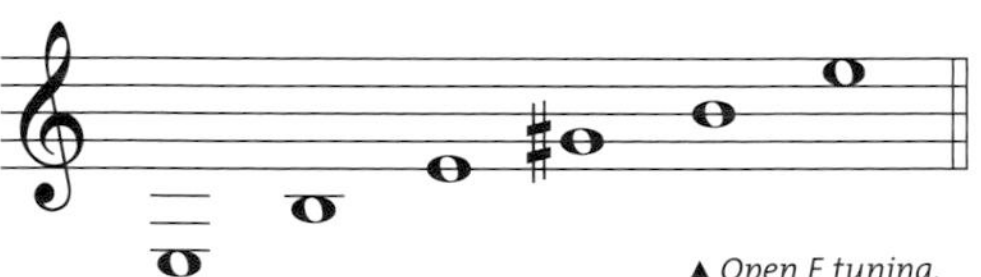

▲ *Open E tuning.*

Open E tuning – E B E G# B E (the third, fourth and fifth strings are tuned higher than normal to make an E major chord).

▲ *Open D tuning.*

Open D tuning – D A D F# A D (the first, second, third and sixth strings are tuned down so that the open strings form a D major chord).

Section One: The Basics

ESSENTIAL TECHNIQUES

INTRODUCTION

Once you've learnt the fundamentals of guitar playing, such as scales and chords, it's time to put these into action in a practical music-making setting. Applying specialist guitar techniques, such as string bending and vibrato, will enhance the sound of your performance and enable you to add your own individuality to both lead and rhythm playing.

LEAD TECHNIQUES

Throughout this chapter the most essential lead guitar techniques will be explained in some depth. Some of these techniques, such as hammer-ons and pull-offs, will help you develop fluency and smoothness in your playing. Others, such as vibrato and string bending, will enable you to make your lead playing more expressive and individual. Guitarists who are renowned for their skill in using string bends include David Gilmour (b. 1946), Gary Moore, Eric Clapton and Buddy Guy.

Blues guitarist B. B. King is widely acknowledged as the master of vibrato playing. Other guitarists who excel with this technique include Peter Green (b. 1946), Albert Collins (1932–93) and Paul Kossoff (1950–76).

► *Blues legend B. B. King uses a well-practised vibrato technique to add richness to his playing.*

Complete Guitar Handbook

An arpeggio is created by playing the notes contained within a chord individually rather than simultaneously. When playing licks or solos, arpeggios can provide just as important a role as scales, in fact, some players – such as Yngwie Malmsteen (b. 1963), Albert Lee and Mark Knopfler (b. 1941) – rely very heavily on arpeggios in their lead guitar playing.

▲ *Dave Davies (far left) used chords in the introductory riff of the Kinks' hit song 'You Really Got Me'.*

RHYTHM TECHNIQUES

Techniques that can make your rhythm guitar playing more creative and exciting are also covered in this chapter. These include topics such as using string damping as a method of extending the dynamic range of your rhythm playing, and playing riffs using chord shapes rather than just single notes. Listen to the guitar playing of Dave Davies of the Kinks (b. 1947), Mick Ronson (1946–93), Angus Young (b. 1953) and Paul Weller for some of the best examples of rhythm guitar techniques in action.

SPECIALIST TECHNIQUES

Exploring some advanced techniques, such as octave playing and harmonics, can really add range and variety to your playing. If your guitar is fitted with a tremolo arm, experimenting with this can lead to some interesting sonic discoveries. Compare the subtle use Hank Marvin (b. 1941) makes of the tremolo arm with the wild sounds made by Steve Vai (b. 1960) and Jeff Beck.

If you don't already own one, try to get hold of a bottleneck (slide). Using one of these will provide you with musical possibilities unobtainable through normal playing. Although their use originated in blues and country music, many rock players also regularly use slides as an alternative to their usual solo styles. Some great slide players include Duane Allman (1946–71), Ry Cooder (b. 1947), Muddy Waters (1915–83) and George Thorogood (b. 1950).

Section One: The Basics

CHANGING CHORDS

It's one thing to know some chord shapes, but it's a far more difficult skill to change fluently between them without leaving any gaps in between. Luckily, there are a few short cuts you can take to make your chord changes easier and faster.

MINIMUM MOVEMENT PRINCIPLE

It's essential that chord changes are crisp and prompt. This might not be too hard when using chords that you're very familiar with, but it can seem daunting with chords that are new to you. However, changing between any chords can be made much easier if you follow the 'minimum movement principle'. This involves making only the smallest finger movement necessary between chords, and avoiding taking fingers off strings or frets only to put them back on again for the next chord. Excess movement between chords is what slows chord changes down; the less your fingers move, the faster your chord changes will be.

	Am	F	Am	C	Am	E	Am
T	0	1	0	0	0	0	0
	1	1	1	1	1	0	1
A	2	2	2	0	2	1	2
	2	3	2	2	2	2	2
B	0		0	3	0	2	0
						0	

▲ *When moving from Am to F, keep the first finger on the second string first fret, but flatten it to cover the first string as well. Between Am and C only move the third finger; keep the others in place. Notice how E major is the same 'shape' as Am – just on different strings.*

Some chords have one or more notes in common. For example, the open position A minor and F major chords both include the note C (first fret on the B string). The C major chord also includes this note and, in addition, has another note in common with the A minor chord (E on the second fret of the D string). The chord progression shown above uses the chords Am, F, C and E: notice the common fingering between each

Complete Guitar Handbook

chord change; in particular, how the first finger stays on the first fret and how the second finger stays on the second fret throughout.

Even if different chords don't contain too many common notes, changing between them can still be made easier if you look out for any possible links. For example, when changing between the D and A major chords the third finger can be slid along the second string (between frets two and three) rather than being taken off the string only to be put back on a fret higher a moment later.

D A D Em D A D

▲ *Try to spot the common links between consecutive chord shapes. For example, between the D and A chords the third finger could just slide along the second string, while the first and second fingers move up or down across the strings.*

Following the principle of minimum movement saves time and makes the chord changes smoother. No matter how remote a chord change appears to be, there will always be some kind of link between the chords; once spotted, this will make changing between them easier.

'OPEN VAMP' STRUM

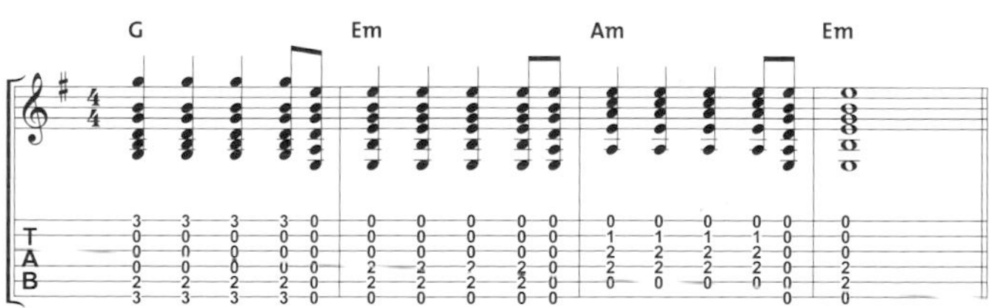

▲ *Chord changes can be made much easier by using an 'open vamp string' between each chord. Strumming the open strings between each chord gives you a little breathing space to move your fingers on to the next chord shape.*

If all else fails, there is a 'pro-trick' you can use that will mask any gap between chord changes: using an 'open vamp' strum. This simply involves strumming the open strings while your fingers move between the chord change. While not ideal, it does mean that, crucially, the overall fluency and momentum of the performance is maintained. In fact, some players actually make a feature of this technique to bring out accents within their rhythm playing. Whatever technique you use, the golden rule in rhythm playing when you come across difficult passages is 'never stop – always keep strumming'.

Section One: The Basics

POWER CHORDS

Playing only selected notes from a chord can actually give a stronger sound than playing the whole chord – especially when you add a touch of distortion. You can get a tighter and more easily controlled sound by just using two or three notes from a chord.

FIFTHS

In rock music, instead of full chords, abbreviated versions just using the root and fifth note are often played. These 'fifth chords' are commonly called 'power chords'. Apart from the tone, one of the main advantages of using fifths is that it's much easier to move quickly from chord to chord because there are only a couple of fingers involved. To play a fifth power chord, simply fret a note on any bass string and add a note two frets up on the adjacent higher string.

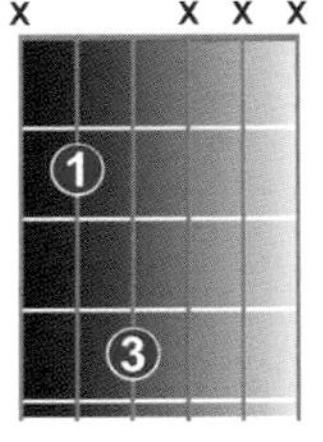

C5 power chord

Songs that use fifths are normally in minor keys, so learn a minor scale in fifths as this will prepare you for the type of progressions commonly used.

▲ *A pentatonic minor scale in fifths.*

To hear the differences in sound between fifths and standard chord shapes, play through the following short chord sequence, first using normal open position chords and then with the chords as fifths. Once you've done this, you could experiment by converting songs that you already play with open chords into a version using fifths.

Complete Guitar Handbook

Seventies rock bands like Judas Priest and Black Sabbath (the heavy metal pioneers) specialized in writing songs based upon riffs played in fifths – often adding an octave note to the chord to get a more powerful sound.

▲ *A typical 1970s rock riff. Octave notes could be used as well as the fifth to give a heavier sound.*

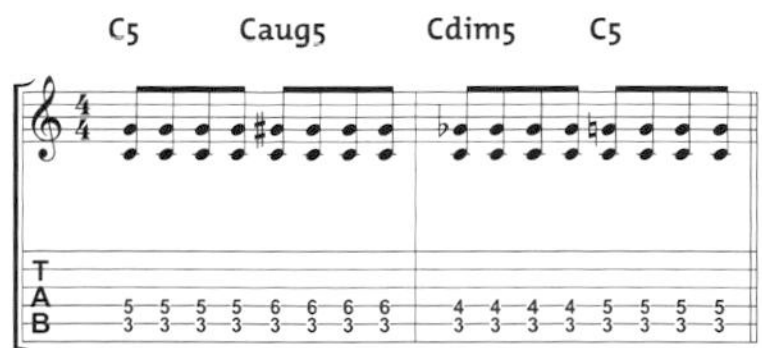

▲ *An 1980s metal riff, using variations on the standard fifth chord.*

Eighties heavy metal bands like Iron Maiden and Metallica used plenty of fifths in their songs, but often varied the fifth shape a little by using augmented or diminished fifths to create a more foreboding sound.

In the early 1990s, the Seattle grunge sound was based on the use of fifths. Bands like Pearl Jam and Nirvana tended to use a less distorted sound than their metal predecessors and also tended to strum using down and up strokes.

▲ *Down and up strums capture the grunge spirit.*

More recent rock bands such as Slipknot and Blink-182 base much of their rhythm playing on fifth power chords, often using dropped tunings to create an even stronger sound.

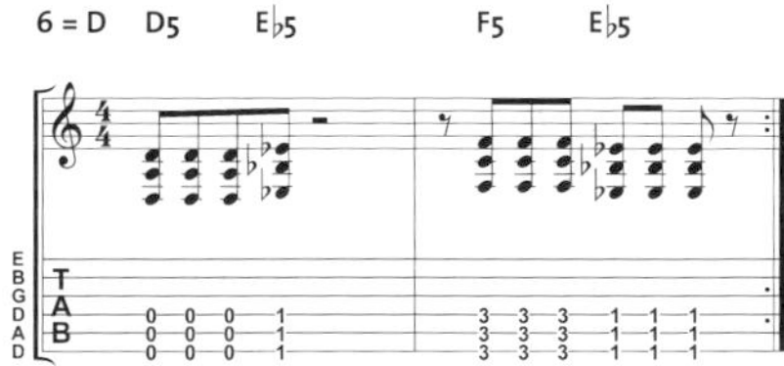

▲ *The low E string is de-tuned to D, enabling fifth power chords to be played on the 6th and 5th strings on a single fret – making fast chord changes much easier.*

To make sure that power chords are played clearly you need to do the following:

- Adapt your hand stretch to the size of the fret at which you're playing (fret-spacing gets narrower as you progress up the fingerboard).
- Move your whole hand (not just reaching with the fingers) when you change fret position.
- Only strum the strings that you are fretting; beware of hitting unwanted open strings.

Section One: The Basics

BARRE CHORDS

Playing open position chords is a great way to begin learning the guitar, but if you take a careful look at any professional players you'll soon notice that most of their chord positions are further up the fretboard; more often than not they'll be playing shapes known as 'barre chords'.

ADVANTAGES OF BARRE CHORDS

Playing a barre chord involves re-fingering an open position chord so as to leave the first finger free to play the barre by fretting all six strings. The whole chord can then be moved up the fingerboard to different pitches. The main advantage of using barre chords is that you can move the same shape up or down the fingerboard to create new chords without the need to memorize a whole host of different fingerings for each chord. Using barre chords will allow you to play more unusual chords (like B♭ minor or F♯ major), which are unobtainable in open position.

MAJOR BARRE CHORDS

To play major chords in barre form, begin by re-fingering an open position E major chord using the second, third and fourth fingers. Then move this up to different fingerboard positions, with the first finger fretting all the strings on the adjacent lower fret. Most guitars have marker dots on frets three, five and seven, and moving the barre of the E major shape to these positions will give the chords of G, A and B major.

▶ G major barre chord – based upon an E major shape. Move this shape to the fifth fret for A major and to the seventh fret for B major.

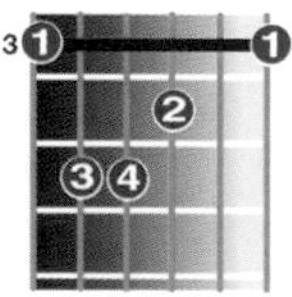

In theory, you could play all major chords with just this one barre chord shape. In practise, however, this would involve leaping around the fingerboard too

Complete Guitar Handbook

much when changing from one chord to another. Therefore, knowing at least two shapes for each chord type will enable you to play through most songs without ever having to shift more than a couple of frets for each chord change. The second major shape you can convert to a barre chord is the open position A major shape; moving this shape with the barre on the marker dots on frets three, five and seven of the A string will give the chords of C, D and E major.

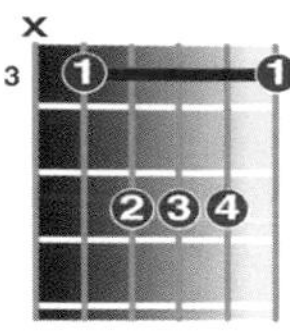

▶ C major barre chord – based upon an A major shape. Move this shape to the fifth fret for D major and the seventh fret for E major.

MINOR BARRE CHORDS

Open position minor chords can also be converted to barre chords. The E minor and A minor shapes can be re-fingered to leave the first finger free to make the barre. When the E minor shape is moved up, the pitch of the chord should be taken from the barre position on the E string. When the A minor chord is moved up, the pitch should be taken from the barre position on the A string.

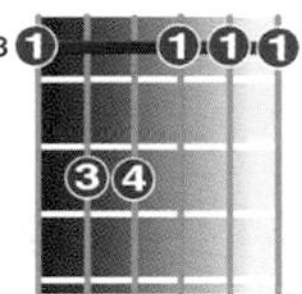

▶ G minor barre chord – based upon an E minor shape. Move this shape to the fifth fret for A minor and to the seventh fret for B minor.

MIXING BARRE CHORDS

Most songs will combine a mixture of major and minor chords. Whether you decide to use an E or A shape barre chord will depend on the position of the previous and the following chord; the trick is to choose the shape that will avoid any large fingerboard shifts.

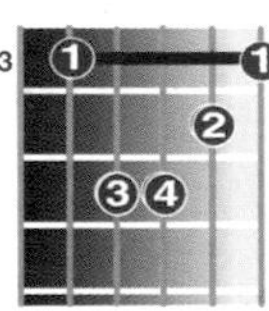

▶ C minor barre chord – based upon an A minor shape. Move this shape to the fifth fret for D minor and to the seventh fret for E minor.

Barre Chord Technique

- Keep the first finger straight and in line with the fret.
- The creases between the joints of the barring finger should not coincide with strings.
- Position all the fretting fingers as close to the fretwire as possible.
- Press down firmly, but avoid using excessive pressure.
- When you move between barre chords ensure your thumb also shifts, so that your whole hand position is moving with each chord change.

Section One: The Basics

CHORD RIFFS

Don't assume that chords are used purely for strumming an accompaniment – in some musical styles chords are quite frequently used to create the main riffs within songs. Some of the strongest and most memorable riffs in the history of rock music have been created using chords rather than single notes.

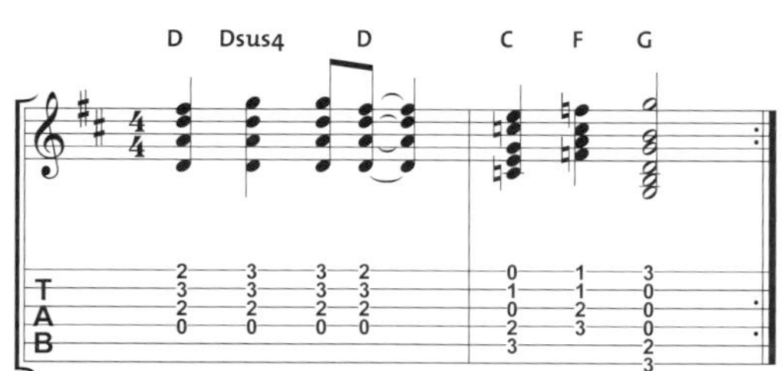

▲ *Example of a riff using open position chords.*

CREATING RIFFS

A riff is a short musical phrase that is repeated many times throughout a song. Using chords to play riffs will nearly always result in a much more powerful sound than a riff played just using single notes. Listen to anything by the Rolling Stones, AC/DC or the White Stripes to hear some fine examples of chordal riffing. When creating riffs with chords, you'll normally need to use more than one chord per measure in order to give a sense of movement. This might mean changing quickly to a totally different chord, or the riffs may just consist of chordal variations (such as major chords changing to suspended chords).

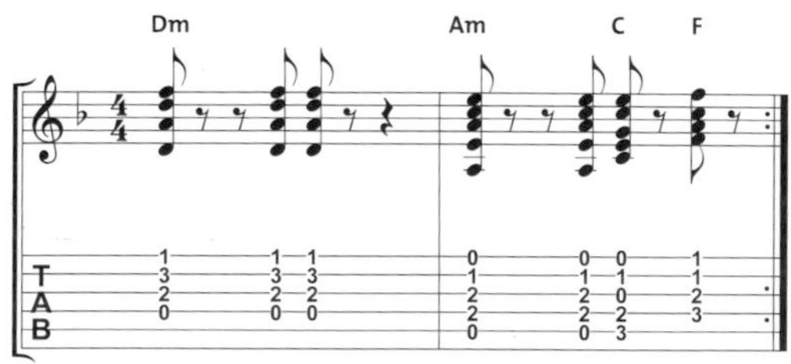

▲ *The rests give this riff its distinct rhythmic character.*

USING RESTS

Using rests (silences) between chords will help add a well-defined rhythm to your riff, giving it musical shape and character. Place the strumming hand against the strings when you wish to mute them.

Complete Guitar Handbook

SEPARATING STRINGS

An effective technique for chord riffing is to separate the bass and treble strings when a chord is played. This will allow you to create a piano-like effect, with the bass part clearly separated from the treble.

▲ *Begin the E and G major chords by striking only the bass strings, followed by just the treble strings of each chord.*

USING POWER CHORDS

When playing chord riffs it's not always necessary to strum all of the strings – often just strumming the root and fifth notes of a chord (normally the bottom two strings of the chord) will suffice. In fact, for riffing, playing 'power chords' often sounds better than strumming all the strings of the complete chord shape as the sound will be tighter and better defined.

▲ *Example of a riff using power chords.*

Tip

Playing chord riffs will inevitably involve the need for some fast chord changes. Practise the chord changes very slowly at first – only speeding up once you are totally secure in moving between the chords.

ADDING SINGLE NOTES

Chord riffs do not need to consist exclusively of chords: adding an occasional single note, particularly an open bass string, can add variety to a riff and often make it easier to play.

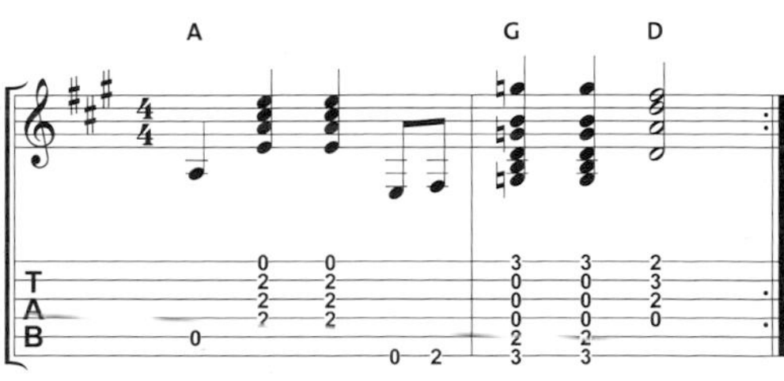

▲ *On the A major chord the bass and treble strings are strummed separately, the E and F# bass notes then facilitate the change to the G major chord.*

Section One: The Basics

STRING DAMPING

Nearly all rock and blues players use string damping as a way of controlling the guitar's volume and tone. By resting the side of the strumming hand lightly on the strings, close to the saddle, a choked or muted sound can be achieved by deadening the sustain of the strings.

DAMPING TECHNIQUE

String damping is an essential technique for varying the tone and volume of your guitar playing. The technique can be used after a note or chord has been played to achieve a short and detached 'staccato' effect. The technique can also be used to bring out accents in a rhythm, by maintaining the muting effect throughout and releasing only intermittently on the beats to be accented.

STRUMMING-HAND DAMPING

To learn this technique, first strum slowly across all the open strings to hear the natural sound of the guitar. Then, place your strumming hand at a 90-degree angle to the strings, close to the saddle, with the side of the hand (in line with the little finger) pressing lightly against all six strings. Maintain contact with the strings with the edge of your hand, and then rotate the hand towards the strings and strum again. The pressure of the hand against the strings will dampen the volume and sustain – this is known as 'palm muting'. Notice how this is very different from the normal sound of strummed open strings. Now try this again with an E minor

► *String damping, using 'palm mute' technique: the edge of the fretting hand rests against the strings next to the bridge; the hand stays in position when you strum, to mute the strings.*

Complete Guitar Handbook

chord. When you use string damping it's not necessary to always strum all the strings of the chord; often – particularly in rock styles – it's better just to strum the bass string and a couple of others. Vary the amount of pressure with which the side of the hand rests on the strings: if you press too hard the notes will just become dead thuds, but if you press too lightly the strings will start to ring and sustain again. Be aware that it's all too easy at first to pull the damping hand away from the strings as you begin to strum, so losing the muting effect. Although it may take a while to gain control of this technique, and to strike the right balance of pressure and release, it's well worth the effort as string damping is an essential tool in any guitarist's technique.

◀ *Palm muting. Measure 1: press firmly against the strings. M. 2: lighten the pressure. M. 3: release damping hand. M. 4: re-apply damping hand, increasing pressure in the final measure.*

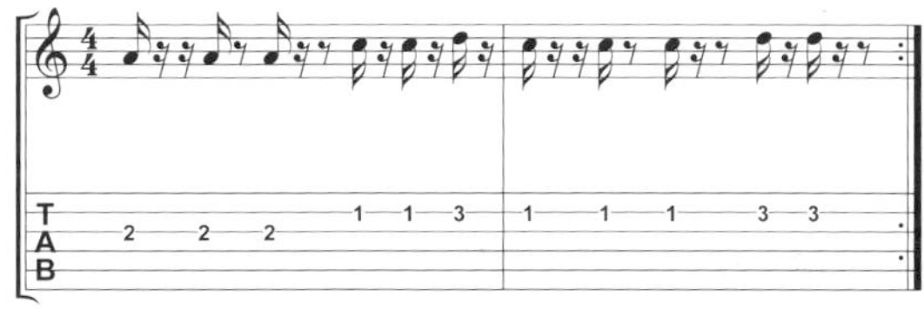

▶ *Palm muting can also be used in lead playing, resulting in a very staccato sound (with all the notes short and detached). This technique is often used in funk music.*

FRETTING-HAND DAMPING

You can also mute the strings by slightly relaxing the pressure on the strings that you are fretting; the fingers still touch the strings, but do not press them all the way down to the fretboard. This technique can be used after a note has been picked to achieve a staccato effect, or after a chord has been strummed to achieve a chord 'chop'. The technique can also be used to bring out accents, by damping the fretting hand continuously while the strumming hand plays a rhythm – the fretting hand only pressing the chord intermittently, so that it sounds only on the beats to be accented.

▶ *Fretting-hand damping: the fretting hand begins by touching, rather than pressing, the strings. This causes the notes to be muted. On the accented beats, the notes of the chord are fretted normally so that the chord sounds clearly when strummed strongly.*

Section One: The Basics

SLURS

Slurring is a method that not only enables you to play much faster than with normal picking, but also provides a much smoother (legato) sound. There are two slurring techniques: 'hammering-on' and 'pulling-off'.

HAMMER-ONS

To 'hammer-on' a note, don't pick the string; instead, rapidly hammer the tip of your finger right next to the fret of the note that you want. It's important to make sure that you hammer-on as close as possible to the fretwire, otherwise it will be very difficult to get the note to sound clearly. Ideally, the note should come out just as though you had picked it normally. If it doesn't, then you're probably not hammering hard enough – the string should leave a slight imprint on your fingertip if you're doing it right.

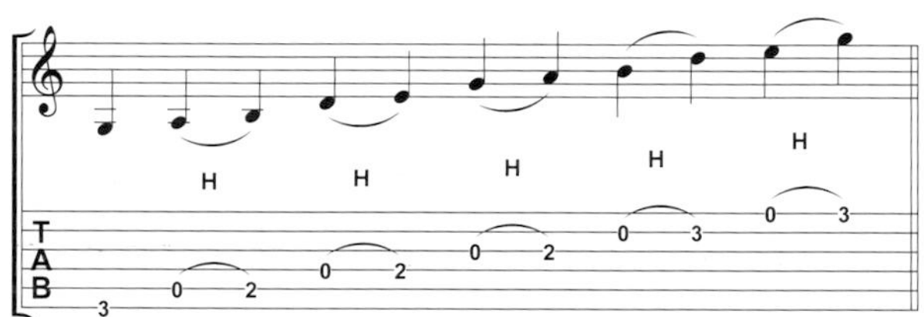

◀ *G pentatonic major scale played ascending using hammer-ons. The curved slur line and the H sign indicate which notes should be hammered-on.*

PULL-OFFS

To 'pull-off', first fret a note, then pull your fretting finger lightly downwards until it plucks the string, and the open string or a lower fretted note, is sounded.

◀ *G pentatonic major scale played descending using pull-offs. The curved slur line and P sign indicate which notes should be pulled off.*

Complete Guitar Handbook

Avoid just lifting your finger off into the air – you have to make a slight downward movement for the note to sound clearly.

COMBINING HAMMER-ONS AND PULL-OFFS

Once you have mastered the basic techniques described above, try the slurring exercises below, which combine both hammer-ons and pull-offs.

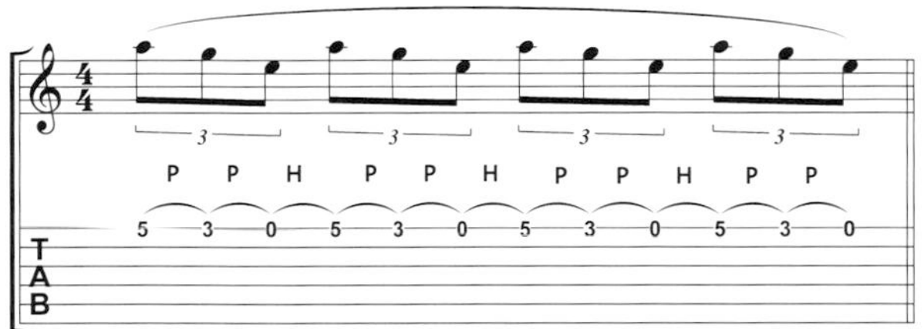

◀ Combination slur, Exercise 1. Two pull-offs lead to an open string, then hammer back on and start again, so that only the very first note is picked.

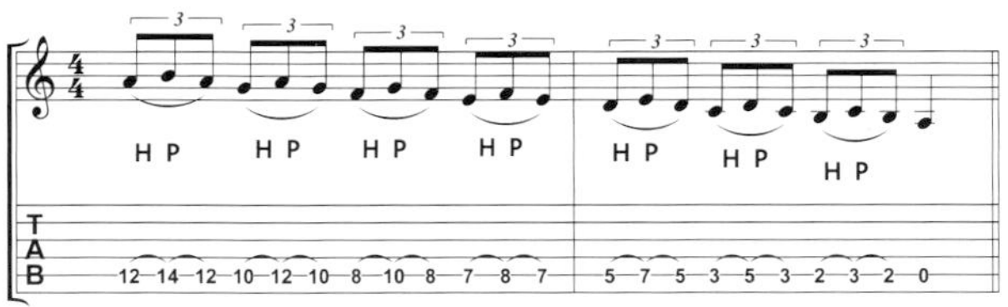

◀ Combination slur, Exercise 2. Use a hammer-on, then a pull-off, on each note of the A natural minor scale descending along the fifth string – picking only the first of each three notes.

TRILL

If you repeatedly hammer-on and pull-off between the same two notes it is known as a 'trill'. This is a technique favoured by many rock guitarists, from Jimi Hendrix to Steve Vai.

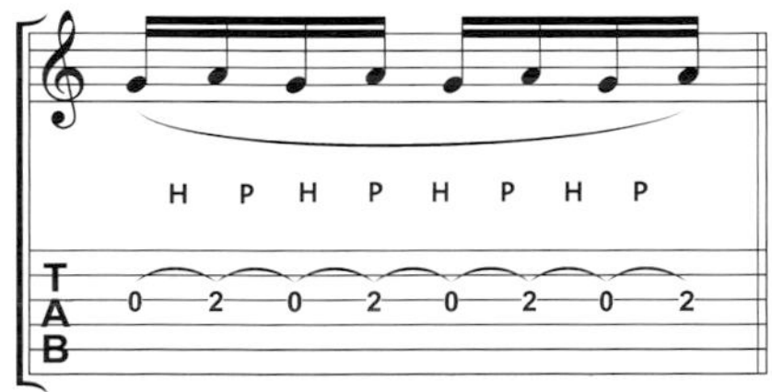

▲ Trill: alternately hammering-on and pulling-off rapidly between the notes G and A.

Tip

Slurring is much easier if your guitar is adjusted to have a low action. Using distortion will also result in less effort being needed when playing slurs.

Section One: The Basics

SLIDES

Sliding from one note or chord to another is a great way of creating a seamless legato sound that can make your playing sound relaxed and effortless. The technique also provides an easy way of adding passing notes to make your playing more individual and inventive.

SLIDE TECHNIQUE

To slide a note means to fret it and then, while maintaining the fretting pressure, to move the finger to another fret on the same string without picking the note again. The second note is sounded only because of the continued pressure of the fretting hand; it is not picked again.

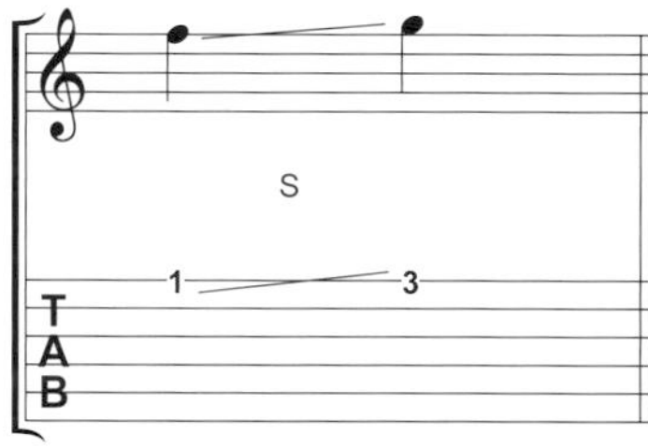

▲ *Slide: pick the F note then, using the force of the fretting finger alone, sound the G note by quickly sliding the first finger along the E string.*

In a standard slide you only hear the first and last notes. However, you can also play a 'glissando' type of slide, in which all the intervening notes are also sounded.

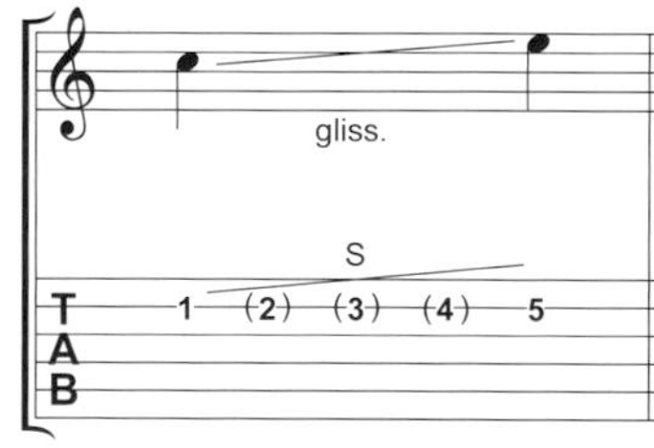

▲ *Glissando slide: pick the C note then, using the force of the fretting finger, slide along the B string up to the E note, allowing the notes in between to sound.*

Controlling the amount of grip with the fretting hand is the secret to good sliding. You should try to ensure that the thumb at the back of the guitar neck relaxes its grip when you are in the process of sliding a note up or down. This doesn't mean that the thumb needs to be released totally, but simply that it shouldn't be squeezing tightly

Complete Guitar Handbook

against the back of the guitar neck. However, just as your hand reaches the note that you want to slide into, the thumb should squeeze the neck slightly harder to act as a brake, preventing your fingers sliding beyond the destination fret.

SLIDING CHORDS

The guitar is one of the few instruments on which you can slide chords up and down, changing their pitch easily and smoothly; the technique creates a fluidity and smoothness of sound that piano players can only dream of! Because slides are so natural to the guitar they form a core component of any good rhythm guitarist's technique. Slides are used by guitarists in nearly all musical styles, from metal and blues to country and ska.

▲ *Example of using slides with power chords. Start with an ascending slide, from two frets below the destination chord, followed by a double slide (sliding down and then back up one fret).*

When sliding chords it is important to ensure that the chord shape is maintained, so that one finger doesn't end up a fret ahead of the rest! The trick is to achieve a neutral balance whereby the chord shape is kept under control, yet at the same time the fingers are relaxed enough to slide up or down the fingerboard.

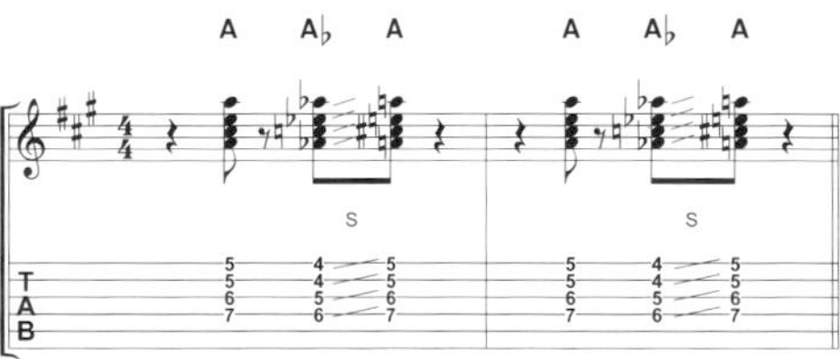

▲ *Example of using slides with major chords. Note that the first finger frets the top two strings. You'll need to keep a strong pressure with the fretting finger in order to maintain volume.*

Playing fifth 'power chords', where only two notes are fretted, is the ideal introduction to sliding chords. Playing power chords with a copious amount of distortion is the easiest way to begin chord sliding, the distortion will provide sustain which will encourage you not to grip too hard when sliding the chords. Using ascending slides (raising the pitch of a chord) is easier at first – the volume tends to disappear quite quickly with descending slides.

Section One: The Basics

VIBRATO

By repeatedly varying the pitch of a note very slightly you can achieve an effect known as 'vibrato'. This is used on most string instruments, but it is particularly useful on electric guitar because of the instrument's potentially long sustain – especially if an overdriven sound is used.

▲ *Paul Kossoff is well known for his excellent use of vibrato.*

Using vibrato can turn a plain solo in something that sounds really classy. Vibrato can help you make the most of the guitar's sustain, and make your playing more expressive.

Vibrato is often confused with string bending (see page 98), but in fact they are two completely different techniques (although the two are sometimes played together within a lick). The main difference between the two techniques is that string bending involves substantially changing the pitch of a note (usually by a half step or more), whereas vibrato is more subtle, with the note being only 'wavered' with a very small variation in pitch (always returning to, and alternating with, the original pitch).

VIBRATO TYPES

There are three main types of vibrato.

1. Horizontal vibrato: rock the fretting hand from side to side, along the direction of the string. Keep the fretting finger in contact with the string, but release the pressure of the thumb on the back of the neck. This type of vibrato will give you increased sustain with just the tiniest variation in pitch. You can rock the hand either slowly or quickly, and for as short or long a time as you

Complete Guitar Handbook

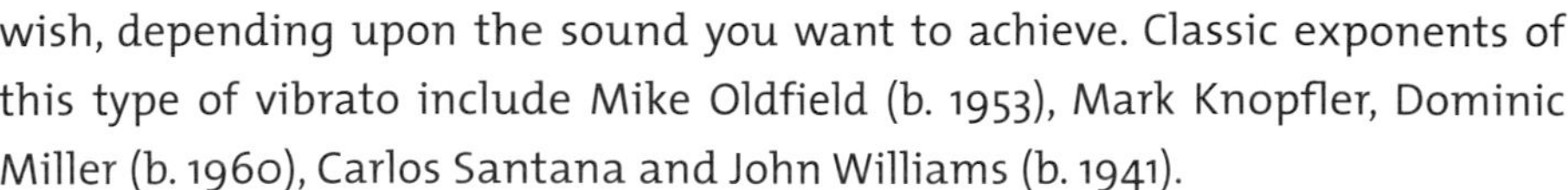

wish, depending upon the sound you want to achieve. Classic exponents of this type of vibrato include Mike Oldfield (b. 1953), Mark Knopfler, Dominic Miller (b. 1960), Carlos Santana and John Williams (b. 1941).

2. Wrist vibrato: while the first finger frets a note, the pitch can be wavered by rotating the wrist away from the fingerboard and back again repeatedly. This is one of the best-sounding vibratos, and can result in a sweet singing tone. However, it can only be used on notes that are fretted by the first finger. The undisputed master of this technique is blues legend B. B. King. Modestly he states: 'I won't say I invented it, but they weren't doing it before I started.' This style of vibrato has been an everyday tool of blues and rock guitar players. B. B. King tends to keep his thumb pressed on the back of the neck to get a fast but short pitch-range, 'stinger' vibrato. Other players, such as Eric Clapton, prefer to release the thumb in order to achieve a slower, wider-ranging vibrato.

3. Vertical vibrato: while fretting a note, repeatedly waggle the tip of the fretting finger to move the string up and down slightly. You don't need to move it too far and you should always make sure that you return the string to its starting position. This type of vibrato is ideal for adding to a string bend. Once a note is bent you can add vibrato to it to add a subtle enhancement to the bend and add sustain. Peter Green and Paul Kossoff were two of the classic exponents of this technique. Other guitarists employed their own variations on the technique: Buddy Guy and Ritchie Blackmore for example, often prefer to use a very fast 'stinging' vibrato after a bend, while Gary Moore and Yngwie Malmsteen tend to use wider, more extreme vibrato.

VIBRATO NOTATION

In music notation, vibrato is indicated by a horizontal wavy line. Sometimes the abbreviation 'vib.' is also written. Occasionally, the word 'wide' might be written to indicate wide vibrato, but generally the type of vibrato used is left to the discretion of the performer.

Section One: The Basics

STRING BENDS

String bending is one of the most essential techniques for any electric guitarist. Nearly every rock or blues guitarist since the 1950s has used string bending as part of their technique, and as a way of expressing emotion through their playing.

String bending is the perfect vehicle for adding emotion, expression and individuality to your lead playing. By carefully pushing a string upwards while fretting it you can alter the pitch of the note that you are playing without needing to move to another fret. Classic exponents include Jimi Hendrix, Eric Clapton, B. B. King, David Gilmour and Ritchie Blackmore, but listen to any guitar-based band today and you'll still hear the technique in regular use in almost every solo.

BENDING TECHNIQUE

In theory, you can bend any note in any scale as long as you bend it up to reach another note in that scale. In practise, most bends will be restricted to the next note in the scale – i.e. a half step (the equivalent of one fret) or a whole step (the equivalent of two frets) higher than the fretted note. You can use any finger to bend a note but, so as not to move out of position and lose fluency, it's best to use the finger that you would normally use to fret the note within the scale. If you're executing the bend with the third or fourth finger, it's really important that you use the remaining fingers, on the same string, to give you added strength when bending. Ignoring this advice will mean that your bends won't go high enough to be in tune, or if they do, then you could end up straining your finger.

BENDING IN TUNE

In order to get your string bends in tune, it's a good idea to practise fretting the higher note first, and then singing that note aloud, while bending the note into tune with your voice. Another method is to repeatedly pick the string while

Complete Guitar Handbook

bending it up very slowly so that you can hear the note gradually bend into tune. The essential thing is to listen as you bend because not much sounds worse than badly out-of-tune string bending! It's important to practise string bends in a range of keys, because the amount of pressure that you need will vary greatly depending upon your position on the fingerboard. For instance, bending a note on the third fret of the third sting will be much harder than bending on the 12th fret on the same string.

Once you feel confident that you are able to bend a note in tune, try playing through these examples, which start with third-finger half-step bends, before progressing to third- and fourth-finger whole-step bends.

▶ Third-finger half-step bend: using the A blues scale, the D note on the G string is bent up a half step to E♭, then let down to D, using the third finger.

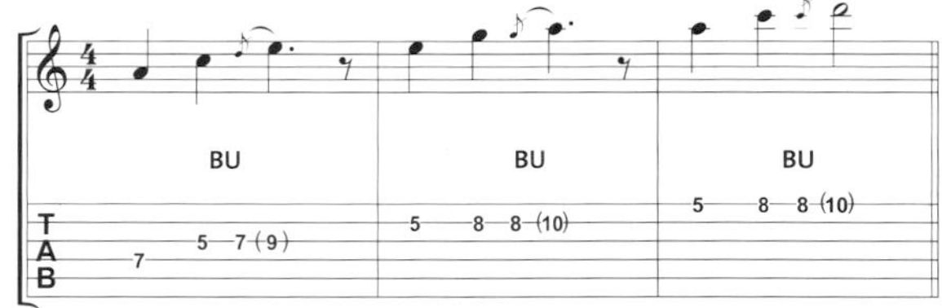

▶ Third- and fourth-finger whole-step bend: using the A pentatonic minor scale, all the bent notes are raised up a whole step. Bend each note slowly until it's in tune, and then hold it there. Use the fourth finger to bend the notes on the second and first string; when doing so, make sure that the second and third fingers are also on the string to give extra strength and support to the fourth finger.

Types of String Bends

- **Choke**: bend the note, and then quickly choke the sound by letting the right hand touch the strings.
- **Hold**: bend the note slowly until it's in tune – then just hold it there.
- **Release**: bend the note up without picking it – then pick it and slowly release it.
- **Up-and-down**: bend the note up and then without re-picking let it down.
- **Double**: bend the note up, let it down, and then bend it up again – but only pick the string the first time.
- **Unison**: while bending a note, fret and play the same note on the next string – or alternate between the two.
- **Vibrato**: bend the note up and then add vibrato by lowering and raising the note repeatedly.
- **Rising**: rapidly pick the string while bending it up very slowly.
- **Harmony**: bend a note while playing or holding a note higher in the scale.
- **Teasing bend**: use several very small bends before fully bending the note into tune. This creates almost a speaking effect – much used by blues players.

Section One: The Basics

PLECTRUM TECHNIQUE

Nearly all electric guitarists want to play fast, but this relies upon having great control over your plectrum. If you start by holding the plectrum the wrong way you can slow down your playing for years to come.

GRIPPING THE PLECTRUM

The best method is to grip the plectrum between the thumb and index finger. Position the plectrum so that its point is about half a centimetre beyond the fingertip. Use only the tip of the plectrum to pick the strings or you will create a physical resistance that will slow down your playing. However, bear in mind that if you show too little plectrum you might end up missing the string altogether. Experiment until you get just the right balance. Also, be careful how tight you grip the plectrum. If you use too much pressure your hand muscles will tighten and so reduce your fluency, but if you hold it too loosely you'll keep dropping it.

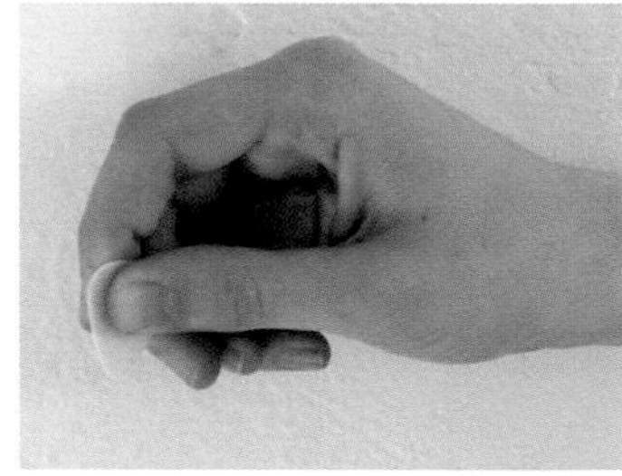

▲ *How to hold your plectrum. Notice the angle and amount of plectrum tip showing.*

Hold the plectrum so that it is in line with your fingernail. Avoid holding it at right angles to your index finger, as this will cause your wrist to lock.

ALTERNATE PICKING

If you want to achieve any degree of speed with the plectrum for lead playing then it's best to use 'alternate picking' as the mainstay of your plectrum technique. This involves alternating downstrokes and upstrokes. Alternate picking is the most logical and economical way of playing, since once you have picked a string downwards, the plectrum will then be ideally positioned to pick upwards, whereas if you try to play two downstrokes in a row you will need to raise the plectrum back up before you can strike the string again.

Complete Guitar Handbook

When alternating down and upstrokes, make sure that the picking action is generated by swivelling the wrist; try to avoid moving the elbow up and down as this will make your picking style much too cumbersome and will hamper your fluency. For fast lead playing, alternate picking and a relaxed wrist action are the fundamental requirements.

PICKING EXERCISES

Begin by practising alternate picking on the open sixth string. Once you have a secure plectrum technique you can make your licks sound faster by doubling, or even quadrupling, your picking on some notes. The fretting hand may be moving quite slowly, but the lick will sound more mobile because of the activity of the picking hand. Practise this technique at first by playing scales with double and quadruple picking.

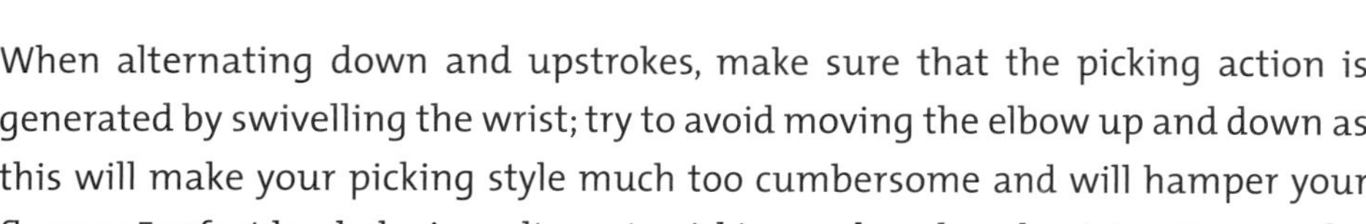

▲ *C major scale, played ascending with double picking and descending with quadruple picking.*

A fast rock sound can be achieved by mixing fretted notes with an open string – while the right hand keeps picking with alternate down and up strokes.

TRIPLET PICKING

A great way of making your playing sound super-fast is to use triplet picking patterns. Because these patterns cut across the standard 4/4 rhythm, they give the impression of being much faster than they really are. This repeated 'down-up-down' picking style can give a rolling or galloping effect to a piece of music. (The term 'triplet' here refers only to the three-part picking action; the rhythm doesn't have to be a triplet in the traditional musical sense.)

▲ *Use a 'down-up-down' picking pattern for each triplet.*

Section One: The Basics

BASIC ARPEGGIOS

Learning arpeggios is a good way of developing a comprehensive knowledge of the guitar fingerboard. But arpeggios aren't just technical exercises – they're great for soloing and can make your lead playing more melodic by emphasizing the harmonic structure of the underlying chord progression.

CONSTRUCTING ARPEGGIOS

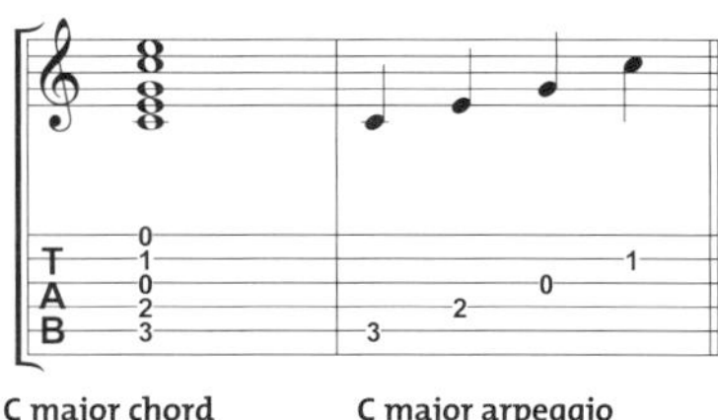

C major chord C major arpeggio

An arpeggio is simply the notes of a chord played individually. Standard major and minor chords, and therefore their arpeggios, contain only three different notes. For example, if you look closely at the open position C major chord you'll notice that although you're playing five strings, there are in fact only three different notes (C E G) in the chord. If you play these notes consecutively, rather than strum them simultaneously, this forms the C major arpeggio.

When you're first learning arpeggios it's helpful to practise them in the set order (1st, 3rd, 5th, 8th), but once you know them you can improvise freely by swapping the notes around, or repeating some, to make up an interesting lick or riff, just as you would when improvising with a scale. The really useful thing is that, because the C major arpeggio contains exactly the same notes as the C major chord, whatever notes you play from the C major arpeggio when improvising will always be totally in tune with a C major chordal accompaniment.

MAJOR AND MINOR ARPEGGIOS

Each basic major or minor arpeggio will only contain three notes; you can work out which notes these are by analyzing the relevant chord shape. Another

Complete Guitar Handbook

method is to take the first, third and fifth notes of the major scale with the same starting note (for example, C E G are the 1st, 3rd and 5th notes of the C major scale and so form the C major arpeggio).

To work out minor arpeggios flatten the third note of the major arpeggio by a half step (e.g. C minor arpeggio contains C E♭ G).

Aim to acquire knowledge of all major and minor arpeggios in as many fingerboard positions as possible. Here are some fingerboard positions for C major and C minor arpeggios. They can be transposed to other pitches by moving them up or down the fingerboard.

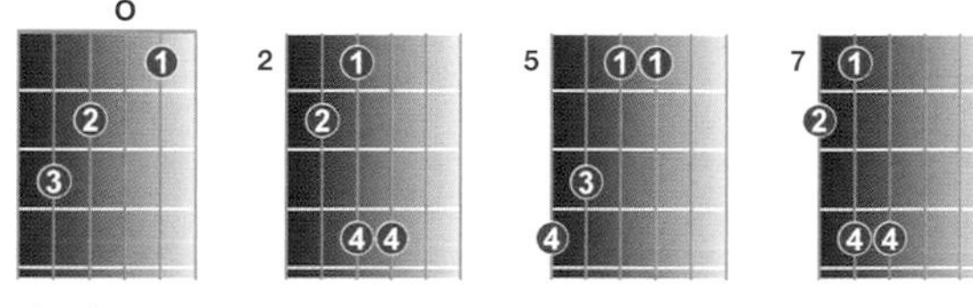

C major arpeggio patterns

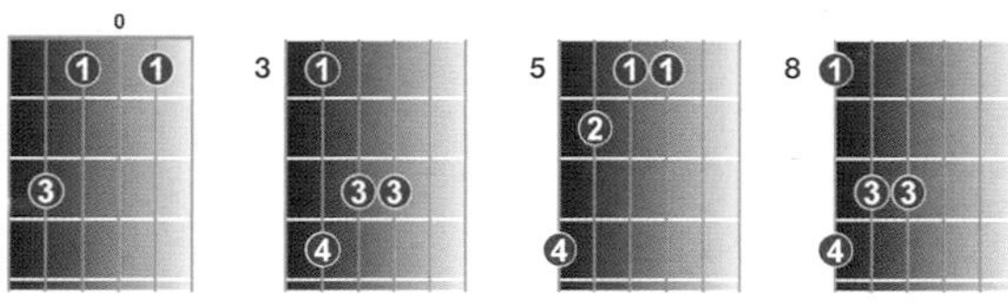

C minor arpeggio patterns

USING ARPEGGIOS

▲ *Lead line using notes only from the arpeggios of each chord.*

You can use arpeggios for riffs and lead playing. When you use a scale for a lead solo you'll have noticed that some notes sound more resolved against certain chords than other notes. This problem disappears when you use arpeggios; because the notes of each arpeggio are taken from the chord they will all sound completely 'in tune' – providing you're playing the right arpeggio for each chord. If you've only used scales before, this takes a little getting used to as you'll need to change arpeggio every time there is a chord change.

In a normal playing situation guitarists rarely use arpeggios throughout a whole solo, as this approach can tend to sound almost too 'in tune'. Instead, arpeggios are used to add colour over just a couple of chords, and the normal key scale is used for the majority of the solo.

Section One: The Basics

MORE ARPEGGIOS

Once you've learnt the basic major and minor arpeggios it's not too difficult to extend these to learn the arpeggios for other chords, such as sevenths and even extended and altered chords. A secure knowledge of arpeggios will mean that you'll always be able to improvise over any chord progression.

SEVENTH ARPEGGIOS

These are formed by taking the notes of the relevant seventh chord and playing them in a scale-like pattern. There are three main types of seventh chord arpeggios: dominant seventh, minor seventh and major seventh. Although they have some notes in common, the sound varies considerably between each one: dominant seventh arpeggios are great for blues and R&B, minor sevenths are used a lot in both rock and funk, and major sevenths give a very melodic sound suited to ballads.

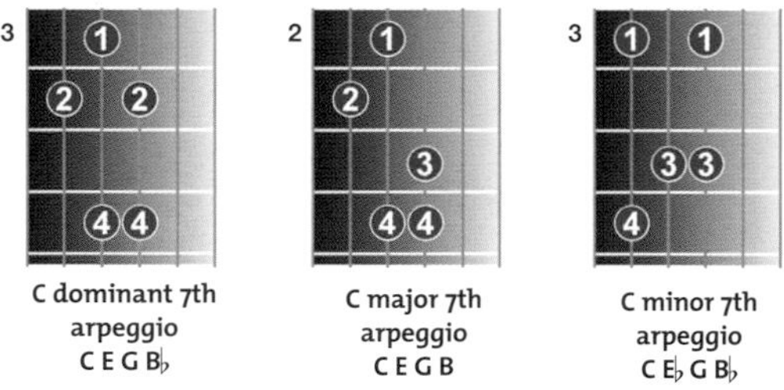

C dominant 7th arpeggio C E G B♭

C major 7th arpeggio C E G B

C minor 7th arpeggio C E♭ G B♭

SIXTH ARPEGGIOS

Major and minor sixth arpeggios are commonly used for creating riffs. The typical rock 'n' roll riff on the right is taken directly from the C major sixth arpeggio.

ALTERED ARPEGGIOS

One of the most useful applications of arpeggios is over altered chords, such as diminished or augmented chords. Although you may have difficultly choosing a

Complete Guitar Handbook

scale to improvise over such chords, arpeggios will always work – because they contain exactly the same notes as the chords you cannot fail to play in tune. Therefore, a thorough knowledge of altered arpeggios will prove highly useful if you wish to improvise over advanced chord progressions, such as those used in jazz and fusion. Here are some of the most useful altered arpeggios. They are all illustrated with a root note of C, but can be easily transposed simply by starting at a different fingerboard position.

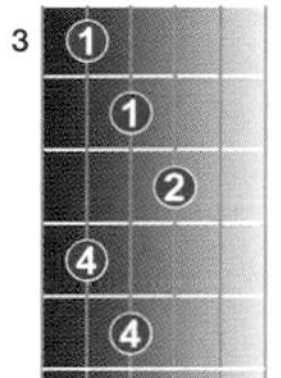

C diminished 7th arpeggio
C E♭ G♭ B♭♭

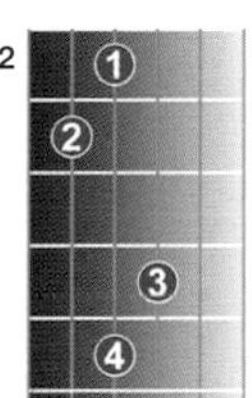

C augmented 5th arpeggio
C E G♯

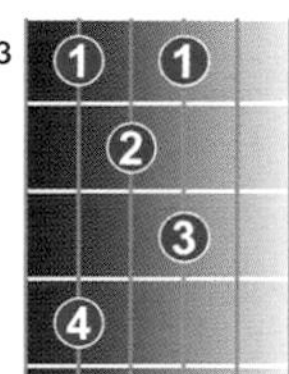

C minor 7th ♭5 arpeggio
C E♭ G♭ B♭

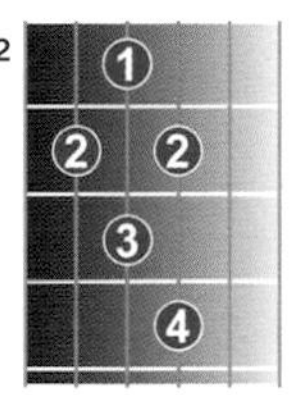

C dominant 7th ♭5 arpeggio
C E G♭ B♭

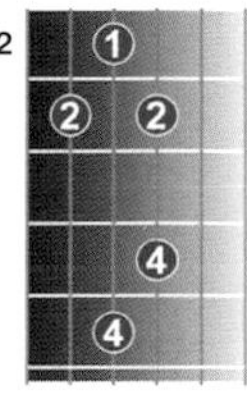

C dominant 7th ♯5 arpeggio
C E G♯ B♭

EXTENDED ARPEGGIOS

When improvising or creating riffs, using arpeggios over extended chords, such as ninths or 13ths, is an ideal way to explore the full melodic potential of these chords. Scale-based lead playing, unlike arpeggio playing, will rarely be able to exploit the full range of chord tones that these extended chords have available. Below you'll find some of the most frequently used extended arpeggios. Remember to shuffle the notes around and play them in a musical and improvised way when using arpeggios in your lead playing. This way they won't sound like a series of technical exercises.

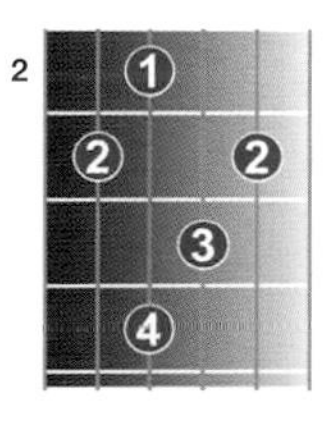

C major 9th arpeggio
C E G B D

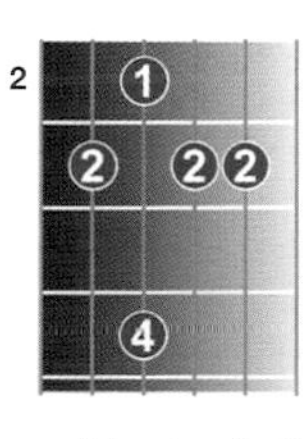

C dominant 9th arpeggio
C E G B♭ D

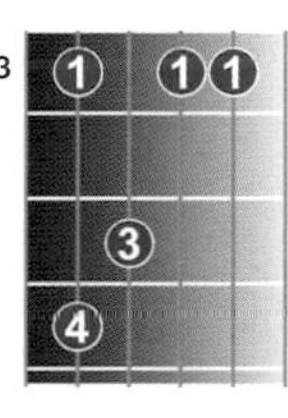

C minor 9th arpeggio
C E♭ G B♭ D

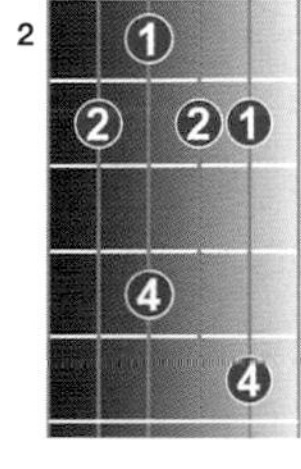

C dominant 11th arpeggio
C E G B♭ D F

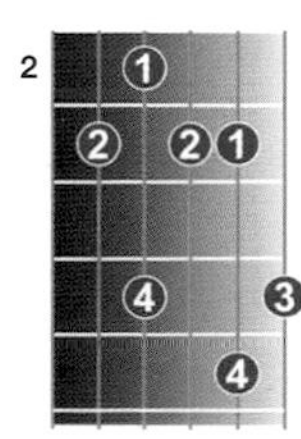

C dominant 13th arpeggio
C E G B♭ D F A

Section One: The Basics

OCTAVES

Octave playing is an instant way of giving more power and solidity to your playing, and because of this it is a technique that is often used by jazz and rock musicians alike. Learning octaves is also one of the quickest ways of getting to know all the notes on the fretboard.

Playing octaves involves playing two of the same notes together (e.g. C and C), but with one of those notes at a higher pitch (i.e. an octave above). The fact that the two notes are the same is what gives octave playing its very powerful sound and avoids any of the sweetness that is often associated with other pairings of notes.

BASS OCTAVES

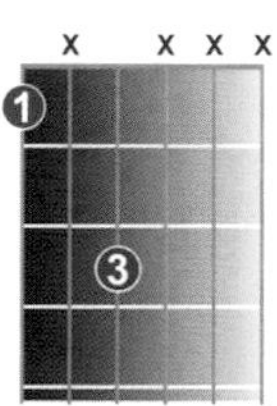

Octave shape based upon the 6th string

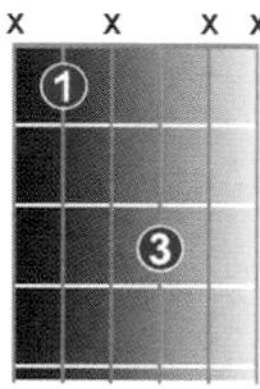

Octave shape based upon the 5th string

There are various ways in which octaves can be played, but for notes on the bass strings by far the most common way is to add a note two frets and two strings higher. For example, if your original note is A on the fifth fret of the sixth string, then the octave A will be on the seventh fret of the fourth string. Similarly, if your original note is D on the fifth fret of the fifth string, then the octave D will be on the seventh fret of the third string. This system, of finding the octave two frets and two strings higher than the original note, will work for all notes on the sixth and fifth strings. The lower note should be played with the first finger, while the octave can be fretted with either the third or the fourth finger.

The most important technique when playing bass octaves is to ensure that the string between the lower note and the octave is totally muted. This should be done by allowing the first finger to lie across it lightly – not fretting the string

Complete Guitar Handbook

but just deadening it. You should also be careful not to strum the strings above the octave note, and as a precaution it's a good idea to mute them by allowing the octave-fretting finger to lightly lie across them.

TREBLE OCTAVES

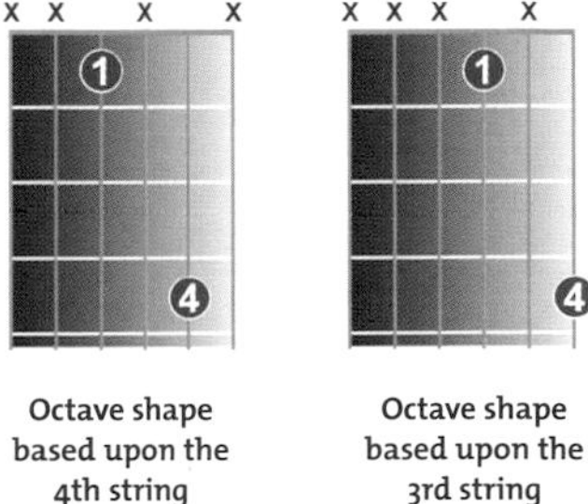

Octave shape based upon the 4th string

Octave shape based upon the 3rd string

The easiest way of playing octaves on the treble strings is to use a similar approach to that described above, but with the octave note requiring a further one-fret stretch. For the fourth and third strings the octave notes can be found by playing three frets and two strings higher. For example, if your original note is G on the fifth fret of the fourth string then the octave G will be on the eighth fret of the second string. This system of finding the octave three frets and two strings higher than the original note will work for all notes on the fourth and third strings.

▶ *Sixth string octave riff. Notice how much stronger this riff sounds when it is played the second time with the octave note added.*

PLAYING OCTAVES

Once you're familiar with the octave shapes shown above, try to play through the examples of octave use given below.

◀ *Sixth and fifth string octaves. Using octaves starting from two strings can minimize the amount of fingerboard movement needed. Just be careful to strum the correct strings and make sure that unwanted strings between the fretted notes are fully muted.*

FINGERBOARD KNOWLEDGE

Once you're familiar with the octave shapes you can use them to learn the notes all across the fingerboard. For example, assuming that you can memorize the notes on the sixth string you can then use your octave shape to work out instantly where the same notes will appear on the fourth string.

Section One: The Basics

HARMONICS

Harmonics can add interesting bell-like chimes to your guitar playing, and are a useful way of sustaining notes. Harmonics are also a great way of adding an extended pitch range to your playing by enabling you to play notes that are much higher than the pitch you can normally reach on the fingerboard.

NATURAL HARMONICS

There are various forms of harmonics that can be played on the guitar, but natural harmonics are the easiest to learn at first. Natural harmonics occur on all strings on frets 12, seven and five (and 12 frets up from these). Natural harmonics also occur on frets nine and four, although making these ring clearly is a bit harder.

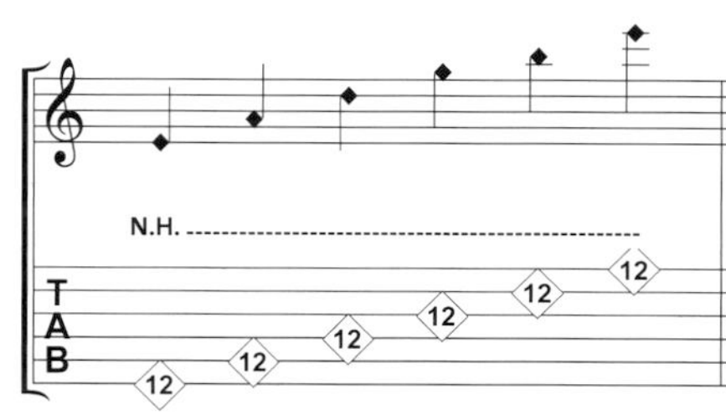

▲ *Natural harmonics at the 12th fret.*

The best way to start playing natural harmonics is to pick the low E string and then touch that string right above the 12th fret. Do not fret the note in the normal way by pressing down on to the fingerboard; instead just lightly touch the string directly over the fretwire.

The harmonics on fret 12 produce the same notes (although with a different tone) as the 12th-fret fretted notes, but harmonics at all other fingerboard positions affect the pitch of the note produced: the harmonic notes on fret seven are an octave higher than the fretted notes;

▶ *Natural harmonics have a chiming bell-like quality.*

Complete Guitar Handbook

the harmonic notes on fret five are the same as the 12th fret fretted notes but an octave higher; the harmonic notes on fret four are two octaves higher than the fretted notes. Natural harmonics also occur on fret nine, and 12 frets up from the previously mentioned fret numbers (e.g. 17, 19, 24).

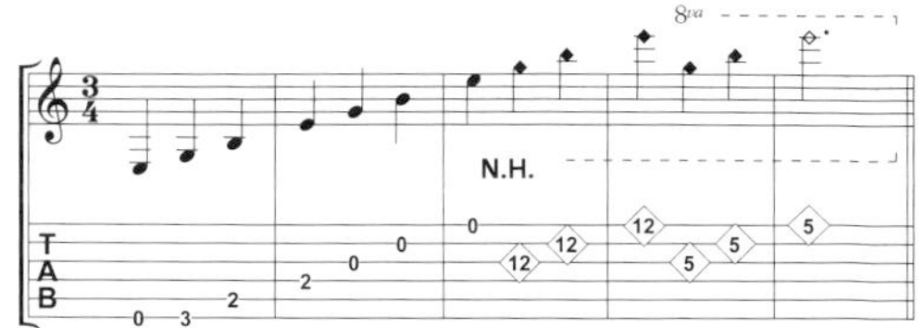

▲ *The E minor arpeggio is extended to four octaves by the use of harmonics. Unless you have a 24-fret guitar, the last note would be impossible without using harmonics.*

OTHER HARMONICS

▲ *Harmonics enable notes higher than those fretted to be played.*

• 'Tapped harmonics' (also known as 'touch harmonics') are most easily played by fretting and picking a note as normal and then touching the same string 12 or seven frets higher.

• 'Artificial harmonics' are similar to tapped harmonics, in that you touch the string 12 frets higher than the fretted note. However, in this technique, instead of picking the fretted note first, you pick the string with the third finger of the picking hand after you have positioned the first finger over the 'harmonic note'.

• 'Pinched harmonics' are often used in rock for making screeching high notes appear out of nowhere in the middle of a lick. The effect is achieved by fretting a note as normal and then picking the string with the side edge of the plectrum while allowing the side of the thumb to almost immediately touch the string – so creating a harmonic. The quality and pitch of the sound that you achieve depends upon where you pick the string. Start by trying to locate the 'nodal point' – that is the equivalent of 24 frets (i.e. two octaves) higher than the note you are fretting.

Tip

Harmonics are easier to execute if you select the treble pickup and turn the treble up on the amplifier. Playing near the bridge (for natural harmonics) and adding some distortion will also help.

BOTTLENECK

A bottleneck (also known as a 'slide') is a tubular device that can be used instead of the fingers for sounding notes. Using a bottleneck is perfect for musical styles such as blues, country and rock music when you want to slide between notes and achieve smooth glissandos.

Originally, the bottleneck guitar sound was created by running a glass neck from a bottle along the strings. Early blues players sometimes used other objects, such as whiskey glasses, knives and beer cans. Nowadays guitarists can benefit from specially manufactured metal, glass or plastic tubes. The metal versions are technically known as 'slides', although in practise the terms 'slide' and 'bottleneck' are often interchanged. Glass bottlenecks give a more rounded tone, but they have less sustain than the metal versions.

▲ *When using a bottleneck, the centre of the tube must rest over the centre of the fret, rather than just behind it.*

USING THE BOTTLENECK

Most players tend to place the bottleneck on the third or fourth finger: using the fourth finger enables the third finger to remain free for normal fretting, but this is dependent upon the fourth finger being large enough to support the bottleneck. To reach the correct pitch,

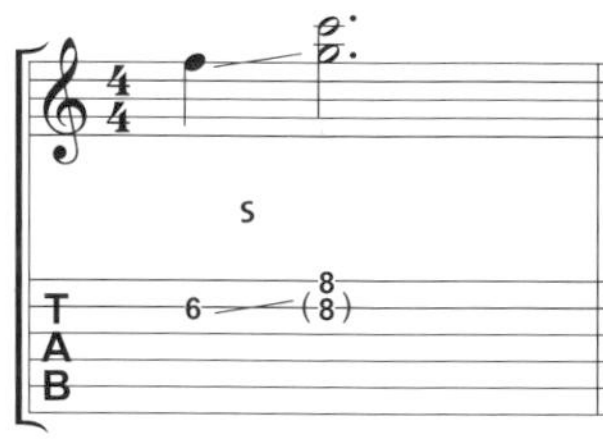

▶ *Bottleneck guitar lick in standard tuning. A slide movement is made on the second string from two frets below up to a two-note chord. Be sure to mute unused strings with either the side of the picking hand or with the lower fingers of the bottleneck hand.*

Complete Guitar Handbook

the middle of the bottleneck should be held directly over the fret, rather than behind it as when fretting a note. The bottleneck only needs to touch the strings; you should not try to press against the frets with the bottleneck as this will cause fretbuzz and result in the notes being out of tune.

Bottleneck is usually played using some vibrato. This is achieved by moving the bottleneck slightly backwards and forwards along the strings above the target fret.

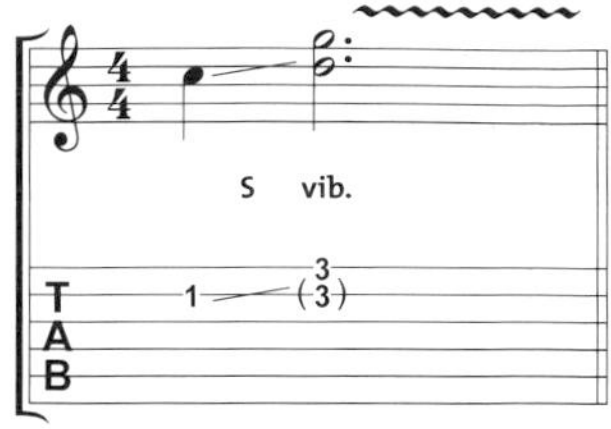

▲ *Vibrato is essential for any bottleneck guitarist. It can be achieved by keeping the bottleneck vertical and moving slightly from left to right above the fret, but always returning to the correct pitch.*

TUNING

So that a full chord can be played with the bottleneck over just one fret, altered tunings are often used when playing bottleneck guitar. The most common bottleneck tunings are D tuning (D A D F♯ A D) and G tuning (D G D G B D). Using a D tuning and placing the bottleneck across all strings over the 12th fret will produce a D major chord. Doing the same on the seventh and fifth frets will produce the two other major chords in the key: A and G. By picking the strings one at a time as arpeggios you can make interesting melodic licks.

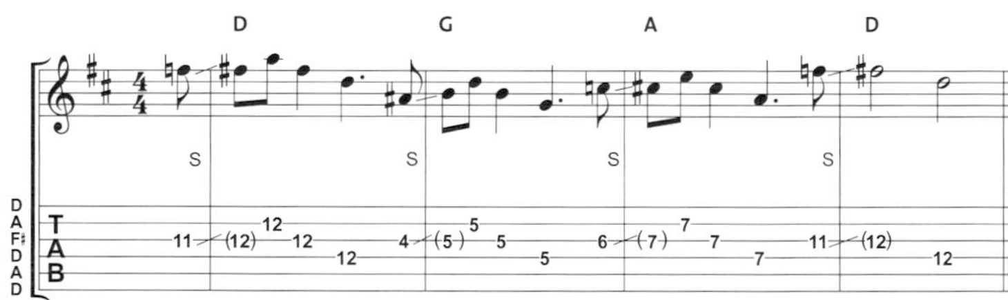

▲ *Bottleneck arpeggio lick using D tuning.*

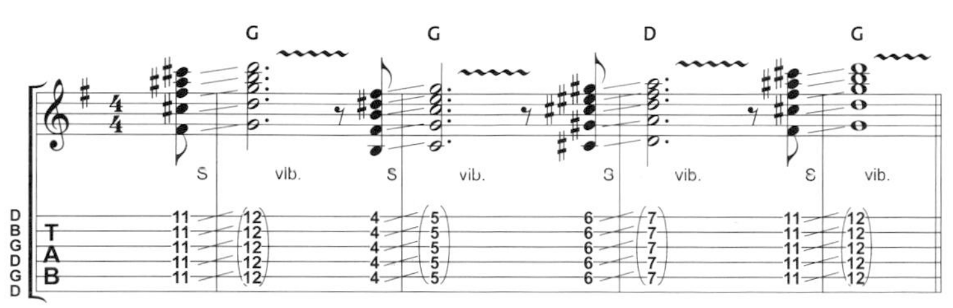

▲ *Bottleneck chords using G tuning.*

To take advantage of the chordal-based tuning, quite often block chords are used in bottleneck playing – usually sliding into a chord from a fret below, as shown to the left.

Section One: The Basics

TREMOLO ARM

The tremolo arm can be one of the most expressive tools available to the electric guitarist. Note that tremolo means a variation in volume, so the arm – which produces a variation in pitch – should really be called a vibrato arm.

To compound the misnomer, the device is often referred to amongst rock guitarists as a 'whammy bar'. The arm or bar can be used in a wide variety of ways, from very subtle vibrato to extreme variations in pitch.

No matter what style of music you might be playing, using the tremolo arm can always add that extra something to give your playing a lift, enabling you to add some extra expression and individuality to your playing. Duane Eddy (b. 1938) and Hank Marvin (of the Shadows) were two of the first guitarists to pioneer the use of the tremolo arm – putting it to good use in their many instrumental hit records of the 1960s. Marvin remains one of the true experts of the technique – often called 'the master of the melody' because of his ability to use the tremolo arm to make his guitar lines expressive and almost vocal-like.

▲ *The tremolo arm (or whammy bar) of an American Deluxe Stratocaster HSS.*

TREMOLO ARM TECHNIQUES

1. The tremolo arm can be used simply as a way of adding vibrato (either subtle or wide) to a note, by gently but repeatedly raising the bar up and down. In fact, this was what the bar was first invented for. This technique generally works best on notes either at the start or end of a phrase, or on any individual

Complete Guitar Handbook

notes that you might wish to emphasize – but, just as with a vocal performance, too much vibrato can sound contrived, so use this technique with care and thought.

▲ *Shake the tremolo arm up and down very slightly to get a typical Shadows-style vibrato.*

2. By pushing or pulling the bar a little further you can actually change the pitch of the note – rather like bending a string. You can lower a note by pushing the bar inwards or you can raise a note by pulling the bar upwards. It takes some practise, but you'll soon begin to get a feel for the amount of pressure required in order to reach the exact pitch of the note you require; notice that less tremolo arm movement is required to alter the pitch of notes higher up the fingerboard compared to lower-fretted notes.

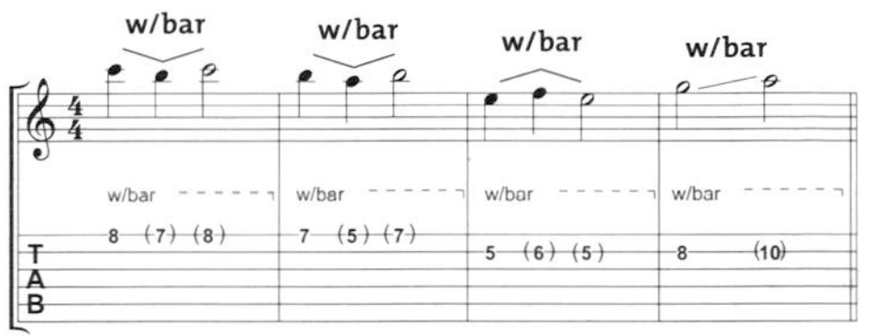

▲ *Depress the tremolo arm bar to achieve the downwards dips in pitch, and then release the bar back to return each note to its original pitch. Pull the tremolo arm upwards to raise notes.*

3. Use of the tremolo arm need not be restricted to single notes – it also works really well with chords, giving a keyboard-like effect to a single strummed chord.

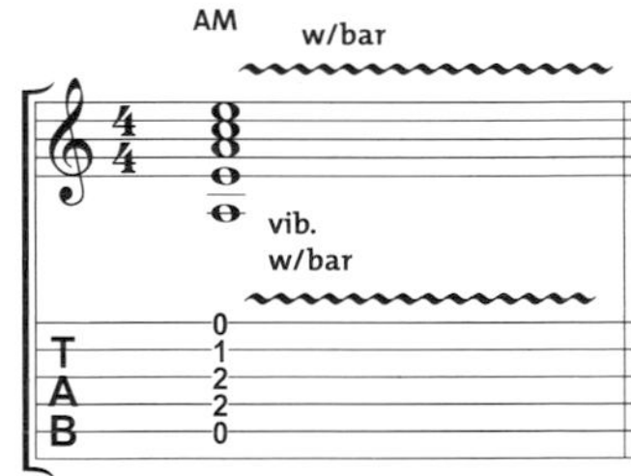

▲ *When striking a single chord, a quite strong but steady movement of the tremolo arm will result in a powerful sweeping sound.*

4. Rock players from Jeff Beck to Eddie Van Halen (b. 1957) and Steve Vai have extended the range of whammy bar techniques with effects like the 'dive bomb' (depressing the bar to lower the note fully until the strings are completely slack).

◀ *The tremolo arm is gradually fully depressed to create a 'dive-bombing' effect.*

Section One: The Basics

TAPPING

Rather than using a plectrum to pick a note, you can play it by tapping the string firmly against the fretboard using a picking-hand finger. Rock guitarists, such as Eddie Van Halen, Randy Rhodes (1956–82), Nuno Bettencourt (b. 1966) and Joe Satriani (b. 1956), use tapping as a regular part of their lead playing.

Tapping allows the guitarist to change between low and high notes on the same string, making possible large interval leaps that are unobtainable in normal playing. Eddie Van Halen was one of the pioneers of tapping. His straightforward approach was 'since you've got fingers on both hands why not use both of them to fret notes?' The world of rock guitar has never looked back, and today tapping is a widely used technique in rock circles.

TAPPING TECHNIQUES

If you intend to play an entire solo with nothing but tapping, you could jettison your plectrum and use your first finger to tap. However, most guitarists prefer to keep the plectrum ready for use between the first finger and thumb, and instead use the second finger to tap notes. Whichever finger you use, make sure that you tap with the bony tip of the finger, rather than the soft fleshy pad to get the clearest sound.

You can angle your tapping finger so that it is in line with the fretboard (horizontal tapping, or position the tapping finger at right angles to the fretboard (vertical tapping) – either method will suffice for basic tapping patterns, but a vertical tapping

▶ *Eddie Van Halen's tapping technique is showcased on 'Eruption' and 'Spanish Fly'.*

Complete Guitar Handbook

▶ *Tapping enables guitarists to mix high and low notes.*

technique will provide you with more possibilities as your playing develops. To get a good tone, tap the fingerboard with a fast, strong action just behind the fretwire.

Although you can perform tapping with a clean sound, it's easier at first to use some distortion because the extra sustain means that you don't need to tap so hard to fret each note.

TAPS AND SLURS

Tapping is often combined with pull-offs to create fast legato licks. These are often based upon arpeggio patterns, with the high tapped notes taken from the same arpeggio as the fretted notes.

T P P H T P P H T P P H T P P H

(8) 3 0 3 (12) 3 0 3 (15) 3 0 3 (12) 3 0 3

T
A
B

▲ *Tapping, Example 1. The tap hand moves, while the fret hand plays the same phrase. The tapped notes are circled.*

GUITAR SET-UP

The lower the action on your guitar the easier you'll find it to produce notes clearly when tapping. Make sure that your guitar's intonation is set up accurately, as the large interval leaps that tapping allows will highlight any intonation problems. Many tap specialists use a string damper near the nut in order to minimize the unwanted ringing of adjacent strings. Tapping is easiest on an electric guitar with powerful pickups; try adjusting your pickups so that they are close to the strings. Using compression will help disguise any volume imbalances between notes.

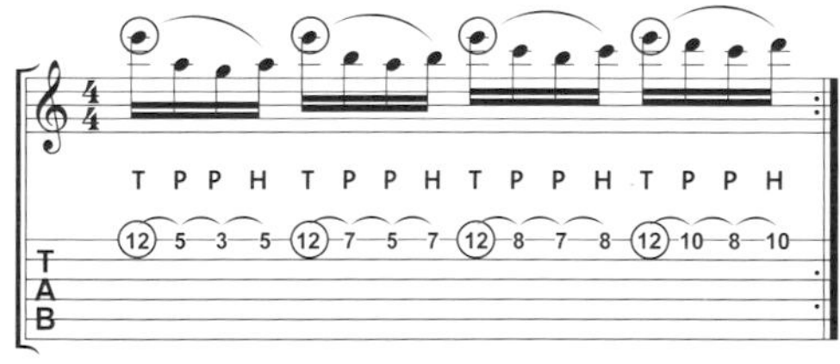

▲ *Tapping, Example 2. The tap hand plays the same note, while the fret hand moves along the fretboard.*

Section One: The Basics

CONSTRUCTING SOLOS

The real benefit of having studied all the scales and lead playing techniques covered in the earlier pages of this book can be realized when you begin to put all this knowledge into action by constructing your own lead guitar solos.

USING SCALES

To solo over any chord sequence you'll need a scale, as this will set the range of notes that will fit with the backing chords. For example, if a song uses chords from the key of C major, all the notes of the C major scale can be used as the basis for your solo. However, you don't need to play all the notes of the scale, or play them in any set order. You should always aim to make your solo sound fresh and inventive, rather than scale-like.

PHRASING

Once you've spent hours practising a scale it's all too easy to keep playing it in a continuous way when soloing. The best method of breaking this habit is to leave spaces between notes so that you start to create short phrases. Within these phrases use notes of different lengths: some long notes that you sustain, balanced by some very quick short notes. This rhythmic variety will add interest and shape to your phrases. To start with, experiment with the C major scale; instead of playing it in strict time, vary the length of some notes and leave some gaps.

▲ *C major scale played ascending and descending with rhythmic shaping. Leave gaps between some notes and make some notes shorter or longer than others.*

Try to incorporate rhythmic variety into your improvisations, remembering that you should also vary the direction in which you play: there's no need to

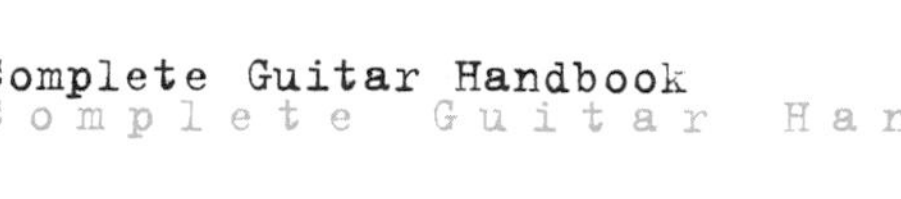

play up the whole range of the scale before you play some descending notes. Adopt a melodic approach in which your improvisation can weave up and down the scale.

▲ Sample melody using the C major scale.

USING INTERVALS

One thing that always makes a solo sound too scale-like is using notes that are adjacent to each other in a scale. This type of playing gives the game away to the listener – they can hear, almost instantly, that the improvisation is derived from a scale. Using interval gaps when playing a scale is a perfect way to break away from this scalic sound.

▲ Use intervals to make a solo less scale-like.

REPETITION

By repeating short series of notes you will begin to establish phrases that will give your solo a sense of structure. By repeating these phrases, or variations on them, you will give the listener something recognizable to latch on to, instead of a seemingly random series of notes with no direction.

▲ Use repetition of phrases to give your solo structure.

SPECIALIST TECHNIQUES

Don't forget to use some of the specialist guitar techniques that have been covered in this chapter. String bends, vibrato, slides or slurs will all help give your solo an individual character and will turn it from a melody into a true guitar solo.

STAGECRAFT

Once you feel confident that you can cope with the technical challenges of rhythm and lead guitar playing covered so far in this book, then it's time to think of joining a band and playing your first gig. Spending a little time thinking about stagecraft will mean you are fully prepared.

CABLES

Avoid cost cutting when it comes to buying guitar cables. For stage work you need a cable you can rely upon: one in which the connections won't pull loose as you leap across the stage. Choose a cable long enought to allow you freedom of movement around a stage. If you're planning a really boisterous stage act you should consider investing in a radio transmitter – this will eliminate the need for a cable between the guitar and amplifier.

▲ *Buy the best cables you can afford to suit your needs, and ensure that they are long enough.*

TUNING

Once you set foot on the stage the show begins – so always get your guitar in tune before you come on stage. Obtain an electronic tuner so that you can tune-up easily in noisy environments. You can even set up the tuner in line between the guitar and amplifier so that you can check the tuning between songs.

NOISE

Consider buying a compressor, or even a volume pedal, so that you can cut down on unwanted signal noise from distortion pedals or high amp settings, both between songs and during quite passages.

Complete Guitar Handbook

▶ *Using a footswitch will allow you to change sounds without stopping playing.*

FEEDBACK

Unless you want to attract feedback (a high-pitched screaming sound) for special effect, try not to stand right next to and facing into the amplifier if the volume is set very high. If your guitar feeds back too easily, ask a guitar technician to check it over.

BALANCE

Adjust the volume of your amplifier and guitar so that it blends well with the other instruments, but don't be scared of turning it up for solos so that you can be heard when playing single notes.

LISTENING

It's essential that you listen to what other musicians in the band are playing, so that you can play together as a cohesive unit. Listen to how your guitar tone and volume blends with or stands out from the band, and adjust this to make it musically appropriate for each song.

FOLDBACK

Get to the venue early and conduct a soundcheck so that levels can be set. If possible, use monitors (small wedge-shaped speakers that face towards the musicians) so that you can hear the vocals clearly. At large venues a sound engineer may provide you with a full foldback mix – if so, make sure the sound is adjusted so that you can hear not only your guitar, but also the rest of the band clearly.

SAFETY

As a gigging musician you could be plugging your amplifier into mains circuits with sometimes dubious wiring. Always use a circuit breaker – it could save your life!

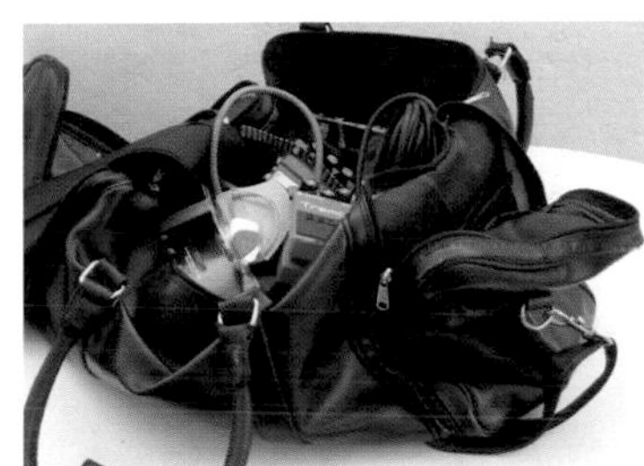

▶ *Be prepared and organize all your gear before you go and play.*

Section One: The Basics

USING EFFECTS

INTRODUCTION

Music starts with sound; the thoughts and emotions you feel when first hearing a live performance or recording are influenced by the sound of the voice or the instruments as much as by the notes they are producing. Part of a guitar sound can be the proper use of effects.

There are few things as stirring as the sound of a great guitar plugged directly into a great amplifier. That said, proper use of effects can add emotional impact for the listener. But improper use can detract as well, so there are a few things to keep in mind when confronting the plethora of sound-altering devices available. Generally the 'less-is-more' principle applies. While lathering on the distortion or delay may sound great when playing alone in your room, it can result in your parts being lost in the mix when competing with bass, drums, keyboards and other guitars. Also, the variety of processors available can be daunting; try to hear the sound that you are seeking in your head or on record first, then look for an effect to create it. This is not to say that just grabbing a pedal and playing with it can't provide musical inspiration of its own sort, but try to avoid using effects just because you can.

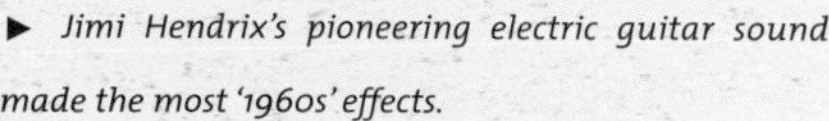

▶ *Jimi Hendrix's pioneering electric guitar sound made the most '1960s' effects.*

Complete Guitar Handbook

THE GREAT MASTERS

▲ *Jeff Beck uses minimum effects for maximum impact.*

The rock history books are full of effects masters, some of whom achieved their marvellous tone with surprisingly few effects. Jeff Beck usually uses just a little distortion and delay to wrest an amazing number of tones out of his Stratocaster. Jimi Hendrix used much less distortion than you might think; tunes like 'Little Wing' were built on clean or only mildly distorted tones. A few pedals – Fuzz Face, Octavia, Uni-Vibe and wah-wah – were all he needed to reinvent the electric guitar. At the other end of the spectrum Pink Floyd's David Gilmour and U2's The Edge's (b. 1961) effects and rigs would take books of their own, and Adrian Belew's (b. 1949) style is largely informed by his use of a car-load of effects that allow him to make his guitar sound like an elephant, rhinoceros, cello, trumpet or seagull – anything but a guitar.

In the following sections we will cover individual types of effects: how they work, how to use them and how some of these artists make magic with them. The more fully you understand the principles of each one, the more easily you will recognize their use by your favourite guitarist.

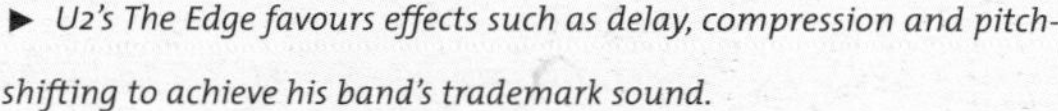

► *U2's The Edge favours effects such as delay, compression and pitch-shifting to achieve his band's trademark sound.*

Section One: The Basics

COMPRESSION

You may have wondered how professional guitarists get their notes to resound so clearly and evenly, or how country guitarists get that 'squeezed-out' sound in their notes. Partly it is the years of practise that has evolved into their technical skill, but another factor is the use of compression.

To understand the use of compressors it helps to understand the difference between distortion and sustain. Distortion is a quality of sound; sustain refers to how long the note, clean or distorted, remains audible. Compression can be used to increase 'apparent' sustain without any distortion.

▲ *Adrian Belew's playing with King Crimson and the Bears, as well as his solo material, has made heavy use of compression.*

It helps if you think of a compressor as an automatic volume pedal; regardless of how hard or how soft you strike the strings, the compressor brings the signal sent to the amplifier to a pre-set level. As the string vibration slows and the guitar volume drops, an amplifier in the compressor raises it back to the same level as the initial attack.

WHAT DOES IT SOUND LIKE?

To illustrate how this works, set your amplifier for a clean sound, strike a note and as the volume falls off, turn up your amplifier volume. You will hear the note appearing to sustain longer. To understand why it is 'appearing', as opposed to actually sustaining, try again without turning up the volume. Listen closely.

Complete Guitar Handbook

▶ *Pedal compressors such as this are used to control volume levels, and reduce dynamic range.*

You will hear that the note ends at the same time; it just doesn't remain as loud for as long.

Pedal compressors usually have controls called sustain or threshold, gain or level, and sometimes an attack control. The first knob adjusts the amount of compression. Since adding compression can initially lower the volume, the gain knob helps raise it back up to compensate. The attack control sets how quickly the compression will begin.

COMPRESSOR APPLICATIONS

1. For clean rhythms, or country 'chicken picking', you can create a squeezing effect by setting a quick attack.
2. The added sustained volume helps to make chorusing and flanging effects much more dramatic.
3. It can provide controlled feedback with minimal distortion and volume.

You can hear these applications used to great effect by Adrian Belew and Andy Summers (b. 1942).

A compressor will also lower the sound of loud notes and raise the volume of the quieter ones, stabilizing an uneven instrument or player. Compressors are often used on acoustic guitars so that the bass strings do not overpower the treble strings, and in the studio to prevent overloading and to help the guitar stand out in the mix.

▶ *Andy Summers' sparse, tasteful rhythm guitar reveals a mastery of effects, including compression, delay and chorus.*

Section One: The Basics

DISTORTION

Distortion is the sound of rock guitar, though even the horn-like tone of Charlie Christian's jazz solos was the product of an amplifier driven to its limits. What is distortion? Without getting into the physics of it, when the ear hears certain overtones surrounding a clean tone it discerns that as distortion.

One way of getting a distorted guitar tone is with a pedal (for the other, see 'Amplifiers', pages 308–323). Discussing these pedals can be confusing because terms like distortion, overdrive and fuzz, are often interchanged; while technically they describe different levels of distorted sound – overdrive being the least amount, distortion next, and fuzz the greatest. For the purposes of this discussion we will use distortion (lower case) as a general term.

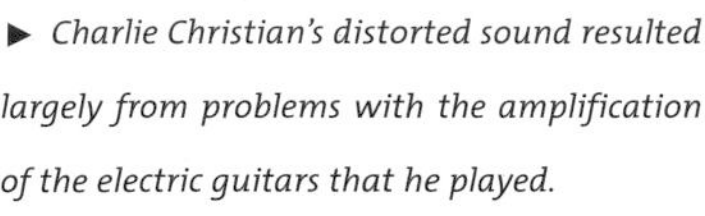

▶ *Charlie Christian's distorted sound resulted largely from problems with the amplification of the electric guitars that he played.*

Complete Guitar Handbook

The sound from an overdrive pedal maintains the character of the original signal.

FUZZTONES

Early distortion boxes sounded very little like an overdriven tube amplifier. Dubbed 'fuzztones' due to their buzzsaw-like tone, they have been used creatively by Jeff Beck, Jimi Hendrix, and later by Adrian Belew who showed that you could produce synthesizer, cello and even animal sounds with a fuzz unit. Fuzz has been used for every kind of pop music, from psychedelia to swamp.

GETTING THE RIGHT EFFECT

To emulate the sound of an overdriven amplifier more accurately you might want a distortion or overdrive effect. Some pedals use an actual tube, while others use increasingly sophisticated chips to offer the feel and sound of an overdriven amp. Most distortion devices come with controls marked distortion, drive or gain; level or volume; and tone.

To get the most out of your distorted sound, remember that the level of the input signal will affect the distorted sound – i.e. single-coil pickups will react differently to higher-powered humbuckers plugged into the same pedal. So if your favourite guitarist plays a Les Paul and you play a Strat, you will have to turn the distortion knob up further on the pedal to achieve a similar effect. Also remember the less-is-more theory: too much distortion can make your notes indistinct, especially if you are playing fast. Check out Van Halen or Hendrix and you will find that they are using less distortion than you might think. If your amplifier is already slightly distorted when your guitar volume is fully up, you only need add a little gain on the pedal to make it sing. Fuzz units tend to sound better through a slightly distorted amplifier and/or with the tone rolled back on the instrument.

A distortion pedal produces a grittier, crunchier sound than an overdrive pedal.

Section One: The Basics

CHORUS

Think about the rich sound of a 12-string guitar, or the sound of two guitars playing identical parts at the same time. Twelve-strings, and the doubling of guitars, have long been used to fill out recordings. To emulate that sonic girth when you are playing live and alone, with only six strings, is where you'll need chorus.

The fullness of sound and chiming characteristics that you experience in the aforementioned situations are created by notes that are out of sync and out of tune. If you were somehow able to get the strings of the 12-string exactly in tune and pluck them all at the same time, they would not sound nearly as rich. Likewise, if two guitarists play perfectly in tune and in time, the sound won't be much bigger than if only one guitar was playing. It is the delay of the pick hitting one of the doubled strings after the other, and the slight tuning variations, that give a 12-string its distinctive sound, and

◀ *Jimmy Page often used a double-neck guitar when playing 'Stairway to Heaven' to achieve a fuller sound.*

Complete Guitar Handbook

it is the timing inconsistencies and tuning differences of two guitarists, or an overdubbed part, that expand the sonic field. The chorus pedal was developed in an effort to duplicate this effect in a live situation and uses delay and pitch-shifting to achieve its end.

HOW DOES IT WORK?

A chorus device, be it analogue pedal or digital rack-mounted unit, delays the original signal by approximately 20 milliseconds, constantly varying this delay time over a range of up to about five milliseconds (plus or minus). If you take a standard delay pedal, and play a note while turning the delay time control knob back and forth, you will hear the pitch of the note vary. A chorus uses a minimal delay fluctuation and mixes it in with the original signal, thus emulating the effect of twice as many strings being played slightly out of time and tune.

▲ *A chorus pedal works by mixing a delayed signal with the original sound.*

Chorus pedals are provided with at least rate and depth controls. The depth control increases the amount of pitch fluctuation, while the rate knob determines how quickly it fluctuates. Some pedals include a blend or level control that allows you to set the amount of effect versus dry signal. This is preferable, especially if you plan to use chorus on solos, where too much can muddy your tone, especially if you are using distortion. Sometimes a feedback control is included to send the delayed signal back to be delayed again for a more intense effect.

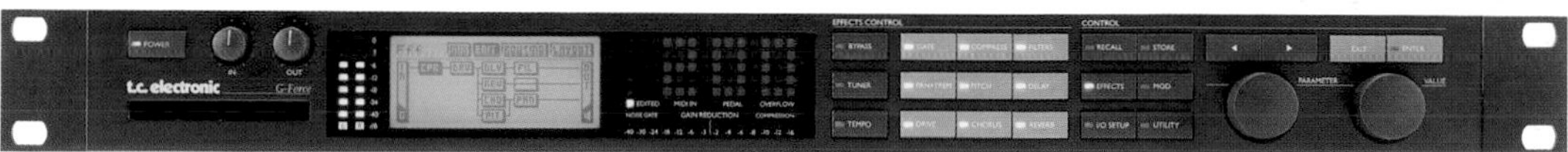

▲ *A digital chorus unit such as this allows you to control the exact amount of delay time you want.*

Section One: The Basics

FLANGING AND PHASING

The accepted explanation of the origin of the term flanging is that an engineer placed a thumb on a recording tape reel, or 'flange', as they are known in the UK, and liked the whooshing sound that it produced. This whoosh became a favourite sound of the psychedelic era – think 'Itchycoo Park' by the Small Faces.

Our engineer's thumb caused a very short, but extremely irregular delay effect that is simulated in flanger devices by sweeping a short delay (shorter than a chorus – about five to 10 milliseconds) over a wide range (from one to 10, or two to 20 milliseconds) with a certain amount of feedback, or recycling of the delay.

▲ *The Small Faces made use of the distinctive 'jet-taking-off' flanging effect that was perfected in the early 1960s.*

DON'T CONFUSE EFFECTS

Flangers are confused with phase shifters due to the similar sweeping sound. Phase shifters use an even shorter delay and almost no feedback; this acts like a filter, sweeping the tone of the signal continually from treble to bass and back. A phase

Complete Guitar Handbook

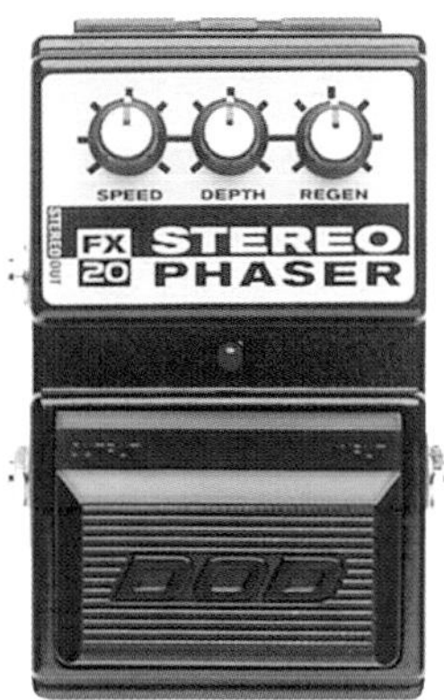

◀ *A phaser has a characteristic swirling sound that can be varied with a speed control to provide colour to a rhythm-guitar part or increased to produce a bubbling effect.*

shifter is desirable over flanging in cases where a more subtle effect is required, or where it is important that the pitch remains unaffected.

A DISTINCTIVE SOUND

In addition to the speed or rate controls found on chorus pedals, flangers often have an added control marked feedback or regeneration. This recycles the delay back through itself. Here, it increases the 'metallic' sound of the effect. Extremely fast rate settings on both flangers and phasers can result in a kind of Leslie speaker effect, à la Stevie Ray Vaughan. Setting a flanger for a medium rate, a lower depth, and minimal feedback can mimic a mild chorus effect. A flanger set like this, rather than a chorus, helped define Andy Summers' sound in the Police. A slow sweep with more intense depth and feedback settings will get closer to the Hendrix or Van Halen sound. Eddie also uses a phaser for this type of effect.

ADVANCED FUNCTIONS

Some more upscale flanging and phasing units will allow you to tap in the time of the sweep to match the tempo of the song that you are playing; some even have a 'trigger' setting that starts the sweep anew each time you strike the strings; this can work well for funk applications.

Stereo versions of these effects (including chorus) can work in one of two ways. One version sends the dry signal to one output and the effect to the other. The other version sends effects to both outputs but sweeping out of phase.

▶ *As well as producing a whooshing sound, the flanger also produces a metallic warbling reminiscent of sci-fi ray guns.*

Section One: The Basics

AMBIENT EFFECTS: DELAY AND REVERB

Your guitar sound does not exist in a vacuum but in the air around it. Musicians are often required to play and record in clubs and studios that are less than acoustically ideal. Luckily, engineers have invented methods of modifying the ambience artificially. (Ambience literally means 'the surrounding air'.)

AMBIENCE

Room ambience is due in part to the time delay between a sound leaving its source (the amplifier) and its return from obstacles in its path. The ear hears the sound first from its source and then again – after various delays – bounced off walls, ceiling and floors. The amount, length and tone of these delays allows the

▲ *Some ambient effects will make it sound as if you are playing in a concert hall, even if you are in your bedroom.*

Complete Guitar Handbook

brain to gauge the size and nature of the room in which the sound is produced. To counteract the effect of close miking and dead-sounding rooms, engineers came up with some effects to restore a natural room ambience. These effects allow the guitar to sound like it is being played in a huge empty hall, even in a small basement-size club or recording room.

TAPE DELAY

Les Paul (b. 1915) not only invented his legendary guitar, but was also one of the first to discover tape delay. Running a signal into a reel-to-reel tape recorder, he recorded it on the 'record' head and played it back as it passed over the same machine's 'playback' head. The signal coming off the playback head was delayed by the distance between the two heads. This delayed signal, added to the original signal on the main recording, creating a delay effect. By recycling the delayed signal over the record and playback heads, additional repeats were achieved.

Varying the length of tape delay is done in a number of ways. The speed of the tape can be changed from seven to 15 to 30 inches per second (ips), causing the delay to get shorter as the speed increases; or the playback head can be moved further away from the record head to lengthen the delay. Multiple playback heads can also be used, allowing multiple delays. Recycling the repeats and mixing them further back is one way of creating the illusion of a much larger room.

The 'slap' echo used on early rockabilly recordings was also produced in this way. Used more as an effect than as a means of recreating ambience, it is one of the earliest examples of using 'effects' in recording.

▶ *Elvis's early singles were noted for their slap-back echo.*

Section One: The Basics

DELAYS

As with flanging, the discovery of the tape delay effect in the studio created a tremendous demand for a unit that could recreate the effect live. Thus the Echoplex, a portable tape echo, was born. Alternatives quickly appeared in the form of analogue and digital delays.

ANALOGUE DELAY

Tape and tape heads have certain attendant problems that caused researchers to seek a way of creating the effect using the budding chip technology. They quickly developed 'analogue' delays, eliminating tape by passing the signal along a series of IC chips. This 'bucket-brigade' technology allows tape-type effects using smaller devices (tape delays are about the size of a desktop stereo speaker, while analogue units are more the size of a trade paperback).

▲ *Analogue delays appeared in the 1970s and are the link between tape and digital delays.*

In analogue delays the sound quality of the echoes diminishes significantly as the delay times and number of repeats increases. They are usable only up to about half a second of delay, after which even the highest-quality units add so much noise and unpleasant distortion that they became pretty worthless. But for many purposes that is plenty. Many guitarists value analogue delays for their warmth, and the fact that the degradation of the signal with each repeat adds naturalness, as well as preventing the ensuing signal from obscuring the original. The Edge and Andy Summers used analogue delays to set up rhythmic patterns, while Adrian Belew placed one on a microphone stand and manipulated the feedback by hand to create insect sounds. Bucket-brigade chips have become increasingly rare, so newly manufactured analogue delays can be quite expensive.

Complete Guitar Handbook

DIGITAL DELAY

Digital technology solved some of the problems inherent in analogue delays. The easiest way to grasp the difference between analogue and digital is to think about it like this: analogue deals with the signal itself, while digital breaks that signal down into a digital code. The code is then processed and translated back into a signal again before sending it to the output. Since the encoded signal is less subject to degradation, it allows longer delays with less distortion.

▲ *You can hear The Edge's use of delay on 'Where The Streets Have No Name'.*

Digital delays allow delay times of 16 seconds, 32 seconds, and beyond. These extremely long delay times have applications like playing along with yourself, much like Robert Fripp's (b. 1946) heavily effected guitar style, his self-styled Frippertronics. The other result is that shorter delay times are extremely clean, to the point where the delayed signal can be virtually indistinguishable from the original.

► *Digital delays sample the guitar's sound and play it back after a defined period.*

Section One: The Basics

USING DELAY

As we have already seen, delays have a number of uses. They can be used for ambience, for doubling, for creating rhythmic patterns, and for many other effects. Delay plays a subtle but distinct role in the sound of artists like Jeff Beck, David Gilmour, Eddie Van Halen and Robben Ford (b. 1951).

Confusion in using delay effects stems from an inability by manufacturers to agree on terminology. Most delays have three controls. One is delay length; this can be called delay time, effect, range or simply delay. Another control affects the number of repeats, from a single repetition of the signal to 'runaway' feedback; this knob can be called feedback, regen (regeneration) or repeat. The third controls the amount of effect added to the original or 'dry' signal (a signal with no effects is called dry; with effects it is wet). This may be called mix, blend, delay or effect, depending on the unit. Many delays will also have a dry output and an effect output, allowing an unaffected signal to be sent to one amplifier or recording track, and just the delay signal or a blend of dry and effected signal to another amplifier or track.

▶ *Robben Ford makes use of a small amount of delay, as well as volume and wah-wah pedals.*

Complete Guitar Handbook

▲ *Ensure that you tailor the amount of delay you use to the room size you are playing, and to monitor this during performance.*

ARTIFICIAL AMBIENCE

To sound like you are playing in a garage or basement with concrete walls there are a couple of things to remember:

1. Use a short delay and a number of repeats, with quite a bit of effect signal in the mix.
2. Increasing the length of the delay increases the room size, but you should reduce the amount of effect or the repeats will obscure your original signal. Also, decrease the number of repeats as you increase the length of the delay or you will sound like you are playing in a cave (unless that is the effect you want).

Too much delay will sink your instrument into the mix, to an indistinguishable level. That said, when playing your guitar alone, it might seem that you have your mix right, but when the rest of the band is added the sound becomes too dry. Be prepared to add delay to your signal as a club fills up, since bodies will absorb the ambience.

Digital delays work well for a doubling effect. For this you need the delay to be as clean as possible since it will be mixed equally, or almost equally, with the original. The delay should be long enough to fatten the sound, but short enough so that it is not a rhythmic pattern. Use a single repeat or it will start to sound like reverb.

◀ *When you are trying to create a natural ambience remember that delay is never louder than the direct signal.*

Section One: The Basics

RHYTHMIC DELAYS AND LOOPING

Digital delays are also good for setting up rhythmic repeat patterns. They can turn your guitar into a sequencer, or result in polyrhythmic patterns like those created by Andy Summers or The Edge. Looping delays can provide a single guitarist with extra parts, or can create highly textured, atmospheric pads.

▲ *When playing in a band with a large drum kit, ensure the drummer can hear the delays otherwise you will lose the beat.*

To use rhythmic delays with a live drummer, he or she must be able to hear you clearly because your delay time will set the tempo. Some digital delays allow you to set the delay length by tapping a switch, so you can make adjustments on the fly if the drummer wavers.

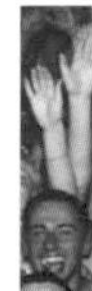

Complete Guitar Handbook

LOOPING EFFECTS

Digital delays with longer delay times (two seconds or more) allow you to create 'looping' effects by playing along with yourself, in the manner of Robert Fripp, Bill Frisell (b. 1951) and others. This can be done in one of two ways. The first is to set a very long delay time, with the mix at near equal, and the feedback at just below 'runaway'. This way, as old patterns fade, you can overlay new ones. The second method is to use the hold button (present on almost all digital delays) to lock in what you have played up until that point (called 'loops'), then perform improvisations that will not be recorded. These improvisations may sound very dry unless you are running your guitar signal through a second delay or reverb. Some delays include specific 'looping' functions, and some devices are meant for looping alone.

Dedicated loopers or combination looper/delay pedals often permit the player to slow the recorded loop to half speed or jump it up to double speed. Some devices also allow the signal to be thrown into reverse, for 'backwards guitar' effects.

▶ *Listen to* Exposure *by Robert Fripp to hear the first recorded evidence of his pioneering looping technique.*

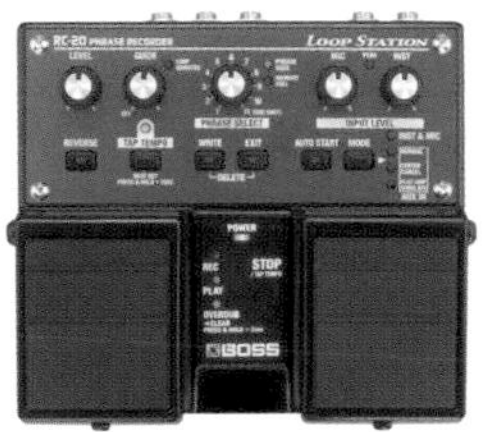

▲ *A looping device can add texture to your playing.*

THE SEQUENCER EFFECT

Emulating a sequencer requires only a short delay time and any sort of device will do.

1. Set the device for a single repeat.
2. Set your delay for 110 to 130 ms. If the device doesn't have a read-out use your ears to set a short slap.
3. Set the blend for the same level delay as original signal (50 per cent).
4. Play an arpeggio with one note on each beat.
5. The delay will double the note, creating a sequencer-like pattern.
6. If you wish to accent the original note, back off the delay blend a little.

Section One: The Basics

REVERB

From surf music to ECM jazz records, reverb plays a major role in defining a guitarist's sound. Even the lack of reverb makes a statement about the kind of music you are making. In general, it is an effect that moves the sound further away from the listener the more it is applied.

WHAT IS REVERB?

Natural ambience is not the result of a single delay length or evenly spaced repeats. Sound is being constantly echoed back at us at various delay times, and the echoes are heard not as repeats, but as the ambience, size, type and emptiness or fullness of the room.

The distinction and the identical nature of their repeats limit delay units in their ability to reproduce ambience. Although they are adequate for sounds with little or no attack, like volume swells and lightly picked or strummed chords, the repeats become too distinct and the regularity of their spacing too pronounced when any hard picking or tight, funky chord work is required. The creation of a space around your sound is more the provenance of reverb.

◄ *The Beach Boys' early recordings give great examples of the all-time classic use of reverb.*

Complete Guitar Handbook

SPRING REVERB

An early type of mechanical reverb was the spring reverb. Found in many guitar amplifiers, it employs a transducer to convert the signal from electrical energy to mechanical energy, then sends it down a spring or springs to another transducer, where it is converted back to electrical energy. The time it takes to travel the length of the spring adds delay. The spring degrades the frequency response in a more uneven manner than analogue or digital delays, creating a more natural effect. More springs means a more natural effect, and longer springs create longer delays. Tube-driven spring reverbs offer extra warmth. Prone to a 'sproi-oi-oing' sound when subjected to hard attack, these are a must when searching for the true Duane Eddy surf tone.

▲ *The spring reverb's sound is created from the physical reverberations of a spring built into the amplifier.*

DIGITAL REVERB

The accuracy of digital reverbs allows them to simulate virtually any size and type of room, and place the sound anywhere in it. This technology gives us the airy ECM jazz sound (Pat Metheny, John Abercrombie (b. 1944), Bill Frisell et al). Similar to digital delays, digital reverbs take the signal and convert it to digital code, then add delays and frequency changes to simulate the desired room size and to place the sound in the desired location within it.

▶ *As well as simulating the sound of different room spaces, digital reverb can also mimic the sound of artificial reverb devices, such as reverb plates and chambers used in studios.*

Section One: The Basics

VOLUME AND WAH-WAH PEDALS

By placing volume and/or tone controls, like those on your guitar, into a pedal, manufacturers have managed to make those quotidian items into creative effects. George Harrison (1943–2001) and Larry Carlton (b. 1948) have turned the simple volume pedal into an expressive tool, while the wah-wah has provided rhythmic and vocal-like effects from Isaac Hayes' 'Shaft' to Hendrix.

VOLUME PEDAL

The volume pedal is simply a passive potentiometer placed in a pedal. Simple though it is, it has myriad uses. At its most basic, it allows you to adjust your volume without interrupting play, maintaining the proper mix with the band. If you are experiencing hum, or buzz, from your guitar, it can act as a noise-gate by instantly lowering your sound during quiet passages.

Many guitarists were inspired to get creative with volume pedals by pedal-steel players, who constantly manipulate one while playing. You will find that your pedal-steel licks sound more authentic if you swell into them with a pedal. You can also create lush

◀ *George Harrison: master of the volume pedal?*

Complete Guitar Handbook

▲ *Mark Knopfler and Dire Straits had great success with a wah-wah pedal.*

GETTING PEDAL-STEEL EFFECTS

1. Plug your guitar into the volume pedal.
2. Plug the pedal into a delay and then into your amplifier.
3. Set the delay for a longer delay (500–700 ms), with six or seven repeats, and the blend at about 30 per cent delay.
4. Play a chord and gradually increase the volume with the pedal from zero to full.
5. If your guitar has a vibrato arm, gently rock it – this will cause modulation as the different pitched notes echo against one another.

pads with a volume pedal and a delay: add distortion and play single low notes for a cello effect, or higher ones for a violin sound.

WAH-WAH

The wah-wah is similar to a volume pedal, but it has tone control. Unlike a guitar tone, the pedal has active circuitry that doesn't merely roll off high end, but actively boosts the highs at one end and the lows at the other. Often rocked in time for rhythmic effect, it can also be used for expressive tonal effects. The riff on the Dire Straits' hit 'Money for Nothing' is the sound of a partially backed-off wah-wah pedal. Accenting the treble on bent notes gives a distinct vocal effect, while slowing sweeping through the range as you play a rhythmic part can emulate a synthesizer filter.

Section One: The Basics

REGGAE

Reggae is a Jamaican style of music with four beats to the measure and the off-beats (beats two and four) strongly accented. It evolved from ska, a music style born in the early 1960s when Jamaican musicians changed the emphasis of the basic R&B rhythm from the first and third beats in the meaure to the second and fourth.

SKA

The most influential ska group was The Skatalites, a collection of classically trained musicians who played to dance-hall crowds in Jamaica's capital, Kingston. They adopted a tight, disciplined rhythm, designed to whip the dancers up into a frenzy, but kept the beat steady so nobody lost their footing.

ROCK STEADY

During the late 1960s, top Jamaican producers Leslie Kong and Coxsone Dodd slowed the beat down to create a more soulful, laid-back reggae style called rock steady. The main exponents of this style included Desmond Dekker, who had the No. 1 hit 'Israelites' (1969), and Jimmy Cliff, singer of 'Wonderful World' (1969). Many of their hits featured charismatic guitar lines from Ernest Ranglin (b. 1932) a renowned reggae session guitarist.

▶ *Officially formed in Jamaica in 1964, the Skatalites were central to the ska era.*

Complete Guitar Handbook

ROOTS

Roots reggae had come along by the early 1970s and it introduced an even more laid-back rhythm with a prominent bass line. Eric Clapton's cover of Bob Marley's 'I Shot the Sheriff' (1974) helped to introduce the style to the UK and the rest of the world, and Marley (1945–81) later became a megastar with songs like 'No Woman No Cry' (1975), 'Jamming' (1977) and 'Is This Love' (1978), before, tragically, he died of cancer in 1981. The roots reggae era has always been associated with heavy cannabis use and this is hardly surprising as practically all of the musicians, Marley included, were regular pot smokers. In fact, reggae artist Peter Tosh (1944–87) made his views clear on his album *Legalise It* (1976).

REGGAE TODAY

▲ *Hugely popular in the 1980s, Madness revived the ska style for a new audience.*

Although the popularity of ska, rock steady and roots reggae styles has waned over the past 20 years, they spawned a number of other sub-genres: dub, an instrumental style with all the vocals (except voice effects) removed; ragga, a harsher, more jagged style; and dance hall, a stripped down version with just drums, bass and vocals. Ska and reggae also influenced groups like Madness, UB40, Aswad, the Police and Musical Youth, who all had considerable chart success during the 1980s, and even pop, punk and alternative artists as diverse as 10cc, The Clash and Frank Zappa have employed catchy reggae rhythms at one time or another. More recently, artists like Ms Dynamite, Roni Size and Massive Attack have been keeping the style alive by mixing it with rock, soul, indie and rap influences.

► *Artists such as Ms Dynamite have brought reggae to the attention of a new audience.*

Section Two: Musical Styles

PLAYING REGGAE GUITAR

Reggae rhythm guitar is usually played as clean 'skanks' (downstrokes), with the strings damped as soon as the chord is sounded, although double-skank rhythms, where the downstrokes are swiftly followed by upstrokes,

▲ *Reggae music is characterized by the emphasis on the off-beat, which pulls the tempo back and gives the music a laid-back feel.*

are sometimes employed. The chord progressions are simple and often major based (e.g. D A D A) or minor based (e.g. Dm Am Dm Am). There is rarely any lead guitar in the style, although a second guitarist will often play repetitive note phrases with note damping (with the palm of the picking hand) to give the groove an even more rhythmic feel. If you have a 'portastudio', software sequencer or other multi-tracking device you can easily record both of these rhythms by yourself.

Guitar-wise, you can use just about any electric solidbody instrument and any reasonable amp to play reggae, but you will probably want to keep the sound clean and turn down your bass and mid-range controls so that your guitar doesn't end up fighting against that heavy bass!

Reggae rhythms can be very repetitive, so you might want to use some effects pedals to create more interest in the rhythm guitar parts. A digital delay unit

Complete Guitar Handbook

with the delay time set to your song's tempo beat can be used to make things sound psychedelic, while a wah-wah pedal, flanger, phaser or chorus unit can create more sonic variety and movement in the rhythm. You can also switch between your guitar's bridge and neck pickups to produce different tones for different songs or sections of a song.

PLAYING SKA GUITAR

Ska is a little trickier to play; while reggae uses two skanks per bar, ska uses four, and each of these is between the beats, so you need to be even more accurate with your strumming and use only upward strums over the guitar's thinner strings.

▲ *Ska features a very simple bass on the beat with the keyboards and guitar bouncing off the beat. The um-ska sound given, which gave ska its name, is the basis for virtually all reggae styles that followed.*

Whenever you're playing any reggae guitar style, you also need to consider how your guitar complements what the bassist and drummer in your band are playing so it sounds like you're working together as one, playing a steady, even rhythm. Listen to recordings by the Wailers, Desmond Dekker, Peter Tosh, Duke Reid or Aswad and you'll soon get the idea!

▲ *Aswad have a unique sound combining jazz, funk, soul and fusion layered over a rock-steady reggae beat.*

Section Two: Musical Styles

FLAMENCO

Flamenco music can be traced back to mid-nineteenth century Spain, when Andalucian musicians developed a 'café cantante' guitar style to accompany singers and dancers at local cafés. Although the earliest Spanish guitar players had relatively unrefined skills, the style evolved over the next half century until Ramon Montoya emerged in the early twentieth century as the first celebrated modern flamenco player.

Ramon was born in Madrid in 1880. He spent his early years cattle trading with his gypsy parents and bought a guitar. Swiftly learning the instrument, he was accompanying singers in Madrid cafés by the time he was 14. He formed a musical allegiance with one of the greatest Spanish singers of the time, Antonio Chacon, and they became a famous act. By then Montoya had developed an unprecedented level of virtuosity on his instrument, and singers had to change the way they sang to accommodate his playing; modern flamenco was born!

Montoya made more than 700 recordings with top cantantes and was a huge influence on the next generation of flamenco guitarists, including his nephew, Carlos Montoya, who developed the style further between the 1940s and 1960s.

◀ *Flamenco dancing was developed by Spanish gypsies in the fifteenth century.*

Complete Guitar Handbook

FLAMENCO TODAY

Today a number of talented flamenco guitarists are recognized worldwide, but the most respected of all these is Paco de Lucía. Born in 1947, Paco took up the guitar at an early age and was performing on Spanish radio by the time he was 12. As a teenager he toured with flamenco dancer José Greco and met Sabicas, an influential guitarist who encouraged Paco to pursue a more personal style. He took this advice and evolved into a highly individual player with a formidable technique, stretching well beyond the boundaries of traditional flamenco.

Paco also made a number of critically acclaimed acoustic guitar trio recordings with jazz-rock maestros Al Di Meola (b. 1954) and John McLaughlin including *Friday Night In San Francisco* (1980) and *The Guitar Trio* (1996). Despite this, his style has always remained decidedly Spanish: 'There was a time when I was concerned about losing myself,' he once said, 'but not now. I realize that, even if I wanted, I couldn't sound like anything other than flamenco.'

▲ *Renowned flamenco guitarist Paco de Lucía has one of the fastest, most intricate finger-picking techniques in the world.*

Section Two: Musical Styles

PLAYING FLAMENCO

While classical guitarists aim for a clean, elegant style, flamenco players tend to favour a more earthy, powerful and dynamic sound. Flamenco guitarists use a number of specialist techniques, including rasgueado, tremolo and golpe. A rasgueado is a unique strumming technique created by fanning or brushing the fingers across the strings to generate a circular effect. To achieve this, hold your strumming hand tightly closed and then strum the strings by releasing the fingers in quick succession. A tremolo involves playing a single note repeatedly and swiftly with the picking-hand fingers to produce long, sustained notes. To play a tremolo, pick a string with your third finger, then your middle finger and then your index finger of the picking hand in quick succession and repeat the pattern again and again. A golpe is a percussive effect performed by tapping the instrument's body with the picking hand to reinforce rhythms and accents in the music.

▲ *The guitar provides the accompaniment to strong, rhythmic, passionate dancing in traditional flamenco.*

There are dozens of different flamenco styles and these are defined by characteristic melodic, rhythmic and harmonic structures. The most popular of these styles include bulerías, soleares, alegrías, fandangos, rondeña and tanguillos. Each one has a distinctive mood, although many are actually regional variants of each other. Flamenco guitarists

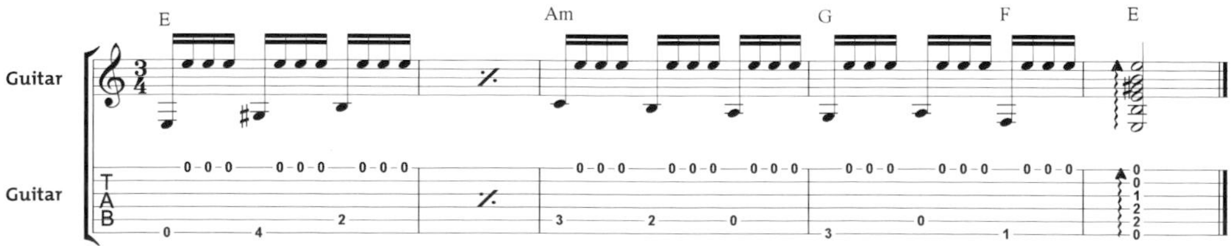

▲ *In flamenco, the exact guitar lines played are normally improvized around a standard theme.*

Complete Guitar Handbook

also play a number of other folk and Latin influenced styles including garrotín, farruca, guajiras and rhumba. The traditional flamenco posture has the guitar resting against the upper part of the body and held tightly between thigh and upper right arm.

▲ *A capo is a simple device that allows the pitch of the guitar's open strings to be changed.*

TECHNIQUES

While the capo is rarely used in classical guitar playing, it is commonly used in flamenco music as it allows the guitarist to change keys while preserving his or her favourite chord voicings. Flamenco players also use the capo because it shortens the vibrating string length and can thus brighten the instrument's sound. Flamenco guitarists also make greater use of their thumbs and fingers than classical players: in classical music, the thumb is usually limited to playing the bass notes, while the next three fingers concentrate on the higher strings; in flamenco, the thumb can range over all six strings and all four picking-hand fingers are usually employed. Flamenco players also mute the strings with their left hand while strumming with the right to produce a percussive rhythmic style.

FLAMENCO GUITAR

Although flamenco guitars look similar to classical instruments, they are actually quite different; classical guitars tend to have deep rosewood bodies while flamenco instruments are thinner and usually constructed from cypress. Flamenco guitars tend to produce a louder, more penetrating sound than classical instruments. They also have their strings set lower and feature a plastic shield on the soundboard to protect the body from damage caused by the energetic finger rasgueados and golpes employed by the players.

► *A flamenco guitar is deceptively similar to but slightly smaller than a typical classical guitar.*

Section Two: Musical Styles

CLASSICAL

Although guitar-like instruments have been around since the Middle Ages, the 'classical' guitar as we know it today didn't appear until the middle of the nineteenth century. And its repertoire was non-existent until Andrés Segovia started performing 50 years later.

Segovia was born in Grenada, Spain in 1893. He started playing guitar at an early age and quickly developed a virtuoso playing style. He created a basic classical guitar repertoire by adapting music composed for other instruments to his own and, by the time he was 20, had arranged pieces by Bach, Handel, Tarrega, Chopin, Schumann and Mozart. By the late 1920s, Segovia's arrangements had become standards and he was performing them in front of Spanish royalty. Composers of the period took note, and the likes of Villa-Lobos, Falla, Castelnuovo-Tedesco and Ponse began to write music specifically for the classical guitar.

▲ *Self-taught, Andrés Segovia plucked the strings with a combination of flesh and nail that helped him produce a wide range of tones.*

Segovia put the classical guitar on the map as a 'serious' instrument and personally taught a further generation of classical virtuosos, including Alirio

Complete Guitar Handbook

Diaz (b. 1923), Julian Bream (b. 1933), Christopher Parkening (b. 1947), Eliot Fisk (b. 1954), John Williams and Alexandre Lagoya (1929–99). These players took the classical technique to new heights and broadened its repertoire further by performing contributions from other new composers.

▲ *Taught by Andrés Segovia, Julian Bream also studied piano, cello, harmony and composition at the Royal College of Music, London.*

PLAYING CLASSICAL GUITAR

To adopt the correct classical guitar posture, sit on a chair and rest the centre of your instrument's body on your left leg. Angle the neck upwards so that your left arm (assuming you're a right-handed player) can reach the fingerboard without any obstructions. Rest your right arm on the upper edge of the guitar's body so that you can position your right hand's fingers directly over the strings near the sound hole. You might also want to place your left foot on a small footstool to bring your left leg up a little to better support the instrument. Practise picking up the guitar and getting into playing position so that it feels natural and easy. Make sure you feel relaxed and there is no tension in your limbs when you do this.

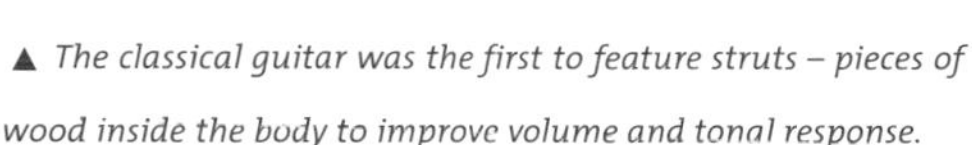

▲ *The classical guitar was the first to feature struts – pieces of wood inside the body to improve volume and tonal response.*

Section Two: Musical Styles

CLASSICAL TECHNIQUES

▲ *Classical guitarists use their thumb and first three fingers to pick strings, as opposed to a plectrum.*

The classical guitar is picked by the tips/nails of the thumb and first three fingers of the right hand (or left hand for left-handed players) so it is important to keep these tidy. These fingers are labelled as follows after their Spanish names: P = pulgar (thumb), I = indice (index finger), M = medio (middle finger) and A = anular (third finger).

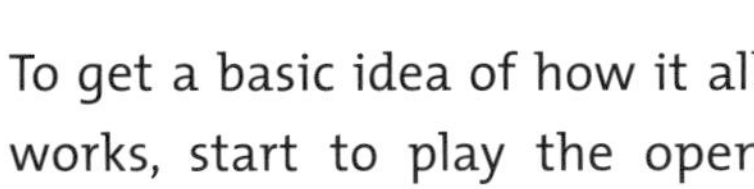

To get a basic idea of how it all works, start to play the open sixth string (the thickest string) with a downward movement of the tip of your thumb, and then, while this low note is still ringing out, strike the open third, second and first strings consecutively with upward movements from your index, middle and third fingers respectively. Repeat this series of movements again and again so that you are following the pattern PIMA PIMA PIMA PIMA. Now start to reverse the order of your finger movements so that your thumb stroke is followed by your third finger, your middle finger and then your index finger: PAMI PAMI PAMI PAMI. Then combine the two exercises so that you alternate between the two: PIMA PAMI PIMA PAMI. Once you feel comfortable with these variations, you'll be in a position to start learning classical guitar music.

▲ *Student Eurico Pereira learns the correct technique from Eliot Fisk.*

Complete Guitar Handbook

The fretting hand is equally important as it has to articulate the notes you are picking. With your thumb behind the neck, position your fingers so that they arch around and their fingertips are perpendicular to the strings. You must have very short fingernails on this hand so that you can press down on the strings and articulate notes cleanly and accurately. The fretting hand switches between chordal positions (for playing arpeggios) and a one-finger-per-fret style (for scalar melodies).

TREMOLO

Classical guitarists also employ a tremolo technique which involves the I, M and A fingers playing a continuous, repeating pattern on a single note, a 'ligado' technique which involves striking a note and then hammering on to another note on the same string with a finger, and rubato, a technique involving the use of subtle tempo changes to accentuate and embellish specific parts of the music.

READING MUSIC

Although you can learn how to play the classical guitar by ear, it is normally taught conventionally with traditional music notation. It is therefore a good idea to familiarize yourself with the notes on the conventional music stave, but bear in mind that to make guitar music easy to read, the notes on the fingerboard are often written one octave higher than their actual pitch. If you're serious about playing classical guitar, we recommend you see a tutor regularly to ensure that you learn to sight-read properly and do not develop any bad playing habits.

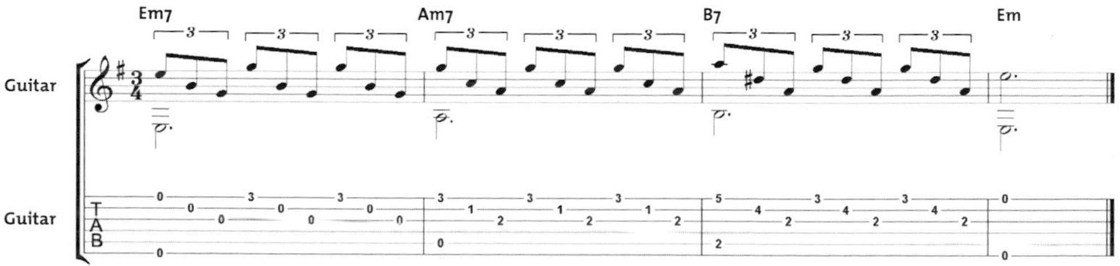

▲ *If you can read music, try playing through this excerpt from Francisco Tárrega's* Étude in E Minor, *for a true idea of how music for the classical guitar can sound.*

Section Two: Musical Styles

COUNTRY

Country music originally grew out of American folk music and it now encompasses a variety of styles, including bluegrass, American folk, hillbilly, country-rock, zydeco (cajun music) and C&W (country and western). At its core, country is a simple music and most of its songs are built around simple chord progressions and melodies played on guitars, fiddles and other instruments.

The country genre was 'born' in the late 1920s when Jimmie Rodgers (1897–1933) and the Carter Family signed recording contracts with Victor Records. Rodgers had a unique voice and the Carters had an impressive repertoire of 'old-style' American folk tunes. They appeared regularly on the Grand Ole Opry, a legendary Nashville-based national radio show.

THE FIRST COWBOY SINGERS

By the 1930s, a number of other country music strands started to become popular: 'cowboy' singers such as Roy Rogers (1911–68) and Gene Autry (1907–98) appeared in popular films; western swing bands like Bob Wills' Texas Playboys successfully fused country-folk with big band, blues, Dixieland and Hawaiian steel sounds; and Bill Monroe introduced a more Celtic-influenced bluegrass style.

◄ *Gene Autry had one of the most visually stunning Martin guitars, the D-45, made for him in 1932.*

Complete Guitar Handbook

HONKY TONK

In the 1940s, a style called 'Honky Tonk' defined two country music clichés: stories about drinking and losing the one you love. Hank Williams' (1923–53) 'Lovesick Blues' (1949) epitomizes this. Ironically his last hit, 'I'll Never Get Out Of This World Alive', was released just before his death on New Year's Day 1953, after a heart attack brought on by drinking.

NASHVILLE

Another milestone was 'the Nashville sound', a blend of country and pop that appeared during the 1950s. It propelled artists such as Jim Reeves, Eddy Arnold and Patsy Cline into the limelight with well-recorded ballads and honky-tonk stories. Then 'outlaw' artists Johnny Cash (1932–2003) and Willie Nelson (b. 1933) added a little danger into the equation during the 1960s, and Lynyrd Skynyrd and Alabama fused country with rock in the 1970s.

▲ *Willie Nelson and Waylon Jennings were the 'most wanted' of the outlaw movement.*

MODERN COUNTRY

During the 1980s and 1990s, artists such as Garth Brooks (b. 1962), Ricky Skaggs (b. 1954), the Judds and Randy Travis (b. 1959) had considerable success, with some of their albums even outselling mainstream pop artists such as Michael Jackson and Madonna.

Country music has had its fair share of guitar virtuosos over the years, and these have included fingerpicking pioneers like Merle Travis (1917–83) and Doc Watson (b. 1923); Hawaiian steel specialists such as Sonny Garrish (b. 1943) and Lloyd Maines (b. 1951); and dynamic electric players like Albert Lee, Danny Gatton (1945–94) and Steve Morse (b. 1954). It is worth checking out recordings by all these great players.

Section Two: Musical Styles

PLAYING COUNTRY

▲ *Randy Travis is a neo-traditionalist, and his music is built on foundations established by the likes of Merle Haggard.*

Much country music is based around the pentatonic major scale (see page 53). This scale is often confused with the pentatonic minor scale (used in blues) as they use the same finger patterns across the guitar neck, but they are in fact different modes in the same scale family.

To explain further, the A pentatonic minor shape between the fifth and eighth frets of the fingerboard is identical to the C pentatonic major shape in the same position. The reason for this is that they both consist of the same notes; C, D, E, G, A and C. The difference is that the A pentatonic minor uses A as its first (tonic) note while the C pentatonic major scale begins on the C note; playing the shape over an A bass note will make it sound bluesy, whereas playing it over a C bass note will make it sound 'country'. The pentatonic major scale is actually the regular major scale ('do-re-mi') with the fourth and seventh notes removed. Because of this it is easier to play and it harmonizes better with the simple chord progressions used in country music.

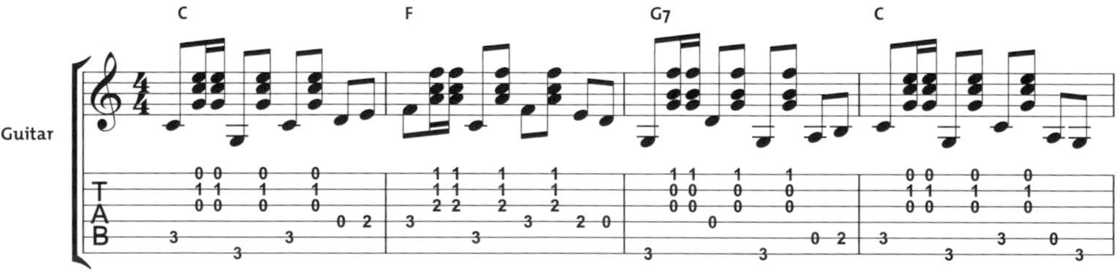

▲ *The classic country music guitar figure would be played on an acoustic instrument, providing a simple but steady melodic and rhythmic structure.*

Complete Guitar Handbook

◀ *Violining: the little finger of the picking hand adjusts the volume while playing.*

ELECTRIC COUNTRY

Electric country guitar players use a lot of note bends in their solos. Of particular importance is the 'harmony bend', a pedal-steel type effect where some notes are held while another is bent. Country players also use double-stops (two-note chords), hammer-ons, pull-offs and slides to add further colour to their solos. Another specialist country technique is 'chicken picking', a damped, staccato right-hand style employed by James Burton (b. 1939) and others for fast, funky phrases.

You can play a basic country rhythm guitar style by separating the bass notes in each chord you play from the rest of the notes in the chord; play the bass notes first and then follow with the rest. Another neat country trick is to use the guitar's volume control (or a volume pedal) to fade chords and notes in from nothing to give a nice, soft attack to the tone – a technique known as 'violining'.

THE RIGHT GUITAR

If you're serious about playing electric country guitar, you should consider getting a Fender Telecaster as it produces a clean, twangy sound and has probably been favoured by more country players than any other electric guitar. If you haven't got a Telecaster, you can approximate its sound by choosing the bridge pickup on any single coil guitar, selecting a clean amplifier sound and cutting back on your mid-range.

▲ *A Fender Telecaster, the first production-made solid electric guitar.*

Section Two: Musical Styles

FOLK

Folk music can be described as 'the natural expression of a people'. It exists in every country, whether it comes in the form of African tribal chants, Irish reels, Indian ragas, nursery rhymes, Hungarian gypsy tunes or Native American ceremonial songs.

Folk music is rarely written for profit and it is passed down from generation to generation, musician to musician. Often lacking the technical sophistication and complexity found in other music styles, it can be extraordinarily beautiful and stirring.

▶ *Prolific songwriter and performer Woody Guthrie sang songs about economic, political and social problems.*

Popular folk music, as we know it today, can be traced directly back to the singer-songwriter Woody Guthrie. Born in 1912 in Okemah, Oklahoma, Guthrie grew up in a poor but musical family. As a teenager he experienced first the tragic death of his older sister, Clara, and then his family's financial ruin when the town's boom period went bust. They moved to Pampa, Texas, where Woody fell in love, married and formed his first band, the Corn Cob Trio.

GUTHRIE'S INFLUENCE

After a great dust storm hit the area (chronicled in John Steinbeck's novel *The Grapes of Wrath*) the Guthrie family headed west with a mass migration of refugees known as 'Okies'. These unemployed workers from Oklahoma, Kansas,

Complete Guitar Handbook

Tennessee and Georgia had all lost their homes and had set out in search of opportunities elsewhere. Penniless and hungry, Woody walked and hitchhiked over to California, where he wrote songs about his experiences. He later travelled all over the US and became a champion for oppressed migrant workers, as well as a controversial critic of politicians, lawyers and businessmen. He made a number of recordings during the 1940s and the honesty, humour and wit expressed in these influenced the likes of Bob Dylan (b. 1941), Joan Baez (b. 1941) and Paul Simon (b. 1941), who all had unprecedented chart success with folk-style songs during the 1960s. Guthrie died after a long struggle with Huntington's Chorea in 1967, and has since been acknowledged as the most important folk artist of the first half of the twentieth century.

▲ *Joan Baez and Bob Dylan were responsible for a folk revival in the 1960s.*

UK FOLK SCENE

Over in the UK, Renaissance lute music and American folk styles inspired the likes of Martin Carthy (b. 1941), Bert Jansch (b. 1943) and John Renbourn (b. 1944) to write strong, original guitar material during the 1960s. Ralph McTell (b. 1944) also helped to popularize English folk with his hit 'Streets of London' (1974).

Although traditional folk has always been popular, the global 'folk scene' has often been in a state of flux, with new musicians adding their own voices to the throng. John Martyn (b. 1948) and Christy Moore (b. 1945) had developed unique and earthy folk styles by the 1970s and influenced many other singer-songwriters, while today artists such as Ani DiFranco (b. 1970), the Levellers and Asian Dub Foundation are all fusing elements of folk with different popular music cultures.

Section Two: Musical Styles

PLAYING FOLK MUSIC

The acoustic guitar is the main instrument used in folk music, and it can either be finger-picked or strummed with a plectrum. Typical folk finger-pickers will normally play the bass strings with the thumb and the treble strings with the index, middle and third fingers of their right hand (assuming they are right-handed), although some just use their index and middle fingers for the treble strings and rest their other two fingers on the guitar body for support.

▲ *With any folk song, the words are the main focus, leaving the melody and structure simple, as in this example.*

Most folk tunes played in this way use the same finger-picking pattern – or a series of variations of it – for the whole song. Some virtuoso players adopt a more elaborate style with all four fingers playing the treble strings, or separate contrapuntal harmonies being played on the bass and treble strings at the same time.

FLAT-PICKING

There are also a number of folk flat-pickers who use a plectrum to play chord arpeggios across the strings, along with scales and licks. Such players use strumming techniques to play the guitar in a rhythmic context and, like finger-pickers, they tend to keep the same rhythm for an entire song. To strum with a plectrum, finger your

▶ *Flat-picking is a playing style where all notes, scalic and chordal, are articulated with a plectrum or thumb pick.*

Complete Guitar Handbook

chord with your left hand and angle the plectrum in towards the strings and pointing slightly upwards with your right hand. Then stroke the plectrum across the strings, making sure that all the notes in the chord ring out cleanly.

Some acoustic flat-pickers can play extremely fast scalar solos with a plectrum by alternating between upstrokes and downstrokes of the right hand, while the left hand is fingering the notes. A number of bluegrass players and 'crossover' guitarists like Al Di Meola (b. 1954), Steve Morse and Ricky Skaggs have used this style to devastating effect.

▲ *Typically, most traditional folk guitar playing is based on finger-picking. The bass strings are usually picked by the thumb, whilst the index, middle and ring fingers are used to pick the treble strings. It is very rare for the little finger to be used.*

AMPLIFICATION

While most traditional folk music can be performed without any amplification, anything in a more modern band context should be performed through a dedicated acoustic amplifier such as the Roland AC60, the Behringer Ultracoustic ACX1000 or one of Marshall's AS series amplifiers. These are specifically designed to bring out the natural characteristics of an acoustic guitar which is playing at a typical 'live band' volume.

▶ *Folk singer Ani DiFranco started her own record label.*

Section Two: Musical Styles

SOUL AND FUNK

Soul music emerged out of R&B during the 1950s, and Ray Charles is widely acknowledged as the first soul star. Born Ray Charles Robinson in Albany, Georgia in 1930, and blind since the age of six, he became interested in gospel and blues music, and developed a unique singing and songwriting style.

Atlantic Records snapped him up and they had an almost instant hit with 'I Got a Woman' (1955). This was followed up with a string of other chart toppers that combined his unmistakably soulful vocal delivery with R&B rhythms.

THE MOTOWN SOUND

By the mid 1960s, Berry Gordy had established the Tamla Motown company in Detroit, and artists such as Smokey Robinson, the Four Tops, Marvin Gaye, the Supremes and Stevie Wonder ensured that soul music was well and truly on the map. The Motown system was both revolutionary and controversial, with the artists signed on salaries and under orders to perform whatever material Gordy wanted. He used an in-house team of producers and

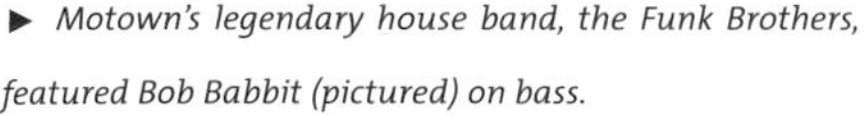

▶ *Motown's legendary house band, the Funk Brothers, featured Bob Babbit (pictured) on bass.*

Complete Guitar Handbook

composers, plus a formidable house band, the Funk Brothers, consisting of Dave Hamilton (guitar), Joe Hunter (piano), Benjy Benjamin (drums) and the legendary James Jamerson (bass, 1936–83). They forged the famous 'Motown sound' that has since been mimicked by countless soul producers worldwide.

▲ *James Brown was key in turning soul music into funk and disco.*

FUNK

Funk also emerged out of R&B and soul during the 1960s, when artists such as James Brown and his guitarist Jimmy Nolan developed a rhythm style so powerful that the melody and harmony were forced to take a back seat. It was popularized even further during the 1970s by acts such as Chic, Funkadelic, the Isley Brothers and Earth Wind And Fire.

GUITARS IN FUNK

Guitars played a more prominent part in funk music than they did in soul, and many funk stars, including Ernie Isley (b. 1952), Prince (b. 1958) and Johnny 'Guitar' Watson (1935–96) were also guitar heroes. Watson grew up listening to bluesmen T-Bone Walker (1910–75) and Clarence 'Gatemouth' Brown (b. 1924), and developed a biting high-treble guitar tone that he already used to effect on albums such as *Gangster Of Love* (1958) and *Johnny Guitar Watson* (1963). He had developed a more funky style by the 1970s and became known for his eccentricities as much as his music; clad in brightly coloured suits with massive flares and lapels, he would play the guitar standing upside down and use a 45-m (150-ft) cord to get on top of the auditorium with his instrument.

Section Two: Musical Styles

PLAYING SOUL GUITAR

Although soul and funk are both primarily played by electric guitarists, the styles are contrasting. Soul guitar is usually simple guitar chords or repetitive licks that fit in with a groove but don't interfere with a song's main focus – the vocals. Funk guitar is usually a series of short licks that form a part of the groove upon which the whole tune is based. These licks are usually syncopated with the rest of the instruments and, along with the bass line, give it that funk 'edge'.

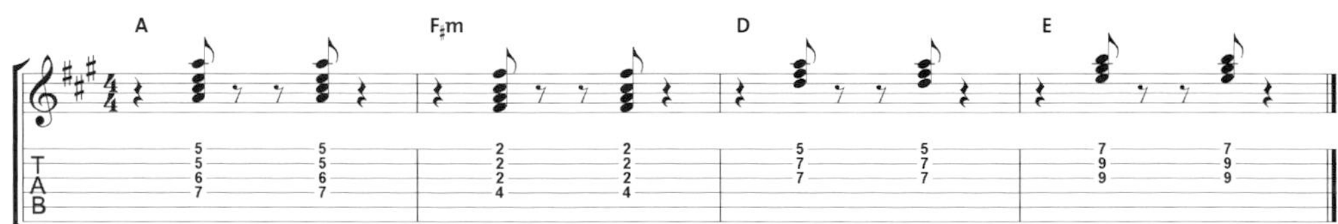

▲ *Playing guitar in a soul music context is all about timing and the interaction between instruments.*

PLAYING FUNK GUITAR

Funk guitar tends to be played on treble strings and away from the chord root notes, as the bass player usually has the job of playing these. Funk guitarists often play extended chords such as ninths, minor ninths and 11ths to give the groove an almost jazzy feel. In fact it is no surprise that 'jazz-funk', a more instrumental style with extended solos, evolved naturally out of funk because of such chords. Guitarists usually play these chords with simple shapes that can be moved all around the guitar neck, and funk tunes are often based around simple chord progressions based on just a couple of these chords; Am9 and Bm9, for example.

▲ *Rather than playing long, elaborate solos, funk players tend to play short, rhythmic riffs, repeated throughout the song.*

Complete Guitar Handbook

Another funk technique is to perform rhythmic strumming on strings muted by the fretting hand. Funk players alternate this with ringing extended chords or simple licks. Isaac Hayes' 'Shaft' is an excellent example of this style.

▲ *This album sold a million copies and proved to be Funkadelic's breakthrough.*

FUNK'N'SOUL EFFECTS

Both soul and funk music require a clean rhythm guitar sound, and this is best obtained by playing a single coil guitar such as a Fender Stratocaster through an amplifier with the bass and mid-range trimmed down and a little bit of compression added. Wah-wah pedals such as the Dunlop Cry Baby have often been used to add more interest (again, listen to Isaac Hayes' 'Shaft'), while some guitarists have even used auto-wah effects like the MXR Auto Q to make things more funky.

Other effects that have been commonly used with funk guitar styles include phasers and flangers. You can easily get these sounds today with the current range of pedals and virtual effects available with computer music programs. Remember, however, the most important ingredient to make your guitar sound really funky is the rhythmic way you play it. Keep to the groove and keep it tight!

▲ *Wah-wah pedals can be used to create a 'wack-wacka' funk rhythm.*

► *Guitarist and singer Curtis Mayfield developed his own style of funk that combined beautiful falsetto vocals with lyrical pleas for social justice.*

Section Two: Musical Styles

LATIN

'Latin' music is a generic term used to describe a diverse range of musical styles from various regions of Central and South America. These include well-known dance rhythms such as the tango, samba, bossa nova, rhumba, mambo, cha cha and salsa, as well as Latin pop and rock.

THE TANGO

The first popular Latin dance rhythm to achieve worldwide recognition was the tango. Characterized by long, gliding steps and sudden pauses, the style was popular with working-class Argentinians during the 1890s and it became internationally established by 1910. The stop-start choreography was erotic and employed close contact between the male and female dancers; in fact, it was originally devised in brothels to mimic the violent relationship between prostitutes, pimps and male rivals.

BOSSA NOVA

By the middle of the twentieth century, a number of more 'regular' Afro-Cuban rhythms, such as the mambo, samba and cha cha had been established, but the guitar did not become a prominent instrument in the genre until Antonio Carlos Jobim

◄ Rio de Janeiro, Brazil, is home to the world-famous carnival, as well as to rhythms such as the samba.

Complete Guitar Handbook

helped popularize the laid-back bossa nova rhythm.

▲ *Santana, in 1968. Their music is a fusion of Latin styles and blues-rock.*

Jobim was born in Rio de Janeiro in 1927. He grew up in a musical family and learned to play the piano and the acoustic guitar. He had started composing his own songs, playing in nightclubs and working in recording studios by the early 1950s, but he remained unknown outside Brazil until Stan Getz and Charlie Byrd scored a surprise hit with his laid-back bossa nova tune 'Desafinado' (1962). The whole world suddenly went mad for the new Brazilian rhythm and Jobim recorded a number of successful easy-listening albums during the early to mid 1960s. The hit trend ran out of commercial steam in the late 1960s, but the bossa nova remains a popular background music style today, played extensively in nightclubs, restaurants and hotels.

The next guitarist to popularize Latin music on a grand scale was Carlos Santana. Born in Mexico in 1947, Carlos started playing the electric guitar at an early age, and performed in Tijuana nightclubs as a teenager before moving to San Francisco in 1962 and forming his own band, Santana. Their music, a unique blend of blues-rock, Latin grooves and psychedelia, brought Latin music rhythms to a wider rock audience and they are still as popular now as they were back in the 1970s. Other notables who have fused rock and blues guitar sounds with Latin grooves include Ry Cooder (b. 1947), an acclaimed multi-genre electric guitarist; Sepultura, the most popular heavy metal band to emerge from Brazil; and Iconoclasta, an influential Mexican prog-rock band.

Section Two: Musical Styles

▲ *Brazilian band Trio Mocoto have been around since the late 1960s, and have created a distinctive samba-soul-rock sound.*

THE SAMBA

The samba is another hugely popular Afro-Cuban rhythm. Unlike the laid-back bossa nova, it is upbeat and projects a party vibe. It is heavily featured at the annual Rio de Janeiro carnivals and has been employed by artists as diverse as Latin band Trio Mocoto, fusion guitarist Pat Metheny and prog-rock keyboardist Patrick Moraz (b. 1948). Latin rhythms have also been featured in many pop hits during the past 40 years, and artists such as Astrud Gilberto (b. 1940), Edmundo Ros (b. 1910), Ruben Blades (b. 1948), Los Lobos, Gloria Estefan (b. 1958) and Ricky Martin (b. 1971) have all enjoyed successful careers as Latin pop stars.

PLAYING LATIN GUITAR

Latin guitar music can be played on both acoustic and electric instruments. If you're an acoustic player, Jobim's bossa nova tunes should be approached on a mellow-sounding guitar, preferably with

▶ *Emulate Carlos Satana's distinctive sound with a guitar such as this solid-body Fender Stratocaster.*

Complete Guitar Handbook

▶ *Pat Metheny is well-know for incorporating Latin styles, such as samba, into his music.*

gut or nylon strings. If you are playing by yourself, you probably won't need an acoustic amplifier, unless you are performing at a nightclub or restaurant. However, if you want to play this music with a band, you will need a decent acoustic amplifier to give your instrument enough volume and reverb to cut through all the other instruments. It is worth pointing out that bossa nova tunes tend to be intimate and understated affairs, so care is needed not to ruin a piece by overplaying!

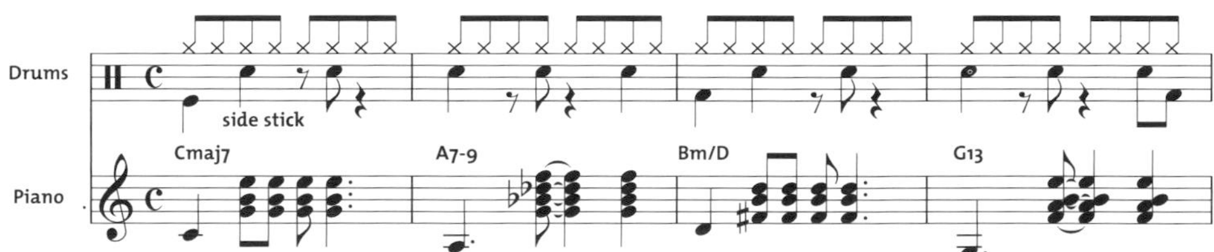

▲ *An example of a typical bossa nova rhythm. The drum pattern is played over the top of an off-beat counter rhythm. The guitar chords are given along with the piano music.*

If you want to get a Santana-style electric sound, you'll need a solidbody guitar with humbucking pickups – Carlos currently uses PRS, but a number of cheaper models will also do the job – and a reasonably powerful amplifier that will allow you to add just enough pre-amp gain to give your sound an edge without throwing it into overdrive. The Santana lead guitar style is pentatonic-based, with additional phrases based upon the Dorian and Mixolydian modes, so all these scales will work well within an electric Latin context. The most important thing to bear in mind while playing any Latin style, though, is to articulate and phrase in a way that emphasizes or complements the underlying groove – because it is this groove that gives all Latin music its distinct vibe.

Section Two: Musical Styles

AFRICAN

Although African music clearly laid down the foundations for the guitar-based genres of blues and rock, relatively few African guitar players have been celebrated outside their own continent. This is mainly because the harmonies and melodies in African musical styles are often different to those that 'western' ears are used to hearing.

The African concept of music is different to that in the west; while western musicians make music that is intended to be pleasing to a listener's ear, traditional African musicians are expressing life as they know it through the medium of sound. Their mixture of complex rhythms, spoken language and natural sounds may sound cacophonous to the uninitiated, but their music does have a meaning.

▲ *Kanda Bongo Man emigrated to Paris from the Congo region to achieve recognition away from the competition.*

SOUKOUS

A number of guitar-based African music styles have appeared since the beginning of the twentieth century and one of the most documented is soukous, a style which emerged from the Congo region 100 years ago. This music style was originally performed on guitar, likembe ('thumb piano') and bottle at European work camps during the first quarter of the twentieth century. From these

Complete Guitar Handbook

humble beginnings it evolved into a popular 'rhumba' style played by extended band line-ups featuring numerous guitars, bass, keyboards, brass, drums and vocals (sung in Lingala, the trade language of the Congo region). Modern performers of this style include Souzy Kasseya (b. 1949), Kanda Bongo Man (b. 1955), Theo Blaise, Fidele Zizi, Victoria and Orchestre Virunga.

The best-known guitarist to hail from the Congo region was Franco (Francois Luambo Makiadi). Born in 1938, Franco began playing a homemade guitar made out of tin cans and stripped electrical wire. He formed the group OK Jazz and became well-known for his social commentary and satire as much as his dexterous guitar playing. His most notable releases include 'Jackie' (1974), a sexually explicit song for which he was briefly sent to jail, and 'Tailleur' (1980), a dance piece lampooning the prime minister of Congo. Franco died of an AIDS-related illness in 1989.

ALI FARKA TOURE

Mali is another important music hotspot in Africa and it boasts the continent's most celebrated electric guitarist, Ali Farka Toure. Toure was born in 1939 into a North Malian noble family that can trace its roots back to the Spanish moors who first crossed the Sahara to control the salt trade. He grew up in Niafunke, a village in the Timbuktu region of Mali, and started to learn the guitar at the age of seven. Deeply rooted in African tradition and mythology, he later claimed that an intense spiritual experience with a snake suddenly resulted in him becoming a better player at the age of 12. At any rate, he practised obsessively and developed his own blues style, characterized by a rhythmic, foot-stomping guitar style and a low vocal delivery.

► *Ali Farka Toure is a blues guitarist often compared to John Lee Hooker.*

Section Two: Musical Styles

▶ *The music of King Sunny Ade and the African Beats is known as 'juju'. They use both traditional African and modern Western instruments.*

Although he became established as a prominent musician while still a young man in Mali, he did not gain worldwide recognition until his eponymous first album was released when he was nearly 50. He has often been called the 'African John Lee Hooker' because of similarities between his style and that of the legendary American bluesman. However, Toure's delivery and song style is smoother than Hooker's. Toure sings in several African languages and only occasionally in English, and his lyrics, according to him, are concerned with the 'education, work, love and society around me'. Toure has recorded and performed with many other internationally acclaimed musicians including Ry Cooder, Taj Mahal (b. 1942) and the Chieftains.

PLAYING AFRICAN GUITAR

Most African guitarists play electric instruments with regular tuning, and a typical African band will have two, three or even four guitar players. A clear tone with a fair amount of treble and mid-range is essential for African popular music, and you can best achieve this with a Fender Stratocaster or Telecaster, or any other instrument fitted with single coil pickups. Amp-wise, just about any decent electric guitar amplifier will do for African-style music, as long as it is capable of projecting a clear treble tone. A generous dash of reverb on top will help to make it sound even more authentic.

A number of African players with limited financial resources made their own guitars out of oil cans, and the idea caught on after it became clear that these guitars produced a surprisingly charismatic sound. The African Guitars company now makes high-specification models, called Afri-cans, on a commercial scale for those who crave that 'homemade' sound.

Complete Guitar Handbook

▲ *Biggie Tembo, lead singer of Zimbabwean guitar band the Bhundu Boys, named the group after his experiences as a runner – or 'bhundu boy' – for the rebels in his country's struggle for liberation.*

Most African guitar playing is rhythm guitar, and this can range from simple strumming to two or three contrapuntal rhythm melodies being played at the same time by different players. Major chords are used extensively and sometimes even in places where you might expect to hear minor chords. This approach lends a bright, optimistic, 'carnival' vibe to the material that makes it very infectious. African pop melodies also tend to be major-scale oriented and this contributes towards the lively, celebratory sound of the music.

◀ *These 'Afri-can' guitars have been made using oil cans for the body.*

Section Two: Musical Styles

BLUES

The blues has played a larger role in the history of popular music than any other genre. It is a direct ancestor to music styles as diverse as rock 'n' roll, rock, heavy metal, soul, funk and pop. Without the blues there would have been no Beatles, Jimi Hendrix, Led Zeppelin, James Brown, Stevie Wonder or Oasis, to name but a few!

▲ *Blind Lemon Jefferson's lack of sight resulted in expressive playing and vocals.*

The blues emerged out of the hardships endured by generations of African-American slaves during the late nineteenth and early twentieth centuries. By 1900, the genre had developed into a three-line stanza, with a vocal style derived from southern work songs. These 'call and response' songs were developed further by early blues guitar players, who would sing a line and then answer it on the guitar. By the 1920s, rural African-Americans had migrated to the big cities in search of work, bringing their music with them. Early street musicians such as Blind Lemon Jefferson (1893–1929), a guitar-playing blues singer, started to make recordings and these inspired the next generation of blues guitar players.

DELTA BLUES

The 1930s were a crucial period in the development of the blues, for it was then that acoustic Mississippi Delta blues performers Charley Patton (1891–1934), Son House (1902–88) and Robert Johnson (1911–38) travelled throughout the southern states, singing about their woes, freedom, love and sex to community after community. Johnson, who allegedly made a mysterious pact with the devil to become a better guitar player, was the first true blues performance artist.

Complete Guitar Handbook

Over on the East Coast, musicians such as Blind Boy Fuller (1907–41), Sonny Terry (1911–86) and Gary Davis (1896–1972) developed a more folky 'Piedmont' blues style.

▲ *The intricate guitar work and unusual tunings of Robert Johnson were a revelation.*

CHICAGO BLUES

By the 1940s, Chicago bluesmen took Mississippi Delta ideas and played them on electric guitars. Lone performers became more scarce while small bands sprang up everywhere. By the 1950s, electric blues was in full swing, with B. B. King, Muddy Waters, John Lee Hooker (1917–2001),T-Bone Walker and Howlin' Wolf (1910–76), all playing to packed houses in major cities. King pioneered across-the-string vibrato and note-bending techniques on his beloved guitar, 'Lucille', and these techniques are now used by all blues lead guitar players. Hooker developed a completely different style, in which he stomped continuously with his right foot while singing and playing. Wolf injected more power and frustration into the blues, and Walker jazzed things up, but it was perhaps Muddy Waters' passionate singing and biting guitar tones that popularized the style more than anyone else from this period. Some bluesmen, such as Big Bill Broonzy (1893–1958), visited England, where their performances inspired British musicians to adopt the style.

◀ *Blues legend Howlin' Wolf contributed to the post-war Chicago blues explosion.*

Section Two: Musical Styles

BRITISH BLUES

The 1960s witnessed a musical and cultural revolution when British guitar players such as Eric Clapton and Peter Green started to mimic American bluesmen. They used solidbody guitars and more powerful amplifiers to get a harder, more driving sound than their American mentors. Clapton's electric guitar sound led to the birth of a number of other styles, including blues-rock, hard rock and even heavy metal.

From the 1970s onwards, artists including Stevie Ray Vaughan, Robert Cray and Robben Ford have added more voices and sounds to the blues repertoire, and the genre is still thriving today.

PLAYING THE BLUES

Blues is based around the blues scale (see page 56), which is a pentatonic minor scale with an added flat fifth note (the 'blue' note). Blues music is usually played in the keys of A, D, E and G as they are all easy keys to play on the guitar. The style has an odd harmonic structure, as the blues scale is usually played or sung over chords that are all dominant sevenths (e.g. A7, D7 and E7 in the key of A) or chords derived from them.

▲ *Buddy Guy was a leading exponent of the Chicago blues sound.*

ACOUSTIC BLUES

There are two main blues styles: traditional acoustic blues and urban electric blues. Acoustic blues normally requires a 'fingerstyle' approach, in which the thumb of the right hand – assuming the player is right-handed – plays a steady bass-note groove while the melody or licks are picked out by the first and second fingers. Most of this is performed quite forcefully, although acoustic blues

Complete Guitar Handbook

players rest the side of their picking hand across the strings at times to make sure the bass notes don't ring out too loudly. Son House, Leadbelly (1889–1949) and Big Bill Broonzy were all masters of this style, so if you want to play it you should familiarize yourself with their recordings. It is important to realize, however, that a lot of their guitar playing was improvised and designed to accompany their own vocal phrasings.

▲ *Acoustic blues finger-style playing. The low E string is played repeatedly with the thumb, establishing a traditional blues rhythm.*

ELECTRIC BLUES

Urban electric blues guitar is usually played within the context of a band, so it is normally restricted to lead or rhythm playing at any one time. Some electric guitar players use a plectrum to achieve accurate pick articulation, while others favour a more earthy fingerstyle approach. Electric blues guitarists play in a wider range of keys than their acoustic counterparts, as they often work with horn players who prefer to play in B♭ and C. Lauded electric blues guitar players include B. B. King, Freddie King, Albert Collins, Buddy Guy, Eric Clapton, Robben Ford and Stevie Ray Vaughan.

▲ *An example of an electric blues solo. A 'lead-in' before the bar, and the use of string bends, makes this a typical Chicago-style solo.*

Section Two: Musical Styles

PLAYING ELECTRIC BLUES

Electric blues stylists often embellish their phrases with expressive techniques such as string bending, sliding and vibrato. String bending should simply be thought of as another way of moving from one pitch to another on the fretboard. To bend a string accurately, you must know your target note – this will usually be a note pitched a half step, a whole step or a step and a half above your unbent note. If your target note is a half step higher, for example, you can play the note behind the next fret up on the same string to hear what it should sound like. When you perform the bend, push the string over towards the bass strings until you hear your target note.

▲ *Bending strings is one of the oldest techniques of lead guitar playing. You can bend one, two, or even three strings at the same time.*

You can produce a blues slide effect when you play a note on a string and, while holding the string firmly down, slide along the fingerboard to another note. You can even slide across two or more strings at a time by barring your fretting finger across the strings and moving it along the neck in the same way. To obtain a vibrato effect, play a fretted note and move the string from side to side – across the fingerboard – with your fretting finger. This makes a sustained note sound more expressive or even aggressive.

|| C7 | C7 | C7 | C7 |

| F7 | F7 | C7 | C7 |

| G7 | F7 | C7 | G7 :||

▲ *Tens of thousands of blues songs are based around the most common chord-progression in the history of popular music: the 12-bar blues sequence.*

GOING SOLO

There are many different approaches to soloing over a blues progression, but the simplest way to learn is to target the root notes of each chord in the progression. In the key of C, for example, the

Complete Guitar Handbook

▲ *Work songs such as this retain a strong African influence, with irregular rhythms that often follow speech patterns.*

main blues chords are C7, F7 and G7. You can begin by playing the C pentatonic minor scale and targeting the notes C, F and G (which are all in the scale) over their respective chords. Try bending or sliding to these notes to make things sound more bluesy.

It is also a good idea to practise blues lead phrasing by using the 'call and response' approach favoured by early blues musicians; sing a phrase and then reply to it with a guitar line, and so on. This should help you to get an authentic blues feel, even if you're not a singer. It will enable you to put comfortable, natural rests between your phrases and notes so it all ends up sounding more musical and logical. You should also jam with other like-minded musicians, as this not only is fun but will also motivate you to become a better player.

◀ *Stevie Ray Vaughan had a stunning, high-energy blues style.*

Section Two: Musical Styles

▲ *Duane Allman of the Allman Brothers was renowned for his use of a bottleneck.*

USING A BOTTLENECK

Some blues players, including Elmore James (1918–63) and Duane Allman, have used a bottleneck made out of glass or metal to obtain a distinctive sliding effect between notes. Bottlenecks are inexpensive and fun to play with, but you'll need a little patience to master the technique properly. Special tunings such as D A D F♯ A D are often used for bottleneck pieces, as they enable the guitarist to play whole chords up the guitar neck with just one finger!

GETTING A BLUES SOUND

To get an authentic blues sound you'll need an appropriate guitar. Almost any acoustic instrument will do for acoustic blues, although resonators, guitars that use thin aluminium cones to mechanically amplify their sound, will give you a

Complete Guitar Handbook

particularly 'bluesy' tone. If you're after an authentic electric blues sound, you should pick an instrument similar to one played by your favourite blues artist. If you want to sound like B. B. King, for example, you should consider a Gibson ES-335, as this is the guitar he has favoured over the years, while a Fender Stratocaster will enable you to sound more like Robert Cray or Stevie Ray Vaughan, and a Telecaster would be essential for that biting Albert Collins sound.

▲ *The wings on a Gibson 335 allow for a rich, jazz tone.*

Amplification is important too, and most blues artists favour valve amplifiers such as the Marshall Bluesbreaker combo or Fender's Twin and Deluxe models as they give a warm, fat sound with a big dynamic range.

Transistor amplifiers are cheaper but they sound more synthetic. If you're just playing guitar in your bedroom you should consider getting an amp modelling box such as a Line 6 POD, or a virtual amp software package such as IK Multimedia's AmpliTube or Native Instruments' Guitar Rig. Each of these comes armed with a surprisingly authentic set of blues presets, and you can use them without upsetting the neighbours.

Tone control settings are important as well; boosting an amplifier's bass and mid-range will give a fat B. B. King sound, while boosting the treble will help to emulate the 'icy' tones of Albert Collins. All in all, it is important to find a guitar tone that you feel comfortable with – if you sound great, you'll play well!

► *The IK Multimedia AmpliTube, an amplifier simulator plug-in.*

Section Two: Musical Styles

ROCK

By the late 1960s, many popular acts had grown tired of producing chart songs, and injected more attitude, experimentation and social conscience into their music. 'Rock' was born. The pioneers of this new style included Eric Clapton, the Rolling Stones and Jimi Hendrix (1942–70), whose music appealed to record buyers who saw mainstream pop as tame.

Clapton first made a name for himself with John Mayall's Bluesbreakers in 1965 when he turned his amp up loud to get a more aggressive, sustained guitar tone. He formed Cream two years later with bassist Jack Bruce and drummer Ginger Baker, and they were the first popular group to feature extended virtuoso solos in their music. By 1967, Hendrix had also extended the range of the electric guitar by coaxing sounds out of it that hadn't been heard before. Clapton and Hendrix based their playing around the blues scale and their solos were often long improvisations. Pop guitar solos were usually brief instrumental fills between vocal passages, but 'classic rock' solos would often take up half of the song.

▲ *In the 1970s, the Rolling Stones moved from their blues roots to a more polished rock sound.*

Complete Guitar Handbook

BIRTH OF THE RIFF

Another prominent feature in early rock music was the riff – a repeated note or chord phrase over which the vocals and solos were projected. A classic example of this is Cream's 'Sunshine of Your Love' (1968), a whole song based upon a simple, grinding riff. Other players such as Jimmy Page, Ritchie Blackmore and Tony Iommi (b. 1948) latched on to the sheer power of this device and started to create even more powerful riffs, such as Led Zeppelin's 'Whole Lotta Love' (1969), Deep Purple's 'Speed King' (1970) and Black Sabbath's 'Paranoid' (1970).

▲ *Ritchie Blackmore of Deep Purple was famous for his complex and lengthy guitar solos.*

Rock music marked a shift away from singles and towards albums; projects such as Led Zeppelin's acclaimed *Led Zeppelin II* (1969), Pink Floyd's psychedelic *Dark Side of the Moon* (1973) and Mike Oldfield's instrumental *Tubular Bells* (1973) were all bestselling albums by artists who rarely recorded singles.

Section Two: Musical Styles

PUNK

In 1976, punk suddenly appeared and bands like the Sex Pistols, the Clash and the Damned introduced a basic rock style that relied more on attitude than technique. However, it was a short-lived trend and by the late 1970s rock began to fragment into a number of sub-genres, including new wave (an offshoot from punk), stadium rock (the likes of Bruce Springsteen and Queen) and the various strands of heavy metal that were beginning to develop in the US and UK.

New wave was essentially a generic term used for the wide range of British bands that followed on from punk. These included idiosyncratic artists such as Elvis Costello (b. 1954) and XTC, straight-ahead rockers like the Pretenders and the Cars, white reggae or ska pop bands including Madness and the Police, and a legion of synthesizer-driven bands. The genre died out when new bands such as the Smiths and REM began to appeal to more alternative rock fans.

◀ *For many, the Clash were the ultimate punk rock band.*

INDIE

The Smiths were the dominant British 'indie' rock band of the 1980s, and this was mainly down to the unique combination of singer Morrissey's forlorn crooning and the uncluttered rhythm guitar work of Johnny Marr (b. 1963). They recorded a number of hit singles and albums that laid down the foundations for the next

Complete Guitar Handbook

generation of British guitar bands, before splitting up in 1987. REM also boasted a unique singer/guitarist combination – Michael Stipe's cryptic vocals and the ringing guitar hooks of Peter Buck (b. 1956). They are still going strong today.

GRUNGE

Despite the influx of fresh indie bands into the album and singles charts during the 1980s, most of the popular bands from this period, including Bon Jovi and Guns N' Roses, were purveyors of straight-ahead rock. By the end of the decade, however, grunge – a vibrant mixture of punk and heavy metal – became a prominent movement with Nirvana, a Seattle-based band, at the helm. Nirvana's success was down to a combination of strong material, stop-start dynamics, and the manic intensity of singer-guitarist Kurt Cobain (1967–94). Unfortunately, Cobain suffered from drug addiction and manic depression, a combination that ended in suicide.

VARIETY OF ROCK STYLES

A number of major song-orientated rock styles emerged during the 1990s including Britpop, which mixed songwriting – inspired by bands like the Beatles – with the more indie vibe of the Smiths. Suede, fronted by the quasi-glam vocals of Brett Anderson and sweeping guitar of Bernard Butler (b. 1970), pioneered this style, and they paved the way for the huge success of Oasis and Blur, bands from the north and south of England respectively. The decade also saw the rise of inventive alternative rock bands including Radiohead, who combined intense guitar sounds with electronic drones and angst-driven lyrics. Today there is an unprecedented variety of rock styles and this range is still growing.

▶ *Bernard Butler helped make Suede a huge success with his virtuoso riffs and squalls.*

Section Two: Musical Styles

PLAYING ROCK

If you want to be a proficient rock guitarist, you'll need to know a variety of basic chord shapes. The most common open chords (ones that include open strings as well as fretted ones) are A, Am, B7, C, C7, D, Dm, D7, E, E7, F, G and G7, which will allow you to play songs in the popular rock keys of A, C, D, E and G. The barre chords you should know are the barred versions of the A and E shapes (major barre chords) and Am and Em shapes (minor barre chords). These will allow you to play in any key you want, as barre shapes can be played anywhere on the fingerboard. Open chords are good for earthy strumming and would suit, for example, an Oasis-style song, while barre chords can be used to create a more powerful, aggressive sound for punk and hard-rock styles. Major chords are ideal for upbeat rock riffs, while minor ones are more suitable for ballads.

POWER CHORDS

You should also familiarize yourself with the basic 'power chords' used in grunge and hard rock. These are two note chords consisting of the first and fifth notes of the major scale, played on any two adjacent strings (such as the sixth and fifth strings, or fourth and third strings) with your index finger fretting the root note (on the thicker string) and your third finger fretting the fifth note (on the lighter string) two frets further up the fingerboard. To play an A power chord on the sixth and fifth strings (E and A strings), for example, place your index finger behind the fifth fret on the sixth string and your third finger behind the seventh fret on the fifth string and then strum those strings only. To play a B power chord on the same two strings, simply move the shape two frets further up the guitar neck and so on.

▲ *Fifth chords are often referred to as 'power chords' because of their solid sound.*

Complete Guitar Handbook

STRUMMING AND PICKING

Rhythmically, rock is fairly straightforward, with emphasis mainly on the first and third beats of the bar. Strumming is usually performed with downstrokes, as these supply more power, although more intricate rhythms might require alternating downstrokes and upstrokes. Many rock guitarists also play chords as arpeggios (playing all the separate notes in ascending or descending order) with a plectrum or the fingers of their picking hand, to produce a more melodious sound. This is used to great effect in rock classics such as Led Zeppelin's 'Stairway to Heaven' and the Animals' 'House of the Rising Sun'.

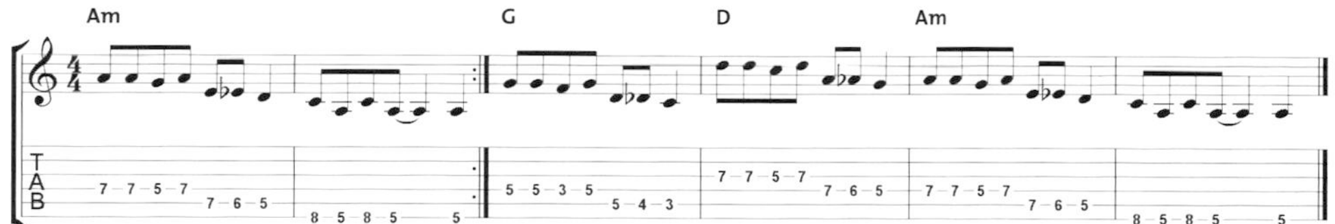

▲ *In classic rock, repetitive guitar riffs such as this one, often open and then form the basis of the songs.*

All rock solos feature the pentatonic minor and blues scales (pages 54–56), and you should familiarize yourself with these scales if you want to play basic rock lead guitar. If you want to take things further, the major scale and the Mixolydian mode (pages 52–53 and 59) will add greater depth to your upbeat solos, and the Aeolian mode will come in handy for those haunting rock ballads.

▲ *Chords in grunge rhythm playing are largely played as fifth chords in order to achieve a controlled, tighter sound.*

Section Two: Musical Styles

GETTING AN AUTHENTIC ROCK SOUND

If you want to get a good rock guitar sound you'll need an electric guitar and some sort of amplifier. The guitar can be a solidbody instrument (one made out of solid wood) or a semi-solid model (hollowed out). Solidbody guitars are great for producing a clear, sustained tone with minimal feedback, while semi-solid instruments produce a fat, warm sound but tend to feedback more when used at higher volumes.

CHOOSING THE RIGHT AMPLIFIER

When it comes to amplifiers, you have a number of options, the most traditional of which would be a hardware amp. These come in two flavours: valve amps, which are expensive but produce a fat, warm sound; and transistor amps, which are more affordable

Complete Guitar Handbook

and reliable but not ideal if you're after a 'vintage' tone. If you do choose to buy a hardware amp, make sure it has a built-in preamp so you can optimize the amount of distortion in your guitar sound.

Hardware amps can get loud, and playing through one at home might upset your neighbours. In such a case, you should consider using an amplifier modelling box such as a Line 6 POD, or a virtual amp software package such as IK Multimedia's AmpliTube. These come with an arsenal of realistic and ready-to-go rock presets, and you can use them at any volume you like. You can even gig with them, as long as the venue at which you're playing has a PA system.

THE RIGHT EFFECTS

Effects pedals have been used extensively by rock players over the years and you too can use them to colour your guitar sound. A wah-wah pedal will come in handy for Hendrix-style soloing, while a phaser or flanger can be used to create psychedelic textures and tones. An overdrive pedal might be useful for adding extra distortion during solos, and a compressor can be great for ironing out excessively loud sounds so that you end up with a more consistent signal. Most virtual amps come with a selection of built-in effects that you can use, so don't forget to try them out if you've got such equipment!

► *Queen, with Freddie Mercury at the helm, are a classic rock act, with soaring guitars and vocals competing for space.*

◄ *The Gibson SG produces a truly great rock sound from its humbuckers. Combine it with a great valve amp like this Fender Deluxe, and you're really rocking.*

◄ *Some people are advocates of effects pedals like the Line 6 POD which can replicate the sounds of different amplifiers.*

Section Two: Musical Styles

JAZZ

Eddie Lang is widely acknowledged as the first significant jazz guitarist. His single-note playing with jazz orchestras during the 1920s marked the beginning of the guitar as a solo instrument in the genre.

Born in Philadelphia in 1902, Lang was the son of a guitar maker. He started learning the violin at an early age but had switched to the guitar by the time he was 10. After working with bands in his home town, he joined the Mound City Blue Blowers in 1924. They toured the US and Europe, and Lang quickly earned a reputation as 'America's best jazz guitarist'. He joined Paul Whiteman's orchestra in 1929 before becoming Bing Crosby's accompanist. He was soon one of the best-paid musicians of the day but, tragically, he died at the peak of his career in 1933, after a 'routine tonsillectomy operation' went wrong.

▲ *Before musicians such as Eddie Lang began to play single-line lead solos, guitars were just part of the rhythm section.*

LANG'S LEGACY

Lang's pioneering guitar work in the 1920s paved the way for the two jazz guitar giants of the 1930s: Django Reinhardt (1910–53) and Charlie Christian (1916–42).

Reinhardt lost the use of two fingers in his left hand after a horrific caravan fire. Astonishingly, he overcame the disability and developed a way of playing the guitar with just the first two fingers of his left hand. He formed the Quintette du Hot Club de France with violinist Stephane Grappelli and other musicians in 1933 and they were a resounding success, recording more than 100 songs and touring all over Europe. Django's soloing set new standards in jazz lead guitar and

Complete Guitar Handbook

▶ *Django Reinhardt developed a unique style of playing after damaging two fingers.*

influenced practically every other jazz guitarist from the 1930s through to the 1950s. Charlie Christian was also hugely influential; he emerged in the early 1940s as the first electric guitar virtuoso, playing saxophone-like lead lines at a volume that could compete with other jazz instruments.

BEBOP

By the 1950s, the more complex bebop style was well established and a number of exciting guitarists began to appear: Barney Kessel was an acclaimed 'bop' soloist who became a session ace and played in bands fronted by Chico Marx and Oscar Peterson; Tal Farlow (1924–98) expanded the jazz guitar chord vocabulary and was one of the first guitarists to be able to play a harmonic note from every fret of the instrument. Johnny Smith (b. 1922) developed a subtle chord-oriented style and had a hit with the mellow 'Moonlight in Vermont' (1952).

◀ *Acclaimed bop guitarist Tal Farlow has influenced everyone from Al Di Meola to Scotty Moore and John McLaughlin.*

Section Two: Musical Styles

JAZZ SUPERSTARS

Jim Hall (b. 1930), Wes Montgomery (1925–68) and Kenny Burrell (b. 1931) were the big jazz guitar names during the 1960s. Hall, unlike most other virtuosos, did not play lots of notes in his solos. In fact, he took the opposite approach and his phrases were usually thoughtful and lyrical, displaying a depth and subtlety that few other guitarists have ever been able to achieve. Wes Montgomery developed an unusual style by using his thumb as a pick. He was one of the first solo guitar players to effortlessly mix single notes with octaves and chords. Kenny Burrell forged a cool, tasteful bop style that established him as one of the most popular instrumental voices in jazz. It was also during the 1960s that the first jazz guitar supergroup, Great Guitars, was born. Featuring Charlie Byrd (1925–99), Herb Ellis (b. 1921) and Barney Kessel, Great Guitars was an eclectic mainstream band that pitted Byrd's Latin and classical style against the other two players' straight-ahead bop.

▲ *Joe Pass began playing the guitar aged nine and covered a huge range of styles, including jazz, bebop, blues and Latin.*

Joe Pass (b. 1929) was another great jazz guitar player to emerge during the 1960s, although he didn't become truly popular until the following decade. Using a phenomenal right-handed finger technique, he was able to play melodies, chords and bass lines all at the same time, and usually performed as a solo player. His album *Virtuoso* (1973), recorded for Norman Granz's Pablo label, made him a jazz star and he later accompanied the likes of Ella Fitzgerald, Count Basie, Duke Ellington and Oscar Peterson.

Complete Guitar Handbook

▲ *Fusion player Allan Holdsworth (left) uses a hammer-on technique for a smooth sound.*

JAZZ FUSION

During the 1970s, a number of guitar players began to fuse jazz with rock; the most influential of these were John McLaughlin, Al Di Meola and Allan Holdsworth (b. 1946). McLaughlin was the lead guitar player on Miles Davis's pioneering jazz-rock album *Bitches Brew* (1969), and he took the direction further with his own band the Mahavishnu Orchestra. Al Di Meola developed a formidable picking technique and fused jazz with Latin and rock styles on his critically acclaimed albums *Elegant Gypsy* (1977) and *Casino* (1978). Allan Holdsworth developed a truly unique and idiosyncratic style, characterized by spectacular chord voicings and fleet, legato solos. He became one of the decade's most sought-after fusion players.

A number of other great jazz guitar players have emerged during the past 30 years, including Pat Metheny, Larry Carlton, Martin Taylor (b. 1956), Stanley Jordan (b. 1959), John Scofield, Bill Frisell and Scott Henderson (b. 1954). Of all these, Pat Metheny has enjoyed the most commercial success. He has forged an earthy and mellow jazz style that appeals to both hardcore jazzers and easy listeners. Few other jazz players have made their music so accessible without sacrificing their integrity.

Section Two: Musical Styles

PLAYING JAZZ GUITAR

All accomplished jazz musicians have a thorough knowledge and understanding of chords and scales, and you will need this too if you want to want to progress with this most demanding of musical styles. Most jazz tunes are based around extended chords (sevenths, ninths, 11ths and 13ths) so make sure you know how to play these all over the fingerboard. Jazz composers also like to raise or lower the fifth and ninth intervals in chords to create more colour within a piece, so it is a good idea to learn these chords as well. Another jazz trick is chord substitution, which is often done by taking a chord with a dominant seventh note, and replacing it with another chord with a root note a tritone (a flattened fifth) higher – for example, substituting a D-flat 7 chord for a G minor chord.

CHORD PROGRESSION

The most common chord progression in jazz is the II-V-I, which uses chords based on the second, fifth and first notes of the major scale respectively. The II chord is a minor 7 chord, while the V is a dominant 7 and the I is a major 7 chord. So in the key of C, the basic II-V-I progression is Dm7, G7, CMaj7. You should familiarize yourself with this chord progression in different keys and in different positions on the fingerboard.

|| C | Am | Dm | G ||

can become:

|| Cmaj9 | Am11 | Dm9 | G13 ||

|| Cmaj9 | Am7♯5 | Dm7♭5 | G 7♯5♯9 ||

|| Cmaj9 | E♭7 | A♭9 | D♭13 ||

▲ *Try playing through these examples of jazz chord extensions, substitutions and altered jazz chords.*

IMPROVISATION

Jazz soloing involves a fair degree of improvisation, and to do this you will need to know a variety of scales and understand which chords they complement. All the major scale modes can be used, but the Dorian, Mixolydian and Ionian modes are of particular importance as they complement the minor 7, dominant 7 and major 7 chords and extensions that are so frequently used in jazz. Most

Complete Guitar Handbook

jazz tunes also feature key changes, so the big challenge in jazz improvisation is to play over these changes without interrupting the melodic flow of a solo.

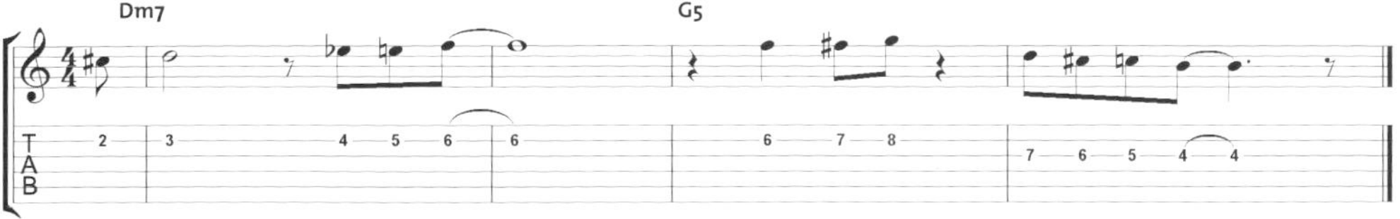

▶ *Play through this example of chromatic playing in jazz improvisation, and then see if you can come up with your own.*

Other scales featured in jazz improvisation include the melodic and harmonic minor scales, the whole tone scale, the diminished scale and the chromatic scale. The latter is often used as it contains notes outside the key scale, which can be used to create extra tension in a melody or solo. Chromatic notes are usually played briefly in phrases that resolve on to key notes, although they can also be sustained to create more tension in the music.

▲ *Jazz guitarist Stanley Jordan employs a unique, two-handed approach to create his sound.*

Section Two: Musical Styles

Improvisation within a set piece is best approached by starting with the basic melody of a tune and playing around with variations of it. You should also jam regularly with other musicians as this will make you comfortable with playing over different chord progressions. Start with simple progressions that allow you to improvise with one or two scales, and then work at jamming over key changes. If you like a real challenge, you can also try 'free improvisation' – trying to create music on the spot with other improvisers without any obvious chord progressions or grooves.

COMPING

Another important jazz guitar skill you should work on is 'comping' – playing chord progressions as an accompaniment while others improvise. When you're comping, try substituting different chords and using different strum patterns to create more harmonic and rhythmic interest. The challenge here is to make the rhythm section sound as cool and varied as possible without losing the underlying groove.

▲ *Guitarists Pat Metheny and John Scofield are known for their fusion sound, a mixture of jazz and rock.*

◀ *Gibson ES-175 guitars were developed in the 1940s. Archtop guitars like this are the favourite instruments of many jazz guitar players.*

Complete Guitar Handbook

GETTING A JAZZ SOUND

Although jazz can be played on just about any type of guitar, you might want to try an electric archtop model such as the Gibson ES-175, as this produces a warm, mellow tone. A relatively clean amplifier such as a Polytone Mini Brute or Roland Jazz Chorus will complement this guitar perfectly. Set your amplifier to boost the low and mid-range frequencies, and cut back on the high frequencies to accentuate the warmth of the guitar.

▲ *A Roland Jazz Chorus amplifier works well with a Gibson ES-175.*

If you want to play jazz-rock, try a solidbody or semi-solid guitar with a rock amplifier as this will allow you to play soaring, sustained solos with minimal feedback. You can also use a chorus pedal to smoothen your chords, and an overdrive unit to make your solos sound more dynamic. Another effect worth trying is the ring modulator, a pedal that produces metallic, atonal sounds, and is great for creating a really 'out there' vibe!

You can also use an amp modelling box like the Line 6 POD, or a virtual amp software package such as IK Multimedia's AmpliTube to create a realistic jazz amp sound. If you're using a software sequencer package such as Cubase SX, Logic or Sonar to make recordings on your computer, you can also use the sequencer's built-in effects to add more colour and spice to your guitar sound.

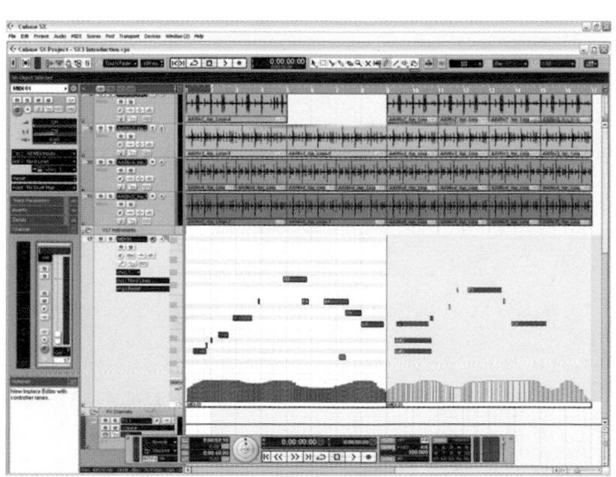

◀ *Cubase has long been one of the most popular MIDI and audio sequencers for home recording.*

Section Two: Musical Styles

METAL

Although the term 'heavy metal' did not become firmly established until the late 1970s, the roots for this popular genre were firmly planted when Led Zeppelin and Black Sabbath formed a decade earlier in the UK. Led Zeppelin was born when the Yardbirds split up and their guitarist, Jimmy Page, assembled a band of his own.

Influenced by the high-volume electric blues-rock guitar styles of Clapton and Hendrix, Page worked on his own ideas and came up with a heavy riff style that featured heavily – alongside Robert Plant's screaming vocals – in Zeppelin's 'Whole Lotta Love' (1969). Black Sabbath formed that same year in Birmingham when guitarist Tony Iommi, singer Ozzy Osbourne, bassist Geezer Butler and drummer Bill Ward decided to start their own band. They developed a more basic heavy riff style that they used on 'Paranoid' and 'Iron Man' (both 1970). Although critics of the time mocked the band's obsession with death, destruction and mental illness, these themes were soon adopted by other bands such as Motörhead, Rainbow and the leather-clad Judas Priest – heavy metal was born!

▲ *Iron Maiden's trademark galloping rhythms and lyrics about fantasy or the devil have changed little over the years.*

Complete Guitar Handbook

NWOBHM

▲ Van Halen revived interest in hard rock after a period of punk music.

By the late 1970s, a number of new British bands began to emerge, including Iron Maiden, Saxon, Def Leppard and Samson. Although their music exuded less depth, range and invention than that of their predecessors, it was a huge commercial success, and later categorized as a distinct sub-genre: the New Wave Of British Heavy Metal (NWOBHM). Meanwhile in the US, Van Halen introduced a new style of technically oriented heavy rock, showcasing the pioneering two-handed tapping techniques of guitarist Eddie Van Halen (b. 1955) and dazzling showmanship of extrovert singer David Lee Roth, while over in Australia, school uniform-clad guitarist Angus Young (b. 1955) and his pals had already forged their own heavy brand of 'no-nonsense rock 'n' roll' in AC/DC.

THRASH

By the middle of the 1980s, the various hard rock and metal styles had evolved further into other styles. Guitarists bored with the NWOBHM style decided they wanted to spice things up by playing harder and faster; thrash metal was born. The six primary thrash bands were Metallica, Slayer, Anthrax, Megadeth, Sepultura and Pantera. Metallica were by far the most successful of these. Their first few albums, *Kill 'Em All* (1983), *Ride the Lightning* (1984) and *Master of Puppets* (1986), expanded the limits of metal by introducing intricately structured compositions played at an unheard-of speed.

◀ Metallica were the most successful of the thrash metal bands, gradually developing their sound into heavy metal.

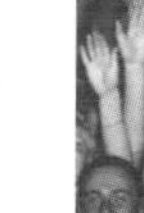

Section Two: Musical Styles

▲ *Dave Grohl, Krist Novoselic and Kurt Cobain of Nirvana, the band that both created and epitomized the grunge movement.*

Despite this, their attitude was refreshingly down-to-earth and unpretentious – they had street cred. Slayer developed an even faster style, delivering a stream of full-throttle metal with formidable chops, manic solos and deranged lyrics. Their fifth album, *Reign in Blood* (1986), is widely regarded as a metal classic. Various other sub-styles later evolved out of thrash, including death metal and black metal.

A SOLO EFFORT

While Kirk Hammett (b. 1962) of Metallica and Kerry King (b. 1964) of Slayer were thrashing their way around the globe, a handful of other heavy rock soloists such as Steve Vai and Yngwie Malmsteen adopted a more 'arty' approach to their soloing. Vai played for Alcatrazz, David Lee Roth and Whitesnake during the 1980s, while releasing a series of solo albums showcasing his then unheard-of whammy bar pyrotechnics and sublime modal soloing. Along with his former mentor, Joe Satriani (b. 1956), Vai raised the standard for rock guitar virtuosity and, while neither of them are considered to be heavy metal players, both have been emulated by lead guitarists within the genre. Malmsteen fused metal with the classical styles of Bach and Paganini, and became the main pioneer of a style that later earned the amusing tag 'baroque and roll'.

Complete Guitar Handbook

NU-METAL

As the 1980s drew to an end, young audiences veered away from thrash and 'flash' and opted for grunge bands like Nirvana and Pearl Jam, but the early 1990s saw a new style emerge; nu-metal bands such as Korn and Slipknot took the best elements of metal and grunge, donned seven-string guitars, with the extra string tuned down to a low B, and played a new style of subversive riff that was hugely popular by the middle of the decade. The novelty of all this wore off after a few years, although offshoot bands including System of a Down, who mix quirky syncopations with political lyrics, and Linkin Park, a rap-influenced nu-rock band, have had success well into the new millennium.

RETURN OF THRASH

As nu-metal began to wane, the thrash style suddenly became cool again, and the metal genre seemed to turn full circle as new American bands such as Shadows Fall, Chimaira, Killswitch Engage and Lamb of God fronted the unimaginatively named New Wave Of American Heavy Metal, while across the Atlantic, the likes of Rhapsody, Soilwork, Lacuna Coil, In Flames and Nightwish have kept the European metal flag flying.

▲ *The hate-driven, theatrical metal of Slipknot fuses jagged, grinding riffs with barbaric percussion.*

▲ *The unpredictability and sheer energy of bands like Lamb of God ensures their continuing appeal.*

Section Two: Musical Styles

PLAYING METAL

Although most metal guitarists know a variety of chord shapes, you can play a lot of music in this style with power chords. The most basic of these are two-note chords consisting of the first and fifth notes of the major scale, played on any two adjacent strings (such as the sixth and fifth strings, or fourth and third strings) with your index finger fretting the root note (on the thicker string), and your third finger fretting the fifth note (on the lighter string) two frets further up the fingerboard. To play a G power chord on the sixth and fifth strings (E and A), for example, place your index finger behind the third fret on the sixth string and your third finger behind the fifth fret on the fifth string and then strum those strings only. To play an A power chord on the same two strings, simply move the shape two frets further up the guitar neck, and so on.

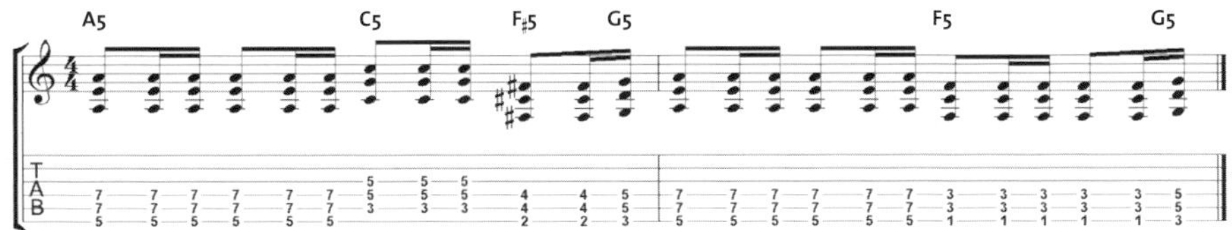

▲ *Try this example of metal rhythm playing which uses sixteenth notes and power chords.*

ADD POWER TO POWER CHORDS

▲ *Power, or fifth chords, are often used in heavy metal and rock music along with distortion.*

You can strengthen your power chords further by adding an extra note, one that is an octave higher than your root note, on the next adjacent string. This is easy to do as it is in the same fret as the fifth interval note; to play a three-note G power chord on the sixth, fifth and fourth strings, adopt the fingering position already described, and place your fourth (little) finger behind the fifth fret on the fourth string to get that octave note. Bear in mind, though, that when you're playing any power chords, you should only strum the strings you are fretting – strumming any of the others will almost certainly produce a dreadful sound!

Complete Guitar Handbook

You should also learn the barred versions of the open A and E shapes and the open Am and Em shapes. These will allow you to play full major or minor chords in any key you want, as the shapes can be used anywhere on the fingerboard. Diminished and augmented chords can also be useful for metal as they produce a dissonant, disturbing effect – ideal for making threatening music!

GETTING IN RHYTHM

Rhythmically, metal is usually relentless, with emphasis on insistent eighth- or sixteenth-note rhythms and a heavy accent on the first and other beats. Strumming is usually performed with downstrokes as these supply more power, although more intricate rhythms will sometimes require alternating downstrokes and upstrokes. Metal guitarists also perform muted versions of their riffs by resting the side of their picking hand against the strings. This creates a great dynamic effect when combined with unmuted versions of the riffs.

▲ *Strumming is an essential technique for the rhythm guitarist to master.*

Section Two: Musical Styles

Scale-wise, you should learn the pentatonic scales and all the common major scale modes. If you want to play a thrash-related style you will have to learn to play them fast with alternate picking – realistically this might take a couple of years. If you want to get quicker results, practise hammer-ons and pull-offs (see pages 92–93), as these can easily be combined with picked notes to create rapid phrases within a solo. Another technique often used in metal is sweep-picking (also called economy-picking). By applying this technique to notes on adjacent strings, you can play an ascending line with a downstroke or a descending line with an upstroke. This works best for arpeggios, which are often one note per string.

GETTING AN AUTHENTIC METAL SOUND

If you want to get an authentic metal guitar sound you'll need a solidbody electric guitar and an amplifier with preamp distortion capabilities. Solidbody guitars are essential for producing a sustained, overdriven tone with minimal feedback at reasonably high volumes. All the classic Gibson models are great for this purpose but there is also a range of dedicated metal instruments available, including the ESP JH2, BC Rich Warlock, PRS Singlecut, Jackson Kelly

▲ *Buying the right equipment is vital if you're trying to achieve an authentic metal sound. Pictured here is a Washburn Special Edition and a Marshall head amplifier.*

Complete Guitar Handbook

and Washburn Dime models. All these guitars have humbucking pickups, which are ideal for an aggressive metal sound. You can also use guitars fitted with traditional single coil pickups if you use an extra distortion pedal.

A thick pick is essential for metal music. A wide one (0.9 mm/0.003 in or thicker) will make a firmer contact with your strings than a thin one, making it easier to play riffs accurately and severely. Try several different picks out before you decide which one is best for you.

WHICH AMPLIFIER IS BEST?

Amp-wise, there are a number of dedicated metal amplifiers which can deliver a truly mean sound. These include valve-style models such as the Mesa Boogie Dual Rectifier, Marshall Mode 4, Hughes & Kettner Warp 7, Peavey 5150 and Randall Warhead models.

Metal can get rather loud, and if you want to play it without upsetting your neighbours, try an amp modelling box such as a Line 6 POD, or a virtual amp software package like IK Multimedia's AmpliTube or Steinberg's Warp VST. All of these feature some great metal presets, and you can use them at any volume you like. Get moshing!

▶ *No logo is more synonymous with heavy rock than the white-on-black Marshall stamp.*

Section Two: Musical Styles

ERIC CLAPTON

English blues-rock legend, born in Ripley, Surrey in 1945. He grew up with his grandparents and became interested in blues music as a teenager. His early influences included Muddy Waters, Robert Johnson, Freddie King and Big Bill Broonzy.

▲ *With John Mayall's Bluesbreakers, Eric Clapton redefined electric blues guitar.*

After a spell with the Yardbirds in the early 1960s, he joined John Mayall's Bluesbreakers in 1965. They released the landmark album *Blues Breakers* (1965), which featured Eric's revolutionary guitar sound heavily; he cranked his amp up and pioneered the use of feedback-assisted sustain and overdrive, playing solos of a previously unheard of intensity. Mayall later recalled 'The things he did with a slow blues could send shivers down your spine.' Eric became an instant cult figure and graffiti proclaiming 'Clapton is God' started to appear on walls, signposts and even rocks in the UK. He left Mayall's band in 1966 to form the supergroup Cream with bassist Jack Bruce and drummer Ginger Baker. They were the first rock band to gain mass appeal through their instrumental abilities, and many of their songs, now regarded as rock classics, featured extended soloing from the band members.

Complete Guitar Handbook

GOING SOLO

▲ *Eric Clapton has enjoyed a hugely successful solo career. The acoustic* Unplugged *album sold millions.*

Cream split up in 1969 and Clapton spent brief periods with Blind Faith (with Stevie Winwood and Ginger Baker) and Delaney & Bonnie & Friends. He formed Derek & the Dominos in 1970 and they recorded the legendary 'Layla' with guest guitarist Duane Allman. Clapton then embarked on a long and successful solo career, although he had considerable problems with drug and alcohol addiction during the 1970s. Standout solo albums include *461 Ocean Boulevard* (1974), which launched the number one hit single 'I Shot The Sheriff', *Slowhand* (1977), which spawned 'Wonderful Tonight' and a great cover of J. J. Cale's 'Cocaine', and *Unplugged* (1992), an acoustic album which featured 'Tears In Heaven', a haunting song about the death of his son.

ENDURING INFLUENCE

More recently, he released *Me & Mr Johnson* (2004), a selection of tunes honouring the legendary Mississippi bluesman Robert Johnson. Eric's blues-style solos and memorable riffs have been a huge influence on many other rock and blues players including Brian May, Paul Kossoff, Gary Moore, Robert Cray, Jimmy Page and Eddie Van Halen. He also helped to introduce the music of the original black blues artists to a wider audience. He has played a number of different electric guitars over the years: a Gibson Les Paul with the Bluesbreakers; a Gibson SG and a Gibson ES-335 with Cream; and a Fender Stratocaster for most of his solo career.

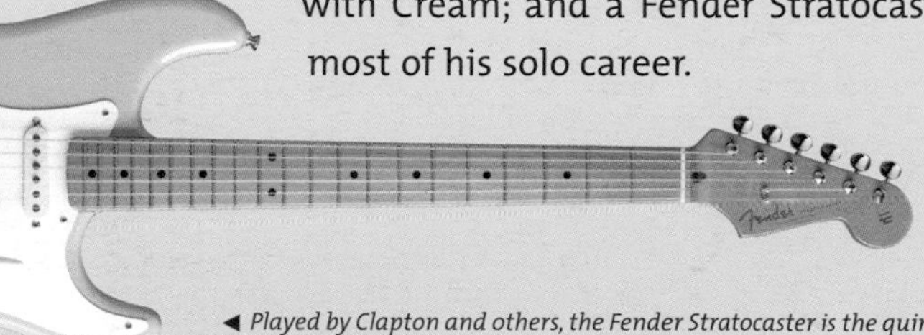

◀ *Played by Clapton and others, the Fender Stratocaster is the quintessential rock guitar.*

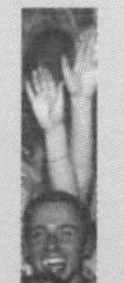

JIMI HENDRIX

Legendary rock guitarist, singer and songwriter, born James Marshall Hendricks in Seattle, Washington in 1942. Jimi grew up in a musical environment – his parents Al and Lucille were professional tap dancers – and had started playing guitar by the time he was 10.

▲ *Hendrix backed the Isley Brothers and Little Richard before forming his own band.*

By this time he had already been exposed to blues artists such as Muddy Waters and B. B. King through his father's record collection. Jimi was left-handed and played a right-handed guitar upside down, with the order of the strings reversed. He enlisted in the US army in 1959, but a parachute jump went wrong and he injured himself and was discharged 26 months later.

A NEW EXPERIENCE

Jimi toured with a variety of acts during the early 1960s and soon earned a reputation as an outstanding sideman. By 1965 he had worked with James

Brown, Ike & Tina Turner, Little Richard, B. B. King, Wilson Pickett and the Isley Brothers. He formed his own band, Jimmy James & the Blue Flames, later that year. Chas Chandler (bass player with the Animals) heard Jimi and was so impressed he brought him over to London and hastily introduced him to drummer Mitch Mitchell and bass player Noel Redding; the Jimi Hendrix Experience was born.

▲ *The ultimate showman, Hendrix embellished his performances with long improvisations.*

The group was an immediate success in Europe and had hits with 'Hey Joe', 'Purple Haze' and 'The Wind Cries Mary' in 1967. Jimi's fame spread back to America when he played at the 1967 Monterey Pop Festival. His use and control of distortion amazed the audience, and their jaws dropped when he set fire to his guitar on stage. The same year, Jimi released *Are You Experienced* (1967), one of the classic rock albums of all time, and followed up with *Axis: Bold As Love* (1967) and *Electric Ladyland* (1968). Although it was a huge success, the band drifted apart by 1969 and Hendrix formed the Band Of Gypsys with bassist Billy Cox and drummer Buddy Miles. They were less successful but talk of reforming the Experience came to nothing.

GONE BUT NOT FORGOTTEN

Hendrix died in London in 1970 after choking in his sleep following a drink and drugs overdose. His death shook the music world, as he had been an exceptionally gifted guitar player who had expanded the instrument's range considerably. He was included in *Guitar Player* magazine's 'Gallery of the Greats' for his lifetime achievement (1983). Posthumous compilations include *The Essential Jimi Hendrix* (1978), *The Singles Album* (1983), *The Ultimate Jimi Hendrix* (1993) and *His Greatest Hits* (1999).

◀ Are You Experienced *was one of only five albums released in Hendrix's lifetime.*

Section Three: Galleries

ANDRÉS SEGOVIA

Classical guitar pioneer, born in Grenada, Spain in 1893. Segovia started playing guitar aged 10, although his parents were concerned because it was not seen as a 'respectable' instrument in those days.

Segovia took a dislike to the region's traditional flamenco style and developed his own formal approach, adapting music composed for other instruments to the guitar, thus creating the basic classical guitar repertoire. Initially he encountered from other musicians and the press, but his reputation as an outstanding performer grew and he was invited to play for Queen Victoria of Spain in 1920. By 1928 he had captivated audiences around the world with his performances, and his arrangements of pieces by Bach, Handel, Tarrega, Chopin, Schumann and Mozart became standards for the classical guitar. He also commissioned works by composers such as Villa-Lobos, Falla, Castelnuovo-Tedesco, Ponse and Tansman, thus broadening the repertoire of the instrument.

▲ *Andrés Segovia increased the popularity of the guitar wherever he went.*

Complete Guitar Handbook

GIFTED TEACHER

The outbreak of the Spanish Civil War forced Segovia to give up his home in Spain in 1936, and he lived by turns in Italy, Uruguay and the United States. During the 1960s and 1970s, he played in many other countries at a rate of around 100 concerts a year. As well as being an exceptional performer, he also had a reputation as an excellent teacher, and his pupils included many outstanding classical guitar players, such as Julian Bream, Christopher Parkening, John Williams, Alirio Diaz, Oscar Ghilia and Alexandre Lagoya. Segovia tirelessly promoted the classical guitar with his own recitals, records and books. However, he was also well-known for his scorn towards popular guitar playing styles and the more radical side of twentieth-century music.

▲ *Segovia taught classical guitarist John Williams among many others.*

AWARD-WINNER

Segovia received countless awards and honours during his lifetime, including the Gold Medal of the Royal Philharmonic Society of London, the Grand Cross of Isabella and Alfonso, and many honorary degrees. He was included in *Guitar Player* magazine's 'Gallery of the Greats' after being voted Best Classical Guitarist by the magazine's readers for five consecutive years (1970–74). King Juan Carlos of Spain knighted him in 1981, and later the Segovia International Guitar Competition was launched in his honour. He died in 1987. Posthumous CD releases include *Guitar Recital* (1995), *The Legendary Segovia* (2000), *The Art of Segovia* (2002), *Complete Bach Recordings* (2002) and *Segovia – The Collection* (2003).

▶ *Segovia was largely responsible for the first nylon guitar strings in 1947.*

Section Three: Galleries

EDDIE VAN HALEN

Heavy metal legend, born in Nijmegen, Holland in 1957. His family moved to Pasadena, California in 1962, and Eddie and his brother Alex developed an early interest in music. Eddie initially started on drums, while Alex played guitar, but they soon swapped instruments and never looked back.

Eddie's early influences included Eric Clapton and Jimi Hendrix, as well as heavy metal pioneers Black Sabbath and Led Zeppelin. The brothers formed Van Halen (originally called Mammoth) in 1973, with bassist Michael Anthony and singer David Lee Roth. They played the LA club circuit during the mid-seventies, and their exciting and flamboyant stage act soon brought in a large following. Eddie stunned audiences with his playing; he was the first rock guitarist to use sophisticated two-handed techniques and squealing harmonics. Gene Simmons (of Kiss) was impressed and convinced Warner Brothers to sign them up.

▲ *Rock legend Eddie Van Halen (right) reinvented how to play the electric guitar.*

EARLY SUCCESS

Their first album, *Van Halen* (1978), made the US Top 20 and sold two million units in a year. It boasted a killer version of the Kinks' 'You Really Got Me' and 'Eruption', an explosive solo guitar track, which became a showcase for the

Complete Guitar Handbook

▶ *Van Halen revived the rock music genre with this eponymous 1978 debut album.*

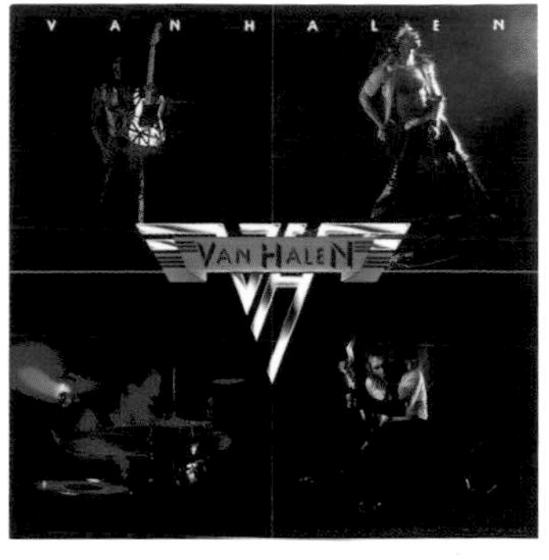

guitarist. They went on to have further success with *Van Halen II* (1979), *Women and Children First* (1980), *Fair Warning* (1981) and *Diver Down* (1982). Eddie then surprised the music world by playing a synthesizer instead of his guitar for the riff of 'Jump' (1984), a huge hit single from their *1984* (1984) album. Egos clashed and Roth left the following year; he was replaced by platinum award-winning star Sammy Hagar on vocals. Van Halen continued with further successful albums: *5150* (1986), *OU812* (1988), *For Unlawful Carnal Knowledge* (1991) and *Van Halen Live: Right Here, Right Now* (1993). Eddie also played the solo on Michael Jackson's 'Beat It' in 1982.

REVOLUTIONARY PLAYER

Alongside Jimi Hendrix, Eddie Van Halen redefined what electric guitar could do, developing an incredibly fast technique with effects that mimicked animals and machines. He influenced a whole new generation of players, including Steve Vai, Joe Satriani, Jennifer Batten, Kirk Hammett (Metallica), Kerry King (Slayer) and Yngwie Malmsteen. In redefining the sound of heavy rock guitar, he secured his place in history as one of the most influential guitar players of all time. He was included in *Guitar Player* magazine's 'Gallery of the Greats' after being voted Best New Talent (1978) and Best Rock Guitarist (1979–83).

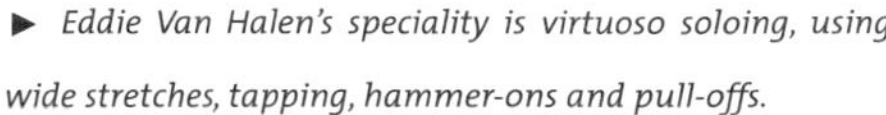

▶ *Eddie Van Halen's speciality is virtuoso soloing, using wide stretches, tapping, hammer-ons and pull-offs.*

Section Three: Galleries

CHET ATKINS

Country fingerstyle pioneer, born in Luttrell, Tennessee in 1924. Atkins took an early interest in country music, and played fiddle with Bill Carlisle's Dixieland Swingers on the radio while he was still at school.

He later switched to guitar and developed an advanced thumb-and-three-fingers technique that inspired many other players. He toured with Archie Campbell and Maybelle Carter during the 1940s and became a radio staff guitarist. RCA signed him up in 1947 and released his debut album, *Chet Atkins Plays Guitar* (1951). He became an A&R director with RCA and helped supervise the careers of Elvis Presley, the Everly Brothers, Jim Reeves, Don Gibson, Charley Pride and many others. Later recordings include *Chet Atkins' Gallopin' Guitar* (1953), *In Three Dimensions* (1956), *Fingerstyle Guitar* (1958), *Chet Atkins' Workshop* (1960), *Down Home* (1961), *Picks on the Beatles* (1965), *Pickin' My Way* (1971), *Work It Out* (1983), *Stay Tuned* (1985), *Sweet Dreams* (1986), *Sails* (1987) and *CGP* (1988).

Atkins also collaborated with Les Paul on *Chester & Lester* (1978), and Mark Knopfler on *Neck & Neck* (1990). He was included in *Guitar Player* magazine's 'Gallery of the Greats' after being Best Country Guitarist for five consecutive years (1970–74). He died in 2001, after a long battle with cancer.

Complete Guitar Handbook

JEFF BECK

Legendary rock player, born in Surrey, England in 1944. As a child, Beck started singing in a church choir and playing violin, cello and piano. Inspired by Les Paul, Muddy Waters and Cliff Gallup, he built his first electric guitar out of wood, homemade frets, wire and a pickup.

Beck played with local bands before replacing Eric Clapton in the Yardbirds in 1965. He left the group during a gruelling 1966 tour of America and went solo with producer Mickey Most. They made the successful hit single 'Hi Ho Silver Lining' (1967). Beck then formed his own band and evolved his unique playing style. By the mid 1970s, he had recorded instrumental jazz-rock albums such as *Blow by Blow* (1975) and *Wired* (1976), whch featured some pioneering lead guitar work, lyrical solos with tasteful bends, unique nuances and brilliant harmonics.

These characteristics grace all his later recordings, including *There And Back* (1980), *Flash* (1985), *Jeff Beck's Guitar Shop* (1989), *Crazy Legs* (1993), *Who Else!* (1999) and *Beck* (2003). Beck is one of the most admired guitarists in the world, drawing equal respect from rock, blues and jazz musicians.

Section Three: Galleries

JULIAN BREAM

English classical virtuoso and lutenist, born in London in 1933. He started playing guitar at age 11, studied piano and cello at London's Royal Academy of Music, and also studied classical guitar with Andrés Segovia.

Although Bream started performing professionally as a classical guitarist during the late 1940s, he joined the British Army in 1952 and spent three years there before resuming his musical career. He later performed extensively in Europe, America and Asia, and was widely acknowledged as a master of renaissance, baroque and romantic music. He also broadened the guitar repertoire by commissioning works from new composers such as Leo Brouwer, Benjamin Britten, William Walton, Lennox Berkley, Hans Werner Henze and Peter Fricker. Standout recordings include *Guitar* (1966), *Classic Guitar* (1968), *The Winds So Wild* (1972), *Lute Music of John Dowland* (1976), *Plays Villa-Lobos* (1977), *Dedication* (1981), *Highlights From The Bream Edition* (1993) and *Popular Classics for Spanish Guitar* (1998).

Bream has won two Grammys (1963 and 1966) and two Edison awards (1964 and 1974). He is one of the giants of classical guitar music, and he is considered by many to be the finest lutenist of his generation.

Complete Guitar Handbook

RY COODER

Multi-genre guitarist, born in Los Angeles in 1947. He started learning the guitar at the age of four and, as a youngster, took lessons from the Reverend Gary Davis, a local blues star.

Cooder formed a duo with Jackie DeShannon as a teenager and later became a successful Hollywood session man, working with Taj Mahal, Captain Beefheart, Randy Newman, Phil Ochs and the Rolling Stones during the late 1960s and early 1970s. He developed a unique and much-admired slide guitar style and recorded a number of critically acclaimed solo albums, including *Ry Cooder* (1970), *Into the Purple Valley* (1971), *Boomer's Story* (1973), *Paradise & Lunch* (1974), *Chicken Skin Music* (1976), *Jazz* (1978), *Bop Till You Drop* (1979), *Borderline* (1980), *Why Don't You Try Me Tonight?* (1986) and *Get Rhythm* (1987). He has also worked on many notable film soundtracks, including *Southern Comfort* (1981), *Alamo Bay* (1985), *Paris, Texas* (1985), *Crossroads* (1986) and *Trespass* (1992).

Cooder is well-known as a collaborator, and has recorded projects with Nick Lowe, Ali Farka Toure, Ruben Gonzalez and many other blues, folk and world musicians. *Guitar Player* magazine included him in their 'Gallery of the Greats' after he won several blues and acoustic guitar categories in readers' polls during the 1980s.

Section Three: Galleries

DAVID GILMOUR

Rock guitarist, born in Cambridge, England in 1944. He developed an early interest in rock 'n' roll and began learning guitar at the age of 14.

Gilmour joined Pink Floyd as a fifth member but ended up replacing Syd Barrett after the band's successful debut, *Piper at the Gates of Dawn* (1967). They recorded the unusual *A Saucerful of Secrets* (1968) and signed to the Harvest label to release other groundbreaking progressive rock albums, including *Ummagumma* (1969), *Atom Heart Mother* (1970), Meddle (1971) and *Obscured by Clouds* (1972). Their big break came with *Dark Side of the Moon* (1973); it was superbly produced and sold over 10 million copies worldwide, staying high in the album charts for more than two years. Two of the album's strongest tracks, 'Time' and 'Money', boasted excellent, soaring rock solos by Gilmour.

Further success followed with *Wish You Were Here* (1975), *Animals* (1977) and *The Wall* (1979), and the band performed massive concerts before splitting up in the early 1980s. Gilmour later reformed the group without Roger Waters and an infamous lawsuit ensued. Gilmour's guitar solos are melodic, spacey and punctuated by tasteful use of the vibrato arm.

Complete Guitar Handbook

JONNY GREENWOOD

British prog-pop guitarist, born in 1971. He became interested in music as a child and started playing guitar while at Abingdon School in Oxfordshire. He formed Radiohead with fellow Oxford University friends Thom Yorke (vocals, guitar), Ed O'Brien (guitar, vocals), brother Colin Greenwood (bass) and Phil Selway (drums) in 1988.

The band drew from influences as diverse as REM, My Bloody Valentine, Pink Floyd and the Pixies. Their debut album, *Pablo Honey* (1993), was well received but greater success and acclaim came with *The Bends* (1995) and *OK Computer* (1997). By then, the band's sound had fully developed into a unique blend of prog rock, angst-ridden lyrics and eldritch electronic textures. They became one of the biggest and most original acts of the nineties, and Greenwood's raw, expressive guitar work was an essential ingredient of their sound. Later recordings *Kid A* (2000) and *Amnesiac* (2001) were more outlandish and a disappointment to many, even though they demonstrated the band's progressive and intelligent nature, but *Hail to the Thief* (2003) was welcomed as a return to form.

Radiohead were clearly the most original, popular guitar band to emerge at the end of the twentieth century, and it looks like they will be around for many years to come.

Section Three: Galleries

ROBERT JOHNSON

Blues pioneer, born in Hazlehurst, Mississippi in 1911. He started to play harmonica as a child and bought a guitar in his teens. Influenced by Son House and Lonnie Johnson, he taught himself to play the instrument.

The story goes that he was an uninspired musician until he 'went down to the crossroads' one day and made a pact with the devil to become a better player. Whatever happened, Johnson excelled at interpreting the songs of others and was considered the first real blues performance artist. He died in Greenwood, Mississippi in 1938 under mysterious circumstances; an early report claimed that he had been stabbed, but it is widely believed that he was poisoned by the jealous husband of a woman he was seeing.

Although Johnson's life came to a premature end and recordings of him are few, he remains one of the most celebrated figures in the history of the blues. His style was mimicked by many other blues artists and his songs have been performed by the likes of Cream, the Rolling Stones and John Mayall. Indigo recently released *Hellhound on my Trail* (1995), a CD compilation of his original recordings.

Complete Guitar Handbook

B. B. KING

Blues legend, born Riley B. King in Itta Bena, Mississippi in 1925. He worked on a plantation from the age of eight and was given a guitar as part of his wages when he was 14.

King became influenced by gospel music and blues players such as Lonnie Johnson, Blind Lemon Jefferson and T-Bone Walker. He moved to Memphis in 1948 and worked as a disc jockey for the WDIA radio station, where he was nicknamed 'Blues Boy from Beale Street' (later shortened to B. B.). He started recording in 1949, soon maturing into an outstanding blues performer, famous for his 'singing' lead lines and pioneering across the-string vibrato and note-bending techniques. His many popular blues albums, include *King of the Blues* (1961), *Live at the Regal* (1965), *Live in Cook County Jail* (1971), *Six Silver Strings* (1985), *Live at the Apollo* (1991), *Blues Summit* (1993), *Live in Japan* (1999) and *Greatest Hits Live* (2003).

King was a huge inspiration to many younger guitar players, including Eric Clapton, Duane Allman, Roy Buchanan and Duane Eddy. He was also winner of a Grammy for Lifetime Achievement (1987). He has played a Gibson ES-335 semi-acoustic guitar since the early 1950s.

Section Three: Galleries

MARK KNOPFLER

Rock guitarist, born in London, England in 1949. He became interested in music while at school and later formed Dire Straits, influenced by Bob Dylan and J. J. Cale, in the mid-1970s.

The group developed an intimate R&B sound, punctuated by Knopfler's dexterous guitar work, and Charlie Gillett played a demo version of one of their early songs, 'Sultans of Swing', on his BBC radio show. The band released an eponymous debut album in 1978, but their big break did not come until they released a more polished version of 'Sultans of Swing' a year later; it reached the Top 10 on both sides of the Atlantic and album sales soared. More success followed with recordings including *Communique* (1979), *Making Movies* (1980), *Love Over Gold* (1982), *Alchemy* (1984), *Brothers in Arms* (1985), *On Every Street* (1991) and *On the Night* (1993).

Knopfler's guitar playing became more sparse and lyrical on later recordings. He headlined the Nelson Mandela Tribute at Wembley (1988), and recorded scores for films such as *Local Hero* (1983) and *Cal* (1984). He also teamed up with country legend Chet Atkins for *Neck & Neck* (1990) and sessioned with Steely Dan, Bob Dylan and many others. He remains a highly respected guitarist.

Complete Guitar Handbook

PACO DE LUCÍA

Flamenco virtuoso, born Francisco Sánchez Gómez in Algeciras, Spain in 1947. He grew up in a musical family – his father was an established flamenco player and his brothers also played guitar.

Paco started playing flamenco guitar at the age of seven, and became influenced by Niño Ricardo, Sabicas and Mario Escudero. He practised for 12 hours a day and developed a formidable technique. His first recording, *Los Chiquitos de Algeciras* (1961), caused a sensation in the flamenco world and his later offerings reinforced his reputation as one of Spain's foremost flamenco players: *The Fabulous Guitar of Paco de Lucía* (1967), *Fuente y Caudal* (1973), *Paco de Lucía en Vivo Desde el Teatro Real* (1975), *Almoraima* (1976), *Solo Quiero Caminar* (1981), *Sirocco* (1987), *Zyryab* (1990) and *Cositas Buenas* (2004). He also recorded three incredible acoustic trio albums, *Friday Night in San Francisco* (1981), *Passion, Grace & Fire* (1983) and *The Guitar Trio* (1996) with fusion virtuosos Al Di Meola and John McLaughlin.

Paco is a supremely gifted player who has redefined flamenco and introduced it to a wider audience. He has influenced countless other flamenco, jazz and world musicians.

Section Three: Galleries

JUAN MARTÍN

A native of Andalucia, Juan is a respected flamenco player. He became interested in the Moorish flamenco, and took up the Spanish guitar at an early age.

He developed a distinctive compositional style that won many admirers and led the US magazine *Guitar Player* to acknowledge him as one of the world's top players. Reviews of his solo compositions such as *The Andalucian Suites* (1991) and *Luna Negra* (1993) have compared him to the great Spanish composers Tárrega and Turina. He has recorded more than 17 albums and his method book, *El Arte Flamenco de la Guitarra*, has helped introduce the world to the techniques behind the complex art of flamenco guitar.

Martín was the first flamenco artist to record with the Royal Philharmonic Orchestra, and has also performed with musicians as diverse as fellow guitarist Paco de Lucía, the legendary jazz trumpeter Miles Davis, and the Nash Ensemble, a highly regarded classical ensemble. He has also performed at major international arts festivals, including Edinburgh, Ludwigsburg, Montreux Jazz, Istanbul, Bosporus, Bergen and Hong Kong, and broadcast on BBC, ITV, Channel 4, Spanish RTE, German ZDF and US CNN television. He continues to perform to receptive audiences around the world.

Complete Guitar Handbook

BRIAN MAY

British rock guitarist, born in Hampton, Middlesex in 1947. May grew up in nearby Feltham and had started learning ukulele, banjo and guitar by the time he was 10.

As a teenager, his influences included Lonnie Donegan, Buddy Holly, the Shadows, Eric Clapton, B. B. King, Jeff Beck and Jimi Hendrix. He made his own guitar at age 17 and studied physics at London University's Imperial College. He formed the group Smile with vocalist Tim Staffell and drummer Roger Taylor. They broke up in 1970 and May and Taylor formed Queen with Freddie Mercury (Staffell's flatmate) and bass player John Deacon. By their second album, *Queen II* (1974), the band had developed a unique sound based around Mercury's quasi-operatic vocals and May's rich multi-layered guitar parts.

Moderate chart success came with singles 'Seven Seas of Rhye' and 'Killer Queen' (both 1974), but the band achieved major success when the epic 'Bohemian Rhapsody' (1975) topped the UK and US singles charts for many weeks. Queen remained a huge, worldwide stadium band until Mercury died of an AIDS-related illness in 1991. May used the same homemade guitar for all Queen's recordings and employed an old English sixpenny piece as a pick.

Section Three: Galleries

PAT METHENY

Guitarist and composer, born in Lee's Summit, Missouri in 1954. He started playing guitar aged 13, influenced by Wes Montgomery, Kenny Burrell, Jim Hall and Jimmy Raney, and later studied at the University of Miami while playing in Gary Burton's band.

He recorded two solo albums before forming the Pat Metheny Group with keyboardist Lyle Mays and others. The first two band albums, *Pat Metheny Group* (1978) and *American Garage* (1980), were successful commercially and artistically; Metheny had forged a new earthy, mellow jazz sound, incorporating elements from bebop, folk and rock. Other notable albums include *Offramp* (1982), *Travels* (1983), *First Circle* (1984), *Still Life Talking* (1987), *Letter from Home* (1989), *We Live Here* (1995) and *Speaking of Now* (2002).

Metheny has also collaborated with many big names in jazz, including Ornette Coleman, John Scofield, Dave Holland and Roy Haynes. He has used many guitars over the years, but his favourites include a Gibson ES-175 semi-acoustic, a Coral electric sitar and a guitar-controlled Synclavier synthesizer. He was included in *Guitar Player* magazine's 'Gallery of the Greats' after being voted Best Jazz Guitarist by the magazine's readers for five consecutive years (1982–86).

Complete Guitar Handbook

JIMMY PAGE

Legendary rock guitarist, born in Heston, London in 1944. He started playing guitar at the age of 14, influenced by Scotty Moore, James Burton and B. B. King.

Page became a successful studio guitarist in London, playing up to three sessions a day with artists as diverse as The Who, Tom Jones and Joe Cocker. He joined the Yardbirds in 1966 and played alongside Jeff Beck. They split up in 1968 and Page formed heavy rock group Led Zeppelin with Robert Plant (vocals), John Paul Jones (bass) and John Bonham (drums). They became one of the most original and successful rock bands of all time and, along with Black Sabbath, paved the way for heavy metal music as it is known today. Highlights include the monster riff of 'Whole Lotta Love', from *Led Zeppelin II* (1969) and the haunting, earthy epic 'Stairway to Heaven' from *Led Zeppelin IV* (1971), although the albums *Led Zeppelin III* (1970), *Houses of the Holy* (1973) and *Physical Graffiti* (1975) all feature quality material.

Led Zeppelin disbanded in 1980 after John Bonham died following an all-day drinking binge. Page later remastered the band's back catalogue for the mammoth 10-disc box set, *The Complete Studio Recordings* (1993).

Section Three: Galleries

LES PAUL

Electric guitar pioneer and inventor, born Lester Polfus in Waukesha, Wisconsin in 1916. Aged nine, he heard a street musician playing a harmonica and allegedly stared at the man until he was given the instrument.

Within a year he was proficient enough to play for money in the streets of Waukesha and was conducting his own experiments with sound. He started playing guitar at age 11 and, by the time he was 18, now playing country music under the name Rhubarb Red. After hearing Django Reinhardt, he switched over to jazz and changed his name to Les Paul. He earned a reputation as a strikingly original and creative guitarist, and soon found himself playing alongside the likes of Nat 'King' Cole and Bing Crosby.

Paul's right arm was shattered in a horrific car crash in 1948, but the doctor was a fan and set his arm in a guitar-playing position. Paul designed a compact solid-body electric guitar to suit his damaged arm and it eventually inspired the Gibson company to produce the first Gibson Les Paul guitars. These became hugely popular when blues-rock and pop artists started playing them during the 1960s, and the Gibson Les Paul remains one of the most popular electric guitar designs to this day.

Complete Guitar Handbook

DJANGO REINHARDT

Gypsy jazz pioneer, born Jean Baptiste Reinhardt in Liverchies, Belgium in 1910. He showed an early interest in music and was a proficient guitar player by his mid-teens.

He settled in Paris, where he discovered American jazz, and made a living there as a street musician. However, tragedy struck at the age of 18, when he lost the use of two fingers in his left hand after a caravan fire. For most guitarists this would have meant the end of a musical career, but Reinhardt not only overcame the disability but also developed a new, unique way of playing the guitar, delivering extraordinary solos with just the first two fingers of his left hand.

In 1933, he formed the Quintette du Hot Club de France with violinist Stephane Grappelli, brother Joseph Reinhardt and Roger Chaput on guitars and Louis Vola on bass. They recorded hundreds of songs and earned international recognition. The band's sound was dominated by Reinhardt's lyrical swing and melodic interplay with Grappelli's violin, and it was a huge influence on younger jazz guitarists during the 1940s and 1950s. Reinhardt favoured French-made Maccaferri guitars, although he did try some electrics during his later years. He died after a stroke in May 1953.

Section Three: Galleries

KEITH RICHARDS

Legendary rock guitarist, born in Dartford, Kent in 1943. 'Keef' received his first guitar at the age of 13.

He went to the same school as singer Mick Jagger and they shared a passion for blues and rock 'n' roll music. They met Brian Jones, a multi-instrumentalist, at Alexis Korner's blues club in London and formed the Rolling Stones, named after a Muddy Waters song.

By 1963 they were joined by bass player Bill Wyman and drummer Charlie Watts, completing the now-famous line-up. After a string of unsuccessful covers, they decided to write some original songs, and developed a fresh and raunchy two-guitar sound. Their single 'Satisfaction' went to No. 1 on both sides of the Atlantic in 1965 and helped popularize the fuzztone guitar sound. They followed it up with a number of instantly recognizable hits, including 'Jumping Jack Flash' (1968), 'Honky Tonk Women' (1969), 'Brown Sugar' (1971), 'Angie' (1973) and 'It's Only Rock 'N' Roll' (1974), and they remain one of the world's most popular live acts.

The Stones became notorious for their drug and alcohol excesses, and earned a 'bad boys of rock' image – a tag that they have always embraced. Richards' rhythm guitar style is basic but devastatingly effective.

Complete Guitar Handbook

CARLOS SANTANA

Rock guitarist and songwriter, born in Mexico in 1947. He started playing the guitar at an early age and performed in Tijuana night clubs as a teenager.

Santana moved to San Francisco in 1962, where he developed a melodic blues-influenced lead guitar style, and formed the band Santana (originally Santana Blues Band). Their debut album *Santana* (1969), a unique blend of blues-rock, Afro-Cuban rhythms and psychedelia, made the US Top 5. *Abraxas* (1970) was even more successful and spawned hits such as 'Black Magic Woman', 'Oye Como Va' and 'Samba Pa Ti'. The next two albums, *Santana III* and *Caravanserai* (both 1972), had a more jazz-rock feel. Carlos became spiritually influenced by guru Sri Chimnoy and recorded *Love, Devotion, Surrender* (1973) with fellow guitarist and fusion pioneer John McLaughlin. *Amigos* (1976) and *Moonflower* (1977), marked a return to his trademark Latin-rock style.

His popularity waned throughout the 1980s and most of the 1990s, but the release of *Supernatural* (1999), a collaboration with contemporary musicians such as Lauryn Hill, Matchbox 20's Rob Thomas, and Eric Clapton, sold more than 20 million copies worldwide. Santana's lead guitar style is blues-rooted, sustained and sensuous.

Section Three: Galleries

JOE SATRIANI

Rock virtuoso, born in Long Island, New York in 1956. He started to play drums as a teenager but switched to guitar after being exposed to Jimi Hendrix, Wes Montgomery and John McLaughlin.

'Satch' soon developed a formidable technique and decided to pass his skills on to others; famous pupils have included Steve Vai, Kirk Hammett of Metallica, Larry LaLonde of Primus, and David Bryson of Counting Crows. Attention quickly came after Vai's success during the mid-1980s, and Satriani made a number of critically acclaimed recordings, including *Not of this Earth* (1986), *Surfing with the Alien* (1987), *Flying in a Blue Dream* (1990), *The Extremist* (1992), *Time Machine* (1993), *Joe Satriani* (1995), *Crystal Planet* (1998), *Engines of Creation* (2000), *Live in San Francisco* (2001), *Strange Beautiful Music* (2002) and *Is There Love in Space?* (2004). He also formed the G3 guitar supergroup with Steve Vai and Eric Johnson (later replaced by Yngwie Malmsteen), and created his own line of signature JS guitars for the Ibanez company.

Satriani was one of the most influential players of the 1980s and 1990s, combining formidable scalar soloing with strong use of the vibrato arm, two-handed techniques, unusual harmonics and other effects.

Complete Guitar Handbook

PETE TOWNSHEND

Rock guitarist and songwriter, born in Chiswick, London in 1945. He started playing guitar when he was 12 and met bass player John Entwistle while playing banjo in a traditional band.

They formed the Who (formerly the Detours) with singer Roger Daltrey and drummer Keith Moon. The band had numerous major hits in the 1960s, including 'My Generation' (1965) and 'Substitute' (1966), and went on to become one of the world's most original and popular rock bands, although they gained notoriety for smashing up their instruments on stage. Townshend's powerful rhythm style was an essential component of the band's sound and he is considered by many to be the inventor of the rock power chord. Highlight albums by the Who include *Tommy* (1969), *Live at Leeds* (1970), *Who's Next* (1971), *Quadrophenia* (1973), *The Who By Numbers* (1975) and *Who Are You* (1978).

Townshend has released a number of solo albums, including *Who Came First* (1972), *Empty Glass* (1980), *All the Best Cowboys Have Chinese Eyes* (1982), *White City* (1986), *Iron Man* (1989) and *Psychoderelict* (1993). His songs have also been recorded by artists as diverse as Elton John, David Bowie, Billy Fury and Tina Turner.

Section Three: Galleries

STEVE VAI

American rock virtuoso, born in Carle Place, Long Island in 1960. He picked up the guitar as a teenager, had lessons with Joe Satriani, and later studied jazz and classical music at the Berklee College of Music in Boston.

Vai transcribed a complex piece by Frank Zappa and sent it in to the rock icon, who promptly hired him as a transcriber and guitarist. Vai played on a number of Zappa albums, including *Shut Up and Play Yer Guitar* (1981), *You Are What You Is* (1981), *Ship Arriving Too Late to Save a Drowning Witch* (1982), *The Man from Utopia* (1983) and *Them or Us* (1984). His own solo projects, including *Flexable* (1984), *Passion & Warfare* (1990), *Alien Love Secrets* (1995), *The Ultra Zone* (1999) and *Alive in an Ultra World* (2001), established him as a superb player; a purveyor of exquisite harmonics, exotic scalar runs and extraordinary tremolo effects.

Vai played with Alcatrazz, David Lee Roth and Whitesnake during the 1980s and, more recently, formed G3, a guitar supergroup with Joe Satriani and Eric Johnson (later replaced by Yngwie Malmsteen). Vai is an outstanding electric guitar player, who has extended the boundaries of rock guitar technique.

Complete Guitar Handbook

STEVIE RAY VAUGHAN

Electric blues guitarist, born in Dallas, Texas in 1954. He started playing guitar aged eight, inspired by his older brother Jimmy, as well as Lonnie Mack, Albert King, Albert Collins and Django Reinhardt.

Vaughan played in a number of bands throughout the 1970s before forming Double Trouble (named after an Otis Rush song) with Tommy Shannon (bass) and Chris 'Whipper' Layton (drums) in 1981. They became a popular live act and received rave reviews after a performance at the Montreux Jazz Festival in 1982. Their debut album *Texas Flood* (1983) featured a strong mixture of originals and covers, and it became an instant blues classic. Around this time, Vaughan also played guitar on Bowie's album *Let's Dance* (1983).

The next Double Trouble album, *Couldn't Stand the Weather* (1984), was also impressive but Vaughan battled with drink and drug addictions during the mid-1980s, giving a number of sub-par performances and recordings. He cleaned up his act and returned to form with *In Step* (1989) but tragically died the following year in a helicopter crash. He had an awesome high-octane approach to lead blues guitar, and many consider him to be the finest player the genre has ever produced.

Section Three: Galleries

JOHN WILLIAMS

Classical virtuoso, born in Melbourne, Australia in 1941. He started playing guitar at the age of seven and his family moved to London in 1952.

As an 11-year-old, Williams impressed Segovia, who agreed to tutor him, and later studied at the Academia Musicale Chigiana in Siena and the Royal College of Music in London. After highly successful debuts in Europe, he toured Russia and the United States throughout 1962–63, and even made several appearances at Ronnie Scott's Jazz Club in London. He became an artistic director of the Wavendon Theatre in 1970 and premiered André Previn's Guitar Concerto in 1971. Williams also recorded a number of successful and critically acclaimed classical albums including *Concerto de Aranjuez* (1976), *Cavatina* (1979), *Paul Hart's Concerto for Guitar and Jazz Orchestra* (1987), *Takemitsu: To the Edge of Dream* (1991), *Vivaldi Concertos* (1991), *The Seville Concert* (1993) and *Schubert and Giuliani* (1999).

He formed the well-known classical-rock fusion group Sky in the late 1970s with other notable UK musicians to record *Sky* (1979), *Sky 2* (1980) and *Sky 3* (1981), and made a number of award-winning collaborations with the respected British classical guitar virtuoso, Julian Bream.

Complete Guitar Handbook

FRANK ZAPPA

Composer-guitarist and rock icon, born Frank Vincent Zappa, Jr. in Baltimore, Maryland in 1940. He started playing drums when he was 12 and switched to guitar at 18.

Early influences included blues guitarists and twentieth-century composers. He formed the Mothers of Invention in the mid 1960s and the group made a number of original and groundbreaking recordings, including *Freak Out* (1966), *We're Only In It For The Money* (1967) and *Uncle Meat* (1968). From the outset, Zappa's material boasted a previously unheard of blend of musical intelligence, adventure and humour. By 1970 the Mothers had split and Zappa assembled more virtuosic line-ups for jazz-rock recordings such as *Hot Rats* (1970), *Overnite Sensation* (1973) and *Roxy & Elsewhere* (1973).

By the early 1980s his music was stretching over from rock through to complex orchestral pieces. He was also a notable guitarist, and *Shut Up and Play Yer Guitar* (1981), a multi-album box set of end-to-end solos, demonstrated this in abundance. Zappa continued recording and archiving his material right up until his death, of prostate cancer, in 1993. He is widely considered to be the most accomplished, original and versatile composer of the rock era.

Section Three: Galleries

FENDER STRATOCASTER

While Fender's Telecaster was an extremely popular model, some players criticized the instrument for its 'Plain Jane' appearance and for its sharp edges, which could be uncomfortable to hold. Heeding these complaints, Leo Fender (1909–91) and colleague Freddie Tavares (1913–90) went back to the drawing board, introducing the Stratocaster in 1954.

Now universally renowned as a classic of twentieth-century design, the Stratocaster is one of the best selling guitars ever made. While it has spawned many imitations, the guitar remains in production some 51 years after its debut; Fender currently offers a full Stratocaster line, from its inexpensive, though high-quality, import versions (under the Squier brand) to the costly, exacting reissues made at the Custom Shop in California.

THE CONSTRUCTION

The Stratocaster was designed with a sleek, sports-car inspired body, smoothly contoured for the player's comfort. Its double-cutaway style afforded players access to high notes and made the guitar more balanced, at the same time as adding visual appeal. The Stratocaster had advanced electronics; it was the first solidbody to incorporate three pickups, enabling an unprecedented variety of sonic options. The pickups possessed staggered polepieces, providing for even volume levels across all six strings. Furthermore, players discovered that the instrument's three-way switch could be set in between

◀ *Jeff Beck plays a signature Strat built according to his specifications with a particularly thick neck. He uses minimal effects and plucks the strings with his fingers.*

Complete Guitar Handbook

positions, activating in tandem either the front and middle or back and middle pickups; this created a unique 'out-of-phase' sound, exploited to excellent effect by Jeff Beck and Jimi Hendrix, among others. Five-way switches were later introduced to make this sound easily accessible.

Another Fender first was represented by the Stratocaster's built-in vibrato device (also called a tremolo bar or whammy bar), which was an all-in-one bridge, tailpiece and tremolo bar. With its six individual saddles – one for each string – moveable in both height and length directions, the new bridge portion was fully adjustable. By releasing tension on the strings, the tremolo bar allowed a player to bend notes with the pick hand, resulting in a shimmering sound effect. This unit worked like a fulcrum, its pivot being six screws that attached it to the guitar's body. Inside the body, the strings were counterbalanced by a series of springs – up to five could be easily removed or installed – accessible via a plastic cavity cover at the back of the guitar.

CARS AND GUITARS

Stratocasters are among the most in-demand guitars on the vintage market. Most desirable are the late-1950s Custom Color models. Inspired by the paint jobs on automobiles, these finishes – including Fiesta Red, Lake Placid Blue (pictured left), Foam Green and Shoreline Gold – are rare; a Custom Color Stratocaster can now command over 20 per cent more than its sunburst- or blonde-coloured counterpoint in identical condition.

GUITAR SPEC

Model Pictured: Daphne Blue Stratocaster

Pickups: Three

Controls: Three-way (later five-way) switch, volume, two tone

Characteristics: wide tonal range, versatile, vibrato arm

Played by: Jeff Beck, Buddy Guy, Jimi Hendrix, Mark Knopfler, Stevie Ray Vaughan

Section Three: Galleries

FENDER TELECASTER

In the late 1940s, inventor Leo Fender set about making an electric guitar that would be resistant to the feedback associated with amplified hollowbodies. His concept was commercially introduced in 1950 with the Fender Esquire, a single-pickup solidbody guitar, followed shortly after by the Broadcaster, a twin-pickup version.

In 1951, the name of the latter guitar was changed to Telecaster, in order to avoid infringing on the Gretsch Company's drum line, as well as to suggest state-of-the-art technology, similar to the name television. The world's first mass-manufactured solidbody, the Telecaster has remained in continuous production for more than five decades.

THE CONSTRUCTION

The Telecaster has a rather plain appearance; its design is a classic example of form following function. In making the Telecaster, Fender set out to create a dependable, minimalist guitar – one that would sound excellent while being cheaply and efficiently manufactured. Accordingly, the Telecaster was devoid of the hand-carved select tone-woods characteristic of acoustic guitars, stripped of superfluous ornamentation, and constructed from easy-to-assemble parts.

Basic as it was, the Telecaster featured a number of innovations in addition to its solid ash body. Attached with four screws, its bolt-on, one-piece maple neck could easily be replaced and the neck's moveable truss rod allowed for precision adjustment. The guitar's 21 frets were set directly into

Complete Guitar Handbook

the neck, precluding the need for a separate fretboard and, to some ears, enhancing the sound. The Telecaster's fully adjustable metal bridge, the first of its kind, could be tweaked lengthwise with three screws, as well as raised or lowered with six screws. Furthermore, the bridge allowed the strings to pass through the body, arguably enhancing the tone.

THE LEGACY

At the time of the Telecaster's introduction, the western lap-steel guitar was extremely popular, and Fender had wanted to create a standard guitar that sounded like a steel version. With its bright, clear tone, the Telecaster ended up producing a sound somewhere between an acoustic guitar and a lap steel. Initially, western swing players were drawn to the instrument's cutting, twangy tone. Guitarist Jimmy Bryant (1929–80), best known for his impossibly swift duets with pedal-steel monster Speedy West (1924–2003), was among the first well-known Telecaster players, and his television appearances helped popularize the new instrument.

As the Telecaster's reputation spread, it became the country and western guitarist's instrument of choice. But due to its straightforward design and durability, the instrument came to be associated with a variety of genres. Bluesman Muddy Waters used a Telecaster to create his signature electric sound, as did a diverse set of other legends including, among others, modern jazzman Mike Stern (b. 1953) and punk rocker Joe Strummer (1952–2002), frontman for the Clash.

◀ *After tuning his Telecaster to open G, Keith Richards explored this alternate tuning and created a whole new style of guitar playing.*

GUITAR SPEC

Model Pictured: 1950s Telecaster
Pickups: Two
Controls: Three-way switch, tone, volume
Characteristics: Versatile; bright, twangy sound
Played by: Jimmy Bryant, Roy Buchanan, James Burton, Danny Gatton, Albert Lee, Keith Richards, Muddy Waters

Section Three: Galleries

GIBSON LES PAUL

Before the Gibson Les Paul was introduced, Les Paul had established himself as one of America's top guitarists. He was also an innovative engineer, having pioneered multi-track recording with his 1948 Capitol release, 'Lover'.

In addition to this, Les Paul had been experimenting with solidbody guitars since the 1930s. Two of his handmade, experimental solidbodies – the 'Log' and the 'Clunker' – led to the 1952 release of the Les Paul model, Gibson's first solidbody, which was to become one of the world's most influential guitar designs.

THE CONSTRUCTION

Relative to the Fender Telecaster (introduced in 1951), the Les Paul's construction was complex. A two-pickup guitar, it was built from a mahogany neck with a rosewood fingerboard, set into a mahogany body with an arched, carved maple top, distinguishing it from a Fender, which had a plain flat top. In addition, the Les Paul's controls – two tone, two volume and selector switch – were mounted on to the top and accessed by two separate plastic covers in the back, necessitating a complex routing system. In any case, the set-neck construction and choice tonewoods, in conjunction with hardware that was screwed directly into the top, made for a warm, creamy tone with considerable sustain. The original Les Paul was completed with a lavish gold-coloured metallic finish, earning it the nickname 'Gold Top', although some models had gold-coloured sides and backs as well.

Complete Guitar Handbook

In response to the popularity of the Gold Top, Gibson created several Les Paul variations. Introduced in 1954, the Custom was an extra-fancy version, with a black-finished all-mahogany body, gold-plated hardware, ebony fretboard, separate tailpiece and ('Tune-o-matic') bridge, and fancier binding. At the other end of the spectrum was the no-frills Les Paul Junior, with a one-piece mahogany body, single pickup, and lack of binding.

▲ *Al Di Meola uses his Les Paul to great effect.*

The most coveted Les Paul is the Standard, introduced in 1958. On that model, the original gold finish was replaced with a transparent cherry sunburst finish – which graduated from red to orange – revealing the instrument's maple top; this was sometimes covered with spectacular 'flames' or figuring in the grain. The Standard featured two powerful humbucking pickups, introduced by Gibson's Seth Lover (1910–97) in 1957. A humbucker had two separate coils, one of which, as the name suggests, was used to cancel out hum. These pickups were louder than their single coil counterparts, and they further enhanced the thick, sustaining tone facilitated by the Les Paul's construction.

Dwindling sales caused the Standard to be discontinued in 1960, but as players like Eric Clapton and Jimmy Page picked up the instrument later that decade, it essentially became the first collectible electric guitar. Owing to its quality and rarity – only 643 models were produced in 1959 – the original Standard is now considered the Holy Grail of electric guitars, with clean examples currently fetching more than $200,000.

GUITAR SPEC

Model Pictured: 1959 Standard

Pickups: Two

Controls: Three-way switch, two volume, two tone

Characteristics: Versatile, rich, powerful tone, excellent sustain

Played by: Duane Allman, Jeff Beck, Mike Bloomfield, Eric Clapton, Al Di Meola, Billy Gibbons, Jimmy Page, Slash

Section Three: Galleries

MARTIN D-45

The Martin guitar company was founded in 1833, when German immigrant Christian Frederick Martin set up shop in the United States. Martin's first instruments were modelled after those made by Johann Stauffer, an Austrian builder under whom he had apprenticed in the 1820s.

Soon, however, Martin began to experiment with his own construction ideas, and created the design principles that would result in the modern flat-top acoustic guitar, ultimately earning the six-string status as a respectable instrument.

THE DREADNOUGHT LINE

Launched in 1931, Martin's dreadnought line of guitars was named after the hulking British battleship of the First World War. With its 15$\frac{5}{8}$-in (40-cm) wide, 4$\frac{5}{8}$-in (11.6-cm) deep body, the dreadnought (first made by Martin for the Ditson company in 1916) was designed with increased volume, tone and projection in mind. The first Martin dreadnoughts were called D-1 and D-2, changed to D-18 and D-28 respectively in 1932. While the plainer D-18 had a mahogany body and the fancier D-28 had a rosewood body, both had a neck that joined the body at the 12th fret; beginning in 1934, the neck joined the body at the 14th fret, effectively extending the guitar's range by a whole step.

▶ *Neil Young playing a Martin Dreadnought, a guitar favoured by folk musicians for the full, expressive sound it produces.*

Complete Guitar Handbook

GUITAR SPEC

Model Pictured: 1988 D-45
Construction: Rosewood body, spruce top, mahogany neck with ebony fretboard
Characteristics: Excellent bass response, full tone, loud, well-balanced, magical sound
Played by: Gene Autry, Stephen Stills, Neil Young

Curiously, the earliest dreadnoughts were marketed as 'bass guitars'. However, these instruments, did not occupy the low range of the bass guitar as known today in its electric incarnation; rather, the designation 'bass guitar' referred to the enhanced low-end response provided by the dreadnought's larger body. Accordingly, the D-28 first gained acceptance amongst country and bluegrass guitars, who needed a massive sound to compete with fiddlers and banjoists. The D-28 eventually became the benchmark for flat-top guitar design; virtually all guitar manufacturers now have a dreadnought line. And having been made continuously since 1932, the D-28 has proven Martin's top-selling model, currently accounting for 80 per cent of its total yearly production.

THE SINGING COWBOY

In 1933, the singing cowboy star and country singer Gene Autry approached Martin with a special request – he wanted a guitar like his hero Jimmie Rodgers' small-bodied 000-45, but with the larger, dreadnought body style. This resulted in the first D-45, an ultra-swanky guitar with fabulously intricate abalone trim, complemented by Autry's name inlaid in pearl script on the fretboard. Five additional D-45s were built before the instrument's formal introduction in 1938. But costing a staggering $200 in the Depression era, the D-45 proved too expensive to manufacture, and it was temporarily discontinued in 1942; at that point only 91 had been made. While the D-45 has been back in production since 1968, the pre-war versions are the most desirable of all flat tops, currently fetching upwards of $100,000.

Section Three: Galleries

BENEDETTO LA CREMONA AZZURRA

Robert Benedetto (b. 1946) is a premier luthier of modern archtops who has been building instruments for over four decades.

His exquisite instruments have been played by such jazz-guitar heavyweights as Johnny Smith, Kenny Burrell and Howard Alden. Among Benedetto's most striking guitars is his Cremona Azzurra (Blue Cremona), commissioned in 1995 for the Blue Guitar project of the late instrument collector Scott Chinery.

FINE CRAFTSMANSHIP

The Blue Cremona was built from the finest of traditional materials, selected for both their sound and beauty. Its 18-in (46-cm) wide top and back were made from very fine old European cello wood, similar to that from which Stradivari were crafted; the two-piece neck from well-seasoned American maple; and the fingerboard, bridge, truss-rod cover and finger rest were all hand-sculpted from select solid ebony.

While crafted in an old-world fashion, the Blue Cremona departs boldly from tradition. As per the commission, the instrument was finished in a striking blue stain. Devoid of superfluous inlays and bindings, the Cremona has a minimalist modern appearance. But more notably, it sports unconventional floral-shaped sound openings – as opposed to conservative f-holes – resulting in both a graceful design and a loud, well-balanced instrument.

GUITAR SPEC

Model Pictured: La Cremona Azzurra
Construction: Fine spruce, maple and ebony
Characteristics: Elegant modernist design, outstanding tone and projection

Complete Guitar Handbook

DANELECTRO CONVERTIBLE

As rock 'n' roll became increasingly popular in the 1950s, more and more teenagers set about mimicking their heroes.

Many of these wannabes picked up Silvertone guitars, manufactured for Sears, Roebuck and Company by Nathan Daniel (1912–94), an electronics buff whose instruments were distributed under the name Danelectro beginning in 1956. 'Danos' were made from inexpensive materials – often Masonite tops affixed to pine frames – but they were undeniably cool, and were occasionally even used by top pros, like Led Zeppelin's Jimmy Page.

GOOD LOOKS

Named for its purported adaptability as an acoustic or electric guitar, Danelectro's Convertible had a hollow, double-horned Masonite body with a bolt-on maple neck. Glued to the instrument's sides, a strip of textured vinyl added a somewhat kitschy appearance. The Convertible could be ordered sans pickup, including pre-drilled notches so that electronics could later be installed, or with a single-coil 'lipstick-tube' pickup, the cover of which was made from an actual cosmetics casing.

GUITAR SPEC

Model Pictured: 1960s Convertible
Pickups: One
Controls: Volume, tone
Characteristics: Retro vibe, quirky tone

In truth, the Convertible – its small, thin body producing a constricted sound – does not quite cut it as an acoustic guitar. When plugged in, though, its single pickup helps produce a wonderfully distinctive tone – halfway between a resonator guitar and a Stratocaster, with all kinds of vintage mojo.

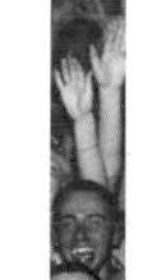

Section Three: Galleries

D'ANGELICO NEW YORKER

In 1932, John D'Angelico (1905–64) set up shop in New York City, repairing stringed instruments.

He also began building 16½-in (42-cm) archtops that were patterned after Gibson's L-5 before branching out with his own style. D'Angelico became a pre-eminent jazz-guitar luthier, known for his unparalleled craftsmanship; he hand-built more than 1,100 guitars – many of which were custom orders. D'Angelico's most identifiable design, the ultra-fancy New Yorker, was introduced in the late 1930s.

GUITAR SPEC

Model Pictured: New Yorker

Construction: 18-in (45.7-cm) wide maple/spruce body, maple neck with ebony fretboard

Characteristics: Ornate, breathtaking design, big, refined sound

Played by: Freddie Green, Bucky Pizzarelli, Russell Malone

SUPERIOR CRAFTSMANSHIP

When Gibson unveiled its top-of-the-line 18-in (45.7-cm) Super 400 in 1934, D'Angelico followed suit with his New Yorker, an archtop with a body of the same spec, X-pattern bracing, and split-block fretboard inlays. While the Super 400 was a very fine guitar in its own right, D'Angelico's handcrafted New Yorker was generally regarded as a superior instrument because it received the sort of attention to detail unobtainable by a large manufacturer such as Gibson.

D'Angelico had a keen aesthetic sense, and his guitars were breathtaking, both as works of art and as musical instruments. With its ornate, gold stair-step tailpiece, art-deco style 'New Yorker' inlay, truss-rod cover, machine heads and fancy binding, the awe-inspiring New Yorker ranks among the most beautiful guitars ever created.

Complete Guitar Handbook

EPIPHONE SHERATON

While known today for sensibly priced imports, in the 1930s the Epiphone Company was the leading manufacturer of archtops. But by the mid-1950s, it was in dire straits and, in 1957, Gibson bought the company and moved it to Kalamazoo, Michigan, when it introduced a new line of 'Epis'.

MORE THAN THEY BARGAINED FOR

Gibson initially thought that Epiphone's $20,000 asking price only included their bass line, but the deal included some Epiphone guitar parts as well. Gibson president Ted McCarty decided to create a new line of Epiphone guitars that could be built with Gibson's existing tooling and production lines, thus relieving the overwhelming dealer demand for Gibson instruments.

Introduced in 1958, a stellar example of a Kalamazoo Epiphone was the Sheraton, essentially a dressed-up version of Gibson's dot-neck ES-335. The early Sheraton had the then-new Gibson semi-hollowbody construction, combined with distinctive Epiphone touches: multi-ply binding, pearl/abalone block-and-triangle fingerboard markers, gold hardware, a split-level 'Frequensator' tailpiece and a floral headstock inlay. Despite it being made alongside Gibsons, the Sheraton never enjoyed the ES-335's elevated status. A fine vintage Epiphone semi-hollow can now be had for a fraction of the price of its Gibson counterpart.

GUITAR SPEC

Model Pictured: Sheraton
Pickups: Two
Controls: Three-way selector, two volume, two tone
Characteristics: Versatile, combintaion of hollowbody warmth with solidbody sustain
Played by: John Lee Hooker

Section Three: Galleries

FENDER PRECISION

In the early 1950s, having created and mass-produced a solidbody electric guitar – the Telecaster – Leo Fender realized that a bass version was in order.

Commercially introduced in 1952, Fender's Precision bass marked the birth of the electric bass guitar, and forever altered the landscape of popular music. The instrument became so commonplace that for many years all electric basses – regardless of make – became known as 'Fender Basses'.

FRETTED WONDER

Prior to the Precision bass, bulky upright contrabasses were used, which were difficult to transport, and hard to make heard amidst other instruments. Lacking frets, these instruments required masterful technique to be played in tune. With its small double-cutaway body, manageable 34-in (83-cm) scale fretted neck and powerful pickup, the radical Precision bass – named for its ease of intonation and clear tone – freed bassists from the problems associated with upright instruments.

The P Bass, as it is known, has a round, crisp sound in all its registers, perfectly complementing the standard rock 'n' roll set-up of electric guitar and drums. It blends well in a variety of genres, including blues, country, and jazz. Much popular music in second half of the twentieth century was indebted to the P Bass's colourful bottom end.

GUITAR SPEC

Model Pictured: Precision Bass
Pickups: One
Controls: Volume, tone
Characteristics: Versatile, crisp, clear tone in all registers
Played by: James Jamerson, Monk Montgomery, Jaco Pastorius, Sting

Complete Guitar Handbook

GIBSON L-5

In 1922, Gibson introduced a masterpiece – the 'Master Line Guitar L-5 Professional Grand Concert Model'.

Priced at $275, this elegant, top-of-the-line model was by far Gibson's most expensive guitar, and its revolutionary, modernistic design represented the birth of the f-hole archtop jazz box.

A JAZZ ADVANCE

Finished in a luxurious Cremona brown sunburst, the debut L-5 had a 16¼-in (41-cm) wide, 3½-in (9-cm) deep body with an arched spruce top and birch back (replaced by maple in 1924); a maple neck with an ebony fingerboard; and a metal tailpiece, which added sustain. The L-5 was the first guitar to feature violin-style f-holes – as opposed to an oval soundhole – which provided a unique tonal response. To further enhance its sonic capabilities, an occasional example was also fitted with a Virzi Tone Producer – a wooden disc suspended inside the guitar's body. But even without this device, the L-5 was essentially America's first orchestra guitar; it possessed a huge, well-balanced sound that effectively cut through the din of horns in a jazz ensemble.

The L-5 has gone through numerous alterations – both cosmetic and structural – throughout the years, and remains one of the most revered jazz guitars. Several versions are currently manufactured in small quantities at Gibson's Nashville, Tennessee Custom Shop.

GUITAR SPEC

Model Pictured: 1924 L-5
Construction: Arched spruce top, maple back and neck, ebony fingerboard
Characteristics: Classic jazz sound, pristine tone and excellent projection
Played by: Eddie Lang, Russell Malone, Wes Montgomery

Section Three: Galleries

GIBSON ES-150

The ES-150 (ES for 'Electric Spanish', 150 for the model's list price – $150 with amplifier, case and cord) was effectively the first mass-produced electric guitar, and was made famous by Charlie Christian, in his work with clarinettist Benny Goodman.

HIGH FIDELITY

With its 16-in (40-cm) carved spruce top, maple back and sides, mahogany neck, and rosewood fretboard, the ES-150 was ultimately an amped-up version of Gibson's mid-level L-50 archtop. The 150's earliest pickup, later called the Charlie Christian model, had one solid, straight pole piece and two magnets. A matching amplifier, the EH-150, was a six-tube, 15-W unit wired to a 10-in (25-cm) High Fidelity Ultrasonic Reproducer (i.e. speaker). This package is primitive by today's standards, but in the late 1930s it was a bold, state-of-the-art rig.

Charlie Christian was quick to exploit the ES-150's voluminous capabilities. 'Amplifying my instrument has made it possible for me to get a wonderful break,' he told *Down Beat* magazine in a feature proclaiming 'Guitarmen, Wake Up and Pluck!' Whereas previous ensemble guitarists had been largely relegated to accompaniment chores, Christian was able to pioneer the horn-like, single-note soloing style to which all modern jazz guitarists are indebted.

GUITAR SPEC

Model Pictured: 1930s ES-150
Pickups: One
Controls: Volume, tone
Characteristics: Historically significant, warm rich tone
Played by: Charlie Christian

Complete Guitar Handbook

GIBSON SJ-200

In the 1930s, as the flat-top acoustic guitar gained increasing popularity, players demanded improved features.

The Martin company responded by introducing big, loud dreadnought models, and in 1934, Gibson followed suit with its first line of jumbo flat-tops, the most fancy of which – the SJ-200 – was introduced in 1938.

THE COWBOY WAY

Hollywood movies of the 1930s were rife with singing cowboys. One of the earliest stars, Ray Whitley, provided Gibson with the ideas – a deeper body, relocated bridge and increased scale length – that resulted in the Super Jumbo model. This advanced flat-top had a 17-in (43-cm) wide spruce top with a new narrow-waist shape. Its 4½-in (11-cm) deep body, combined with a 26-in (66-cm) scale-length fretboard, provided a deep booming sound perfectly suited to cowboy strumming, blues riffing, and a variety of other applications.

The Super Jumbo was available in two versions: a fairly simple, mahogany-bodied SJ-100 and the fancier, rosewood-bodied SJ-200 (later replaced with maple), which has remained in continuous production. With its pearl fingerboard inlays, nine-ply binding, elaborate bridge and decorated pickguard, the opulent SJ-200 was, according to Gibson literature, 'The King of the Flat-Top Guitars'.

GUITAR SPEC

Model Pictured: 1952 SJ-200
Construction: Rosewood body, spruce top, maple neck with ebony fretboard
Characteristics: Versatile, excellent bass response, loud, well-balanced sound
Played by: Reverend Gary Davis, Emmylou Harris, Ray Whitley

Section Three: Galleries

GIBSON ES-335

In 1958, Gibson unveiled yet another brilliant innovation – the ES-335 TD ('ES' stood for 'Electric Spanish'; 'T' for thinline; and 'D' for double-cutaway).

In continuous production since its introduction, the ES-335 has proven one of Gibson's most enduring designs, and vintage ES-335s are highly collectible – only 209 TDNs (the model in natural finish) were made between 1958 and 1960, and a clean example can now fetch upwards of $40,000.

NOVEL CONSTRUCTION

In the late 1950s, solidbody electrics were becoming increasingly popular as they offered sustaining tone and resistance to feedback. Hollowbody electrics, on the other hand, possessed a certain tonal warmth. So Gibson created a neat hybrid – the ES-335 was built from a laminated, 16-in (40-cm) wide, 1¾-in (4-cm) thick hollow maple body with a solid maple block in its centre. The guitar's semi-solid, double-cutaway construction allowed its mahogany neck (with rosewood fingerboard) to be joined to the body at the 19th fret, which permitted access to the uppermost registers. Two humbuckers, controlled by a three-way switch, afforded a number of timbral possibilities. In short, the ES-335 had the best of both worlds – the warmth of a hollowbody with the sustain and feedback resistance of a solidbody.

GUITAR SPEC

Model Pictured: ES-335 TDN
Pickups: Two
Controls: Three-way selector, two volume, two tone
Characteristics: Versatile, hollowbody warmth with solidbody sustain
Played by: B. B. King, Eric Clapton, Larry Carlton

Complete Guitar Handbook

GIBSON FLYING V AND EXPLORER

With the rise of rock 'n' roll the late 1950s, Gibson began to lag behind as players gravitated towards Fender's more radical designs, like the Stratocaster and the Jazzmaster.

Gibson responded in 1958 by supplementing its line with audacious 'modernistic' models, breaking away from conventional curves with oddly shaped guitars, including the Flying V and the Explorer.

ART GUITAR

A solidbody guitar produces sound primarily through the interaction of its strings and pickups, so it needn't be crafted in a traditional shape to produce a decent tone. Capitalizing on this principle, Gibson's Ted McCarty, in conjunction with a local Michigan artist, designed several unconventional guitars; one was fashioned after an arrow, but a staff member at Gibson thought it looked more like a 'flying v', hence the name.

Initially, the guitars were commercial disasters; players found the instruments too radical. Only 98 Flying Vs were shipped in 1958–59, and fewer than 25 Explorers were made during the same period. Nonetheless, these guitars, which have been continuously reissued, inspired the radical shapes of experiments by later manufacturers. And today, due to their scarcity, they are among the most collectible of electric guitars.

GUITAR SPEC

Model Pictured: 1950s Flying V
Pickups: Two
Controls: Two volume, one tone
Characteristics: Bold design, classic humbucker tone
Played by: Dave Davies, Rick Derringer, Lonnie Mack

Section Three: Galleries

GIBSON SG

By 1960, sales of the now iconic Les Paul Standard had become sluggish. So in 1961, Gibson gave the instrument a thorough redesign.

With its double-cutaway, light, thin mahogany body, long-looking mahogany neck, twin humbuckers, vibrato unit and deep cherry finish, the new Les Paul was at first known as the new Standard. It was renamed the SG (solid guitar) in 1963, when Paul's contract with Gibson expired.

GUITAR SPEC

Model Pictured: SG

Pickups: Two

Controls: Three-way switch, two volume, two tone

Characteristics: Lightweight and versatile, powerful, honking sound

Played by: Duane Allman, George Harrison, Tony Iommi, Derek Trucks, Angus Young

LES NO MORE

Paul was not impressed with his new namesake guitar. As he related to guitar historian Tom Wheeler: 'I didn't like the shape – a guy could kill himself on those sharp horns. ... The neck was too skinny and I didn't like the way it joined the body; there wasn't enough wood.' So Paul called Gibson and had his name removed from the instrument.

Despite Paul's disapproval, the SG has remained in continuous production since 1961. The guitar is now a rock 'n' roll icon. Its pointy, devil-horned silhouette and raw sound have proved indispensable for heavy acts such AC/DC and Black Sabbath. A comfortable, versatile instrument, the SG has also been employed to excellent effect by slide guitarists such as Duane Allman and Derek Trucks.

Complete Guitar Handbook

GRETSCH WHITE FALCON

Founded by German immigrant Friedrich Gretsch in New York in 1883, Gretsch Guitars is best known for its instruments of the 1950s and 1960s. By far the flashiest Gretsch was the White Falcon.

NOT-SO-FREE BIRD

Intended as a promotional item, the White Falcon was designed to impress visitors at a trade show in Chicago in the mid-1950s. It was so spectacular, though, that it was demanded as a production model. In 1955, the ultra-expensive ($600) White Falcon was commercially introduced; this mono guitar featured a hollow, single-cutaway 17-in (43-cm) wide body, twin DeArmond pickups, Cadillac-inspired tailpiece and a nifty, falcon-emblazoned pickguard. Lacquered in white and trimmed in sparkling gold, complemented by 24-K hardware, this was exactly the showpiece for which guitarists had hoped.

While maintaining its overall opulent appearance, the White Falcon saw a number of variations: in 1959, a stereo version was issued; the 1963 model was a double-cutaway; and in 1965, a number of knobs and switches were added, affording access to new tonal variations. The rarest of these birds, however, was the semi-solid White Penguin, made in extremely small quantities between 1955 and 1961.

GUITAR SPEC

Model Pictured: 1950s White Falcon

Pickups: Two

Controls: Three-way selector, volume for each pickup, master volume, master tone

Characteristics: Flashiness, classic Gretsch twang

Played by: Stephen Stills, John Frusciante, Neil Young

Section Three: Galleries

HOFNER 500/1

In their eight years together, the Beatles amassed many fabulous instruments, the most famous of which was Paul McCartney's violin-shaped electric bass guitar.

McCartney played a 500/1 throughout the Beatles' career; so synonymous was the instrument that it became known as the 'Beatle' or 'Cavern' bass, after the Liverpool club where the Beatles got their start.

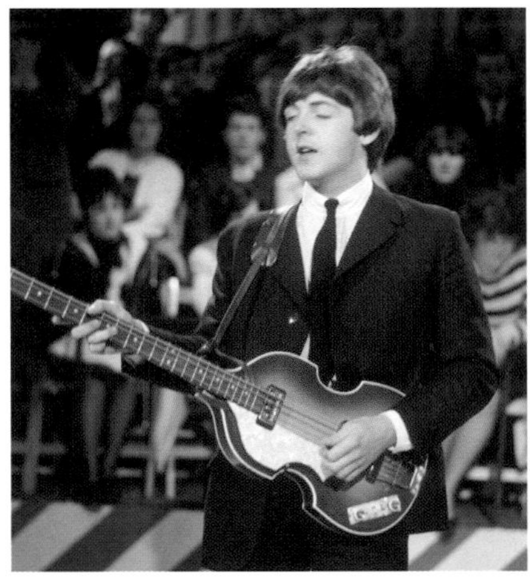

BASIC NECESSITY

In the early 1960s, Paul McCartney apparently couldn't afford a Fender bass, so he opted for the less expensive, more distinctive Hofner 500/1, which he first encountered in Hamburg's Steinway shop in 1961. As an added bonus, with its symmetrically shaped body, the 500/1 looked normal when played left-handed, as required by McCartney.

Made from a small, hollow spruce/maple body and a thin maple neck with a short-scale (30-in/76-cm) rosewood fretboard, the 500/1 is extremely comfortable to play. Its two pickups are controlled by individual on/off switches and volume knobs, plus a master boost knob, allowing for subtle tonal variation. The 500/1's basic tone is rich and round, with a pronounced mid-range; in its upper register, the instrument sounds especially heavy – as heard on the bass line from the Beatles' 'Come Together' (1969).

GUITAR SPEC

Model Pictured: 1960s 500/1

Pickups: Two

Controls: Two on-off switches, two volume, master boost

Characteristics: Excellent playability, warm, round tone

Complete Guitar Handbook

IBANEZ JEM

In the 1980s there emerged an extreme type of guitar playing, often referred to as 'shred'.

This over-the-top style was characterized by impossibly swift picking, two-handed tapping and crazed whammy-bar manipulation. Such pyrotechnics necessitated specialized instruments. In the late 1980s, guitar hero Steve Vai collaborated with the Ibanez company to produce the JEM – a 'Superstrat' based upon traditional Fender principles, coupled with modern advances.

A GEM OF A GUITAR

First available in 1987, the JEM was built to Vai's exacting specifications – a contoured, lightweight basswood body with a 'monkey grip' (i.e. a built-in handle for doing 'stupid stuff', as Vai once put it); high-output DiMarzio pickups and a 24-fret rosewood fingerboard. The guitar also featured a recessed Ibanez 'Edge' whammy bar with locking nut, so that pitch could be radically lowered and raised without creating any tuning problems.

GUITAR SPEC

Model Pictured: 1980s JEM
Pickups: Two
Controls: Five-way selector, volume, tone
Characteristics: Versatile, crisp, clear tone in all registers, advanced tremolo bar
Played by: Steve Vai

An early, limited edition of the JEM – painted green and known as 'Loch Ness' models – were signed, numbered, and decorated with tiny drawings by Vai, making them instant collector's items. Regular production versions included a yellow model with pink pickups, a shocking-pink one with disappearing pyramid inlays and a floral-patterned one with vine inlays, fashioned after the curtains in Vai's home. JEMs have proved to be wildly successful over the years, and they're still in production, albeit with toned-down finishes.

Section Three: Galleries

KAY BARNEY KESSEL ARTIST

Based in Chicago, the Kay company manufactured affordable guitars in all styles – including a number of archtop variations – from the 1930s through to the 1960s.

In the late 1950s, in an attempt to bolster its chintzy image, Kay teamed up with leading jazz guitarist Barney Kessel to create several artist models.

WE THREE KINGS

Made from 1957–60, Kay's three Kessels included the 13-in (33-cm), semi-solid Pro ($200), the 15½-in (39-cm), single-cutaway Artist ($300) and the 17-in (43-cm) single-cutaway Jazz Special ($400). Each version had a number of fun touches, including Kessel's gold signature on the pickguard, and an art-deco style 'Kelvinator' headstock overlay, named after a similar-looking refrigerator. This piece of ornamentation was injection-moulded from clear plastic and studded with gold dots.

While outfitted with good hardware, the Kessels were all made from inexpensive veneered bodies and therefore lacked the full tone of a traditional archtop; tellingly, Kessel was never known to perform or record with one of his models. Yet these striking instruments tend to have an attractive punch and an indisputably cool vintage vibe, and in recent years they have become quite collectible.

GUITAR SPEC

Model Pictured: Kay Barney Kessel Artist
Pickups: Two
Controls: Three-way switch, two volume, two tone
Characteristics: Vintage vibe, punchy tone
Played by: Sarah McLachlan

Complete Guitar Handbook

NATIONAL STYLE O

Before the advent of amplification, guitarists struggled to be heard above woodwinds and brass in popular ensembles.

Consequently, in the mid-1920s, the Los Angeles guitarist George Beauchamp had an idea for a built-in 'ampliphonic system', which he took to John Dopyera and his brother Rudy – Czechoslovakian immigrants known for their sonic improvement of banjos. From this meeting came the National Triple Resonator – a guitar amplified by three metal cones, enhanced by a metal body – which debuted in 1927, followed several years later by a single-cone version, the Style O.

HOW DO THEY WORK?

On a tri-cone guitar, three thin, 6-in (15-cm) aluminium speaker cones – two on the bass side and one on the treble side – are arranged in a triangle. An aluminium, T-shaped bridge with a wooden saddle connects the centre of each cone. When the strings' vibrations excite the saddle, the bridge and the cones are in turn vibrated, creating a sweet, sustaining tone with complex harmonics, perfectly suited to Hawaiian-style slide guitar.

Single-resonator models feature a 9½-in (24-cm) cone topped with a maple 'biscuit'; the strings pass over a wooden saddle attached to the biscuit. As there is a more direct course from the strings to the cone on a single-resonator guitar, it is a louder instrument than the tri-cone version. Preferred by blues players, the single-resonator guitar produces a harsher, more staccato sound, rather like a banjo.

GUITAR SPEC

Model Pictured: Style O
Construction: Brass alloy body, mahogany neck, cone resonator
Characteristics: Loud, aggressive tone
Played by: Son House, Tampa Red, Bukka White

Section Three: Galleries

OVATION ADAMAS

In the twentieth century the guitar was subject to many innovations; one of the most visible was the rounded back of the Ovation guitar, developed by Charles H. Kaman (b. 1919).

An engineer who had founded an aircraft company, Kaman introduced his first round-back guitar in 1966. At first slow to catch on, Ovation guitars began to gain acceptance when singer/songwriter Glen Campbell was seen playing one on his TV show in 1969.

THE SYNTHETIC CONSTRUCTION

Before he designed the first Ovation, Kaman had been advised that a guitar made of synthetics would be unmarketable but he designed a prototype anyway. After many experiments with high-tech sonic equipment, Kaman devised a one-piece body shell, or Lyrachord bowl, made from fibres that were also used to cover helicopter blades. Coupled with a solid spruce top, one of Ovation's first models, the Balladeer, was an effective marriage of radical and traditional design.

GUITAR SPEC

Model Pictured: Adamas
Construction: Lyrachord bowl body, birch/carbon top
Characteristics: Bright tone, exceptional projection
Played by: Glen Campbell, Al Di Meola, Rick Nielsen

Introduced in 1976, the Adamas was Ovation's top-of-the-line guitar. Its synthetic top was made of a thin 1/32-in (0.8-mm) birch core, with thinner layers of carbon graphite fibres. A series of small soundholes at the body's top end facilitated greater projection than a traditional, centred round hole. Surrounding the soundholes, a wooden epaulette in the shape of leaves, added a rustic touch to this space-age instrument.

Complete Guitar Handbook

PARKER FLY

Introduced in 1992, the Parker Fly embodied a complete rethinking of the electric guitar.

Developed over a decade of experiments by luthier Ken Parker and electronics guru Larry Fishman, the innovative Fly incorporated a number of new technological and manufacturing patents in a streamlined, space-age design.

THE CONSTRUCTION

While the Fly is radical in its conception, the most traditional of materials – wood – is at the heart of the instrument, which possesses a gracefully slender poplar body and a lightweight basswood neck. But, departing from tradition, the neck is reinforced with a skin of glass/carbon epoxy. Another revolutionary feature is that the instrument's hardened stainless steel frets are resistant to the wear and tear associated with traditional nickel/steel fretwire.

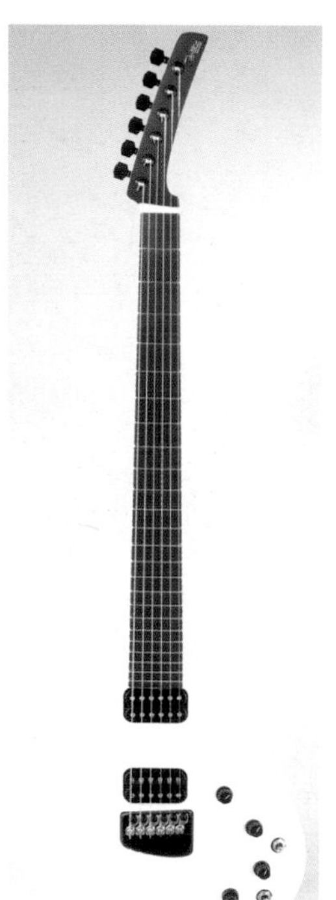

The Fly combines two magnetic humbucking pickups with a bridge-mounted piezo-electric unit (fed to an active stereo preamp), for access to a full range of electric tones and an amplified-acoustic guitar simulation. These sounds can be blended to create a unique electric/acoustic tone, and the guitar's split-stereo output allows for further depth of sound.

GUITAR SPEC

Model Pictured: Fly
Pickups: Two magnetic, one piezo
Controls: Three-way switch, two volume, two tone, master volume
Characteristics: Versatile, edgy, immediate tones, bright, spirited and funky
Played by: The Edge, Eddie Van Halen, Joni Mitchell, Keith Richards

Section Three: Galleries

PRS CUSTOM 24

In the summer of 1975, a young Paul Reed Smith set up a workshop in his parents' home and began making guitars.

Before long, he was peddling his creations at local concerts, to legendary guitarists like Al Di Meola, Ted Nugent and Carlos Santana. By the mid-1980s, Smith, having absorbed the traditional principles of Fender and Gibson guitars, arrived at his own strikingly modern design. Now made at a state-of-the-art facility in Maryland, PRS guitars are legendary in their own right.

THE BEST OF BOTH WORLDS

Basically the same instrument that Smith shopped at his first trade show in 1985, the Custom 24 is at the core of the PRS line. The guitar effectively combines elements of Gibson- and Fender-style design: its double-cutaway silhouette was inspired by Gibson's Les Paul Special, and its mahogany body with maple top and mahogany neck is informed by the Les Paul Standard. The Custom 24's vibrato bar updates that of the Fender Stratocaster; a five-way pickup selector includes coil-tap positions, converting the guitar's humbuckers to single coils and thus facilitating both Gibson- and Fender-like tones.

The Custom 24 has been offered in a dazzling array of finishes, and a number of other special touches. For a surcharge, the rosewood fretboard can be inlaid with abalone birds in flight (a PRS hallmark), and the top can be upgraded to highly figured maple. Some variations have proved less inspiring. The Custom 24 Metal – a heavy metal version with a custom striped finish – was only made from 1985–87.

GUITAR SPEC

Model Pictured: Custom 24
Pickups: Two
Controls: Five-way rotary selector, volume, tone
Characteristics: Versatile, robust creamy tone
Played by: Nils Lofgren, Al Di Meola, Carlos Santana

Complete Guitar Handbook

RICKENBACKER 360-12

Having produced a 'Frying Pan' electric guitar in 1931 and an Electro Spanish archtop in 1932, the Rickenbacker company helped usher in the era of amplification.

Overshadowed by Fenders and Gibsons, Rickenbacker electrics were obscure until the early 1960s, when the Beatles' John Lennon picked up his 325 model. Soon after, bandmate George Harrison got an early 12-string version, as did the Byrds' Roger McGuinn, who used a 360-12 to create his trademark jingle-jangle sound.

THE BASIC CONSTRUCTION

First made in 1964, the 360-12 was a deluxe mono/stereo guitar, constructed of a slender, semi-hollow maple body and a set-in maple neck with rosewood fretboard, inlaid with white triangles. Commonly sprayed with a Fireglo (pink-to-red sunburst) finish, the guitar was outfitted with twin high-output 'Toaster Top' pickups, a two-tiered white pickguard, and a custom 'R' tailpiece.

GUITAR SPEC

Model Pictured: 1964 360-12
Pickups: Two
Controls: Three-way selector, two volume, two tone, one balance
Characteristics: Jangly, shimmering tone
Played by: George Harrison, Roger McGuinn, Peter Buck

The 360-12 employs an unconventional tuning-knob configuration – its machine heads are alternately placed slotted (classical-guitar style) and in the regular perpendicular fashion. This allows for a conventionally sized headstock, ensuring that the instrument is balanced. The 360-12 has the six strings of a standard guitar, doubled at the octave on the bottom four strings, and at unison on the top two, resulting in a big, chorusing sound, like that of two guitars being played at once.

Section Three: Galleries

SELMER/MACCAFERRI JAZZ

A colleague of Andrés Segovia, Mario Maccaferri (1900–93) was a renowned classical guitarist during in the 1920s.

But Maccaferri began to find the classical style stifling; reportedly, he told Segovia that playing the instrument was 'like a monkey scratching his belly'. So Maccaferri turned to instrument design, hoping to remove the guitarist from a primate-like state.

THE SOUND CHAMBER

Maccaferri's wooden guitars are best known for their sound chambers. Inside the guitar, Maccaferri built a discrete free-floating sound device, which attached to the instrument's sides at four points; mounted above the soundhole, a reflective plate projected the sound outwards. This configuration negated any loss of resonance caused by the player's abdomen contacting the back of the guitar. Among other innovations that are now commonplace, Maccaferri is also credited with pioneering self-contained tuning gears and the single-cutaway body style.

GUITAR SPEC

Model Pictured: Jazz
Construction: Laminated rosewood body, solid spruce top, sound chamber
Characteristics: Crisp, bright tone, excellent projection
Played by: Django Reinhardt

In the early 1930s, Maccaferri began producing his new designs in a guitar line through Selmer. With its laminated rosewood body, solid spruce top, D-shaped soundhole, extended fretboard and floating bridge, the Selmer/ Maccaferri Jazz became the instrument of choice for Belgian guitarist Django Reinhardt, whose Gypsy-jazz stylings have profoundly impacted guitarists.

Complete Guitar Handbook

STEINBERGER GL

In 1981, the industrial designer Ned Steinberger (b. 1948) introduced the sleek, unconventional L-2 electric bass, the most radical update of the instrument since its introduction by Leo Fender three decades earlier.

A six-string guitar version, the GL, followed in 1983. Initially Steinberger's instruments were objects of ridicule, but they soon came to be praised by both musicians and design journals.

SPACE-AGE CONSTRUCTION

The GL's conventionally sized neck and diminutive body were made from a lightweight composite of epoxy resin, carbon graphite and glass fibres – twice as strong and 10 times denser than wood. This consistent, synthetic material precluded the tonally inactive spots found in wood, the vibration of which soaks up the strings' energy. The GL's most striking element was its lack of a headstock; the tuners were relocated to the end of the body (necessitating double-ball-ended strings), creating a total physical balance. When played in a seated position, a folding leg-rest provided further ergonomic support.

Many top players, including Eddie Van Halen, were drawn to the GL. But perhaps due to its disorientating shape, the guitar did not achieve widespread appeal. Subsequently – compromising Steinberger's original design – more conventionally shaped wooden models were introduced, including the Sceptre, which had a headstock.

GUITAR SPEC

Model Pictured: Steinberger GL
Pickups: Two
Controls: Three-way switch, volume, tone
Characteristics: Clear and resonant, piano-like attack
Played by: Allan Holdsworth, Mike Rutherford (Genesis), Eddie Van Halen

VOX MK VI

In the 1960s, England produced some of the most famous rock bands, but the country's guitar manufacturers had difficulty competing with American brands like Fender, Gibson and Gretsch.

One British company to achieve a measure of success was Vox, which in addition to a fine line of valve amplifiers, made guitars in England between 1961 and 1964, later outsourcing them to Italy.

FAMILIAR CONSTRUCTION, NEW SHAPE

With its bolt-on maple neck, three single-coil pickups controlled by a five-way switch, and vibrato unit, the Mk VI was clearly inspired by Fender's Stratocaster. But with its egg-shaped body and headstock, the instrument, nicknamed the 'Teardrop' was one of the most unconventional-looking guitars of the early 1960s.

The Mk VI gained considerable exposure when a rare, two-pickup white version was seen being played by Rolling Stones guitarist Brian Jones on *The Ed Sullivan Show*. While this appearance did not create instant, overwhelming demand for the instrument, the guitar steadily gained interest amongst players and collectors alike; since the 1980s the Mk VI has been reissued in several different versions, and original 1960s models perform well on the vintage market.

GUITAR SPEC

Model Pictured: 1960s Mk VI

Pickups: Three

Controls: Five-way switch, volume, two tone

Characteristics: Bright, clear tone; novel body shape

Played by: Ian Curtis (Joy Division), Tony Hicks (the Hollies), Brian Jones

ZEMAITIS DELUXE METAL FRONT

A cabinet-maker originally, Englishman Tony Zemaitis (1935–2002) made his first guitar – a nylon-string acoustic – in 1955.

GUITAR SPEC

Pictured: Metal Front
Pickups: Two
Controls: Three-way selector, two volume, two tone, two coil tap
Characteristics: Object of art, Les Paul style features, penetrating tone
Played by: Bob Dylan, George Harrison, Keith Richards

He continued building instruments as a hobby until 1965, when he became a self-employed luthier. Until his retirement in 2000, Zemaitis built only a handful of guitars per year, for clients such as Bob Dylan, George Harrison and Keith Richards.

HEAVY METAL

Zemaitis found that a typical guitar's pickups were too close to the strings, so he decided to equip his guitars with preamps, allowing the pickups to be lowered. Perusing an electronics catalogue for a suitable preamp, Zemaitis noticed that each model possessed a metal chassis, inspiring him to decorate the faces of his custom instruments with metal plates.

In the early 1970s, one of Zemaitis' customers began decorating the fronts of Zemaitis guitars. Ronnie Wood played one of these on television in 1971, and Zemaitis began to receive a huge number of orders, most of which he declined. Today, these handsome instruments, decorated with flowers, geishas, dragons and the like, are highly coveted, both as objects of art and musical instruments.

Section Three: Galleries

THE ELECTRIC GUITAR

The electric guitar is a marriage of twentieth-century technology and design with a simple plucked instrument from ancient Persia. These first gut-stringed instruments were carried along trade routes from Asia to Europe.

The guitar as we recognize it now was developed from these first instruments, and electric versions of the acoustic guitar were made in the early 1900s. In the 1950s Leo Fender developed the first mass-produced and affordable electric guitar.

The electric guitar is the result of half a century of ideas and imagination. But the first commercially successful electric guitars – the Fender Stratocaster and Telecaster – are still produced today.

Anyone transported in time from 1950 to today would see nothing unusual in a guitar built in a South Korean factory just the day before. The design classic has stood the test of time.

HOW DO THEY WORK?

Electric guitars make sound by creating electromagnetic induction through pickups containing copper wire wrapped around a magnet. The discovery by Michael Faraday and Joseph Henry in 1831 of electro-magnetic induction brought about many technological benefits, including the invention of the telephone some 45 years later. Some say that it was not long before guitar players were experimenting with telephone receivers attached to acoustic guitars in an effort to become amplified.

THE FIRST ELECTRIC GUITARS

True or not, guitar players have spent forever trying to find ways to get their acoustic guitars heard above the stomping 88-key acoustic piano and doghouse bass at

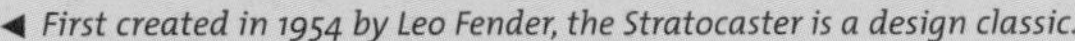

◄ *First created in 1954 by Leo Fender, the Stratocaster is a design classic.*

► *The National Style O is the most famous style of guitar produced by the National (Dobro) company.*

Complete Guitar Handbook

▲ *Single-coil pickups on a Fender Stratocaster. These are used to detect the vibrations of a guitar string that can then be amplified.*

gin joints somewhere in the Southern states of the US. Some players even tried to attach a gramophone horn to the front of the guitar. This development, turned inside out, became the 'Dobro' – an all-metal guitar with a resonator inside the body. During the 1940s, a magnetic guitar pickup was developed and finally mass produced by Leo Fender for the Telecaster (first called a Broadcaster) guitar in 1949 and the Stratocaster in 1954. These designs have become classics. Seth Lover patented his high powered 'PAF' (patent-applied-for) pickup in 1955.

FUTURE DEVELOPMENTS

More recent developments in technology have brought us instruments such as the Line 6 Variax; a guitar with a computer inside able to instantly recreate the sound of any guitar you need to use at the time. Who knows what developments are around the corner? But one thing is for sure, guitar players will experiment for as long as the guitar is around.

If the fundamental design and components of the electric guitar are so old fashioned, why it is still so popular? Why hasn't the guitar become another retro trademark like an old car or a toaster oven? The answer is that nobody ever created a heartbreaking tune on a toaster and that old cars just rust and die. The electric guitar is still young, fun and sexy after more than 50 years in mass production.

▲ *The future of guitar playing? Variax 500 guitars have computers inside them that recreate the sound of any guitar.*

Section Four: Reference

ANATOMY OF AN ACOUSTIC GUITAR

The acoustic guitar in all its forms has been around for about as long as we have. From simple instruments made from gut and turtle shell to the highly ornamental seventeenth-century lute and chittara, our love affair with the most portable and still the most lyrical of all acoustic instruments remains undiminished.

WOODS

The wood used for body, top and neck of the guitar has an enormous effect on the tone and performance of the instrument. Mahogany has been a traditional material for back and sides as it has strength and tone.

The top of the guitar can be made from spruce, which has a warm sound, maple with a brighter sound or koa wood, which has a similar sound to mahogany but with an enhanced mid-range. Rosewood, alder, poplar, basswood and even bamboo can all be used in the manufacture of acoustic instruments.

Complete Guitar Handbook

1 TOP

The top of the guitar is usually made of one piece of close-grained spruce, split in two and laid in half over the top. This process is called 'book-matching'. To enhance the appearance of the guitar a rosette may be inlaid around the soundhole or a thin strip of darker wood may sometimes be inlaid along the guitar behind the bridge.

2 BRIDGE

Steel string guitars have non-adjustable bridges fixed to the guitar top. The function of the bridge is to transmit the string vibrations to the guitar top, which will vibrate in turn and amplify the sound of the guitar. The bridge is often made of rosewood or ebony and is fitted with a bone or plastic saddle. The acoustic guitar bridge doesn't compensate for intonation.

3 BRACING

Braces, or 'ribs', are thin pieces of wood glued to the top and back of the guitar inside the guitar body. The braces add strength to the guitar and, depending on the number and positioning of the ribs, can greatly affect the guitar tone. The steel string guitar uses the traditional 'X' brace pattern, with the centre of the X just below the soundhole.

4 BODY

The acoustic guitar has a hollow body, usually of mahogany. The body has waisted sides and, depending on the model, may also have a cutaway on the lower bout to enable access to the higher frets. Binding is inlaid around the body at the point where the top and back meet the sides of the guitar. The guitar is finished with polyester, polyurethane or nitro-cellulose lacquer depending on model and maker.

5 NECK

Necks are traditionally made of the same wood as the guitar's back and sides. The neck has an adjustable truss rod running from the nut to the heel of the guitar where the body meets the neck. Nylon string acoustic guitars are not subject to as much tension as steel string guitars and so do not require a truss rod. Acoustic guitars are built to the same scale as the electric guitar, but the neck normally meets the body at the 14th fret.

6 FRETS AND FINGERBOARD

The rosewood or ebony fingerboard is laid on top of the neck and is fitted with 20 or 21 frets. As with the electric guitar, position markers are inlaid into the fingerboard to aid the guitarist. Dots are also laid into the edge of the fingerboard at the same position.

Part Two: Reference

ANATOMY OF AN ELECTRIC GUITAR

The electric guitar is not complex, but the pieces of the electric guitar must fit together and match each other perfectly or the guitar will never reach its potential to move mountains. Here are some of the most important ingredients.

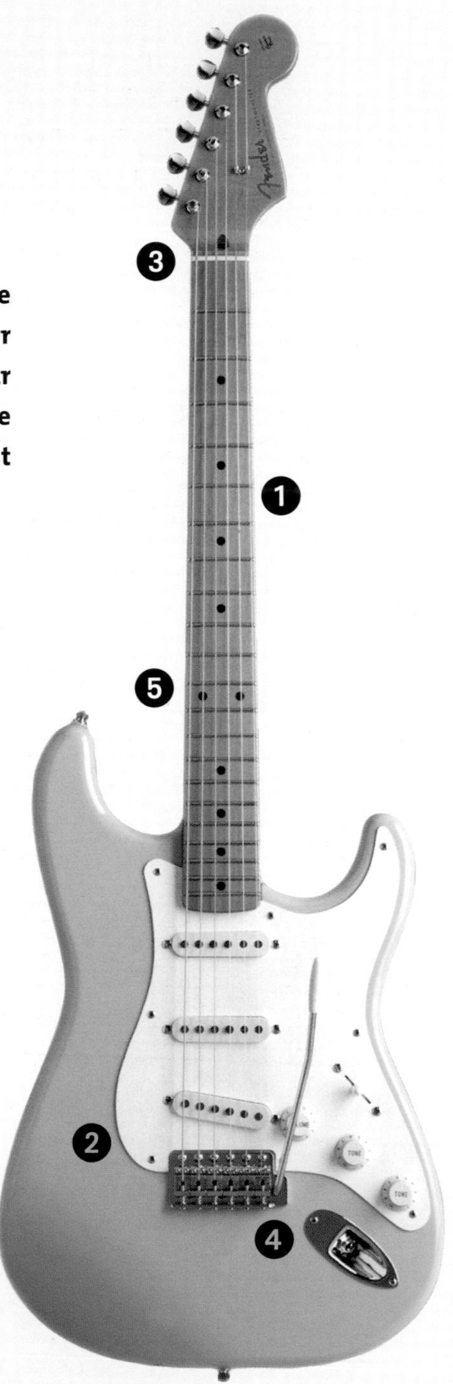

1 FINGERBOARD

The fingerboard covers the face of the neck and provides a playing surface for the guitarist. The fingerboard can be made of any suitable material but they are usually made of rosewood or maple. Frets are set into the fingerboard to enable the guitarist to find and stop the string at the desired point quickly.

The fingerboard can have 21, 22 or 24 frets, depending on the model of guitar. Fingerboard material also influences the tone of the guitar. Maple and ebony produce a brighter tone while rosewood has a darker tone. Some manufacturers are making fingerboards from synthetic materials such as graphite these days.

Complete Guitar Handbook

2 BODY

This is usually wooden, made of ash, elder or basswood depending on the origin of your instrument. Expensive US-produced guitars are made of rare hardwoods such as mahogany and maple. As good-quality wood becomes harder to obtain, guitars are nearly always made of one or more pieces of wood sandwiched together to create a body of the required depth. Modern guitar manufacturers such as Ibanez have created guitars with no wooden parts, while Gibson has a range of 'Smart Wood' guitars made from wood cut from sustainable forests.

3 NUT AND FRETS

The nut of the guitar is placed at the end of the fingerboard just below the headstock, where it provides one of the two anchor points (the other being the bridge saddle) for the string. Nickel silver frets are fitted to the fingerboard underneath the strings. The frets are placed at precise points on the fingerboard to enable the guitarist to play in tune. Frets wear down over time and change the tone of the guitar as they do so. The distance between the nut and the bridge saddle is extremely important and dictates the scale of the guitar. Fender instruments have a 25-in (63.5-cm) scale while Gibson instruments have a slightly smaller 24-in (61-cm) scale.

4 HARDWARE

Pickups, bridge and electronics are fundamental to the tone of the electric guitar. Single-coil pickups produce a very bright sound; twin-coil pickups have a warmer, less defined sound. Bridges are either fixed or vibrato models (aka tremolo). Vibrato models enable the player to produce amazing sounds by pressing on the vibrato arm to lower the tension in the strings. Tension is returned when the player releases the arm and springs pull the bridge back into place.

5 NECK

The neck of the guitar is often made from dense maple or ash. The wood needs to be hard and stable as the neck is under tension. Depending on the model of guitar the neck may either be joined to the body with three or four long screws, or by a traditional wood joint and string glue. If the neck is screwed to the body it is called a 'bolt-on neck'. Necks that are jointed to the body are called 'set-in'. Bolted and jointed necks have different tonal characteristics: bolted necks are thought to be brighter while set-in neck guitars have a rounded tone.

Section Four: Reference

CHOOSING STRINGS

Strings are the voice of your guitar. The right strings will make your guitar sound great, feel fantastic and last much longer than a cheaper set. The wrong strings will sound terrible, will turn your expensive guitar into an unplayable plank and, worst of all, will break just at the worst moment. So buy the most expensive set you can afford. Your guitar and your ears will thank you for it.

Strings for electric and acoustic guitars are either 'wound' (rhymes with round) or 'plain'. The difference is that wound strings are in fact two separate strings, one wound around the other. Plain strings are simply a single length of wire. Both wound and plain strings have a ball attached to one end of the string. This enables the string to be attached to the guitar bridge. Nylon strings mostly do not have this ball end, although some beginner's sets do have a ball as it makes the string easier to attach.

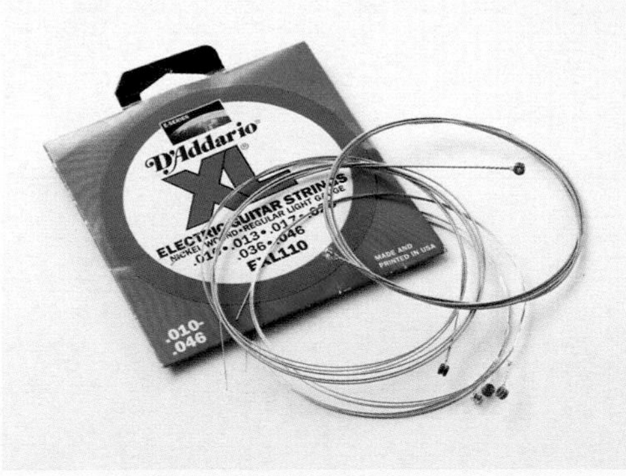

▲ *Light gauge strings aren't the only size: try any set for a week or two to see if they are comfortable.*

STRINGS FOR ELECTRIC GUITARS

If playing an electric guitar choose a medium set of .009-gauge nickel-steel strings and play with them for a week or so. If they do not feel quite right change up a gauge to .010 or down a gauge to .008.

Strings are sold in packs of six and described by the weight of the first (thinnest or highest in pitch) string. A set of .009 gauge strings will have a top E just nine-thousandths of an inch thick. The other strings are graded to suit. Each of the strings in a .010-gauge set will be heavier than their equivalent in a .009 set and much heavier than in a .008-gauge set.

Ernie Ball and other manufacturers make hybrid sets. For instance, a 'heavy bottom/skinny top' set has the three highest strings from a light-gauge set (.008) and the lower strings from a heavier set. Some players like this bottom-heavy feel and sound. The trade-off is always feel against stability.

Complete Guitar Handbook

Thinner .008 or even .007 strings feel easy on your fingers but quickly go out of tune and break. Heavier .010 or .011 strings are harder work but last much longer and sound louder. One thing that Jimi Hendrix, Stevie Ray Vaughan and many other fantastic players have in common is that they all had big, strong fingers and used heavy strings.

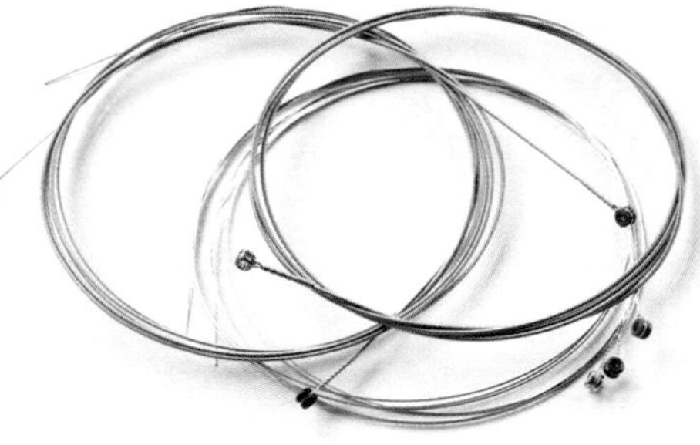

▲ *The gauge of a string is the technical term for its width.*

STRINGS FOR ACOUSTIC GUITARS

Acoustic guitar strings are also sold in light, medium and heavy sets. However, acoustic sets are always heavier than electric. An extra-light set of .010 acoustic strings is a medium-weight electric set and so on. Acoustic string sets have two other major differences. Firstly, the wound strings are usually made of bronze and steel alloy instead of nickel-silver. This has a brighter sound more suited to acoustic music. Secondly, the third string (G) is wound instead of the plain G in an electric set.

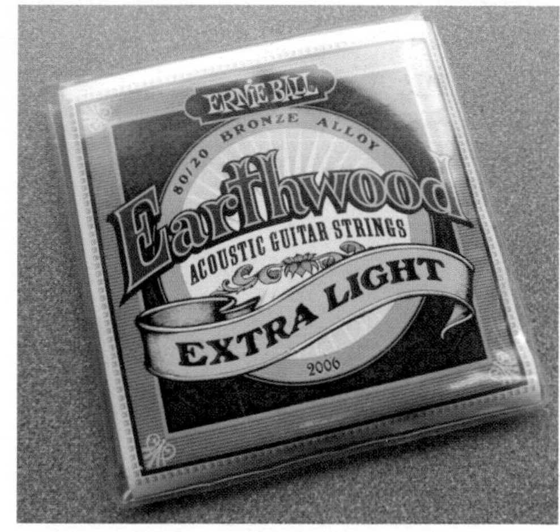

▲ *Bronze string are usually used with acoustic guitars.*

Nylon strings are used on classical guitars. Nylon produces a round, mellow sound which is preferred for classical, Latin and many pop/folk styles. This type of string requires a lower string tension, making a classical guitar easier to play than a steel-string acoustic. The longer string length from saddle to nut enhances the bass response and sustain.

▲ *Nylon strings are used on classical guitars for a softer tone.*

Section Four: Reference

FITTING STRINGS: ACOUSTIC

To fit new strings on an acoustic guitar, place the instrument on a clean, flat surface – a workbench, table or even your knee. Loosen the strings using the (tuning) machine heads until the end of the string can be pulled back through the centre hole. At the other end of the guitar remove the wooden or plastic bridge pin using a bridge-pin remover/string-winding tool and keep safely. The ball end can now be pulled out of the bridge and the string is free from the guitar.

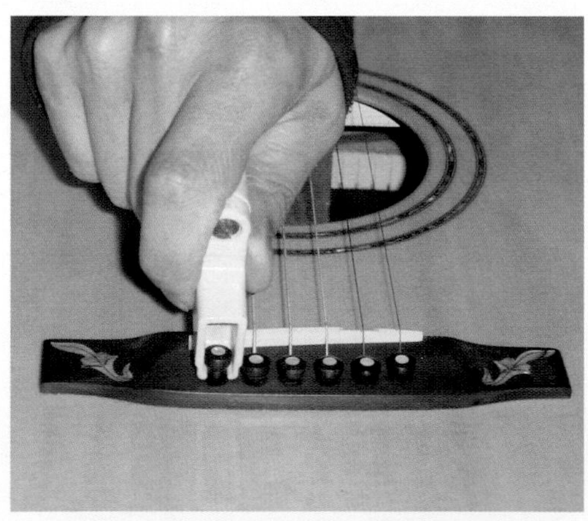

▲ *When changing a string on an acoustic guitar, first remove the pin that holds it in place.*

CLEAN IT UP

Repeat this process for each string and discard the old set safely. Before fitting the new set, take a few minutes to wipe down the fingerboard. Use a soft cloth with some lemon or olive oil, or even a specialist fingerboard cleaner, to remove the dirt from between the frets. Buff the fingerboard and frets with a soft cloth but resist the urge to take metal cleaner or polish to the frets. If shiny frets are a must, wipe frets gently with 000-gauge synthetic steel wool and buff with cotton cutting cloth available from specialist carpentry or finishing suppliers (or an old cotton shirt will do).

ATTACH THE STRING

Take the thickest string from the packet of new strings and uncoil. Bend the new string 30 degrees, one inch from the ball end and push the ball end into the first hole in the bridge. Seat the bridge pin in the hole and pull the string gently. Remember that the bridge pin is not there to hold the string down. The pin simply pushes the string against the side of the hole, thereby trapping the ball end under the bridge. If the pin keeps slipping out, buy a new set from your local guitar store. Wooden pins are always better than plastic.

Complete Guitar Handbook

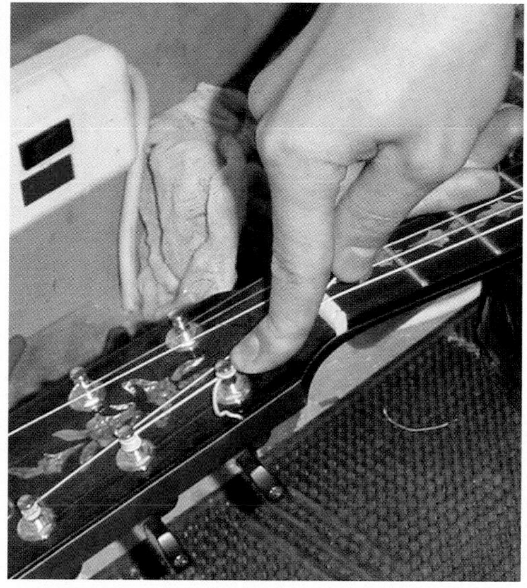

▲ *Once the new string has been inserted through the capstan, ensure enough slack has been left to wind it round the post.*

WIND IT THROUGH

With the string attached under the bridge it's time to take the other end of the string over the bridge saddle, up the fingerboard, over the nut and then push it through the hole in the first machine-head. Turn the machine-head key until the hole is pointing towards the string, then pass the first few inches of string through the head. The actual amount of string to pass through the head depends on which string it is in the set, the scale of your guitar, the weight of the string and even the manufacturer. Only experience will give you that perfect 'one, three, three, five, eight, eight' winding – and even guitar players with many years experience get it badly wrong sometimes. Always aim for at least four windings on any plain string, two windings on any wound string. Ensure that the windings are neat and placed on top of each other; never leave so much loose that the new winding is lying on top of the string already wound round the post.

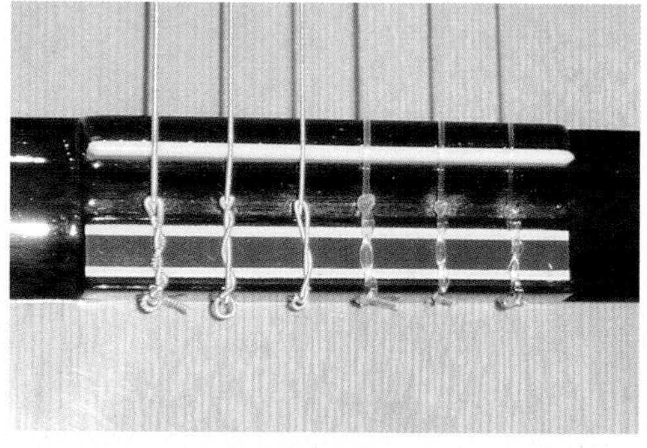

▲ *This is how the strings on an acoustic guitar should appear once secured.*

FINISHING OFF

Finally, when all the strings are fitted to the guitar take a pair of side cutters and give your guitar a haircut. Six inches of wire in the eyeball is enough to take the edge off anyone's day!

◄ *A fast winder is a simple device that lets you quickly wind the capstan of the tuning peg, wrapping the string evenly.*

Section Four: Reference

FITTING STRINGS: ELECTRIC

Electric guitar players love to abuse and destroy their strings as quickly as possible. Unlike acoustic players, electric guitar players believe that two gigs is a very long time between string changes and that 'medium weight' .013 strings are best left to bass players. Fit your electric guitar strings so that they will come up to tune quickly, stay there and can be replaced just as quickly – ideally in the time it takes to sing a chorus of 'Living on a Prayer' and at the same time!

ATTACH THE STRING

Pass the ball end through the bridge of the guitar, either from the back if you have a Stratocaster, Telecaster or some other model with a through-body bridge, or through the back of the bridge as fitted to Les Paul, PRS and other solid-top models. Tug the string firmly a couple of times to seat the ball end and pass the string up to the machine heads. As usual, turn the machine head key until the hole in the shaft is pointing down at the string.

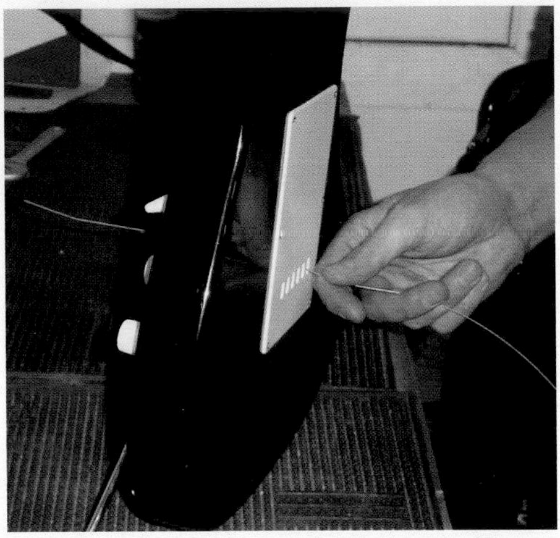

▲ *Push the string through the bridge block in the back of the guitar and up through the hole in the centre of the saddle.*

WIND IT THROUGH

Pass the string through the machine head but leave enough slack to enable the string to be pulled about three inches from the fingerboard. Bring the loose end clockwise around the shaft and tuck it under the string as it enters the string post. Turn the key so the string is wound on to the post, trapping the loose end under the new winding. This is tricky but

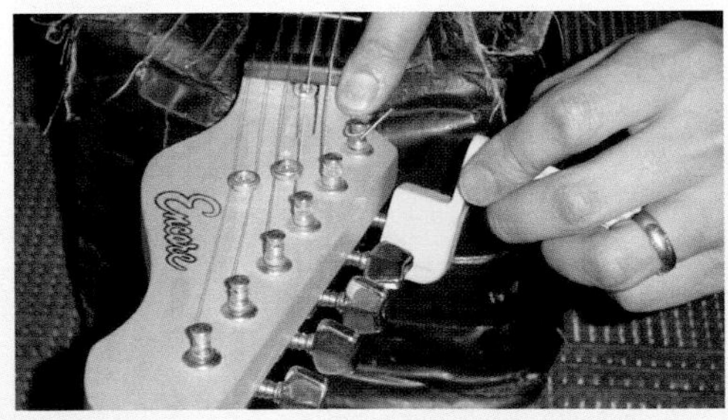

▲ *Fast winders can help you wind new strings round the post.*

Complete Guitar Handbook

it comes with practise and when you have the knack you'll find that strings fitted like this are easier to tune and stay in tune. Repeat for each of the other strings. If your headstock is 'three a side', you'll need to pass the loose end clockwise around the post for the G, B and E strings to trap the end successfully.

STRETCH YOUR STRINGS

Stretch the new strings immediately after fitting. Place the guitar on your knee in the playing position and place the flat of your thumb under the low E string. Push the string firmly away from the guitar and repeat for each string. Now retune and stretch again. You should find that you can repeat this three or four times before the guitar remains roughly in tune after stretching. Replace any broken strings immediately. If a string is poor enough to break during this procedure, it's a safe bet that it would not have lasted until the end of your first song.

▲ *Stretching new strings once fitted helps tuning stability.*

MAKING STRINGS LAST LONGER

To increase the life of your new strings, as well as stretching them, you could try applying a very thin coat of three-in-one oil to each saddle before fitting the new strings. This fine layer of oil will prevent moisture from creeping between the string and the saddle. When you have fitted the new strings, wipe a soft cloth dipped in three-in-one over the strings and saddle. This will prolong the life of your strings and also keep intonation and height adjustment screws from seizing up. After playing, wipe down the strings with a piece of soft cotton, and use a string-care product such as Fast Fret to remove grease and grime from the strings.

▲ *Cleaning your strings helps reduce grime building up.*

Section Four: Reference

SETTING THE ACTION

Action is incorrectly known as the height of the string above the fingerboard. In truth, the 'action' of the guitar is a combination of string height, intonation and neck relief, and it refers to how the guitar feels when played.

The great majority of guitar players prefer a comfortable action, though some jazz players are proud of the difficult action of their instruments as it enables the purity of tone that jazz players prefer. Rock players could not use a heavily strung jazz instrument, as rock relies on super-fast playing with extreme hammering and pull-offs that are only possible on a guitar with a very low and comfortable action.

STRING HEIGHT

String height on all electric and some acoustic guitars can be adjusted at the bridge. Optimum string height is dictated by player preference and the physical characteristics of the guitar, such as fret height or the angle of the neck. Generally, players prefer to have the strings as close as possible to the fingerboard without buzzing or false tones that are produced when the vibrating string meets the frets or even the top of the pickup.

Depending on the model of the guitar, the individual saddles or even the whole bridge can be adjusted to whatever height is suitable. Adjustments should

▲ *The action of a guitar significantly affects the sound – the higher the action, the louder the volume.*

▲ *The gap between the bottom of the low E string and the top of the seventh fret should be about 0.013 inches.*

Complete Guitar Handbook

▶ *The saddle is the place on a guitar's bridge for supporting the strings. Acoustic guitars tend to have a one-piece saddle.*

always be made with the guitar tuned to concert pitch. Make small changes to the height of the bridge saddles before retuning and playing at the top of the neck close to the pickups. Listen closely for rattles caused by the strings meeting the frets and if possible, check with the guitar through an amplifier. Stratocasters and other guitars with individual bridge saddles, can be adjusted to produce a profile at the bridge that mirrors or closely resembles the camber (curved radius) of the fingerboard. Some guitars have bridges that may only be raised or lowered using wheels or screws at each bridge pillar. Height adjustment with this kind of bridge can only be a compromise and if you find that you are unable to get the adjustment you need it may be time to talk to a repairman about a more adjustable bridge for your guitar. Often the strings will appear to mysteriously rattle or buzz around the 13th or 14th fret. This is caused by fret wear or even a poorly fitted fret behind the point where the buzz is heard. If you do not have the tools or experience to put it right yourself, the only option is to raise the bridge until the string stops buzzing and make plans to take the guitar for a service.

Guitar bridges trap muck and grease from your hands and if left for a while they will rust and eventually stick. Adjusting a stuck bridge saddle is difficult and sometimes destructive as the small grub screws inside the saddle are easily broken. Use a small amount of penetrating oil or 'Plus Gas' on the screws and other moving parts, then set aside for a couple of hours before trying again. A stuck bridge probably needs more maintenance than just a simple wipe over with a little oil, but a can of WD-40 in the guitar case comes in handy for emergencies.

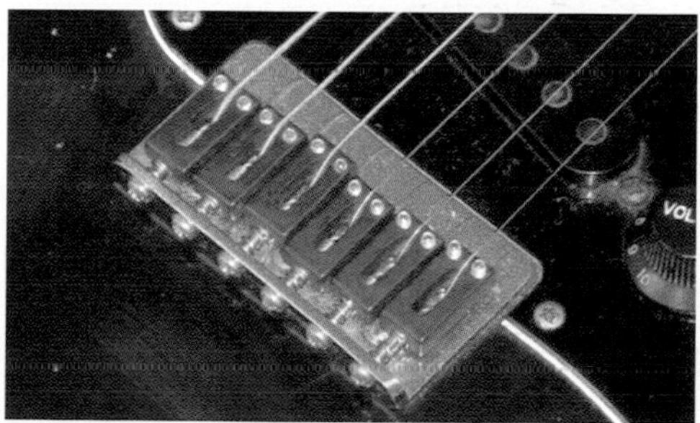

▲ *Electric guitar saddles usually have six substructures, each with a groove over which a string passes.*

Section Four: Reference

SETTING THE BRIDGE FOR INTONATION

The electric guitar bridge has a moveable string saddle under each string. These saddles can be adjusted in two ways – backwards or forwards for intonation or up and down for string height. Bridge adjustment involves correctly setting both string height and intonation for each string to make the guitar comfortable to play and to play in tune.

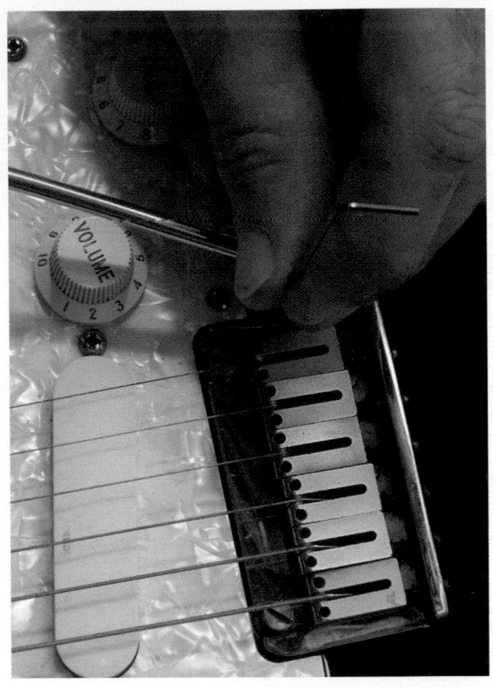

▲ *Use a hex key to raise or lower the bass and treble side of the bridge by screwing or unscrewing each of the retaining pillars.*

Some bridges do not have height-adjustable saddles. For these guitars the whole bridge must be moved up or down using screws set into the bridge posts. Height adjustment in this way is not as precise but it is easier than setting the height for each string.

▲ *Raise or lower the height of the bridge by turning the milled thumb wheel under the bass or treble sides.*

DIFFERENT BRIDGES

Because each string is larger than the next, the distance between the string and the top of the fret is greater or smaller depending on the thickness of the string. This tiny difference causes the guitar to go gradually out of tune as the notes are fretted higher up the neck. Electric guitars have bridge saddles that can be moved

Complete Guitar Handbook

▶ *Adjusting the intonation should be done whenever changes are made to string gauge, neck relief or string height.*

forwards or backwards to compensate for this difference. Acoustic guitars have the same problem, but bridges with this kind of correction are not common on acoustic guitars as notes above the 12th fret are not as easy to play. It is important to correctly adjust the bridge as the guitar will permanently be 'out of tune' above the 12th fret if this is not done. This adjustment should also be checked each time the strings are changed as the new set may have different characteristics.

CHECK THE INTONATION

To check the intonation you will need an electronic tuner and a screwdriver or 'Allen wrench', depending on the model of bridge. Prepare to move the string saddle using the screwdriver or key to turn the adjustment screw behind each string saddle. Play the harmonic note at the 12th fret and note the reading on the tuner. Tune to concert pitch (a=440) if necessary and recheck the harmonic note – it should be reading dead centre on the tuner. Now play the fretted note at the 12th fret and check the reading. If the fretted note is lower (flat) the saddle must be moved forward by 1/16 in (1–2 mm). If the fretted note is sharp, the saddle must be moved back towards the bottom of the guitar. Retune and check that the harmonic and fretted notes are the same, then move on to the next string.

TINY ADJUSTMENTS

Following this adjustment you may find that the string height has also changed. After adjusting the string height you will have to recheck the intonation. Either the string height or the intonation of the guitar will change each time the saddle or the bridge is moved. Optimum bridge adjustment involves making tiny adjustments and then checking both height and intonation. Eventually the bridge will be balanced and your guitar will play in tune and feel great. It is a hassle, and it may take some time, but it will be worth the trouble.

Section Four: Reference

ADJUSTING THE NECK RELIEF

The neck of the guitar has a slight concave bow in it. This bow is there by design to allow for the vibrating string at its widest excursion above the seventh fret. If the bow was not there, or if it was not deep enough, the vibrating string would catch on the frets causing the guitar to rattle as it was played.

The amount of bow set into the neck is called the 'relief'. The relief is held by a metal rod, which lies at tension under the fingerboard. This is called the truss rod. One end of the truss rod has a key or nut allowing for more or less tension to be applied to the neck. Neck relief is the third most important adjustment you have to make to your guitar. It must also be made in conjunction with string height and intonation and, most importantly, the bridge must be reset following adjustment of neck relief.

▲ *A Gibson Les Paul-style truss rod (pictured top) and a Fender Stratocaster-style truss rod (pictured bottom).*

HOW MUCH RELIEF?

If your guitar is not rattling when played it may be that your neck relief is perfectly set. On the other hand if your guitar feels 'stiff' when playing around the seventh fret it may be that there is too much relief. To check the amount of relief you must tune the guitar to concert pitch and hold it in the playing position. Lay a steel ruler on its edge along the neck of

Complete Guitar Handbook

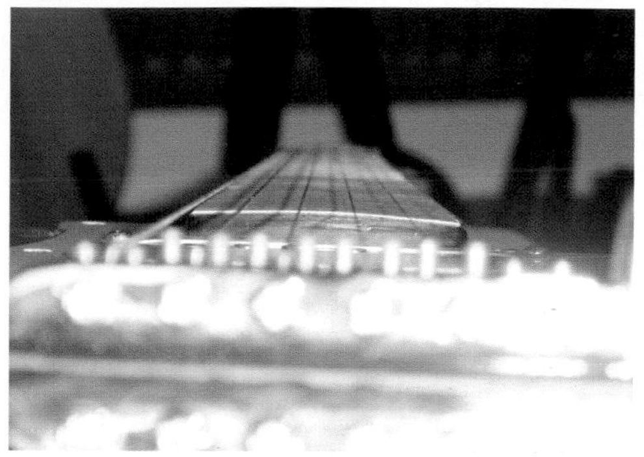

◀ *Check for faults in the guitar's neck by looking along it.*

the guitar between the low E and A strings. Examine the gap between the ruler and the seventh fret. There should be enough space to slip a thin piece of card or even a .010 flatpick between the ruler and the fret. Any thin material will do. If this gap appears to be too large you may be able to reduce the gap and so ease the playing of the guitar without causing string rattle.

TRUSS-ROD ADJUSTMENT

Depending on the model of your guitar, use a nut spinner or Allen wrench to loosen the truss-rod adjustment screw by a very small amount. The adjustment screw is normally found at the headstock just behind the nut and is often covered with a plastic plate. Check the measurement again, play the guitar and see how it has reacted to this adjustment. You may have to adjust and play several times before you have the optimum neck relief. Check string height (action) and intonation at the bridge following the final adjustment.

The truss-rod adjustment key may be stiff and difficult to turn. This could indicate that the guitar neck has suffered some damage (maybe from extreme changes in heat or humidity, causing warping) or it may be that the truss rod is damaged. If the adjustment cannot be made you must take the guitar to a professional repair shop. Truss-rod adjustment is always made with the guitar tuned to concert pitch and in the playing position. Allowances should also be made for further changes in the neck in the hours following adjustment; any adjustment that is made should always following a change in choice of string gauge.

◀ *Measure the guitar's action with a ruler. It should be no more than 0.013 inches.*

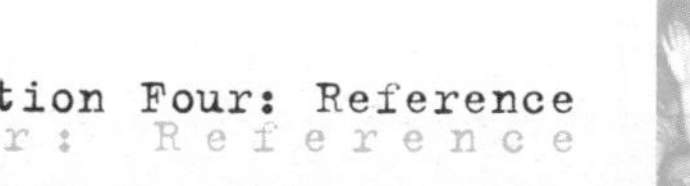

Section Four: Reference

GUITAR CARE

Your guitar is a living, breathing instrument. The wood of your guitar contains hundreds of thousands of tiny holes. These holes trap moisture, swell and contract, and can make your guitar change its mood overnight if not carefully looked after.

The golden rule is never keep your guitar anywhere that you would not be happy yourself. That means not storing it under the bed, hung on a wall above a radiator or put at the back of the garage for the winter. Seasonal change spells danger for the guitar. Your instrument can experience extreme changes in temperature just on the journey from the house to the car. Invest in a moulded case with a waterproof seal to check the ingress of moisture into the case (SKB and Hiscox have a fine selection).

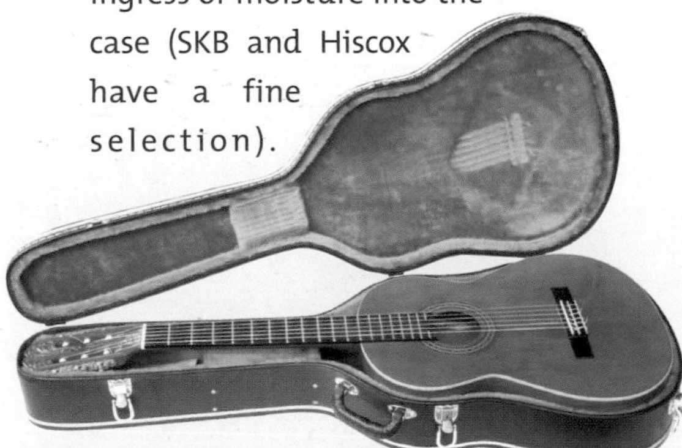

▲ *A glass of water left in a centrally heated room can stop guitars drying out.*

A packet or two of silica gel can be placed inside the case to absorb the moisture evaporating from the guitar. In winter, travel with your guitar in the car rather than the unheated boot or trunk.

Inside the house your guitar should be on a guitar stand away from radiators or sources of heat. In dry conditions place a glass of water near the guitar stand and, if you do have to leave the guitar in storage for more than a few months, do not take the strings off! Your guitar was made to be under tension and removing the strings will enable the neck to twist and warp. In short, make your guitar as comfortable as you would be yourself. But do not forget that the best thing you can do to keep your guitar in premium condition is to regularly pick it up and play it!

◀ *A hard case is the heaviest but most sensible option for transporting your instrument safely.*

Complete Guitar Handbook

KEEP IT CLEAN

When cleaning your guitar, use as little domestic cleaning product (furniture spray or silicone-based polish) as possible. Use a little white automotive polishing compound to take off the grease and grime, then use clean cotton cutting cloth to bring up the original finish. Use a tack rag (a cotton cloth moistened with light machine oil) to wipe down the bridge and other hardware. The tack rag will also do a good job on the metal pickup covers, but watch out for metal pieces that will stick to the magnets and fur up your tone. A clean tack rag moistened with a little WD-40 is as good as any shop-bought product when used along a dirty string. Unfinished fingerboards of ebony or rosewood can be helped with a little lemon oil or olive oil rubbed well into the grain. Finished maple fingerboards can be treated like the body of the guitar.

The plastic parts of your guitar can be treated with the same white automotive compound but may need a little silicone spray polish on a soft cloth when buffing back. Be careful with the control surfaces that may be screen printed 'Rhythm/ Treble' or similar. The printed words can be rubbed off if you use too much force and can't be rubbed back into view.

▲ *Cleaning your guitar every time you play is an important habit to get into to prolong the life of your instrument.*

▲ *Wipe the strings down after every performance or practise.*

Section Four: Reference

FRET CARE

Frets are both hardwearing and fragile at the same time. With normal use your guitar will last for years without needing a re-fret. Drop it on its face and those nickel frets will quickly acquire more grooves than your dad's record collection. Dented or badly worn frets can, with care, be brought back into line with a crowning file (available from any good luthier) and some fine needle files and steel wool.

▲ *Fret files are used to sand down uneven or protruding frets.*

REPLACING FRETS

The key is to carefully draw the needle files over the fret, taking as little material off the fret as possible. When the top of the fret is as smooth you can get it, take the crowning file over the top of the fret to bring back the rounded shoulder of the fret. Finish off with same fine steel wool. This process takes a lot of time and is not easy. The problem is that taking material off the fret means lowering its height.

▶ *Frets are metal strips placed across the radius of a guitar's fingerboard to mark out notes a half tone apart.*

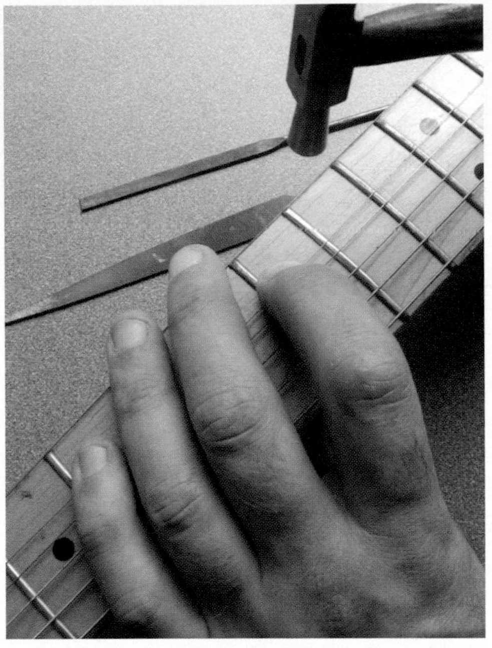

▲ *A loose fret can cause string buzzing. Tap the loose fret into place with a small hammer or remove carefully with pliers.*

Complete Guitar Handbook

A string stopped at this fret will probably buzz on the fret in front because it can no longer clear it. If this is happening you have a choice. You could lower all the frets on the neck, but this is a bad choice as it will take a lot of time, is highly destructive, completely irreversible and will probably be disastrous for your guitar. The other thing to do is to raise or re-adjust the string height to clear all the frets. This is much simpler, is completely non-destructive and could even improve the sound of your guitar. It will be harder to play – but at least it will be playable and you can spend your time making enough money from all those gigs to pay for a complete re-fret.

CLEANING FRETS

Polished frets are impressive and one of the best ways to get a great reaction from a customer is to make sure that when you open the case on their newly set-up instrument, the frets are polished enough to see your face in them. Shop polishes like this are simple to achieve and can look fantastic.

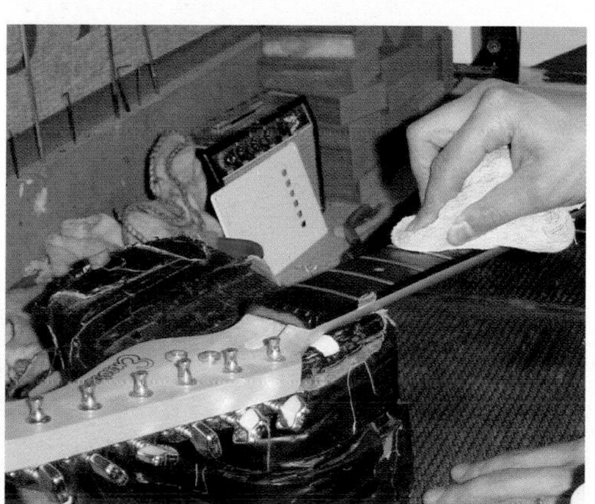

Start by taping between the frets with low-tack masking tape until you can't see the wooden fingerboard and only the crowns of each fret are exposed. Use a pad of very fine 000-grade synthetic steel wool, available from DIY stores. Wipe (do not rub) over the tops of the frets along the length of the guitar neck using minimal pressure. Brush off the grime that has collected by each fret and carefully polish the sides of each fret using a soft toothbrush if necessary. Do not be tempted to use any metal polish, particularly Brasso or anything with abrasive qualities. This kind of polish is too much for the nickel silver. Even worse, the residue will work its way on to the fingerboard – a nightmare on an open-grained rosewood board. Use only hard cotton cutting cloth and some firm rubbing to bring the nickel silver right up.

Remove the tape, wipe the fingerboard over with lemon oil, wipe down again, restring, check action, intonation and relief ... and you are done!

◀ *Your guitar's fretboard can accumulate a lot of dirt and grease from your fingers, so it is important to clean it regularly.*

Section Four: Reference

CUSTOMIZE YOUR GUITAR

NEW PICKUPS

Pickups are simple to replace and offer the very best return for your money. Most stock guitars, including famous name models, aren't fitted with the very best pickups for a number of reasons. Replacing the stock pickups with beefed-up 'aftermarket' parts will give your guitar a better tone and provide you with a better experience. Replacement pickups are designed to slot straight into the holes left by the other pickups. You can often use the old screws and springs too. Stock single coil pickups may be 'two-wire' pickups – hot and ground. Replacement pickups for the same guitar may be two- or even five-wire pickups. The latter can simply be attached using two-wire instructions. It's not necessary to use all five conductors if you do not want to. Choose a new pickup from Seymour Duncan, DiMarzio or one of the new manufacturers such as Bare Knuckle.

NEW HARDWARE

After pickups, the second most popular aftermarket part is a new bridge.

▲ *Bridges can be replaced fairly easily, but you should check with a professional that you have chosen the right size.*

Replacement bridges are available for all models of guitar and are very popular, which is surprising. After all – when did you last wear a hole in a solid steel bridge? Replacement bridges are popular because a new bridge can be easier to adjust and will probably hold the adjustment longer than a stock bridge. Fitting is easy, but take your guitar to the dealer when you choose your bridge just in case there is a difference in dimensions. Guitars from the Far East often have parts that are slightly smaller than similar parts from Europe or the USA. A worthwhile alternative to a whole new bridge is a new set of bridge saddles. Special saddles are now available that will actually help your strings to last longer (String Savers), and they are well worth the minimal expense.

Complete Guitar Handbook

CUSTOM CONTROL KNOBS, SCRATCHPLATES AND OTHER HARDWARE

Check out suppliers Pincotts, Stewart Macdonalds or Allparts for groovy multi-coloured control knobs and scratchplates. Replacing a scratchplate takes about an hour of your time and the results can be truly spectacular.

▲ *Scratchplates stop damage occurring to the guitar's body and can also add decoration to the instrument.*

A NEW PAINT JOB

An old Stratocaster-style guitar is like an artist's canvas just waiting to be turned into something beautiful. Take off all the hardware, remove the neck and rub down the old finish with very fine steel wool until the guitar is extremely smooth to the touch. Then attach the body to a piece of wood using the bolt holes in the heel, and let go with a few cans of your favourite automotive spray paint. Take a tip from the experts and always spray outside on a windless day (unless you have a very expensive custom spray booth in your house). Use short, even strokes and do anything to avoid drips or runs in the paint. Wait 12 hours between coats and at least 48 hours after the final coat before you go near it with finishing compound. Practise makes perfect, so do not use your favourite guitar. Old American, English or Japanese guitars are also a bad choice for a re-spray, as the best-selling prices always go to un-refinished instruments.

► *Guitar bodies can be completely refinished using automotive spray paint.*

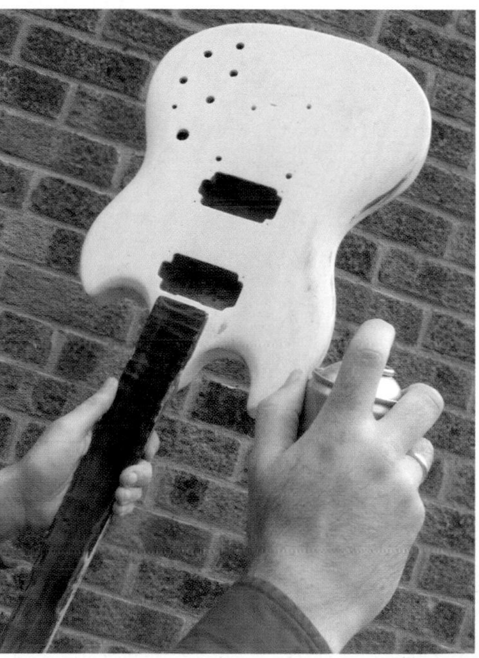

Section Four: Reference

HOW THE ELECTRICS WORK

The standard electric guitar contains a few relatively simple components. Electromagnetic pickups harness the vibrating metal string to produce energy, which is attenuated (made weaker) if desired by rotary controls called potentiometers further along the signal chain. These are called volume controls on the guitar.

Very similar potentiometers attached to capacitors bleed more energy from the signal in the form of tone controls. If the guitar has more than one pickup, a switch is placed in the path between the pickups and the tone and volume controls to enable the guitarist to select which pickup is activated. Finally, the signal appears at a jack socket which mates very closely with a jack or 'phone' plug, which is attached to high-quality copper strands protected by a rubber or cloth sleeve. The other end of the copper is attached to another phone plug, which connects the guitar to an amplifier. The purpose of the amplifier is to take the signals from the guitar and make them into something you want to hear.

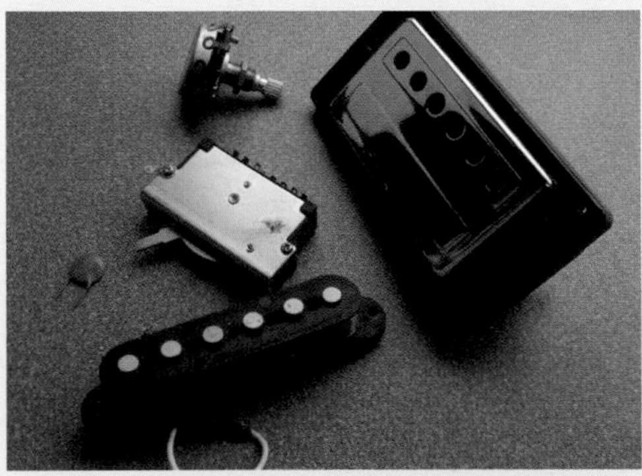

▲ *Switches and pickups are the basic electronic components of the electric guitar.*

ACTIVE TECHNOLOGY

Modern guitars take these basic principles and add more switching or tone controls to enable a wider range of tones to be achieved from the guitar. Active guitars boost the signal after it leaves the pickups using power from a battery situated in the guitar. Active pickups are fitted to non-active guitars to achieve the same thing. Some pickup manufacturers use high technology to produce clean, glassy sounds from the guitar (EMG, Actodyne). Many pickup manufacturers pride themselves on using very old equipment and NOS (New Old Stock) components to produce brand-new pickups that look, sound and feel exactly like pickups made 40 years ago (Seymour Duncan).

Complete Guitar Handbook

◀ *Most electric guitars have a selector switch that allows the player to choose whichever pickup is desired.*

IN WITH THE NEW

During the 1980s some innovative manufacturers began to experiment with computer music technology to create guitars that were more like keyboards than stringed instruments (Bond guitars). In the early Eighties, Ned Steinberger produced the 'L-2' guitar with a wholly carbon-graphite composite body. Guitars such as the Parker Fly Mojo, featuring a mahogany body and composite neck, offer the best of traditional and modern.

In the new millennium the crown belongs to 'modelling' guitars such as Line 6 Variax. These computer-aided instruments create convincing real-time guitars using the characteristics of sounds stored in their memory blended with the artist's own performance. Because the sounds are created from a list of instructions held in the computer's memory the guitarist is able to produce a rock sound, then a country sound, even an acoustic guitar or banjo sound one after the other without having to put down a plectrum. Instruments like the Variax offer so much in the way of convenience to the player that it's difficult to believe guitarists will lose sight of these instruments in the way that previous innovations have gone by the wayside. But however popular the Variax might get, it's still never going to be as easy to fix or as much fun to customize as an old electric guitar. The pickup isn't dead yet!

▲ *The Parker Fly Mojo guitar is made using an effective mix of traditional and modern.*

▶ *The Variax 500 may be the future for guitarists, but don't write off the Fender just yet.*

Section Four: Reference

TOOLS

Some say that all you need to fix an electric guitar is a sharp knife and a roll of gaffa tape. That's true up to a point, but lasting repairs are made by skilled technicians and these guys need a few simple tools to get the job done.

SCREWDRIVERS

Get a Philips #2 and flat-bladed screwdriver with a high-quality tip that won't blunt and leave the tops of domed screws in a mess. Fender bolt-on necks need a larger Philips tip, while Gibson AB-1 bridges and stop-bar tailpieces need a large, good-quality flat-bladed tip. Rubber grips are much more pleasant to bounce off a glassy finish than hard plastic.

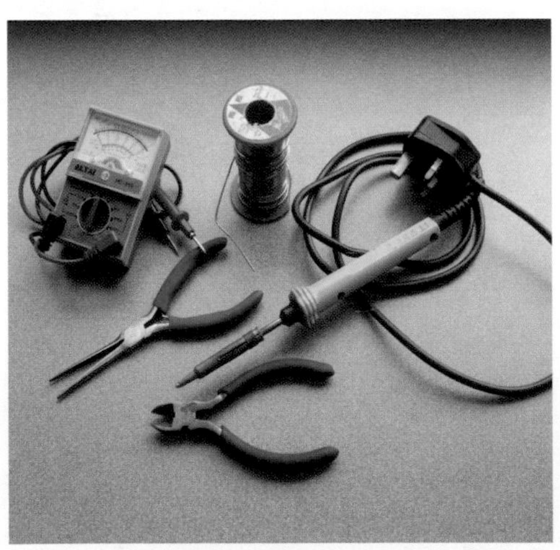

▲ *It is possible to equip yourself to handle the majority of electrical tasks with just a few inexpensive tools.*

KEYS

A complete set of 'Allen' or hex keys in US (inches) and European (metric) sizes. Allen keys hold everything together, from bridges to locking nuts to control knobs. Many guitars have hex nuts at the truss rod too. Many US guitars need a ½-in (1.2-cm) key for bridge adjustment and a ⅛-in (3-mm) hex key for truss-rod adjustment. A set of nut drivers or box spanners is also useful for truss-rod adjustments on Gibson guitars and some others.

NEEDLE FILES

A set of fine modeller's files is vital for removing burrs from bridges and nuts. Other abrasives such as 000-gauge synthetic steel wool and glass paper are also useful for fretwork and for removing very shallow scratches. Deeper scratches and dents require filling with specialist materials available from luthier suppliers. A very fine modeller's saw is also useful for cutting nut slots.

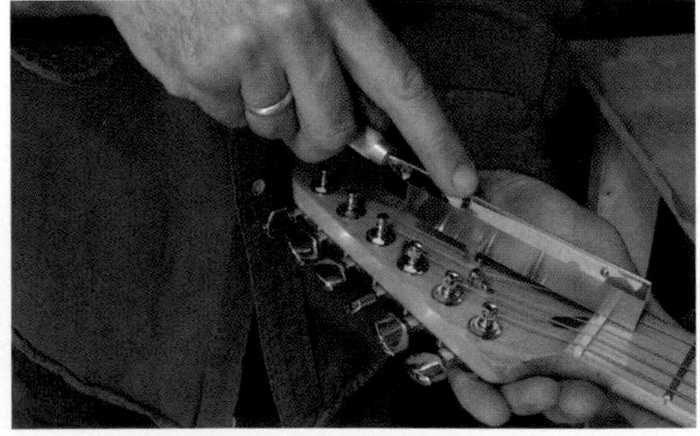

▲ *You may need an Exacto saw to deepen the B and E string slots when replacing a nut.*

Complete Guitar Handbook

▲ *Have the right tools to hand so you can make vital repairs.*

FILLERS AND LIQUID ABRASIVES

Holes can be filled with automotive fibreglass filler then rubbed smooth before spraying. Liquid abrasives are good for cutting back around shallow scratches but should never be used on unfinished wood such as fingerboards.

SOLDERING IRON

A good-quality soldering iron with variable heat is vital for perfect solder joints. Resin flux solder is required along with the hot iron to make the joint. Always use safety glasses when working with hot solder and a mask to avoid directly inhaling the fumes. If you are considering a lot of soldering, make a rig at the right height with enough light to see by, and ventilation to bring clean air into the room and to extract the fumes that may build up.

SIDE CUTTERS AND THIN PLIERS OR PINCERS

Side cutters are essential for trimming excess wire and snipping the untidy guitar strings from the headstock. Needle nose pliers are useful if you have to hold cables within a cavity. Crocodile clips or locking clamps can make tricky wiring jobs much easier.

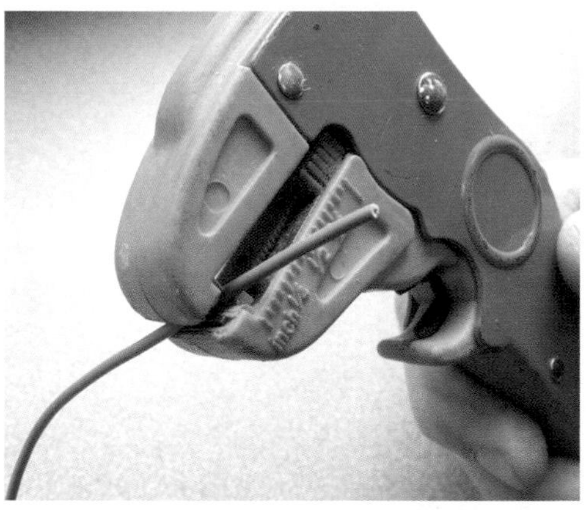

▲ *A useful tool for cutting wires and trimming strings.*

TAPE AND GLUES

Low-tack masking tape is essential for masking areas around the working point. High-speed glue is occasionally useful for repairs to pickups or other parts inside the body, but has very low shear strength and doesn't stand up well to handling or moisture. High-speed glue repairs are often highly visible as well. If you need to join two plastic parts use Araldite and smooth the excess if you can with glass paper.

Section Four: Reference

PICKUPS

Pickups create the sound of the electric guitar. Every guitar has at least one pickup placed under the strings and, depending on the model of the guitar, there may be two or even three pickups. The function of the pickup is to detect the vibrating string of the guitar and turn the vibrations into electric current that can be amplified enough to move a speaker cone. The electric guitar pickup does this by electro-magnetic induction.

Each pickup is a coil of some 7,000 turns of copper wire wrapped around a magnet. The vibrating metal strings of the guitar push and pull the magnetic field created by the magnet and so create an alternating electric current in the coil of wire. Stronger magnets, combined with a greater number of turns of wire, will produce a more powerful pickup but will eventually lose definition. Smaller magnets and fewer turns produce a more musical sound but are lower in power. Pickup manufacturers use these characteristics to produce a range of pickups for country, rock or metal players. This simple explanation can't take into account the decades of experimentation and innovation that have produced the amazing electric guitar pickups available today. However, the principle of wires and magnets remains at the heart of every electric guitar.

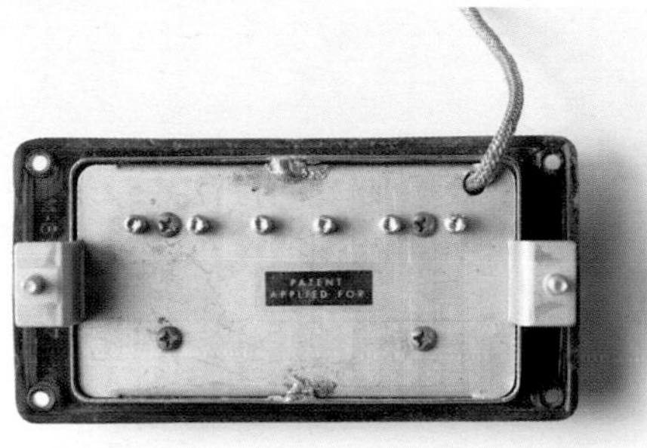

▲ *The Patent Applied For (PAF) humbucker pickup is perhaps the most sought-after of all Gibson electric guitar pickups.*

HUMBUCKERS

Electric guitar pickups have one or two coils of wire. Pickups with a single coil have a bright, clean sound which is full of detail and popular with country and blues players. Pickups with two coils are much more powerful and can overdrive

▲ *The inside view of a humbucker pickup.*

▶ *Piezo pickup systems are fitted to most electro-acoustic and some purely electric guitars.*

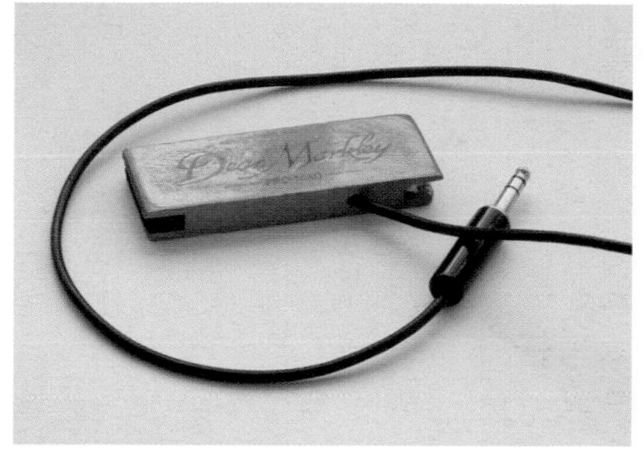

an amplifier to produce a distorted sound which is associated with rock. Pickups are sensitive to electromagnetic noise or 'hum', which is amplified along with the strings causing the sound to be unclear. While working on ways to avoid this interference, an engineer working with the Gibson guitar corporation of America found that by reversing the polarity of one of the coils in a double-coil pickup, the hum would almost disappear. This became the famous 'humbucking' pickup, the design of which has been copied many times over.

▲ *A humbucking pickup can translate vibrations into energy.*

PICKUPS FOR ACOUSTIC GUITARS

The sound of acoustic guitars, pianos, violins and every sort of acoustic instrument can also be amplified using transducers or contact microphones. This kind of pickup also uses electro-magnetism but, instead of relying on the strings to disturb the magnetic field, these pickups sense acoustic vibration. The magnet and coil is mounted underneath a small metal plate placed against the instrument's soundboard. When the soundboard vibrates, the vibrations are converted by the electromagnet into small electric currents, which are amplified in the same way as electric guitar pickups.

MAGNETIC MAGIC

Inventors and engineers have stretched the simple principle of electro-magnetism almost to breaking point. Pickups can be single or twin coil at the touch of a switch. The electric guitar bridge can also be turned into a pickup by placing transducers below each bridge saddle. The pickups can be battery powered to produce massive distortion and can be placed underneath the wooden top of the guitar to aid its appearance.

Section Four: Reference

TROUBLE-SHOOTING

Guitar electronics lend themselves to simple troubleshooting. Here are a few common problems and remedies....

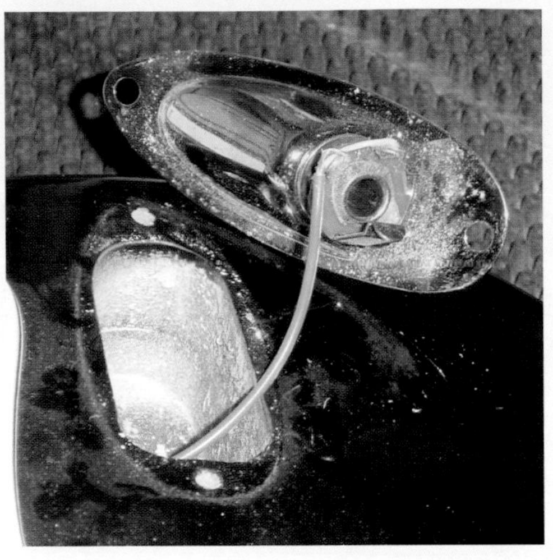

▲ *The jack sockets are the parts of your guitar most vulnerable to damage and should be replaced whenever necessary.*

NOISY SWITCHING

Pickup selector switches fail over time as the point of contact inside the switch becomes dirty or broken. This usually results in pickups not seeming to work, a big problem but one that can easily be resolved. Spray contact cleaner (Servisol) inside the switch and move the selector to work the fluid into the contacts. If the problem doesn't go away you will have to remove the rear cover or scratchplate and examine the switch. Check for loose or missing wiring. Finally, consider having the switch replaced with a new one.

PROBLEMS WITH THE JACK SOCKET

The jack socket is a weak point on the guitar. If the instrument appears to work only when the barrel of the jack plug is pushed to one side you have a bent or corroded socket. Remove the control plate or scratchplate and gently squeeze the long spring arm towards the centre hole. Gently rub with a little fine glass paper to remove corrosion, then test.

DULL OR SCRATCHY VOLUME AND TONE CONTROL

Carbon tracks inside the tone control become worn with age and use. Remove the scratchplate or rear cover and apply contact cleaner to the inside of the potentiometer through the small space in the metal can above the solder connections. Work the control backwards and forwards to ease the fluid along the track. The pot will have to be replaced if this procedure fails to solve the problem.

HUMMING OR NOISE THAT STOPS WHEN THE STRINGS OF THE GUITAR ARE TOUCHED

This problem indicates poor grounding of the guitar. Remove the rear cover or scratchplate and look for a grounding

Complete Guitar Handbook

wire connecting the metal can of the volume pot to the bridge of your guitar. Replace if this connection is missing or broken on your Stratocaster or Telecaster guitar. This ground wire is missing on Les Paul-style guitars. Unfortunately most copy Les Paul guitars have a hum problem because the electronics in these instruments are shielded with a metal can. Copy Les Paul guitars don't have the can and also don't have the ground wire.

Adding a ground wire between the bridge and ground will help protect your copy Les Paul from noise. Electric foil or conductive paint should completely cover the walls of the cavity containing the electronics. A few strips attached to the scratchplate won't be enough. Check out Stewart-Macdonald or any good electronic parts supplier. Some players also add a 0.022uF capacitor to the ground wire. This will help to protect you from lethal mains voltage if your amplifier should have a poor or missing ground. Ensure that the capacitor is taped or wrapped in bubble wrap to avoid touching and shorting on any other components.

'FURRY' PICKUPS

Pickups attract metal particles from strings and other metal parts of the guitar. Over time these can cause the pickup to lose definition. Use Bluetack to remove the metal particles by dabbing around the pickups, paying attention to the small gaps between the cover and the pole pieces.

▲ *Copper tape can be used to deal with humming or any other noise that stops when the strings are touched.*

▲ *Dab Bluetack around the pickups to remove accumulated metal particles.*

Section Four: Reference

CABLES

The electric guitar and amplifier are usually connected by a guitar lead or cable. The typical guitar cable has a stranded copper core screened with stranded or braided steel wire, called a 'screen', as a protection against atmospheric radio waves.

The screen is always connected to a solid pathway to ground through the metal chassis of the amplifier and the ground wire of the electric cord connecting the amp to the power supply. The small amount of energy created when the stray radio waves reach the screen is channelled to ground rather than being amplified along with the guitar signal. It is vitally important to make sure that your amplifier has a good-quality earth connection. Doing so will clean up your tone and may also save your life.

COPPER CABLES

The 'hot' stranded copper wire core of the guitar cable needs to be both flexible and high quality. Treble sounds can quickly be degraded by passing the signal through poor-quality cable, so the guitar lead must use high-purity copper for the signal path. Some manufacturers, such as Planet Waves, sell guitar cables with two very high-quality cores. The central cores overlap to encourage noise cancellation along the length of the cable. Planet Waves also has cables with connectors labelled 'guitar' and 'amp'. When connected as directed the guitar cable is almost noise free and will reject noise created by 'earth loops'.

▲ *Most guitar cables have a stranded copper core screened with stranded or braided steel wire.*

JACK PLUGS

Each end of the guitar cable is terminated with a metal connector called a 'jack plug'. These connectors

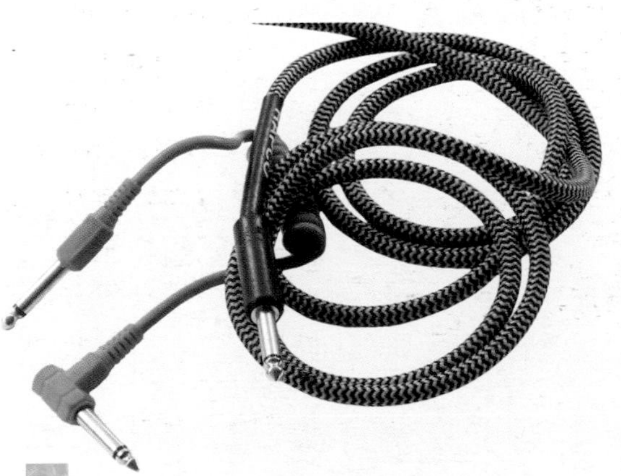

◄ *Jack plugs: the standard cable connection for most effects and guitars.*

Complete Guitar Handbook

have two signal paths: the ground connection is made along the shaft of the jack plug, while signal connections are made through the very tip of the plug. The dark band between the shaft and the tip is insulating material separating the signal from the ground. A short circuit would be created if these were to be connected, and the guitar cord would stop working. Some bass guitars use 'balanced' leads terminating in a round connector with three pins. These leads are for use with special 'low-impedance' instruments or microphones. A balanced cable has two signal wires and a ground wire, sometimes with an additional screen. These cables are able to carry a high-quality signal along a longer distance than a normal guitar cable with very little signal loss.

FIXING BROKEN CABLES

Guitar cables fail either because one or more of the jack connectors has been damaged or because the wire itself has become broken. It's simple to check the plugs by unscrewing the metal barrel and examining the connections. If the hot connection has come away it will need to be soldered back on or else a new lead must be obtained. A broken wire is more difficult to detect as the connections will be fine even though the lead appears to be broken. Sometimes 'waggling' or stretching the cable will tell you where the break is. In this case the cable could be cut behind the break and a new plug fitted. However, it's usually more efficient to simply buy a new cable. Guitar cables with moulded plugs cannot be repaired without replacing the jack plugs and are usually discarded after breaking.

◀ *The sound from a typical guitar-and-amplifier setup such as this relies on good-quality cables being used.*

Section Four: Reference

CUSTOMIZE YOUR ACTIVE ELECTRONICS

The best way to change the sound of your guitar and increase its value is to replace the factory pickups with high-output replacements. There are replacement pickups available for nearly every guitar, but all fit into just three general categories.

SINGLE COIL
• *STRATOCASTER, TELECASTER AND OTHER MODELS*

Single-coil pickups have one coil for each pickup. Vintage-style replacement pickups have one single-coil but more windings and hotter magnets. Vintage-style pickups such as Seymour Duncan's SSL-1, have similar staggered pole pieces and simple wiring like their factory equivalents – but they sound much better. Other options for single-coil replacements include pickups featuring long 'blade' style magnets such as Seymour Duncan's SHR-1 Hot Rails pickup. These have more output than vintage-style pickups and don't suffer from dropout as the blade magnet extends across all six strings. Further away from vintage-style pickups are DiMarzio's hum-cancelling four-conductor HS2 and virtual vintage DP405 extremely low-noise, high-output pickups.

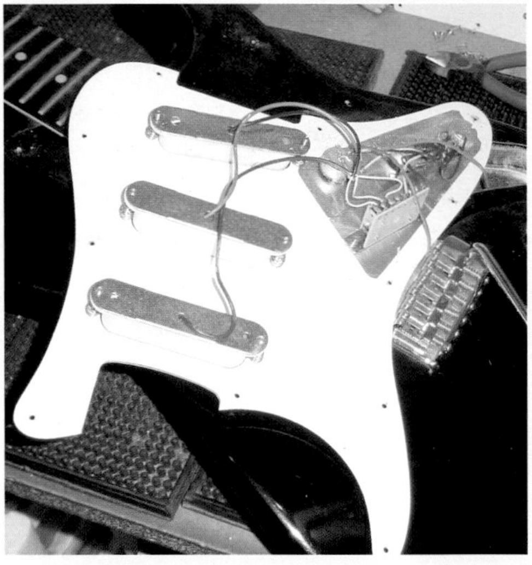

▲ *Before fitting new pickups to Stratocaster-style guitars, you should first remove the scratchplate.*

▲ *A new single-coil pickup before being assembled and fitted.*

Complete Guitar Handbook

HUMBUCKING PICKUPS • *LES PAUL AND OTHER SIMILAR MODELS*

Humbucking pickups have two coils arranged to reduce noise and produce a hotter output than single-coil pickups. Replacement options for humbucking pickups include UK-made Bare Knuckle pickups featuring extreme tone shaping and very high output. Bare Knuckle's Warpig model has distressed metal covers and Allen bolts for pole pieces. Humbucking pickups have five-conductor wiring (four conductors and ground). Switches can be placed between the conductors and the guitar electronics to enable one of the coils to be switched off (coil tapping) or the polarity of pickups to be reversed. By replacing your pickups you can also increase the range of sounds available from your guitar.

▲ *Ensure that the new pickup is mounted and orientated correctly before re-attaching the pickup assembly to the guitar.*

HUM-CANCELLING PICKUPS FOR STRATOCASTER AND TELECASTER

The limitations of the single-coil pickup are low output and high noise. These limitations have been overcome by hum-cancelling pickups that fit single-coil body cavities without the need for additional routing or woodwork. Hum-cancelling pickups, such as the Seymour Duncan JB Jnr, are miniature humbucking pickups in single-coil shapes. Both these pickups offer full four-conductor wiring and high output without the requirement for destructive work on your guitar.

Other options for customizing your guitar electronics include active preamp kits for enhanced and expanded tone.

- Active kits need a battery, which requires additional circuitry being zinstalled into the guitar.
- Consider additional switching for the pickups already in place.
- A simple 'on-off' mini-toggle switch can produce the 'missing' pickup combination of all pickups on neck and bridge only. Connect one side of the switch to the pickup selector switch at the connection for the hot wire from the treble pickup. Connect the other side to the hot connection leading to the volume control. Use the switch to turn the bridge pickup on or off independently of the pickup selector switch.

Section Four: Reference

THE AMPLIFIER

The electric guitar amplifier has generated almost as much mythology as the instrument itself. Beginning with the radio-like amps of the 1940s, up through the Fender Tweed amps of the 1950s, and on to the coveted Blackface Fenders, Marshall combos or stacks, and the Beatlesque Vox AC15s and 30s.

When it comes to playing electric guitar, the amplifier is an extension of the instrument itself. As the guitar replaced banjo in the dance bands of the 1930s and 1940s, guitarists began experimenting with pickups in order to equal and surpass the louder banjo, and ultimately to be able to solo above the horns and piano.

HOW DO THEY WORK?

We have seen how a guitar pickup works. In order for the relatively low electrical output generated by the coil windings to drive the cone of a speaker (see page 312), it must be increased – or 'amplified'. A guitar amplifier takes power from an external electrical source (outlet or battery) and controls the delivery of that power to the speaker according to the level of the voltage from the pickups. This can be accomplished by using valves (tubes), solid-state chips or a combination of both.

The first amplifiers were of relatively low wattage (10–20 watts), while some of the early pickups were quite powerful, easily capable of driving those fledgling combos into a mild distortion. Tales of slashed speakers and loose tubes notwithstanding, you can hear Charlie Christian's Gibson guitar pushing his amplifier hard on his famous records with Benny Goodman. The guitars on blues and western swing records from that era were also usually breaking up

▶ *The hard bop music of performers such as Wes Montgomery benefitted from the cleaner tone of a more powerful amp.*

Complete Guitar Handbook

▲ *Although you may not need as many amplifiers as AC/DC, choose one that will suit your specific playing requirements.*

the amp to some degree. It was only later, as the amps got more powerful, and some of the single-coil pickups less so, that you began to hear cleaner tones in the surf music of the Ventures, the instrumental pop of the Shadows, the be-bop of Wes Montgomery, the funk of Chic and the country guitar of James Burton.

NEW AMP TECHNOLOGY

As popular music became more, well, popular, venues got larger and amplifiers continued to grow into the multiple stacks of heads and speakers that you sometimes see today. For over half a century after its invention, the guitar amplifier remained virtually unchanged. Only with the advent of cheap DSP (digital signal processing) chips have we started to see some new twists on the old formula. Multiple onboard effects and amp modelling have become possible, but certain things still remain the same: for the most part, more volume requires a bigger amplifier. The trend towards more power in smaller cheaper packages that has swept through most technologies has not quite overtaken the art of guitar amplification. In the quest for guitar tone, bigger still produces louder and better still tends towards being more expensive.

▲ *Mackie's UAD-1 digital signal processor (DSP) card comes with Nigel, a guitar-amp simulator and effects suite.*

Section Four: Reference

TUBE (VALVE) AMPLIFIERS

In the beginning, there were only tube amplifiers. Initially they were adapted from radio and record players, though unlike hi-fi buffs and radio operators, guitarists were not concerned with strictly accurate transmission of sound. Instead they found that they liked the colouration and distortion that tubes added; this tone that became touchstone for years to come.

HOW DOES IT WORK?

In simplest terms, a tube amplifier takes the electricity generated by your guitar's pickups into a control grid. The grid reads the fluctuations of electricity that represent your playing, sending this voltage to the tubes to be amplified by the first stage of preamp tubes. It is then passed through (usually) passive tone controls that can roll off bass, treble and sometimes mid-range (some amplifiers have active tone controls that add as well as subtract these frequencies). The next stage of preamp tubes brings back the voltage lost in the passive tone roll-off. The power tubes then turn the increased voltage into current before sending it to the speakers.

TYPES OF TUBE AMPLIFIERS

The sound of a tube amplifier can be determined by a number of factors. One is the type of power tubes used in the design. The four most common types used are the 6V6, the 6L6, the EL84 and the EL34; we will discuss the sonic differences later (see pages 318–319).

PROS AND CONS

Even though the tube sound has been the industry standard for many years, tube amplifiers are far from a perfect solution. For starters, tubes are made of glass,

◄ *Valve amplifiers are the preferred choice of many guitarists as they respond particularly well to playing dynamics. Companies such as Groove Tubes (see inset) currently produce sought-after valves for guitar amps.*

Complete Guitar Handbook

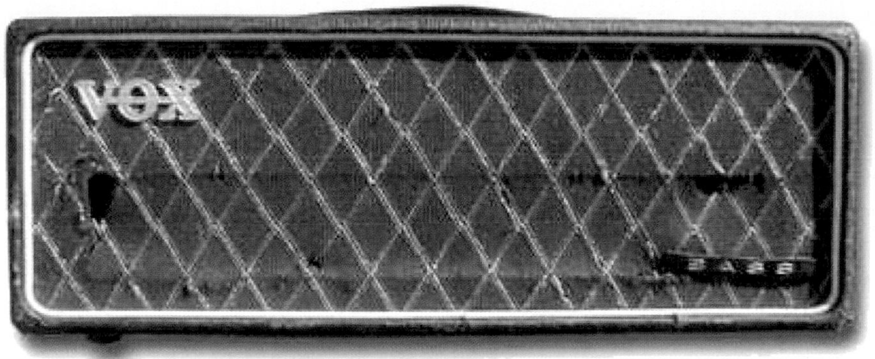

▲ *The Vox company was started by Tom Jennings and Dick Denny, who manufactured small combos for the UK market.*

making them somewhat fragile when it comes to road work; even if they don't actually break, the shock of bouncing up and down in the band bus can wear them out over time. They are also sensitive to heating up and cooling off, so it is best to leave the amplifier on during a gig rather than turning it off between sets; many amplifiers have standby switches that allow you to kill the sound without shutting down the tubes. That said, some amplifiers can also sound different after being left on for a length of time, so if you are trying to match sounds in the studio and your amplifier is one of these you should shut it off between takes. You should try to replace all your tubes at the same time so that they match; if a tube goes out on an amplifier that has four tubes, and you are low on cash, you can replace the outside two or the inside two.

Despite its faults the tube amplifier is still the most popular amplifier design. Solid-state and digital amplifiers attempt to emulate it, and guitarists worldwide put up with its quirks in exchange for its warmth and character. As much as its sound appeals, so does the elusive 'feel' of playing through a great tube amplifier. The 'give' one experiences in reaction to a hard attack, and the natural tube compression that kicks in when the amplifier is pushed, are an integral part of the electric guitar experience.

◄ *Vox amplifiers are made today by Japanese electronics giant Korg, and are claimed to be every bit as good as the originals.*

Section Four: Reference

SOLID-STATE AMPLIFIERS

In the late 1960s solid-state technology replaced tubes in most electronic devices, and amplifier design got swept up in the trend. Despite some advantages it was not universally welcomed as these fledgling designs suffered in the tone department. Solid-state has come along way since then.

In solid-state amplifiers, transistors take over from tubes to convert the voltage from the pickups into the current necessary to drive the speakers. The elimination of tubes allows for lighter weight, cooler, more reliable amplifiers. In early designs this was weighed against the fact that transistors produce 'hard clipping', as opposed to the 'soft clipping' of tubes. This means that a solid-state amplifier would remain clean up to a certain volume and then suddenly begin to distort, whereas tubes gradually shift from a clean sound to a more distorted one. Once distorted, the quality of tube distortion was found to be much more pleasing by most guitarists. Later developments in solid-state design have led to a more tube-like response.

Today solid-state amplifiers are favoured by players seeking maximum clean headroom for jazz or funk, and some heavy metal guitarists for the tightness of the low end when playing in drop-tunings. Jazz player George Benson still uses Polytone solid-state amplifiers for his music, and Jim Hall will often use a small Walter Woods transistor amp. In proper hands, some solid-state amplifiers can produce a smooth distortion as well.

SPEAKERS

An often-overlooked part of the tone chain is the guitar amplifier's speaker. Different speakers can alter your sound as much as changing guitars or even

◄ *Early transistor amplifiers had a bad reputation for their limited dynamic range, but modern designs are much improved.*

Complete Guitar Handbook

◀ *Marshall speakers are iconic and have graced the stages of everyone from Eric Clapton to the Who.*

amplifiers. Speaker cabinet design can also influence the sound, so let's look at this important link.

A speaker works like a pickup in reverse: the fluctuating current created by the amplifier is passed through a coil and magnet – the 'voice coil' – that reacts with a magnet on the speaker diaphragm. As your playing causes the level of current to change, the diaphragm moves back and forth, moving air and creating sound.

The size of the speaker, the number of speakers, the size of the magnets, the design of the cabinets and the material of the diaphragm all influence the quality and volume of the sound that ultimately ensues. Some speakers are more efficient than others; that is, they produce more volume from the same wattage amplifier. Guitar speakers tend to come in 10-in (25.4-cm) and 12-in (30.5-cm) diameters (and the occasional 15-in/38-cm). Speakers have impedance ratings, expressed in Ohms – either 8 or 16.

SPEAKER WIRING

Speakers can be wired together in series, parallel, or both.

1. Series doubles the impedance: 8 Ohms + 8 Ohms in series = 16 Ohms.
2. Parallel halves the impedance: 8 Ohms + 8 Ohms in parallel = 4 Ohms.
3. In a speaker cabinet with four or more speakers, both wirings are employed to bring the impedance back to the Ohm-age of the original single speaker: 8 Ohms + 8 Ohms = 16 Ohms, 16 Ohms + 16 Ohms in parallel = 8 Ohms.
4. This impedance should be matched to the amplifier output Ohms.

Section Four: Reference

CLASSIC AMPLIFIERS

Despite advances in electronic technology, guitarists gravitate to the same basic tube amplifier sounds. Most amplifiers are judged on how well they reproduce the sounds of a few classic archetypes from the 1950s and 1960s. The Big Three are Fender, Marshall and Vox.

FENDER

Fender represents the 'American' sound: sparkling, full-range clean tones and smooth, warm distortion, suitable for blues, country, surf and jazz. Leo Fender began by developing amplifiers for lap-steel guitarists and his original tweed-covered amps from the late 1940s and early 1950s still sound great today, with tweed Bassmans being sought after by rock and blues guitarists. Later models, covered in black Tolex, with black control panels, are called Blackface Fenders and are also prized. The Super Reverb was an integral part of Stevie Ray Vaughan's sound, and the Twin reverb helped define the country twang of James Burton and others. The powerful Showman models were developed for surf artists like Dick Dale, who loved to play clean but loud! Classic Fender amplifiers use 6V6 and 6L6 power tubes. Amplifiers like the affordable Peavey Classic series and the more expensive, early Mesa Boogies and boutique Victoria amplifiers are based upon Fender designs.

In the 1960s, Leo sold his company to CBS. During this period, the control panels changed to silver and the power of many models was increased. These Tweed, Blackface and early Silverface amps are all hand-wired (most current production amps use printed circuit boards), and are extremely rugged. Even at collectors' prices, they can still be cheaper than many boutique amplifiers.

MARSHALL

In the early 1960s Jim Marshall owned a music shop in London, where the Fender Bassman combo was a favourite amongst guitarists. As the sound of rock 'n' roll was becoming louder and edgier, the players expressed a wish

▶ *Mesa Boogie amps have a harmonically sweet distortion.*

Complete Guitar Handbook

for 'dirtier' amplifiers. Marshall developed an amplifier based upon the Bassman, replacing the 12AY7 preamp tubes with the hotter 12AX7 model. In addition, he moved the tone controls from before the preamp stage to after, and eventually began using EL34 tubes instead of Fender's 6L6s. Fortunately for him, in 1965 Eric Clapton and John Mayall's Bluesbreakers virtually invented the sound of modern rock guitar using a Marshall JTM45 2 x 12 combo (on the so-called *Beano* album). Marshall had originally designed the amplifer as a separate head and 4 x 12 cabinet combination. At the behest of Pete Townshend, Marshall then created a 100-watt head, stacking a slanted 4 x 12 on top of a straight 4 x 12 cab. This 'stack' configuration became synonymous with the heavy metal and hard rock sound of artists such as Jimi Hendrix, Joe Satriani, Kiss and Deep Purple. Amplifiers in the Marshall tradition include, Soldano, Mesa Boogie (Rectifier) and Peavey Triple XXX.

VOX

In the 1960s, a battle raged between Jim Marshall's new amplifiers and the Vox amplifiers being sold by the British Jennings Musical Industries. The Beatles were the most visible users of Vox amplifiers, but the company's classic AC30 2 x 12 combo was put to good use by Jeff Beck, the Rolling Stones, and later by Queen's Brian May. The EL84 powered AC30 and AC15 combos remained fashionable among the pop and softer rock bands for a while but eventually the lower-priced and louder Marshalls gained sway. The AC30 regained popularity in the 1980s as artists like Tom Petty tried to recapture the sound of 1960s' pop groups. What few originals there were available were notoriously unreliable, giving rise to companies like Matchless, which were able to create workhorse amplifiers with the AC30 sound.

OTHER CLASSICS

If you want a vintage amplifier and can't afford one of the Big Three, there are other old amplifiers that offer hand-wiring and classic tube tones of their own. Look out for old Ampeg Jets, Geminis and Rockets, as well as Silvertone and Supro amps, as played by Jimmy Page on Led Zeppelin records. Early Gibson amplifiers can also sound great. They are all increasing in value but are not yet priced like vintage Fender, Vox and Marshall amplifiers.

► *Ampeg is best known for its Portaflex bass guitar amps.*

Section Four: Reference

AMPLIFIER MODELLING

Having used various rented classic amplifiers for use in making a record, players find themselves unable to produce those sounds live. With the rise of home recording, many urban-dwelling guitarists own great amplifiers but risk eviction trying to record them in the usual fashion. Hence the rise of amplifier modelling.

▲ *Known now as the SansAmp Classic, this pedal was the first analogue amplifier modeller available to guitarists.*

HARDWARE

In 1982 Tom Scholz, guitarist for the band Boston, began manufacturing the Rockman, a device that permitted players to plug directly into the mixing board (deck) and still sound a bit like the guitar was plugged into a miked amplifier. In 1989, Tech 21 brought out the first SansAmp, an analogue, pedal-sized device that offered more varied and more realistic amp tones. In 1996, the company also began offering a line of amplifiers that incorporated their technology. Shortly afterwards, the Line 6 company began to make use of the increasingly powerful and increasingly inexpensive DSP technology in their amplifiers to create software that modelled the interaction of guitar amp components and their effect on the signal. In the late 1990s, they placed this software in a red, kidney-shaped container called the POD. It gave guitarists emulations of numerous amplifier sounds, cabinet and speaker types, as well as a range of vintage and modern effects. Other companies followed suit, and soon Vox, DigiTech, Johnson, Fender, Behringer and others were offering tabletop modellers

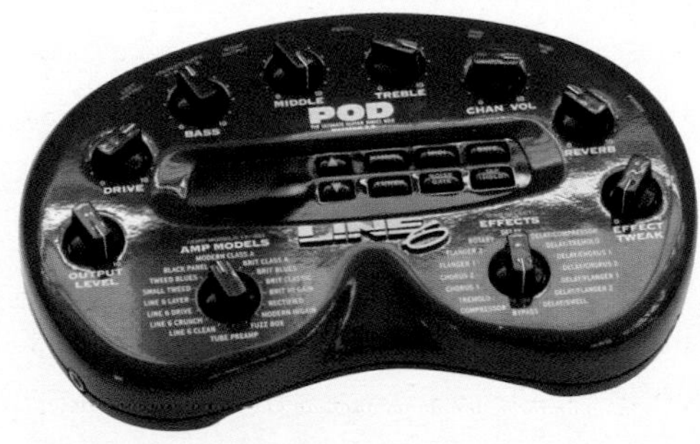

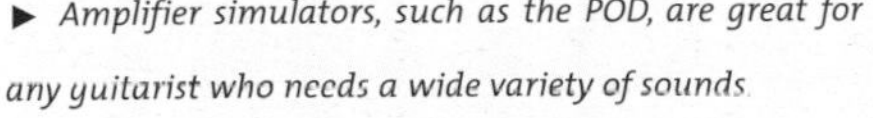

▶ *Amplifier simulators, such as the POD, are great for any guitarist who needs a wide variety of sounds.*

Complete Guitar Handbook

and/or amplifiers, making it possible to reproduce various sounds live without carting a van of amps.

SOFTWARE

The first Line 6 product was actually Amp Farm, a plug-in for Pro Tools TDM recording systems (exclusively). Plug the guitar into the board, and Amp Farm displays pictures of virtual Fenders, Marshalls and Vox amplifiers as it changes straight guitar tone into one resembling the results of plugging into a miked

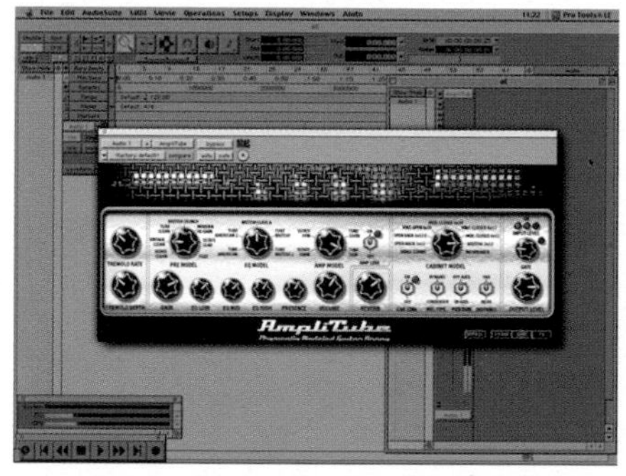

▲ *IK Multimedia AmpliTube is a popular amplifer simulator.*

amplifier. An advantage of software modelling is that it is possible to record guitar parts and not commit to the final amplifier, or tone, until the final mix. For other recording systems, there is now similar software available, like IK Multimedia's Amplitube and Native Instruments' Guitar Rig. In fact, modelling software has become a part of most recording packages, hardware or software.

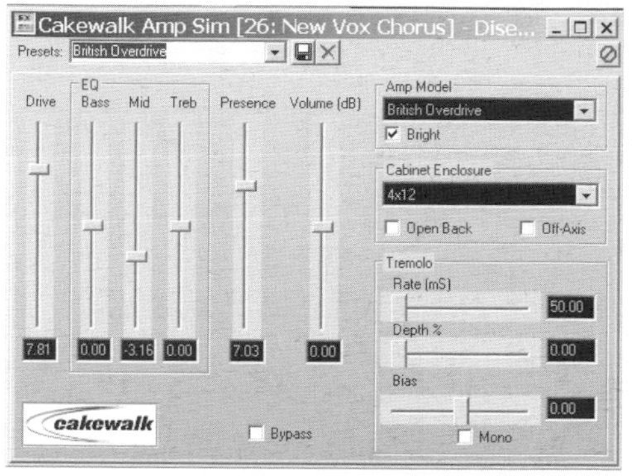

▲ *Cakewalk features Amp Sim, a guitar amplifier simulator.*

The reaction to modelling has been much the same as the one to digital recording. Just as die-hard tape fanatics are yielding to the convenience and affordability of digital recording, amplifier aficionados have caved in to the convenience of modelling. Does it sound like the real thing? Played solo, head to head, few will contend that a modelled vintage amplifier sounds exactly like the original. But in a mix or played live with a band, it sounds close enough – at least millions think so.

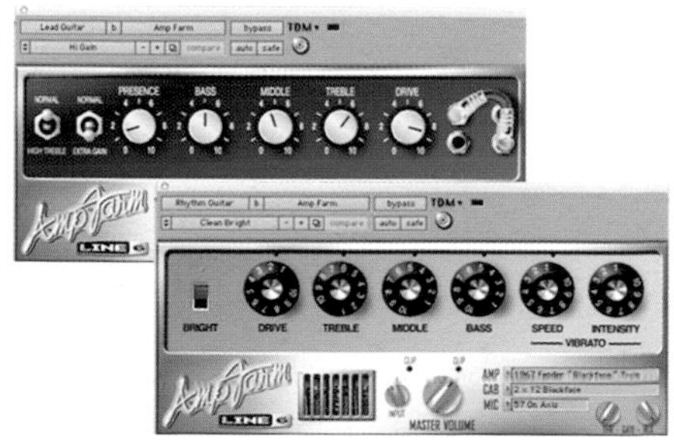

▲ *Software modelling using a plug-in like Amp Farm allows you to record guitar parts and not commit until the final mix.*

Section Four: Reference

SET-UPS AND SOUNDS

Which amplifiers you buy depends on many factors. Do you have money, or room, for only one? Are you playing with a band or playing just for fun at home? Do you play just one kind of music or many?

▲ *Combo amplifiers are a combination of amplifier and loudspeaker and as a result are more portable and convenient.*

WHAT SOUND DO YOU WANT?

Different styles of music require different amplifiers. Country, jazz and funk need clean tones, often at high volume – an amplifier with plenty of 'headroom' (60–100 watts), such as Fender's Twin Reverb, works best. Rock or pop rock requires good crunch tones, and warm distortion. The amp should clean up

▲ *For metal, a Peavey Triple XXX amplifier will provide the necessary high output and edgy distortion.*

◀ *A Fender Twin Reverb amplifier works best with any music that requires clean tones at high volumes.*

Complete Guitar Handbook

when guitar volume is backed off, and distort smoothly when it is turned up. Examples include the Fender Super Reverb, Vox AC30 and the Marshall 50-watt heads or combos. For metal, especially live, you want high output and edgy distortion, so consider Marshall 100-watt stacks, Mesa Boogie Rectifiers or Peavey Triple XXX models.

REMEMBER YOUR GUITAR!

When buying an amplifier, be sure to bring the main guitar that you will be playing. You don't want to judge it with a guitar that doesn't sound like yours. If there is a return policy, try to play it in your rehearsal space or on a gig – you never really know how an amplifier sounds until you play it in context. If not, try to go to the shop early on a weekday – at a quiet shopping time they might let you crank up the volume a little.

Don't get hung up on price, brand or mystique. There are plenty of relatively inexpensive amplifiers, like Fender's Junior and Hot Rod series or Marshall and Vox's solid-state amplifiers, that sound terrific at bargain prices. There are also pricey boutique amps that don't cut it.

SAY NO TO GIMMICKS

Remember that great basic tone is far more important than bells and whistles. You can always add distortion and other outboard effects later, but if the amplifier's unadorned sound doesn't do it for you, no amount of add-ons will make it better. Actually, the best test of an amplifier is to play through it clean, without any reverb or other effects. If you are not tempted to reach for the reverb knob, you have a winner.

Finally, trust your ears; if you think that it sounds good, it does sound good. There is no arbiter of tone. This is part of your musical voice and should reflect your particular taste, not some consensus.

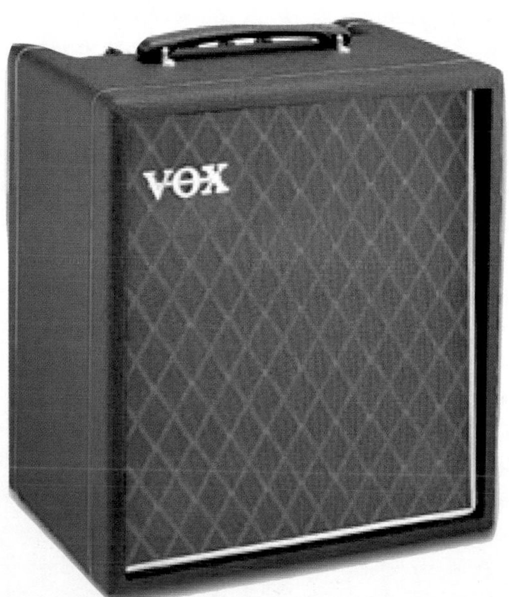

◀ *Vox amps, used by everyone from Status Quo to Suede, range from the affordable to the pro.*

Section Four: Reference

REAL WORLD RIGS

Most professionals agree that the ideal guitar tone comes from owning the perfect amplifier for the music and playing it at its optimum volume. Ideally you would own amplifiers in different sizes and tonal colours, bring them all to each gig, and play the one that matches the tune and the venue. Unfortunately, few of us have that luxury.

If you play primarily only one style of music you should start with an amplifier that is best suited to that style. It is better to have too much headroom than too little; you don't want to be caught in a situation where the amp is distorting more than you wish.

POWER ATTENUATOR

Amplifiers – even solid-state ones – sound best when they are pushing their output stages. Sometimes achieving this requires louder volume than the venue permits. One solution is a Power Attenuator. This plugs in between your speaker output and your speakers, allowing you to push your output stage, then lower the final volume. If you use a separate amp head, another trick is to use a cabinet with higher impedance than is recommended for the amp, this will act similarly to an attenuator. (NEVER use a cabinet rated lower than the amp.) If you tour with a band in a controlled sound situation, using a lower wattage amp put through the PA will result in a better overall band sound, giving the engineer more control over the mix. Also, keep in mind that a small amp can sound huge in the studio.

For players who cover many musical styles, manufacturers offer versatile amplifiers that can handle any and all of them, as well as many playing situations. They feature master volumes that permit high gain distortion sounds at low volumes, and plenty of effects options. As we have seen, modelling amplifiers also offer different amplifer tones in one package.

▶ *Even a small practise amplifier can come to life with a microphone in front of it.*

Complete Guitar Handbook

Most multipurpose amplifiers feature multiple channels with control knobs marked gain, volume and/or master. Usually one channel will be optimized for clean sounds and the other for distortion. Sometimes the 'clean' channel has both gain and volume controls so that you can get mild distortion sounds from it as well, and still higher gain sounds from the overdrive channel.

▲ *A metal player, such as Steve Harris of Iron Maiden, would most likely select a clean or distorted channel on his amplifier.*

SAMPLE SETTINGS

STYLE: COUNTRY

Channel: Clean

Settings: Gain-3 Treble-7 Mid-5 Bass-5 Master-10

STYLE: JAZZ

Channel: Clean

Settings: Gain-2 Treble-3 Mid-7 Bass-7 Master-10

STYLE: FUNK

Channel: Clean

Settings: Gain-4 Treble-9 Mid-4 Bass-5 Master-10

STYLE: ROCK

Channel: Clean

Settings: Gain-9 Treble-6 Mid-7 Bass-7 Master-8

Channel: Distortion

Settings: Gain-3 Treble-6 Mid-7 Bass-7 Master-6

STYLE: POP

Channel: Clean

Settings: Gain-5 Treble-6 Mid-4 Bass-7 Master-10

Channel: Distortion

Settings: Gain-7 Treble-6 Mid-7 Bass-7 Master-8

STYLE: METAL

Channel: Clean

Settings: Gain-8 Treble-6 Mid-4 Bass-7 Master-10

Channel: Distortion

Settings: Gain-10 Treble-9 Mid-3 Bass-9 Master-10

These settings are all starting points – feel free to experiment. Virtually all major amplifier manufacturers offer a variety of channel-switching amplifiers, in all sizes, making it easy to find one to suit your needs.

Section Four: Reference

SET-UPS OF THE STARS

▲ *Fender amplifiers have been used by many guitar legends.*

Below you will find information about the equipment used to help create the classic tones of some the world's most famous guitarists. Like the rest of us, these players often try out new and different rigs; but their signature tone came from a combination of this gear and their distinctive touch.

JEFF BECK

Beck has played Les Pauls, Stratocasters and Telecasters through very few effects, including a Pro-Co Rat, a delay, a wah-wah and either Fender or Marshall amplifiers.

ERIC CLAPTON

Clapton has often changed musical styles, at times playing a Les Paul into a Marshall 2 x 12 combo, a Stratocaster through a Pignose portable amplifier and a Fender Champ ('Layla'), and in more recent years, a Stratocaster through Soldano and Fender-style amplifiers.

KURT COBAIN

Cobain's basic set-up consisted of plugging left-handed Fender Jaguars and Mustangs with humbuckers installed at an angle to the bridge into a Boss DS-2 Turbo Distortion and an Electro-Harmonix Poly-Flange, Poly-Chorus or Small Clone. He used a Big Muff pedal for distortion. His amplification consisted of a Mesa Boogie Studio or Quad preamp set clean, wired into a Crest 4801 power amplifer and a number of 4 x 12 speakers.

THE EDGE

U2's The Edge used an Electro-Harmonix Deluxe Memory Man to add multiple rhythmic delays to the signal put out by his Gibson Explorers or Fender Strats. More recently his huge rack has housed an array of analogue and digital effects, routed into multiple Vox AC30s.

ROBBEN FORD

Robben originated the smooth LA guitar tone playing a Gibson Super 400 archtop through a Fender Bassman. He later switched to Gibson ES-335s, the Fender Robben Ford model, and Baker guitars.

Complete Guitar Handbook

These go through a wah-wah and a volume pedal into a T.C. Electronic 2290 for chorus and delay, and a Lexicon PCM-70 for reverb, into a Howard Dumble amplifier.

JIMI HENDRIX

Jimi used his upside-down Fender Stratocaster through Fender, Sunn and Marshall amplifiers, creating an astonishing array of sounds with relatively few effects: Fuzz Face, Octavia, Uni-Vibe, and wah-wah, tape delay and flanging among them.

MARK KNOPFLER

Mark Knopfler, associated with the 'out-of-phase' Stratocaster sound, used a stock Strat early on but has since employed Schecter Custom Shop Strat copies, Strat style Pensa-Suhr guitars and a Gibson Les Paul. He has used Fender, Soldano, Jim Kelly and other amplifiers over the years.

PAT METHENY

Metheny modernized jazz guitar by adding ambience. Using multiple delays and amplifiers, he spreads his sound across the stage. His guitar synthesizer goes into a Synclavier for his harmonica and trumpet sounds. Originally using Acoustic solid-state amplifiers he now uses a Digitech multi-effects unit and his own monitors.

◄ *Pat Metheny uses a Digitech multi-effects unit.*

ANDY SUMMERS

Summers revolutionized pop guitar tone with an Electro-Harmonix Electric Mistress flanger, a Memory Man and an MXR Dynacomp compressor through mostly Marshall amplifiers.

EDDIE VAN HALEN

Eddie began playing his home-built guitars through Marshalls. Later he employed Peavey, Music Man and Charvel guitars bearing his name through Peavey 5150 amplifiers, along with MXR phasers and flangers.

STEVIE RAY VAUGHAN

An important ingredient in SRV's sound was his use of heavy-gauge (.013–.058) strings on his '63 Strat. He tuned down to E♭, and ran his signal through a Fuzz Face, Octavia, Ibanez TS808 Tube Screamer, wah-wah and Leslie rotating speaker cabinets on its way to combinations of Fender Vibroverbs or Super Reverbs, Marshalls and Dumble amplifiers.

Section Four: Reference

TO BEGIN

Whether your taste runs to Charlie Christian or Good Charlotte, there's a particular recording method that can make your guitar sound as good on playback as it does through your amplifier, though it will take practise and experience to achieve results similar to those of famous artists.

You probably first heard a guitar in a recording rather than a live performance. The second half of the twentieth century saw the guitar replace the piano as the dominant musical instrument in the western world, and the success of rock 'n' roll ushered in the big business of creating as many different guitar 'tones' as there are colours in a paint store.

▲ *Les Paul, guitar inventor and pioneer of multi-tracking recording techniques.*

Many thousands of records exist with guitar sounds for you to study, emulate and duplicate. Of course, the great guitar heroes came up with their own unique sounds, and your primary task when you're ready to record is to accurately capture the sound you've already created with either your chosen acoustic guitar or your preferred combination of electric guitar, amplifier and effects.

EAR TRAINING

Learning to recognize the relationship between notes on the scale by their sound is called ear training. But another kind of ear training is crucially important in becoming an accomplished guitar stylist, producer or recording engineer: learning to analyze the sound of your own gear and the guitar sounds you hear on records.

For example, you may know that Eric Clapton played a Gibson ES-335 when he was in Cream, but in later years he preferred the Fender Stratocaster. If you rush out and buy a 335 or a Strat 'off the

Complete Guitar Handbook

► *A good producer can turn a lacklustre performance of a song into a polished gem.*

shelf' and start recording with them, you'll have little chance of emulating Clapton's sound, let alone his reputation and success.

More study will inform you that the guitar sound of Cream came not only from the model of guitar, but also from the year it was made (1964), the type and design of its pickups, the string gauge, Clapton's preferred amplifier and of course the guitarist's style and technique. Repeated listening to the records of your favourite player will help train your ear to recognize the variety of tones the artist created with his own gear. But the guitar sound you hear is influenced by other factors as well.

THE RECORDING CHAIN

Because you know your favourite player best from his recordings, you must also factor in the equipment used at the recording sessions. This will include the type of microphone that captured the sound, the microphone preamp that was used to boost the level of the signal, the type of mixing console that was used to route the signal, and any number of outboard effects units used to enhance its quality.

The system of electronic devices through which the signal flows on its journey from guitar to tape (or, more likely, computer) is called the recording chain. A chain is only as good as its weakest link, so attention must be paid at every stop along the signal's way. The first stop – the selection and maintenance of your instrument – is the most important stage of recording. You should make sure your sound is at its best before you get anywhere near a recording studio. The rules are different for each guitar, but we can take a general look at the recording challenges facing players of electric and acoustic guitars.

◄ *Large-diaphragm microphones are versatile and will serve you better than lower-cost dynamic or condenser microphones.*

Section Four: Reference

ELECTRIC OR ACOUSTIC?

Although the acoustic guitar dates back centuries, the sound of electric guitar dominates modern records.

Electric guitar sound, which is often heavily processed by stompboxes and outboard effects devices, can create a wide variety of tones, but acoustic guitar typically creates a wider frequency response – the range of sound to which our ears can respond. Generally, in an acoustic guitar recording the 'lows' are lower and the 'highs' are higher. This is an important distinction when you begin to understand how recording engineers approach a mix.

▶ *Many of Joe Pass's great tracks were recorded using the simple combination of archtop guitar and amplifer.*

ELECTRIC GUITAR SOUND

Electric guitar used to sound similar to acoustic guitar. The earliest electrics sported pickups designed simply to amplify the natural acoustic tone of the guitar. Pioneer recordings by Charlie Christian and Django Reinhardt exhibit the result of this early approach as well as primitive recording technology.

Traditional jazz guitarists often play a semi-hollowbody archtop guitar that follows this tradition, such as the Gibson L-5. This type of guitar is usually matched with a simple amplifier designed to reproduce the rich archtop sound. It is almost never processed with extra effects, and emphasizes bass tones, sounding 'dark'. Classic examples can be heard on records by the jazz greats Joe Pass and Wes Montgomery.

The vast majority of modern players, however, prefer the solidbody electric. Thousands of recordings illustrate the endless range of solidbody tones, from the sultry fire of Carlos Santana, to the bright plucking of Nashville 'chicken pickers' like Brent Mason, to the seven-string thunder of virtuosos like Steve Vai. Despite the wide range of tones these electric players create, the universally

Complete Guitar Handbook

▼ *A versatile industry standard dynamic microphone like the Shure SM57 is an excellent investment.*

preferred way of capturing these sounds is to place a simple dynamic microphone in front of the amplifier's grille cloth.

Dynamic microphones work best with limited frequency ranges like those produced by snare drums and individual vocalists. Most modern electric guitar tones occupy a similar space in the middle of the audible frequency spectrum. This keeps guitar chords from competing with lower-frequency sounds like bass or higher-frequency sounds like female vocals or cymbals. It also helps an electric guitar 'cut through' a mix during a solo.

ACOUSTIC GUITAR SOUND

Conversely, acoustic guitar is more like a piano in that its bass notes can be very bass-y indeed and its high notes can approach a frequency range only dogs can appreciate. Although the *pitch* of notes is the same in electric and acoustic guitar, the *tones* are very different.

▲ *Use your ear to decide how to mike an acoustic guitar.*

The guitars of well-known players can sound as unique as those of electric guitarists, though typically with far less effects processing. Acoustic guitars can sound so thin and bright as to resemble an autoharp, an effect seemingly favoured by a number of Nashville producers, or comparatively dark, such as on classic rock recordings by the Beatles or Yes.

The most popular method for recording an acoustic guitar is to place at least one condenser microphone in an effective area between the lower body and neck of the guitar. Condenser microphones are more sensitive to tones at the extreme ends of the frequency spectrum.

▶ *Small-diaphragm condenser mikes record sensitive sounds.*

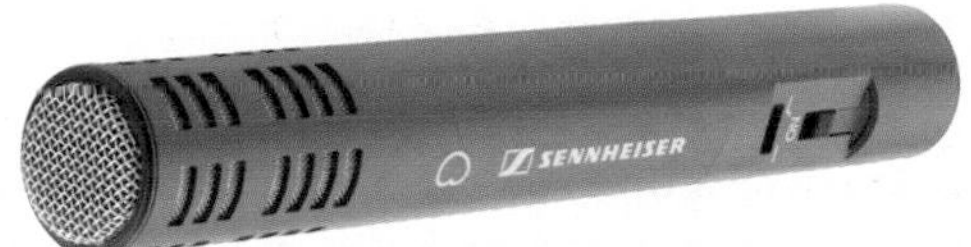

Section Four: Reference

PREPARING FOR THE STUDIO

Recording a performance or a song you've composed can be one of the most rewarding experiences of your musical life. The process is fun, and the recorded result can be an accomplishment in which you take a lot of pride – if everything goes well.

The trick is to determine the type of project early on in the process, and your exact role as a guitar player. Are you a sideman who's been hired to enhance someone else's work? Are you adding a crucial guitar part to your own demo, which has to be in the record company's hands tomorrow morning? Are you sitting around your own studio informally jamming with friends?

Different mindsets are required for these varying roles. The first example in the list given above, recording guitar parts for a producer in an outside studio, requires the most preparation on your part. Look at yourself and your guitar as an element of the process known as pre-production.

▲ *Recording in a professional studio can be a great experience.*

SHIPSHAPE

If you've been hired to work on a commercial recording, in some ways you have the easiest role. You don't have to worry about engineering, studio mechanics or gear maintenance (other than your own). In all likelihood you've been hired because your sound is good and the producer, songwriter or contractor who hired you likes your work.

In this case focus on your equipment and your playing. If you're an experienced session musician you're already prepared. Your guitar is in top shape, with new strings that are already stretched and broken in. The guitar's controls and pots are clean and noise-free. Your frets are well maintained, your neck is unbowed, and your head is on straight, so to speak.

Complete Guitar Handbook

▲ *Ensure your pickups are clean before entering the studio.*

Your guitar also stays in tune, and you can correct it quickly if it goes out. The poles of your pickups are matched, creating no uneven volumes between strings and no noise, other than what's expected with single-coil pickups. You may have even modified your guitar with hotter pickups or 'silent' single-coils from companies like EMG, Seymour Duncan or DiMarzio.

READY TEDDY

Your amplifier and accessories are also in top condition. Your amplifier sounds as clean and noise-free as the day it came off the assembly line. Your cables are short-run for the least signal degradation and you have high-quality spares, as you do of picks, straps and strings. (It is not a pretty sight when a commercial recording session stops dead because a guitarist has no spare high E string, or has left his strap at home.)

Most important, you are ready to play. You have warmed up before arriving at the studio or have done so unobtrusively during other studio pre-session activity. If you're not already familiar with the material to be recorded you are looking over a chart (printed music) of the piece.

Once your amplifer has been positioned and miked by the assistant engineer, you have positioned yourself where you can hear your amplifer and play comfortably. You have indicated any adjustments that need to be made to the mix in the headphones you've been given for monitoring the other musicians or previously recorded tracks. You know and are ready for your cues. It's time for the engineer to start rolling and press Record.

► *Make sure that you have fully prepared for your session in the recording studio in order to get the most out of it.*

Section Four: Reference

THE COMMERCIAL STUDIO

▲ *You can make gobos out of foam or any other thick material.*

A professional recording studio offers every aid a guitarist needs to make his or her sound the best it can be.

Some guitarists are much more than sidemen, handling the roles of engineer or producer as well. Even if you only want to work in a modest home-recording studio, you'll want to know your way around a professional facility.

THE LIVE ROOM

The live room – sometimes just called the studio – is a vanishing breed in the world of computer-based recording studios, but as long as live bands make records we'll still need the big galoots. Developed in the days when all recorded music required an orchestra, the live room is where musicians make noise. It is separated from the control room, where engineers can supposedly work in peace.

◀ *You may not need as much hardware as percussionist Evelyn Glennie, but some kit will be very useful.*

The band, ensemble, or orchestra sets up in the live room; microphones are set up to capture the individual instruments; and the microphones' cables connect to a multi-connector 'mic box', usually mounted on a wall in the live room. The cables connect to the mixing console in the control room.

Usually, all the studio's microphone stands are kept in the live room, as is the studio's grand piano, if it owns one. Often, you'll find tall moveable baffles known as

Complete Guitar Handbook

▶ *Even small studios may need a patch bay for routing signals.*

gobos, which are very important for controlling bleed from say, one extremely loud amplifier into the microphone of another extremely loud amplifier nearby, and vice versa. Since bleed can ruin a good recording, if a gobo doesn't provide enough isolation from other instruments a guitarist may have to set up in a different area, such as a vocal booth.

THE CONTROL ROOM

Every guitarist probably knows that the giant structure in the middle of a studio control room is the mixing console (see Signal Flow, page 336), but other elements in the control room are just as important to a successful guitar recording.

OUTBOARD GEAR

Usually housed in racks on a sidewall or in an island, outboard gear includes the standard 19-in (48.3-cm) wide 'effects boxes' that are used to enhance all audio signals. Rackmount effects include dynamics processors such as compressors and noise gates, along with true effects such as reverbs and digital delay lines. You will also find instruments such as samplers and synthesizer modules, as well as power amplifiers and sometimes even modified computers in racks.

THE PATCH BAY

The patch bay lets the engineer connect ('patch') any audio signal in the control room or live room to any other device that can accept the signal. This means you can hear your sound through the megabucks outboard reverb in the control room instead of the cheap reverb in your amplifier, if you wish, without moving from your playing position. The patch bay makes things much more convenient; without it you'd have to crawl into the tight spaces behind those racks every time you wanted to plug in a different piece of gear.

THE COMPUTER

The newest member of the standard studio control room – the computer – is now frequently the most important element of the commercial recording studio – as it is in the home studio. Besides replacing the tape recorder, the computer stores sounds, automates the mixing console, saves all the settings of gear used in the session and provides fun and entertainment during 'down time'. It still doesn't make the coffee though; that's what assistant engineers are for.

Section Four: Reference

HOME RECORDING

Guitar tracks are now frequently recorded in home studios, which provide relaxed, low-pressure environments for creating music.

In a home studio you can usually spend more time experimenting with various sounds, techniques and mix decisions. You can mix one section while you're tracking another. You can record whenever inspiration hits you rather than conform to a set schedule. Best of all, you can leave your Marshall stack set up and not have to haul it to another studio!

▲ *A computer with the appropriate sound card, sequencer software, virtual instruments and plug-in effects is essential.*

However, staying focused on an important project when the distractions of home and family are close by can be difficult. To be as efficient as possible, approach a home-recording project as you would a session at an outside studio.

ORGANIZE YOUR WORKSPACE

It's easy to let your home studio become as dishevelled as your bedroom. But a messy, disorganized workspace inhibits the music-making process. You may feel completely at home with that old pizza box underfoot, but do your band-mates or clients feel the same way?

A knack for tidiness is even more important when it comes to session-critical items like computer files, CDs of important data, adaptor plugs and other recording paraphernalia. Designate an identifiable space for similar items (like a drawer for unlabelled CDs and tapes), and use it!

CONTROL YOUR ROOM

Although a thorough discussion of studio design, acoustic treatments and soundproofing is beyond the scope of this book, an acceptable recording

Complete Guitar Handbook

▶ *Commercial studios use professional gobos, but even hanging heavy blankets will help keep signals in and noise out.*

environment can be set up without you having to make a major investment in either labour or materials.

For starters, most residential living rooms and bedrooms are usable natural recording spaces. Rooms with carpets, couches, drapes and other absorbent materials control unwanted reflections and enable an average guitar or voice to sound pretty good.

Commercial recording studios have an advantage in the areas of sound isolation and treatments for problems like bass build-up in the corners of a room. Of course there are other reasons your bedroom won't sound as good as Abbey Road, but for recording demos, some simple tasks can improve the results:

1. Choose your work area wisely. If you're setting up a studio in a bedroom, use a corner (preferably against exterior walls) for your workstation and monitors. Try various placements for your amplifier, angling it up if necessary to hear its sound at ear level. Keep blankets handy to help isolate an amplifier microphone from any ambient noise in the room.

2. Find the 'sweet spot'. Keep your monitors at least a foot or two from surrounding walls. Listen to a familiar CD in various parts of the room. If the sound is different every few steps or in one particular area, experiment with workstation and furniture placement until you find the best spot for your monitors.

3. Use a small amplifier. These days, combo amps with one small speaker can sound frighteningly similar to concert stacks. Consider using a guitar processor such as the Line 6 POD to avoid miking an amplifier at all. Chances are the convenience and quality will more than make up for the loss of your beloved amplifier's sound.

For more on studio set-up techniques, see the companion volume, *The Illustrated Home Recording Handbook*.

Section Four: Reference

STUDIO RECORDING

Your role as a guitarist in a recording session may be as simple as adding a syncopated single-note background rhythm to a complex production, or it may be to perform multiple parts in a completely guitar-based arrangement. Either way, getting the sound on tape involves the same process.

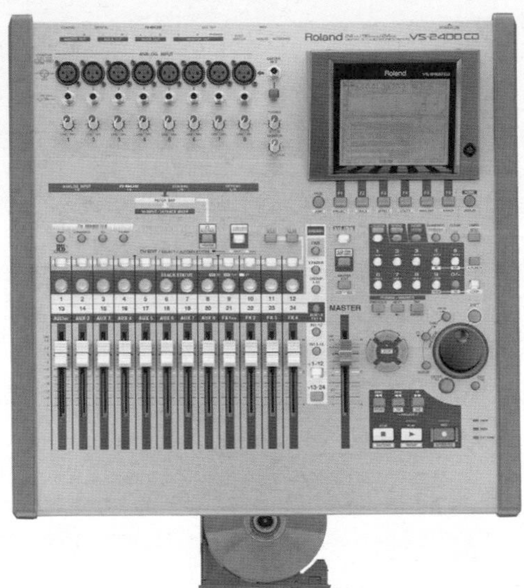

▲ *The Roland VS-2400 CD, which can record up to 24 tracks of 24-bit/48-kHz audio simultaneously.*

With your equipment ready to go and the music in your head or in print on a music stand, you will begin recording at the beginning of the song or punch in (resume recording somewhere in the middle of a track you've already begun).

Two methods of working have dominated the way guitarists record: working with engineers in a commercial studio and recording by themselves in a home studio. The environment may dictate the type of equipment you use.

If you have prepared wisely, your instrument, amplifier and effects already form an efficient system that sounds exactly the way you and the producer want it (see pages 342–343). It is now the recording engineer's job to get that sound on to a recording medium, most likely a digital audio recorder or workstation (DAW). The DAW may be a dedicated personal digital workstation (PDW) such as Yamaha's AW2816 or Roland's VS-2400CD. However, it's more likely that you'll be recording to a computer application with supporting hardware, such as one of Digidesign's Pro Tools systems, Steinberg's Cubase or Nuendo, or MOTU's Digital Performer.

GOING DIGITAL

Any digital recording system converts the analogue signals created by your guitar rig into binary code, the ones and zeros that computers understand. These

Complete Guitar Handbook

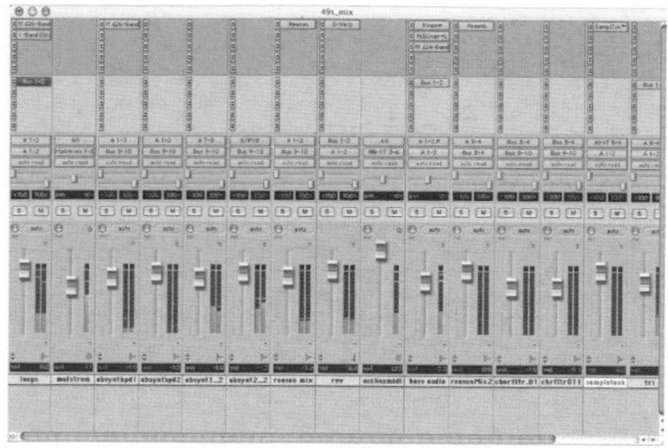

◀ *Digidesign's Pro Tools is the market leader, and is able to record and play back multiple audio tracks simultaneously.*

days that conversion may take place in the computer, in an add-on card, in a separate unit (audio interface) that is connected to the computer, or in the guitar rig itself.

While you are playing along with the song, the digital converters are doing their job and the recording application is sending the converted data to the computer's hard drive. The recording application is designed to function just like a multi-track tape recorder, allowing you to record on individual tracks and perform overdubs as you listen to previously recorded tracks. The application also works like a conventional analogue mixer, allowing you to route individual tracks to digital signal processors (DSP) called plug-ins, before combining these processed tracks into a final stereo or surround mix.

▶ *Many engineers prefer the sound of tape reproduction over digital, as produced by the Otari MTR90 24-track tape recorder.*

STICKING WITH ANALOGUE

You might own or work at a studio that still uses an analogue recording system based upon a multi-track tape recorder. Many people feel that printing analogue signals on tape imparts a warm quality to the audio signal that is preferable to the sound created by digital recorders. However, the guitar sound you've created is more likely to become altered and possibly degraded by all but the most sophisticated (and increasingly rare) analogue recorders.

Successful analogue recording requires wide tape (2-in/5-cm tape for multi-track recording) and a fast tape speed (15 or 30 in/38 or 76 cm per second) or a noise-reduction system such as those made by Dolby or dbx to compensate for noise and loss of fidelity generated by thin, slow-moving tape. Maintenance issues and the high cost of supplies are all factors that have made analogue recording an unattractive option in an age of more affordable and pristine-sounding digital equipment.

Section Four: Reference

SIGNAL FLOW

The various paths your guitar sound can take through a recording system before it becomes part of a final mix on a CD are determined by your mixing console or computer, depending on which one gets the signal from your guitar rig first.

Recording engineers must learn the concept of signal flow, which is crucial to understanding how a mixing console (or the mixing console simulation in your software) works.

The diagram on page 337 shows how an audio signal like that from your guitar rig travels through a mixer and is routed to various destinations to enhance the signal's quality before being deposited on one or more tracks of a multi-track recorder. The same pathways are also options after recording, when the recorded signal is combined with other signals to produce a final mix.

If you are recording from the direct output of an amplifier or guitar processor, the line-level signal enters the input section of a mixer channel. If your amplifier is miked the weaker microphone-level signal enters the preamp section of that mixer channel, where the signal is boosted before continuing its journey. Some mixers provide an instrument-level input for plugging your guitar directly into the board. But most modern guitarists prefer some sort of extra processing of the sound before the signal reaches the mixer or computer, so this is a less common option.

After you've chosen the correct output from your rig and connected the proper cable to it, the signal enters a channel of your mixer or the recording interface connected to your computer. If you're using a mixer, you have the option of further analogue processing before routing the signal to the recorder. If you're using a computer audio interface, the signal will be digitized at this point and all processing will now take place in the digital domain, usually through the use of plug-ins – small auxiliary programs that open within your recording application.

The Focusrite TrackMaster is a good purchase as it possesses both pre-amplifier and channel-strip functions.

Complete Guitar Handbook

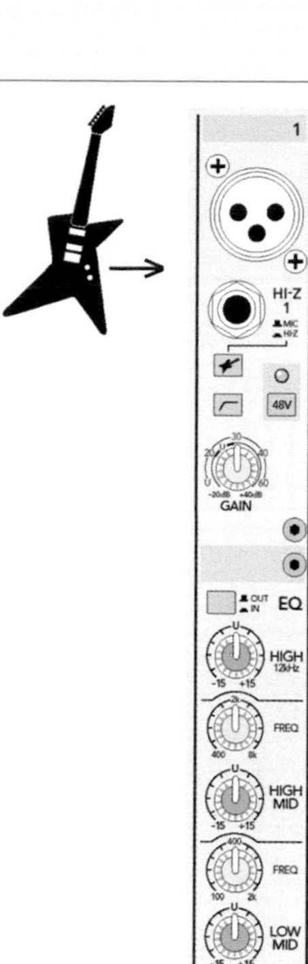

PREAMP SECTON
The signal from your guitar rig enters a mixer's preamp.

If a guitar or amplifier is miked, the signal enters a mixer channel at the 3-pin XLR input.

The signal from a guitar processor or amp's 'direct out' enters the channel's Line Input.

Some mixers have Instrument Inputs, into which a guitar can be plugged directly.

The incoming level can be boosted or cut on modern mixer channels.

EQ SECTION
After the preamp section, the signal enters the EQ section, where its tone can be adjusted.

Modern mixer channels allow control over several frequency bands to shape the sound of the guitar.

The EQ circuitry can usually be defeated or bypassed to ensure the cleanest possible signal.

AUX SECTION
At this point the signal can be sent out of the mixer along with signals from other channels.

This is usually done to send several channels to one device, such as a reverb unit or headphone amplifier.

This mixer can provide four different sub-mixes to external devices.

OUTPUT SECTION
The output section determines the final status of the signal before it reaches the main mix or 'stereo bus'.

The signal may be panned to position the sound in the stereo field, or it may be assigned to an 'aux bus', usually used to control the level being sent to an external recorder.

On this mixer, pressing the Mute button sends the signal to the aux bus.

Finally, the channel fader controls the level sent to the stereo bus or, on this mixer, to the aux bus when the Mute button is pressed.

Section Four: Reference

PERFORMING

The quality of your playing can sometimes suffer when you're also wearing the hats of producer and recording engineer. Simplify your recording system so it requires as little attention as possible when you're recording that important track.

Inexperienced guitarists often find the pro recording studio a daunting experience. But when you trade the pressure for the control you exercise in your own studio, another set of problems arises. How do you operate the controls of a recording system when you're playing your instrument? How can you hear the mix in your monitors when your amplifier is so loud? How do you communicate with your band and engineer at the same time?

ON LOCATION

The easy solution to most of these problems is to enlist the help of others. If you're a sideman working in an outside studio, let the engineer or producer handle the logistics of recording while you concentrate on your performance. Good preparation is the best prescription. Make sure you and your rig are ready to go, learn the material in advance, and set up your rig according to the engineer's instructions.

When recording, bear in mind that technical flaws like squeaky strings, noisy pots and badly voiced chords generate noises that will show up in the mix. These may not have been apparent when you were playing in your bedroom or jamming with the band. You don't want a producer, engineer or fellow musician staring at you wondering why all your retakes are slowing down the work and costing somebody (perhaps you) time and money. Thoroughly practising and preparing before the session starts avoids that nightmare.

HOME SWEET HOME

If you are the producer and engineer you will not only have to get a good performance but also solve the technical problems that occur in the session.

Here are some tips for handling common challenges when recording at home.

1. Use guitar processors or modellers for recording. Units like the Line 6 POD have revolutionized guitar recording by giving the player access to dozens of simulated guitars, amplifiers, speaker cabinets and effects in small desktop cases that can be transported anywhere. They generate great

Complete Guitar Handbook

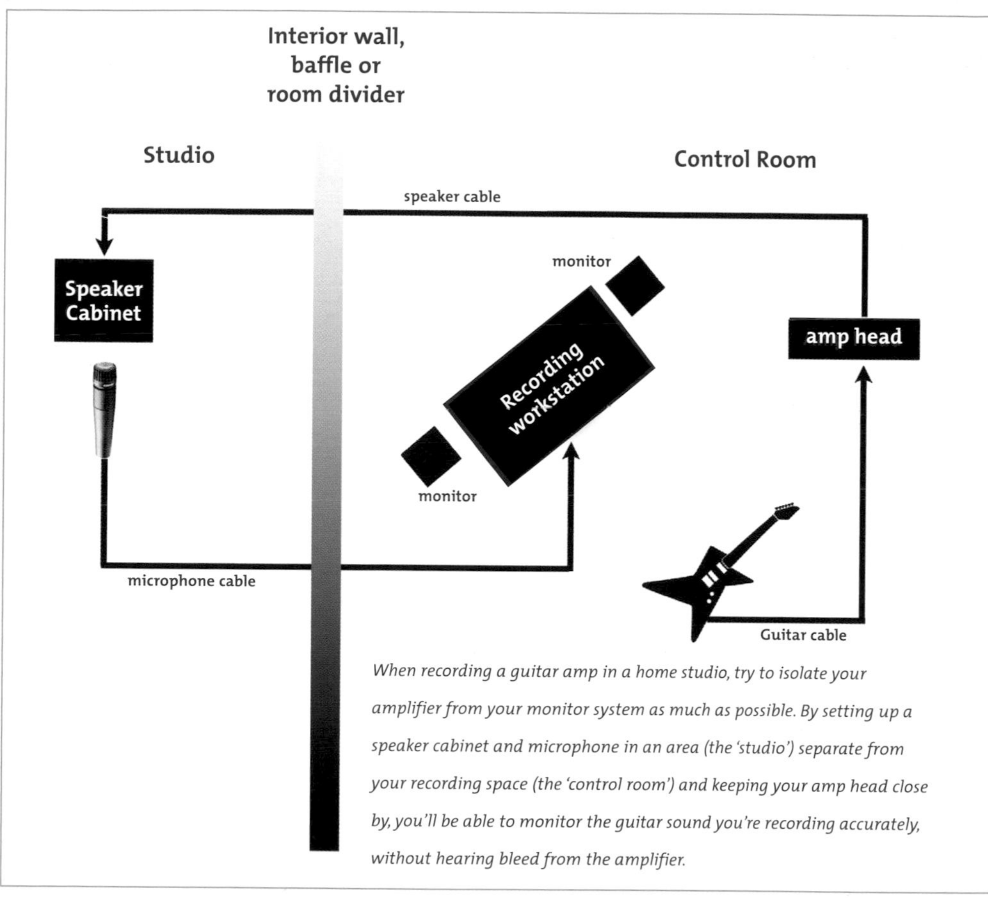

When recording a guitar amp in a home studio, try to isolate your amplifier from your monitor system as much as possible. By setting up a speaker cabinet and microphone in an area (the 'studio') separate from your recording space (the 'control room') and keeping your amp head close by, you'll be able to monitor the guitar sound you're recording accurately, without hearing bleed from the amplifier.

sounds that could take you days to duplicate when miking an amp in your home studio. It is easy to sit at your recording workstation and alternate between operating the recorder and playing.

2. Isolate your amplifier. If you're only happy with the sound of your own amp and speaker cabinet, you'll get the best results by placing the amp in a room separate from your recording area. This works best with a two-piece amp like a Marshall stack, because you can keep the head with you in the control room and run speaker cable to the cabinet. Place the speaker cabinet in a closet or bathroom, position microphones and run the cables back to your recorder or mixer. Now you can control the amplifier's sound by listening to it through your studio monitors. You'll only need to leave the control room if you have to reposition the microphone.

MIXING

Creating a final mix has always been more art than science, but the modern guitarist has more options than ever for getting his sound right before recording and during mixdown.

Assuming your sound was the best it could be before recording and you've executed your parts to your or the producer's satisfaction, what other options will be present for fine-tuning your sound after recording?

PLUG-INS

Traditionally, guitarists got the best sound they could before recording, sometimes using stompbox versions of signal-processing tools like compression and gating to even out and clean up the signal. Although a more dramatic effect like phase shifting or flanging would be considered so crucial to the sound that it would be recorded with the guitar part, usually these effects would be reserved for mixdown, where they could be better controlled while maintaining the fundamental guitar part that was recorded.

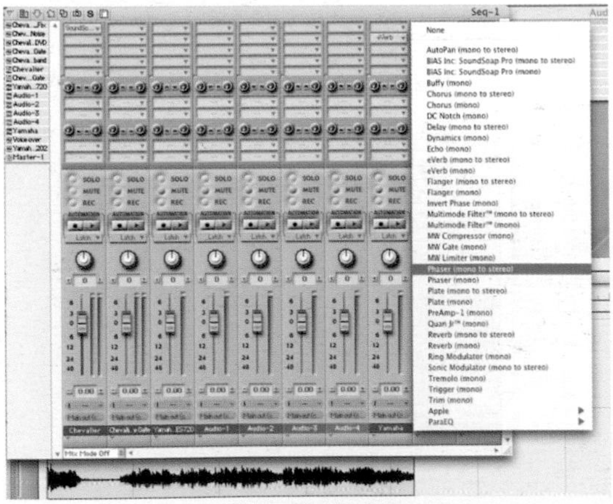

Digital recording allows scores of effects to be auditioned and employed at any step of the process. (See pages 346–347.) A guitar can be recorded 'bone dry' into the computer and processed later by dynamics or effects plug-ins, completely altering the character of the original guitar sound.

Because digital recording is a 'non-destructive' process, the original part can be referred to at any time. An effect will be accessed during a mix by selecting it from a list of effects that accompanies the guitar track in the recording application. A recordist has access to any effect imaginable without keeping a roomful of outboard effects on the premises.

◀ A channel strip pull-down menu allows you to add any number of effects to your original recording.

Complete Guitar Handbook

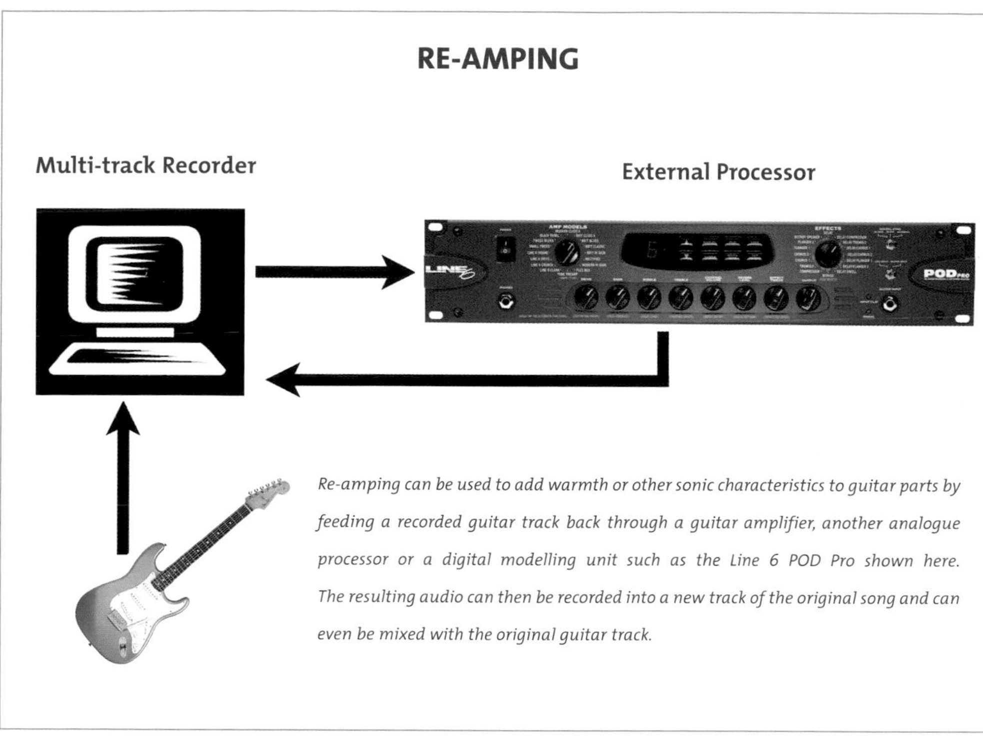

RE-AMPING

During mixdown, guitar tracks can also be routed back to amplifiers from a recorder. This is increasingly becoming a popular method for injecting a warmer sound created by analogue equipment into digitally recorded tracks. If the processing amp has digital inputs and outputs, re-amping means you can use a digital amplifier to reprocess a signal without converting it back to analogue, thereby maintaining the integrity of the digital signal. This might be a good option when taking previously recorded tracks to a different studio for mixing.

▲ *A mixer, hard or soft, can be intimidating. Nuendo's mixer allows the user to configure it to his or her own needs.*

Section Four: Reference

GETTING A GOOD SOUND

A successful recording session begins the same way as a successful performance – by getting not only a good sound but also a sound that's right for the project at hand.

As with any other technique related to guitar performance, a thorough command of your sound requires practice, and well-known recording stars who are guitarists have practised for years, honing their sound and making adjustments to enhance their identifiable style or to fit new music trends. Today, because of 'modelling' devices, a guitarist can have an unprecedented wealth of sounds for recording at his fingertips.

ACOUSTIC GUITAR

If you play acoustic guitar exclusively, you may own a collection of guitars with unique tones. That makes it much easier to pick the right sound for a recording session. Body size, body shape, type of strings and string gauge all affect the guitar's sound. Certain acoustic guitars are more 'boxy' sounding than others, which means that the guitar's tone exhibits greater response in the lower mid-range frequencies around 400 Hz. Other guitars, such as large dreadnoughts and jumbo models with a deeper bass, a brighter high-frequency response and a subdued mid-range can sound full and rich in a solo setting.

However, the full, rich solo sound is not necessarily the best choice for recording with other instruments, a fact that illustrates one of the cardinal rules of

Complete Guitar Handbook

recording: a sound that is beautiful by itself, or when 'soloed' in a mix, is not necessarily the best sound *in* the mix, where an instrument needs to occupy its own sonic 'space'. A guitar with lots of bass or high-frequency content can interfere with other instruments in those frequency ranges and turn the entire mix to mud!

If you don't own a collection of acoustic guitars, be prepared to modify your guitar's tone during the miking or mixdown process. Either process may require some trial and error to get the right sound for the job. The process starts with the guitar itself.

ACOUSTIC-ELECTRIC GUITAR

Before you tackle the art and science of miking an acoustic guitar, consider an alternative that may provide the sound you want – the acoustic-electric guitar. These guitars have built-in electronics and an output jack that enables you to connect the guitar directly to a mixer or audio interface. The primary means of creating the signal is either through the use of a specialized magnetic pickup mounted in the guitar's soundhole or a piezo transducer mounted in the bridge.

The acoustic-electric is very popular for stage use because it allows the player freedom of movement from a microphone stand. Its unique character is often fine for recordings where an aggressive, biting acoustic sound is appropriate. However, many acoustic players, especially those playing traditional folk or country styles, would never consider an acoustic-electric for studio work.

Still, the convenience of a direct output, the ability to adjust EQ from the guitar itself, and its unique sound all add up to make the acoustic-electric a viable choice in many cases. It can work very well in mixes that require some acoustic guitar flavour rather than authenticity.

► *Acoustic-electric guitars produce a crisp, acoustic sound with plenty of sustain and little feedback.*

◄ *Acoustic artists such as James Taylor will have different guitars to suit different musical styles and playing requirements.*

Section Four: Reference

ACOUSTIC GUITAR MIKING

The most important decision in recording acoustic guitar, besides picking the guitar itself, is choosing the right microphone.

There are as many ways to mike an acoustic guitar as there are guitars themselves. However, getting a pro-quality sound has become easier in recent years as the price of high-quality condenser microphones has come down.

DIAPHRAGM MICROPHONES

Condenser microphones in general capture a wide frequency response with excellent detail, and have traditionally been the preferred choice for acoustic guitars. A condenser with a small diaphragm (less than 1-in/2.5-cm diameter) generally has a faster transient response than a microphone with a large one. Engineers associated the large-diaphragm microphone with a warmer sound, and those microphones became the most popular choice for vocals. Small-diaphragm condensers enjoy a similar popularity for recording acoustic guitar.

For many years Neumann was the acknowledged leader in producing high-quality small and large diaphragm condensers, such as the KM 184 and U 87. Today there are many high-quality, affordable alternatives including those from AKG, Audio-Technica, Shure, Soundeluxe, Studio Projects and many others. Both types of condenser can provide excellent results on acoustic guitar.

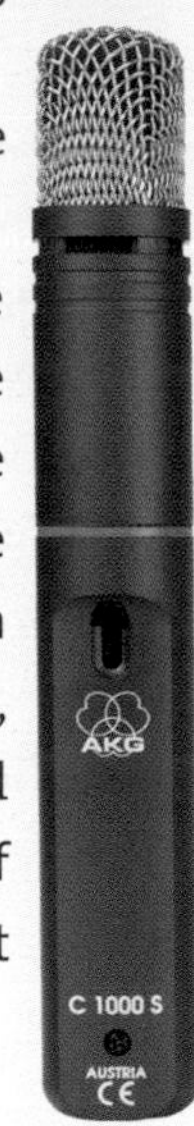

▲ *Condenser microphones are perfect for acoustic recordings.*

POSITIONING

The best microphone position for an acoustic guitar will depend on your style of playing, the ambience of the room, and the guitar itself. Because you cannot totally isolate yourself from the guitar in order to monitor its sound in your control room, recording the acoustic guitar yourself is one of the most challenging tasks for the guitarist and/or engineer. Some trial and error is therefore unavoidable.

◀ *Condenser microphones are far more sensitive than dynamic microphones and so are used to record quiet or subtle sounds.*

Complete Guitar Handbook

A standard procedure for miking acoustic guitar involves using two small-diaphragm condenser microphones. One microphone is placed about 6–8 in (15–20 cm) from, and pointed at, the soundhole. Another microphone is positioned opposite the neck and pointed towards the upper frets. If a third microphone is available, it can be placed 3 ft (1 m) or further away to pick up some of the natural reverberation in the room. All three microphones are mixed to create one composite signal that is recorded.

This is only a starting point . Most home recordists cannot dedicate three microphones to this task, and many have to use the same large-diaphragm condenser for acoustic guitar that they use for vocals. There is no magic 'sweet spot' for microphones. The most important job in placing the microphone is getting the sound as good as it can be in the room first. That may involve wall coverings to control reflections, several changes of playing position, and lubricants to control squeaky chairs, microphone stands or visitors.

ACOUSTIC GUITAR MIKING

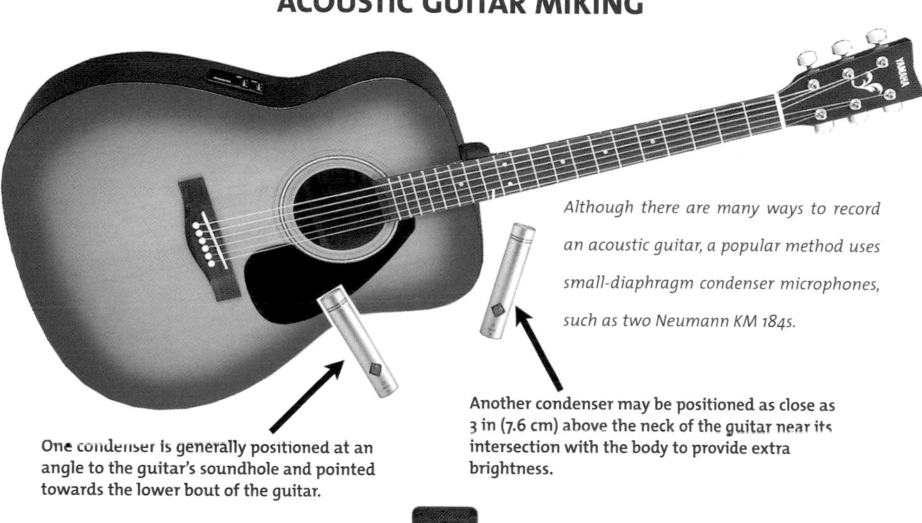

Although there are many ways to record an acoustic guitar, a popular method uses small-diaphragm condenser microphones, such as two Neumann KM 184s.

One condenser is generally positioned at an angle to the guitar's soundhole and pointed towards the lower bout of the guitar.

Another condenser may be positioned as close as 3 in (7.6 cm) above the neck of the guitar near its intersection with the body to provide extra brightness.

In some cases, a large-diaphragm condenser, such as a Neumann U 87 will be positioned 6 ft (1.8 m) or more away to capture room ambience. The signals from all three microphones will be mixed to create the recorded sound.

Section Four: Reference

ELECTRIC GUITAR MIKING

Practise will introduce nuance into your playing and give you a range of tones that can be created by the simple interaction of your fingers, your pickups and your amplifiers. After that, it's stompbox time!

By now you have learned many different ways to start off with the guitar sound you want. Single-coil pickups with five-position selector switches on Stratocaster-style guitars sound very different from dual-humbucker Les Pauls and the model's various knockoffs, which sound very different from single pickup archtops.

But your chosen guitar does not start to shine until you've matched it with the right amplifier, solid-state or tube, piggyback or combo. Even with the right amplifier (see pages 308–323), your guitar sound will come alive when you begin to understand and develop a knack for using a whole range of effects, which might include compression, distortion and delay (see pages 120–143).

Of course, effects don't have to come from stompboxes like the popular ones made by BOSS and others. You can use a studio's outboard compressor or digital delay unit. Often, though, guitarists consider these units too clean and prefer to use an effect they've tailored to their playing style on live gigs. If that's your method (and if your amplifier is like one of your children, never to be separated from its instrument and effect siblings) then you'll want to mike the amplifier.

MIKING YOUR AMP

Most studio engineers prefer to use a small dynamic microphone (or two), such as the hugely popular and time-tested Shure SM57 on a combo amp or cabinet stack. Dynamic microphones are rugged and are able to handle high sound pressure levels (SPL), which make them well-suited for loud sound sources like 1,000-watt amplifiers and 200-pound drummers! Though generally able to capture less detail than condenser microphones, dynamic microphones often don't need to. Heavily compressed and distorted lead guitar sounds and crunchy rhythm parts tend to occupy a limited frequency range in the middle of the spectrum. Dynamic microphones seem to enhance the warmth and fire that most electric guitarists want.

Complete Guitar Handbook

▲ *Most recording engineers get good results miking a combo amplifier such as the Fender Twin reverb with a single dynamic microphone, like a Shure SM57, positioned about 3 in (7.6 cm) in front of the amp's grille and pointed towards the outside area of the speaker's cones. With larger amplifiers, multiple-microphone set-ups may be used, and as with acoustic guitars, a condenser microphone may be used to capture some of the natural room ambience contributing to the amplifier's sound.*

Dynamic microphones like the SM57 are 'front address', meaning that the capsule faces out the end of the microphone. (Large diaphragm condensers like the Neumann U 87 or AKG C 414 models are 'side address' microphones.) Generally a dynamic microphone will be placed on a stand 6–12 in (15–30 cm) from the amplifier or speaker cabinet's grille cloth. Best results are often obtained by angling the microphone toward the outside edge of a speaker's cone rather than dead centre, but once again, experimentation, trial-and-error and experience will be necessary to optimize your guitar sound in your studio.

Different styles of music create different amplifier requirements.

Section Four: Reference

THE FINAL MIX

In the modern studio, many new options are available for creating an entirely unique sound that separates you from other guitarists.

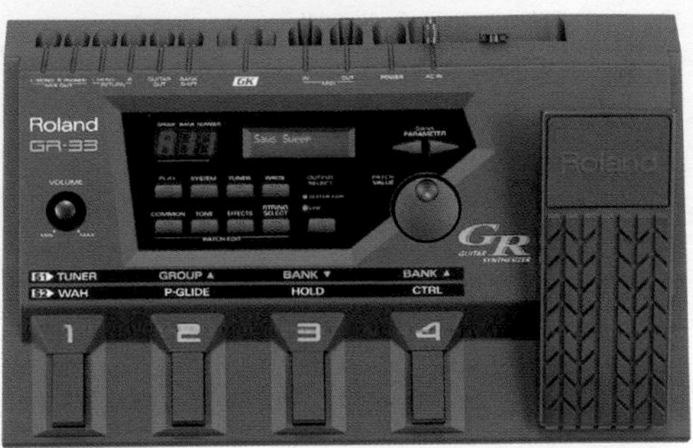

▲ *A Roland GR-33 guitar synth deals with the problem of string vibrations in a very compact package.*

Though traditional acoustic guitar and amp miking techniques still dominate record production, a guitarist has many new tools for modifying his or her sound and creating new ones.

GUITAR SYNTHESIZERS AND CONTROLLERS

For decades companies have sought to free creative guitarists from the sonic limitations of string vibrations. Early versions of guitar synthesizers suffered from tracking problems, the inherent latency in converting a string vibration into a signal (and later a computer instruction) that could control the broad palette of sounds available through synthesizers. But Roland achieved the greatest refinement of the process and success with its GR series of guitar synthesizers. At the beginning of 2005, the company's GR-33 guitar synthesizers possessed the internal architecture of an entire JV-1080 synthesizer module.

Roland also developed emulation technology that brought the sounds of multiple guitars, amplifiers, speaker cabinets and even pickup models and alternate tunings to players using the company's VG (virtual guitar) line of processors and amps with the GK series add-on pickups.

The VG devices could also be driven by the built-in piezo bridge pickup of other guitars with 13-pin outputs, such as the Brian Moore Guitars' iGuitar. This set-up enables you to summon up realistic versions of the sound of any guitarist from Jimi Hendrix to Joe Satriani and beyond while playing your favourite axe.

SOFTWARE HEAVEN

Whether your recorded guitar sound comes from a miking job or a guitar processor or synthesizer, the development of digital processing gives the computer-

Complete Guitar Handbook

◀ *Guitar amp plug-ins, such as Guitar Rig, give a technology friendly guitarist more options then ever before..*

savvy guitarist more tools than ever before. After concentrating on conventional effects like reverbs and delays, software programmers turned their attention to guitar-oriented plug-ins. Pro Tools, the first and most popular digital audio platform in commercial studios, led the way with Line 6's Amp Farm for Pro Tools TDM-based systems.

TDM requires costly external hardware, but many guitar plug-ins and stand-alone applications are now available for host-based audio programs such as Cubase, Logic and Digital Performer, which may be able to utilize various plug-in platforms such as VST, AU or MAS. In early 2005, some of these plug-ins included IK Multimedia's Amplitube, Native Instruments' Guitar Rig and Apple's Guitar Amp.

These plug-ins allow you to bypass hardware amps and effects, and create or remix your sound using only the plug-in's processing power either before or after recording. After assigning your guitar input to a track in the recording application, a pull-down menu is generally the means of selecting the plug-in you wish to use. You can also record a dry guitar signal and call up the plug-in during mixdown to select amp models, compression and distortion levels and other effects.

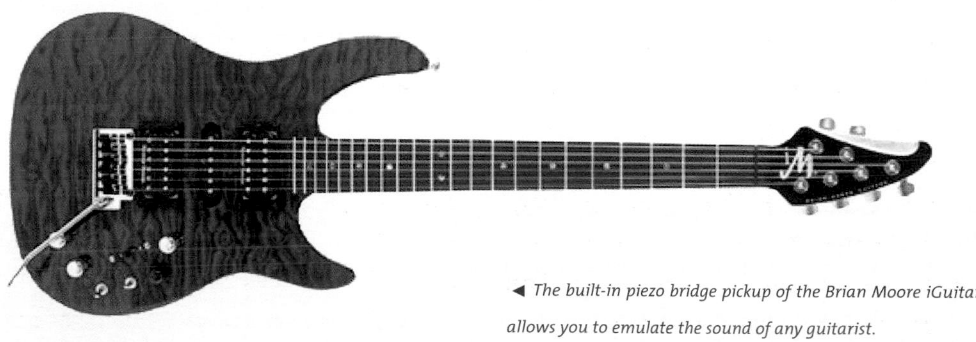

◀ *The built-in piezo bridge pickup of the Brian Moore iGuitar allows you to emulate the sound of any guitarist.*

Section Four: Reference

SECTION FIVE

CHORD DICTIONARY

The chord fretboxes in this section will help you learn the shapes of hundreds of chords, and will be a useful reference guide when you are playing and composing your own music. These next few pages are by no means comprehensive, but should contain enough chord formations for you, whatever your needs.

While learning the fingerings might not seem particularly interesting, you should remember that the wider your chord vocabulary becomes, the more you will be able to vary your compositions and your playing style. If you jam with other musicians, it is very important to know your chords – you don't want to be struggling to find the right fingering when the leader shouts 'G'!

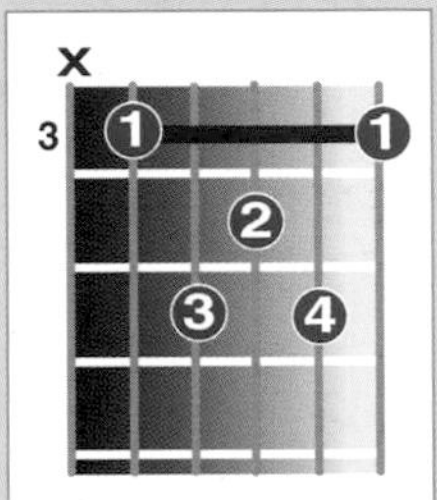

Cmaj7 C Major 7th
1st (C), 3rd (E), 5th (G), 7th (B)

The chords are divided by key, from A to G♯, with the key's notes shown at the bottom of the right-hand page. There are two double-page spreads devoted to each key. The first spread outlines the main chords you will need to learn, each shown in three different fingerings or positions. It can be useful to know a variety of positions for each chord, especially when fitting them into a progression – when you are playing in high fingerboard positions, you do not want to have to stop and scramble about, trying to find a chord position back on the first few frets.

The second spread shows some of the more advanced chords that can be useful when playing progressions, for linking chords or for use when you are improvising. There are only two positions shown for these, so as to include a greater variety of chords.

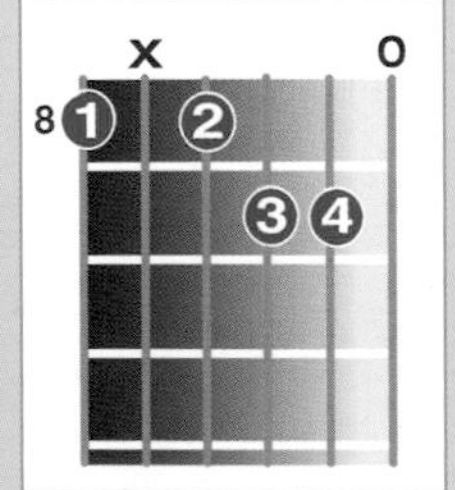

C7♯5 C Dominant 7th ♯5
1st (C), 3rd (E), ♯5th (G♯), ♭7th (B♭)

Complete Guitar Handbook

All the diagrams show the guitar fretboard in an upright position, with high E on the right. The nut appears at the top if the chord is played on the lower frets. If the chord is in a higher position, the fret number on which it begins is given to the left of the diagram.

The notes to be played are shown as circles, with the finger number that should be used for each note (❶= index finger; ❷ = middle finger; ❸ = ring finger; ❹ = little finger). An **X** above the string indicates that the string should not be played in the chord and should be muted to prevent it sounding accidentally. An **O** above the string shows that it should be played as an open string.

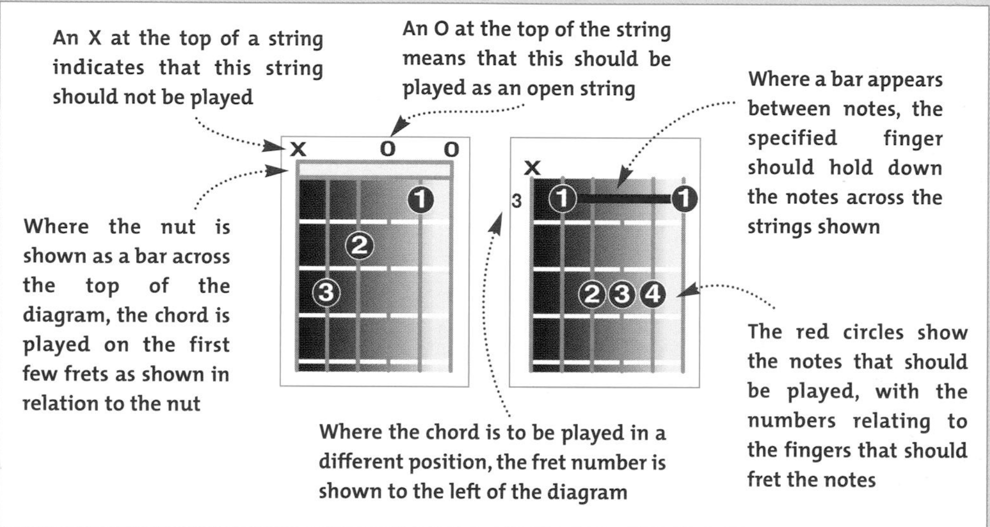

This section should not be difficult to use. Where there is a choice of note name (e.g. C♯ or D♭) we have selected the one that you are more likely to come across in your playing.

Where a chord contains a flattened (♭) or sharpened (♯) interval (e.g. ♯5th), you can find the notes by playing a fret lower (for a flat) or a fret higher (for a sharp) than the interval note indicated at the top of the page. In the keys that contain a large number of sharps or flats, double flats (♭♭) and double sharps (x) sometimes occur in the augmented or diminished chords. A double flat is the note two frets below the named note, while a double sharp is two frets up.

A MAIN CHORDS

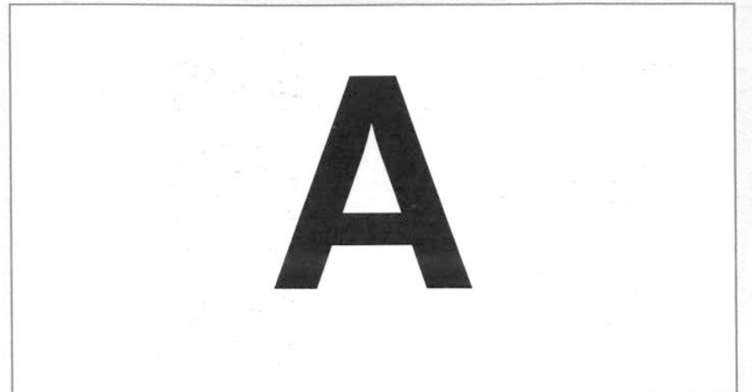

A A Major
1st (A), 3rd (C♯), 5th (E)

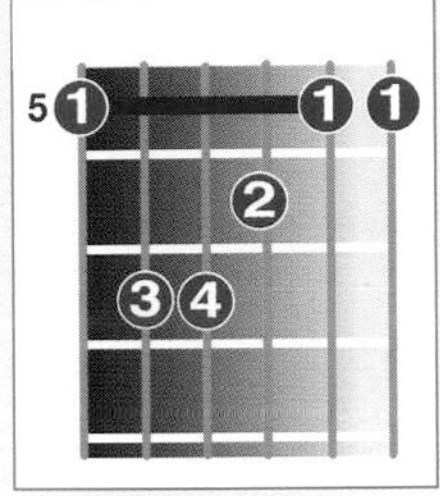

A A Major
1st (A), 3rd (C♯), 5th (E)

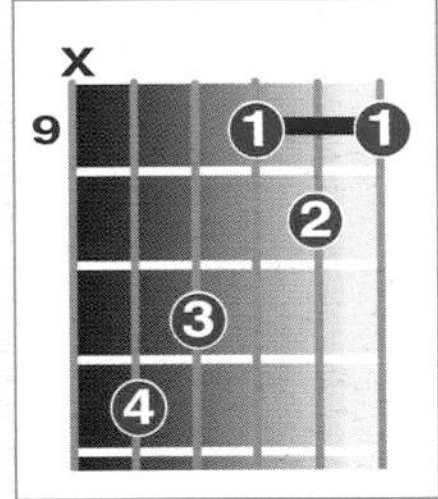

A A Major
1st (A), 3rd (C♯), 5th (E)

Am A Minor
1st (A), ♭3rd (C), 5th (E)

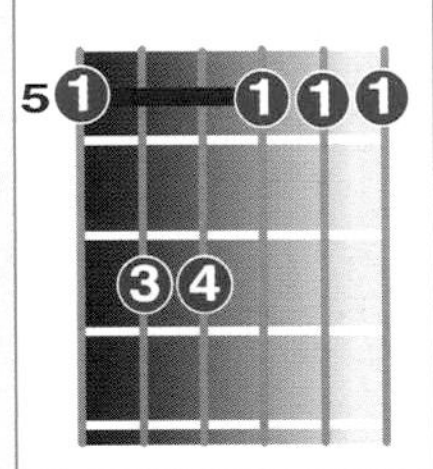

Am A Minor
1st (A), ♭3rd (C), 5th (E)

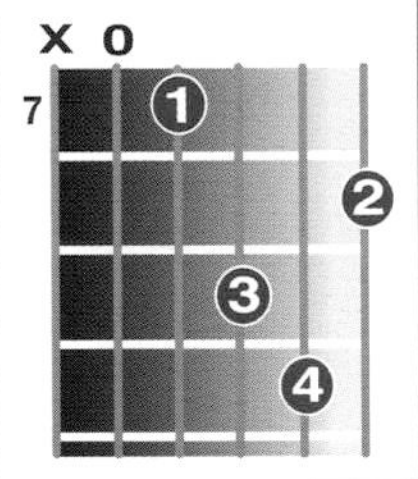

Am A Minor
1st (A), ♭3rd (C), 5th (E)

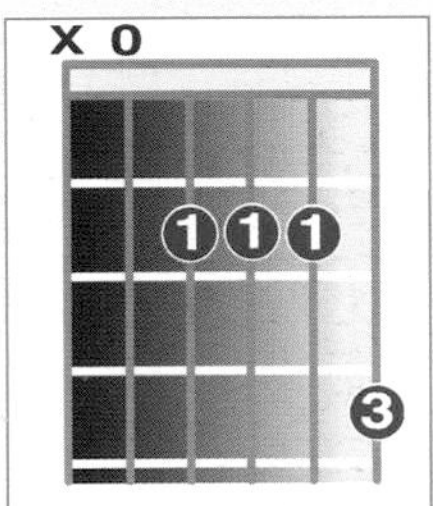

Amaj7 A Major 7th
1st (A), 3rd (C♯), 5th (E), 7th (G♯)

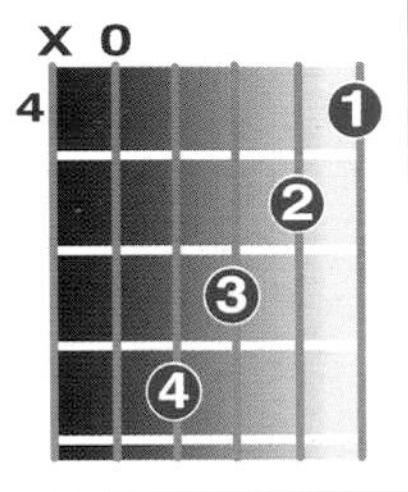

Amaj7 A Major 7th
1st (A), 3rd (C♯), 5th (E), 7th (G♯)

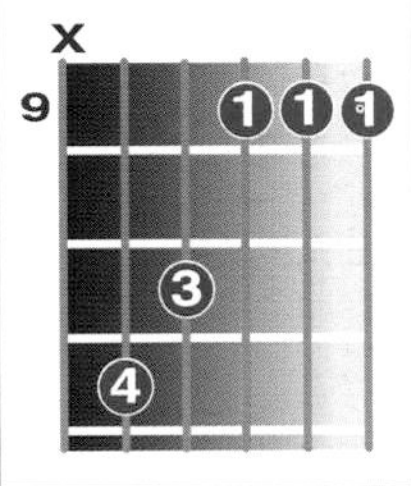

Amaj7 A Major 7th
1st (A), 3rd (C♯), 5th (E), 7th (G♯)

Am7 A Minor 7th
1st (A), ♭3rd (C), 5th (E), ♭7th (G)

Am7 A Minor 7th
1st (A), ♭3rd (C) 5th (E), ♭7th (G)

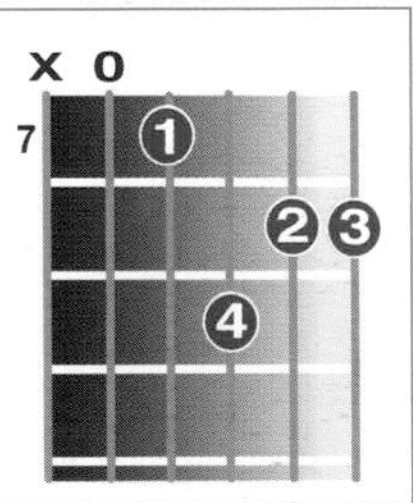

Am7 A Minor 7th
1st (A), ♭3rd (C),5th (E), ♭7th (G)

Asus4 A Suspended 4th
1st (A), 4th (D), 5th (E)

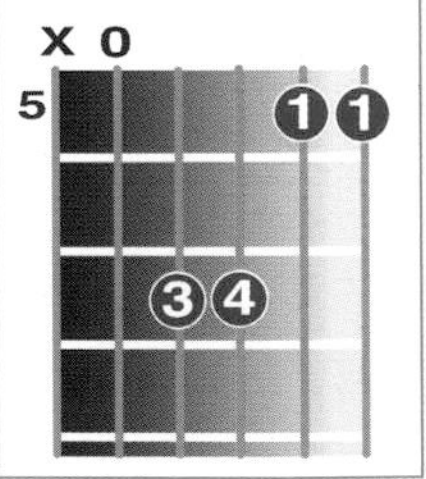

Asus4 A Suspended 4th
1st (A), 4th (D), 5th (E)

Complete Guitar Handbook

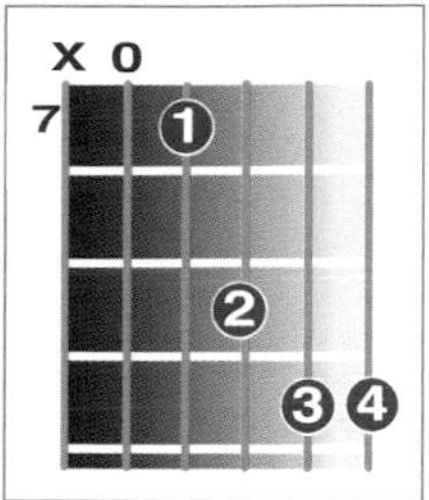

Asus4 A Suspended 4th
1st (A), 4th (D), 5th (E)

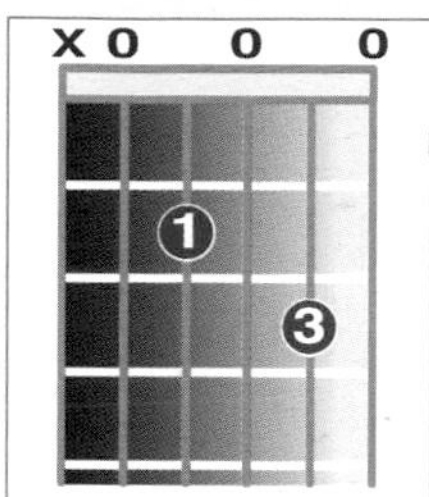

A7sus4 A Dominant 7th sus4
1st (A), 4th (D), 5th (E), ♭7th (G)

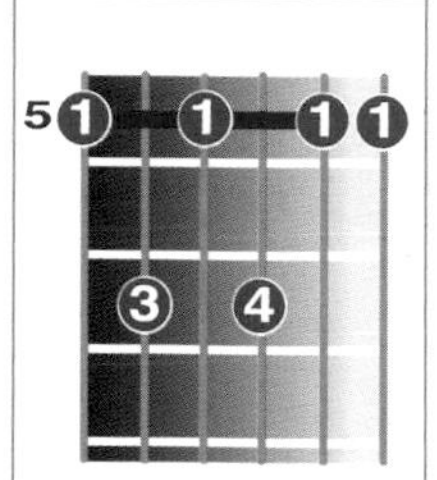

A7sus4 A Dominant 7th sus4
1st (A), 4th (D), 5th (E), ♭7th (G)

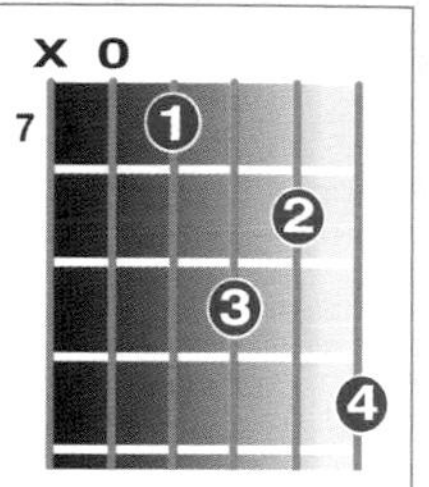

A7sus4 A Dominant 7th sus4
1st (A), 4th (D), 5th (E), ♭7th (G)

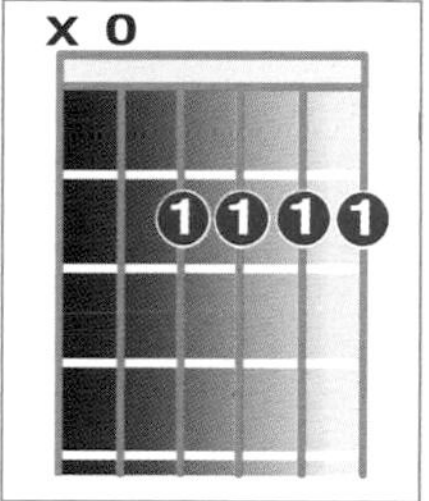

A6 A Major 6th
1st (A), 3rd (C♯), 5th (E), 6th (F♯)

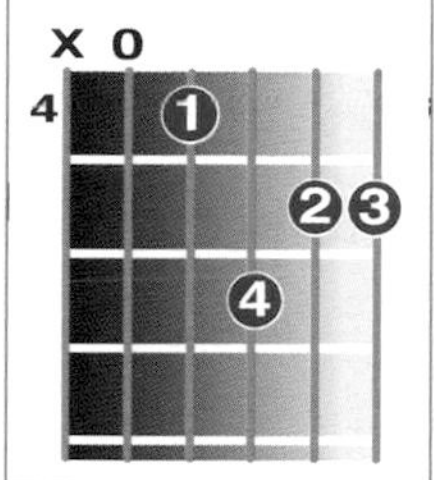

A6 A Major 6th
1st (A), 3rd (C♯), 5th (E), 6th (F♯)

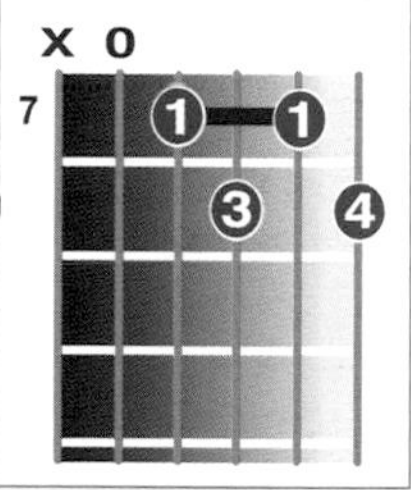

A6 A Major 6th
1st (A), 3rd (C♯), 5th (E), 6th (F♯)

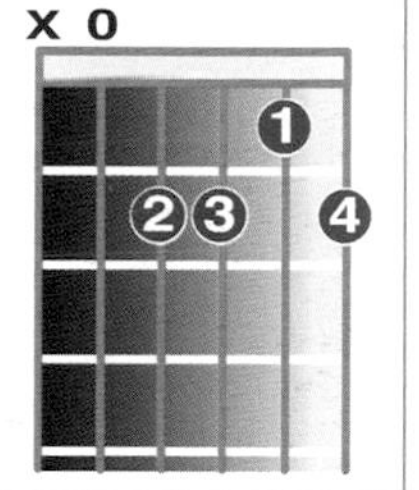

Am6 A Minor 6th
1st (A), ♭3rd (C), 5th (E), 6th (F♯)

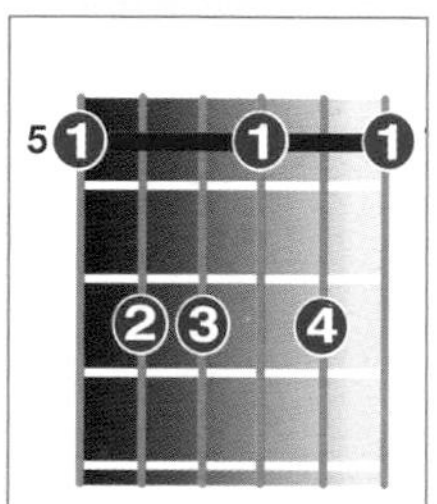

Am6 A Minor 6th
1st (A), ♭3rd (C), 5th (E), 6th (F♯)

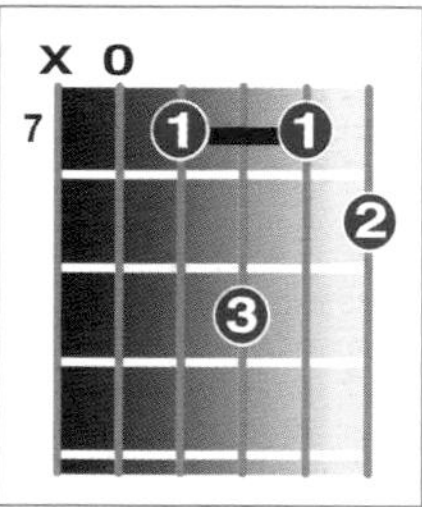

Am6 A Minor 6th
1st (A), ♭3rd (C), 5th (E), 6th (F♯)

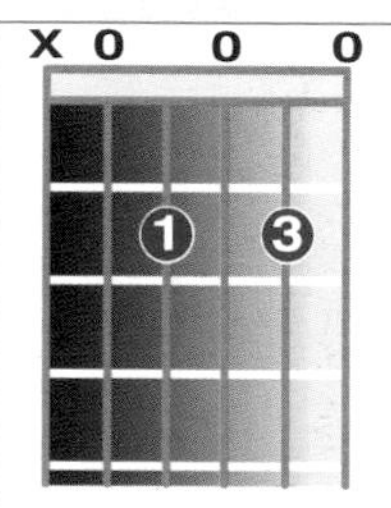

A7 A Dominant 7th
1st (A), 3rd (C♯), 5th (E), ♭7th (G)

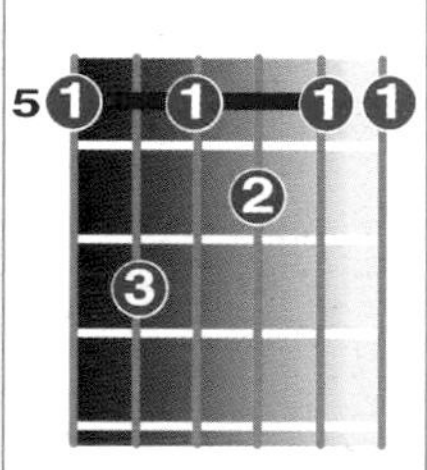

A7 A Dominant 7th
1st (A), 3rd (C♯), 5th (E), ♭7th (G)

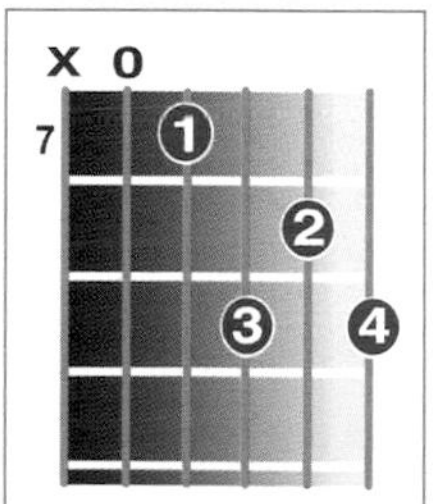

A7 A Dominant 7th
1st (A), 3rd (C♯), 5th (E), ♭7th (G)

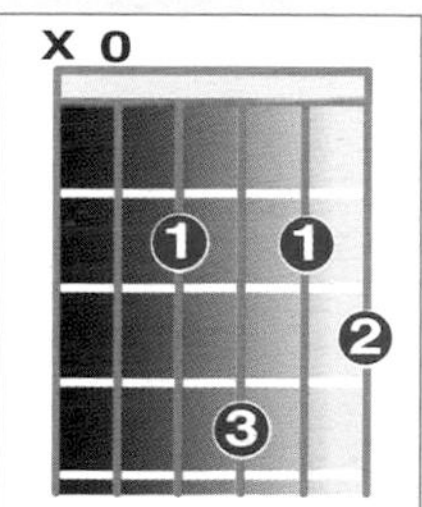

A9 A Dominant 9th
1st (A), 3rd (C♯), 5th (E), ♭7th (G), 9th (B)

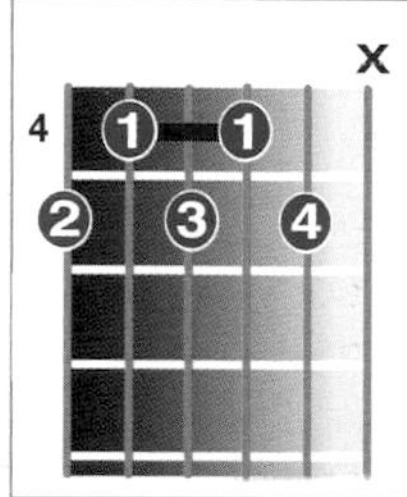

A9 A Dominant 9th
1st (A), 3rd (C♯), 5th (E), ♭7th (G), 9th (B)

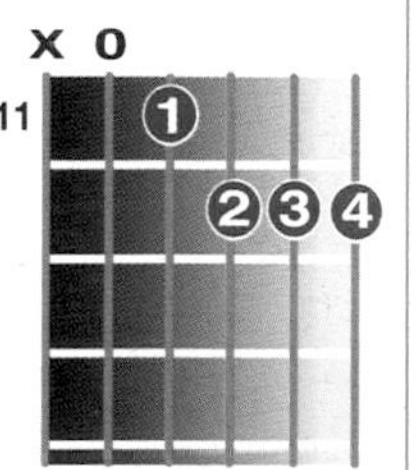

A9 A Dominant 9th
1st (A), 3rd (C♯), 5th (E), ♭7th (G), 9th (B)

Section Five: Chord Dictionary

A ADVANCED CHORDS

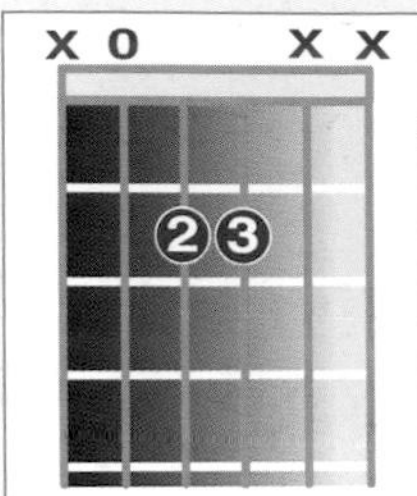

A5 A 5th (power chord)
1st (A), 5th (E)

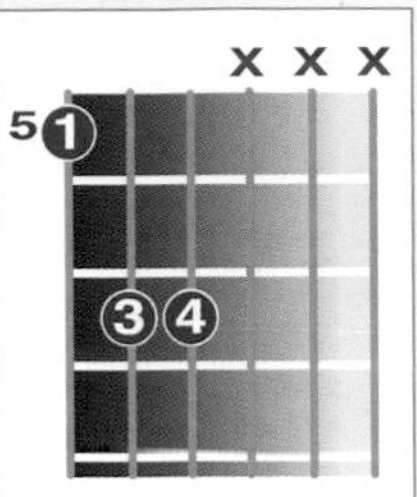

A5 A 5th (power chord)
1st (A), 5th (E)

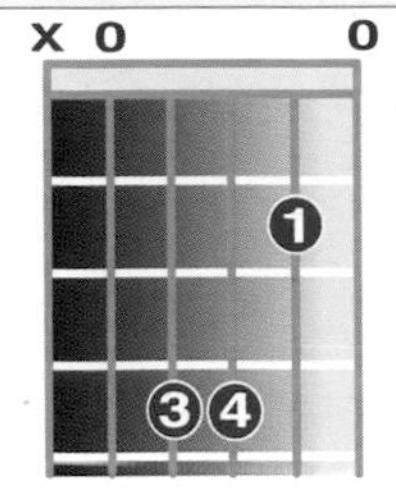

A 6/9 A Major 6th add 9th
1st (A), 3rd (C♯), 5th (E), 6th (F♯), 9th (B)

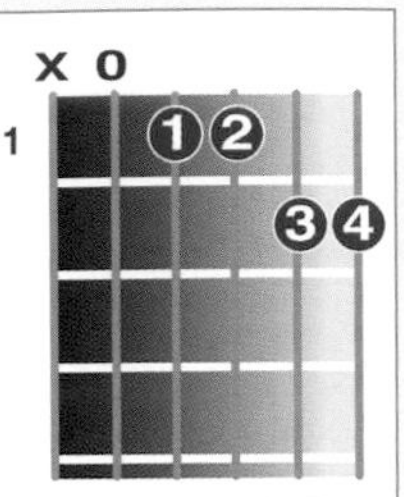

A 6/9 A Major 6th add 9th
1st (A), 3rd (C♯), 5th (E), 6th (F♯), 9th (B)

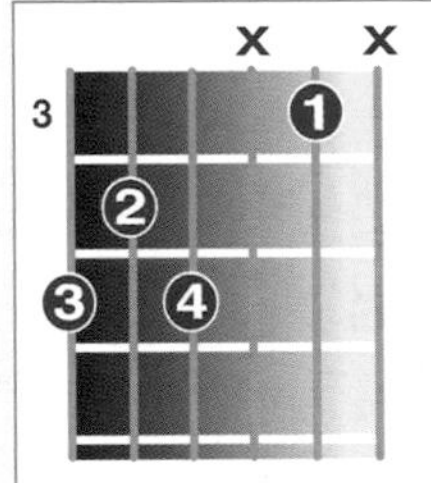

A11 A Dominant 11th
1st (A), 3rd (C♯), 5th (E), ♭7th (G), 9th (B), 11th (D)

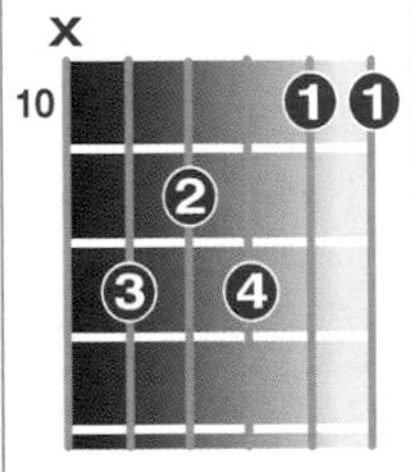

A11 A Dominant 11th
1st (A), 3rd (C♯), 5th (E), ♭7th (G), 9th (B), 11th (D)

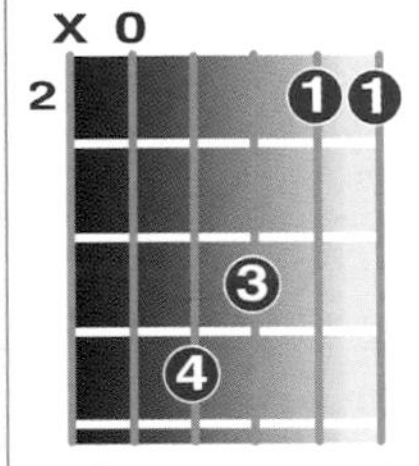

A13 A Dominant 13th
1st (A), 3rd (C♯), 5th (E), ♭7th (G), 9th (B), 13th (F♯)

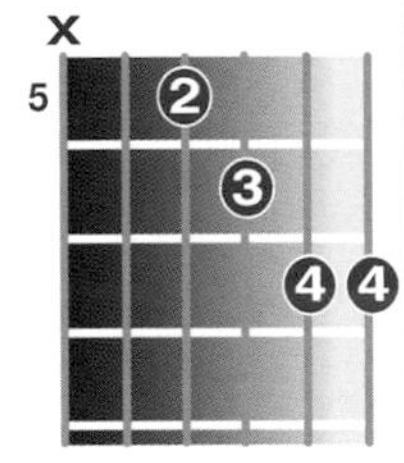

A13 A Dominant 13th
1st (A), 3rd (C♯), 5th (E), ♭7th (G), 9th (B), 13th (F♯)

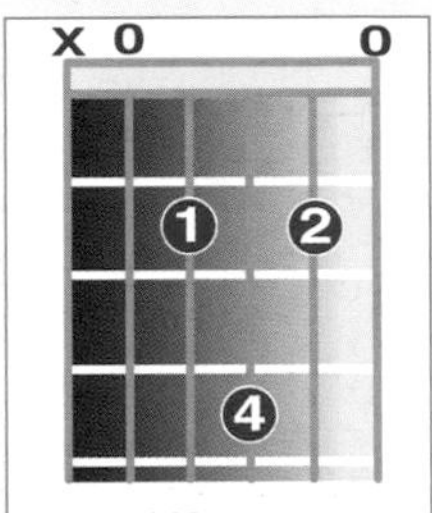

Aadd9 A Major add 9th
1st (A), 3rd (C♯), 5th (E), 9th (B)

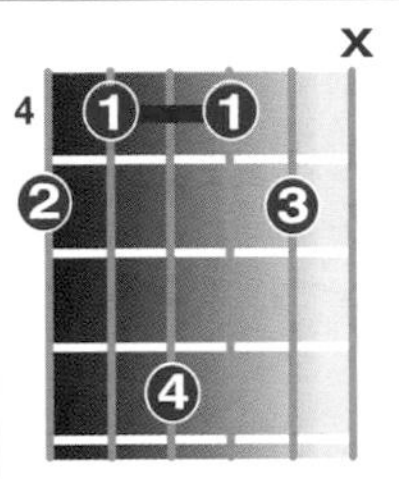

Aadd9 A Major add 9th
1st (A), 3rd (C♯), 5th (E), 9th (B)

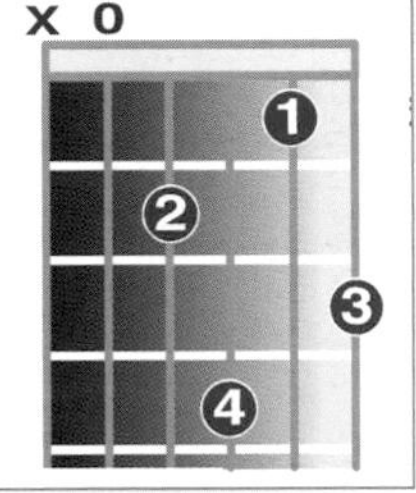

Am9 A Minor 9th
1st (A), ♭3rd (C), 5th (E), ♭7th (G), 9th (B)

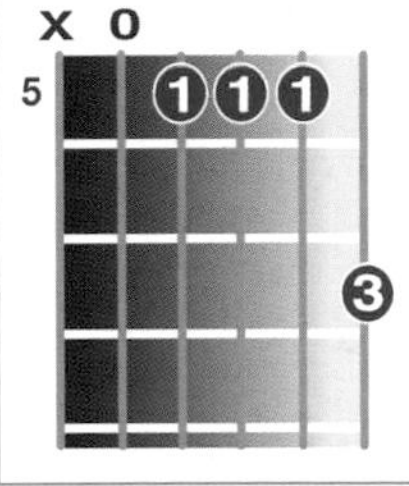

Am9 A Minor 9th
1st (A), ♭3rd (C), 5th (E), ♭7th (G), 9th (B)

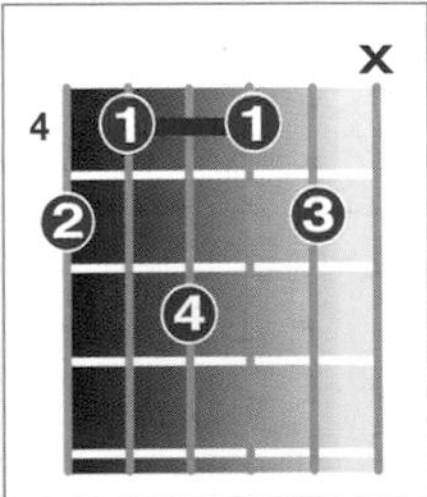

Amaj9 A Major 9th
1st (A), 3rd (C♯), 5th (E), 7th (G♯), 9th (B)

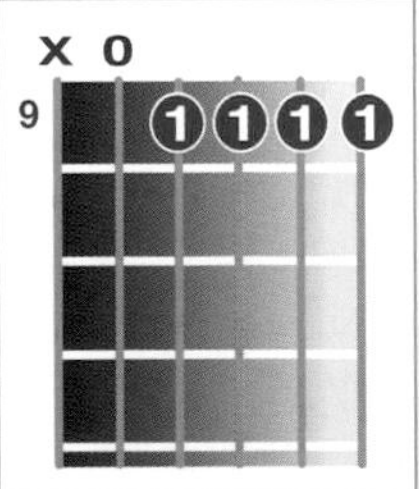

Amaj9 A Major 9th
1st (A), 3rd (C♯), 5th (E), 7th (G♯), 9th (B)

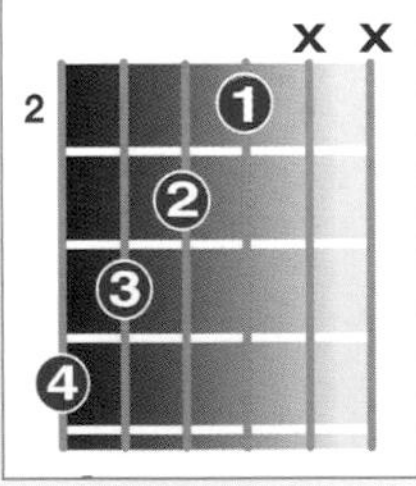

A+ A Augmented
1st (A), 3rd (C♯), ♯5th (E♯)

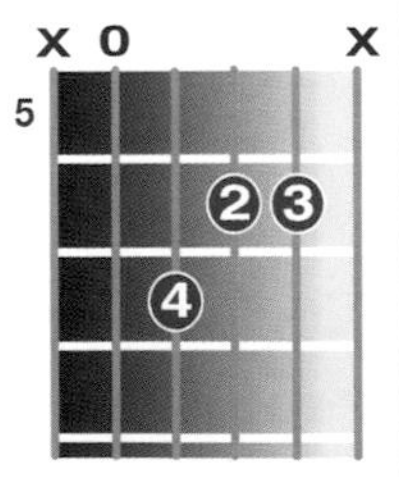

A+ A Augmented
1st (A), 3rd (C♯), ♯5th (E♯)

Complete Guitar Handbook

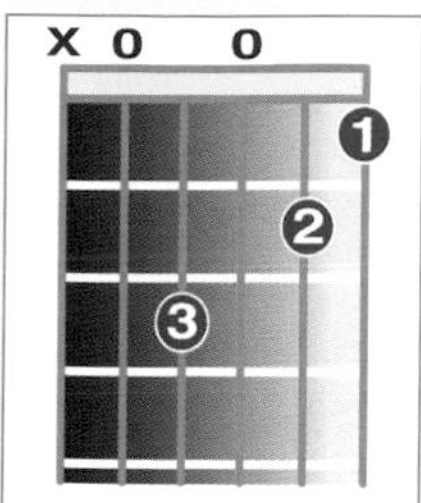

A7♯5 A Dominant 7th ♯5
1st (A), 3rd (C♯), ♯5th (E♯), ♭7th (G)

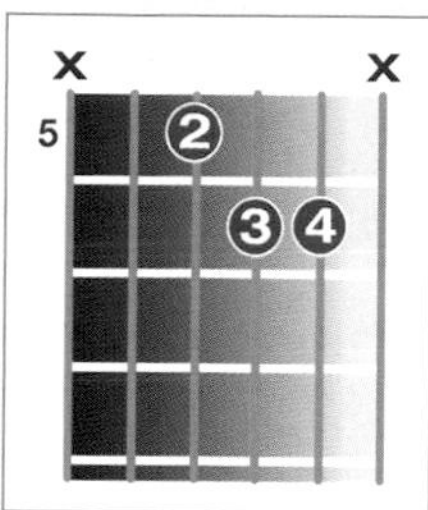

A7♯5 A Dominant 7th ♯5
1st (A), 3rd (C♯), ♯5th (E♯), ♭7th (G)

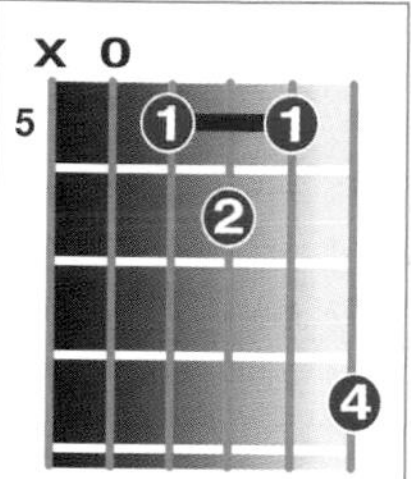

A7♯9 A Dominant 7th ♯9
1st (A), 3rd (C♯),
5th (E), ♭7th (G), ♯9th (B♯)

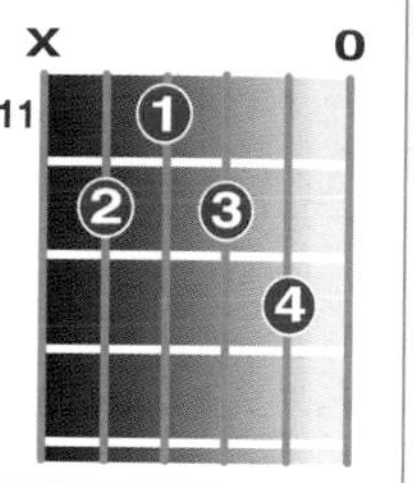

A7♯9 A Dominant 7th ♯9
1st (A), 3rd (C♯),
5th (E), ♭7th (G), ♯9th (B♯)

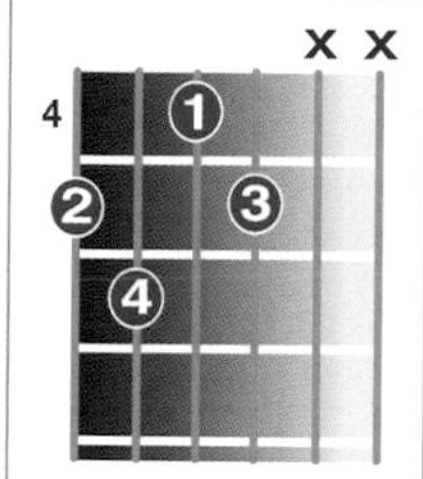

Ao7 A Diminished 7th
1st (A), ♭3rd (C), ♭5th (E♭), ♭♭7th (G♭)

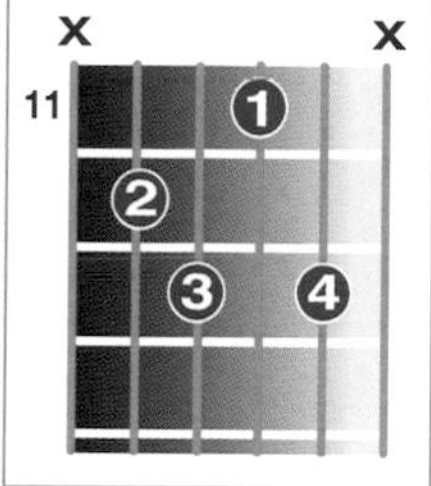

Ao7 A Diminished 7th
1st (A), ♭3rd (C), ♭5th (E♭), ♭♭7th (G♭)

Ao A Diminished triad
1st (A), ♭3rd (C), ♭5th (E♭)

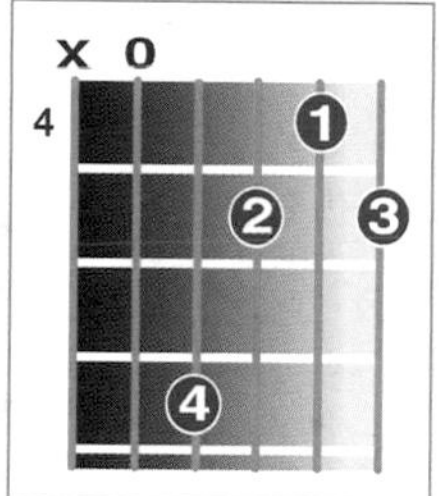

Ao A Diminished triad
1st (A), ♭3rd (C), ♭5th (E♭)

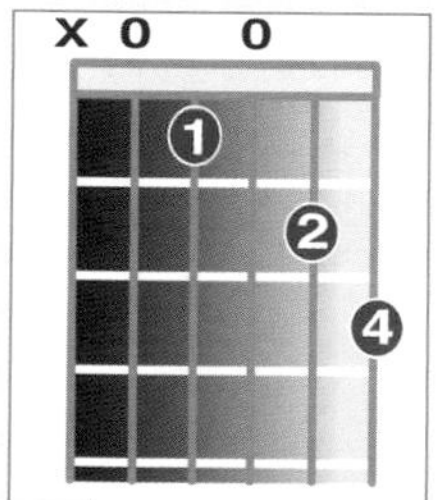

A7♭5 A Dominant 7th ♭5
1st (A), 3rd (C♯), ♭5th (E♭), ♭7th (G)

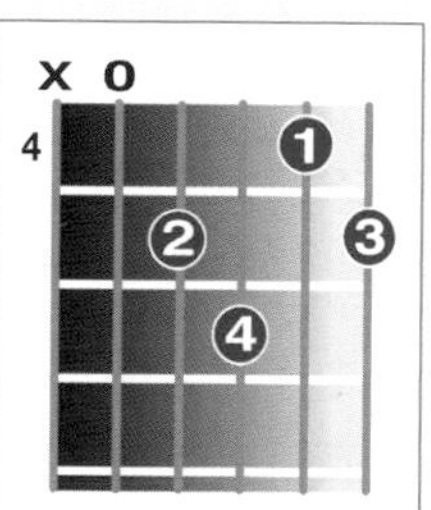

A7♭5 A Dominant 7th ♭5
1st (A), 3rd (C♯), ♭5th (E♭), ♭7th (G)

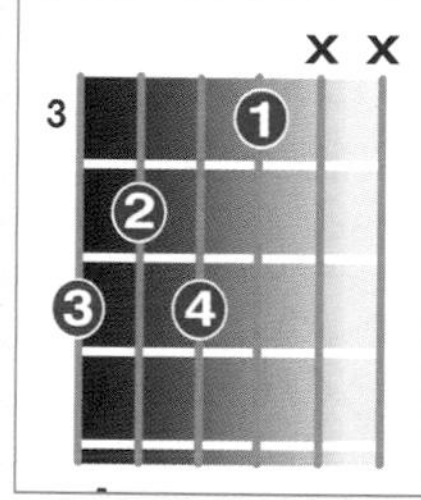

A7♭9 A Dominant 7th ♭9
1st (A), 3rd (C♯),
5th (E), ♭7th (G), ♭9th (B♭)

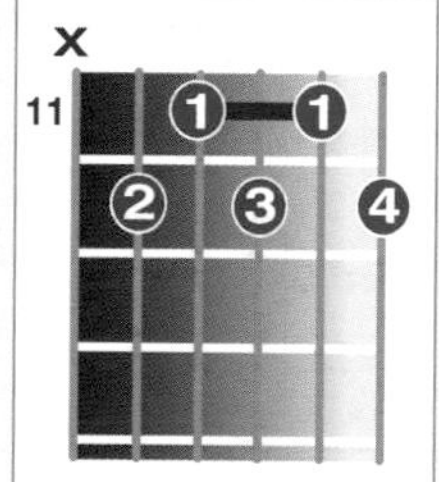

A7♭9 A Dominant 7th ♭9
1st (A), 3rd (C♯),
5th (E), ♭7th (G), ♭9th (B♭)

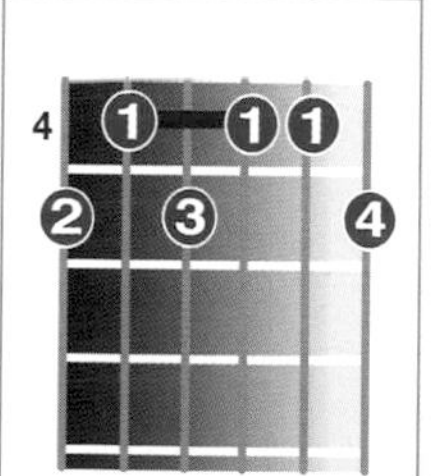

A9♭5 A Dominant 9th ♭5th
1st (A), 3rd (C♯),
♭5th (E♭), ♭7th (G), 9th (B)

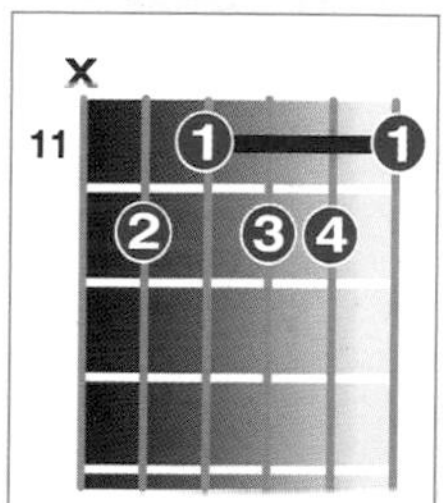

A9♭5 A Dominant 9th ♭5th
1st (A), 3rd (C♯),
♭5th (E♭), ♭7th (G), 9th (B)

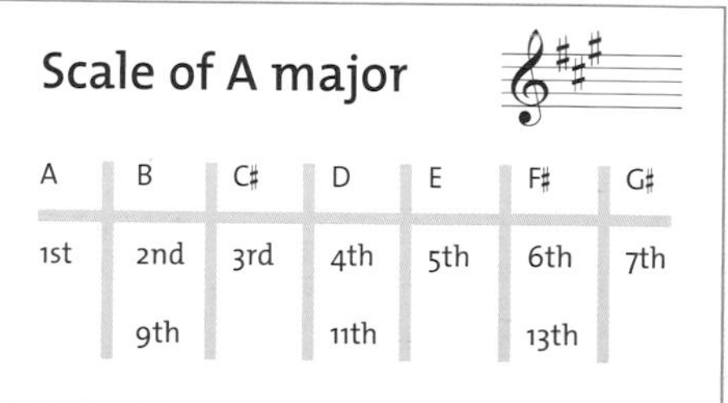

Scale of A major

A	B	C♯	D	E	F♯	G♯
1st	2nd	3rd	4th	5th	6th	7th
	9th		11th		13th	

Section Five: Chord Dictionary

B♭/A♯ MAIN CHORDS

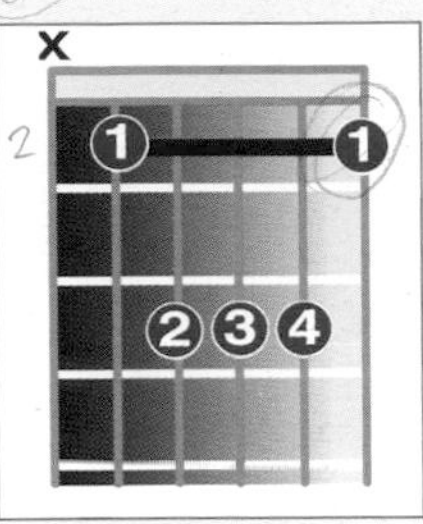

B♭ B♭ major
1st (B♭), 3rd (D), 5th (F)

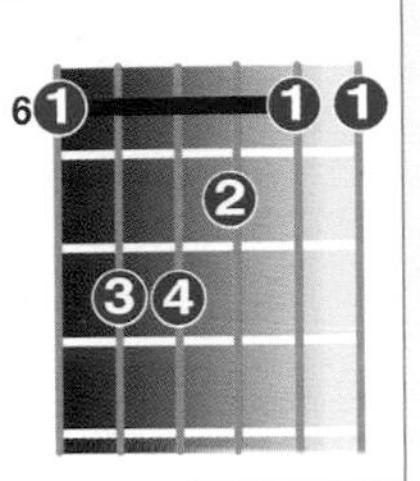

B♭ B♭ major
1st (B♭), 3rd (D), 5th (F)

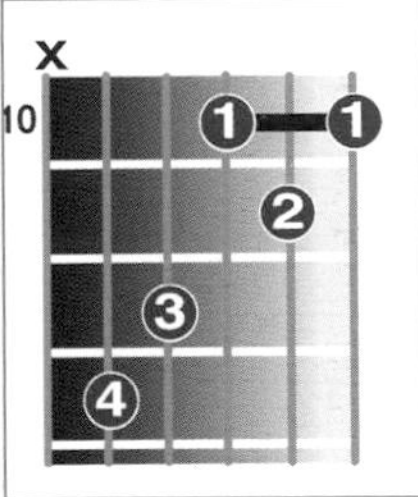

B♭ B♭ major
1st (B♭), 3rd (D), 5th (F)

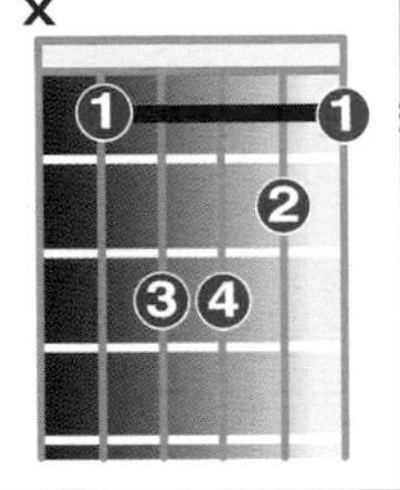

B♭m B♭ Minor
1st (B♭), ♭3rd (D♭), 5th (F)

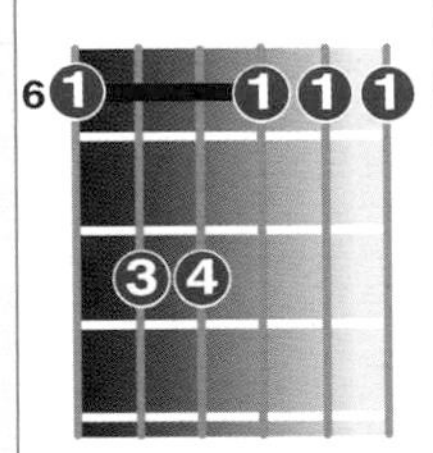

B♭m B♭ Minor
1st (B♭), ♭3rd (D♭), 5th (F)

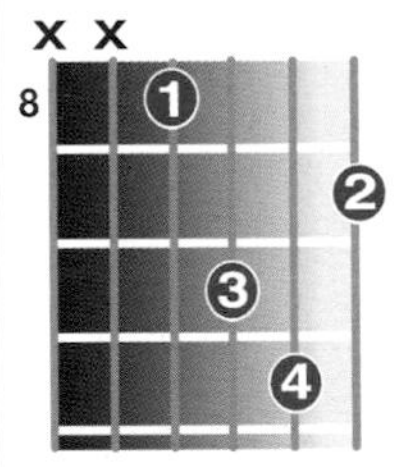

B♭m B♭ Minor
1st (B♭), ♭3rd (D♭), 5th (F)

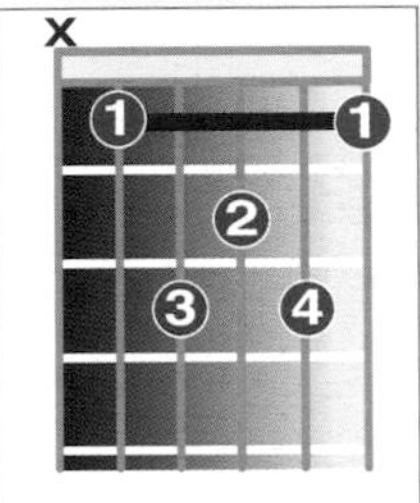

B♭maj7 B♭ Major 7th
1st (B♭), 3rd (D), 5th (F), 7th (A)

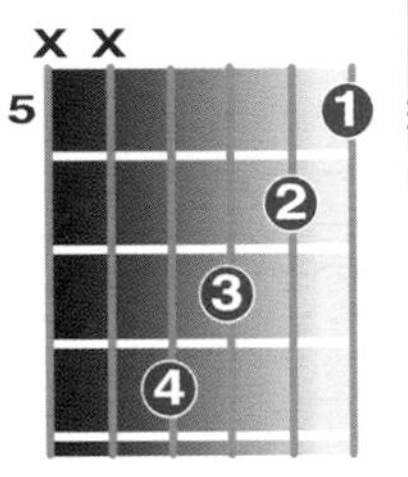

B♭maj7 B♭ Major 7th
1st (B♭), 3rd (D), 5th (F), 7th (A)

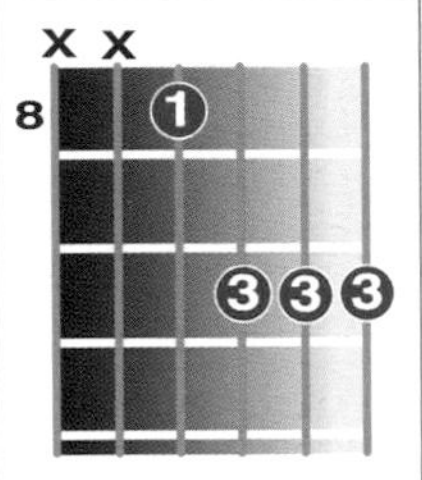

B♭maj7 B♭ Major 7th
1st (B♭), 3rd (D), 5th (F), 7th (A)

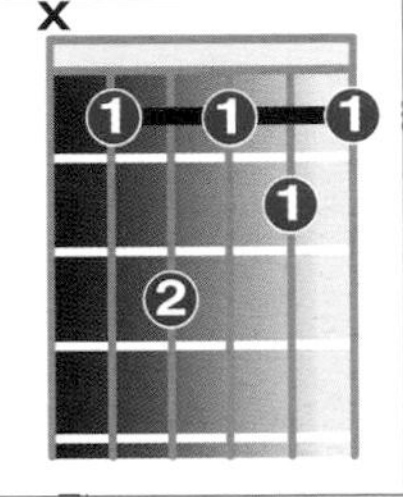

B♭m7 B♭ Minor 7th
1st (B♭), ♭3rd (D♭), 5th (F), ♭7th (A♭)

B♭m7 B♭ Minor 7th
1st (B♭), ♭3rd (D♭), 5th (F), ♭7th (A♭)

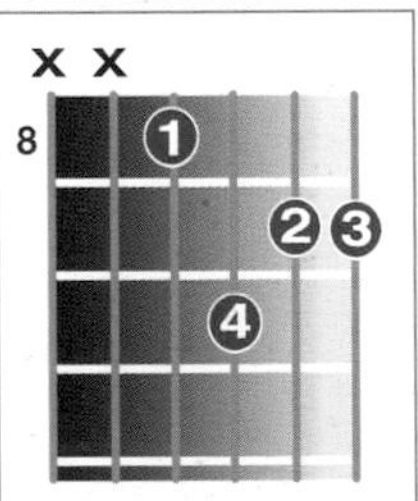

B♭m7 B♭ Minor 7th
1st (B♭), ♭3rd (D♭), 5th (F), ♭7th (A♭)

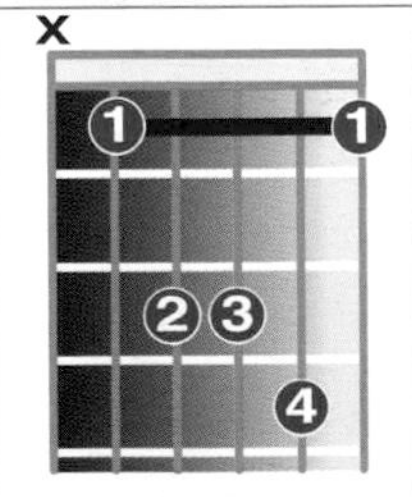

B♭sus4 B♭ Suspended 4th
1st (B♭), 4th (E♭), 5th (F)

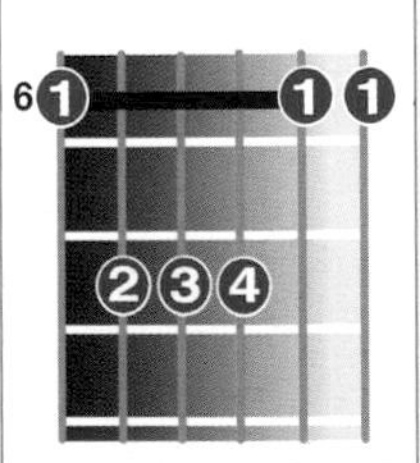

B♭sus4 B♭ Suspended 4th
1st (B♭), 4th (E♭), 5th (F)

Complete Guitar Handbook

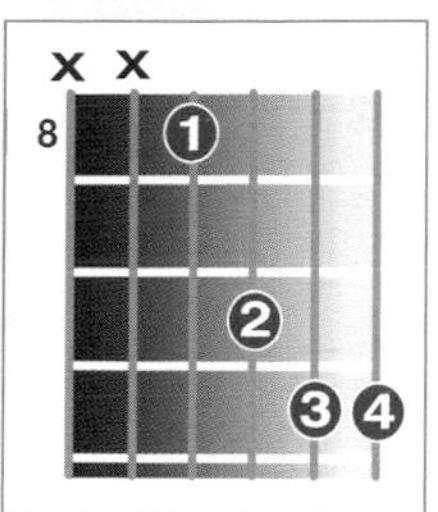

B♭sus4 B♭ Suspended 4th
1st (B♭), 4th (E♭), 5th (F)

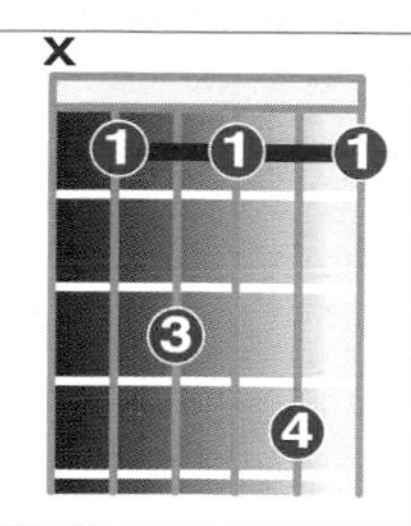

B♭7sus4 B♭ Dominant 7th sus4
1st (B♭), 4th (E♭), 5th (F), ♭7th (A♭)

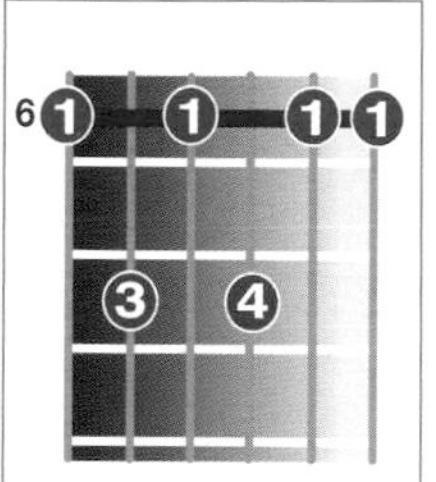

B♭7sus4 B♭ Dominant 7th sus4
1st (B♭), 4th (E♭), 5th (F), ♭7th (A♭)

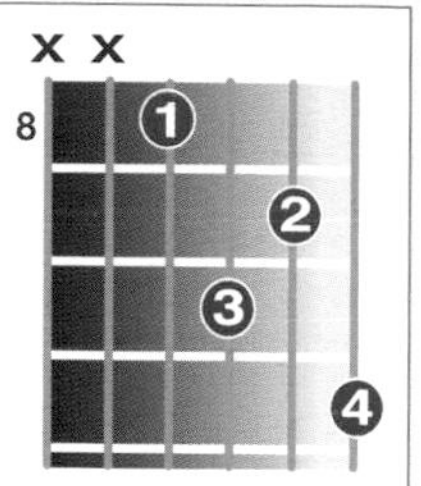

B♭7sus4 B♭ Dominant 7th sus4
1st (B♭), 4th (E♭), 5th (F), ♭7th (A♭)

B♭6 B♭ Major 6th
1st (B♭), 3rd (D), 5th (F), 6th (G)

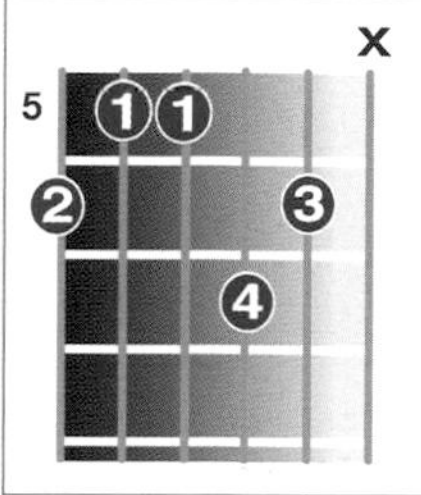

B♭6 B♭ Major 6th
1st (B♭), 3rd (D), 5th (F), 6th (G)

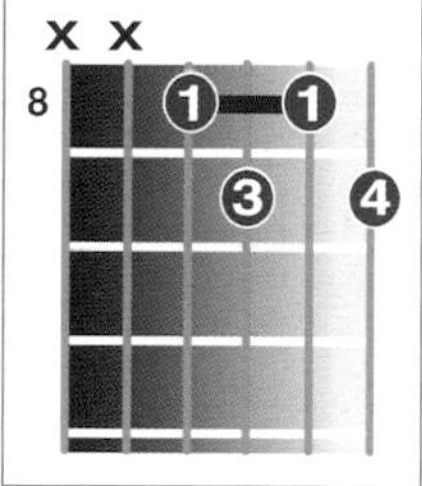

B♭6 B♭ Major 6th
1st (B♭), 3rd (D), 5th (F), 6th (G)

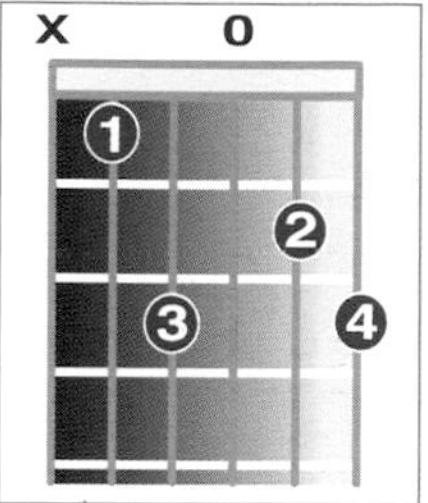

B♭m6 B♭ Minor 6th
1st (B♭), ♭3rd (D♭), 5th (F), 6th (G)

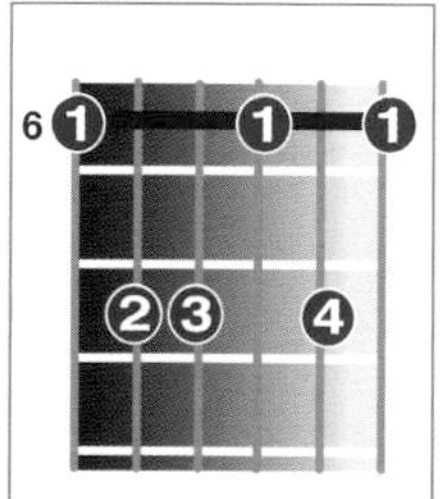

B♭m6 B♭ Minor 6th
1st (B♭), ♭3rd (D♭), 5th (F), 6th (G)

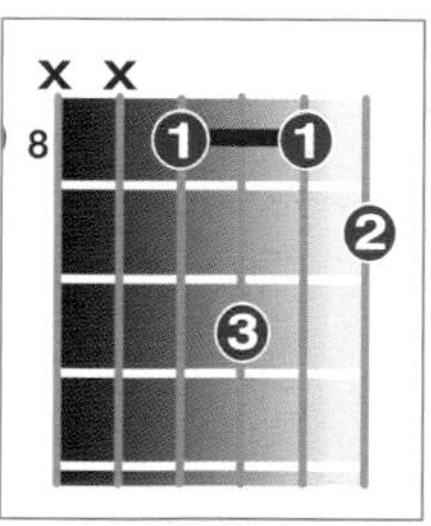

B♭m6 B♭ Minor 6th
1st (B♭), ♭3rd (D♭), 5th (F), 6th (G)

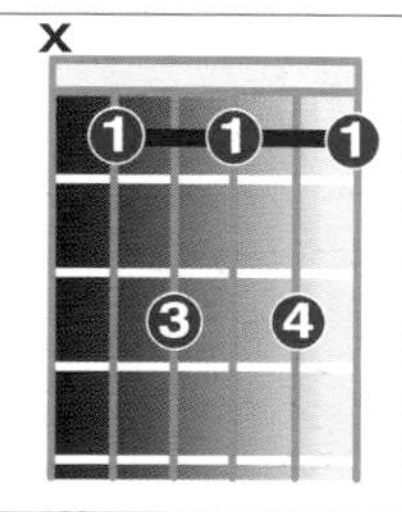

B♭7 B♭ Dominant 7th
1st (B♭), 3rd (D),
5th (F), ♭7th (A♭)

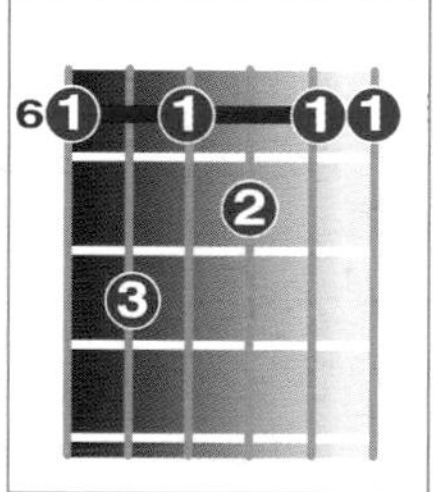

B♭7 B♭ Dominant 7th
1st (B♭), 3rd (D),
5th (F), ♭7th (A♭)

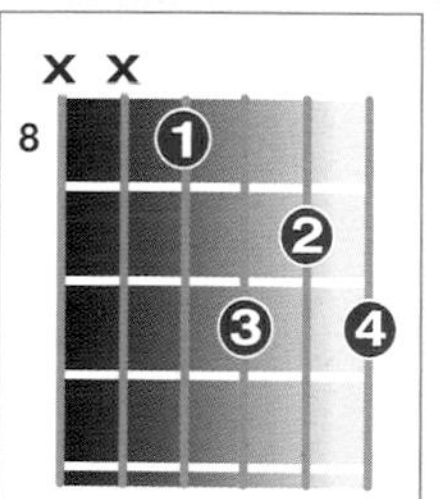

B♭7 B♭ Dominant 7th
1st (B♭), 3rd (D),
5th (F), ♭7th (A♭)

B♭9 B♭ Dominant 9th
1st (B♭), 3rd (D), 5th (F),
♭7th (A♭), 9th (C)

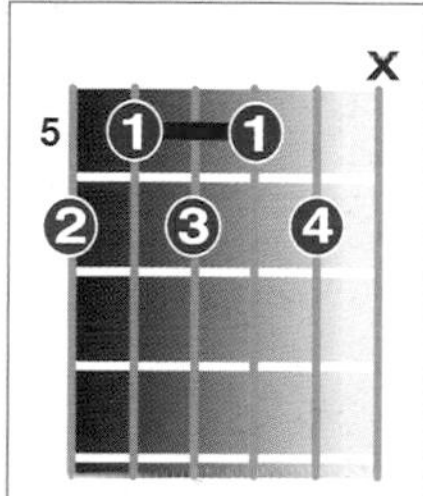

B♭9 B♭ Dominant 9th
1st (B♭), 3rd (D), 5th (F),
♭7th (A♭), 9th (C)

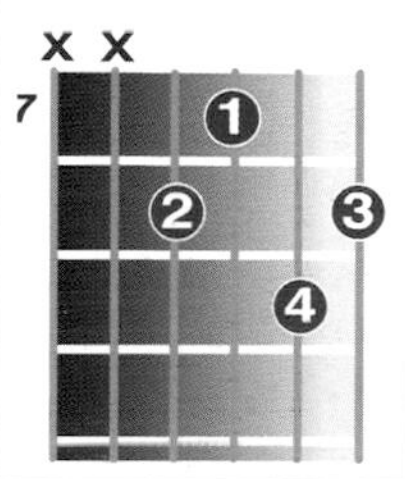

B♭9 B♭ Dominant 9th
1st (B♭), 3rd (D),
5th (F), ♭7th (A♭), 9th (C)

Section Five: Chord Dictionary

B♭/A♯ ADVANCED CHORDS

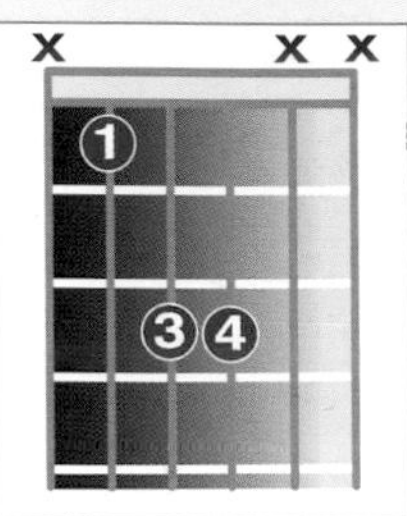

B♭5 B♭ 5th (power chord)
1st (B♭), 5th (F)

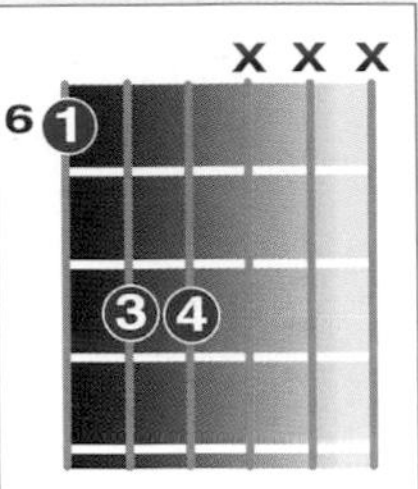

B♭5 B♭ 5th (power chord)
1st (B♭), 5th (F)

B♭6/9 B♭ Major 6th add 9th
1st (B♭), 3rd (D), 5th (F), 6th (G), 9th (C)

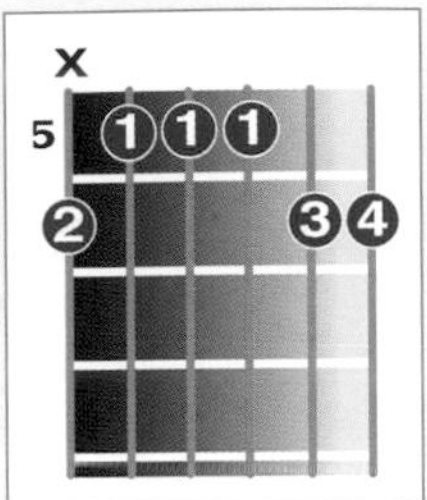

B♭6/9 B♭ Major 6th add 9th
1st (B♭), 3rd (D), 5th (F), 6th (G), 9th (C)

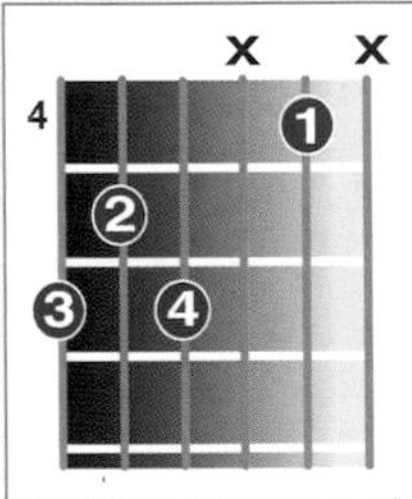

B♭11 B♭ Dominant 11th
1st (B♭), 3rd (D), 5th (F), ♭7th (A♭), 9th (C), 11th (E♭)

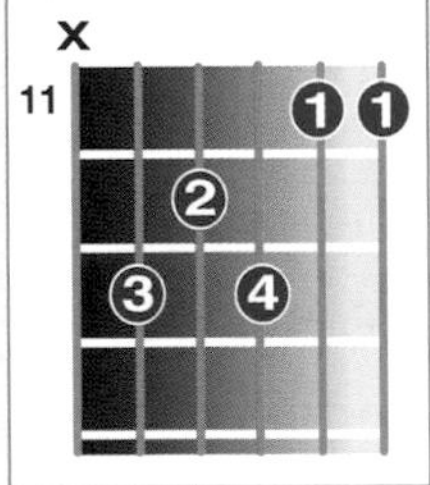

B♭11 B♭ Dominant 11th
1st (B♭), 3rd (D), 5th (F), ♭7th (A♭), 9th (C), 11th (E♭)

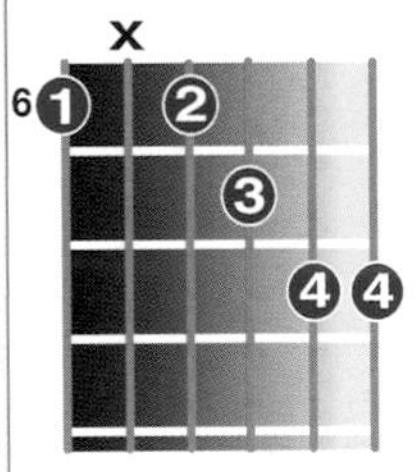

B♭13 B♭ Dominant 13th
1st (B♭), 3rd (D), 5th (F), ♭7th (A♭), 9th (C), 13th (G)

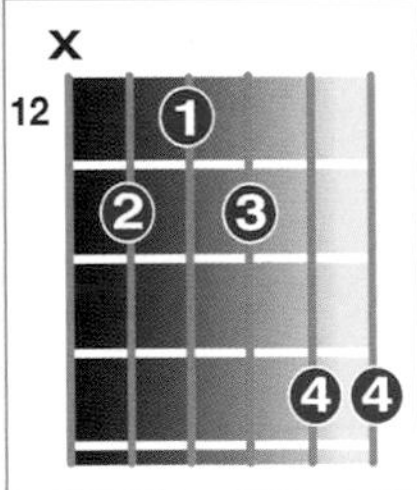

B♭13 B♭ Dominant 13th
1st (B♭), 3rd (D), 5th (F), ♭7th (A♭), 9th (C), 13th (G)

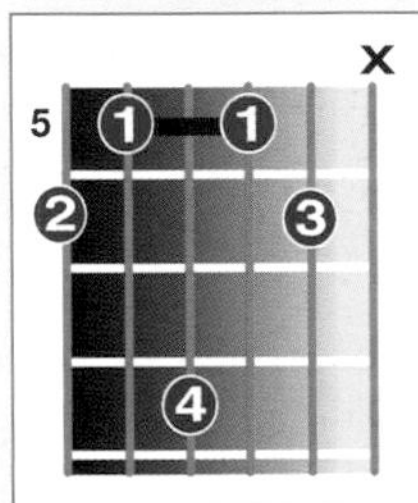

B♭add9 B♭ Major add 9th
1st (B♭), 3rd (D), 5th (F), 9th (C)

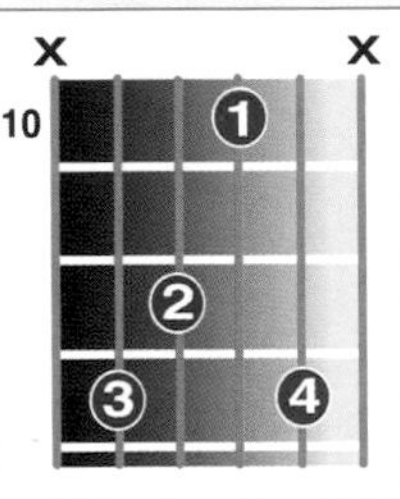

B♭add9 B♭ Major add 9th
1st (B♭), 3rd (D), 5th (F), 9th (C)

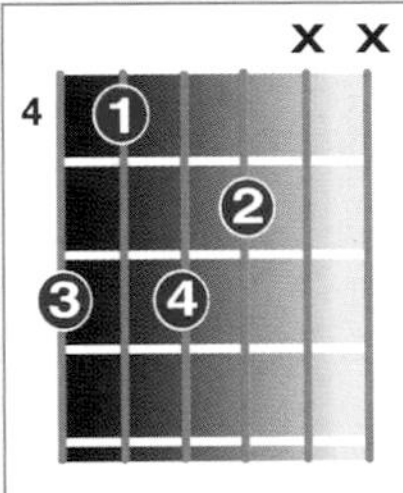

B♭m9 B♭ Minor 9th
1st (B♭), ♭3rd (D♭), 5th (F), ♭7th (A♭), 9th (C)

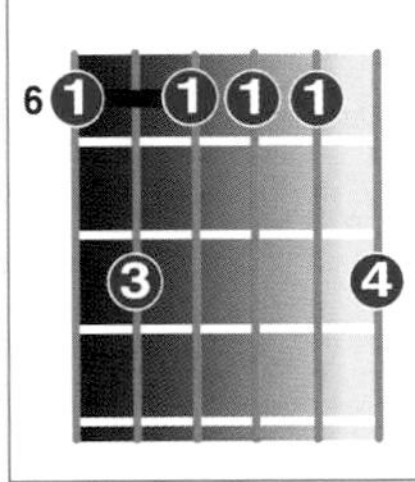

B♭m9 B♭ Minor 9th
1st (B♭), ♭3rd (D♭), 5th (F), ♭7th (A♭), 9th (C)

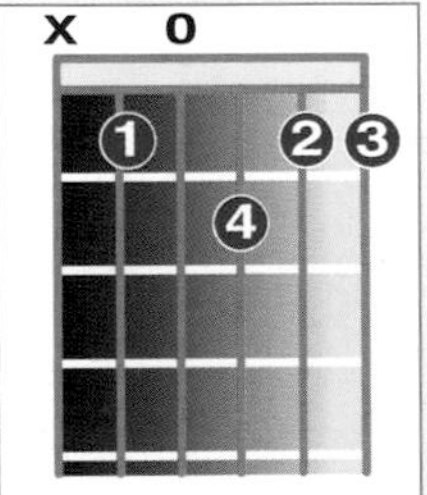

B♭maj9 B♭ Major 9th
1st (B♭), 3rd (D), 5th (F), 7th (A), 9th (C)

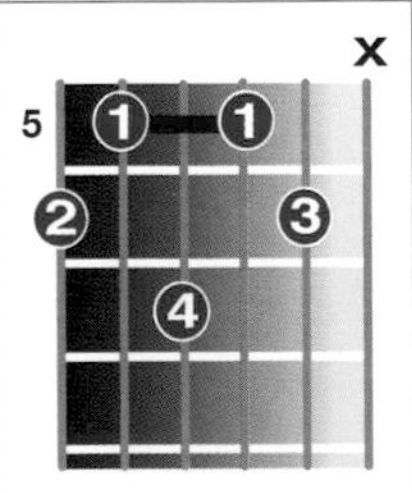

B♭maj9 B♭ Major 9th
1st (B♭), 3rd (D), 5th (F), 7th (A), 9th (C)

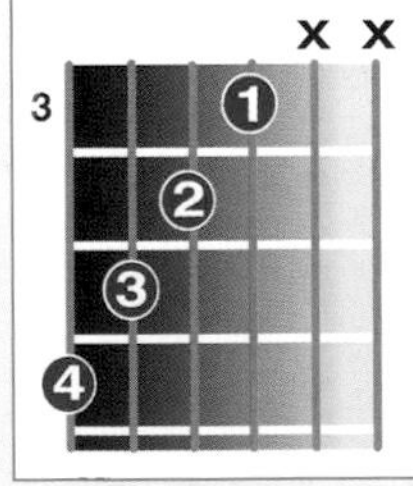

B♭+ B♭ Augmented
1st (B♭), 3rd (D), ♯5th (F♯)

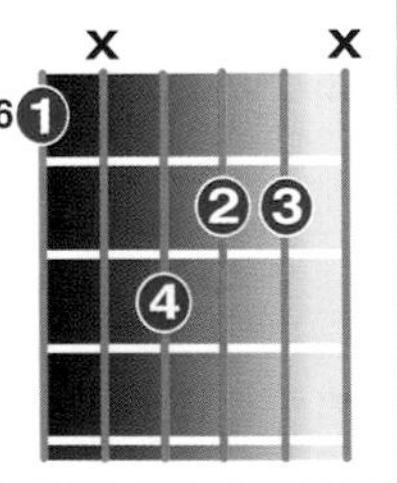

B♭+ B♭ Augmented
1st (B♭), 3rd (D), ♯5th (F♯)

Complete Guitar Handbook

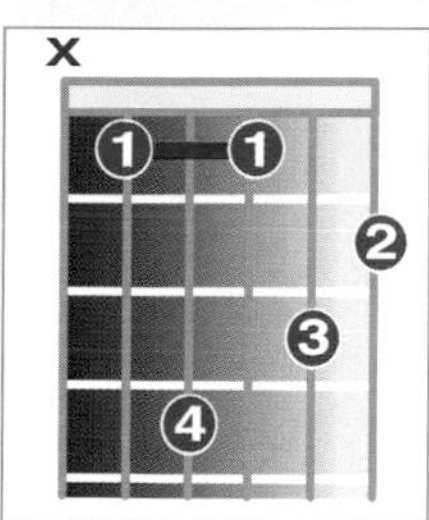

B♭7♯5 B♭ Dominant 7th ♯5
1st (B♭), 3rd (D), ♯5th (F♯), ♭7th (A♭)

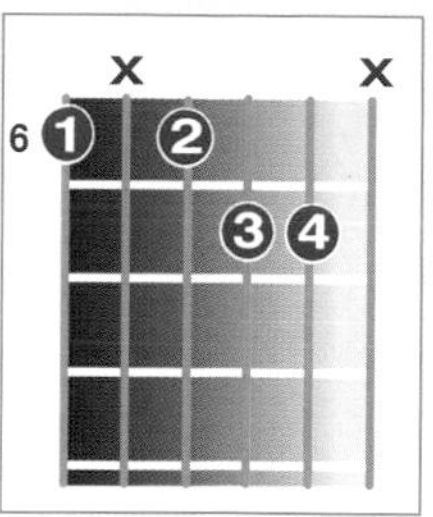

B♭7♯5 B♭ Dominant 7th ♯5
1st (B♭), 3rd (D), ♯5th (F♯), ♭7th (A♭)

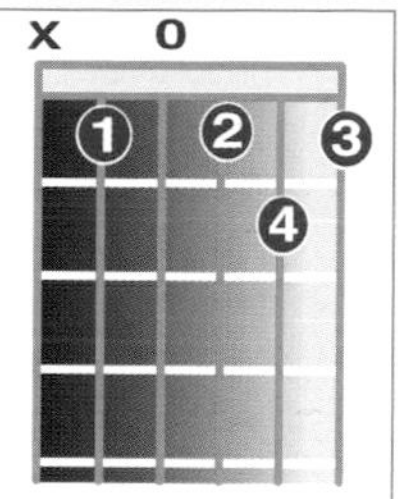

B♭7♯9 B♭ Dominant 7th ♯9
1st (B♭), 3rd (D), 5th (F), ♭7th (A♭), ♯9th (C♯)

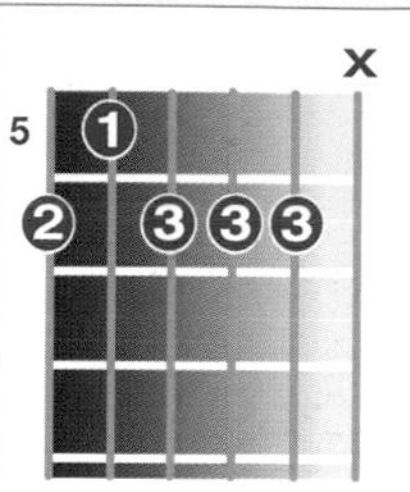

B♭7♯9 B♭ Dominant 7th ♯9
1st (B♭), 3rd (D), 5th (F), ♭7th (A♭), ♯9th (C♯)

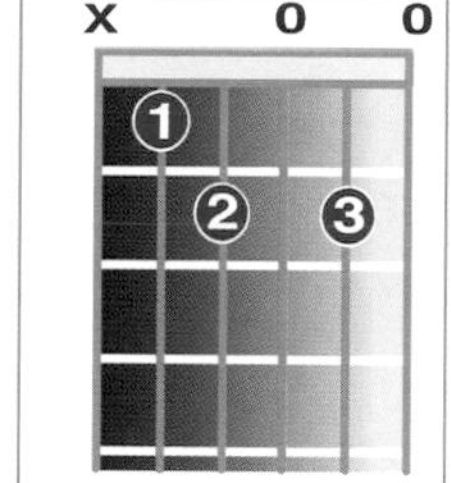

B♭o7 B♭ Diminished 7th
1st (B♭), ♭3rd (D♭), ♭5th (F♭), ♭♭7th (A♭♭)

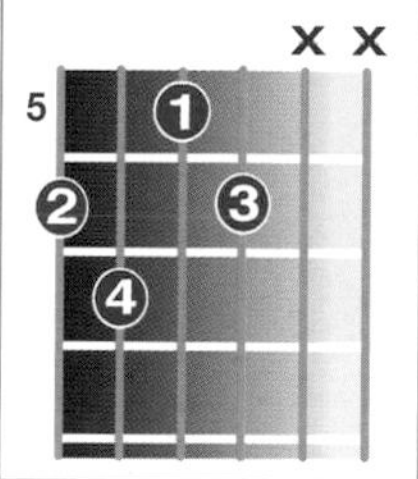

B♭o7 B♭ Diminished 7th
1st (B♭), ♭3rd (D♭), ♭5th (F♭), ♭♭7th (A♭♭)

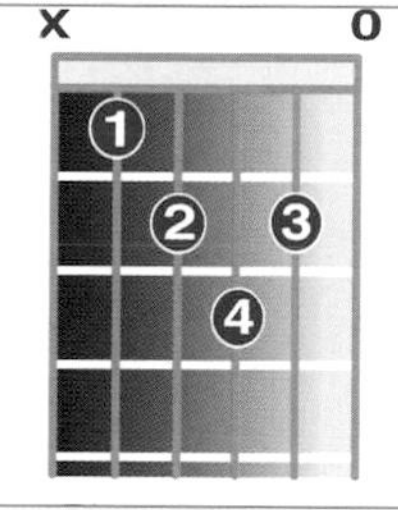

B♭o B♭ Diminished triad
1st (B♭), ♭3rd (D♭), ♭5th (F♭)

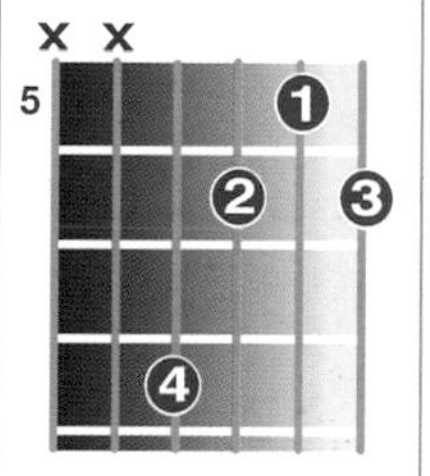

B♭o B♭ Diminished triad
1st (B♭), ♭3rd (D♭), ♭5th (F♭)

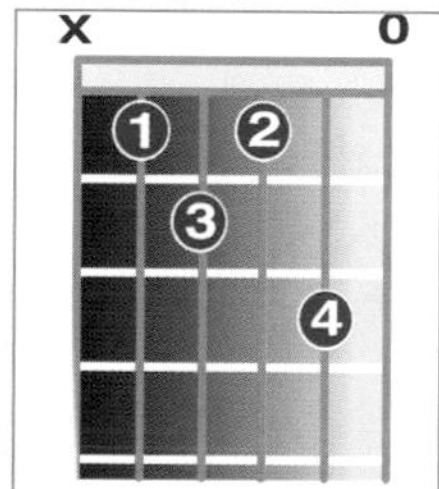

B♭7♭5 B♭ Dominant 7th ♭5
1st (B♭), 3rd (D), ♭5th (F♭), ♭7th (A♭)

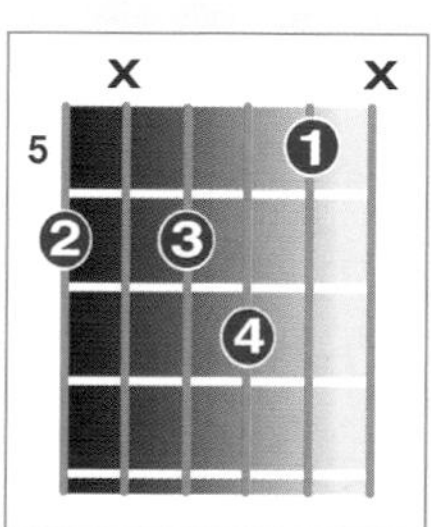

B♭7♭5 B♭ Dominant 7th ♭5
1st (B♭), 3rd (D), ♭5th (F♭), ♭7th (A♭)

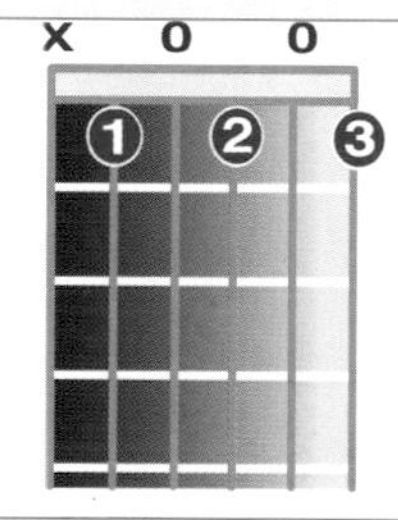

B♭7♭9 B♭ Dominant 7th ♭9
1st (B♭), 3rd (D), 5th (F), ♭7th (A♭), ♭9th (C♭)

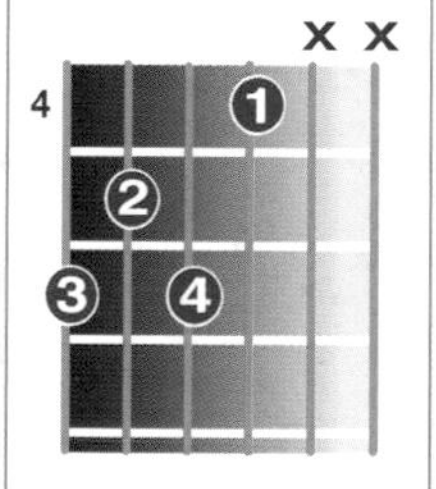

B♭7♭9 B♭ Dominant 7th ♭9
1st (B♭), 3rd (D), 5th (F), ♭7th (A♭), ♭9th (C♭)

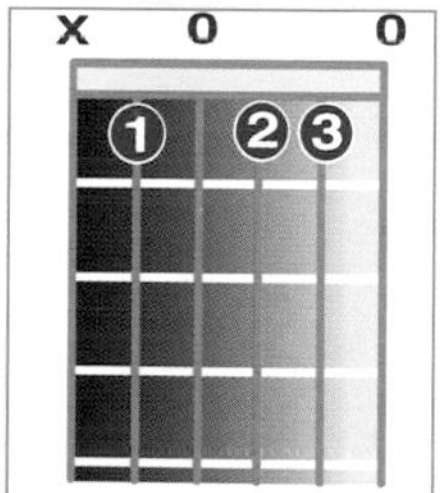

B♭9♭5 B♭ Dominant 9th ♭5th
1st (B♭), 3rd (D), ♭5th (F♭), ♭7th (A♭), 9th (C)

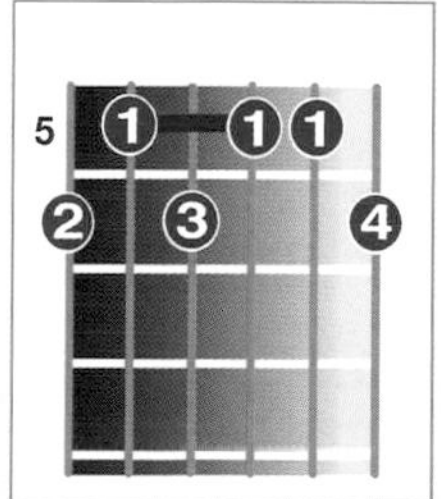

B♭9♭5 B♭ Dominant 9th ♭5th
1st (B♭), 3rd (D), ♭5th (F♭), ♭7th (A♭), 9th (C)

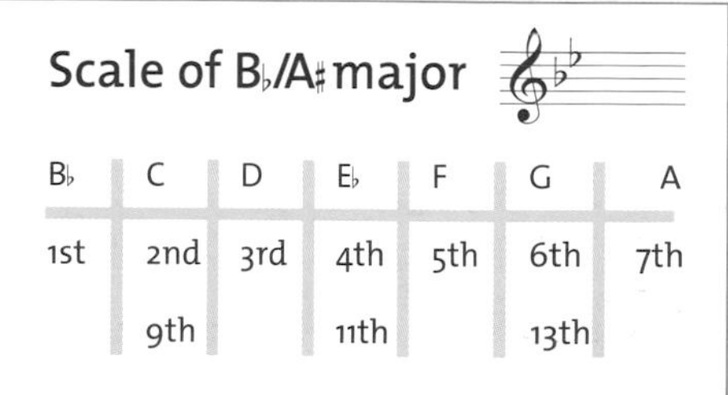

Scale of B♭/A♯ major

B♭	C	D	E♭	F	G	A
1st	2nd	3rd	4th	5th	6th	7th
	9th		11th		13th	

Section Five: Chord Dictionary

B MAIN CHORDS

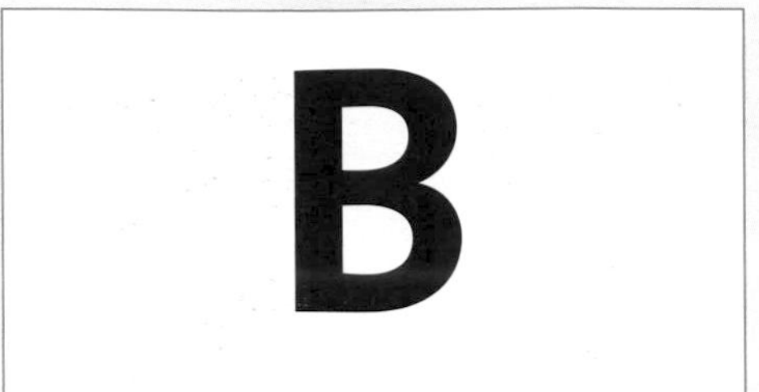

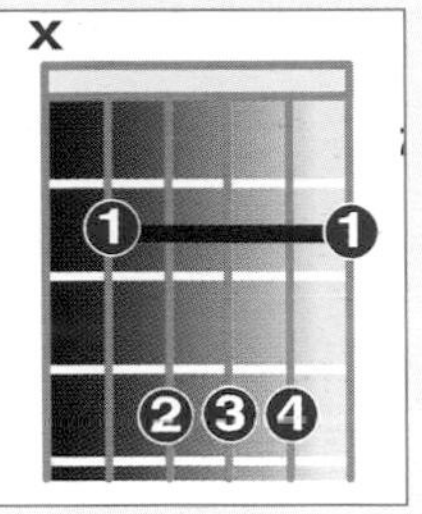

B B Major
1st (B), 3rd (D♯), 5th (F♯)

B B Major
1st (B), 3rd (D♯), 5th (F♯)

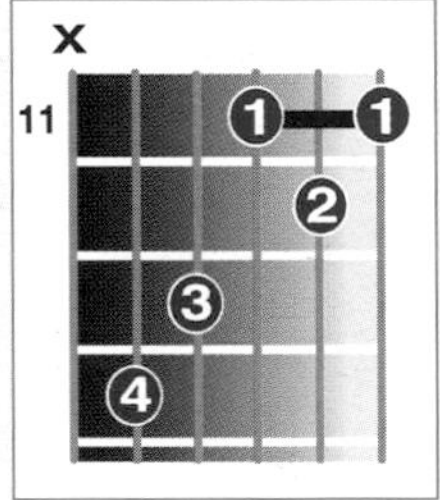

B B Major
1st (B), 3rd (D♯), 5th (F♯)

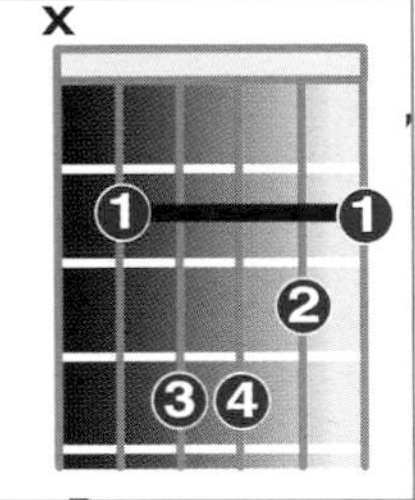

Bm B Minor
1st (B), ♭3rd (D), 5th (F♯)

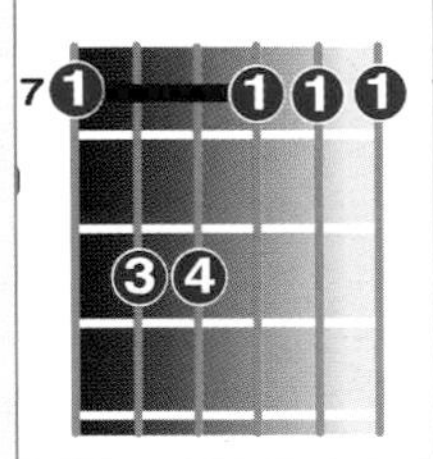

Bm B Minor
1st (B), ♭3rd (D), 5th (F♯)

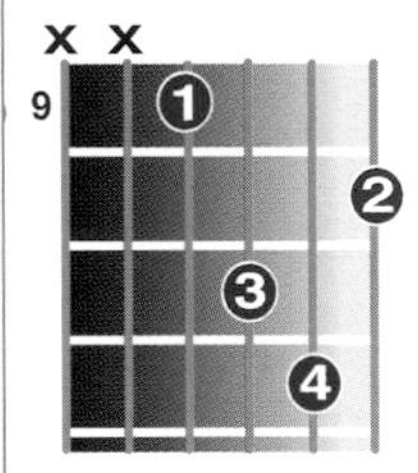

Bm B Minor
1st (B), ♭3rd (D), 5th (F♯)

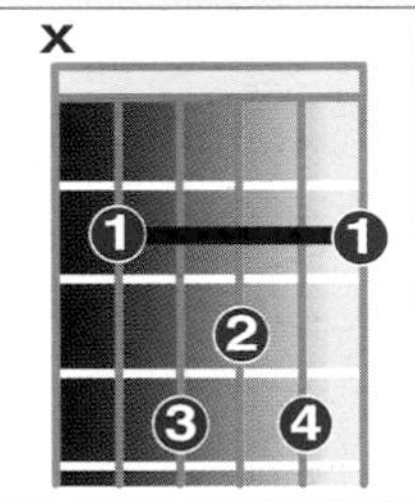

Bmaj7 B Major 7th
1st (B), 3rd (D♯),
5th (F♯), 7th (A♯)

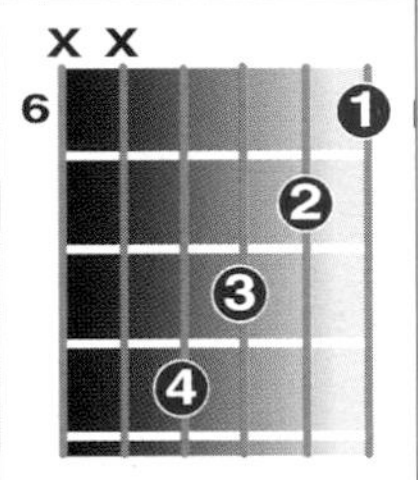

Bmaj7 B Major 7th
1st (B), 3rd (D♯),
5th (F♯), 7th (A♯)

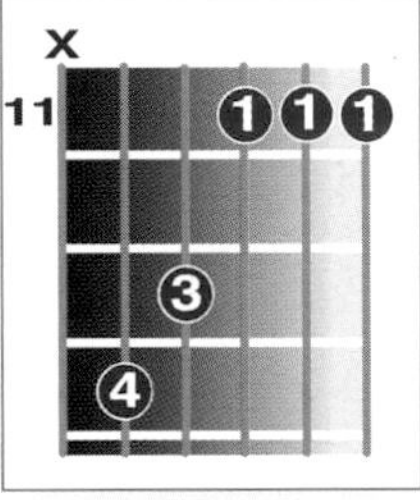

Bmaj7 B Major 7th
1st (B), 3rd (D♯),
5th (F♯), 7th (A♯)

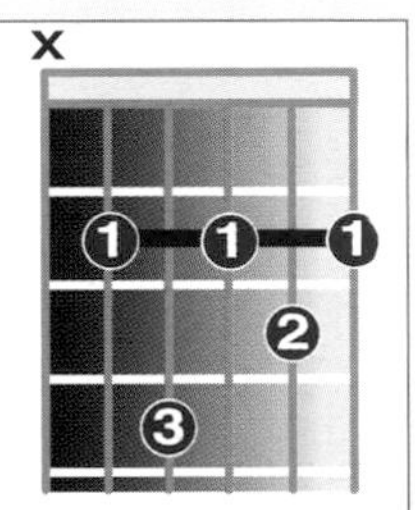

Bm7 B Minor 7th
1st (B), ♭3rd (D),
5th (F♯), ♭7th (A)

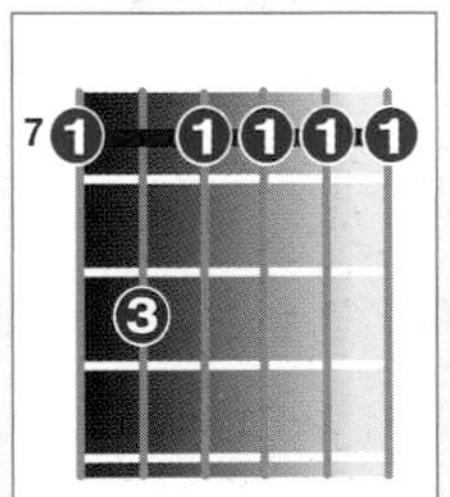

Bm7 B Minor 7th
1st (B), ♭3rd (D),
5th (F♯), ♭7th (A)

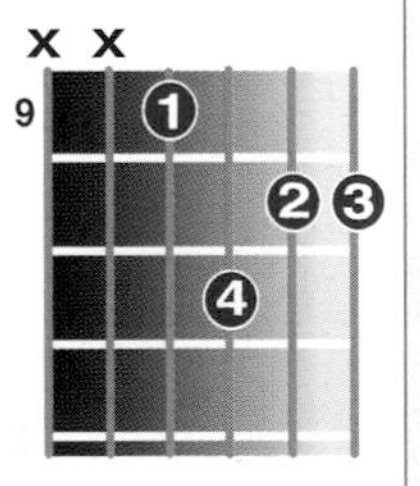

Bm7 B Minor 7th
1st (B), ♭3rd (D),
5th (F♯), ♭7th (A)

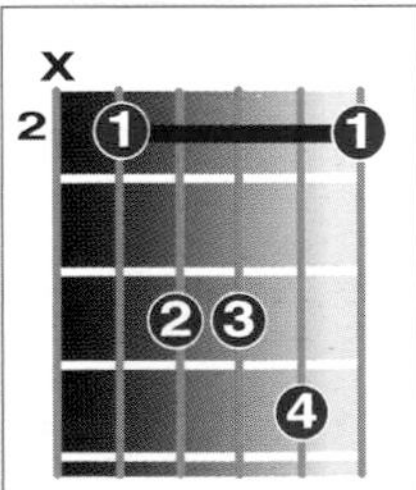

Bsus4 B Suspended 4th
1st (B), 4th (E), 5th (F♯)

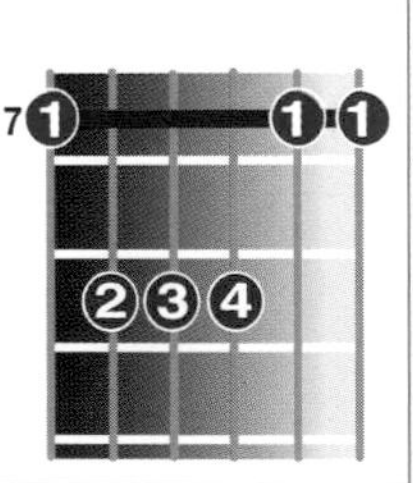

Bsus4 B Suspended 4th
1st (B), 4th (E), 5th (F♯)

Complete Guitar Handbook

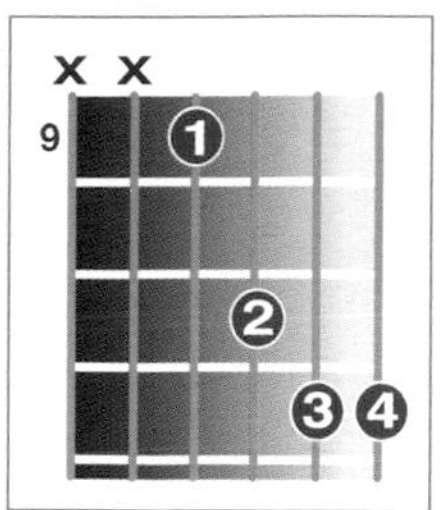

Bsus4 B Suspended 4th
1st (B), 4th (E), 5th (F♯)

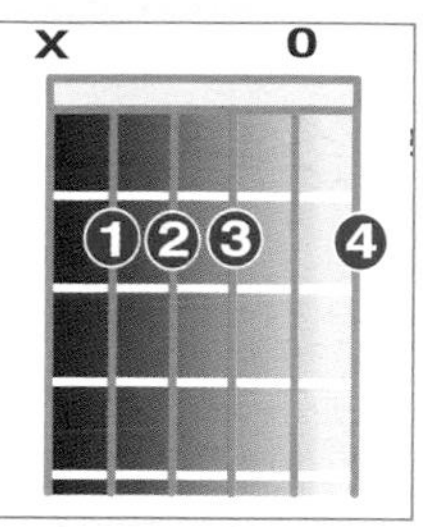

B7sus4 B Dominant 7th sus4
1st (B), 4th (E), 5th (F♯), ♭7th (A)

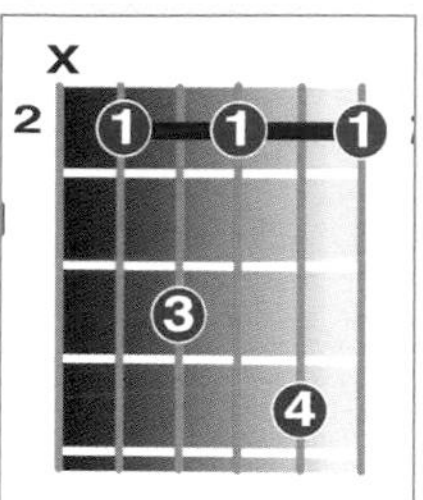

B7sus4 B Dominant 7th sus4
1st (B), 4th (E), 5th (F♯), ♭7th (A)

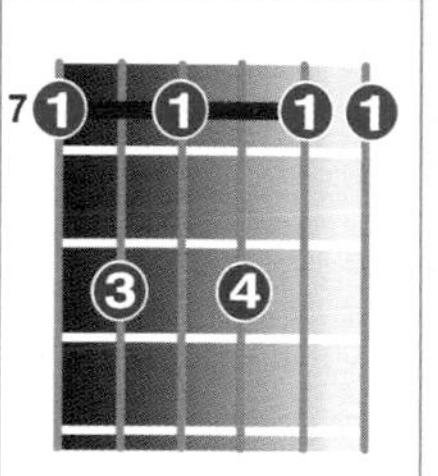

B7sus4 B Dominant 7th sus4
1st (B), 4th (E), 5th (F♯), ♭7th (A)

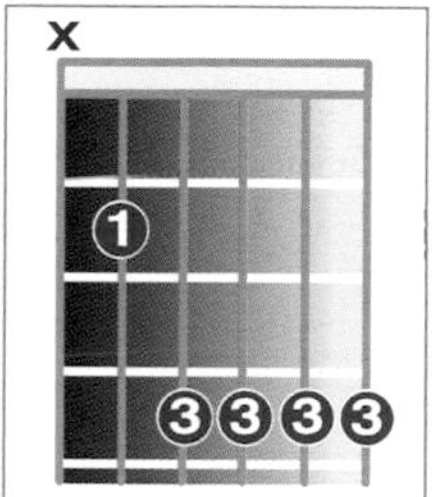

B6 B Major 6th
1st (B), 3rd (D♯), 5th (F♯), 6th (G♯)

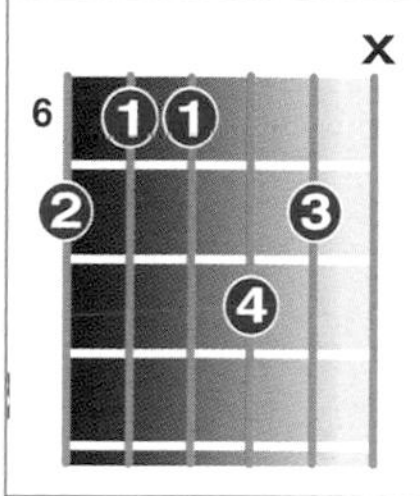

B6 B Major 6th
1st (B), 3rd (D♯), 5th (F♯), 6th (G♯)

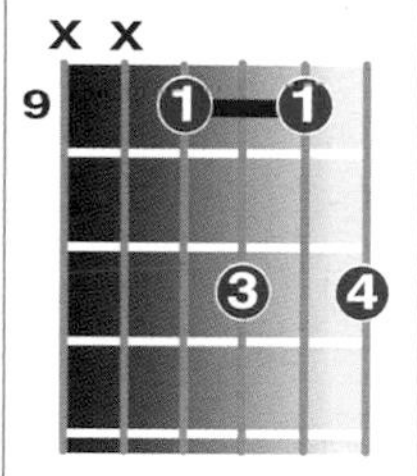

B6 B Major 6th
1st (B), 3rd (D♯), 5th (F♯), 6th (G♯)

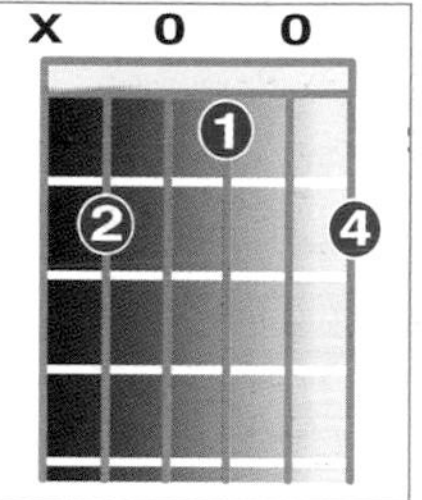

Bm6 B Minor 6th
1st (B), ♭3rd (D), 5th (F♯), 6th (G♯)

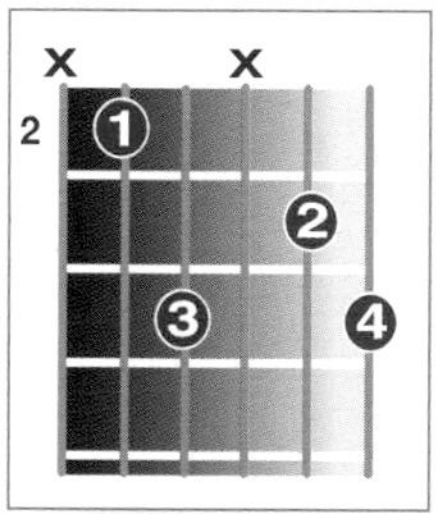

Bm6 B Minor 6th
1st (B), ♭3rd (D), 5th (F♯), 6th (G♯)

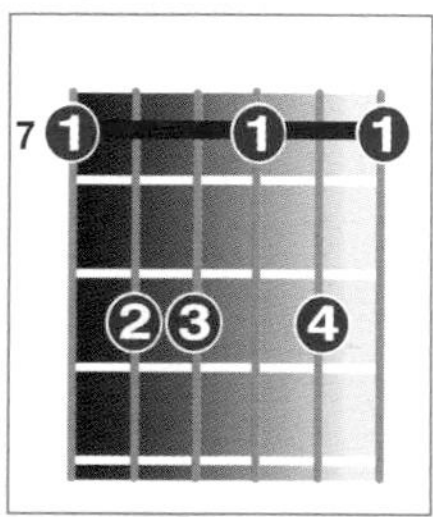

Bm6 B Minor 6th
1st (B), ♭3rd (D), 5th (F♯), 6th (G♯)

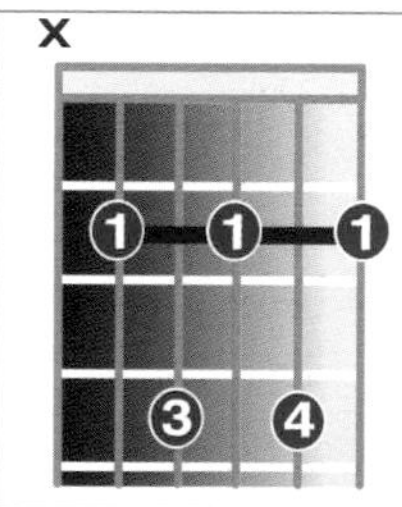

B7 B Dominant 7th
1st (B), 3rd (D♯), 5th (F♯), ♭7th (A)

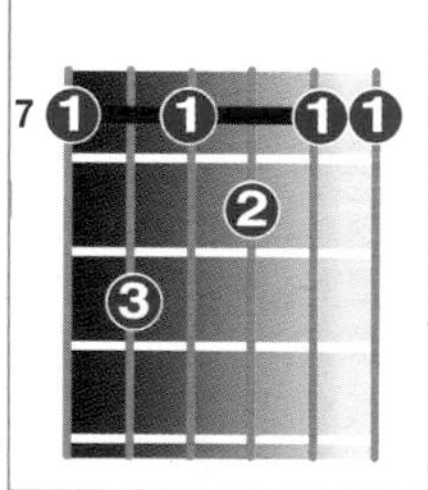

B7 B Dominant 7th
1st (B), 3rd (D♯), 5th (F♯), ♭7th (A)

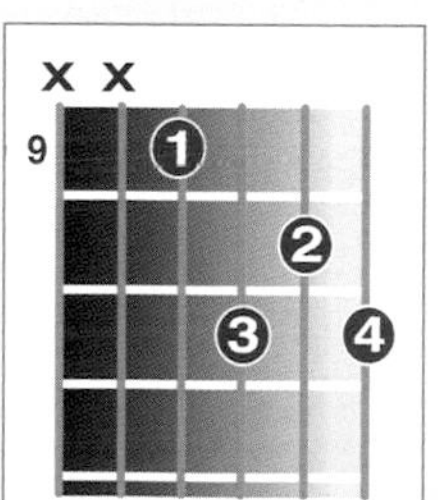

B7 B Dominant 7th
1st (B), 3rd (D♯), 5th (F♯), ♭7th (A)

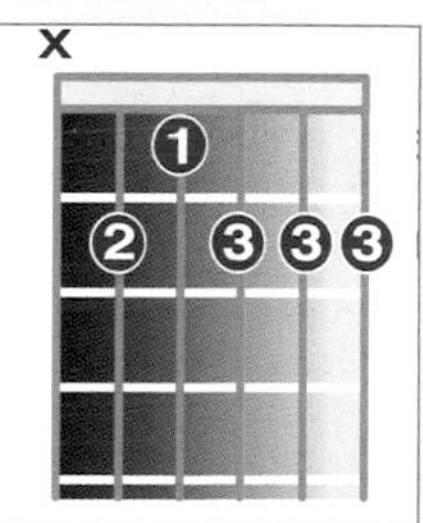

B9 B Dominant 9th
1st (B), 3rd (D♯), 5th (F♯), ♭7th (A), 9th (C♯)

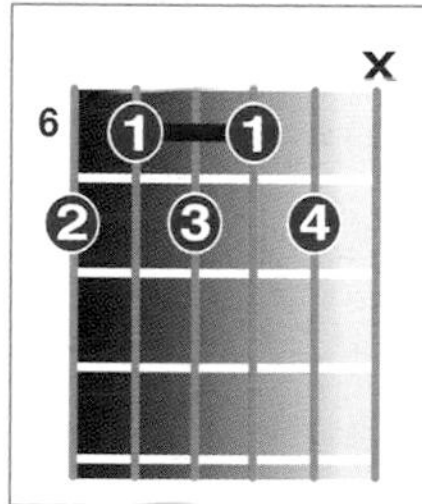

B9 B Dominant 9th
1st (B), 3rd (D♯), 5th (F♯), ♭7th (A), 9th (C♯)

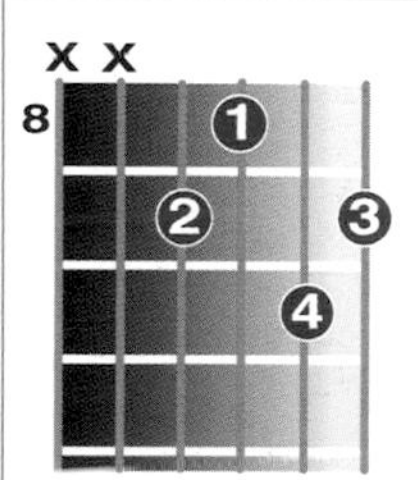

B9 B Dominant 9th
1st (B), 3rd (D♯), 5th (F♯), ♭7th (A), 9th (C♯)

Section Five: Chord Dictionary

B ADVANCED CHORDS

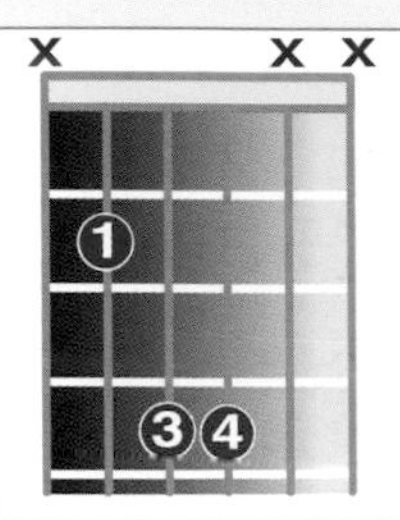

B5 B 5th (power chord)
1st (B), 5th (F♯)

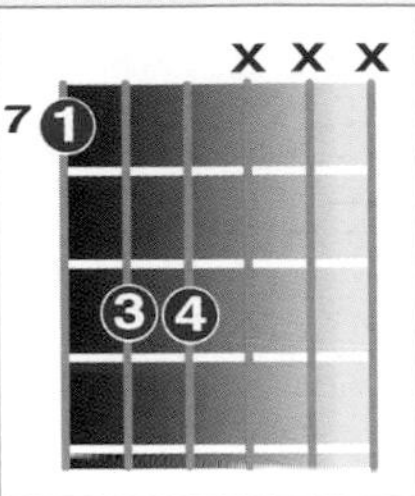

B5 B 5th (power chord)
1st (B), 5th (F♯)

B 6/9 B Major 6th add 9th
1st (B), 3rd (D♯), 5th (F♯), 6th (G♯), 9th (C♯)

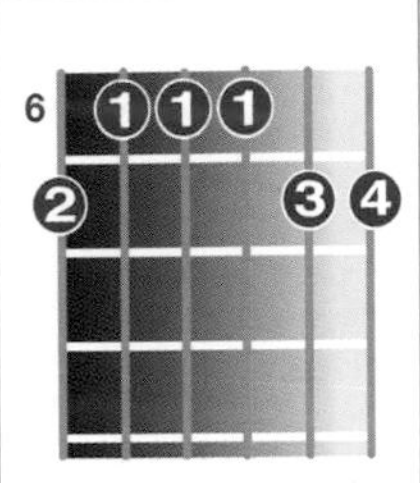

B 6/9 B Major 6th add 9th
1st (B), 3rd (D♯), 5th (F♯), 6th (G♯), 9th (C♯)

B11 B Dominant 11th
1st (B), 3rd (D♯), 5th (F♯), ♭7th (A), 9th (C♯), 11th (E)

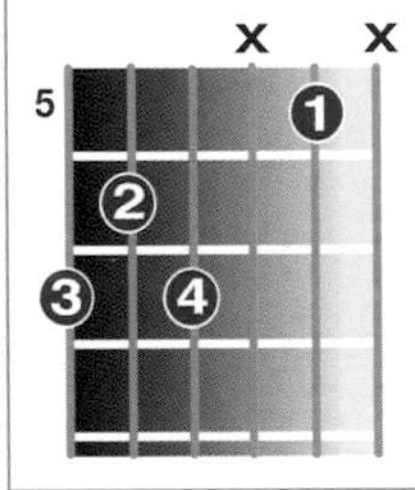

B11 B Dominant 11th
1st (B), 3rd (D♯), 5th (F♯), ♭7th (A), 9th (C♯), 11th (E)

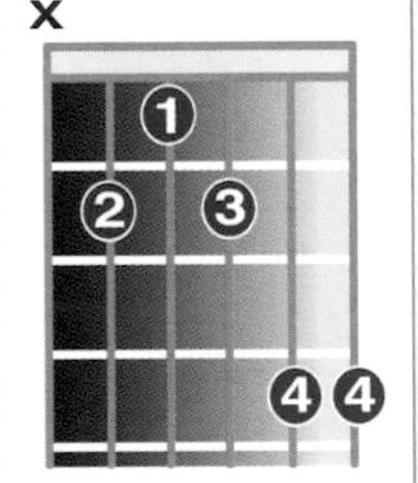

B13 B Dominant 13th
1st (B), 3rd (D♯), 5th (F♯), ♭7th (A), 9th (C♯), 13th (G♯)

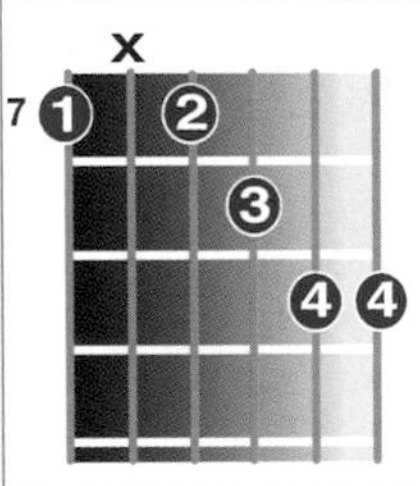

B13 B Dominant 13th
1st (B), 3rd (D♯), 5th (F♯), ♭7th (A), 9th (C♯), 13th (G♯)

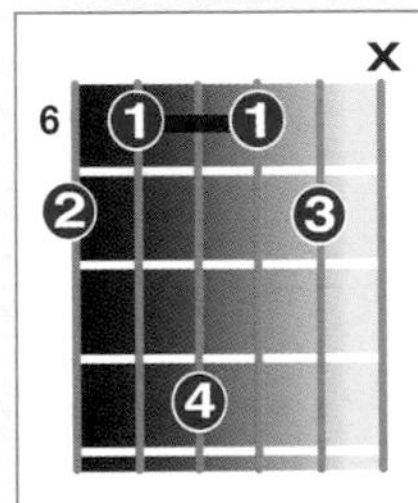

Badd9 B Major add 9th
1st (B), 3rd (D♯), 5th (F♯), 9th (C♯)

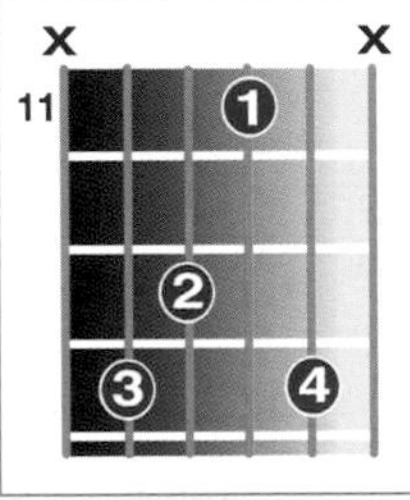

Badd9 B Major add 9th
1st (B), 3rd (D♯), 5th (F♯), 9th (C♯)

Bm9 B Minor 9th
1st (B), ♭3rd (D), 5th (F♯), ♭7th (A), 9th (C♯)

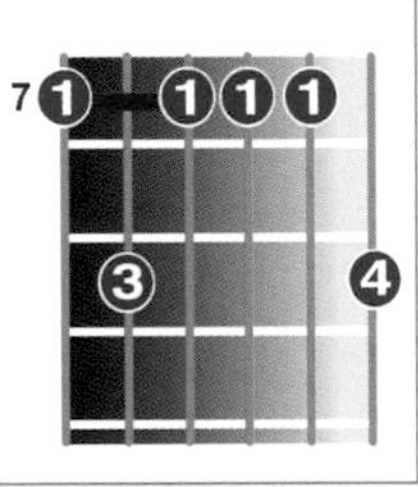

Bm9 B Minor 9th
1st (B), ♭3rd (D), 5th (F♯), ♭7th (A), 9th (C♯)

Bmaj9 B Major 9th
1st (B), 3rd (D♯), 5th (F♯), 7th (A♯), 9th (C♯)

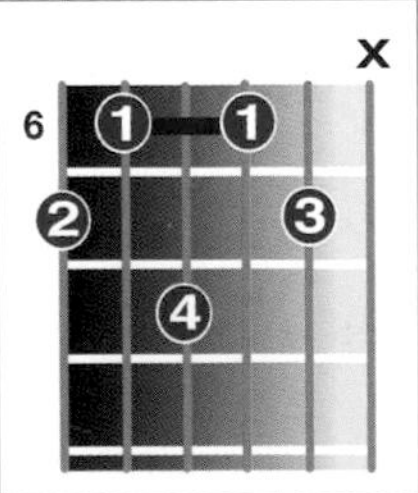

Bmaj9 B Major 9th
1st (B), 3rd (D♯), 5th (F♯), 7th (A♯), 9th (C♯)

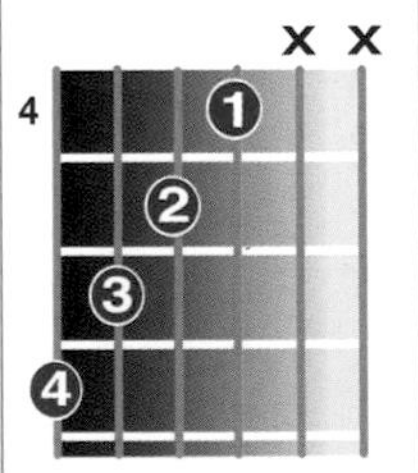

B+ B Augmented
1st (B), 3rd (D♯), ♯5th (Fx)

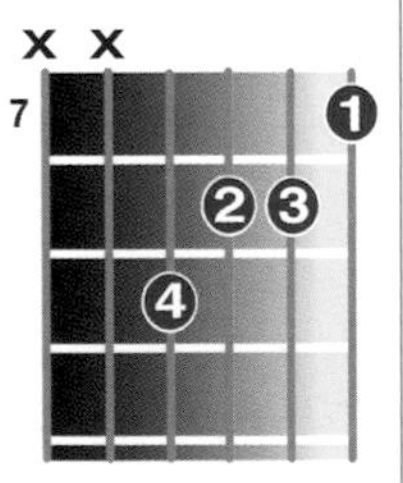

B+ B Augmented
1st (B), 3rd (D♯), ♯5th (Fx)

Complete Guitar Handbook

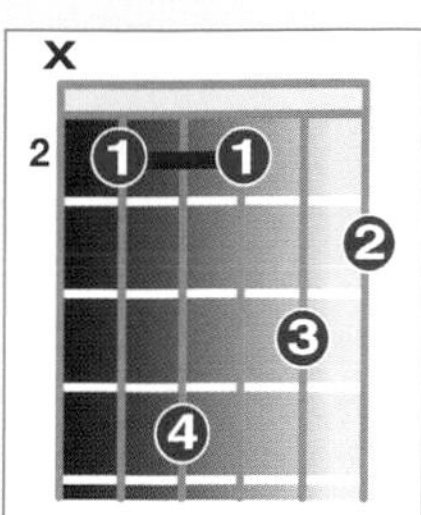

B7♯5 B Dominant 7th ♯5
1st (B), 3rd (D♯), ♯5th (Fx), b7th (A)

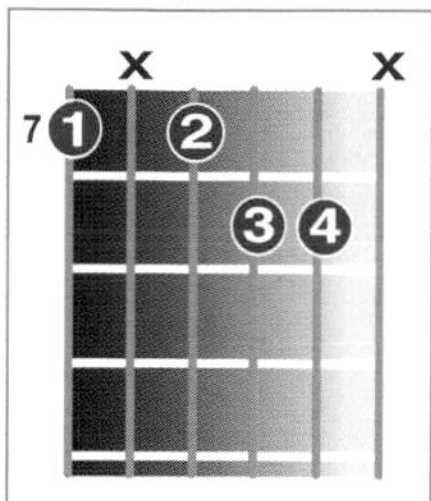

B7♯5 B Dominant 7th ♯5
1st (B), 3rd (D♯), ♯5th (Fx), b7th (A)

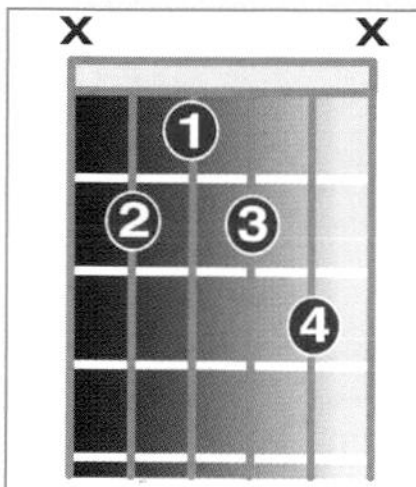

B7♯9 B Dominant 7th ♯9
1st (B), 3rd (D♯), 5th (F♯), ♭7th (A), ♯9th (Cx)

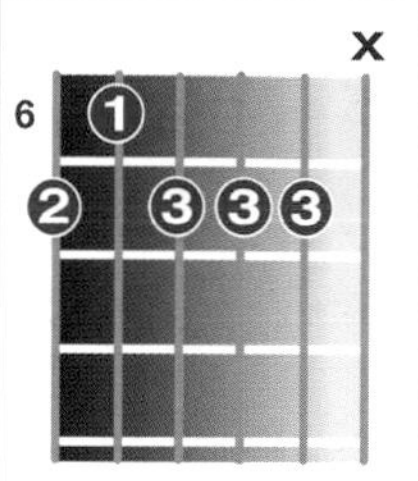

B7♯9 B Dominant 7th ♯9
1st (B), 3rd (D♯), 5th (F♯), ♭7th (A), ♯9th (Cx)

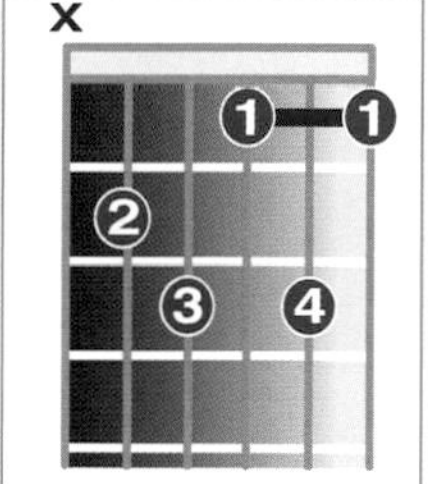

Bo7 B Diminished 7th
1st (B), ♭3rd (D), ♭5th (F), ♭♭7th (A♭)

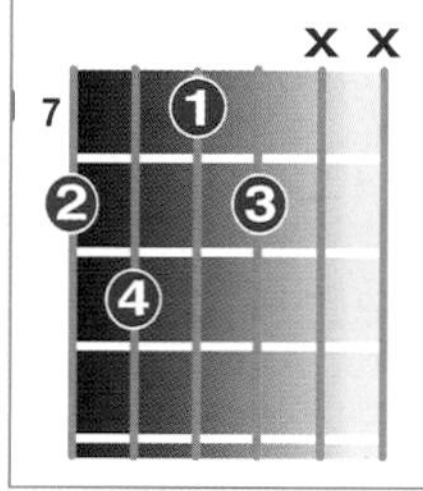

Bo7 B Diminished 7th
1st (B), ♭3rd (D), ♭5th (F), ♭♭7th (A♭)

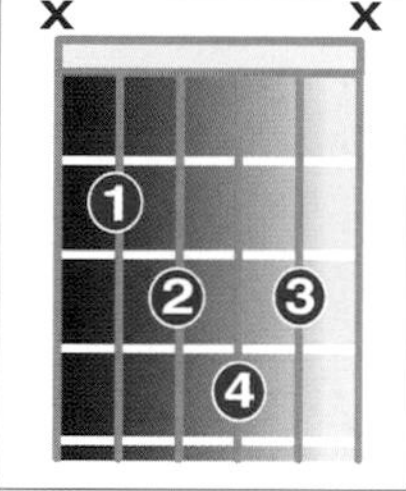

Bo B Diminished triad
1st (B), ♭3rd (D), ♭5th (F)

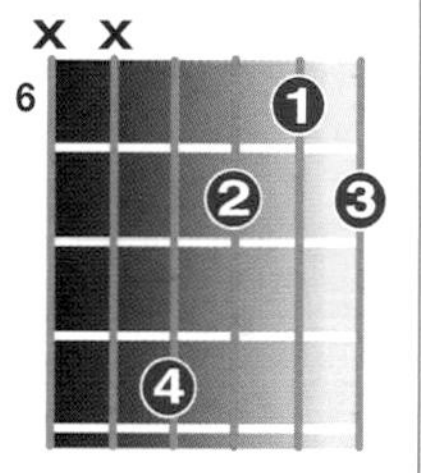

Bo B Diminished triad
1st (B), ♭3rd (D), ♭5th (F)

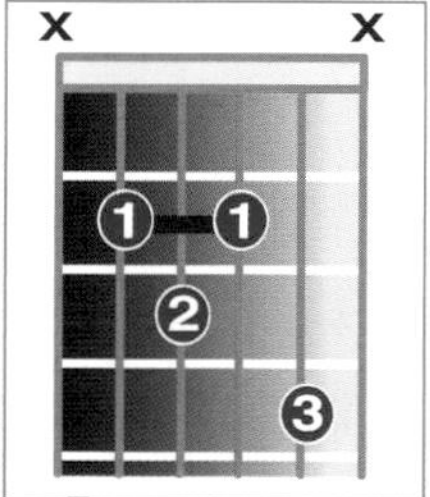

B7♭5 B Dominant 7th ♭5
1st (B), 3rd (D♯), ♭5th (F), ♭7th (A)

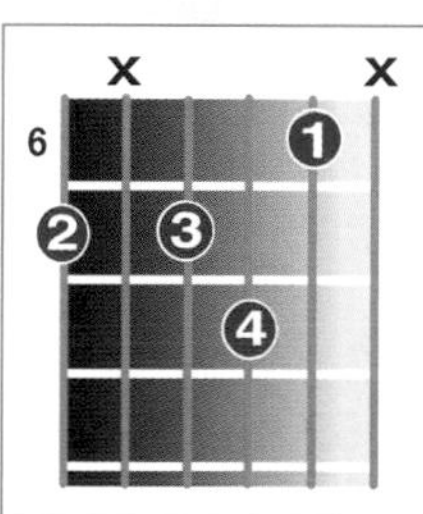

B7♭5 B Dominant 7th ♭5
1st (B), 3rd (D♯), ♭5th (F), ♭7th (A)

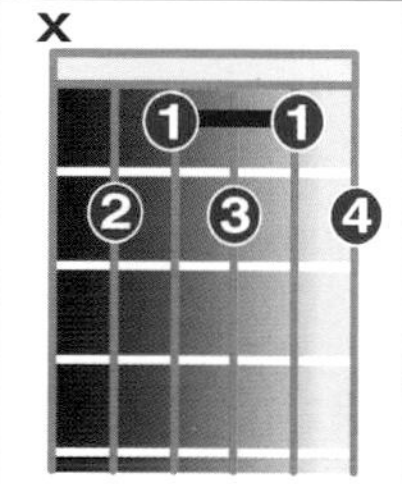

B7♭9 B Dominant 7th ♭9
1st (B), 3rd (D♯), 5th (F♯), ♭7th (A), ♭9th (C)

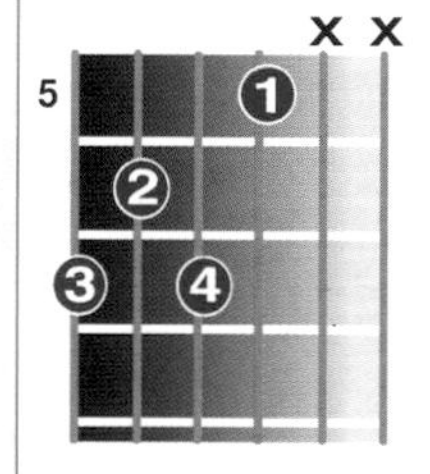

B7♭9 B Dominant 7th ♭9
1st (B), 3rd (D♯), 5th (F♯), ♭7th (A), ♭9th (C)

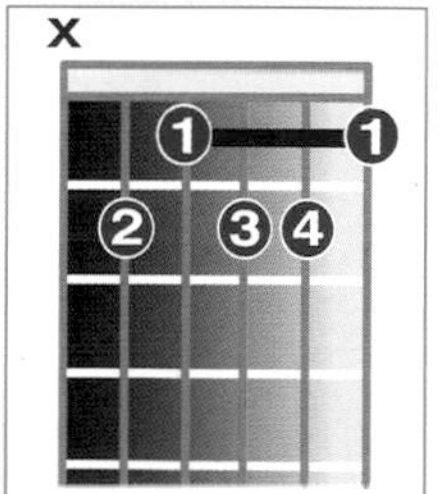

B9♭5 B Dominant 9th ♭5th
1st (B), 3rd (D♯), ♭5th (F), ♭7th (A), 9th (C♯)

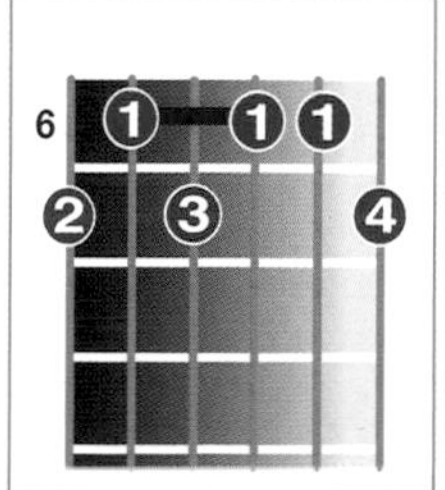

B9♭5 B Dominant 9th ♭5th
1st (B), 3rd (D♯), ♭5th (F), ♭7th (A), 9th (C♯)

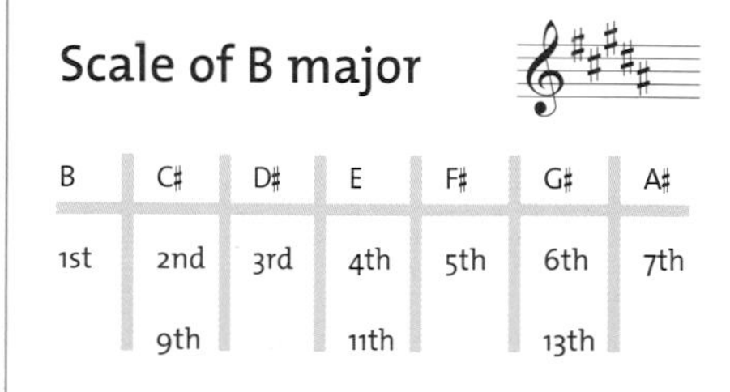

Scale of B major

B	C♯	D♯	E	F♯	G♯	A♯
1st	2nd	3rd	4th	5th	6th	7th
	9th		11th		13th	

Section Five: Chord Dictionary

C MAIN CHORDS

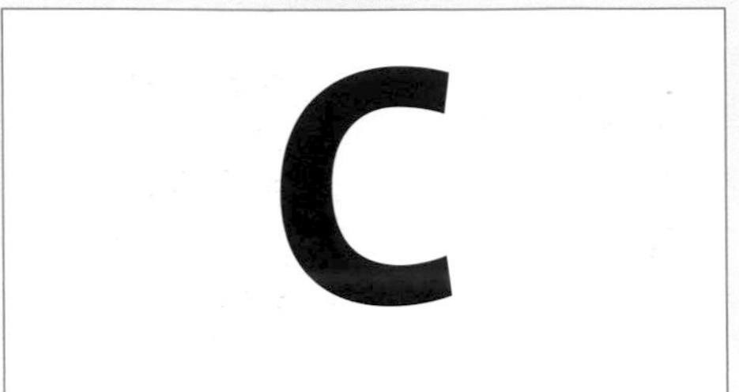

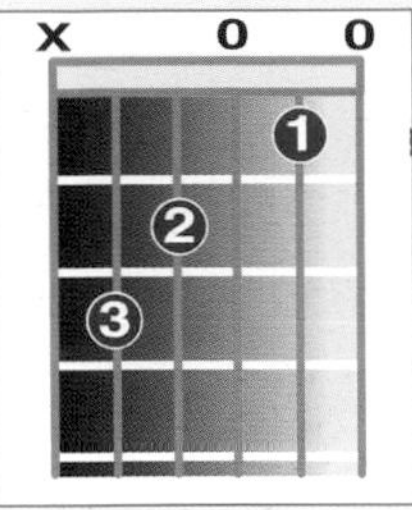

C C Major
1st (C), 3rd (E), 5th (G)

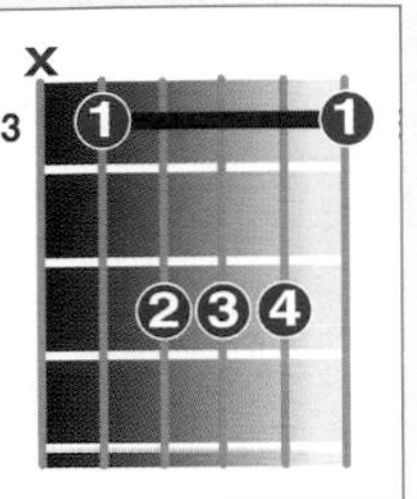

C C Major
1st (C), 3rd (E), 5th (G)

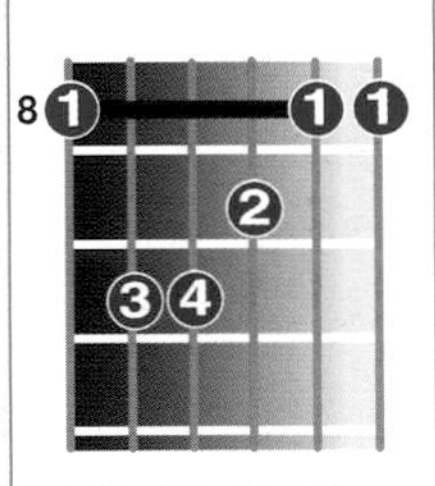

C C Major
1st (C), 3rd (E), 5th (G)

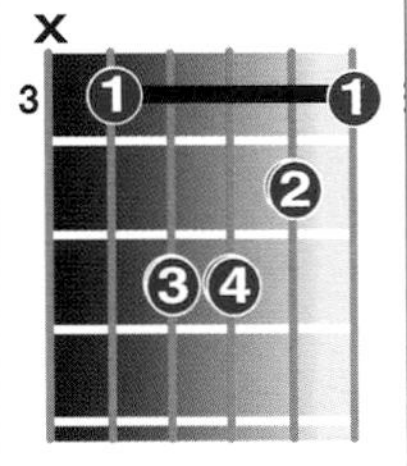

Cm C Minor
1st (C), ♭3rd (E♭), 5th (G)

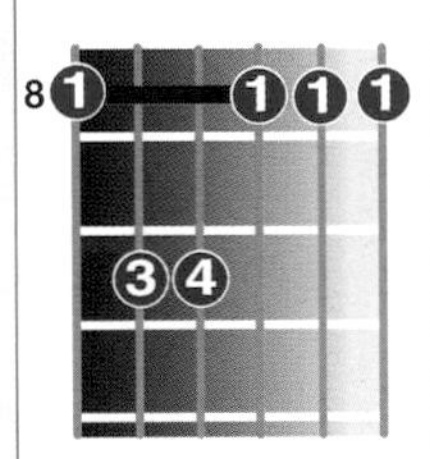

Cm C Minor
1st (C), ♭3rd (E♭), 5th (G)

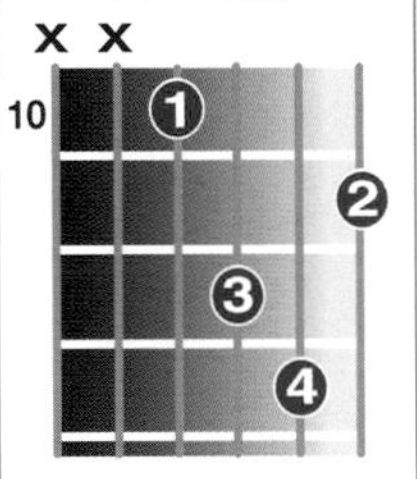

Cm C Minor
1st (C), ♭3rd (E♭), 5th (G)

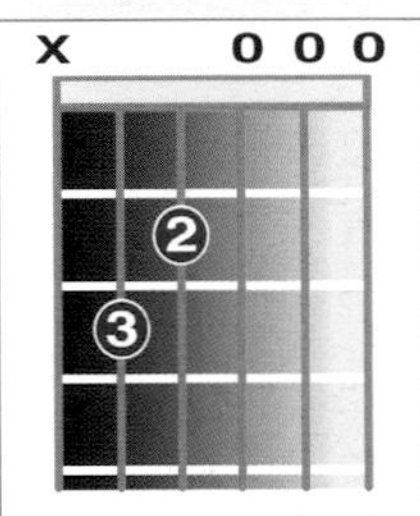

Cmaj7 C Major 7th
1st (C), 3rd (E), 5th (G), 7th (B)

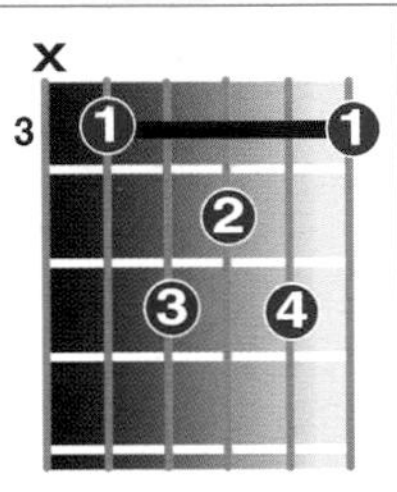

Cmaj7 C Major 7th
1st (C), 3rd (E), 5th (G), 7th (B)

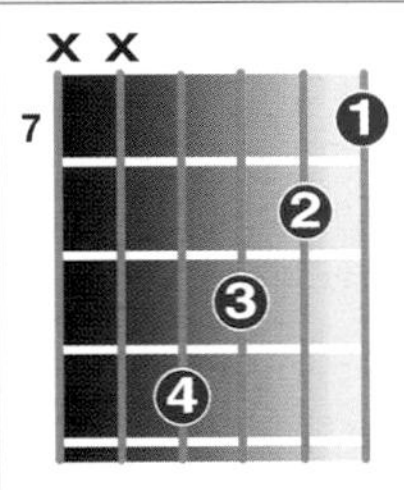

Cmaj7 C Major 7th
1st (C), 3rd (E), 5th (G), 7th (B)

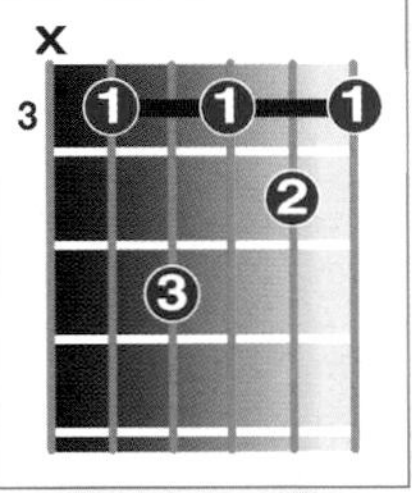

Cm7 C Minor 7th
1st (C), ♭3rd (E♭),
5th (G), ♭7th (B♭)

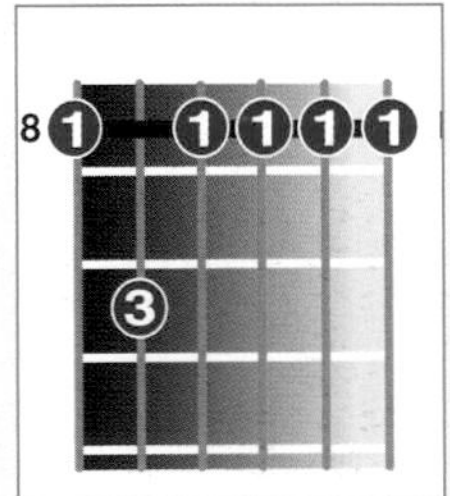

Cm7 C Minor 7th
1st (C), ♭3rd (E♭),
5th (G), ♭7th (B♭)

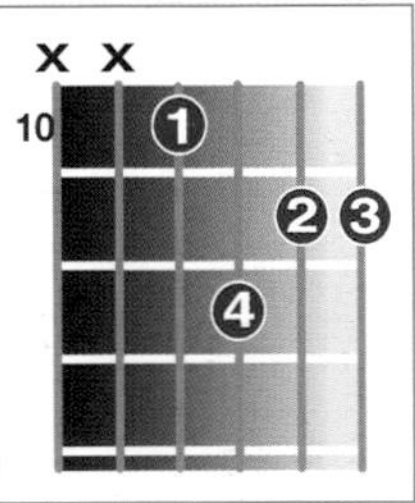

Cm7 C Minor 7th
1st (C), ♭3rd (E♭),
5th (G), ♭7th (B♭)

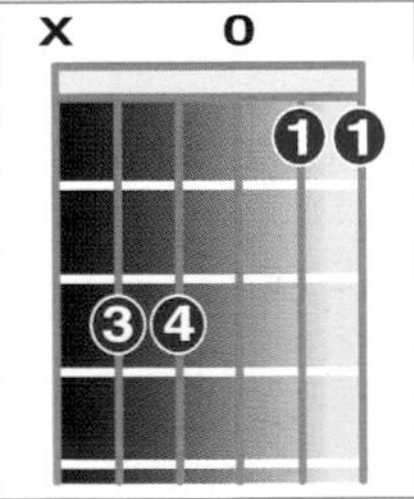

Csus4 C Suspended 4th
1st (C), 4th (F), 5th (G)

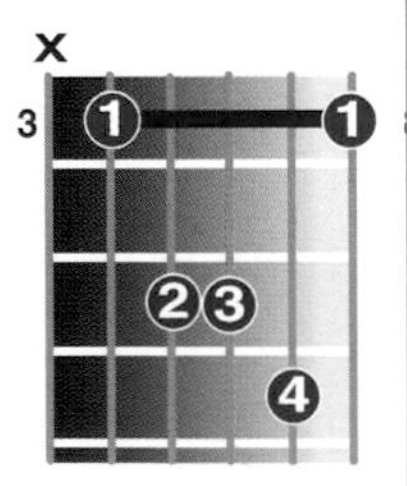

Csus4 C Suspended 4th
1st (C), 4th (F), 5th (G)

Complete Guitar Handbook

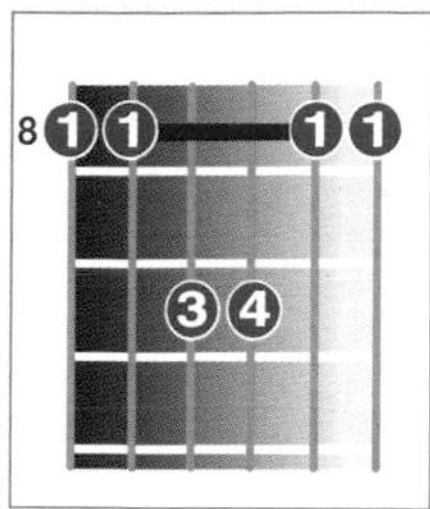

Csus4 C Suspended 4th
1st (C), 4th (F), 5th (G)

C7sus4 C Dominant 7th sus4
1st (C), 4th (F), 5th (G), ♭7th (B♭)

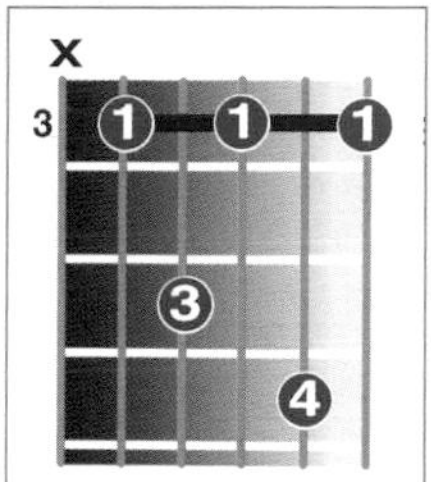

C7sus4 C Dominant 7th sus4
1st (C), 4th (F), 5th (G), ♭7th (B♭)

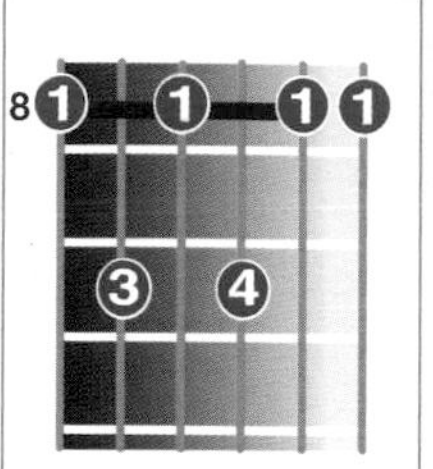

C7sus4 C Dominant 7th sus4
1st (C), 4th (F), 5th (G), ♭7th (B♭)

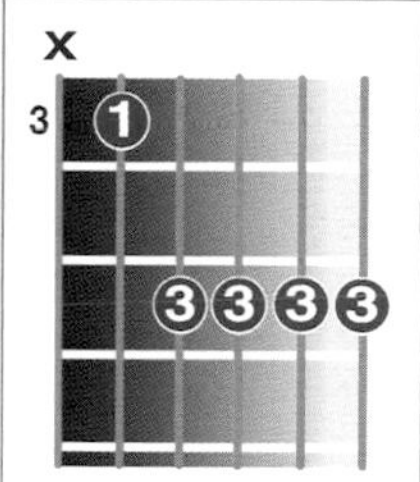

C6 C Major 6th
1st (C), 3rd (E), 5th (G), 6th (A)

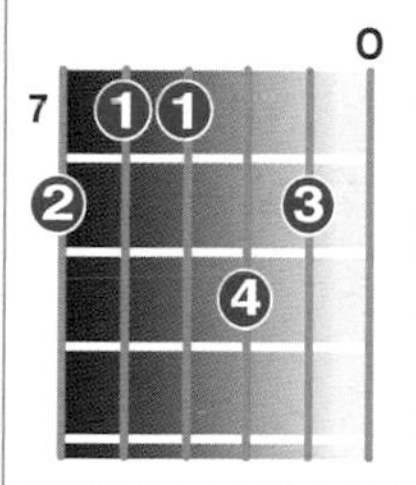

C6 C Major 6th
1st (C), 3rd (E), 5th (G), 6th (A)

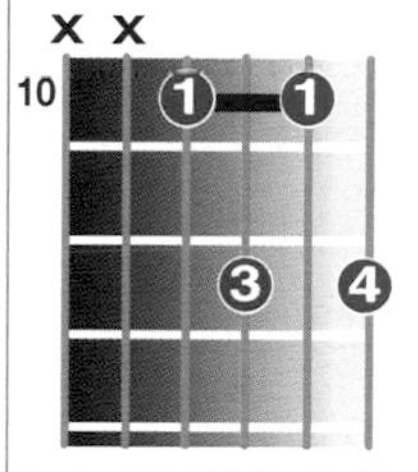

C6 C Major 6th
1st (C), 3rd (E), 5th (G), 6th (A)

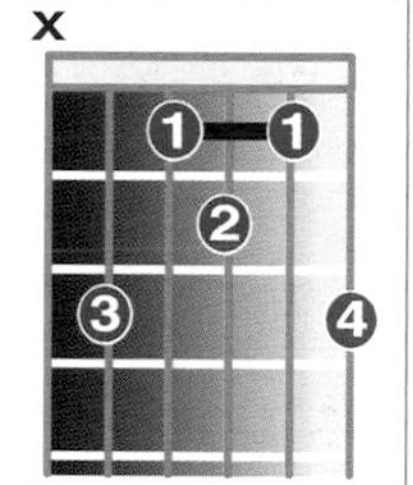

Cm6 C Minor 6th
1st (C), ♭3rd (E♭), 5th (G), 6th (A)

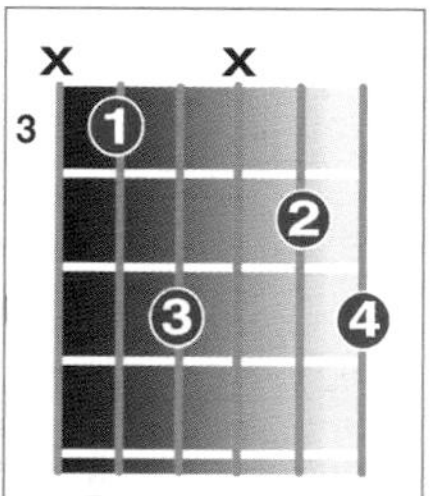

Cm6 C Minor 6th
1st (C), ♭3rd (E♭), 5th (G), 6th (A)

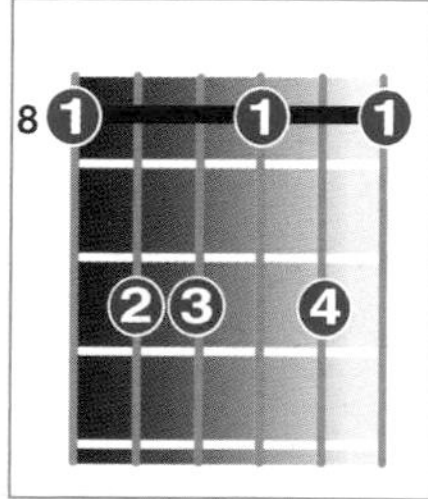

Cm6 C Minor 6th
1st (C), ♭3rd (E♭), 5th (G), 6th (A)

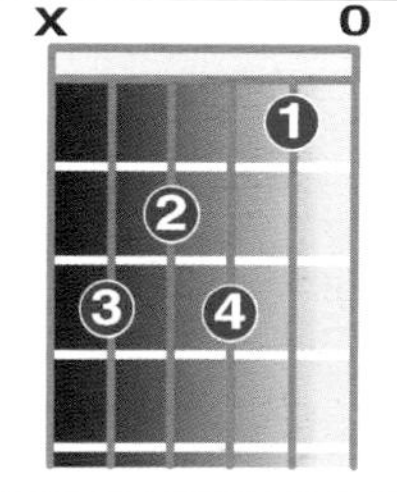

C7 C Dominant 7th
1st (C), 3rd (E), 5th (G), ♭7th (B♭)

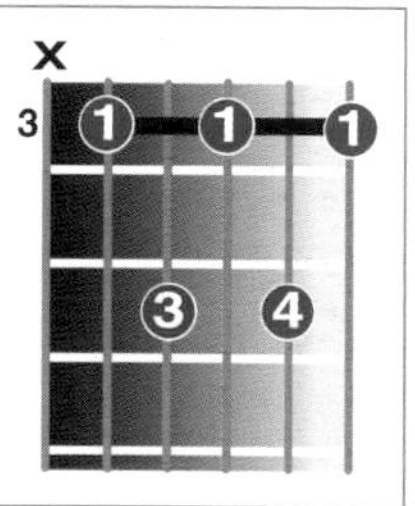

C7 C Dominant 7th
1st (C), 3rd (E), 5th (G), ♭7th (B♭)

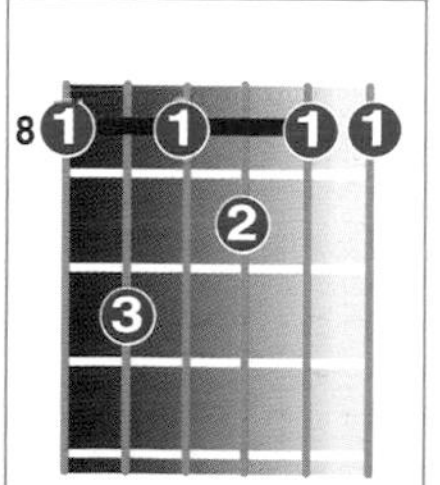

C7 C Dominant 7th
1st (C), 3rd (E), 5th (G), ♭7th (B♭)

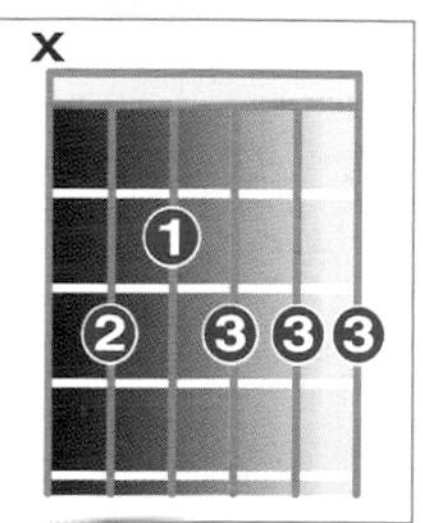

C9 C Dominant 9th
1st (C), 3rd (E), 5th (G),
♭7th (B♭), 9th (D)

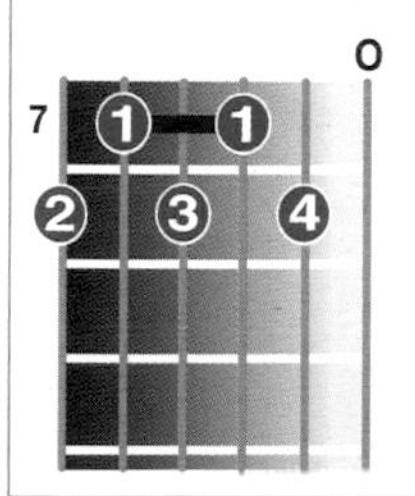

C9 C Dominant 9th
1st (C), 3rd (E), 5th (G),
♭7th (B♭), 9th (D)

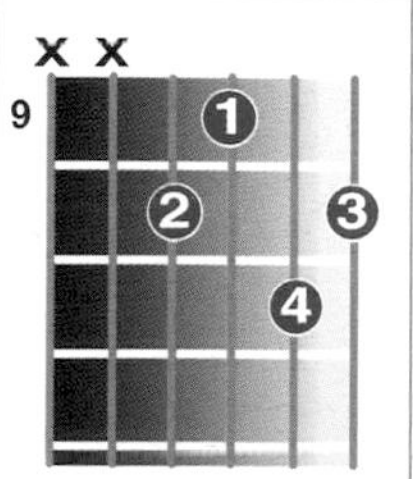

C9 C Dominant 9th
1st (C), 3rd (E), 5th (G),
♭7th (B♭), 9th (D)

Section Five: Chord Dictionary

C ADVANCED CHORDS

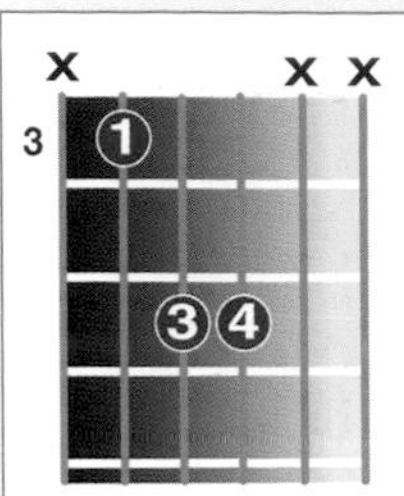

C5 C 5th (power chord)
1st (C), 5th (G)

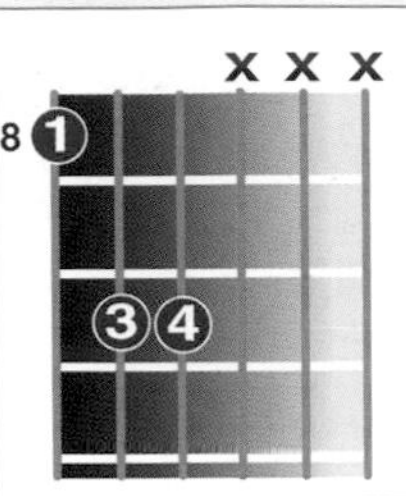

C5 C 5th (power chord)
1st (C), 5th (G)

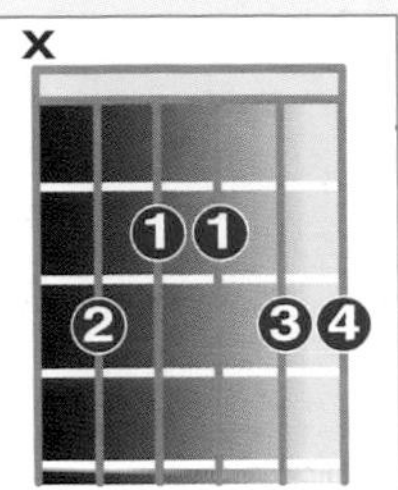

C 6/9 C Major 6th add 9th
1st (C), 3rd (E), 5th (G), 6th (A), 9th (D)

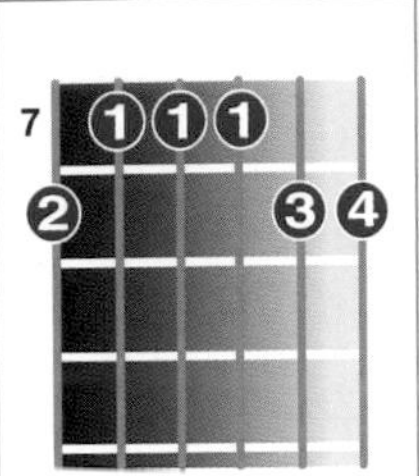

C 6/9 C Major 6th add 9th
1st (C), 3rd (E), 5th (G), 6th (A), 9th (D)

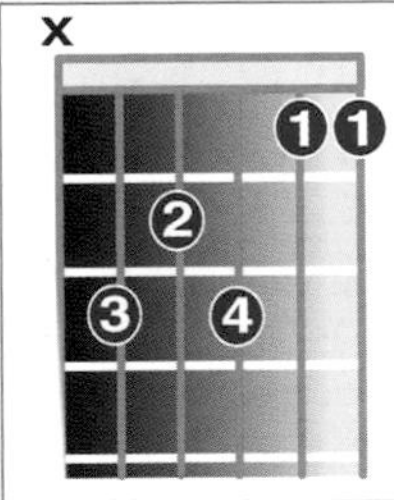

C11 C Dominant 11th
1st (C), 3rd (E), 5th (G), ♭7th (B♭), 9th (D), 11th (F)

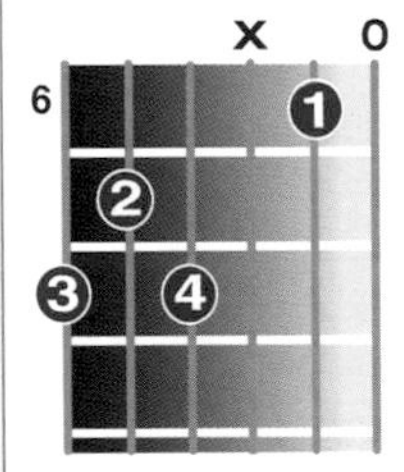

C11 C Dominant 11th
1st (C), 3rd (E), 5th (G), ♭7th (B♭), 9th (D), 11th (F)

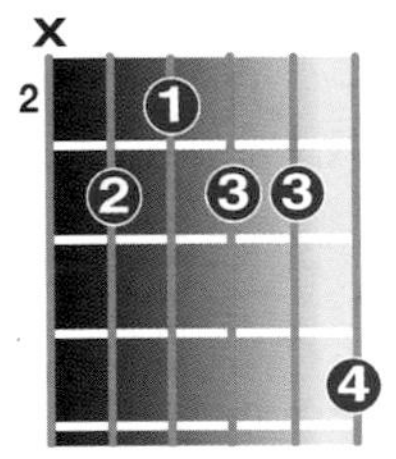

C13 C Dominant 13th
1st (C), 3rd (E), 5th (G), ♭7th (B♭), 9th (D), 13th (A)

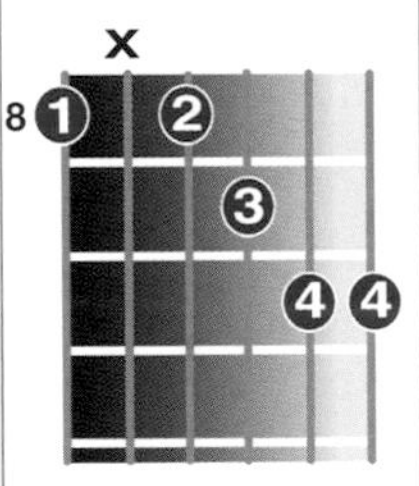

C13 C Dominant 13th
1st (C), 3rd (E), 5th (G), ♭7th (B♭), 9th (D), 13th (A)

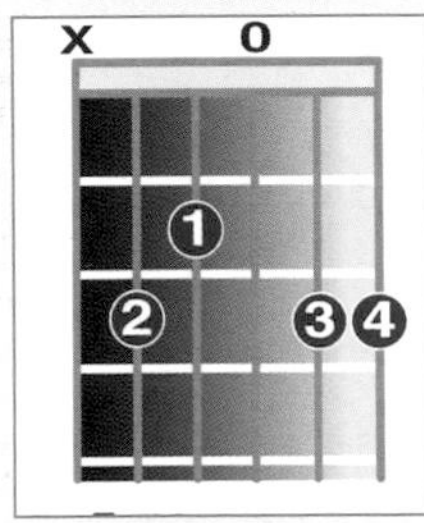

Cadd9 C Major add 9th
1st (C), 3rd (E), 5th (G), 9th (D)

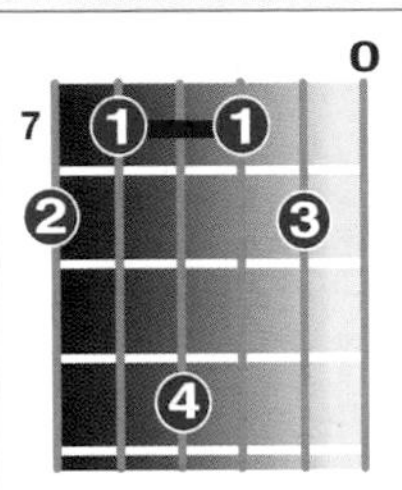

Cadd9 C Major add 9th
1st (C), 3rd (E), 5th (G), 9th (D)

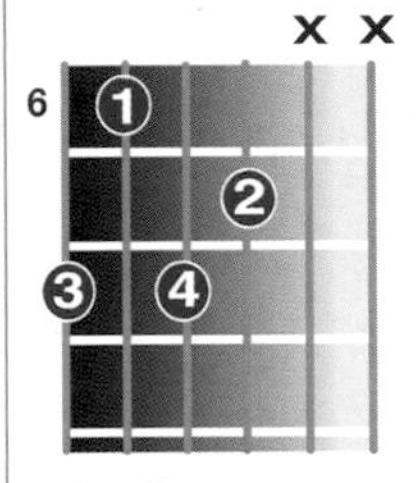

Cm9 C Minor 9th
1st (C), ♭3rd (E♭), 5th (G), ♭7th (B♭), 9th (D)

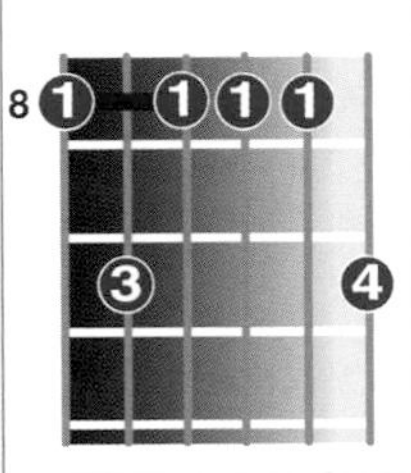

Cm9 C Minor 9th
1st (C), ♭3rd (E♭), 5th (G), ♭7th (B♭), 9th (D)

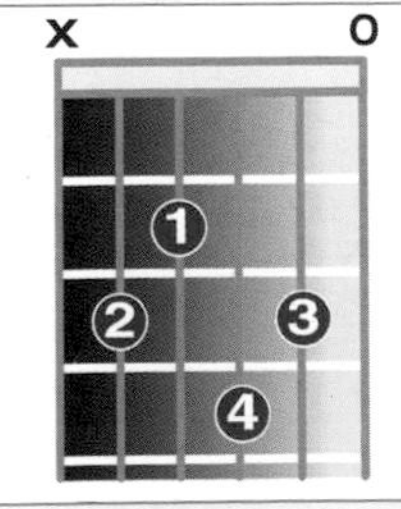

Cmaj9 C Major 9th
1st (C), 3rd (E), 5th (G), 7th (B), 9th (D)

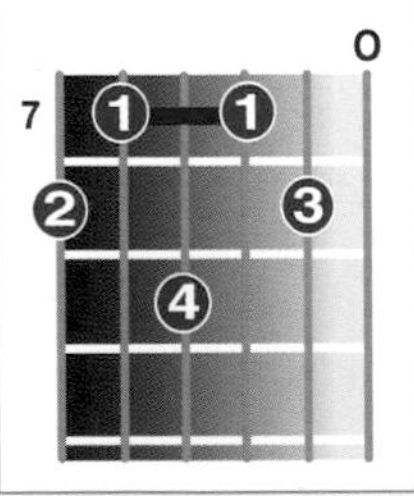

Cmaj9 C Major 9th
1st (C), 3rd (E), 5th (G), 7th (B), 9th (D)

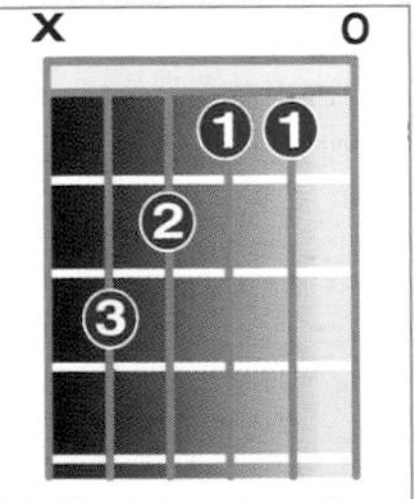

C+ C Augmented
1st (C), 3rd (E), ♯5th (G♯)

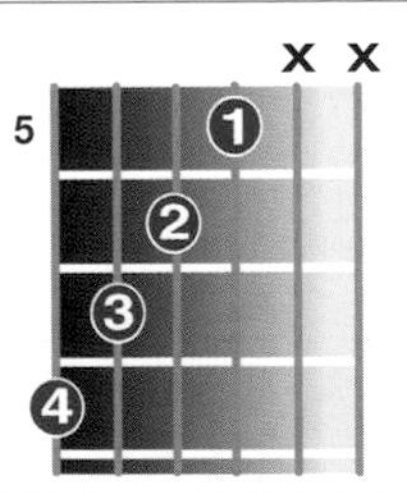

C+ C Augmented
1st (C), 3rd (E), ♯5th (G♯)

Complete Guitar Handbook

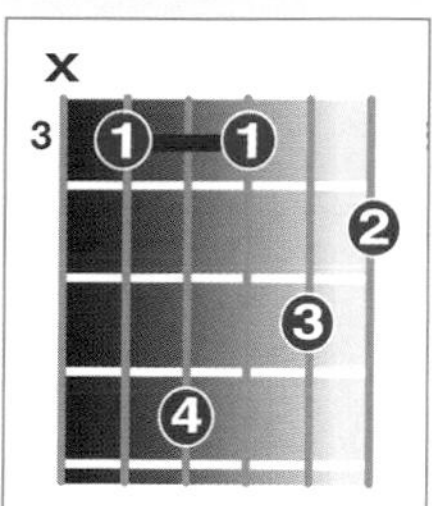

C7♯5 C Dominant 7th ♯5
1st (C), 3rd (E), ♯5th (G♯), ♭7th (B♭)

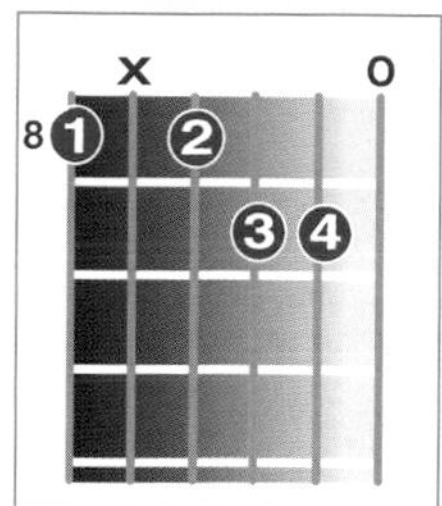

C7♯5 C Dominant 7th ♯5
1st (C), 3rd (E), ♯5th (G♯), ♭7th (B♭)

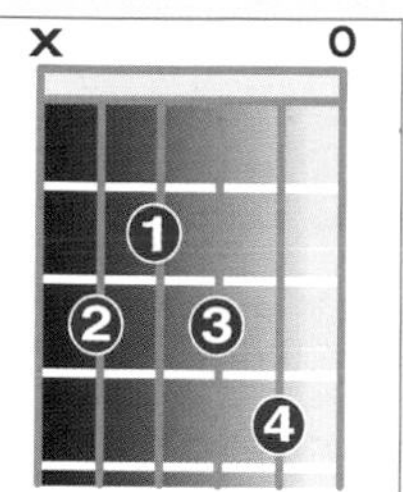

C7♯9 C Dominant 7th ♯9
1st (C), 3rd (E), 5th (G), ♭7th (B♭), ♯9th (D♯)

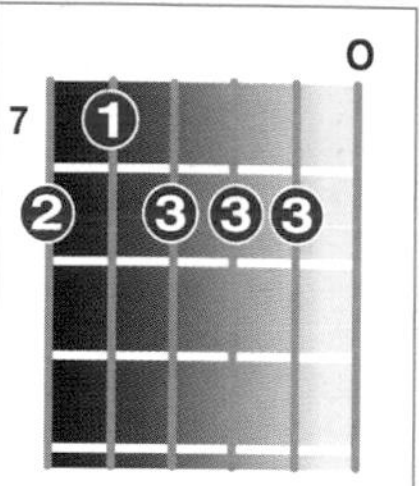

C7♯9 C Dominant 7th ♯9
1st (C), 3rd (E), 5th (G), ♭7th (B♭), ♯9th (D♯)

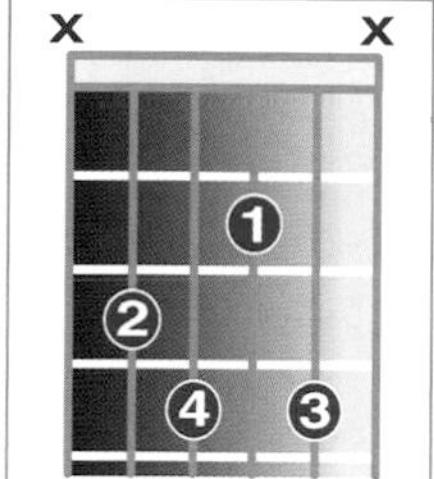

Co7 C Diminished 7th
1st (C), ♭3rd (E♭), ♭5th (G♭), ♭♭7th (B♭♭)

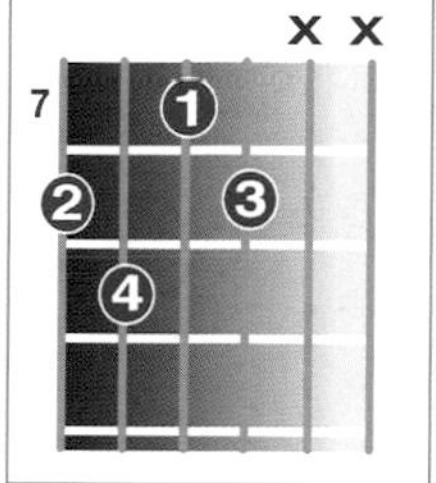

Co7 C Diminished 7th
1st (C), ♭3rd (E♭), ♭5th (G♭), ♭♭7th (B♭♭)

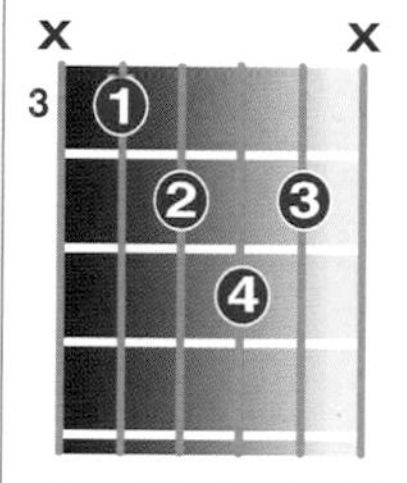

Co C Diminished triad
1st (C), ♭3rd (E♭), ♭5th (G♭)

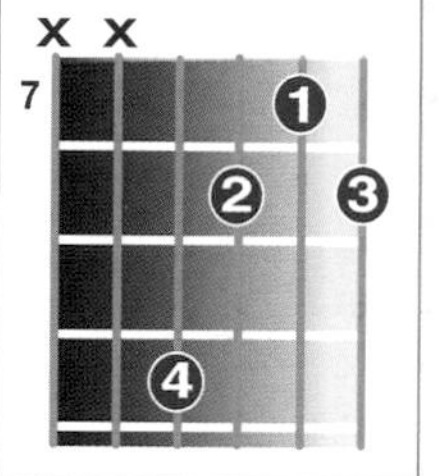

Co C Diminished triad
1st (C), ♭3rd (E♭), ♭5th (G♭)

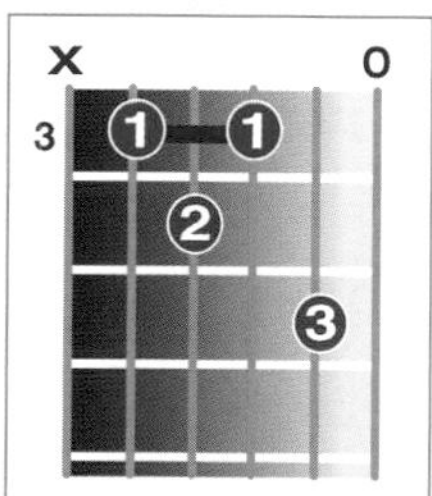

C7♭5 C Dominant 7th ♭5
1st (C), 3rd (E), ♭5th (G♭), ♭7th (B♭)

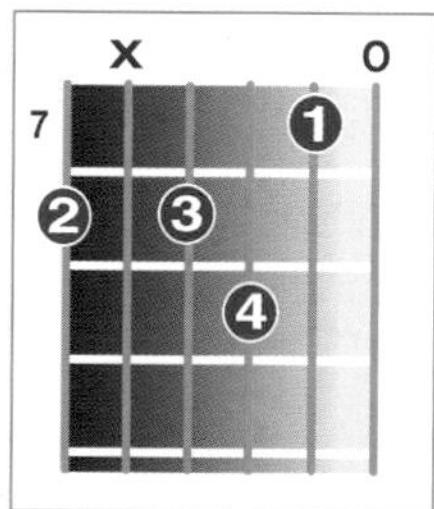

C7♭5 C Dominant 7th ♭5
1st (C), 3rd (E), ♭5th (G♭), ♭7th (B♭)

C7♭9 C Dominant 7th ♭9
1st (C), 3rd (E), 5th (G), ♭7th (B♭), ♭9th (D♭)

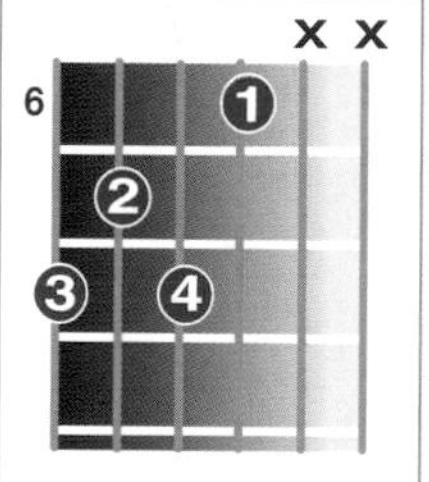

C7♭9 C Dominant 7th ♭9
1st (C), 3rd (E), 5th (G), ♭7th (B♭), ♭9th (D♭)

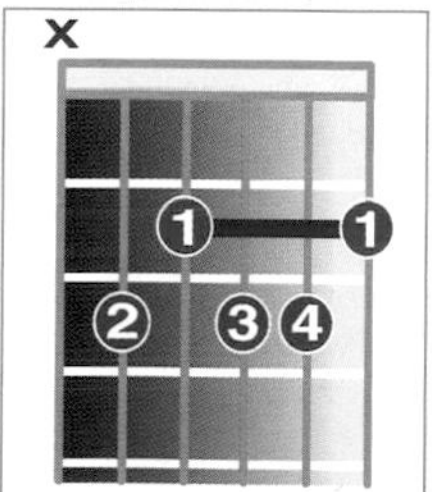

C9♭5 C Dominant 9th ♭5th
1st (C), 3rd (E), ♭5th (G♭), ♭7th (B♭), 9th (D)

C9♭5 C Dominant 9th ♭5th
1st (C), 3rd (E), ♭5th (G♭), ♭7th (B♭), 9th (D)

Scale of C major

C	D	E	F	G	A	B
1st	2nd	3rd	4th	5th	6th	7th
	9th		11th		13th	

Section Five: Chord Dictionary

C♯/D♭ MAIN CHORDS

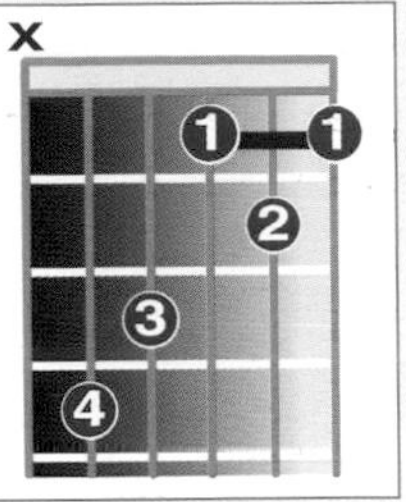

C♯ C♯ Major
1st (C♯), 3rd (E♯), 5th (G♯)

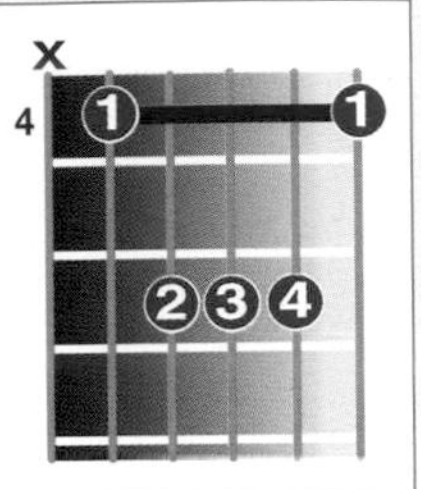

C♯ C♯ Major
1st (C♯), 3rd (E♯), 5th (G♯)

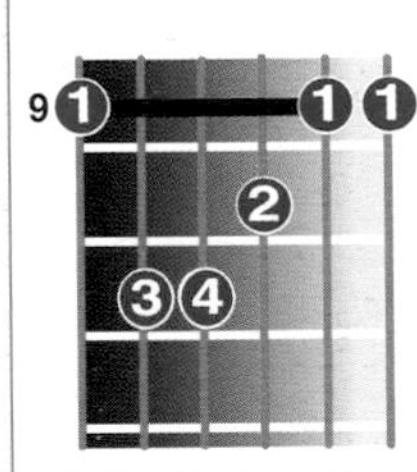

C♯ C♯ Major
1st (C♯), 3rd (E♯), 5th (G♯)

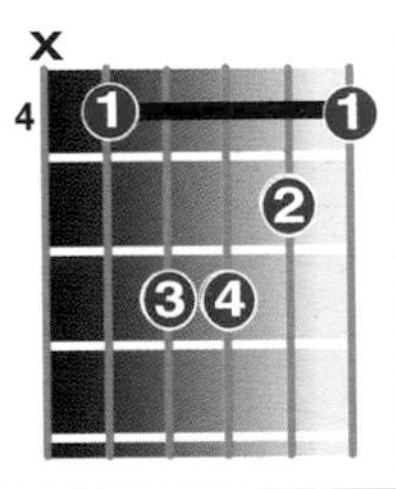

C♯m C♯ Minor
1st (C♯), ♭3rd (E), 5th (G♯)

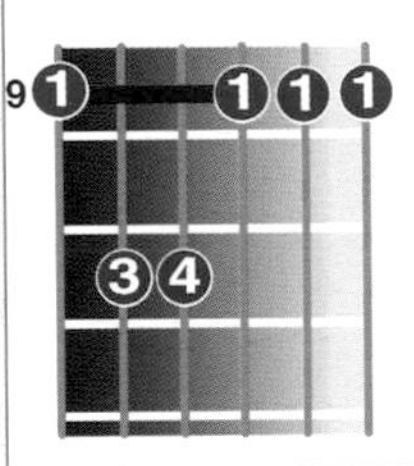

C♯m C♯ Minor
1st (C♯), ♭3rd (E), 5th (G♯)

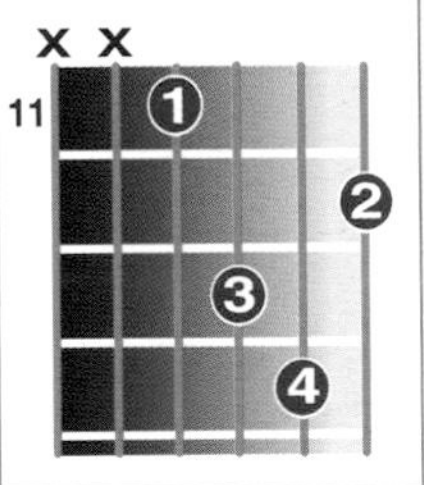

C♯m C♯ Minor
1st (C♯), ♭3rd (E), 5th (G♯)

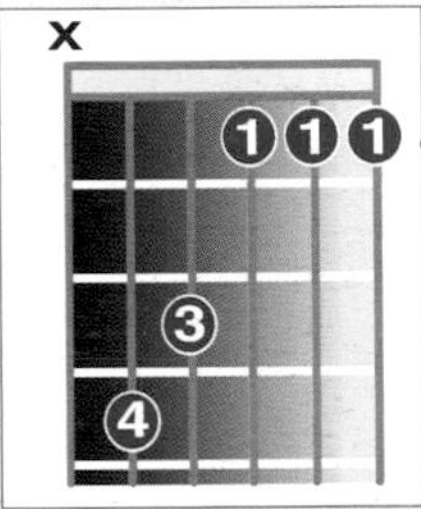

C♯maj7 C♯ Major 7th
1st (C♯), 3rd (E♯), 5th (G♯), 7th (B♯)

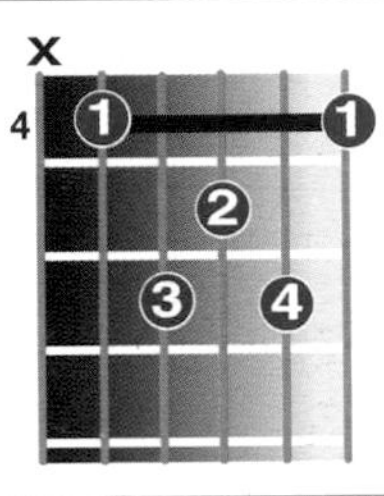

C♯maj7 C♯ Major 7th
1st (C♯), 3rd (E♯), 5th (G♯), 7th (B♯)

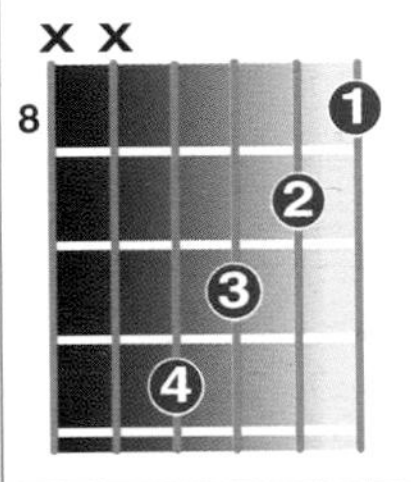

C♯maj7 C♯ Major 7th
1st (C♯), 3rd (E♯), 5th (G♯), 7th (B♯)

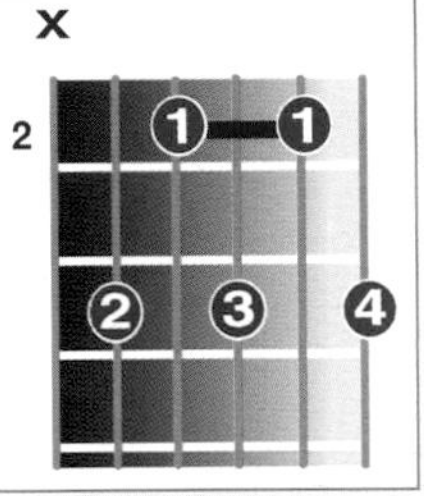

C♯m7 C♯ Minor 7th
1st (C♯), ♭3rd (E), 5th (G♯), ♭7th (B)

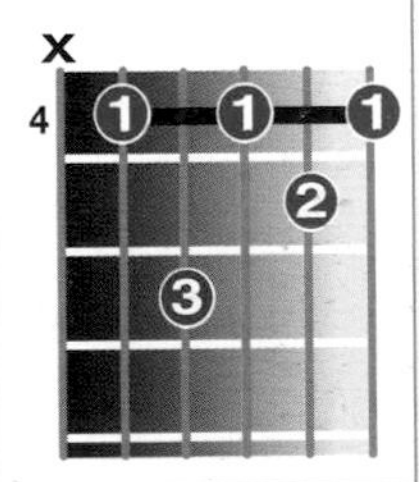

C♯m7 C♯ Minor 7th
1st (C♯), ♭3rd (E), 5th (G♯), ♭7th (B)

C♯m7 C♯ Minor 7th
1st (C♯), ♭3rd (E), 5th (G♯), ♭7th (B)

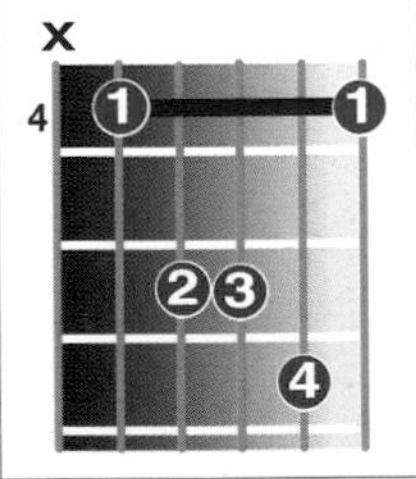

C♯sus4 C♯ Suspended 4th
1st (C♯), 4th (F♯), 5th (G♯)

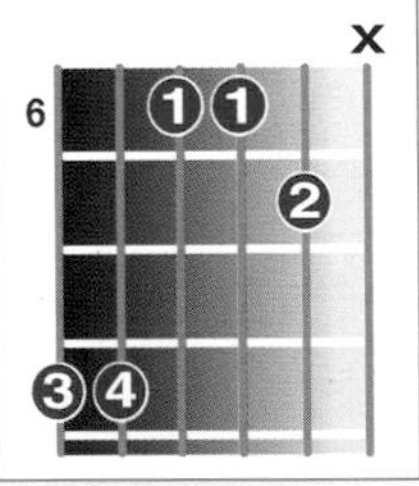

C♯sus4 C♯ Suspended 4th
1st (C♯), 4th (F♯), 5th (G♯)

Complete Guitar Handbook

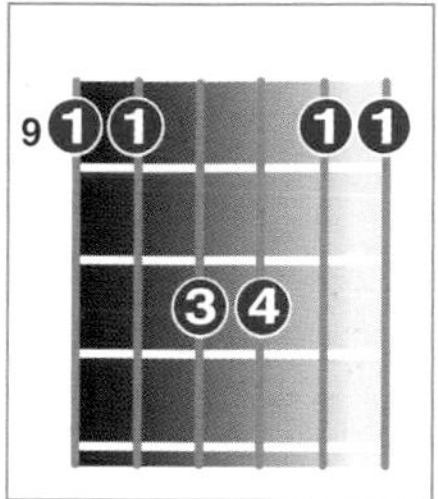

C♯sus4 C♯ Suspended 4th
1st (C♯), 4th (F♯), 5th (G♯)

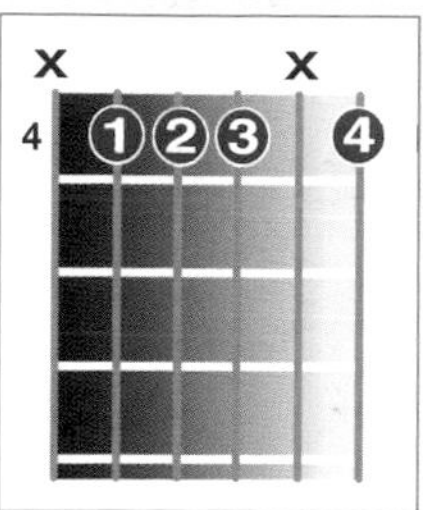

C♯7sus4 C♯ Dominant 7th sus4
1st (C♯), 4th (F♯), 5th (G♯), ♭7th (B)

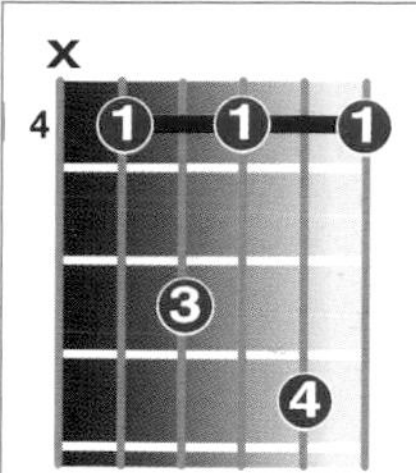

C♯7sus4 C♯ Dominant 7th sus4
1st (C♯), 4th (F♯), 5th (G♯), ♭7th (B)

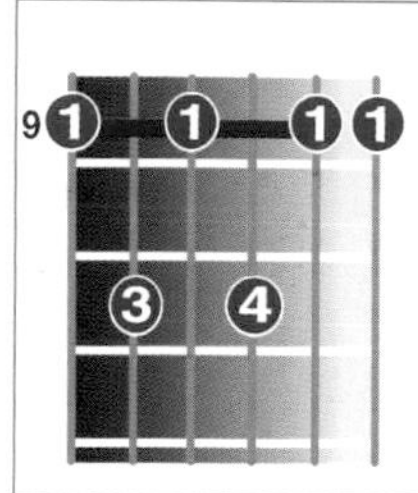

C♯7sus4 C♯ Dominant 7th sus4
1st (C♯), 4th (F♯), 5th (G♯), ♭7th (B)

C♯6 C♯ Major 6th
1st (C♯), 3rd (E♯),
5th (G♯), 6th (A♯)

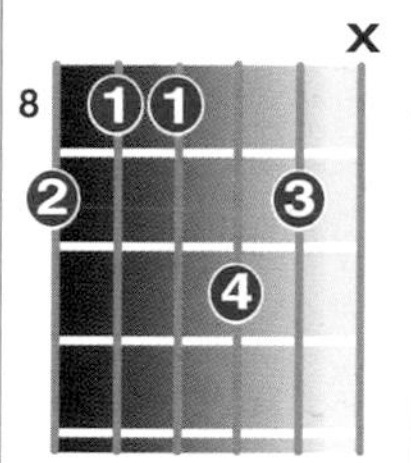

C♯6 C♯ Major 6th
1st (C♯), 3rd (E♯),
5th (G♯), 6th (A♯)

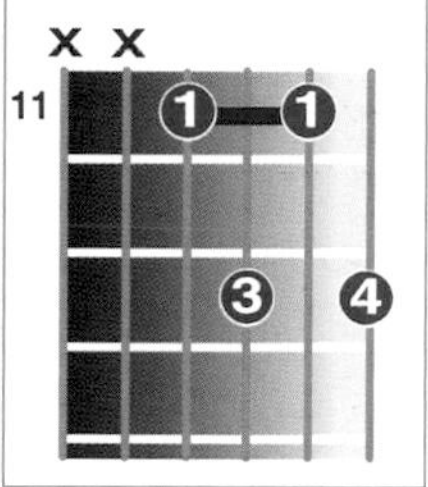

C♯6 C♯ Major 6th
1st (C♯), 3rd (E♯),
5th (G♯), 6th (A♯)

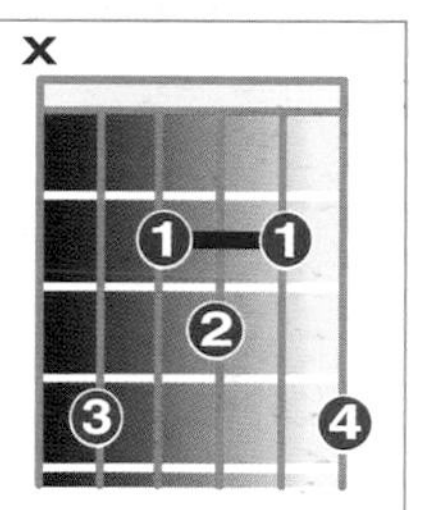

C♯m6 C♯ Minor 6th
1st (C♯), ♭3rd (E),
5th (G♯), 6th (A♯)

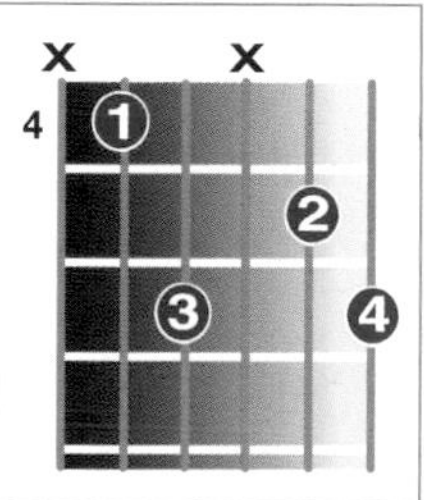

C♯m6 C♯ Minor 6th
1st (C♯), ♭3rd (E),
5th (G♯), 6th (A♯)

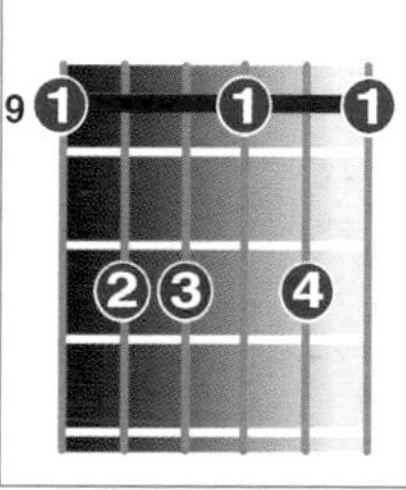

C♯m6 C♯ Minor 6th
1st (C♯), ♭3rd (E),
5th (G♯), 6th (A♯)

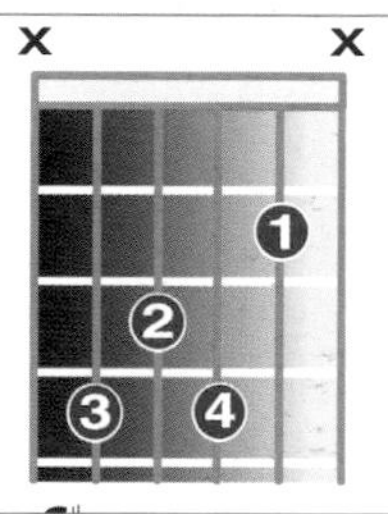

C♯7 C♯ Dominant 7th
1st (C♯), 3rd (E♯),
5th (G♯), ♭7th (B)

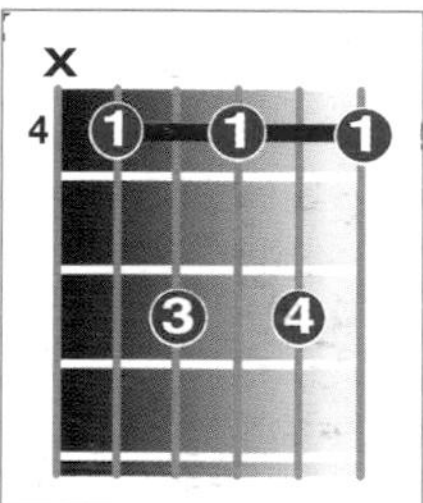

C♯7 C♯ Dominant 7th
1st (C♯), 3rd (E♯),
5th (G♯), ♭7th (B)

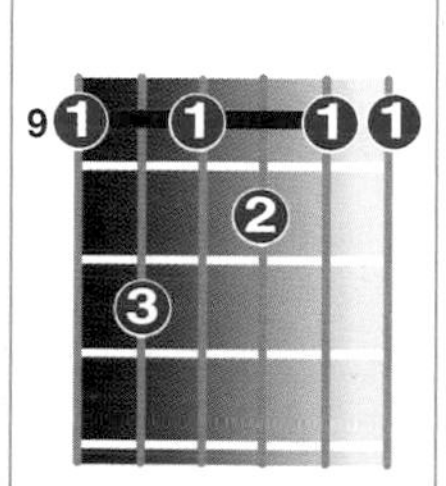

C♯7 C♯ Dominant 7th
1st (C♯), 3rd (E♯),
5th (G♯), ♭7th (B)

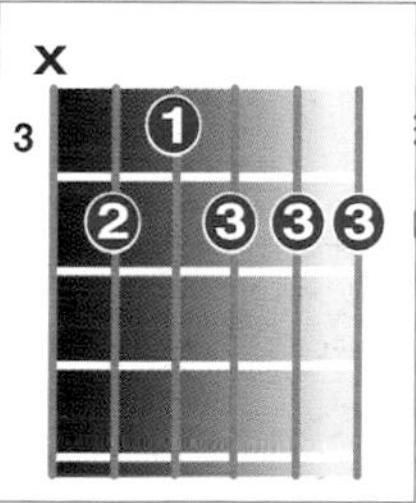

C♯9 C♯ Dominant 9th
1st (C♯), 3rd (E♯), 5th (G♯),
♭7th (B), 9th (D♯)

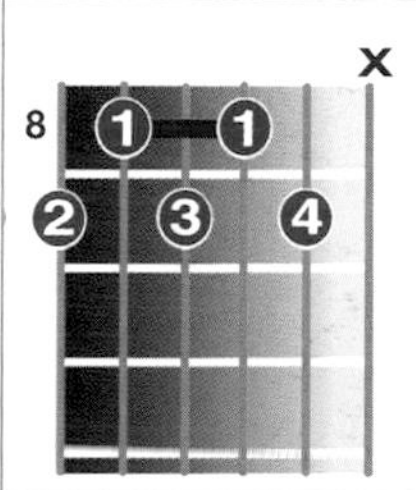

C♯9 C♯ Dominant 9th
1st (C♯), 3rd (E♯), 5th (G♯),
♭7th (B), 9th (D♯)

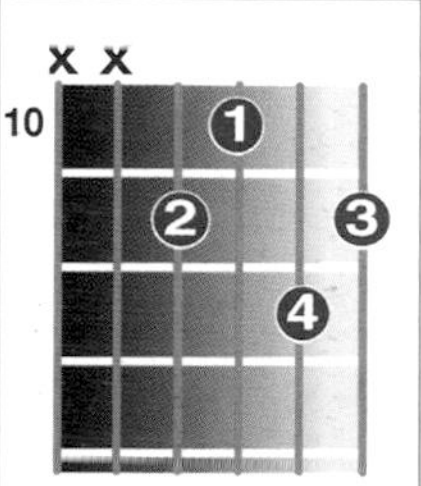

C♯9 C♯ Dominant 9th
1st (C♯), 3rd (E♯), 5th (G♯),
♭7th (B), 9th (D♯)

Section Five: Chord Dictionary

C♯/D♭ ADVANCED CHORDS

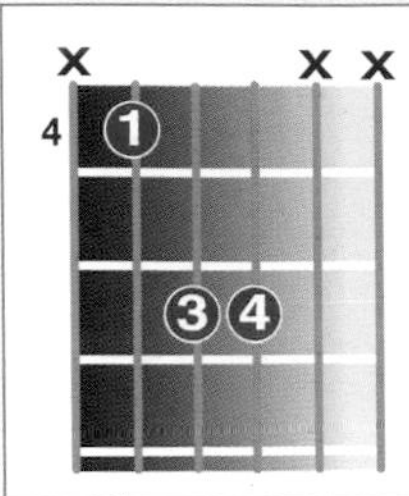

C♯5 C♯ 5th (power chord)
1st (C♯), 5th (G♯)

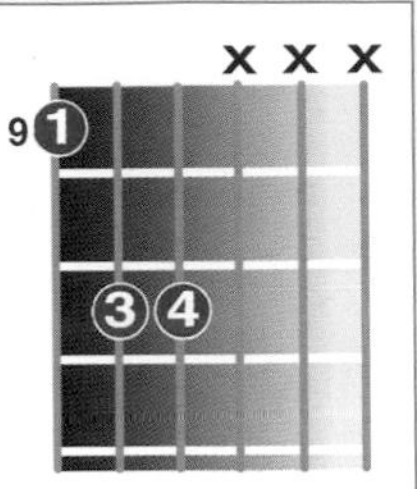

C♯5 C♯ 5th (power chord)
1st (C♯), 5th (G♯)

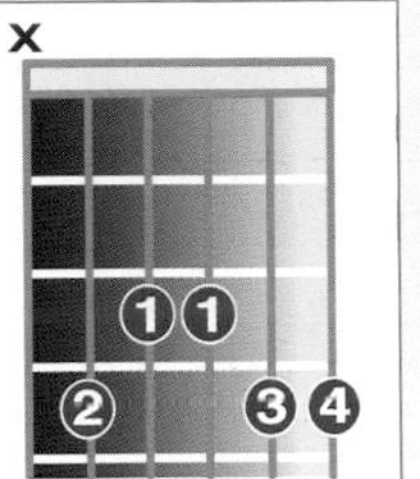

C♯ 6/9 C♯ Major 6th add 9th
1st (C♯), 3rd (E♯), 5th (G♯), 6th (A♯), 9th (D♯)

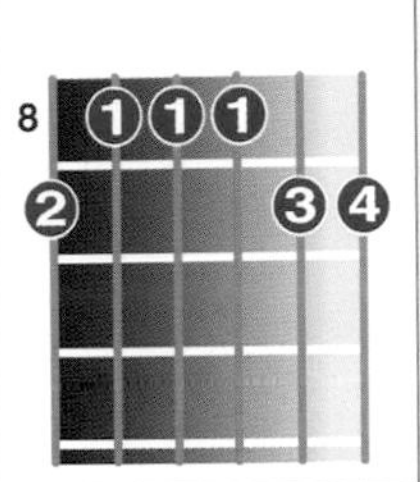

C♯ 6/9 C♯ Major 6th add 9th
1st (C♯), 3rd (E♯), 5th (G♯), 6th (A♯), 9th (D♯)

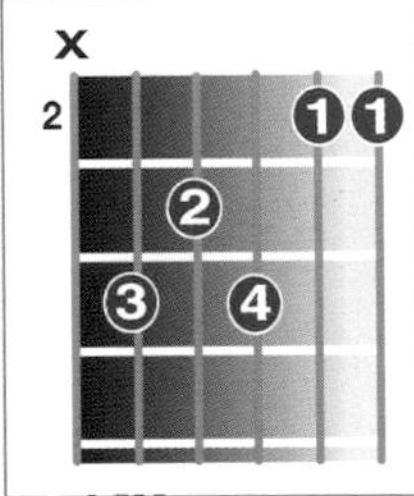

C♯11 C♯ Dominant 11th
1st (C♯), 3rd (E♯), 5th (G♯), ♭7th (B), 9th (D♯), 11th (F♯)

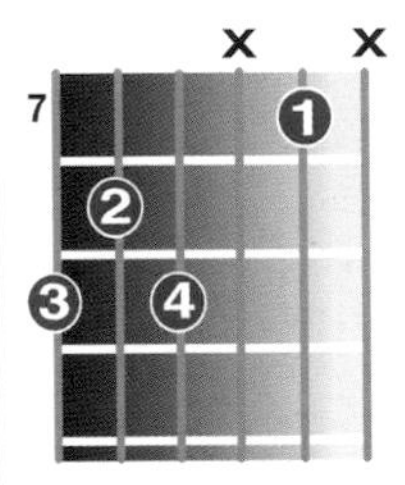

C♯11 C♯ Dominant 11th
1st (C♯), 3rd (E♯), 5th (G♯), ♭7th (B), 9th (D♯), 11th (F♯)

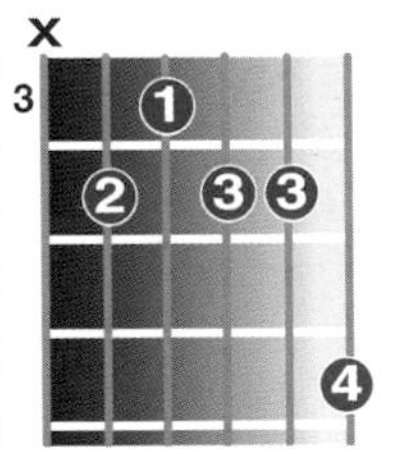

C♯13 C♯ Dominant 13th
1st (C♯), 3rd (E♯), 5th (G♯), ♭7th (B), 9th (D♯), 13th (A♯)

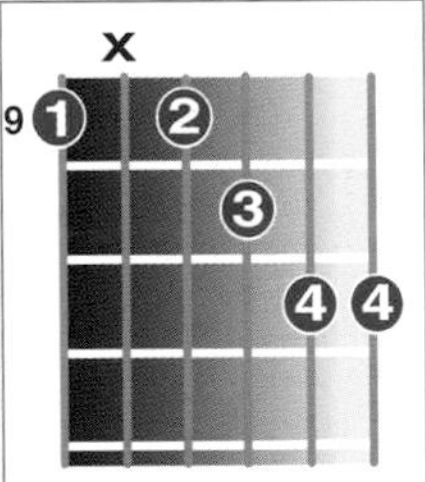

C♯13 C♯ Dominant 13th
1st (C♯), 3rd (E♯), 5th (G♯), ♭7th (B), 9th (D♯), 13th (A♯)

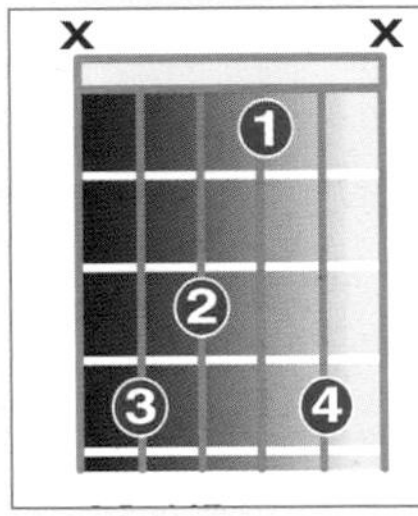

C♯add9 C♯ Major add 9th
1st (C♯), 3rd (E♯), 5th (G♯), 9th (D♯)

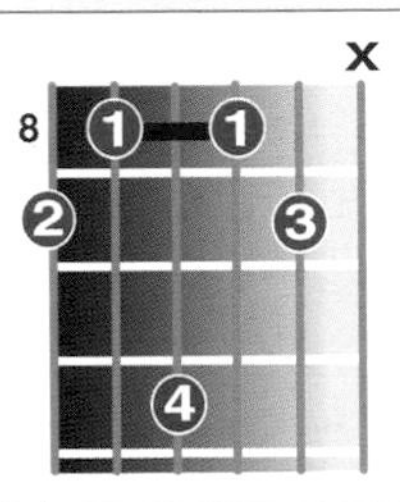

C♯add9 C♯ Major add 9th
1st (C♯), 3rd (E♯), 5th (G♯), 9th (D♯)

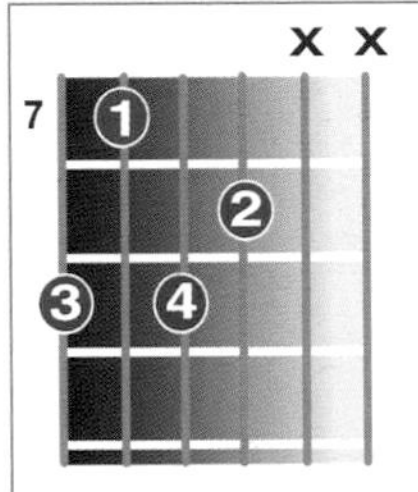

C♯m9 C♯ Minor 9th
1st (C♯), ♭3rd (E), 5th (G♯), ♭7th (B), 9th (D♯)

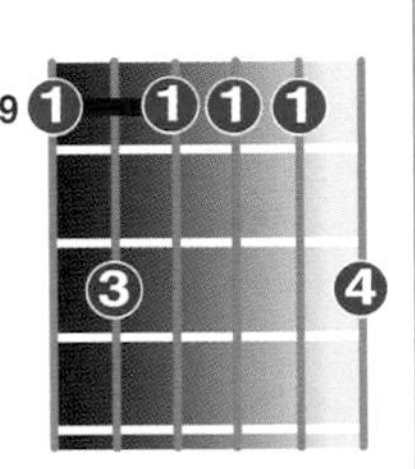

C♯m9 C♯ Minor 9th
1st (C♯), ♭3rd (E), 5th (G♯), ♭7th (B), 9th (D♯)

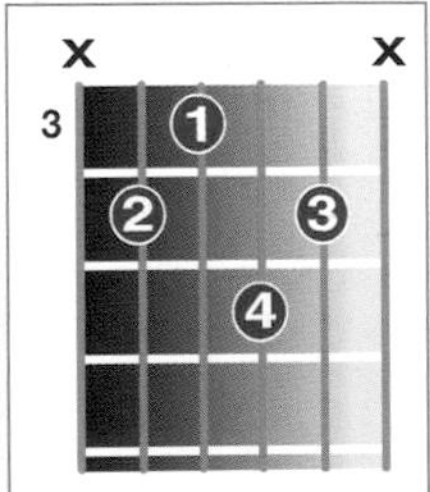

C♯maj9 C♯ Major 9th
1st (C♯), 3rd (E♯), 5th (G♯), 7th (B♯), 9th (D♯)

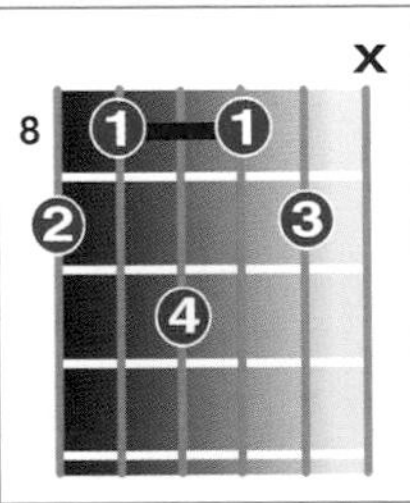

C♯maj9 C♯ Major 9th
1st (C♯), 3rd (E♯), 5th (G♯), 7th (B♯), 9th (D♯)

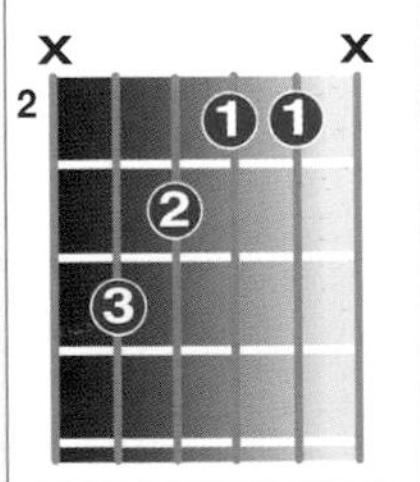

C♯+ C♯ Augmented
1st (C♯), 3rd (E♯), ♯5th (Gx)

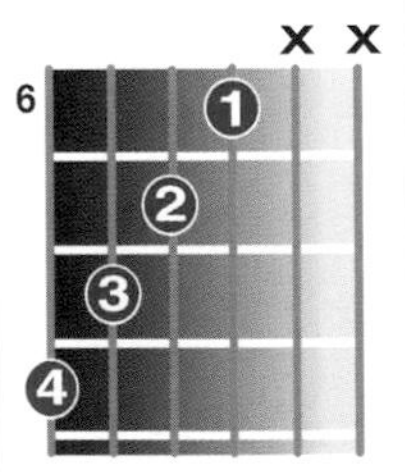

C♯+ C♯ Augmented
1st (C♯), 3rd (E♯), ♯5th (Gx)

Complete Guitar Handbook

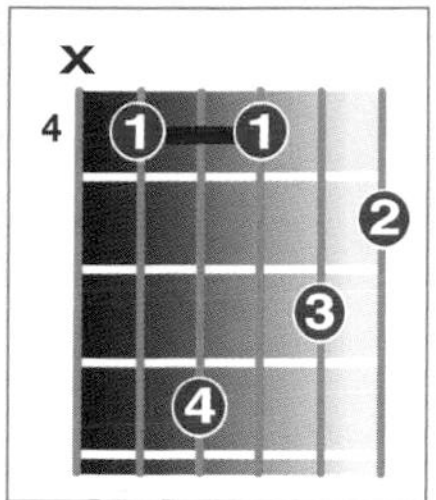

C♯7♯5 C♯ Dominant 7th ♯5
1st (C♯), 3rd (E♯), ♯5th (Gx), b7th (B)

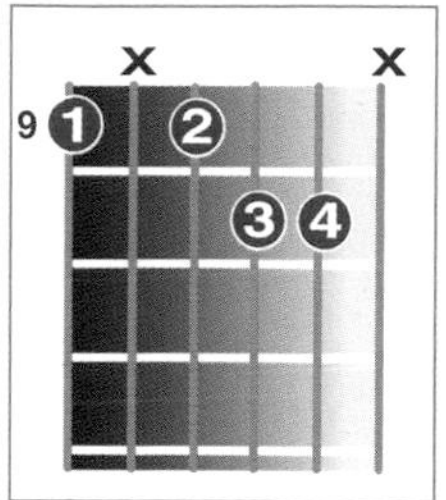

C♯7♯5 C♯ Dominant 7th ♯5
1st (C♯), 3rd (E♯), ♯5th (Gx), b7th (B)

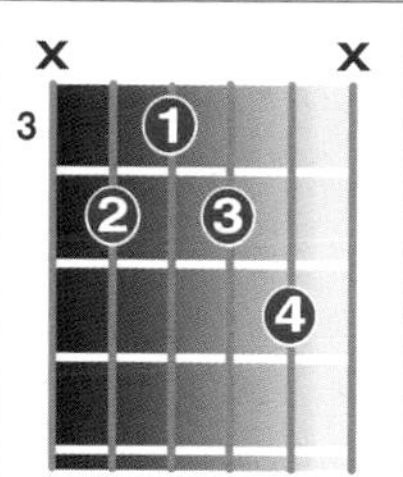

C♯7♯9 C♯ Dominant 7th ♯9
1st (C♯), 3rd (E♯), 5th (G♯), ♭7th (B), ♯9th (Dx)

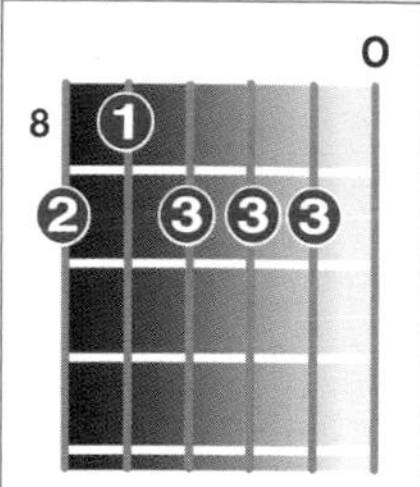

C♯7♯9 C♯ Dominant 7th ♯9
1st (C♯), 3rd (E♯), 5th (G♯), ♭7th (B), ♯9th (Dx)

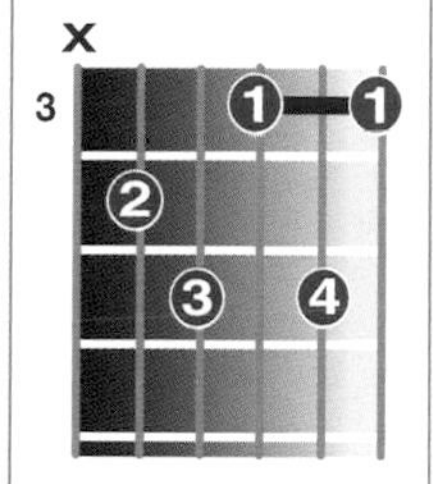

C♯o7 C♯ Diminished 7th
1st (C♯), ♭3rd (E), ♭5th (G), ♭♭7th (B♭)

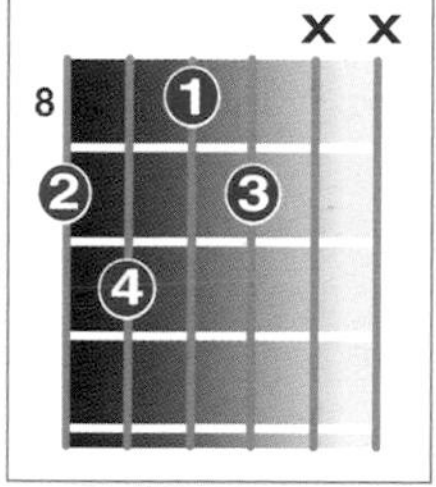

C♯o7 C♯ Diminished 7th
1st (C♯), ♭3rd (E), ♭5th (G), ♭♭7th (B♭)

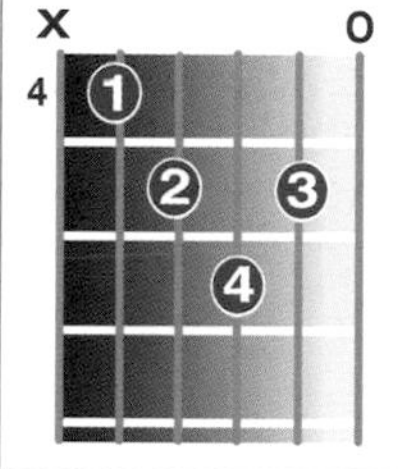

C♯o C♯ Diminished triad
1st (C♯), ♭3rd (E), ♭5th (G)

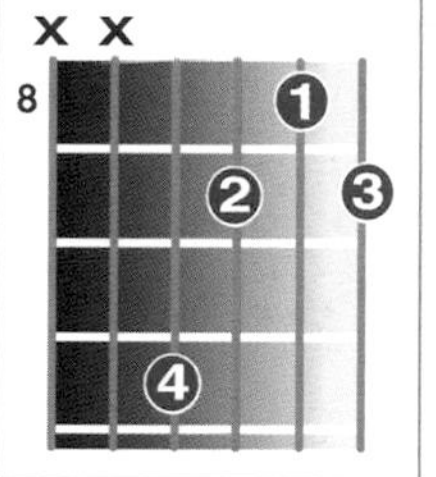

C♯o C♯ Diminished triad
1st (C♯), ♭3rd (E), ♭5th (G)

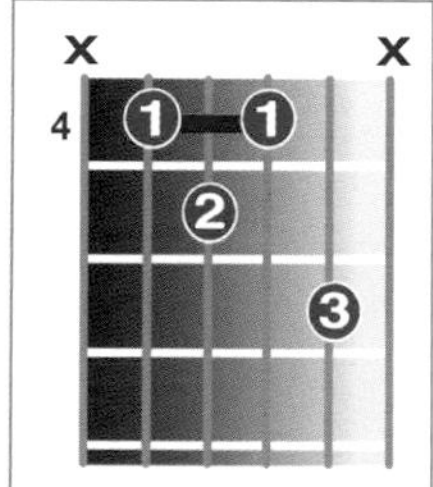

C♯7♭5 C♯ Dominant 7th ♭5
1st (C♯), 3rd (E♯), ♭5th (G), ♭7th (B)

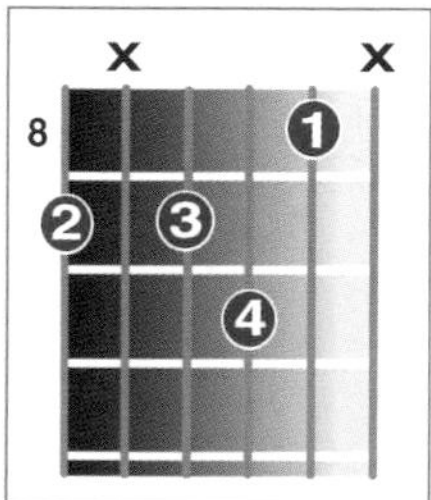

C♯7♭5 C♯ Dominant 7th ♭5
1st (C♯), 3rd (E♯), ♭5th (G), ♭7th (B)

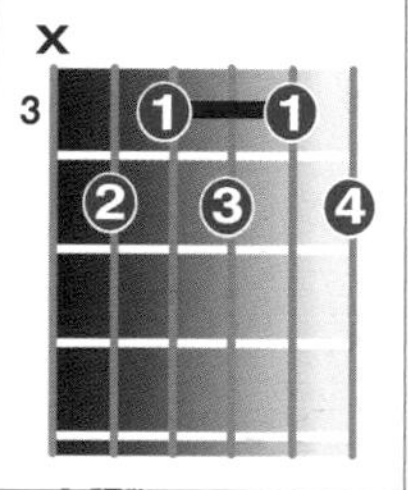

C♯7♭9 C♯ Dominant 7th ♭9
1st (C♯), 3rd (E♯), 5th (G♯), ♭7th (B), ♭9th (D)

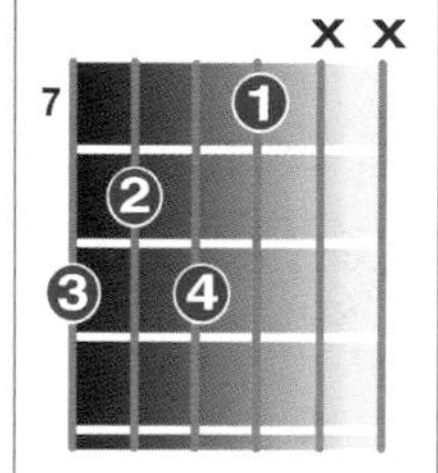

C♯7♭9 C♯ Dominant 7th ♭9
1st (C♯), 3rd (E♯), 5th (G♯), ♭7th (B), ♭9th (D)

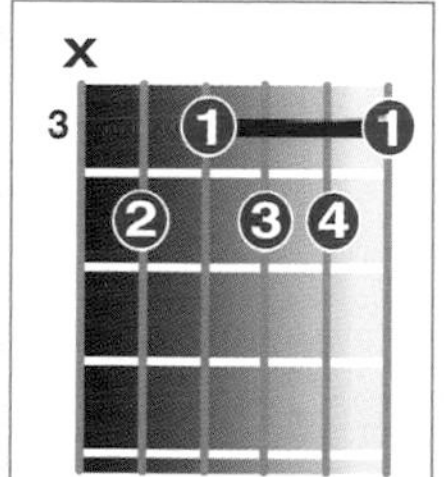

C♯9♭5 C♯ Dominant 9th ♭5th
1st (C♯), 3rd (E♯), ♭5th (G), ♭7th (B), 9th (D♯)

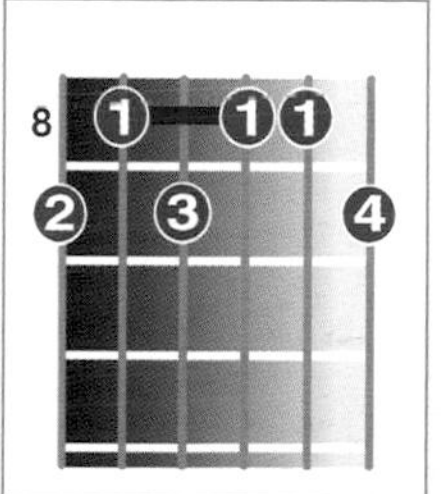

C♯9♭5 C♯ Dominant 9th ♭5th
1st (C♯), 3rd (E♯), ♭5th (G), ♭7th (B), 9th (D♯)

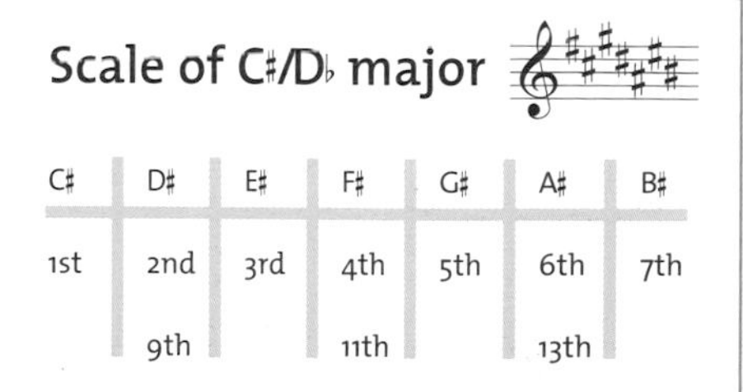

Scale of C♯/D♭ major

C♯	D♯	E♯	F♯	G♯	A♯	B♯
1st	2nd	3rd	4th	5th	6th	7th
	9th		11th		13th	

Section Five: Chord Dictionary

D MAIN CHORDS

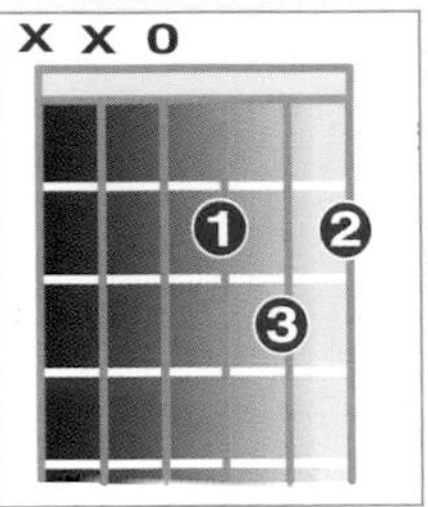

D D Major
1st (D), 3rd (F♯), 5th (A)

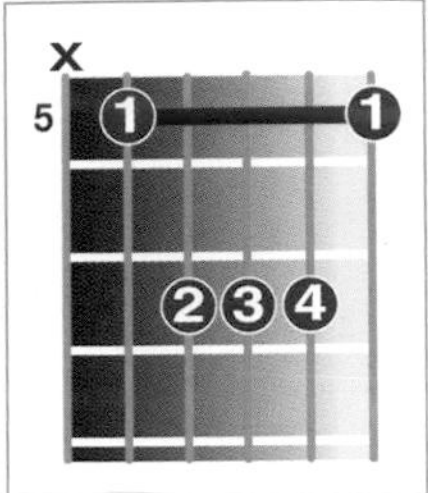

D D Major
1st (D), 3rd (F♯), 5th (A)

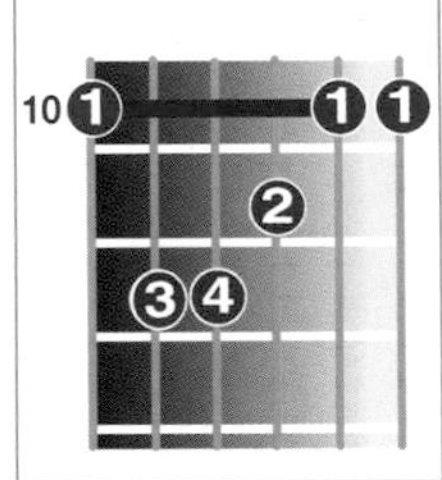

D D Major
1st (D), 3rd (F♯), 5th (A)

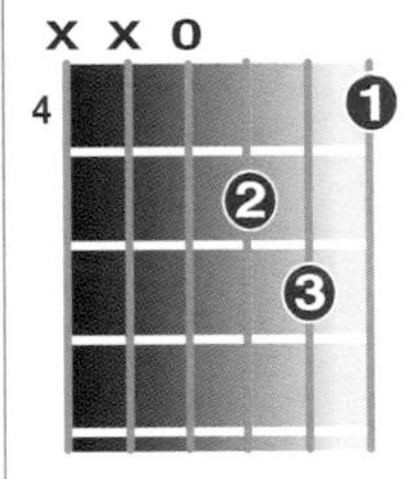

Dm D Minor
1st (D), ♭3rd (F), 5th (A)

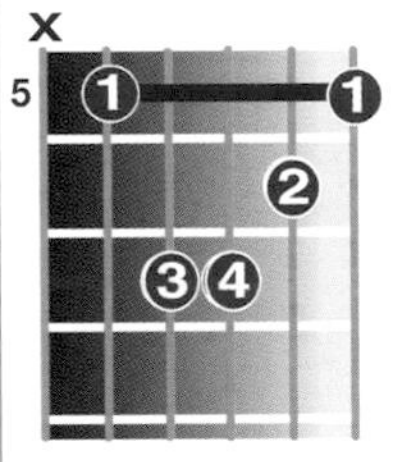

Dm D Minor
1st (D), ♭3rd (F), 5th (A)

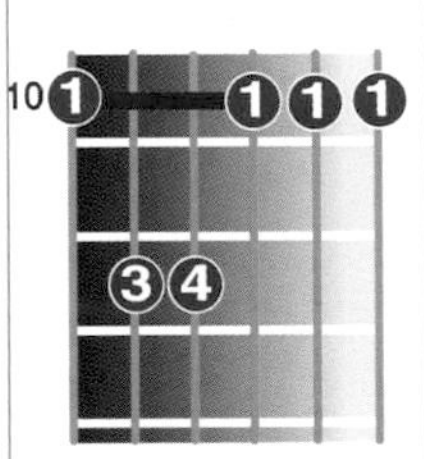

Dm D Minor
1st (D), ♭3rd (F), 5th (A)

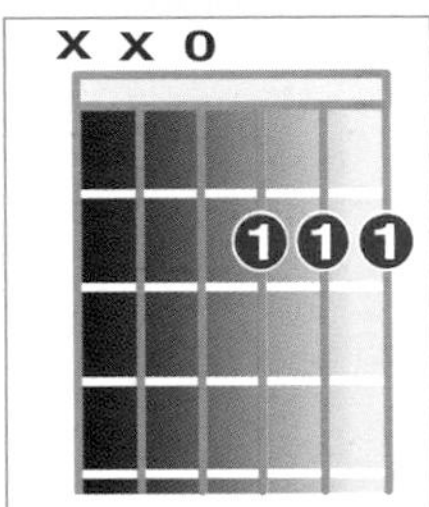

Dmaj7 D Major 7th
1st (D), 3rd (F♯), 5th (A), 7th (C♯)

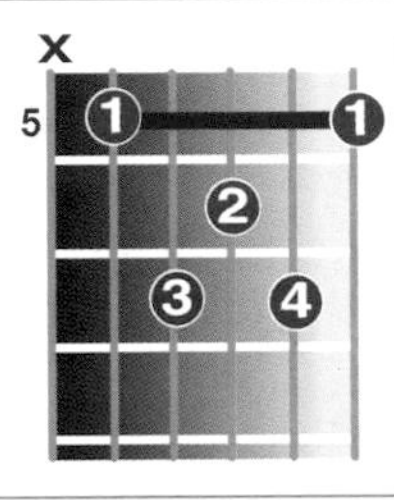

Dmaj7 D Major 7th
1st (D), 3rd (F♯), 5th (A), 7th (C♯)

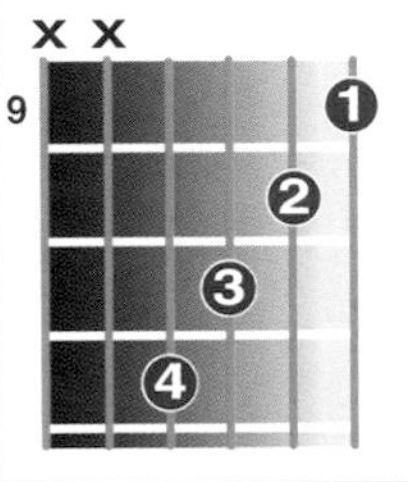

Dmaj7 D Major 7th
1st (D), 3rd (F♯), 5th (A), 7th (C♯)

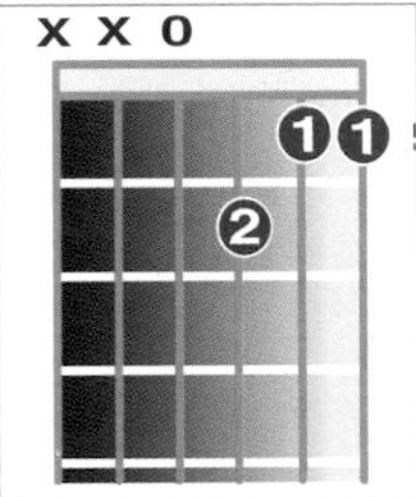

Dm7 D Minor 7th
1st (D), ♭3rd (F), 5th (A), ♭7th (C)

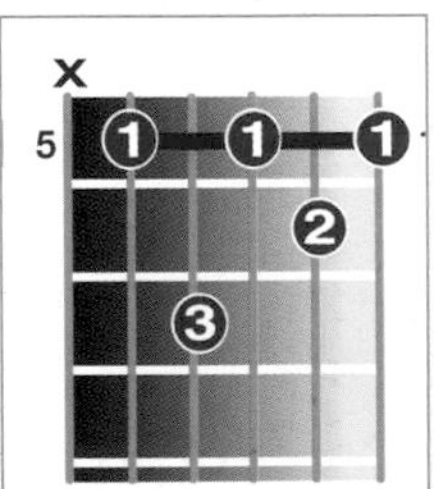

Dm7 D Minor 7th
1st (D), ♭3rd (F), 5th (A), ♭7th (C)

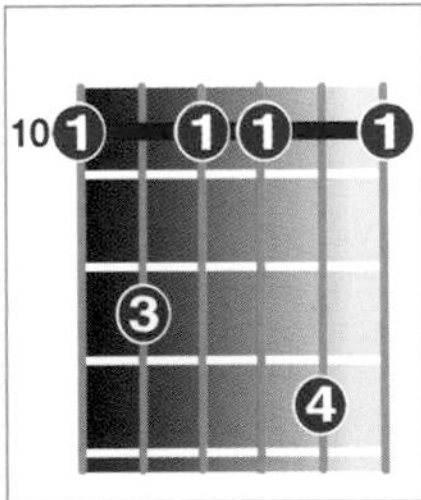

Dm7 D Minor 7th
1st (D), ♭3rd (F), 5th (A), ♭7th (C)

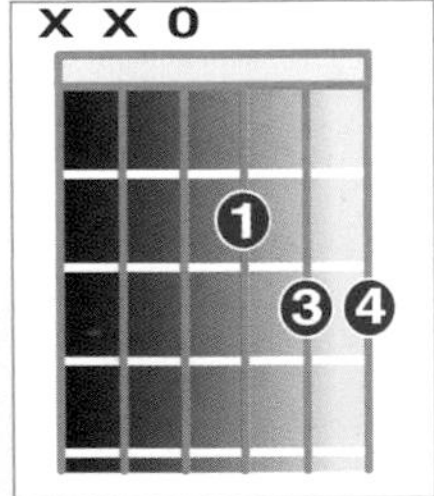

Dsus4 D Suspended 4th
1st (D), 4th (G), 5th (A)

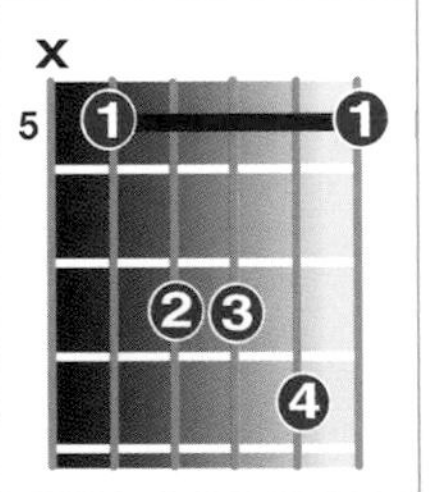

Dsus4 D Suspended 4th
1st (D), 4th (G), 5th (A)

Complete Guitar Handbook

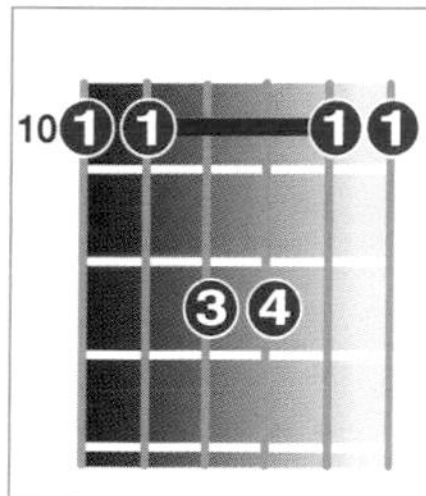

Dsus4 D Suspended 4th
1st (D), 4th (G), 5th (A)

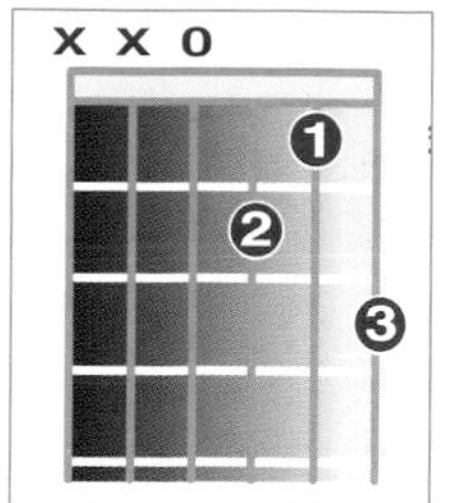

D7sus4 D Dominant 7th sus4
1st (D), 4th (G), 5th (A), ♭7th (C)

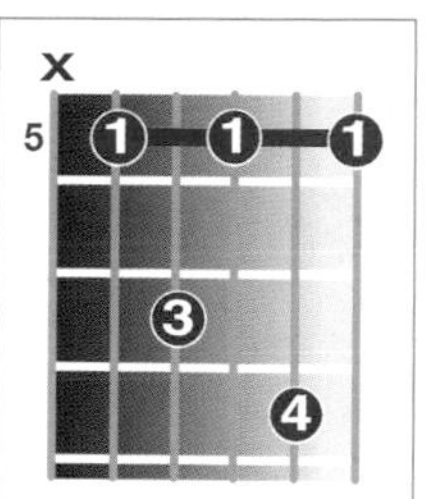

D7sus4 D Dominant 7th sus4
1st (D), 4th (G), 5th (A), ♭7th (C)

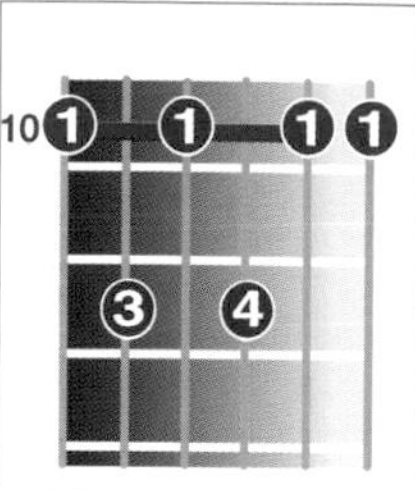

D7sus4 D Dominant 7th sus4
1st (D), 4th (G), 5th (A), ♭7th (C)

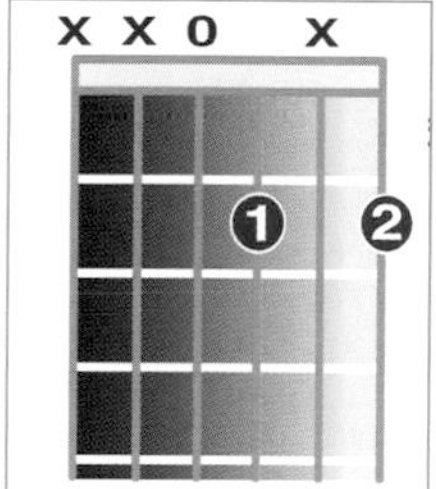

D6 D Major 6th
1st (D), 3rd (F♯), 5th (A), 6th (B)

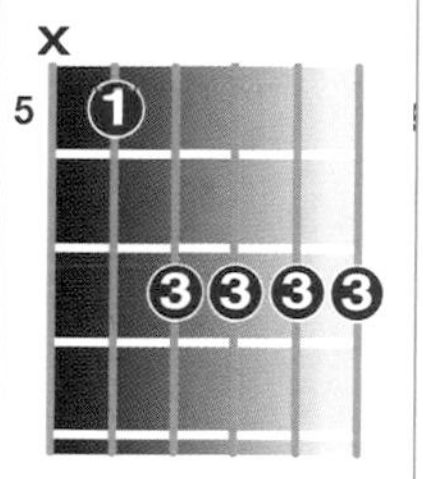

D6 D Major 6th
1st (D), 3rd (F♯), 5th (A), 6th (B)

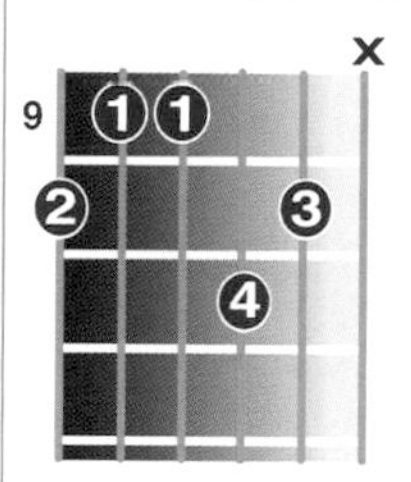

D6 D Major 6th
1st (D), 3rd (F♯), 5th (A), 6th (B)

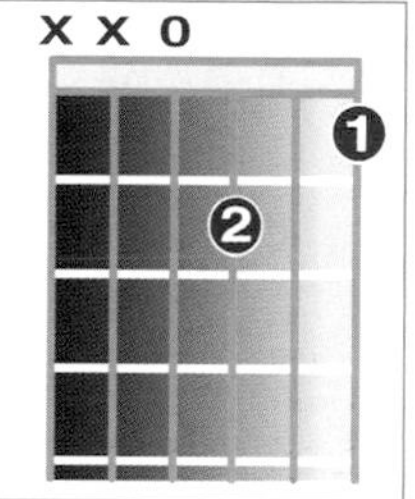

Dm6 D Minor 6th
1st (D), ♭3rd (F), 5th (A), 6th (B)

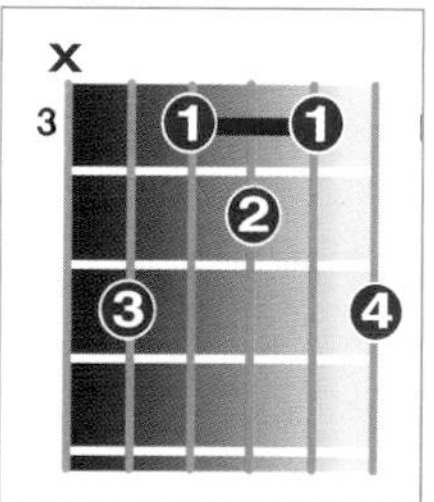

Dm6 D Minor 6th
1st (D), ♭3rd (F), 5th (A), 6th (B)

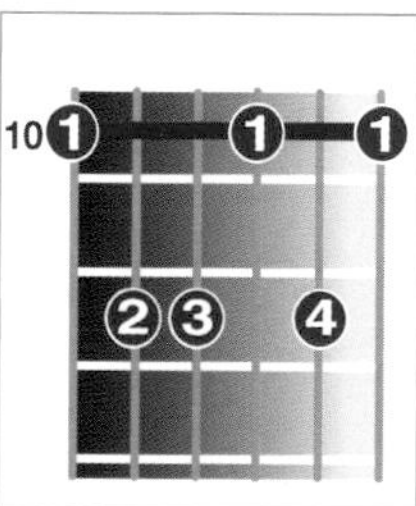

Dm6 D Minor 6th
1st (D), ♭3rd (F), 5th (A), 6th (B)

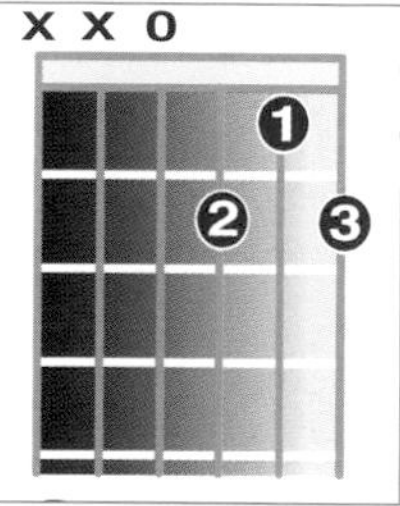

D7 D Dominant 7th
1st (D), 3rd (F♯),
5th (A), ♭7th (C)

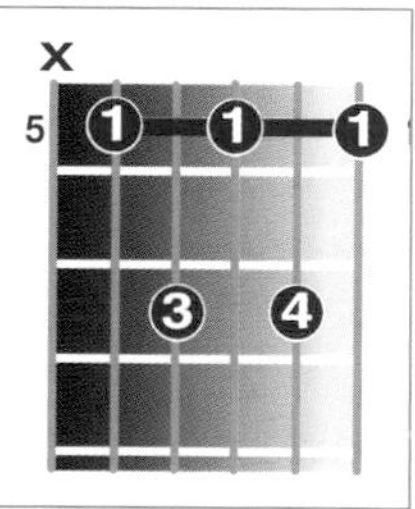

D7 D Dominant 7th
1st (D), 3rd (F♯),
5th (A), ♭7th (C)

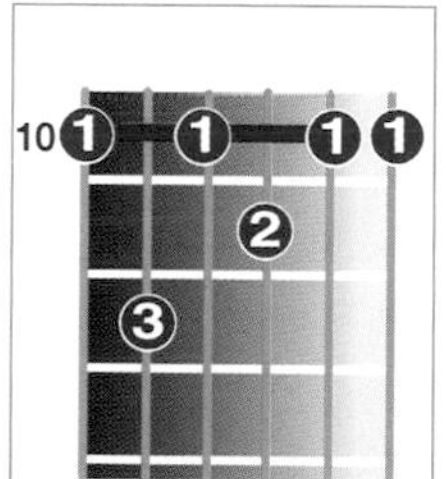

D7 D Dominant 7th
1st (D), 3rd (F♯),
5th (A), ♭7th (C)

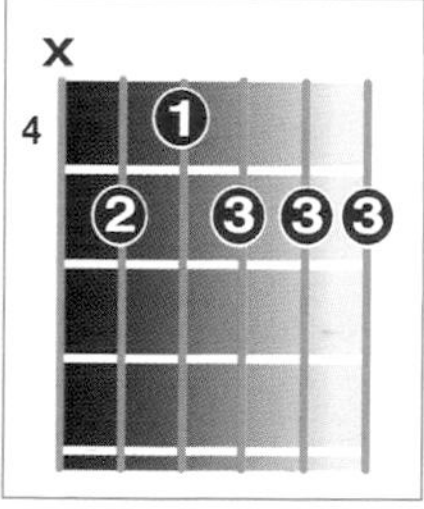

D9 D Dominant 9th
1st (D), 3rd (F♯), 5th (A),
♭7th (C), 9th (E)

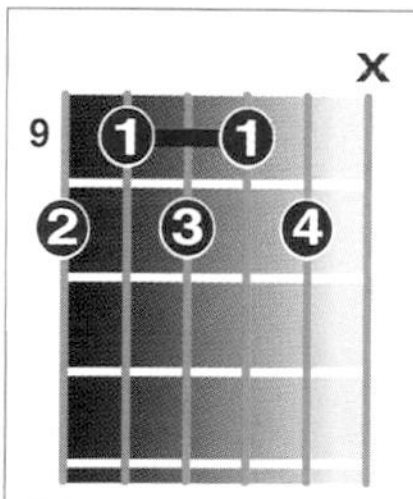

D9 D Dominant 9th
1st (D), 3rd (F♯), 5th (A),
♭7th (C), 9th (E)

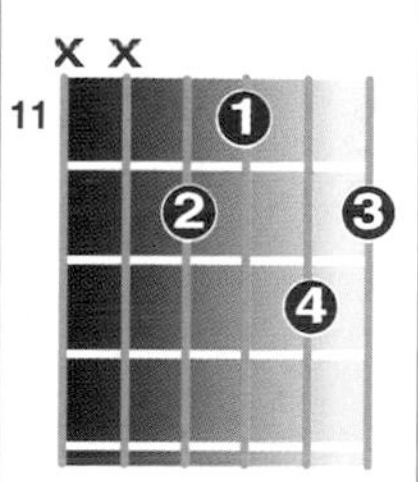

D9 D Dominant 9th
1st (D), 3rd (F♯), 5th (A),
♭7th (C), 9th (E)

Section Five: Chord Dictionary

D ADVANCED CHORDS

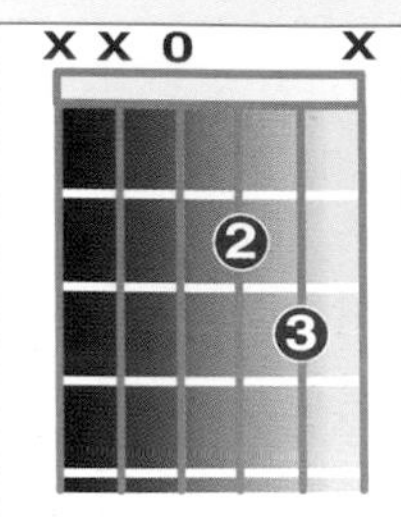

D5 D 5th (power chord)
1st (D), 5th (A)

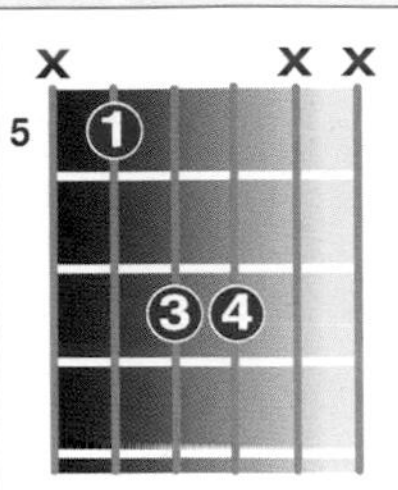

D5 D 5th (power chord)
1st (D), 5th (A)

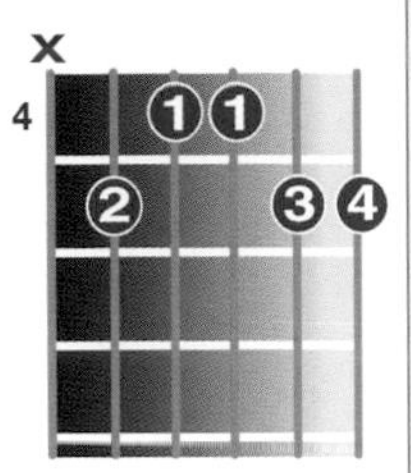

D 6/9 D Major 6th add 9th
1st (D), 3rd (F♯), 5th (A),
6th (B), 9th (E)

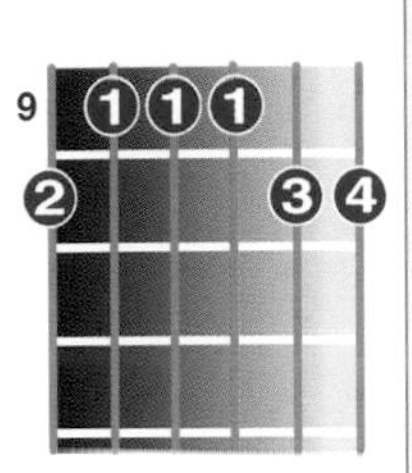

D 6/9 D Major 6th add 9th
1st (D), 3rd (F♯), 5th (A),
6th (B), 9th (E)

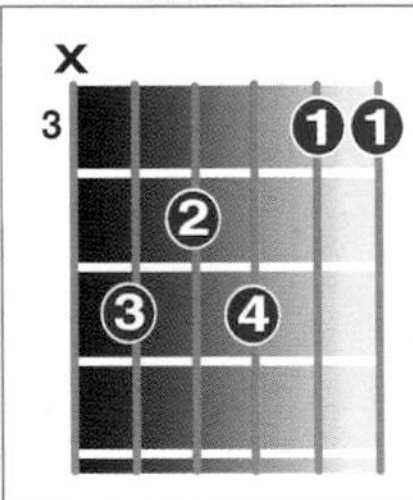

D11 D Dominant 11th
1st (D), 3rd (F♯), 5th (A),
♭7th (C), 9th (E), 11th (G)

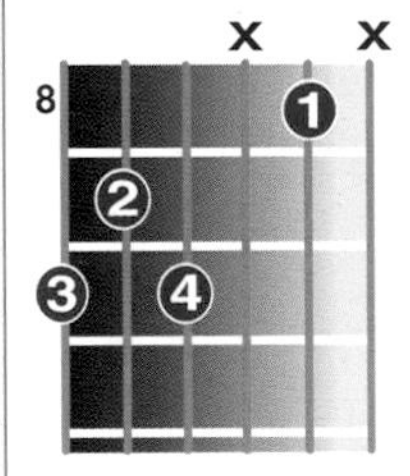

D11 D Dominant 11th
1st (D), 3rd (F♯), 5th (A),
♭7th (C), 9th (E), 11th (G)

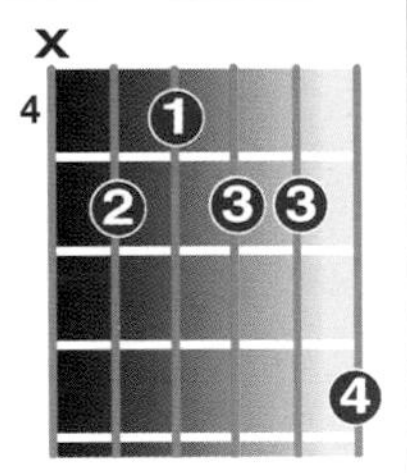

D13 D Dominant 13th
1st (D), 3rd (F♯), 5th (A),
♭7th (C), 9th (E), 13th (B)

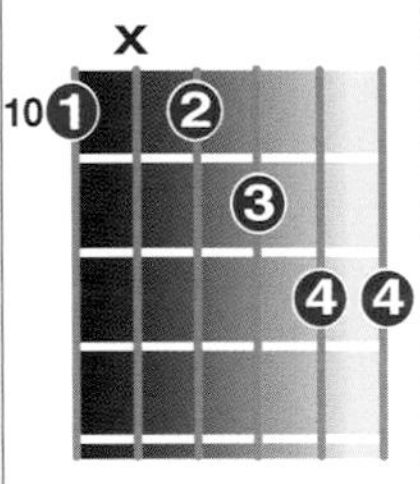

D13 D Dominant 13th
1st (D), 3rd (F♯), 5th (A),
♭7th (C), 9th (E), 13th (B)

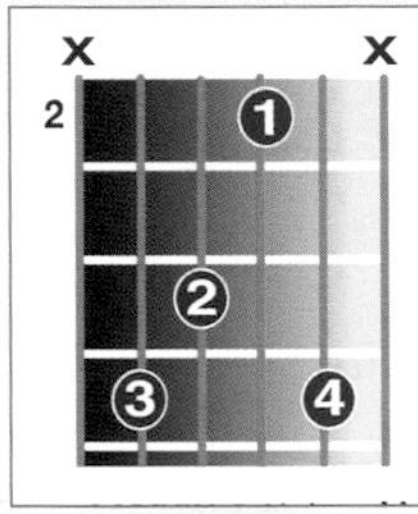

Dadd9 D Major add 9th
1st (D), 3rd (F♯), 5th (A), 9th (E)

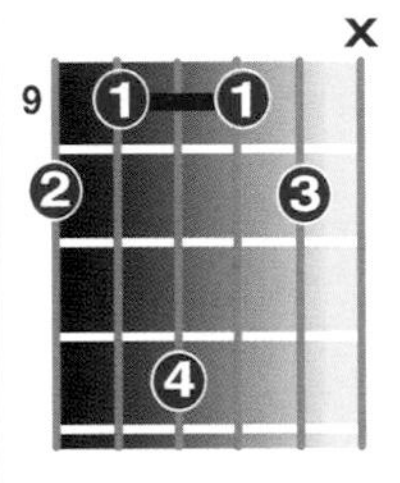

Dadd9 D Major add 9th
1st (D), 3rd (F♯), 5th (A), 9th (E)

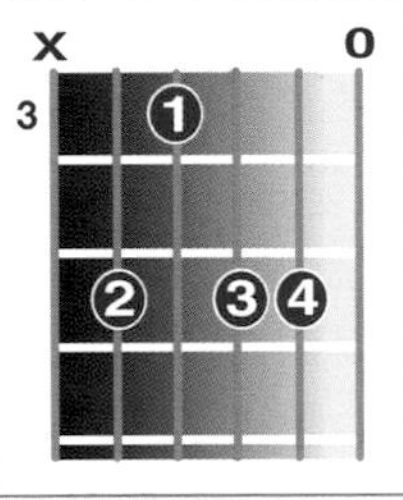

Dm9 D Minor 9th
1st (D), ♭3rd (F), 5th (A),
♭7th (C), 9th (E)

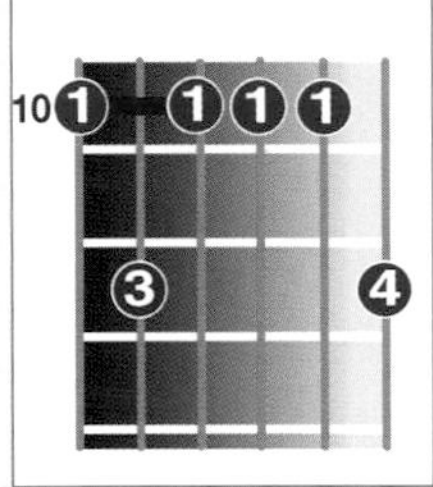

Dm9 D Minor 9th
1st (D), ♭3rd (F), 5th (A),
♭7th (C), 9th (E)

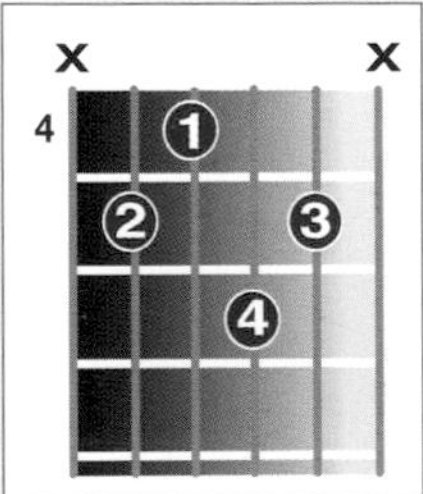

Dmaj9 D Major 9th
1st (D), 3rd (F♯), 5th (A),
7th (C♯), 9th (E)

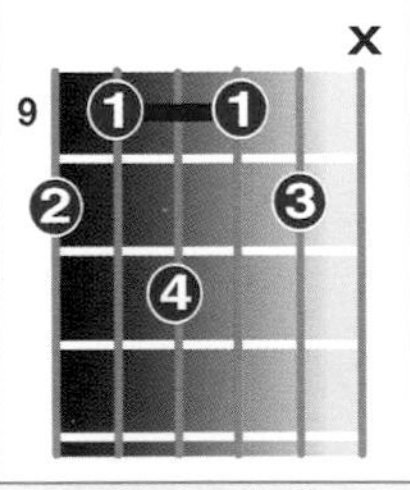

Dmaj9 D Major 9th
1st (D), 3rd (F♯), 5th (A),
7th (C♯), 9th (E)

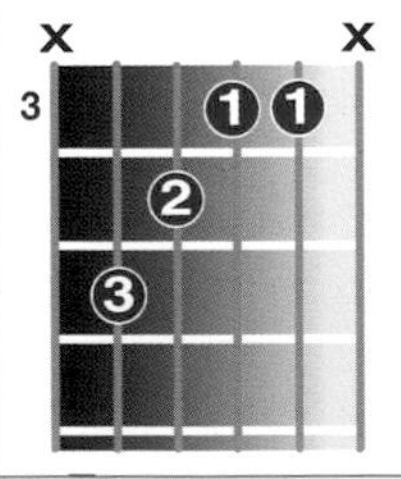

D+ D Augmented
1st (D), 3rd (F♯), ♯5th (A♯)

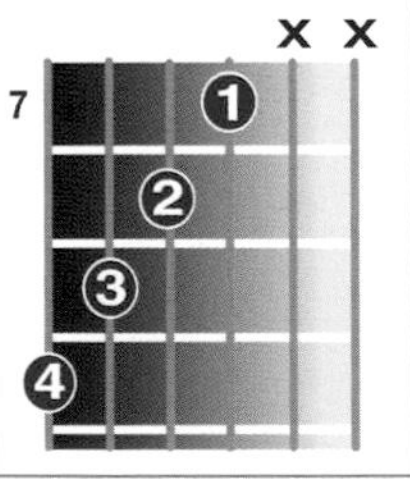

D+ D Augmented
1st (D), 3rd (F♯), ♯5th (A♯)

Complete Guitar Handbook

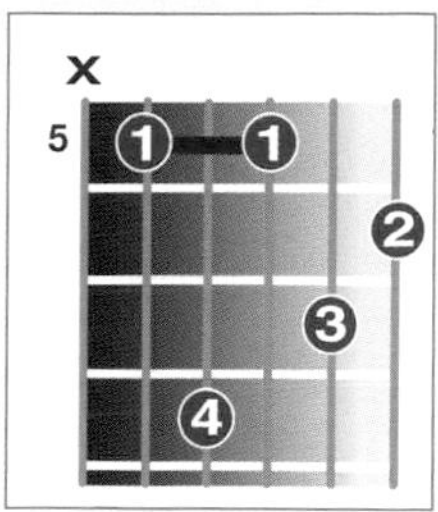

D7♯5 D Dominant 7th ♯5
1st (D), 3rd (F♯), ♯5th (A♯), ♭7th (C)

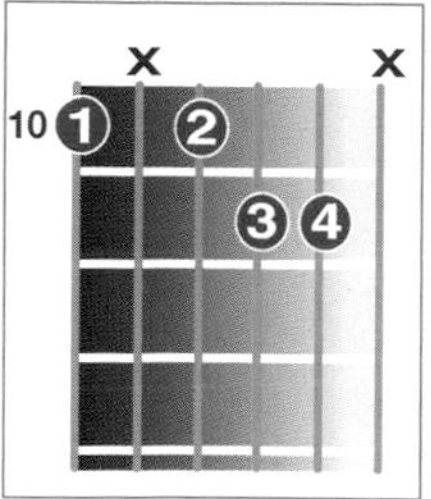

D7♯5 D Dominant 7th ♯5
1st (D), 3rd (F♯), ♯5th (A♯), ♭7th (C)

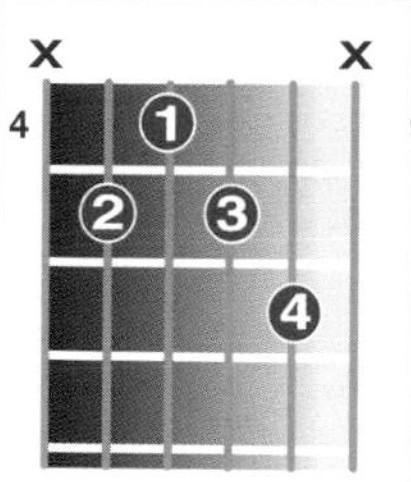

D7♯9 D Dominant 7th ♯9
1st (D), 3rd (F♯), 5th (A), ♭7th (C), ♯9th (E♯)

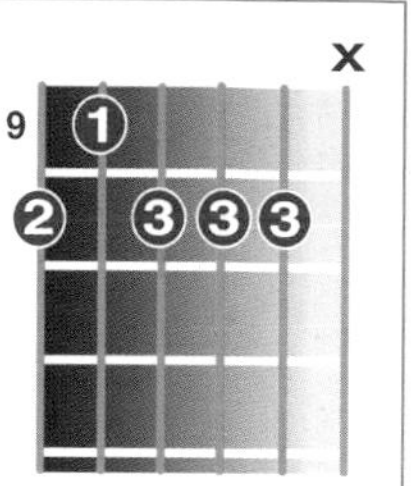

D7♯9 D Dominant 7th ♯9
1st (D), 3rd (F♯), 5th (A), ♭7th (C), ♯9th (E♯)

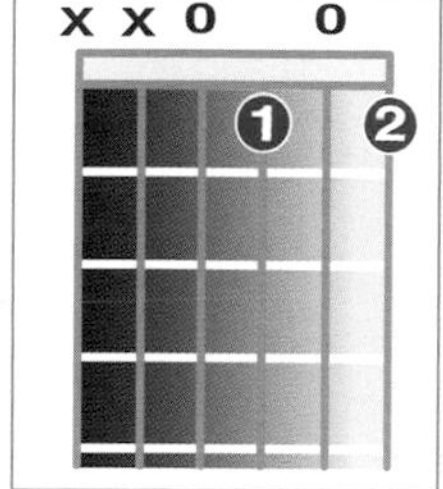

Do7 D Diminished 7th
1st (D), ♭3rd (F), ♭5th (A♭), ♭♭7th (C♭)

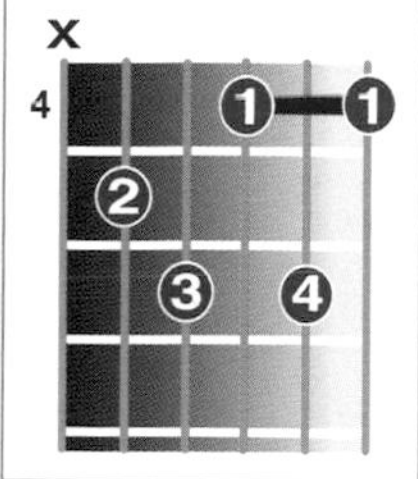

Do7 D Diminished 7th
1st (D), ♭3rd (F), ♭5th (A♭), ♭♭7th (C♭)

Do D Diminished triad
1st (D), ♭3rd (F), ♭5th (A♭)

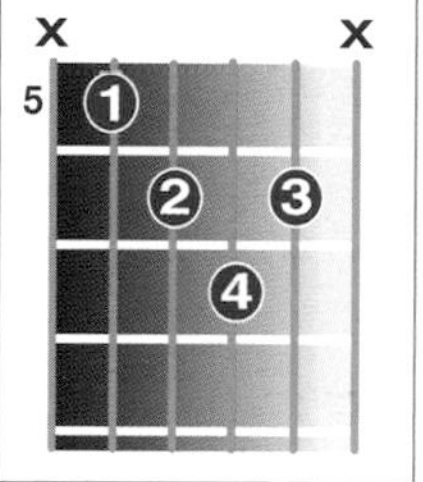

Do D Diminished triad
1st (D), ♭3rd (F), ♭5th (A♭)

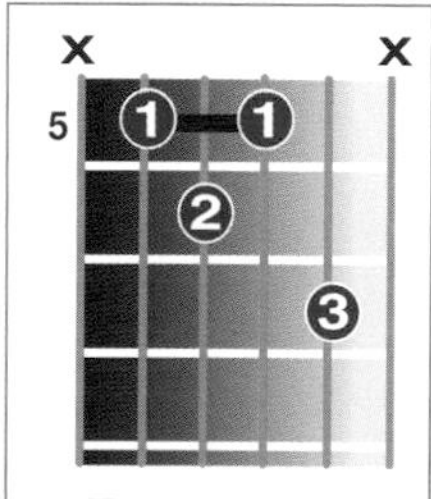

D7♭5 D Dominant 7th ♭5
1st (D), 3rd (F♯), ♭5th (A♭), ♭7th (C)

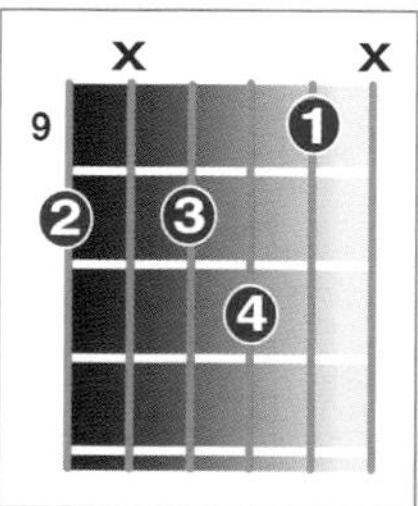

D7♭5 D Dominant 7th ♭5
1st (D), 3rd (F♯), ♭5th (A♭), ♭7th (C)

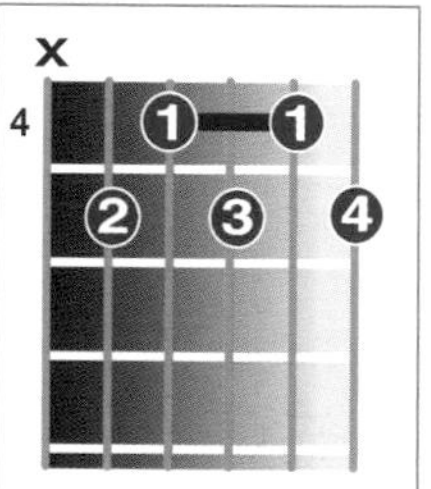

D7♭9 D Dominant 7th ♭9
1st (D), 3rd (F♯), 5th (A), ♭7th (C), ♭9th (E♭)

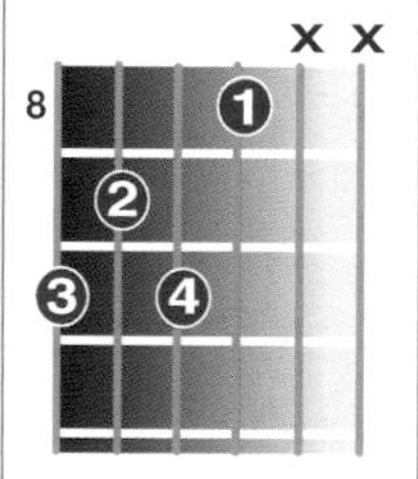

D7♭9 D Dominant 7th ♭9
1st (D), 3rd (F♯), 5th (A), ♭7th (C), ♭9th (E♭)

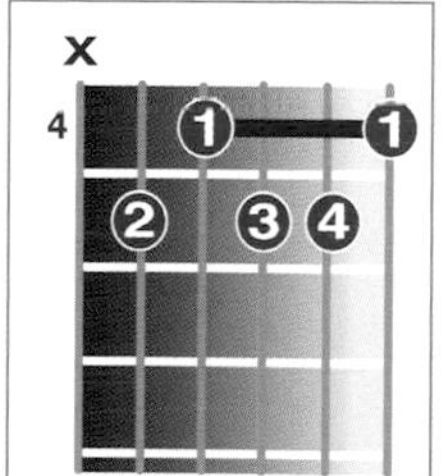

D9♭5 D Dominant 9th ♭5th
1st (D), 3rd (F♯), ♭5th (A♭), ♭7th (C), 9th (E)

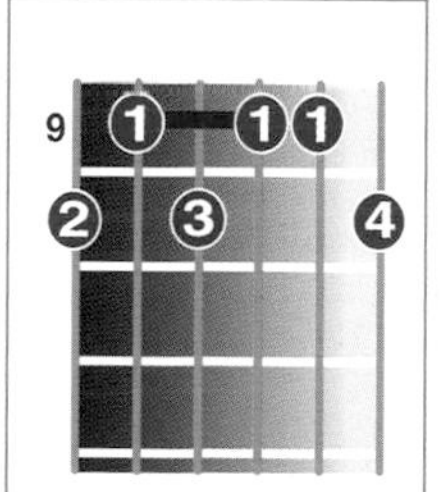

D9♭5 D Dominant 9th ♭5th
1st (D), 3rd (F♯), ♭5th (A♭), ♭7th (C), 9th (E)

Scale of D major

D	E	F♯	G	A	B	C♯
1st	2nd	3rd	4th	5th	6th	7th
	9th		11th		13th	

Section Five: Chord Dictionary

E♭/D♯ MAIN CHORDS

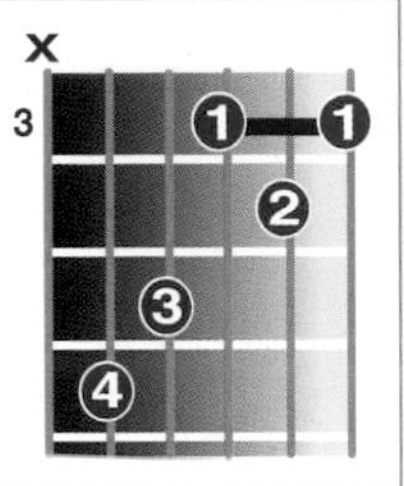

E♭ E♭ Major
1st (E♭), 3rd (G), 5th (B♭)

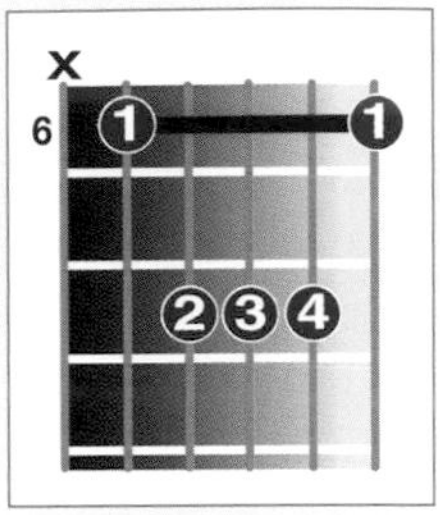

E♭ E♭ Major
1st (E♭), 3rd (G), 5th (B♭)

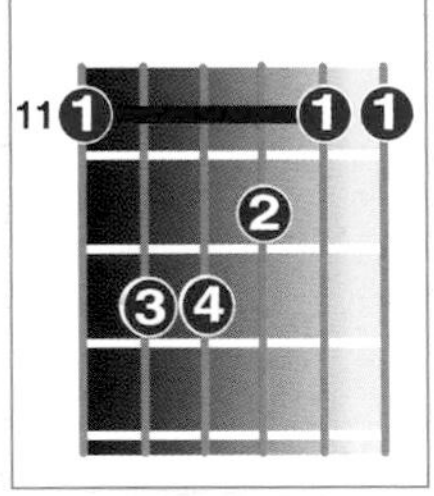

E♭ E♭ major
1st (E♭), 3rd (G), 5th (B♭)

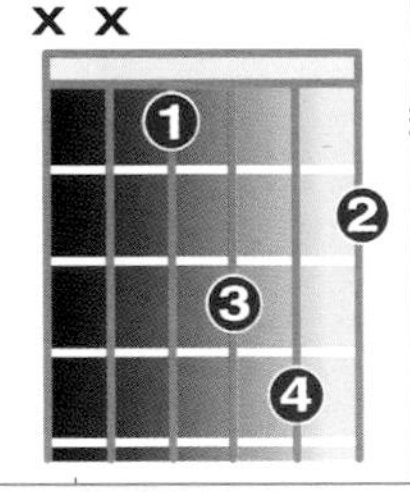

E♭m E♭ Minor
1st (E♭), ♭3rd (G♭), 5th (B♭)

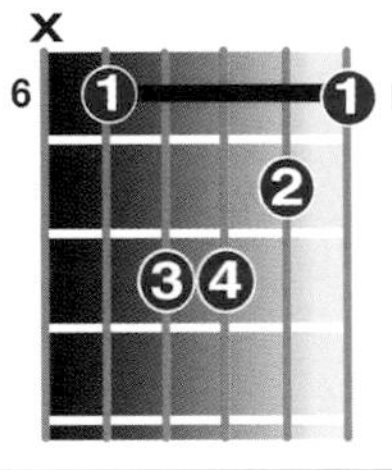

E♭m E♭ Minor
1st (E♭), ♭3rd (G♭), 5th (B♭)

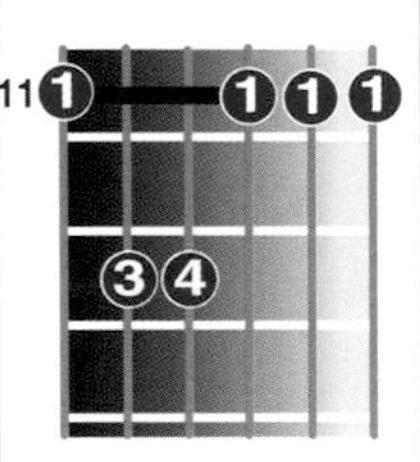

E♭m E♭ Minor
1st (E♭), ♭3rd (G♭), 5th (B♭)

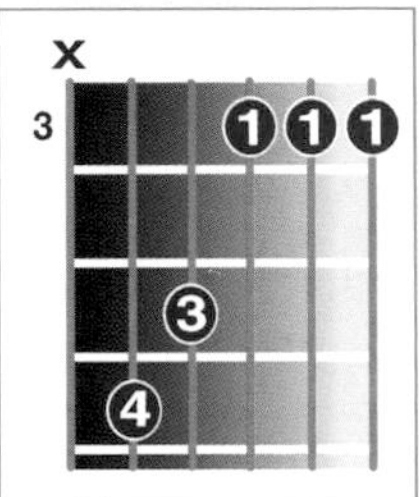

E♭maj7 E♭ Major 7th
1st (E♭), 3rd (G),
5th (B♭), 7th (D)

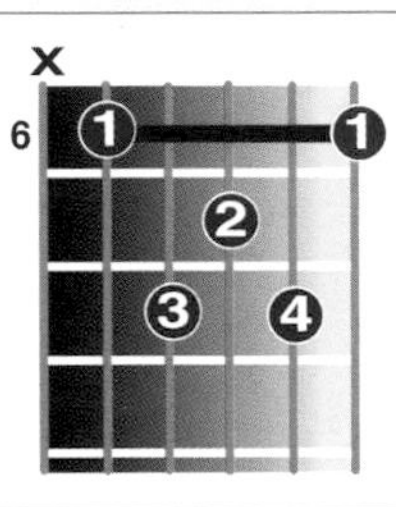

E♭maj7 E♭ Major 7th
1st (E♭), 3rd (G),
5th (B♭), 7th (D)

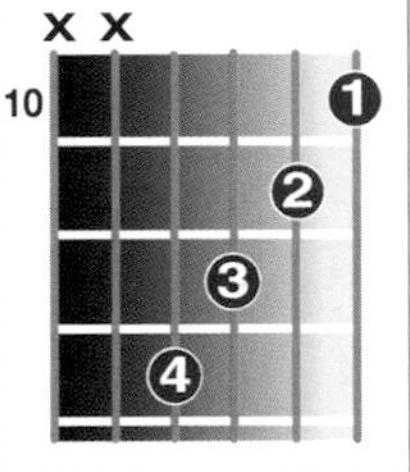

E♭maj7 E♭ Major 7th
1st (E♭), 3rd (G),
5th (B♭), 7th (D)

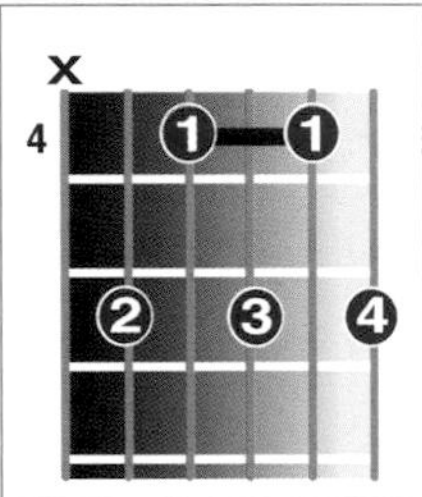

E♭m7 E♭ Minor 7th
1st (E♭), ♭3rd (G♭), 5th (B♭), ♭7th (D♭)

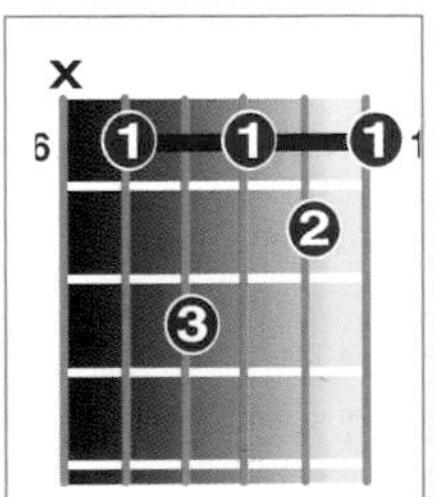

E♭m7 E♭ Minor 7th
1st (E♭), ♭3rd (G♭), 5th (B♭), ♭7th (D♭)

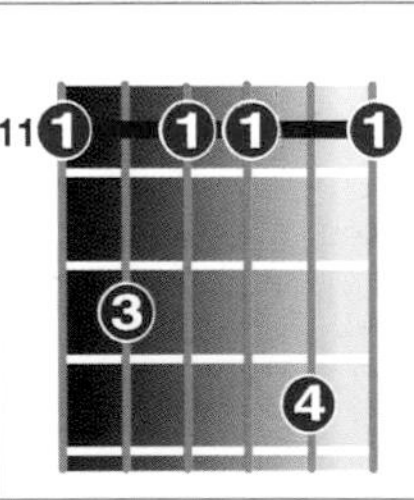

E♭m7 E♭ Minor 7th
1st (E♭), ♭3rd (G♭), 5th (B♭), ♭7th (D♭)

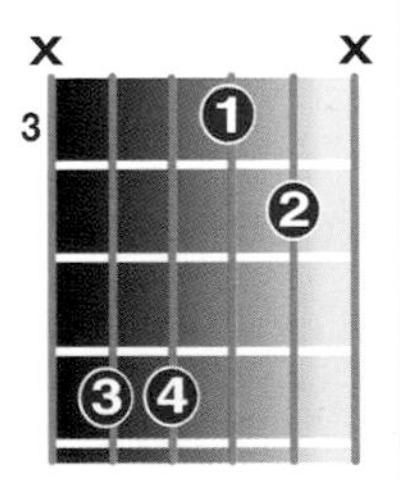

E♭sus4 E♭ Suspended 4th
1st (E♭), 4th (A♭), 5th (B♭)

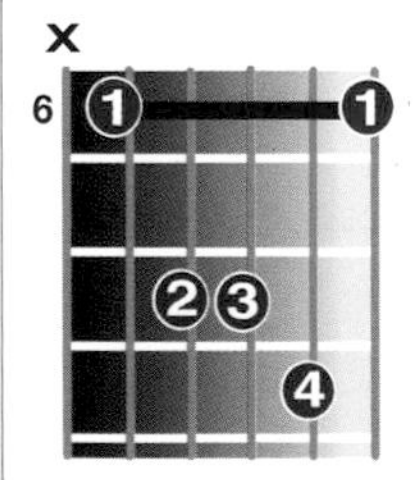

E♭sus4 E♭ Suspended 4th
1st (E♭), 4th (A♭), 5th (B♭)

Complete Guitar Handbook

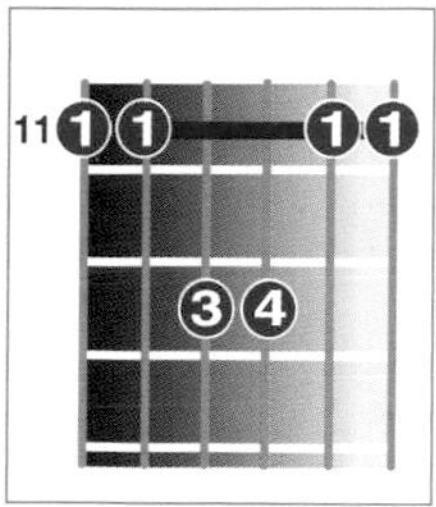

E♭sus4 E♭ Suspended 4th
1st (E♭), 4th (A♭), 5th (B♭)

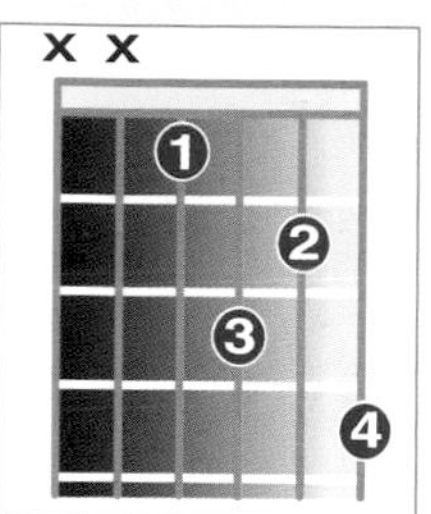

E♭7sus4 E♭ Dominant 7th sus4
1st (E♭), 4th (A♭), 5th (B♭), ♭7th (D♭)

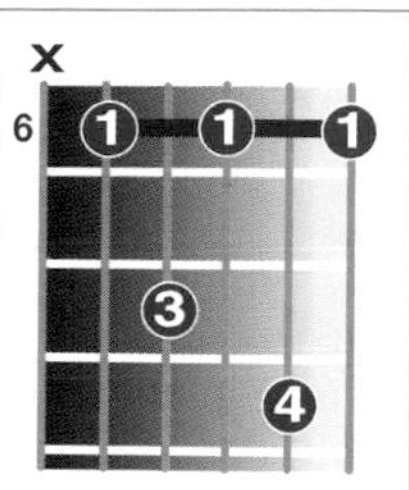

E♭7sus4 E♭ Dominant 7th sus4
1st (E♭), 4th (A♭), 5th (B♭), ♭7th (D♭)

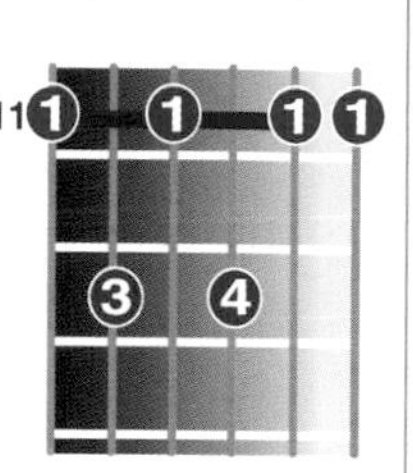

E♭7sus4 E♭ Dominant 7th sus4
1st (E♭), 4th (A♭), 5th (B♭), ♭7th (D♭)

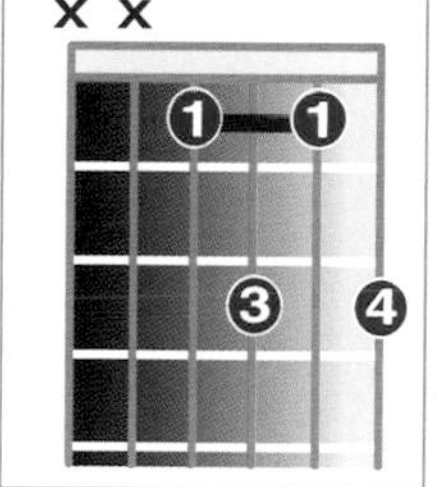

E♭6 E♭ Major 6th
1st (E♭), 3rd (G),
5th (B♭), 6th (C)

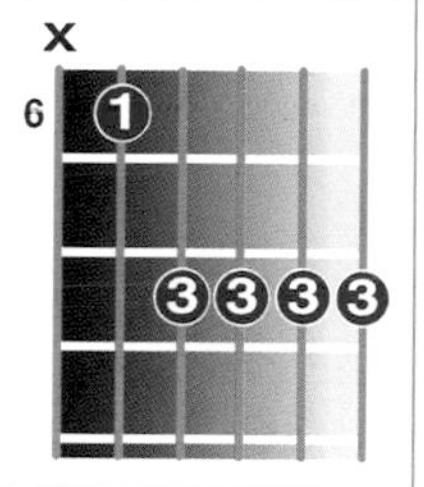

E♭6 E♭ Major 6th
1st (E♭), 3rd (G),
5th (B♭), 6th (C)

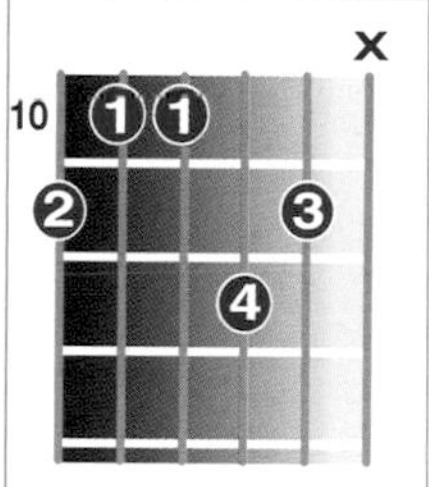

E♭6 E♭ Major 6th
1st (E♭), 3rd (G),
5th (B♭), 6th (C)

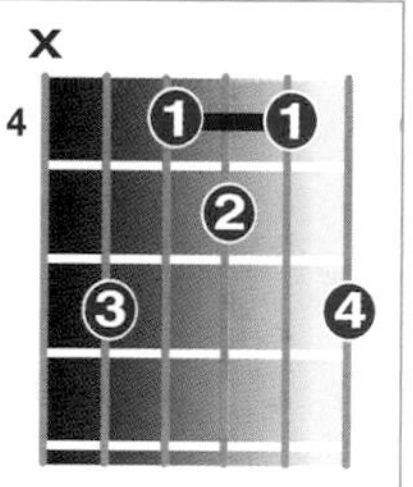

E♭m6 E♭ Minor 6th
1st (E♭), ♭3rd (G♭),
5th (B♭), 6th (C)

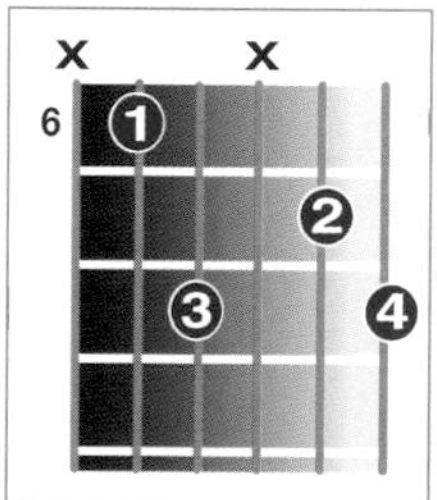

E♭m6 E♭ Minor 6th
1st (E♭), ♭3rd (G♭),
5th (B♭), 6th (C)

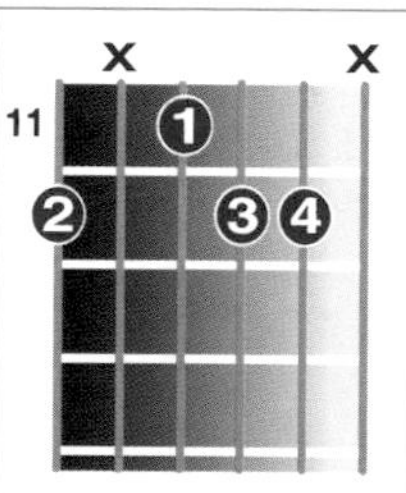

E♭m6 E♭ Minor 6th
1st (E♭), ♭3rd (G♭),
5th (B♭), 6th (C)

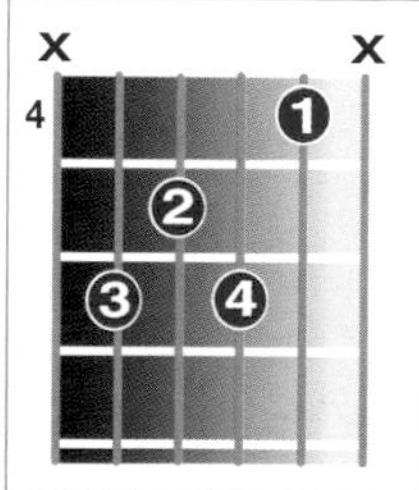

E♭7 E♭ Dominant 7th
1st (E♭), 3rd (G), 5th (B♭), ♭7th (D♭)

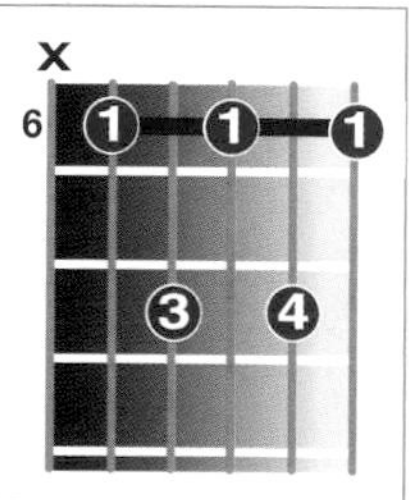

E♭7 E♭ Dominant 7th
1st (E♭), 3rd (G), 5th (B♭), ♭7th (D♭)

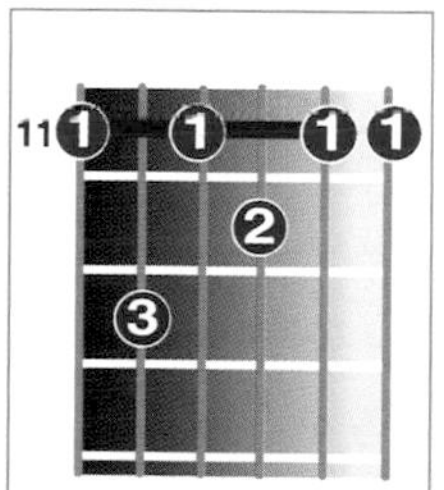

E♭7 E♭ Dominant 7th
1st (E♭), 3rd (G), 5th (B♭), ♭7th (D♭)

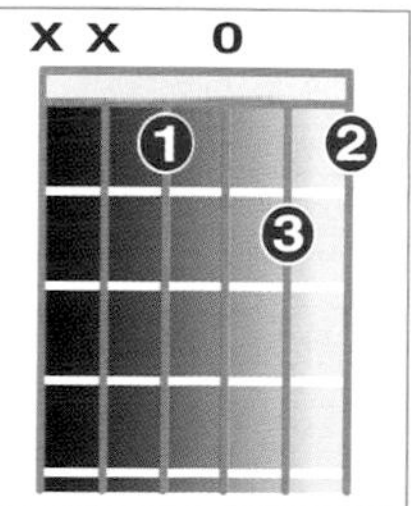

E♭9 E♭ Dominant 9th
1st (E♭), 3rd (G), 5th (B♭),
♭7th (D♭), 9th (F)

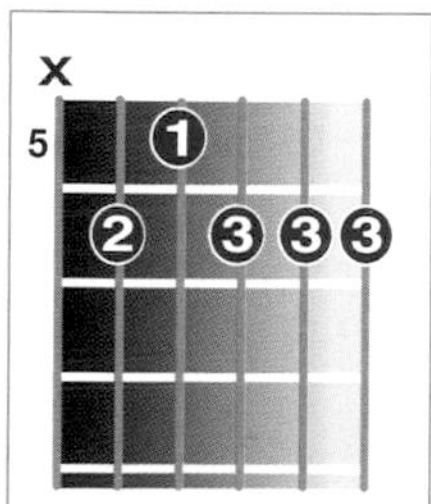

E♭9 E♭ Dominant 9th
1st (E♭), 3rd (G), 5th (B♭),
♭7th (D♭), 9th (F)

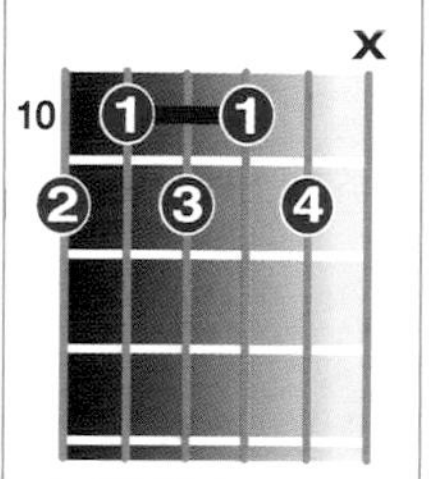

E♭9 E♭ Dominant 9th
1st (E♭), 3rd (G), 5th (B♭),
♭7th (D♭), 9th (F)

Section Five: Chord Dictionary

E♭/D♯ ADVANCED CHORDS

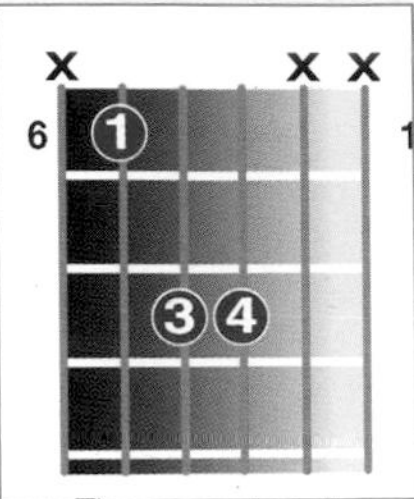

E♭5 E♭ 5th (power chord)
1st (E♭), 5th (B♭)

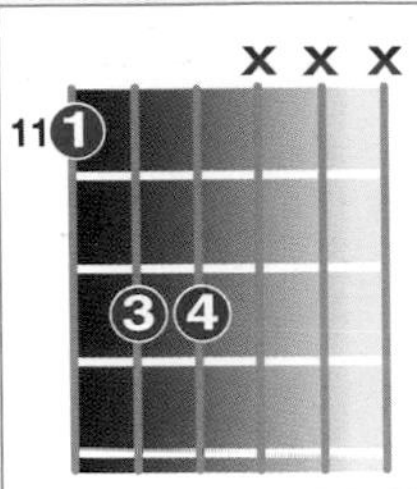

E♭5 E♭ 5th (power chord)
1st (E♭), 5th (B♭)

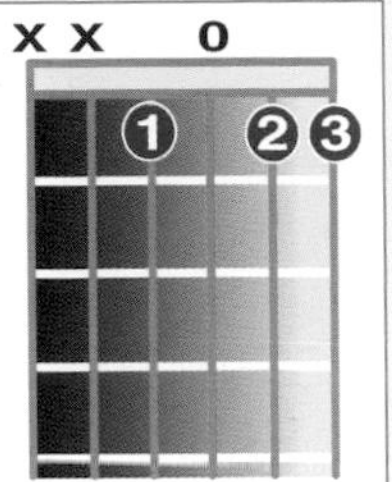

E♭6/9 E♭ Major 6th add 9th
1st (E♭), 3rd (G), 5th (B♭),
6th (C), 9th (F)

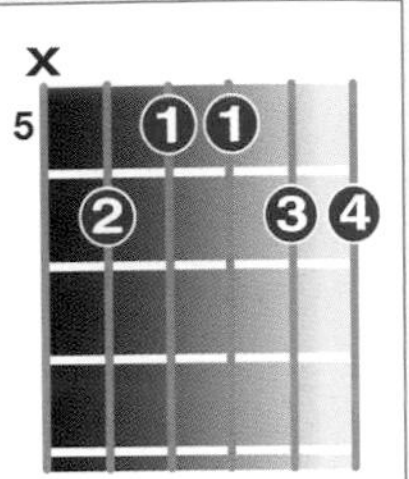

E♭6/9 E♭ Major 6th add 9th
1st (E♭), 3rd (G), 5th (B♭),
6th (C), 9th (F)

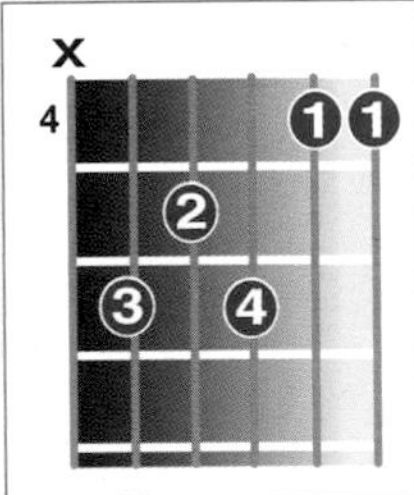

E♭11 E♭ Dominant 11th
1st (E♭), 3rd (G), 5th (B♭),
♭7th (D♭), 9th (F), 11th (A♭)

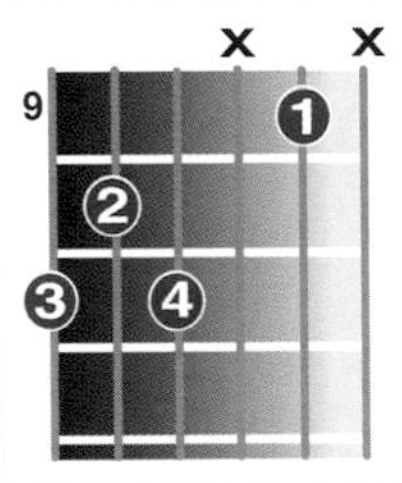

E♭11 E♭ Dominant 11th
1st (E♭), 3rd (G), 5th (B♭),
♭7th (D♭), 9th (F), 11th (A♭)

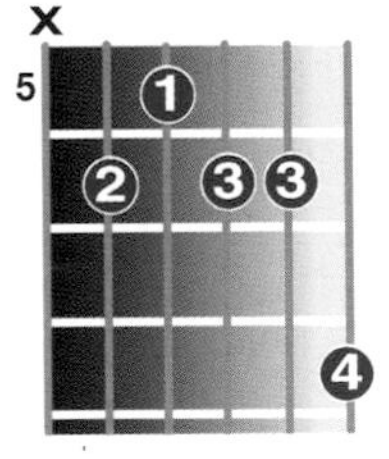

E♭13 E♭ Dominant 13th
1st (E♭), 3rd (G), 5th (B♭),
♭7th (D♭), 9th (F), 13th (C)

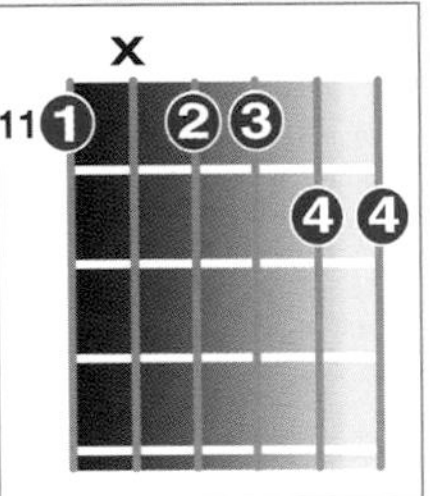

E♭13 E♭ Dominant 13th
1st (E♭), 3rd (G), 5th (B♭),
♭7th (D♭), 9th (F), 13th (C)

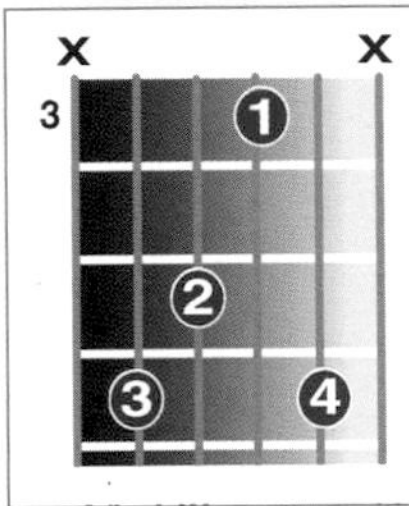

E♭add9 E♭ Major add 9th
1st (E♭), 3rd (G), 5th (B♭), 9th (F)

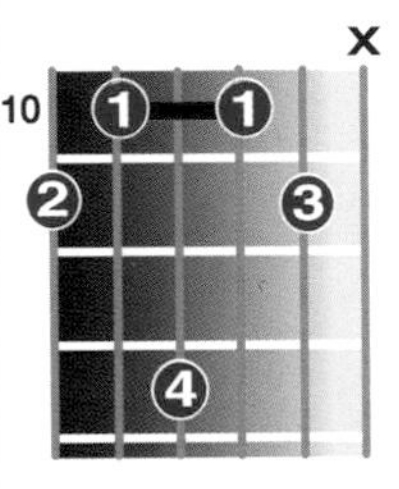

E♭add9 E♭ Major add 9th
1st (E♭), 3rd (G), 5th (B♭), 9th (F)

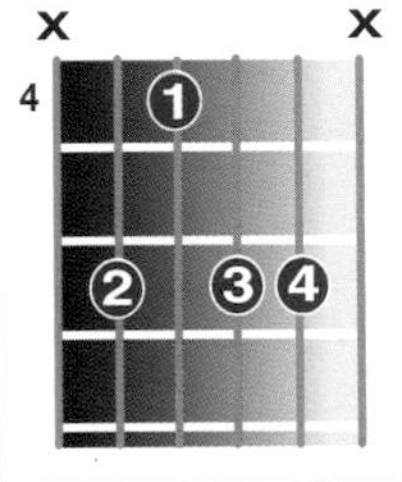

E♭m9 E♭ Minor 9th
1st (E♭), ♭3rd (G♭), 5th (B♭),
♭7th (D♭), 9th (F)

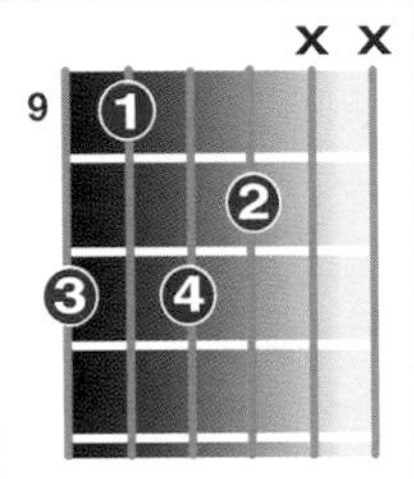

E♭m9 E♭ Minor 9th
1st (E♭), ♭3rd (G♭), 5th (B♭),
♭7th (D♭), 9th (F)

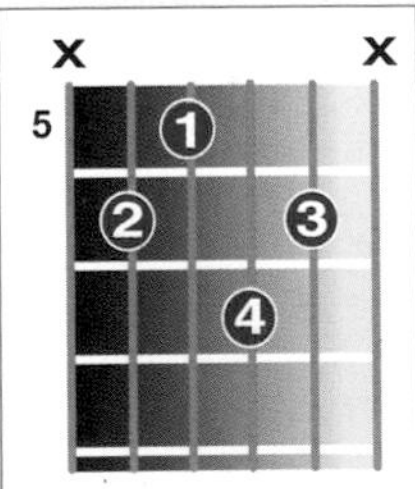

E♭maj9 E♭ Major 9th
1st (E♭), 3rd (G), 5th (B♭),
7th (D), 9th (F)

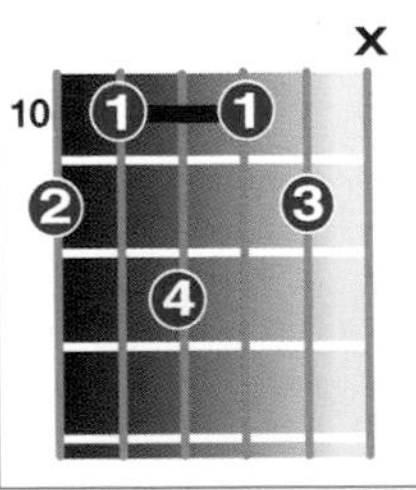

E♭maj9 E♭ Major 9th
1st (E♭), 3rd (G), 5th (B♭),
7th (D), 9th (F)

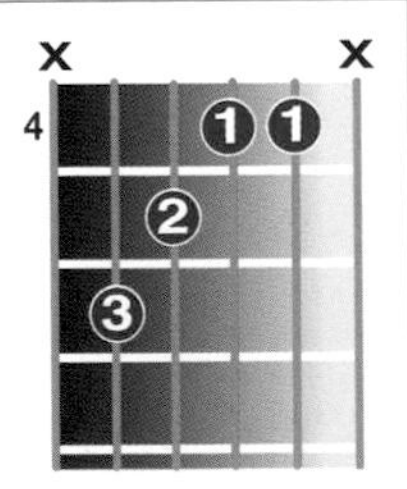

E♭+ E♭ Augmented
1st (E♭), 3rd (G), ♯5th (B)

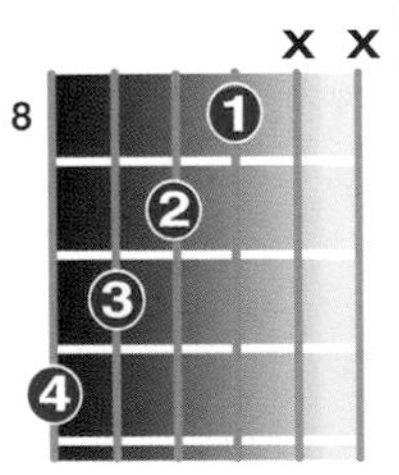

E♭+ E♭ Augmented
1st (E♭), 3rd (G), ♯5th (B)

Complete Guitar Handbook

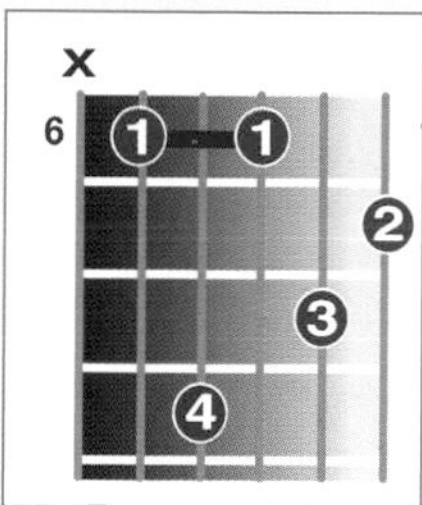

E♭7♯5 E♭ Dominant 7th ♯5
1st (E♭), 3rd (G), ♯5th (B), ♭7th (D♭)

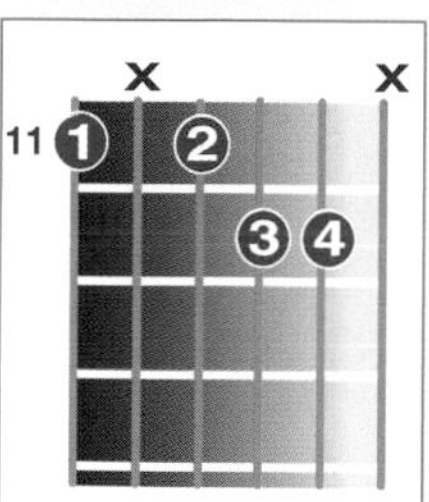

E♭7♯5 E♭ Dominant 7th ♯5
1st (E♭), 3rd (G), ♯5th (B), ♭7th (D♭)

E♭7♯9 E♭ Dominant 7th ♯9
1st (E♭), 3rd (G), 5th (B♭), ♭7th (D♭), ♯9th (F♯)

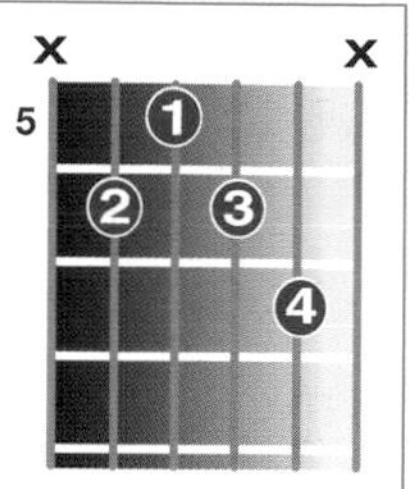

E♭7♯9 E♭ Dominant 7th ♯9
1st (E♭), 3rd (G), 5th (B♭), ♭7th (D♭), ♯9th (F♯)

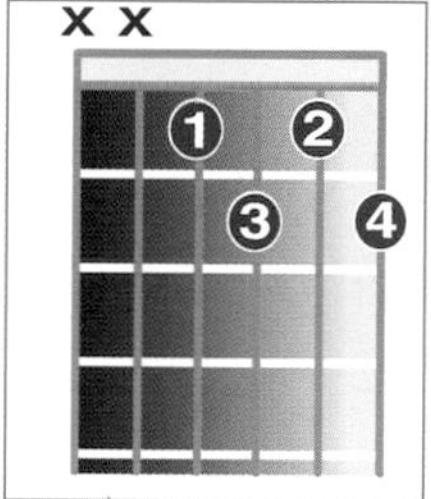

E♭o7 E♭ Diminished 7th
1st (E♭), ♭3rd (G♭), ♭5th (B♭♭), ♭♭7th (D♭♭)

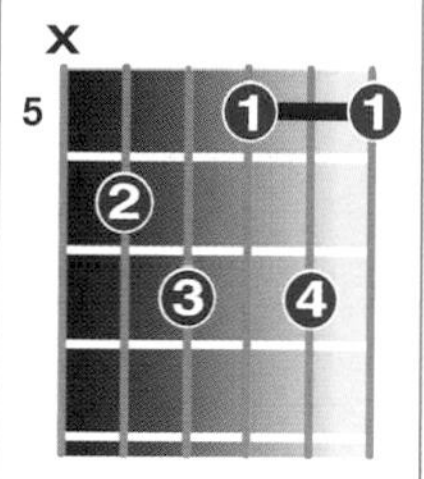

E♭o7 E♭ Diminished 7th
1st (E♭), ♭3rd (G♭), ♭5th (B♭♭), ♭♭7th (D♭♭)

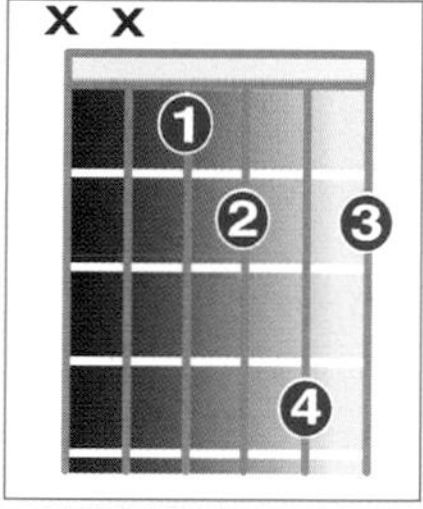

E♭o E♭ Diminished triad
1st (E♭), ♭3rd (G♭), ♭5th (B♭♭)

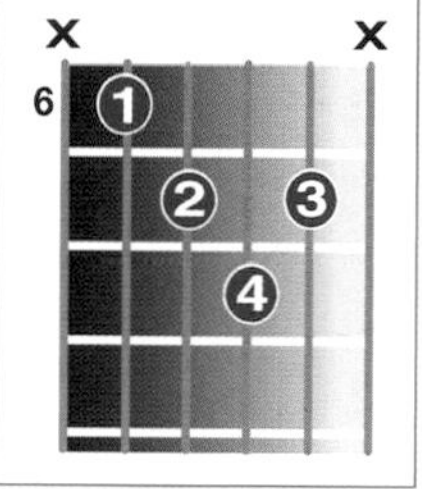

E♭o E♭ Diminished triad
1st (E♭), ♭3rd (G♭), ♭5th (B♭♭)

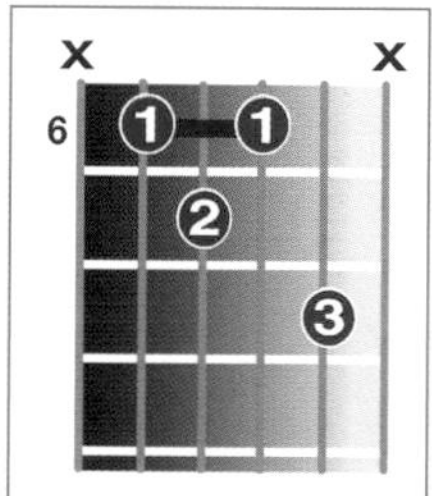

E♭7♭5 E♭ Dominant 7th ♭5
1st (E♭), 3rd (G), ♭5th (B♭♭), ♭7th (D♭)

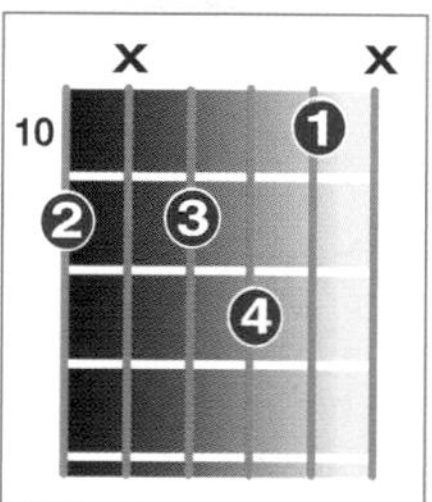

E♭7♭5 E♭ Dominant 7th ♭5
1st (E♭), 3rd (G), ♭5th (B♭♭), ♭7th (D♭)

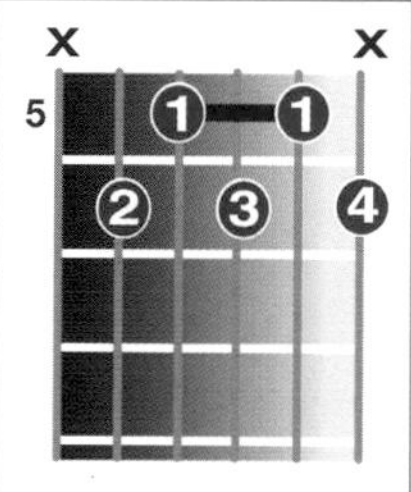

E♭7♭9 E♭ Dominant 7th ♭9
1st (E♭), 3rd (G), 5th (B♭), ♭7th (D♭), ♭9th (F♭)

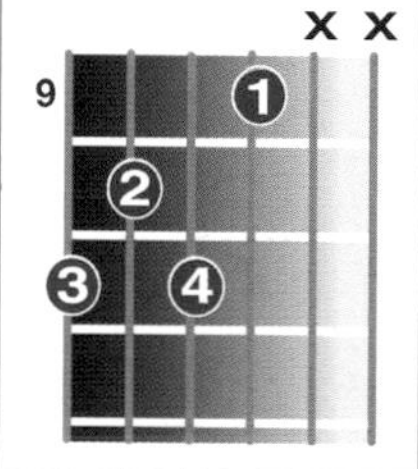

E♭7♭9 E♭ Dominant 7th ♭9
1st (E♭), 3rd (G), 5th (B♭), ♭7th (D♭), ♭9th (F♭)

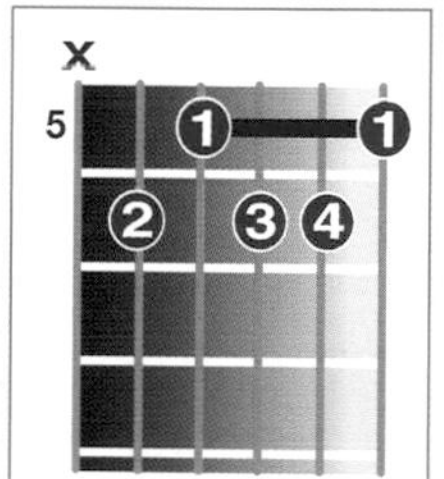

E♭9♭5 E♭ Dominant 9th ♭5th
1st (E♭), 3rd (G), ♭5th (B♭♭), ♭7th (D♭), 9th (F)

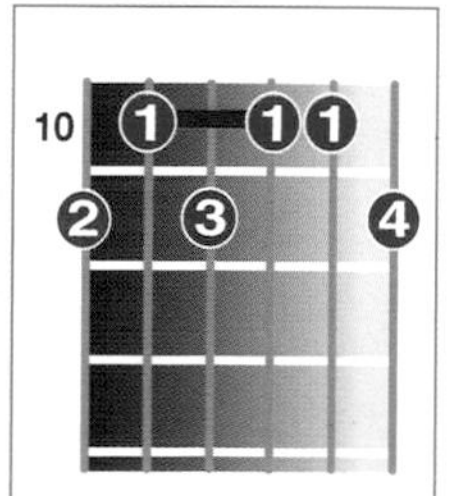

E♭9♭5 E♭ Dominant 9th ♭5th
1st (E♭), 3rd (G), ♭5th (B♭♭), ♭7th (D♭), 9th (F)

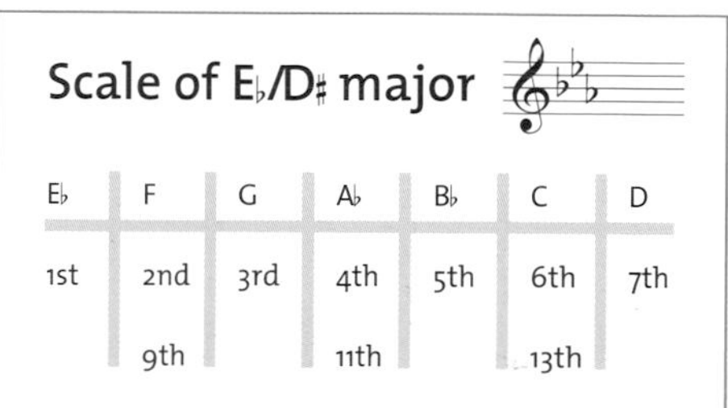

Scale of E♭/D♯ major

E♭	F	G	A♭	B♭	C	D
1st	2nd	3rd	4th	5th	6th	7th
	9th		11th		13th	

Section Five: Chord Dictionary

E MAIN CHORDS

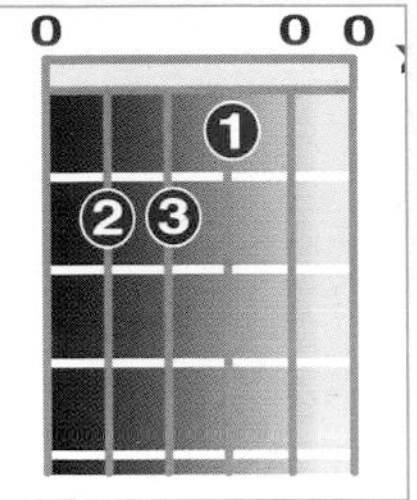

E E Major
1st (E), 3rd (G♯), 5th (B)

E E Major
1st (E), 3rd (G♯), 5th (B)

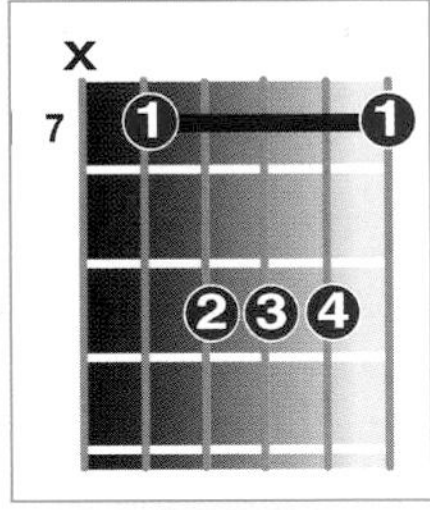

E E Major
1st (E), 3rd (G♯), 5th (B)

Em E Minor
1st (E), ♭3rd (G), 5th (B)

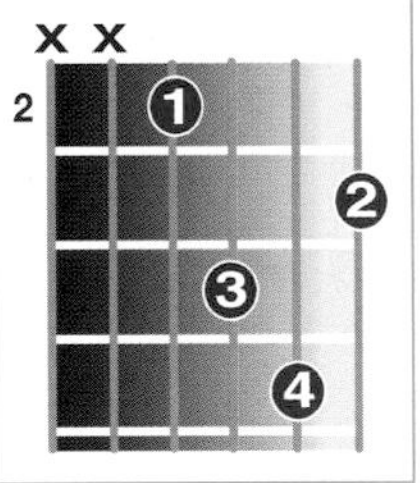

Em E Minor
1st (E), ♭3rd (G), 5th (B)

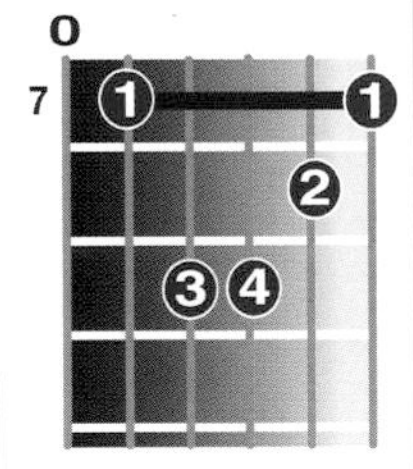

Em E Minor
1st (E), ♭3rd (G), 5th (B)

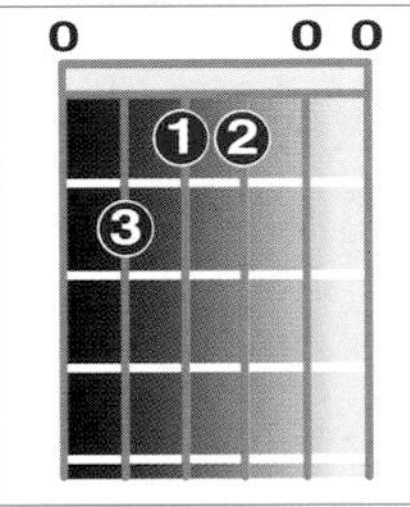

Emaj7 E Major 7th
1st (E), 3rd (G♯), 5th (B), 7th (D♯)

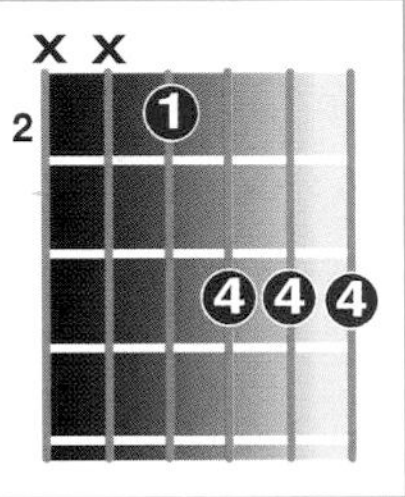

Emaj7 E Major 7th
1st (E), 3rd (G♯), 5th (B), 7th (D♯)

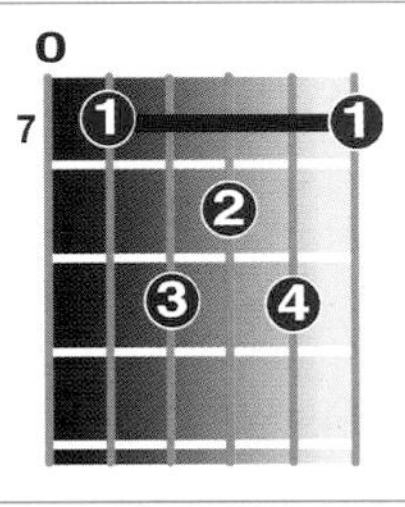

Emaj7 E Major 7th
1st (E), 3rd (G♯), 5th (B), 7th (D♯)

Em7 E Minor 7th
1st (E), ♭3rd (G), 5th (B), ♭7th (D)

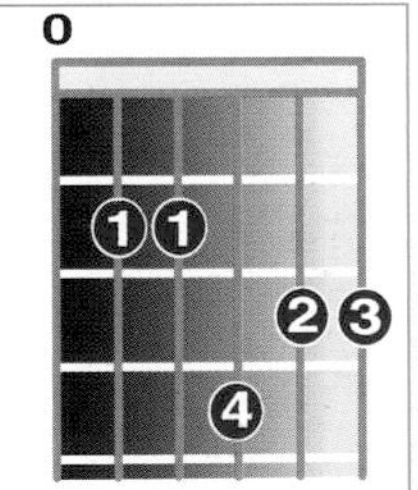

Em7 E Minor 7th
1st (E), ♭3rd (G), 5th (B), ♭7th (D)

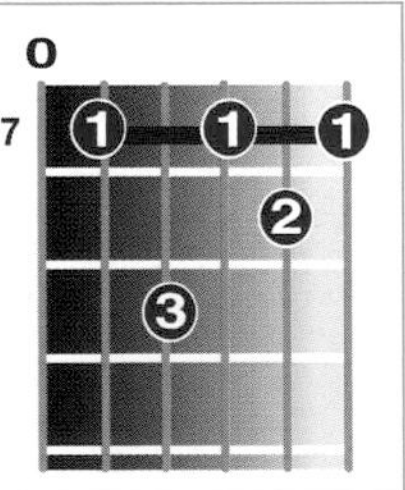

Em7 E Minor 7th
1st (E), ♭3rd (G), 5th (B), ♭7th (D)

Esus4 E Suspended 4th
1st (E), 4th (A), 5th (B)

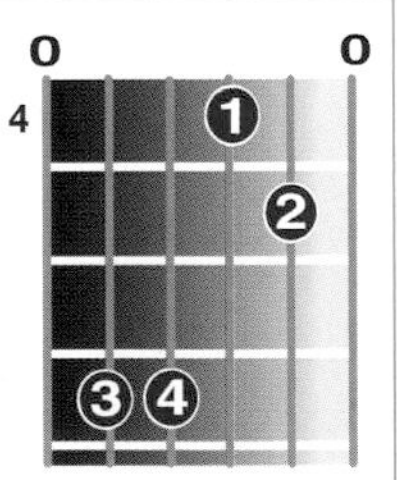

Esus4 E Suspended 4th
1st (E), 4th (A), 5th (B)

Complete Guitar Handbook

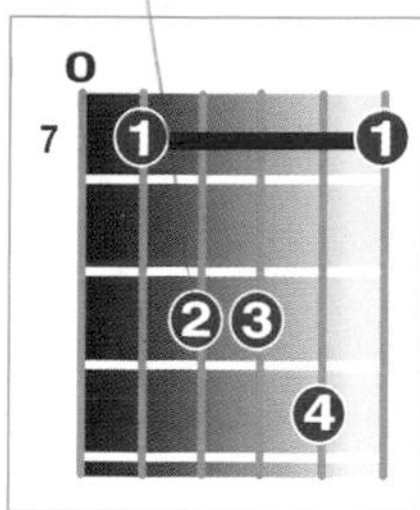

Esus4 E Suspended 4th
1st (E), 4th (A), 5th (B)

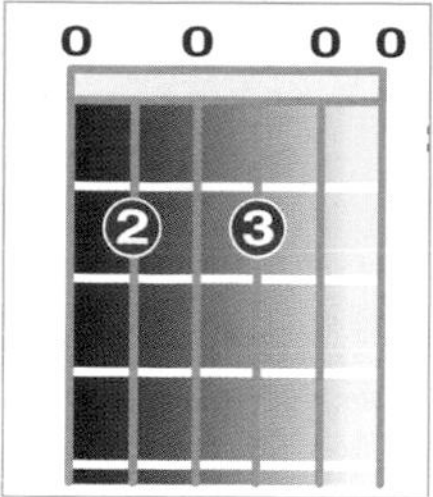

E7sus4 E Dominant 7th sus4
1st (E), 4th (A), 5th (B), ♭7th (D)

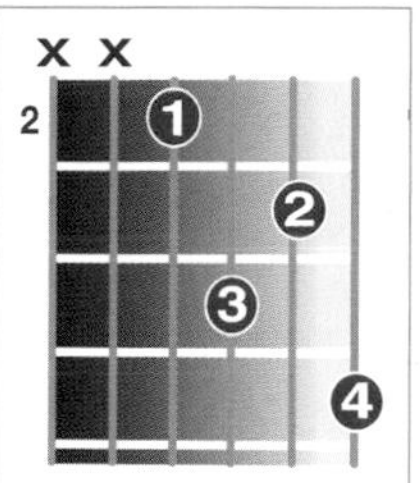

E7sus4 E Dominant 7th sus4
1st (E), 4th (A), 5th (B), ♭7th (D)

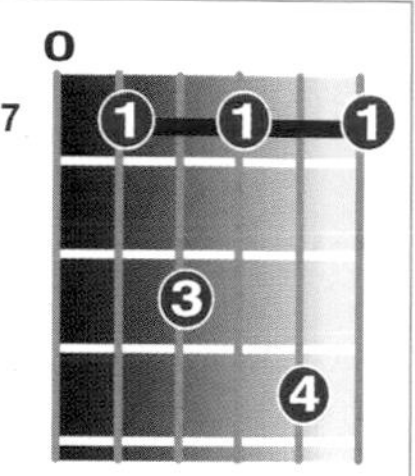

E7sus4 E Dominant 7th sus4
1st (E), 4th (A), 5th (B), ♭7th (D)

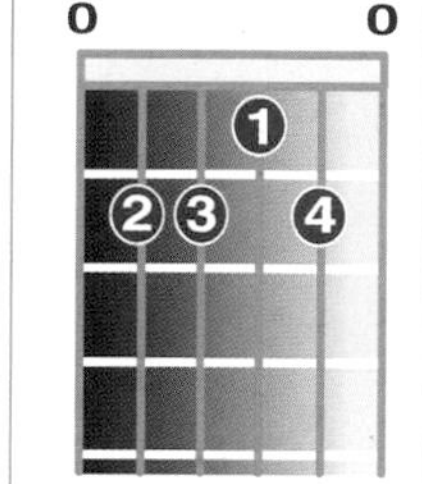

E6 E Major 6th
1st (E), 3rd (G♯),
5th (B), 6th (C♯)

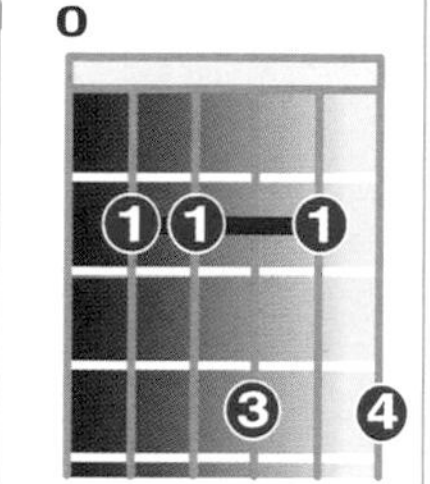

E6 E Major 6th
1st (E), 3rd (G♯),
5th (B), 6th (C♯)

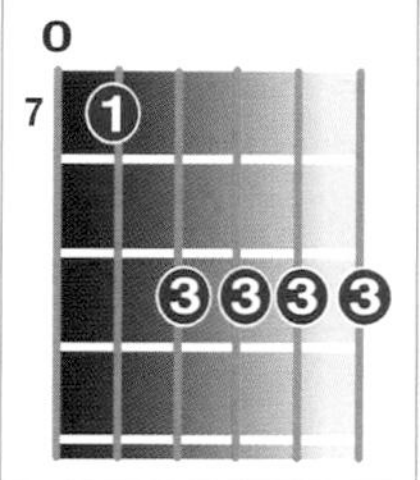

E6 E Major 6th
1st (E), 3rd (G♯),
5th (B), 6th (C♯)

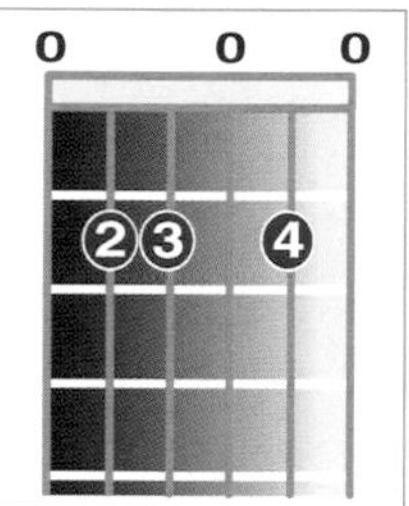

Em6 E Minor 6th
1st (E), ♭3rd (G), 5th (B), 6th (C♯)

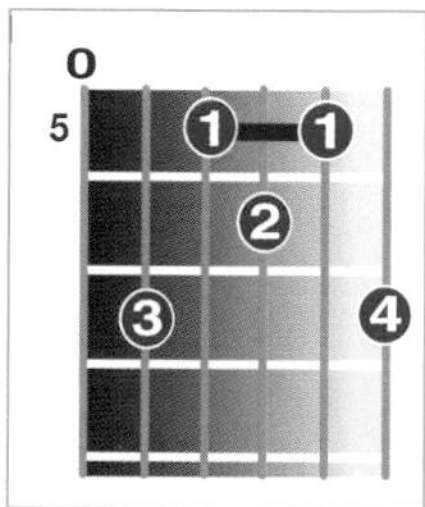

Em6 E Minor 6th
1st (E), ♭3rd (G), 5th (B), 6th (C♯)

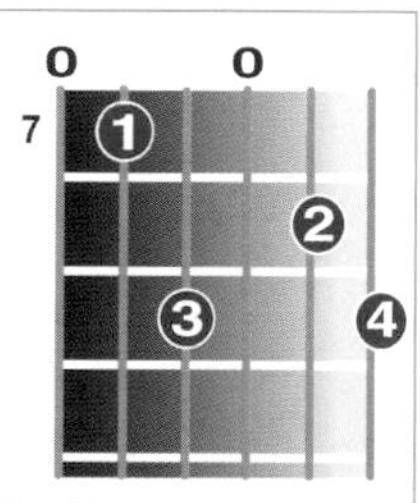

Em6 E Minor 6th
1st (E), ♭3rd (G), 5th (B), 6th (C♯)

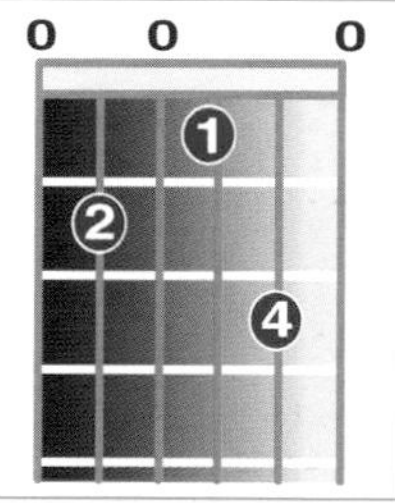

E7 E Dominant 7th
1st (E), 3rd (G♯),
5th (B), ♭7th (D)

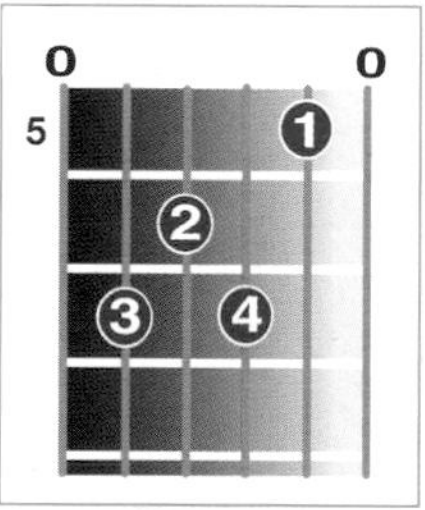

E7 E Dominant 7th
1st (E), 3rd (G♯),
5th (B), ♭7th (D)

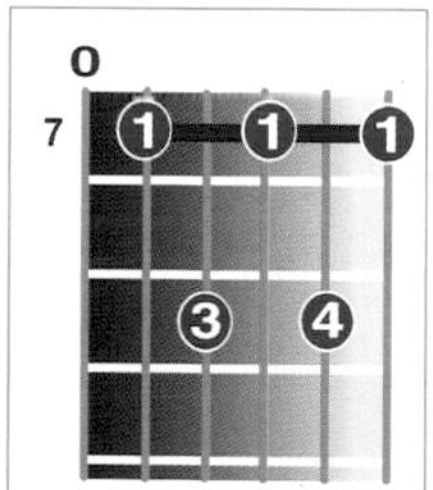

E7 E Dominant 7th
1st (E), 3rd (G♯),
5th (B), ♭7th (D)

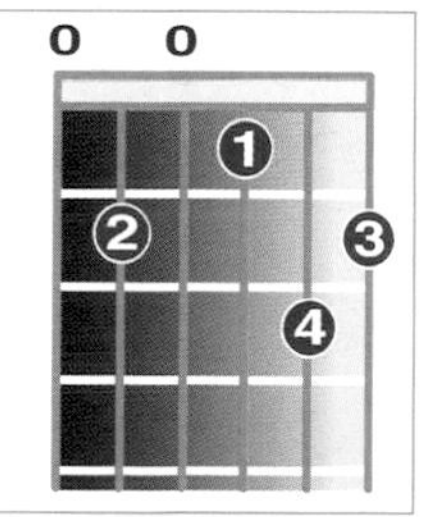

E9 E Dominant 9th
1st (E), 3rd (G♯), 5th (B),
♭7th (D), 9th (F♯)

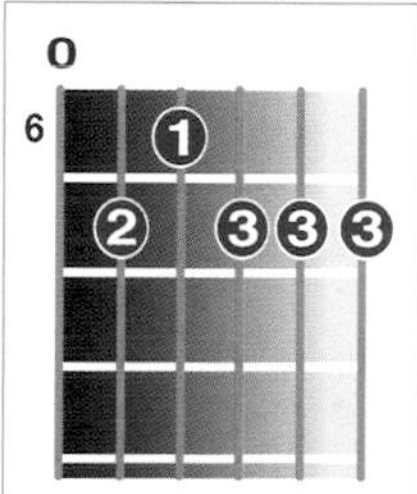

E9 E Dominant 9th
1st (E), 3rd (G♯), 5th (B),
♭7th (D), 9th (F♯)

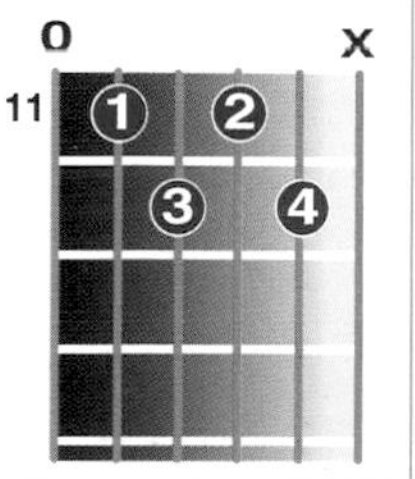

E9 E Dominant 9th
1st (E), 3rd (G♯), 5th (B),
♭7th (D), 9th (F♯)

Section Five: Chord Dictionary

E ADVANCED CHORDS

E5 E 5th (power chord)
1st (E), 5th (B)

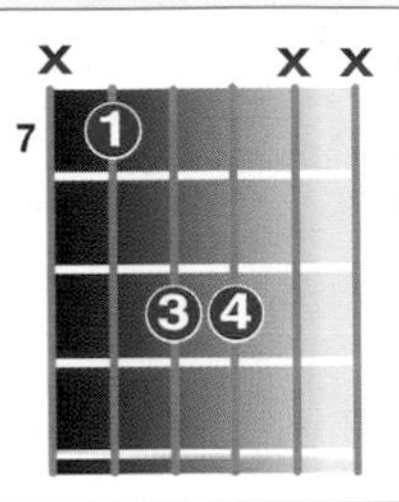

E5 E 5th (power chord)
1st (E), 5th (B)

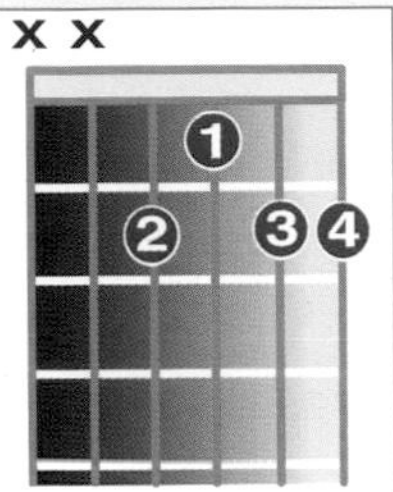

E 6/9 E Major 6th add 9th
1st (E), 3rd (G♯), 5th (B), 6th (C♯), 9th (F♯)

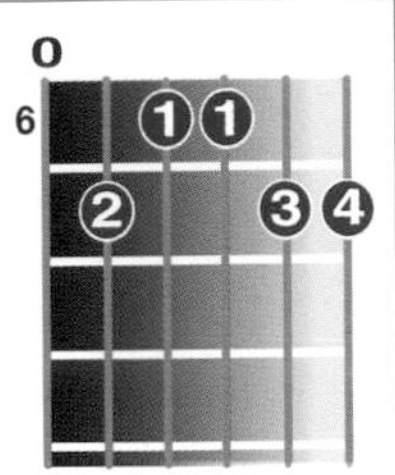

E 6/9 E Major 6th add 9th
1st (E), 3rd (G♯), 5th (B), 6th (C♯), 9th (F♯)

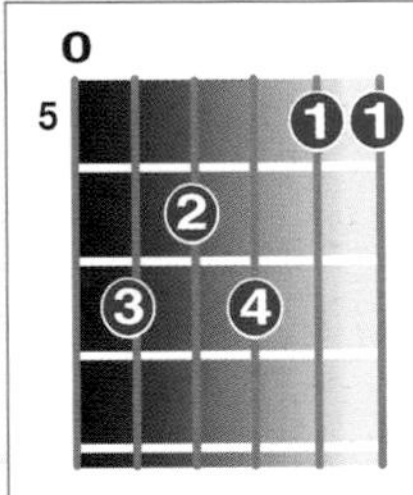

E11 E Dominant 11th
1st (E), 3rd (G♯), 5th (B), ♭7th (D), 9th (F♯), 11th (A)

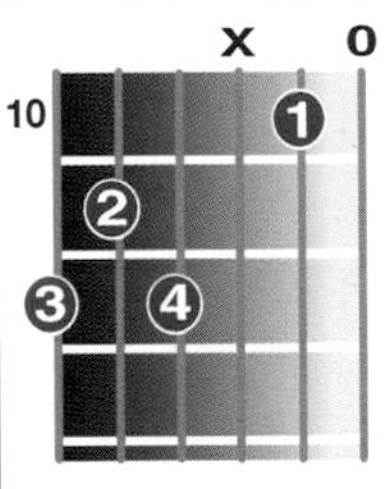

E11 E Dominant 11th
1st (E), 3rd (G♯), 5th (B), ♭7th (D), 9th (F♯), 11th (A)

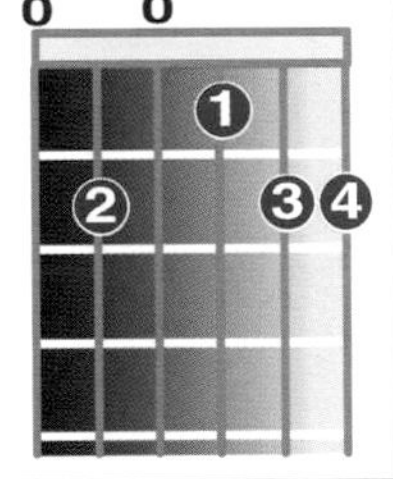

E13 E Dominant 13th
1st (E), 3rd (G♯), 5th (B), ♭7th (D), 9th (F♯), 13th (C♯)

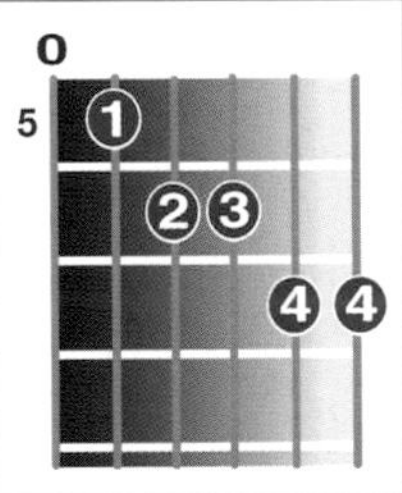

E13 E Dominant 13th
1st (E), 3rd (G♯), 5th (B), ♭7th (D), 9th (F♯), 13th (C♯)

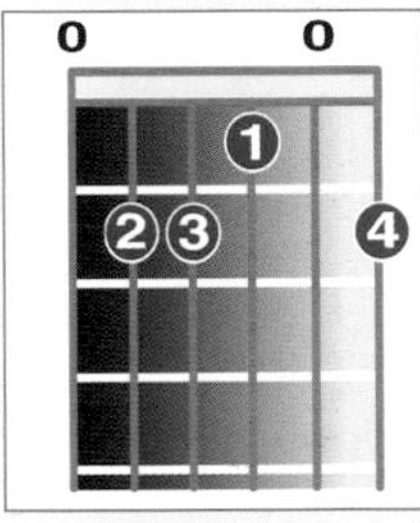

Eadd9 E Major add 9th
1st (E), 3rd (G♯), 5th (B), 9th (F♯)

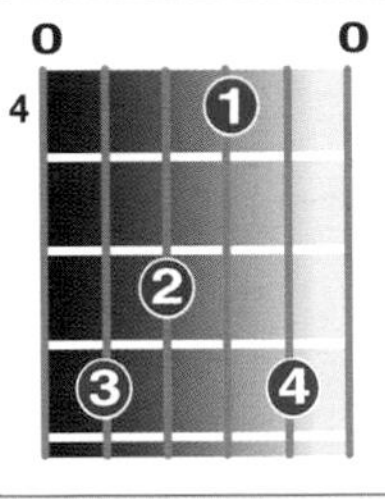

Eadd9 E Major add 9th
1st (E), 3rd (G♯), 5th (B), 9th (F♯)

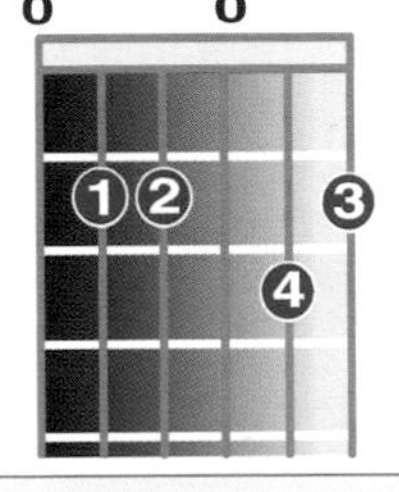

Em9 E Minor 9th
1st (E), ♭3rd (G), 5th (B), ♭7th (D), 9th (F♯)

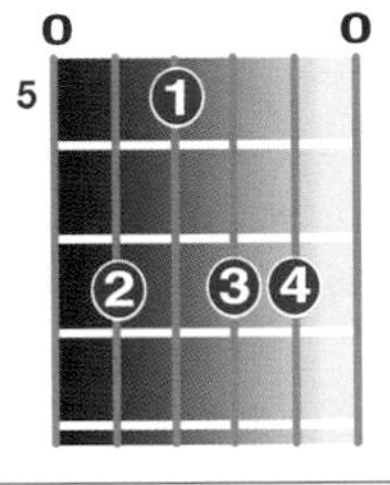

Em9 E Minor 9th
1st (E), ♭3rd (G), 5th (B), ♭7th (D), 9th (F♯)

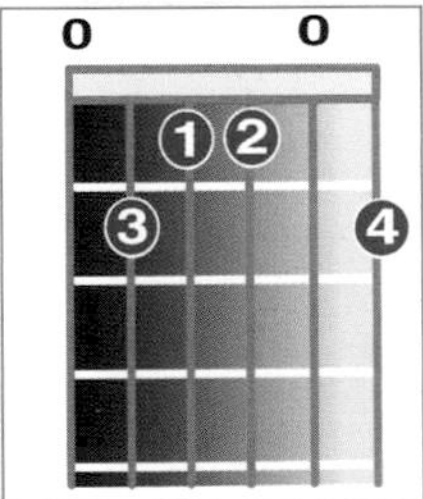

Emaj9 E Major 9th
1st (E), 3rd (G♯), 5th (B), 7th (D♯), 9th (F♯)

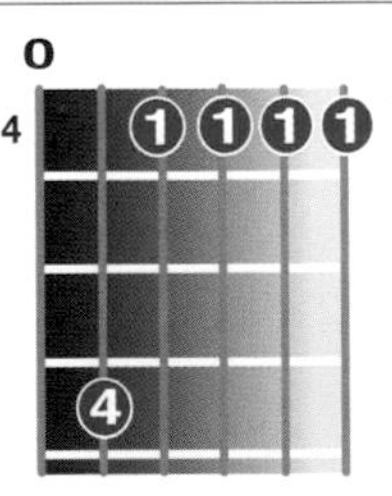

Emaj9 E Major 9th
1st (E), 3rd (G♯), 5th (B), 7th (D♯), 9th (F♯)

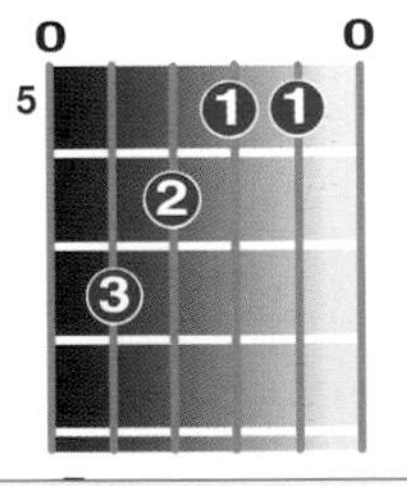

E+ E Augmented
1st (E), 3rd (G♯), ♯5th (B♯)

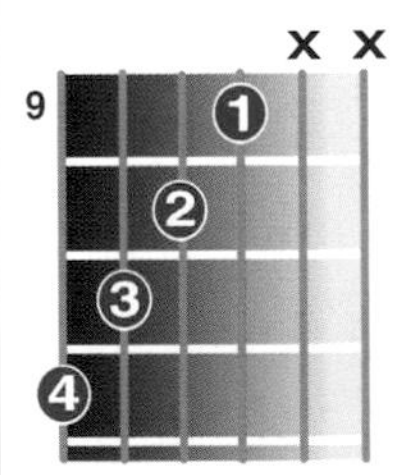

E+ E Augmented
1st (E), 3rd (G♯), ♯5th (B♯)

Complete Guitar Handbook

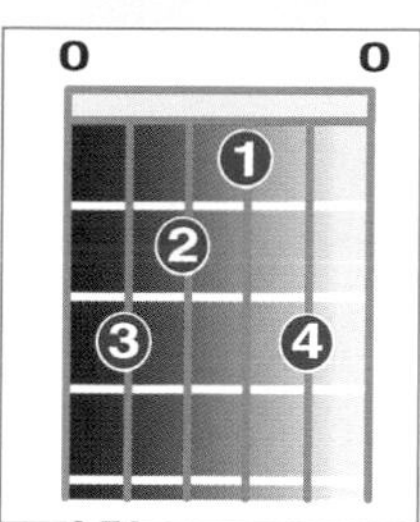

E7♯5 E Dominant 7th ♯5
1st (E), 3rd (G♯),
♯5th (B♯), ♭7th (D)

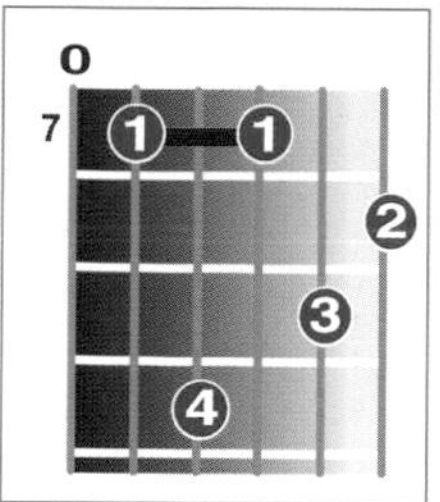

E7♯5 E Dominant 7th ♯5
1st (E), 3rd (G♯),
♯5th (B♯), ♭7th (D)

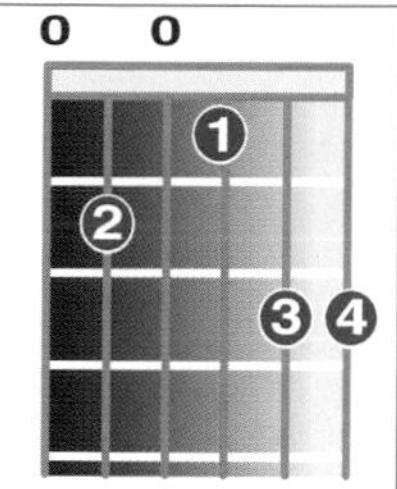

E7♯9 E Dominant 7th ♯9
1st (E), 3rd (G♯), 5th (B),
♭7th (D), ♯9th (Fx)

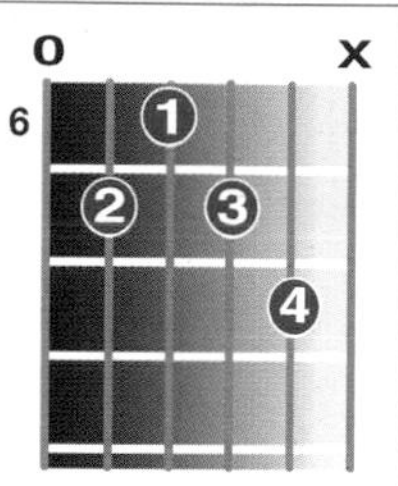

E7♯9 E Dominant 7th ♯9
1st (E), 3rd (G♯), 5th (B),
♭7th (D), ♯9th (Fx)

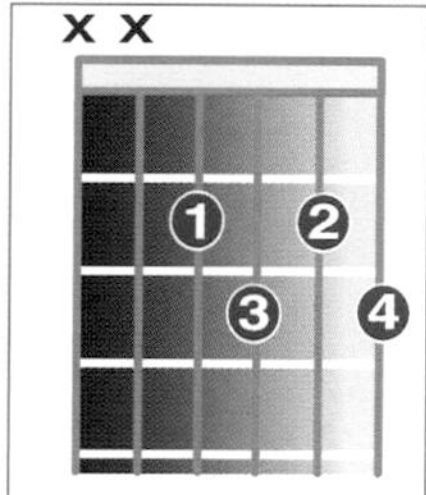

Eo7 E Diminished 7th
1st (E), ♭3rd (G),
♭5th (B♭), ♭♭7th (D♭)

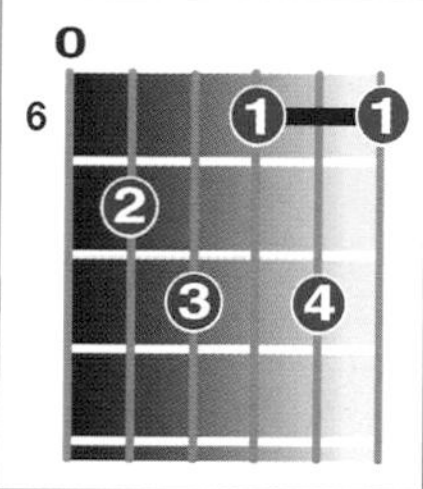

Eo7 E Diminished 7th
1st (E), ♭3rd (G),
♭5th (B♭), ♭♭7th (D♭)

Eo E Diminished triad
1st (E), ♭3rd (G), ♭5th (B♭)

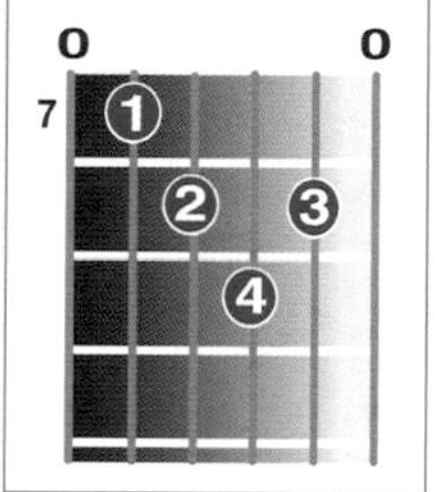

Eo E Diminished triad
1st (E), ♭3rd (G), ♭5th (B♭)

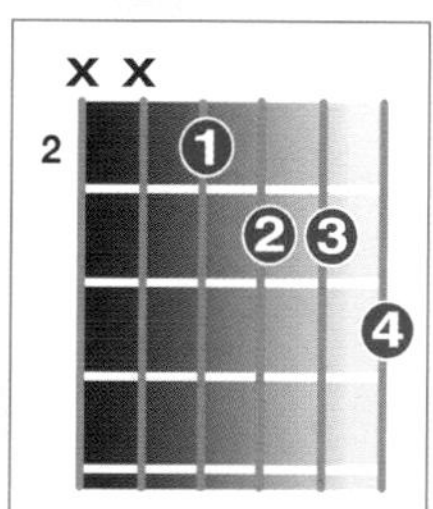

E7♭5 E Dominant 7th ♭5
1st (E), 3rd (G♯),
♭5th (B♭), ♭7th (D)

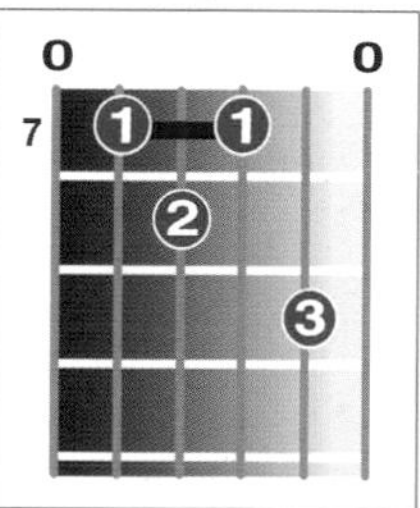

E7♭5 E Dominant 7th ♭5
1st (E), 3rd (G♯),
♭5th (B♭), ♭7th (D)

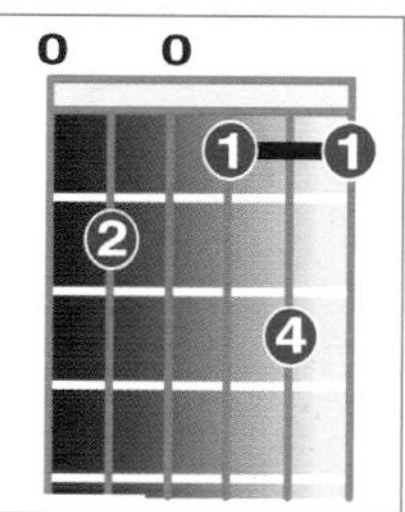

E7♭9 E Dominant 7th ♭9
1st (E), 3rd (G♯), 5th (B),
♭7th (D), ♭9th (F)

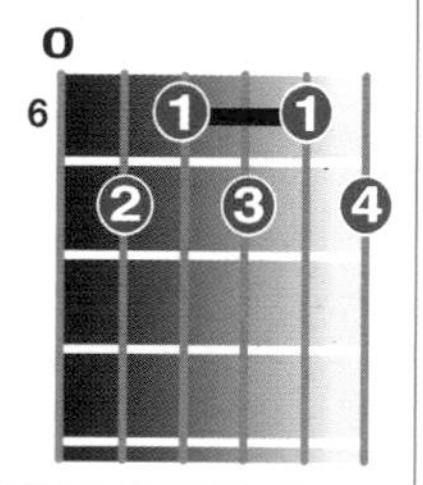

E7♭9 E Dominant 7th ♭9
1st (E), 3rd (G♯), 5th (B),
♭7th (D), ♭9th (F)

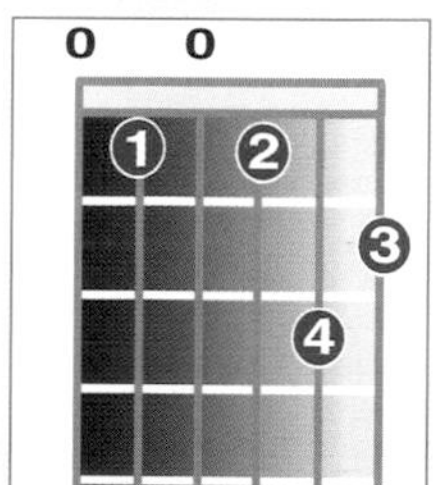

E9♭5 E Dominant 9th ♭5th
1st (E), 3rd (G♯), ♭5th (B♭),
♭7th (D), 9th (F♯)

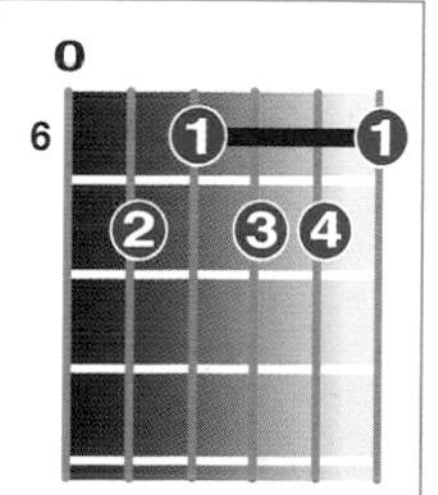

E9♭5 E Dominant 9th ♭5th
1st (E), 3rd (G♯), ♭5th (B♭),
♭7th (D), 9th (F♯)

Scale of E major

E	F♯	G♯	A	B	C♯	D♯
1st	2nd	3rd	4th	5th	6th	7th
	9th		11th		13th	

Section Five: Chord Dictionary

F MAIN CHORDS

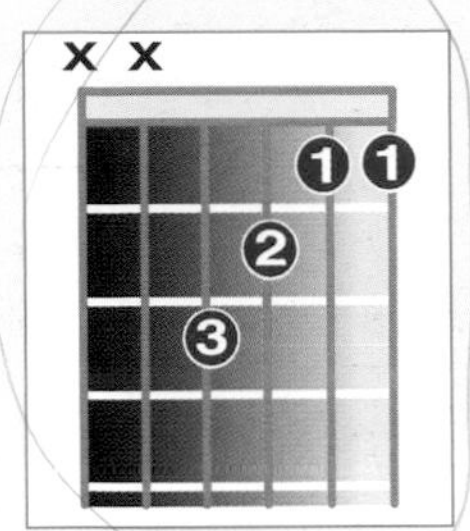

F F Major
1st (F), 3rd (A), 5th (C)

F F Major
1st (F), 3rd (A), 5th (C)

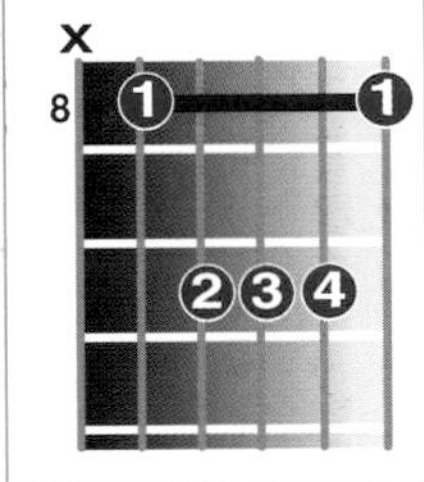

F F Major
1st (F), 3rd (A), 5th (C)

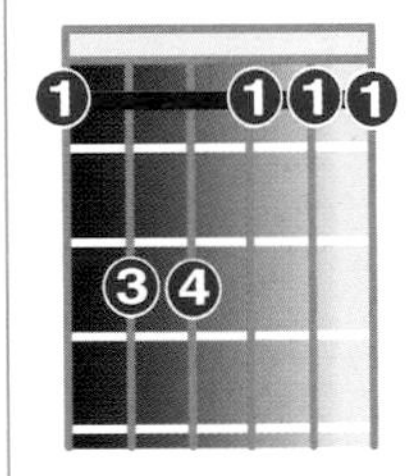

Fm F Minor
1st (F), ♭3rd (A♭), 5th (C)

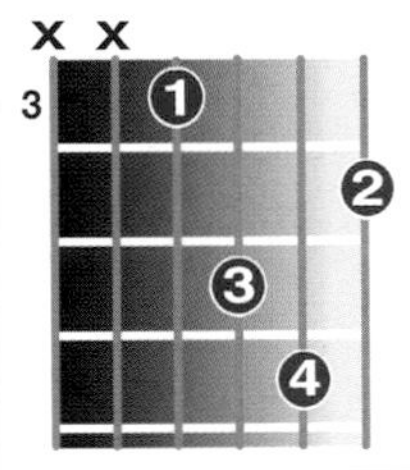

Fm F Minor
1st (F), ♭3rd (A♭), 5th (C)

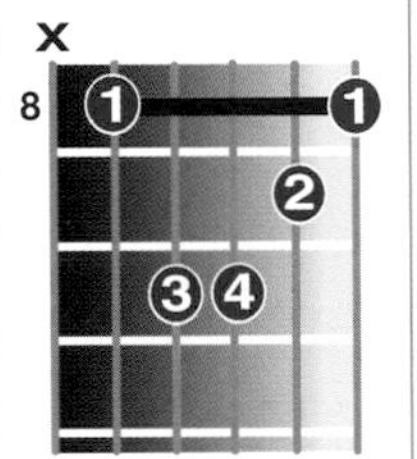

Fm F Minor
1st (F), ♭3rd (A♭), 5th (C)

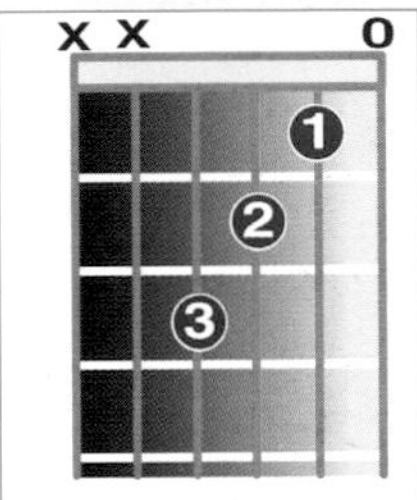

Fmaj7 F Major 7th
1st (F), 3rd (A), 5th (C), 7th (E)

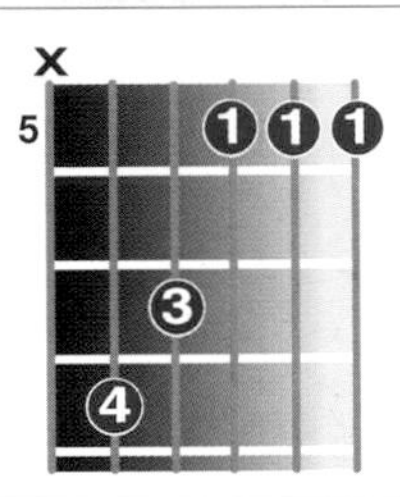

Fmaj7 F Major 7th
1st (F), 3rd (A), 5th (C), 7th (E)

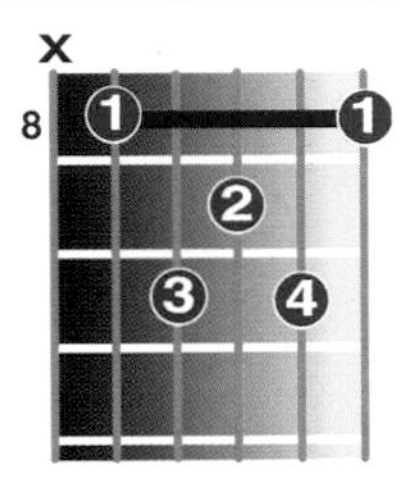

Fmaj7 F Major 7th
1st (F), 3rd (A), 5th (C), 7th (E)

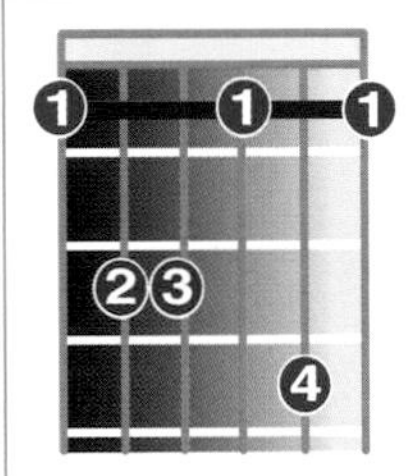

Fm7 F Minor 7th
1st (F), ♭3rd (A♭),
5th (C), ♭7th (E♭)

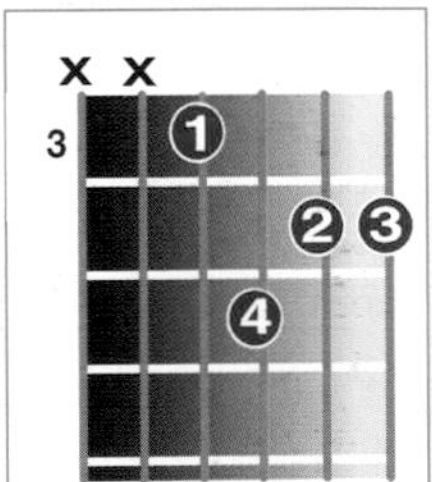

Fm7 F Minor 7th
1st (F), ♭3rd (A♭),
5th (C), ♭7th (E♭)

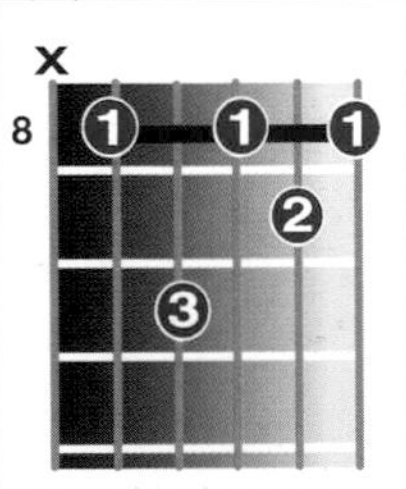

Fm7 F Minor 7th
1st (F), ♭3rd (A♭),
5th (C), ♭7th (E♭)

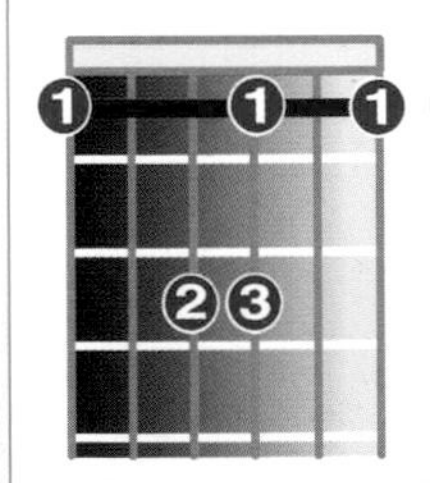

Fsus4 F Suspended 4th
1st (F), 4th (B♭), 5th (C)

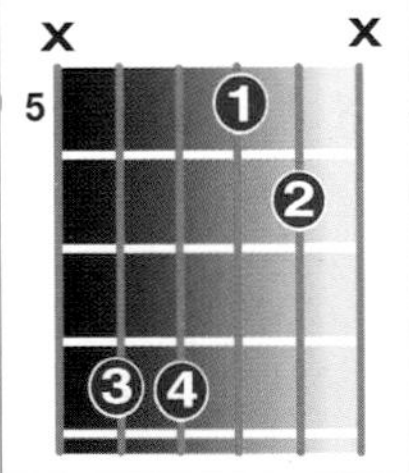

Fsus4 F Suspended 4th
1st (F), 4th (B♭), 5th (C)

Complete Guitar Handbook

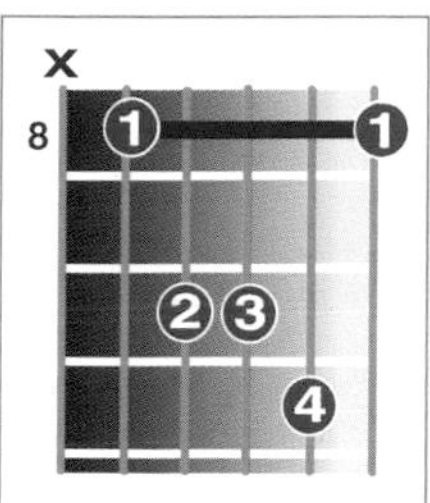

Fsus4 F Suspended 4th
1st (F), 4th (B♭), 5th (C)

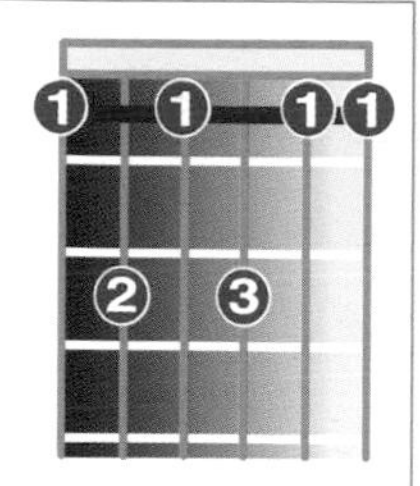

F7sus4 F Dominant 7th sus4
1st (F), 4th (B♭), 5th (C), ♭7th (E♭)

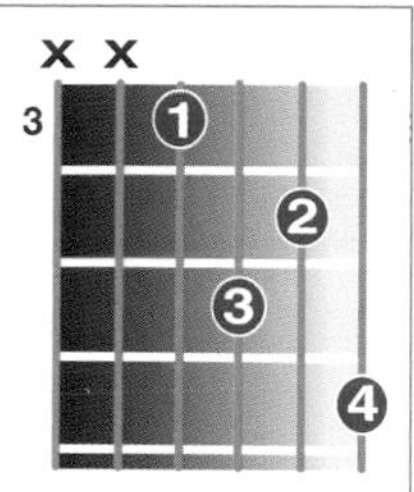

F7sus4 F Dominant 7th sus4
1st (F), 4th (B♭), 5th (C), ♭7th (E♭)

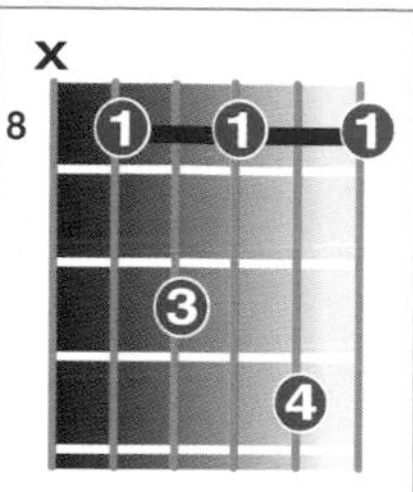

F7sus4 F Dominant 7th sus4
1st (F), 4th (B♭), 5th (C), ♭7th (E♭)

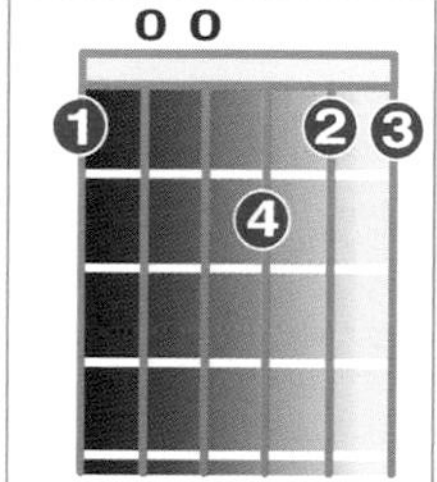

F6 F Major 6th
1st (F), 3rd (A), 5th (C), 6th (D)

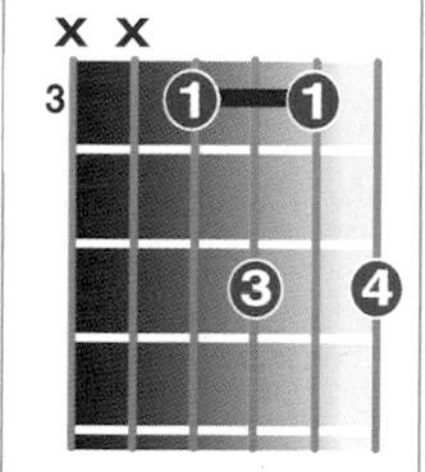

F6 F Major 6th
1st (F), 3rd (A), 5th (C), 6th (D)

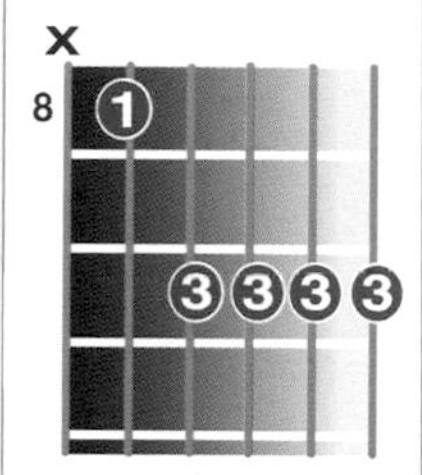

F6 F Major 6th
1st (F), 3rd (A), 5th (C), 6th (D)

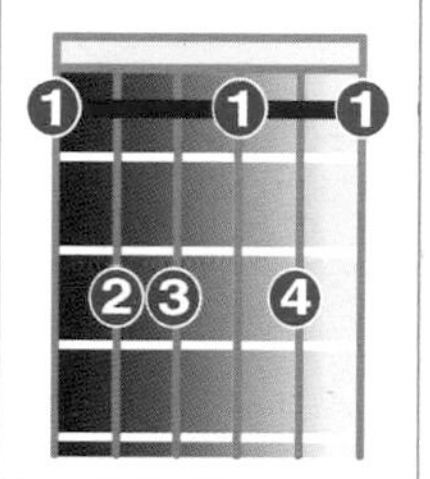

Fm6 F Minor 6th
1st (F), ♭3rd (A♭),
5th (C), 6th (D)

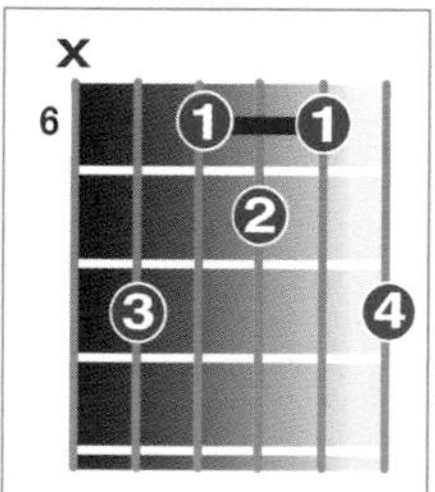

Fm6 F Minor 6th
1st (F), ♭3rd (A♭),
5th (C), 6th (D)

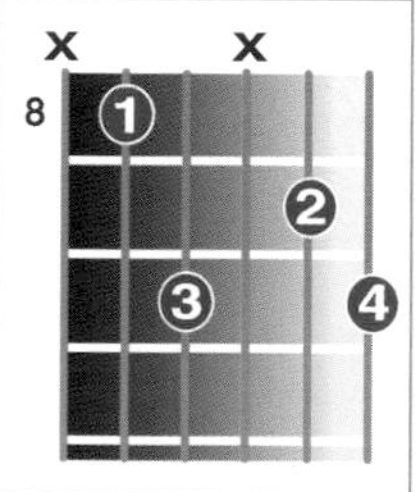

Fm6 F Minor 6th
1st (F), ♭3rd (A♭),
5th (C), 6th (D)

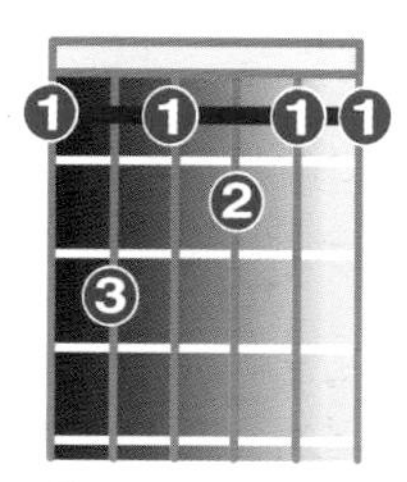

F7 F Dominant 7th
1st (F), 3rd (A), 5th (C), ♭7th (E♭)

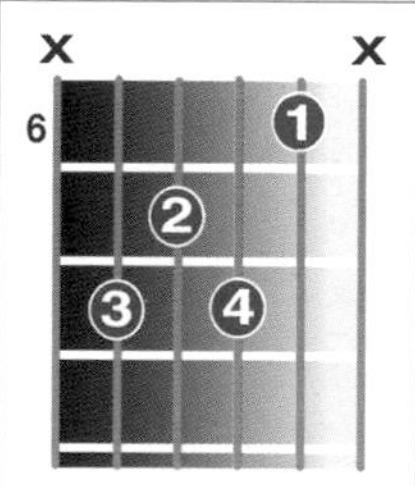

F7 F Dominant 7th
1st (F), 3rd (A), 5th (C), ♭7th (E♭)

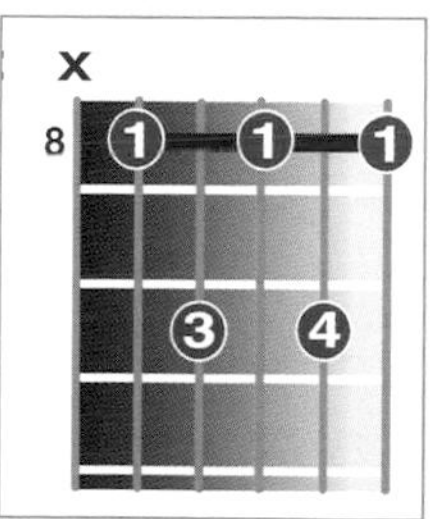

F7 F Dominant 7th
1st (F), 3rd (A), 5th (C), ♭7th (E♭)

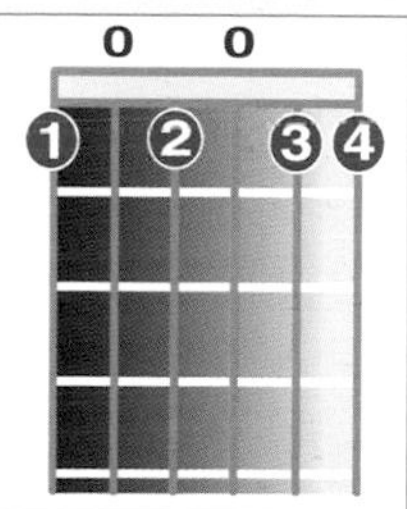

F9 F Dominant 9th
1st (F), 3rd (A), 5th (C),
♭7th (E♭), 9th (G)

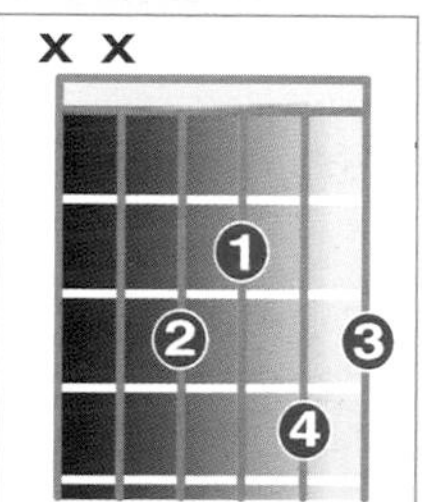

F9 F Dominant 9th
1st (F), 3rd (A), 5th (C),
♭7th (E♭), 9th (G)

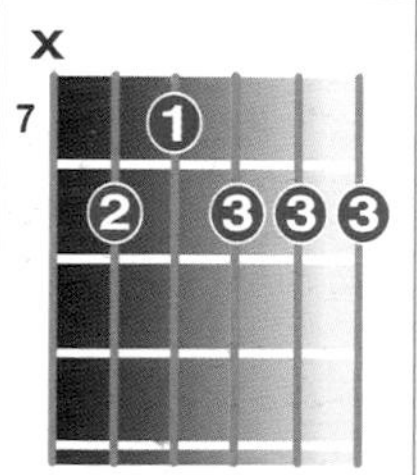

F9 F Dominant 9th
1st (F), 3rd (A), 5th (C),
♭7th (E♭), 9th (G)

Section Five: Chord Dictionary

F ADVANCED CHORDS

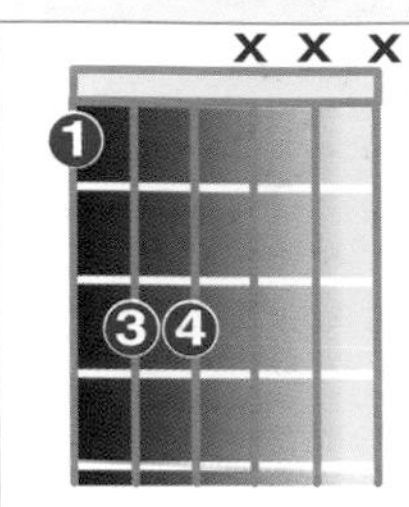

F5 F 5th (power chord)
1st (F), 5th (C)

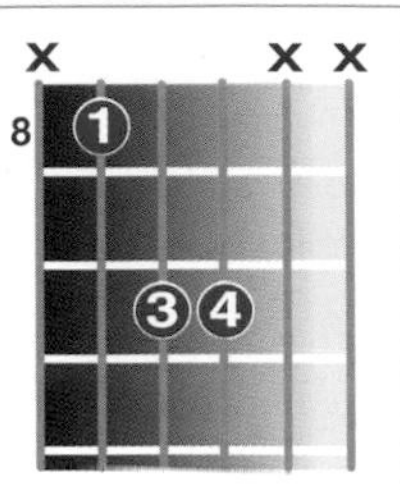

F5 F 5th (power chord)
1st (F), 5th (C)

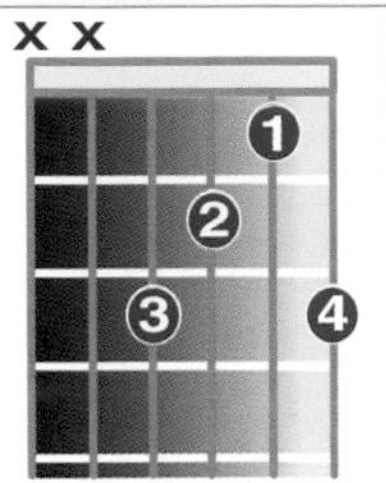

F 6/9 F Major 6th add 9th
1st (F), 3rd (A), 5th (C), 6th (D), 9th (G)

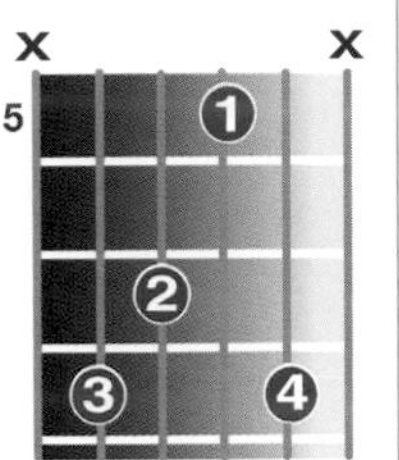

F 6/9 F Major 6th add 9th
1st (F), 3rd (A), 5th (C), 6th (D), 9th (G)

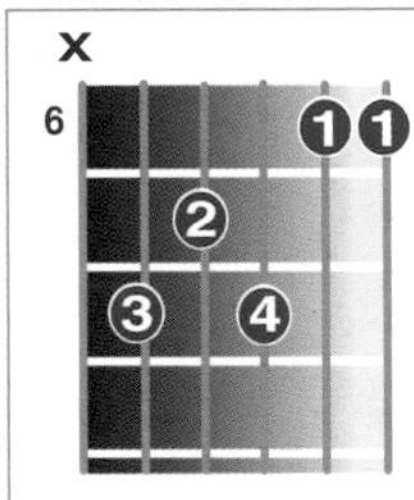

F11 F Dominant 11th
1st (F), 3rd (A), 5th (C), ♭7th (E♭), 9th (G), 11th (B♭)

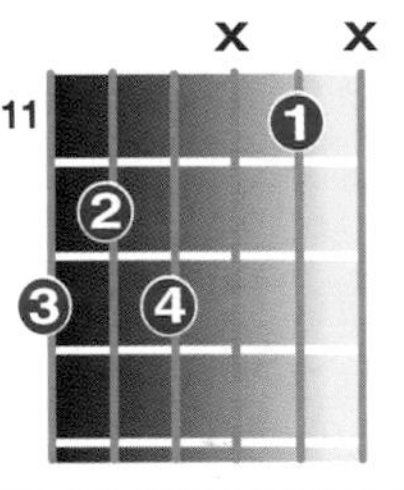

F11 F Dominant 11th
1st (F), 3rd (A), 5th (C), ♭7th (E♭), 9th (G), 11th (B♭)

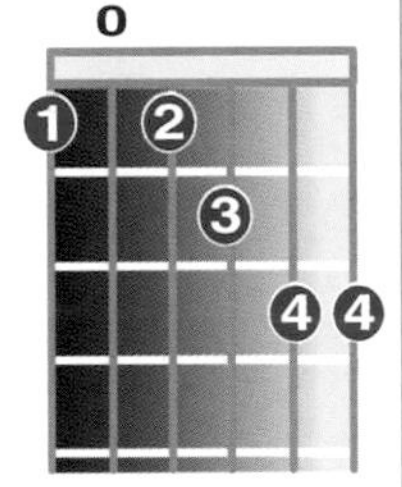

F13 F Dominant 13th
1st (F), 3rd (A), 5th (C), ♭7th (E♭), 9th (G), 13th (D)

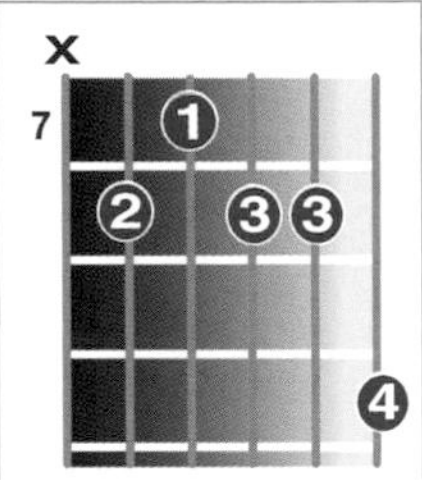

F13 F Dominant 13th
1st (F), 3rd (A), 5th (C), ♭7th (E♭), 9th (G), 13th (D)

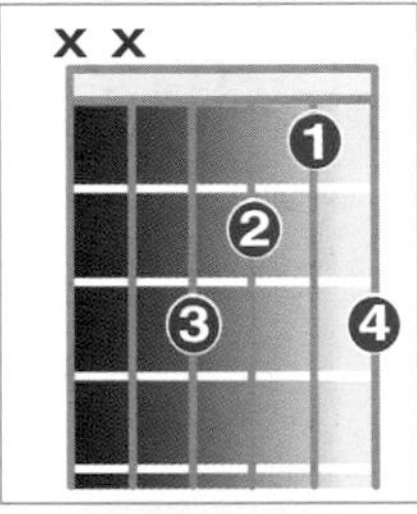

Fadd9 F Major add 9th
1st (F), 3rd (A), 5th (C), 9th (G)

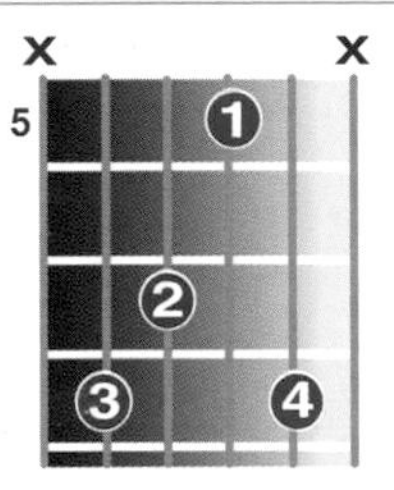

Fadd9 F Major add 9th
1st (F), 3rd (A), 5th (C), 9th (G)

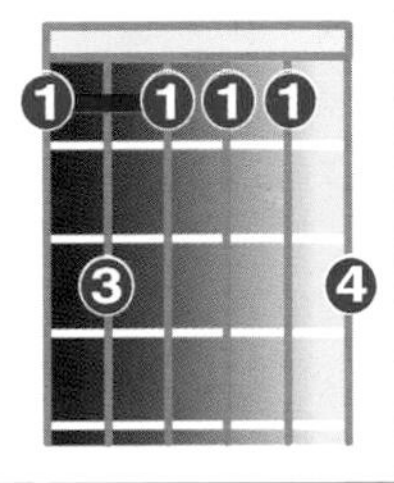

Fm9 F Minor 9th
1st (F), ♭3rd (A♭), 5th (C), ♭7th (E♭), 9th (G)

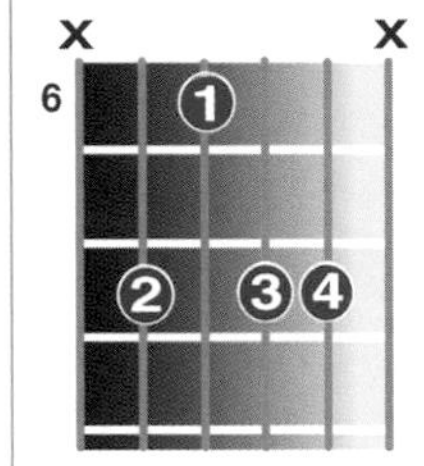

Fm9 F Minor 9th
1st (F), ♭3rd (A♭), 5th (C), ♭7th (E♭), 9th (G)

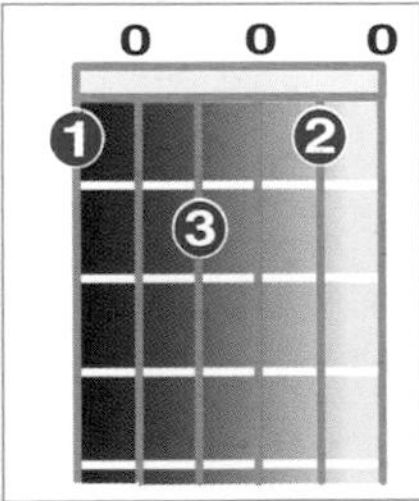

Fmaj9 F Major 9th
1st (F), 3rd (A), 5th (C), 7th (E), 9th (G)

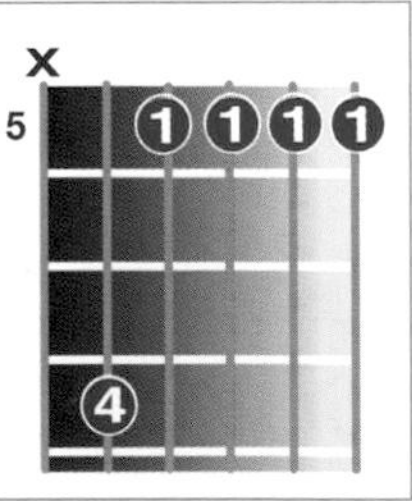

Fmaj9 F Major 9th
1st (F), 3rd (A), 5th (C), 7th (E), 9th (G)

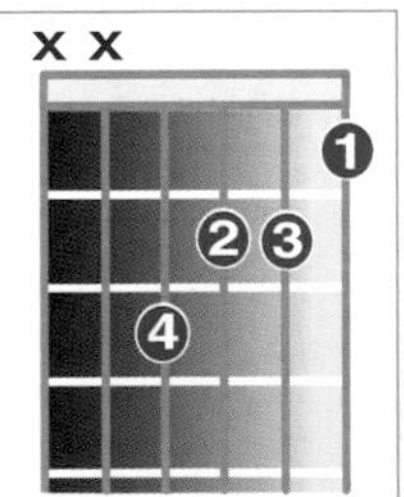

F+ F Augmented
1st (F), 3rd (A), ♯5th (C♯)

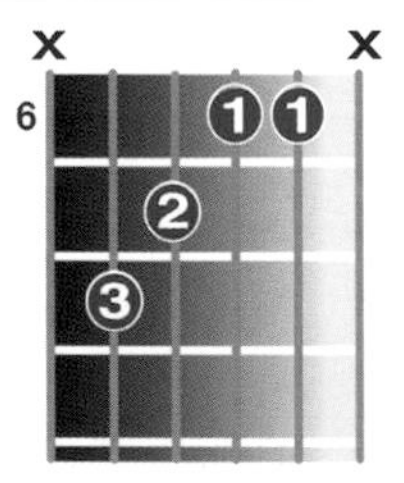

F+ F Augmented
1st (F), 3rd (A), ♯5th (C♯)

Complete Guitar Handbook

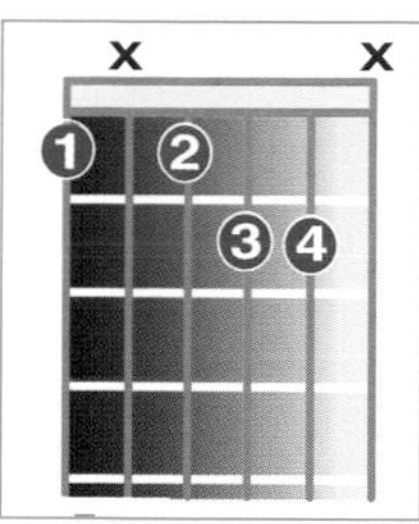

F7♯5 F Dominant 7th ♯5
1st (F), 3rd (A), ♯5th (C♯), ♭7th (E♭)

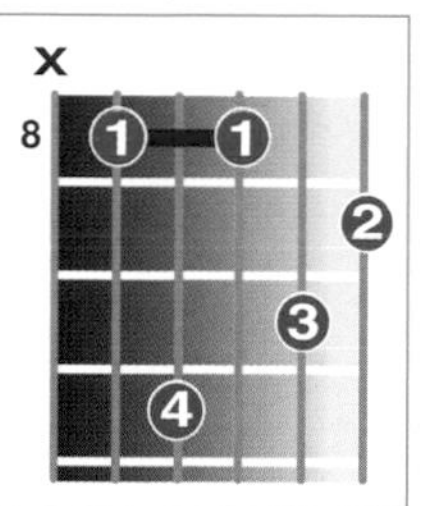

F7♯5 F Dominant 7th ♯5
1st (F), 3rd (A), ♯5th (C♯), ♭7th (E♭)

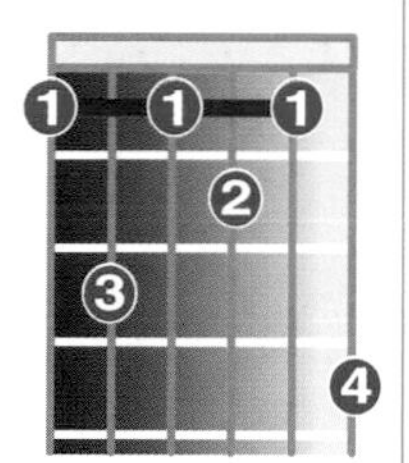

F7♯9 F Dominant 7th ♯9
1st (F), 3rd (A), 5th (C), ♭7th (E♭), ♯9th (G♯)

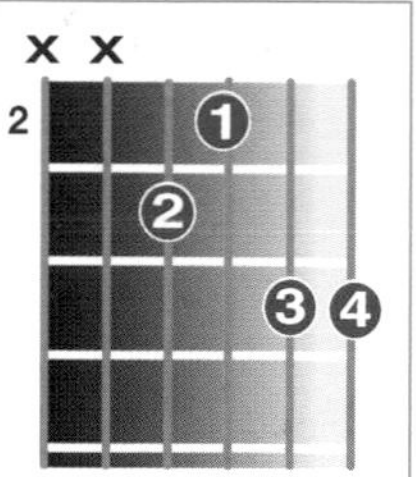

F7♯9 F Dominant 7th ♯9
1st (F), 3rd (A), 5th (C), ♭7th (E♭), ♯9th (G♯)

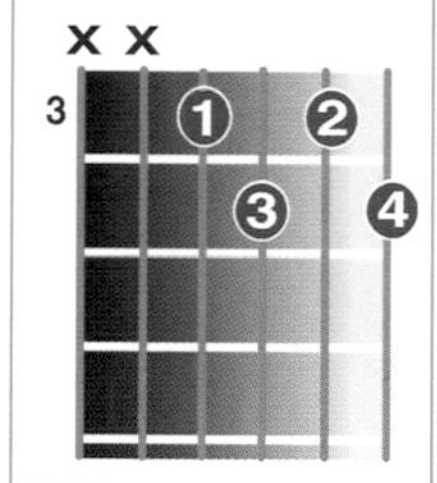

Fo7 F Diminished 7th
1st (F), ♭3rd (A♭), ♭5th (C♭), ♭♭7th (E♭♭)

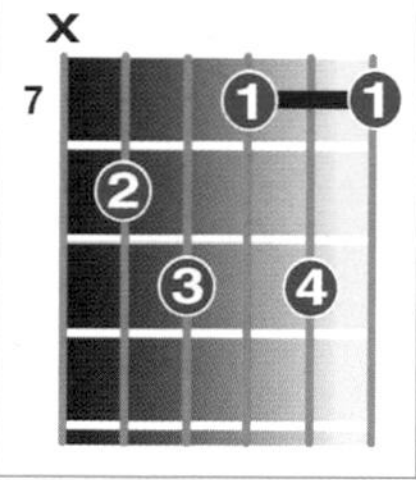

Fo7 F Diminished 7th
1st (F), ♭3rd (A♭), ♭5th (C♭), ♭♭7th (E♭♭)

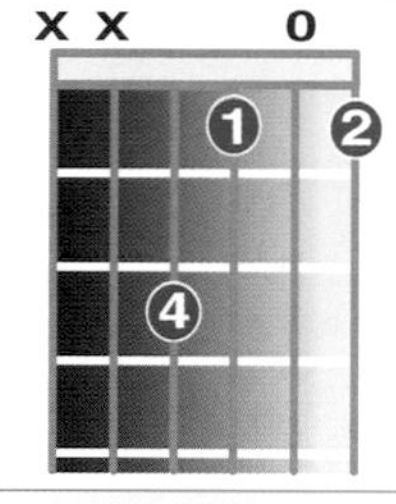

Fo F Diminished triad
1st (F), ♭3rd (A♭), ♭5th (C♭)

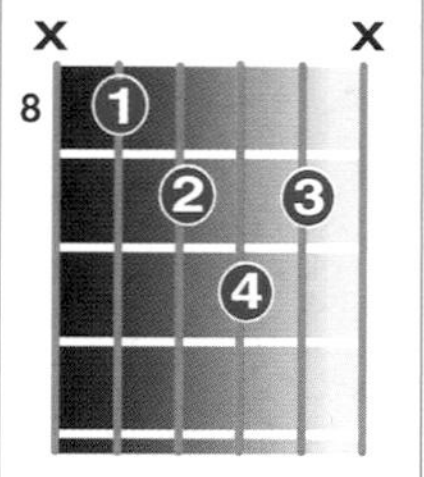

Fo F Diminished triad
1st (F), ♭3rd (A♭), ♭5th (C♭)

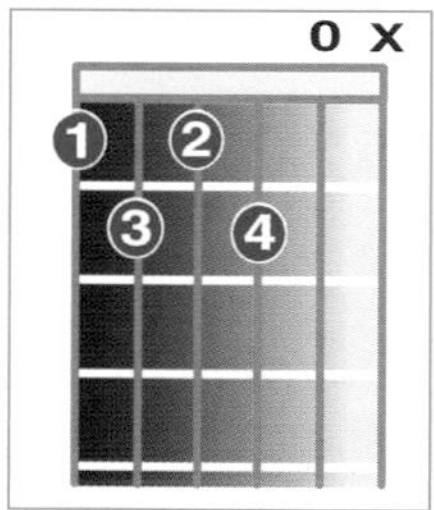

F7♭5 F Dominant 7th ♭5
1st (F), 3rd (A), ♭5th (C♭), ♭7th (E♭)

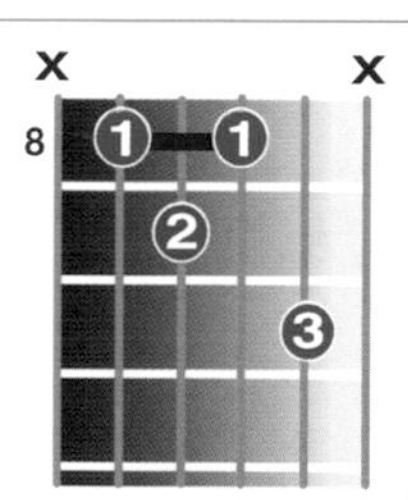

F7♭5 F Dominant 7th ♭5
1st (F), 3rd (A), ♭5th (C♭), ♭7th (E♭)

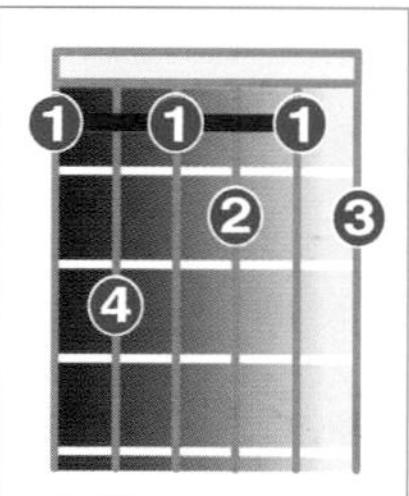

F7♭9 F Dominant 7th ♭9
1st (F), 3rd (A), 5th (C), ♭7th (E♭), ♭9th (G♭)

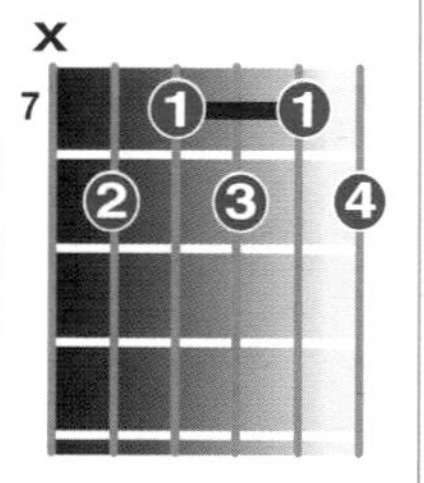

F7♭9 F Dominant 7th ♭9
1st (F), 3rd (A), 5th (C), ♭7th (E♭), ♭9th (G♭)

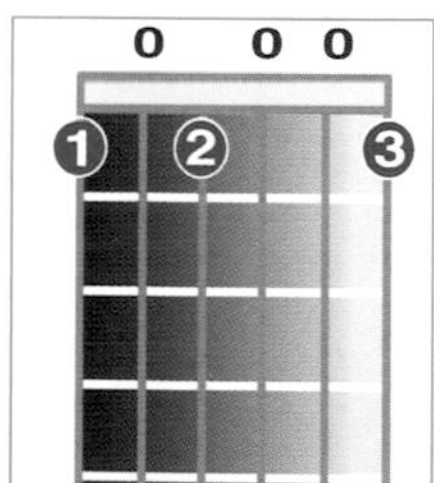

F9♭5 F Dominant 9th ♭5th
1st (F), 3rd (A), ♭5th (C♭), ♭7th (E♭), 9th (G)

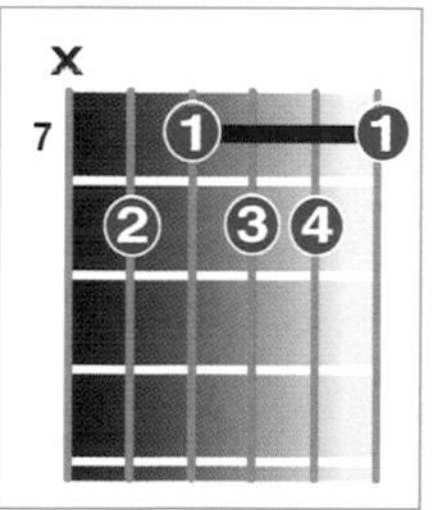

F9♭5 F Dominant 9th ♭5th
1st (F), 3rd (A), ♭5th (C♭), ♭7th (E♭), 9th (G)

Scale of F major

F	G	A	B♭	C	D	E
1st	2nd	3rd	4th	5th	6th	7th
	9th		11th		13th	

Section Five: Chord Dictionary

F♯/G♭ MAIN CHORDS

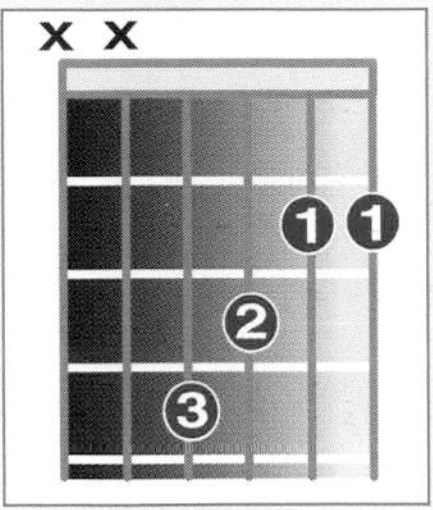

F♯ F♯ Major
1st (F♯), 3rd (A♯), 5th (C♯)

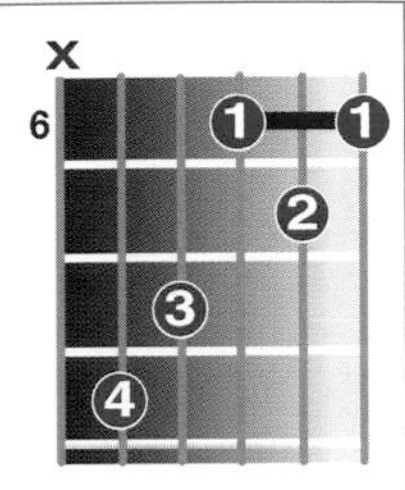

F♯ F♯ Major
1st (F♯), 3rd (A♯), 5th (C♯)

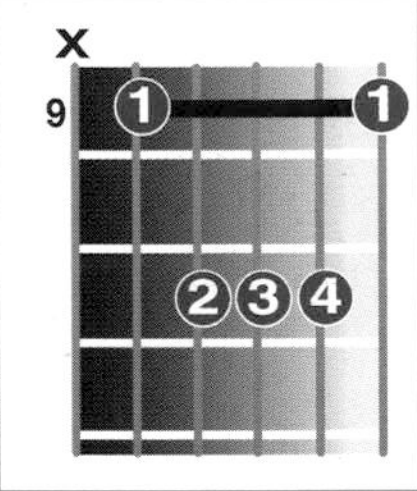

F♯ F♯ Major
1st (F♯), 3rd (A♯), 5th (C♯)

F♯m F♯ Minor
1st (F♯), ♭3rd (A), 5th (C♯)

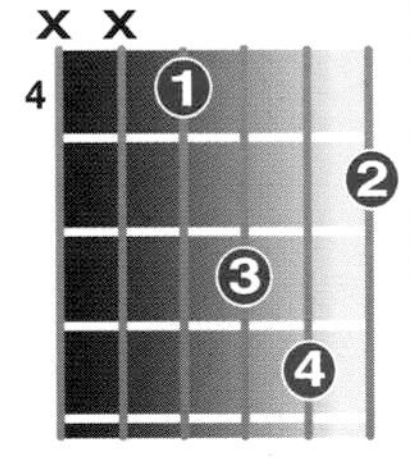

F♯m F♯ Minor
1st (F♯), ♭3rd (A), 5th (C♯)

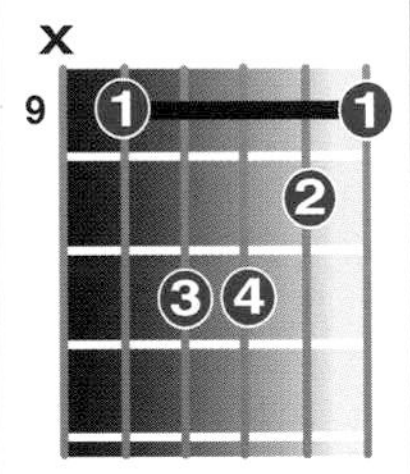

F♯m F♯ Minor
1st (F♯), ♭3rd (A), 5th (C♯)

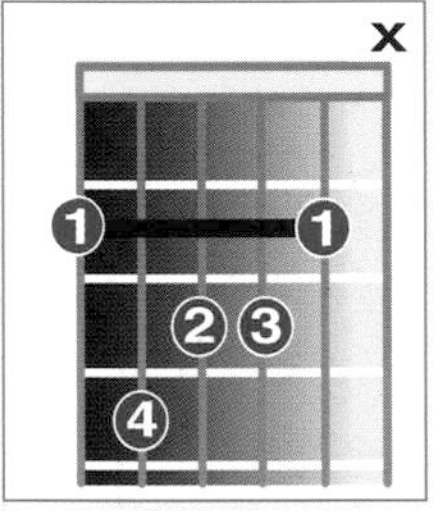

F♯maj7 F♯ Major 7th
1st (F♯), 3rd (A♯),
5th (C♯), 7th (E♯)

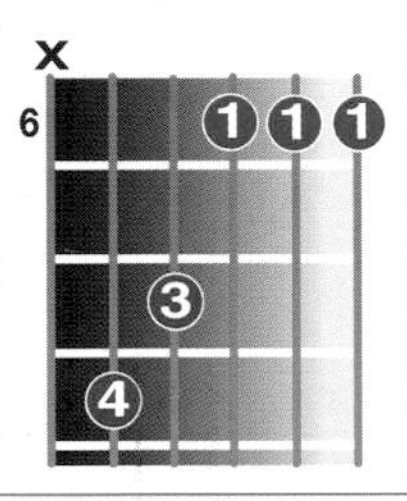

F♯maj7 F♯ Major 7th
1st (F♯), 3rd (A♯),
5th (C♯), 7th (E♯)

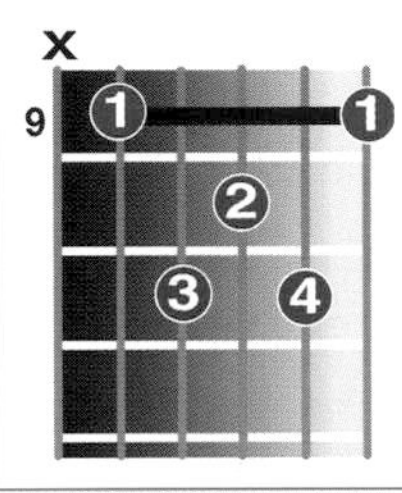

F♯maj7 F♯ Major 7th
1st (F♯), 3rd (A♯),
5th (C♯), 7th (E♯)

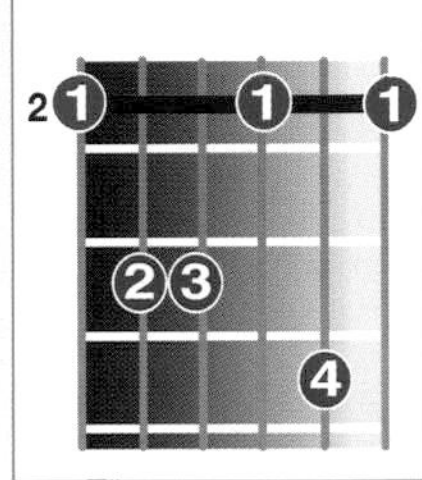

F♯m7 F♯ Minor 7th
1st (F♯), ♭3rd (A),
5th (C♯), ♭7th (E)

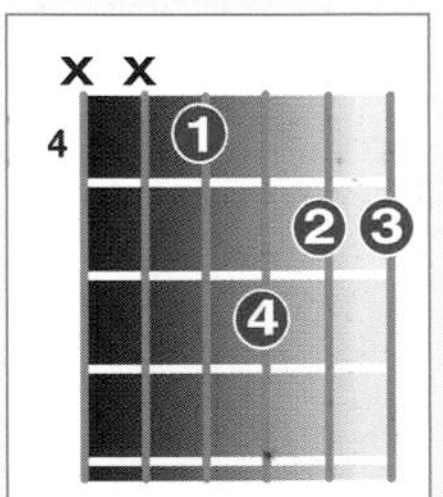

F♯m7 F♯ Minor 7th
1st (F♯), ♭3rd (A),
5th (C♯), ♭7th (E)

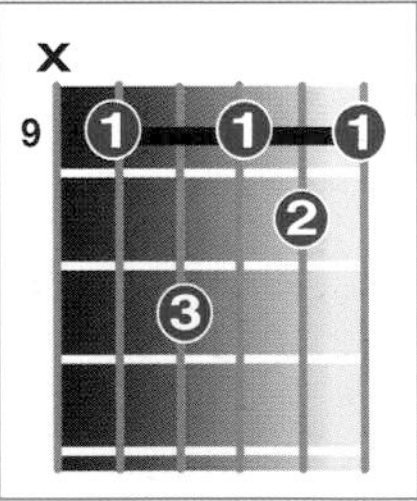

F♯m7 F♯ Minor 7th
1st (F♯), ♭3rd (A),
5th (C♯), ♭7th (E)

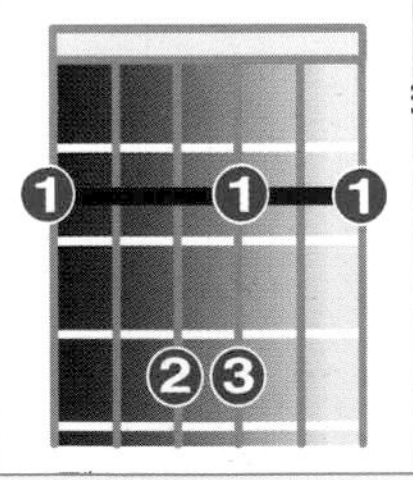

F♯sus4 F♯ Suspended 4th
1st (F♯), 4th (B), 5th (C♯)

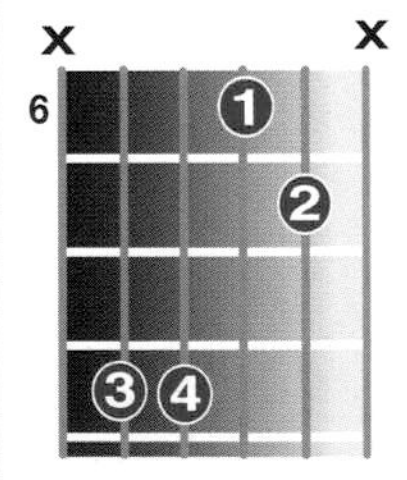

F♯sus4 F♯ Suspended 4th
1st (F♯), 4th (B), 5th (C♯)

Complete Guitar Handbook

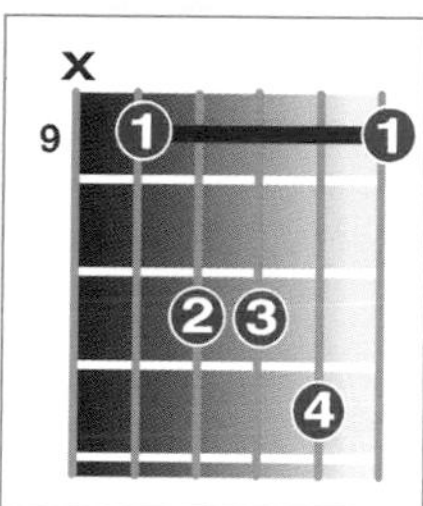

F♯sus4 F♯ Suspended 4th
1st (F♯), 4th (B), 5th (C♯)

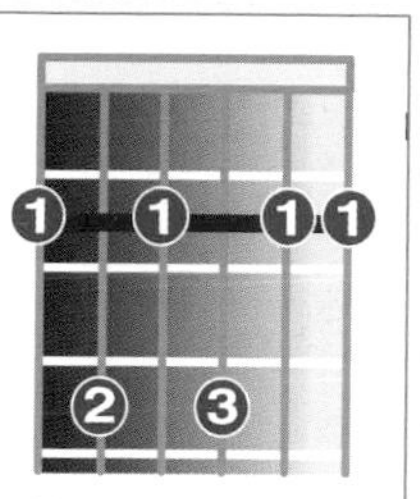

F♯7sus4 F♯ Dominant 7th sus4
1st (F♯), 4th (B), 5th (C♯), ♭7th (E)

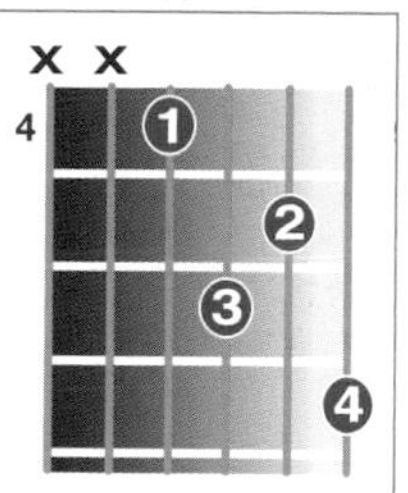

F♯7sus4 F♯ Dominant 7th sus4
1st (F♯), 4th (B), 5th (C♯), ♭7th (E)

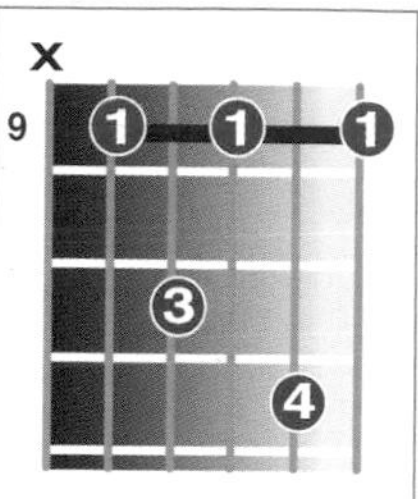

F♯7sus4 F♯ Dominant 7th sus4
1st (F♯), 4th (B), 5th (C♯), ♭7th (E)

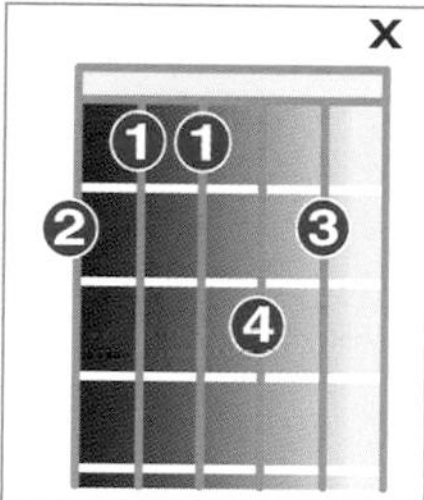

F♯6 F♯ Major 6th
1st (F♯), 3rd (A♯),
5th (C♯), 6th (D♯)

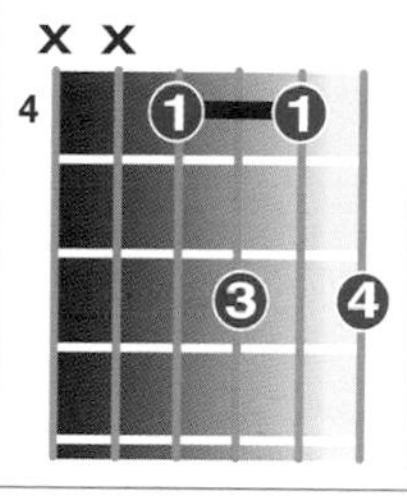

F♯6 F♯ Major 6th
1st (F♯), 3rd (A♯),
5th (C♯), 6th (D♯)

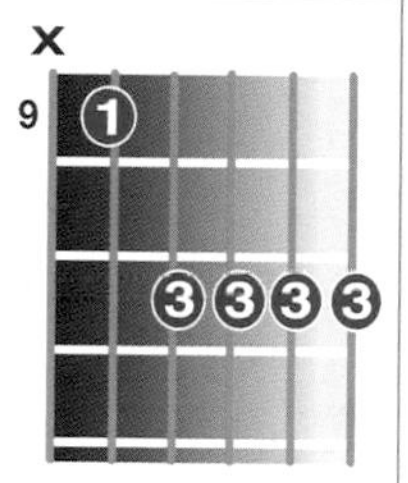

F♯6 F♯ Major 6th
1st (F♯), 3rd (A♯),
5th (C♯), 6th (D♯)

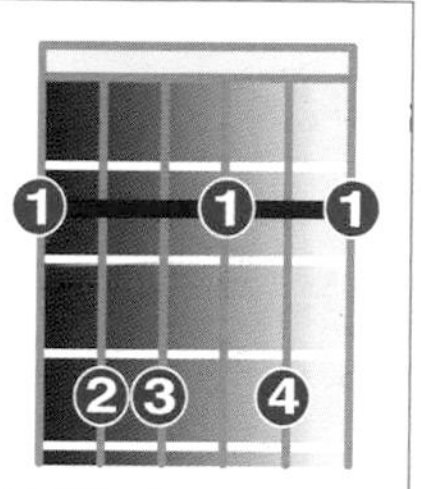

F♯m6 F♯ Minor 6th
1st (F♯), ♭3rd (A), 5th (C♯), 6th (D♯)

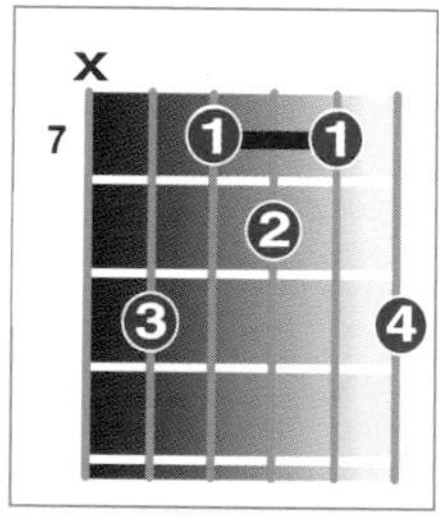

F♯m6 F♯ Minor 6th
1st (F♯), ♭3rd (A), 5th (C♯), 6th (D♯)

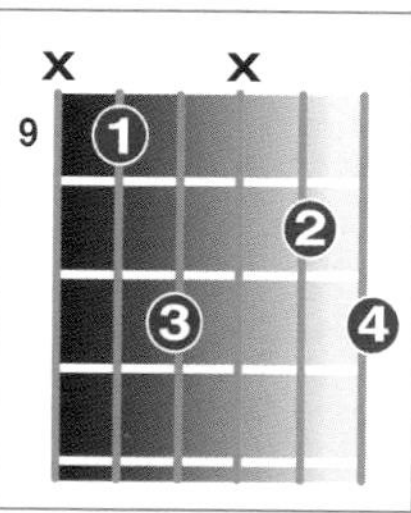

F♯m6 F♯ Minor 6th
1st (F♯), ♭3rd (A), 5th (C♯), 6th (D♯)

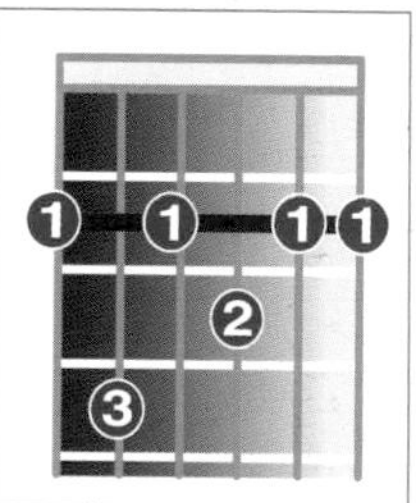

F♯7 F♯ Dominant 7th
1st (F♯), 3rd (A♯),
5th (C♯), ♭7th (E)

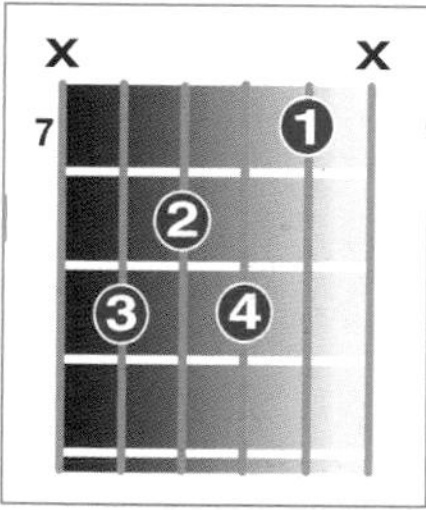

F♯7 F♯ Dominant 7th
1st (F♯), 3rd (A♯),
5th (C♯), ♭7th (E)

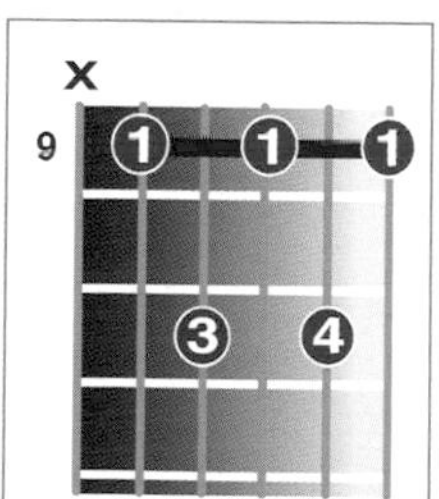

F♯7 F♯ Dominant 7th
1st (F♯), 3rd (A♯),
5th (C♯), ♭7th (E)

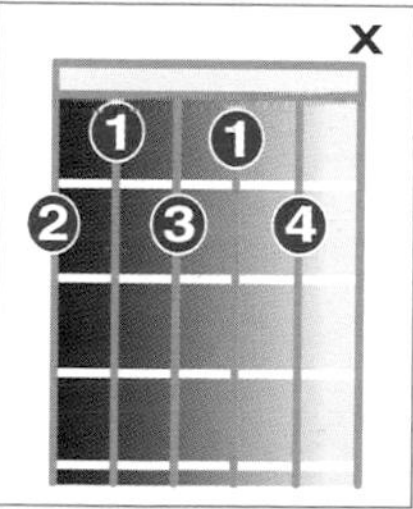

F♯9 F♯ Dominant 9th
1st (F♯), 3rd (A♯), 5th (C♯),
♭7th (E), 9th (G♯)

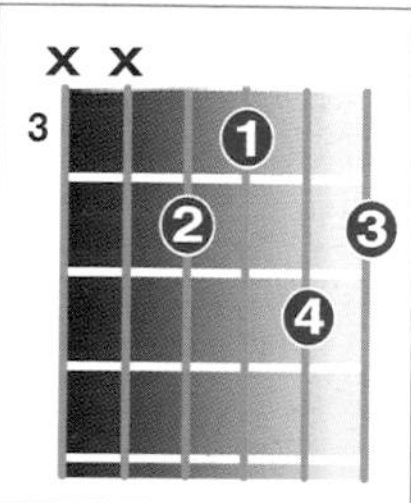

F♯9 F♯ Dominant 9th
1st (F♯), 3rd (A♯), 5th (C♯),
♭7th (E), 9th (G♯)

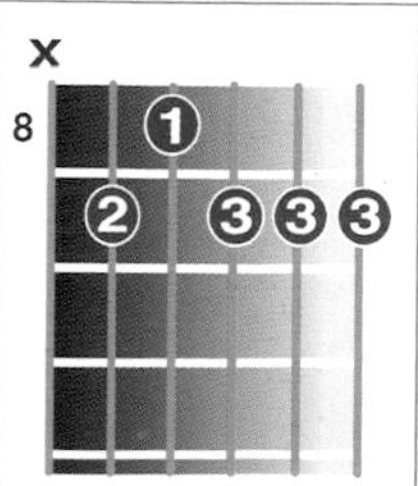

F♯9 F♯ Dominant 9th
1st (F♯), 3rd (A♯), 5th (C♯),
♭7th (E), 9th (G♯)

Section Five: Chord Dictionary

F♯/G♭ ADVANCED CHORDS

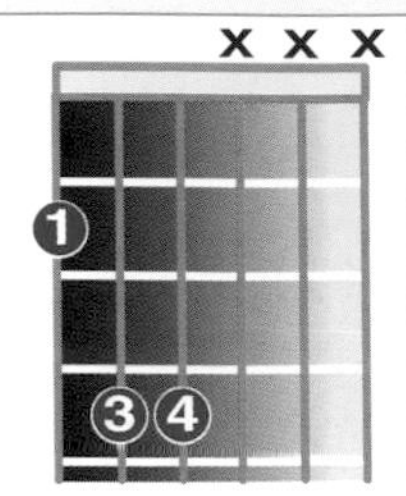

F♯5 F♯ 5th (power chord)
1st (F♯), 5th (C♯)

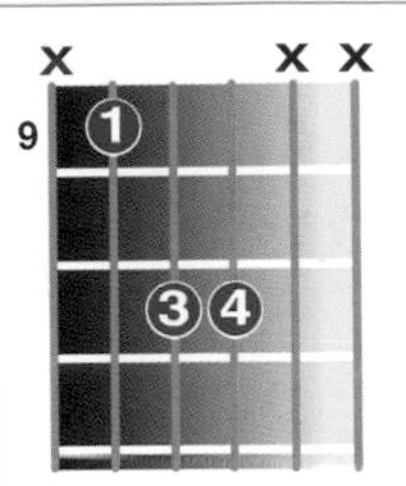

F♯5 F♯ 5th (power chord)
1st (F♯), 5th (C♯)

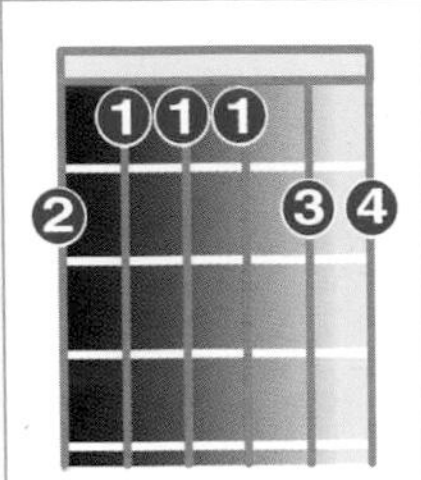

F♯ 6/9 F♯ Major 6th add 9th
1st (F♯), 3rd (A♯), 5th (C♯), 6th (D♯), 9th (G♯)

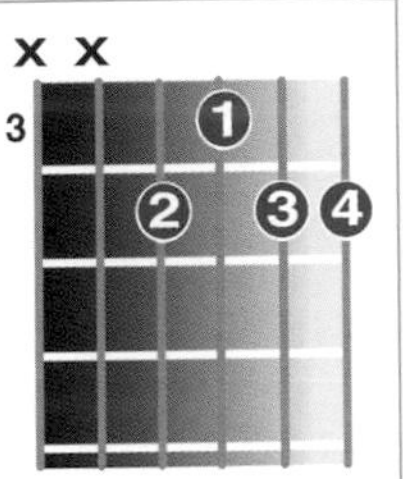

F♯ 6/9 F♯ Major 6th add 9th
1st (F♯), 3rd (A♯), 5th (C♯), 6th (D♯), 9th (G♯)

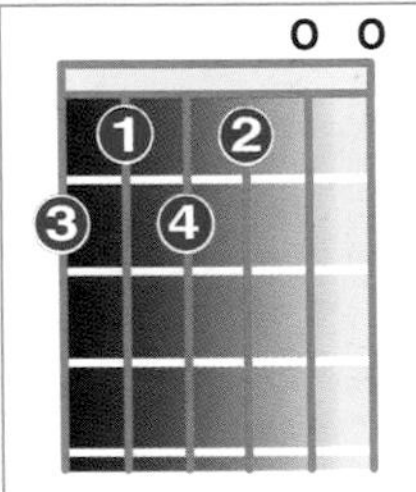

F♯11 F♯ Dominant 11th
1st (F♯), 3rd (A♯), 5th (C♯), ♭7th (E), 9th (G♯), 11th (B)

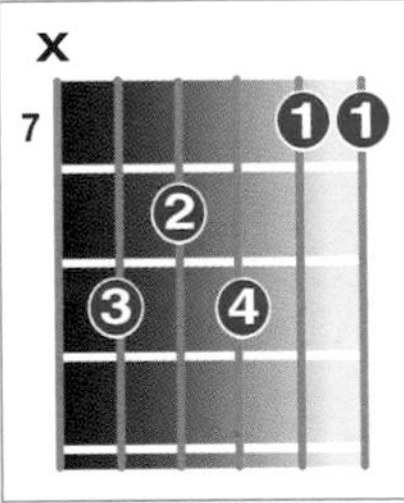

F♯11 F♯ Dominant 11th
1st (F♯), 3rd (A♯), 5th (C♯), ♭7th (E), 9th (G♯), 11th (B)

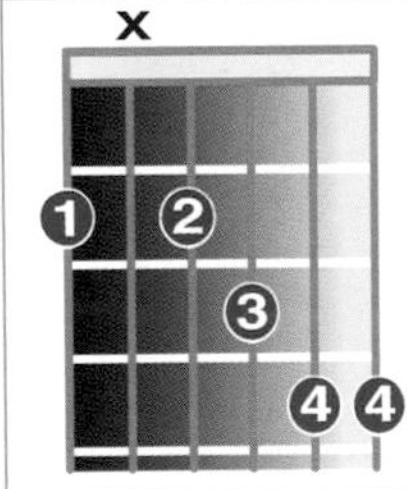

F♯13 F♯ Dominant 13th
1st (F♯), 3rd (A♯), 5th (C♯), ♭7th (E), 9th (G♯), 13th (D♯)

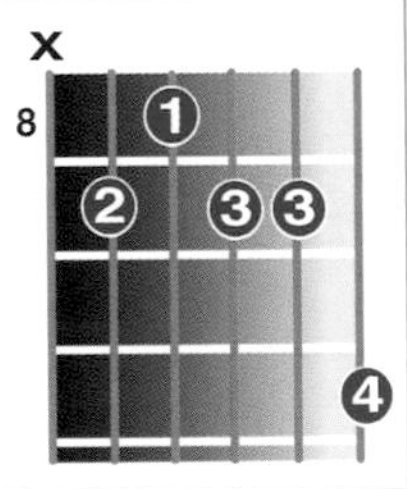

F♯13 F♯ Dominant 13th
1st (F♯), 3rd (A♯), 5th (C♯), ♭7th (E), 9th (G♯), 13th (D♯)

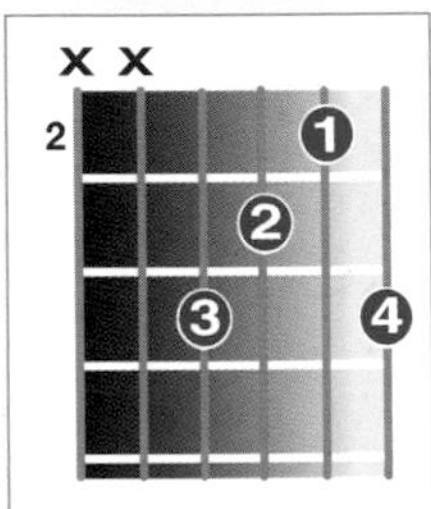

F♯add9 F♯ Major add 9th
1st (F♯), 3rd (A♯), 5th (C♯), 9th (G♯)

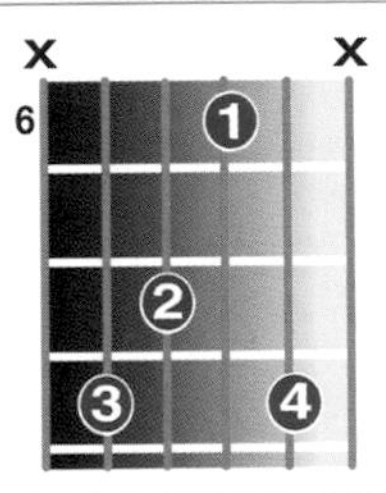

F♯add9 F♯ Major add 9th
1st (F♯), 3rd (A♯), 5th (C♯), 9th (G♯)

F♯m9 F♯ Minor 9th
1st (F♯), ♭3rd (A), 5th (C♯), ♭7th (E), 9th (G♯)

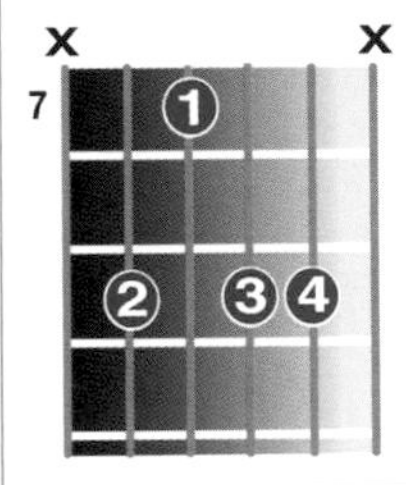

F♯m9 F♯ Minor 9th
1st (F♯), ♭3rd (A), 5th (C♯), ♭7th (E), 9th (G♯)

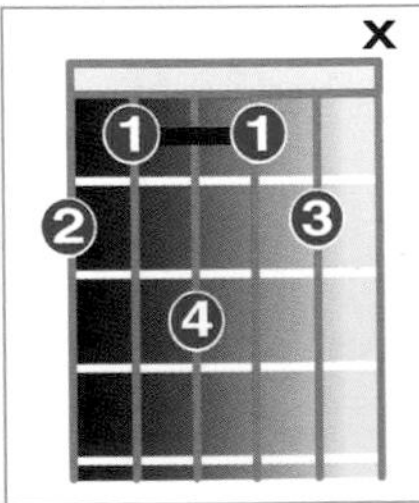

F♯maj9 F♯ Major 9th
1st (F♯), 3rd (A♯), 5th (C♯), 7th (E♯), 9th (G♯)

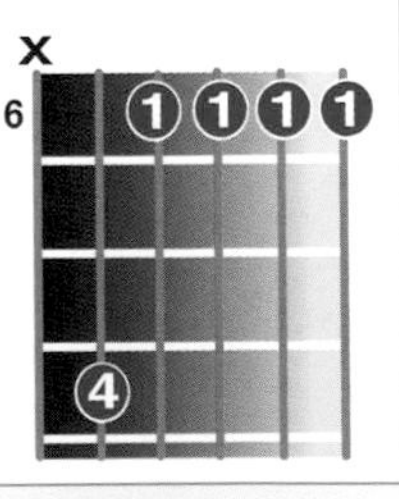

F♯maj9 F♯ Major 9th
1st (F♯), 3rd (A♯), 5th (C♯), 7th (E♯), 9th (G♯)

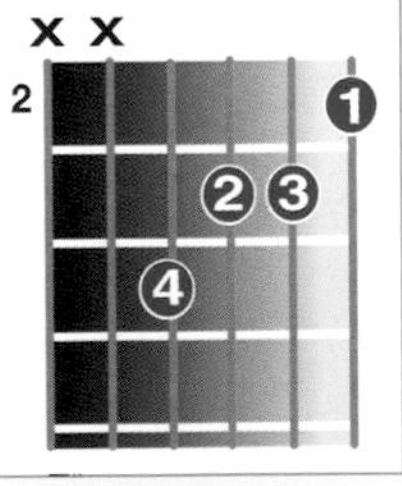

F♯+ F♯ Augmented
1st (F♯), 3rd (A♯), ♯5th (Cx)

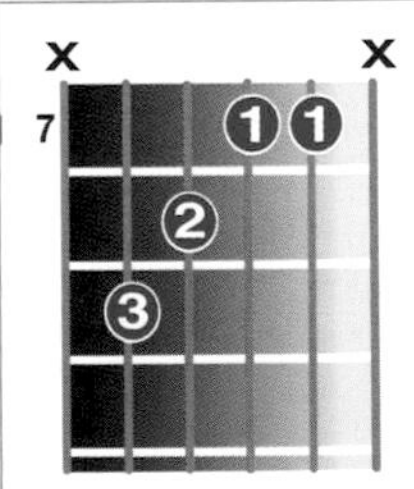

F♯+ F♯ Augmented
1st (F♯), 3rd (A♯), ♯5th (Cx)

Complete Guitar Handbook

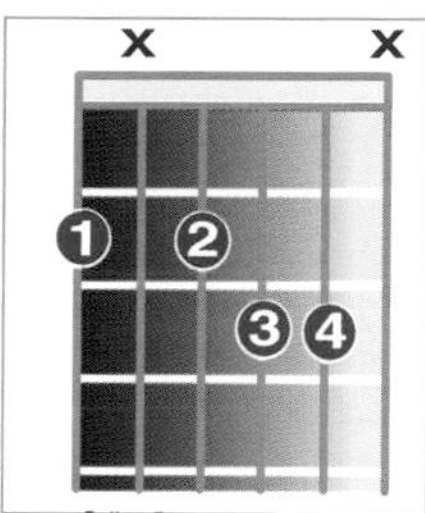

F♯7♯5 F♯ Dominant 7th ♯5
1st (F♯), 3rd (A♯), ♯5th (Cx), b7th (E)

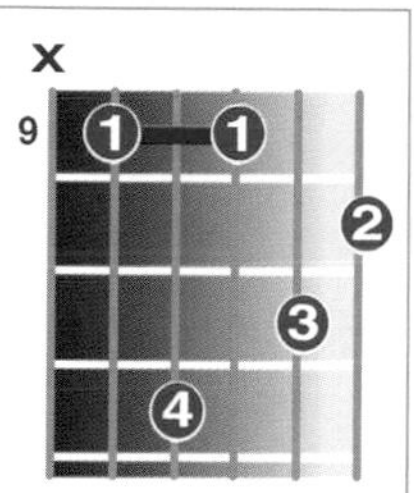

F♯7♯5 F♯ Dominant 7th ♯5
1st (F♯), 3rd (A♯), ♯5th (Cx), b7th (E)

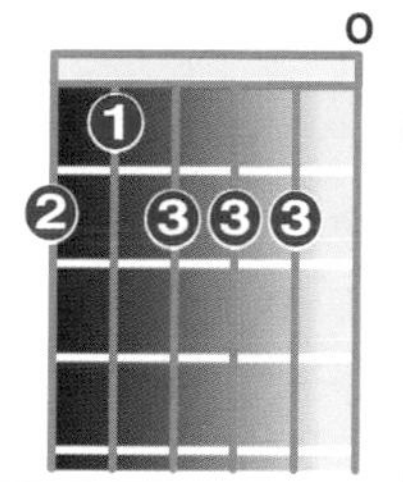

F♯7♯9 F♯ Dominant 7th ♯9
1st (F♯), 3rd (A♯), 5th (C♯), ♭7th (E), ♯9th (Gx)

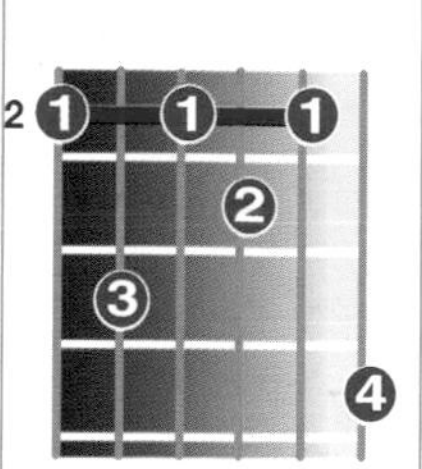

F♯7♯9 F♯ Dominant 7th ♯9
1st (F♯), 3rd (A♯), 5th (C♯), ♭7th (E), ♯9th (Gx)

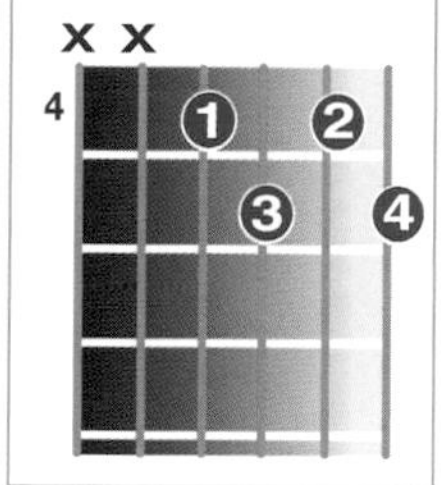

F♯o7 F♯ Diminished 7th
1st (F♯), ♭3rd (A), ♭5th (C), ♭♭7th (E♭)

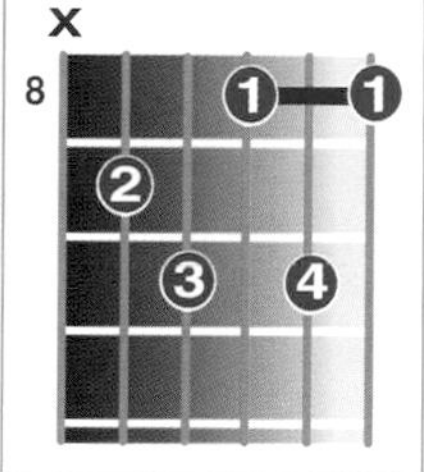

F♯o7 F♯ Diminished 7th
1st (F♯), ♭3rd (A), ♭5th (C), ♭♭7th (E♭)

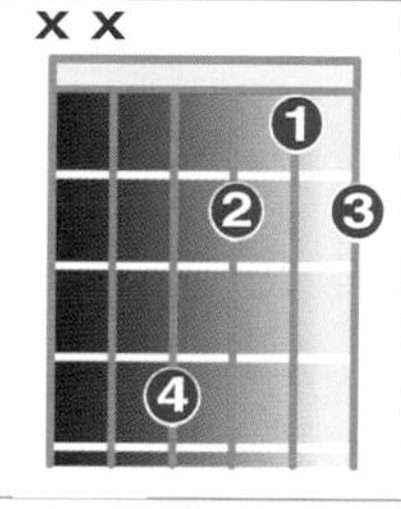

F♯o F♯ Diminished triad
1st (F♯), ♭3rd (A), ♭5th (C)

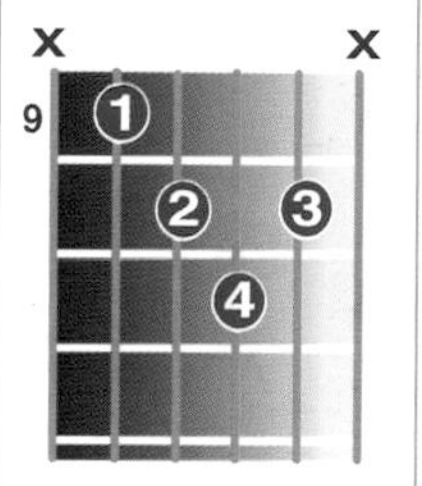

F♯o F♯ Diminished triad
1st (F♯), ♭3rd (A), ♭5th (C)

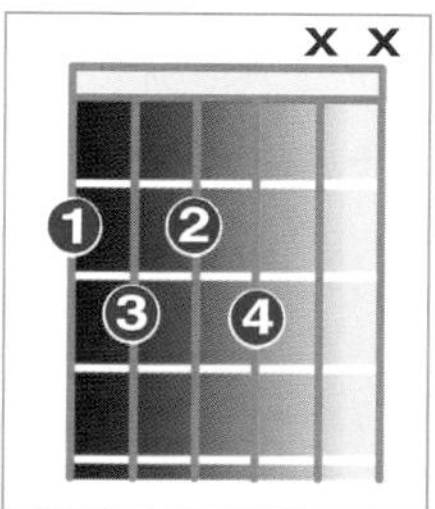

F♯7♭5 F♯ Dominant 7th ♭5
1st (F♯), 3rd (A♯), ♭5th (C), ♭7th (E)

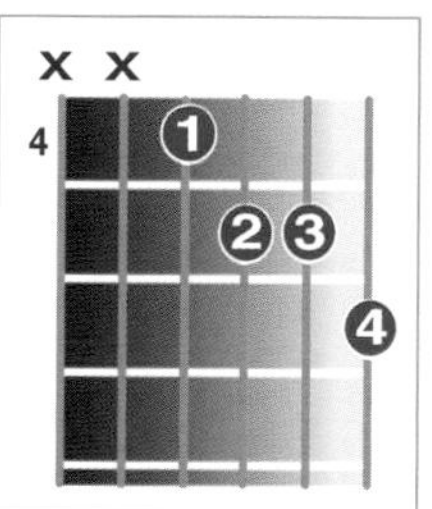

F♯7♭5 F♯ Dominant 7th ♭5
1st (F♯), 3rd (A♯), ♭5th (C), ♭7th (E)

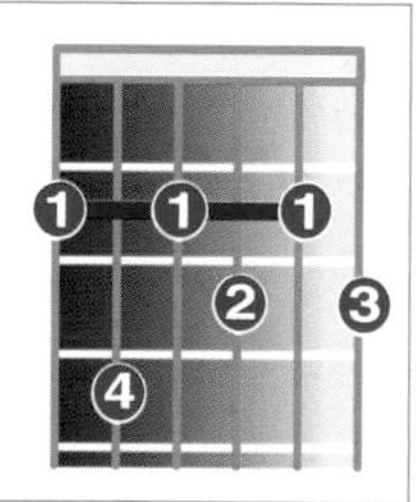

F♯7♭9 F♯ Dominant 7th ♭9
1st (F♯), 3rd (A♯), 5th (C♯), ♭7th (E), ♭9th (G)

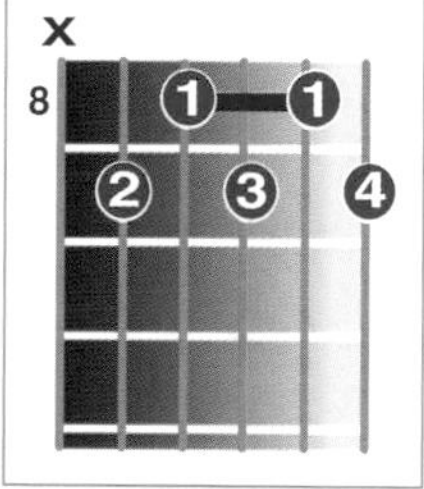

F♯7♭9 F♯ Dominant 7th ♭9
1st (F♯), 3rd (A♯), 5th (C♯), ♭7th (E), ♭9th (G)

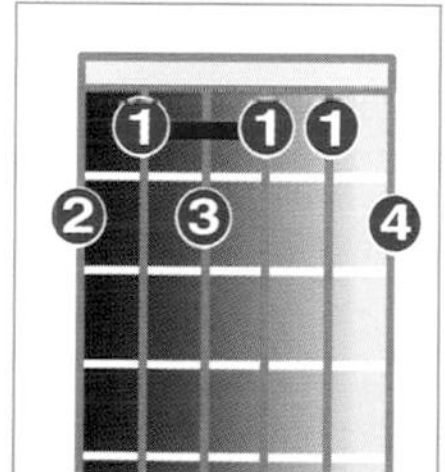

F♯9♭5 F♯ Dominant 9th ♭5th
1st (F♯), 3rd (A♯), ♭5th (C), ♭7th (E), 9th (G♯)

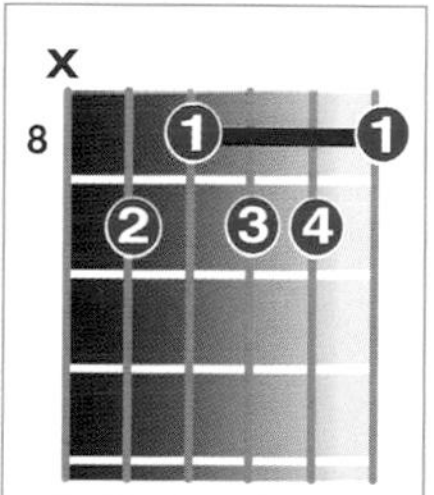

F♯9♭5 F♯ Dominant 9th ♭5th
1st (F♯), 3rd (A♯), ♭5th (C), ♭7th (E), 9th (G♯)

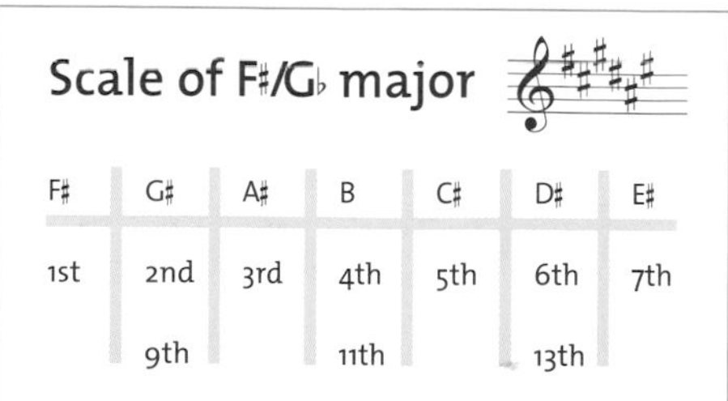

Scale of F♯/G♭ major

F♯	G♯	A♯	B	C♯	D♯	E♯
1st	2nd	3rd	4th	5th	6th	7th
	9th		11th		13th	

Section Five: Chord Dictionary

G MAIN CHORDS

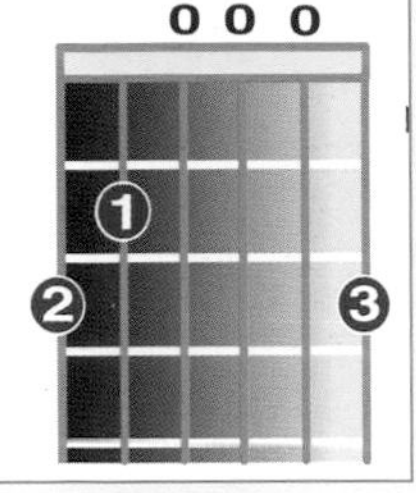

G G Major
1st (G), 3rd (B), 5th (D)

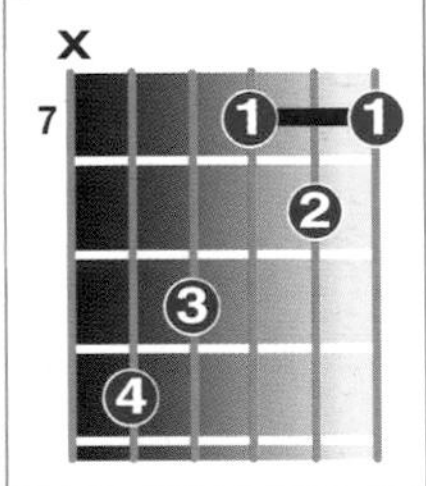

G G Major
1st (G), 3rd (B), 5th (D)

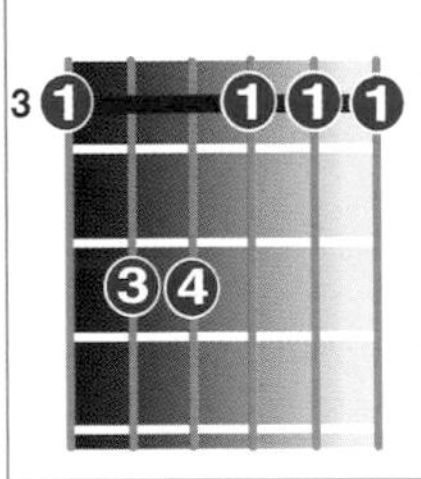

Gm G Minor
1st (G), ♭3rd (B♭), 5th (D)

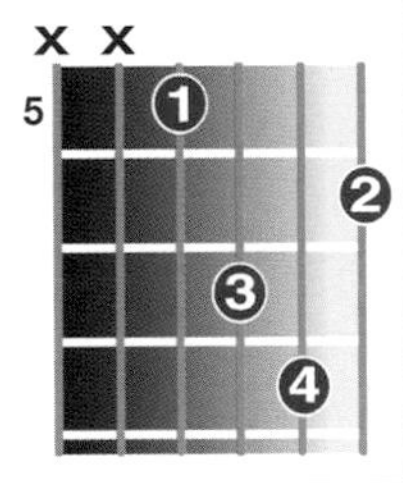

Gm G Minor
1st (G), ♭3rd (B♭), 5th (D)

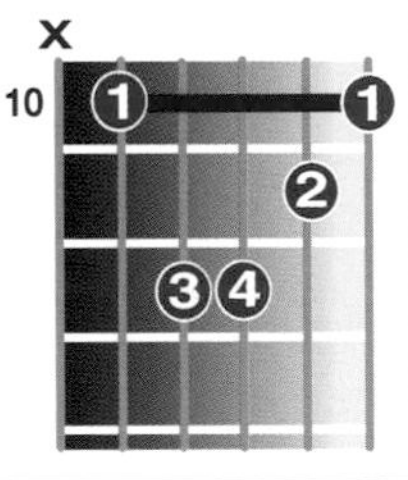

Gm G Minor
1st (G), ♭3rd (B♭), 5th (D)

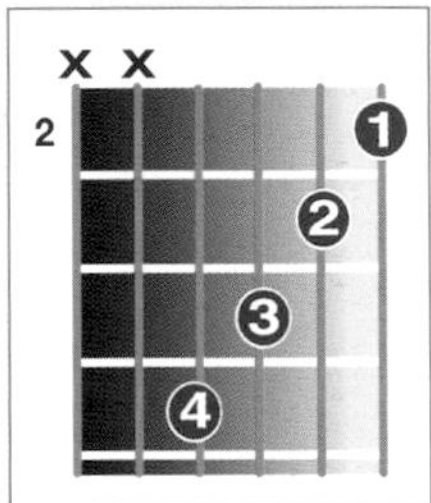

Gmaj7 G Major 7th
1st (G), 3rd (B), 5th (D), 7th (F♯)

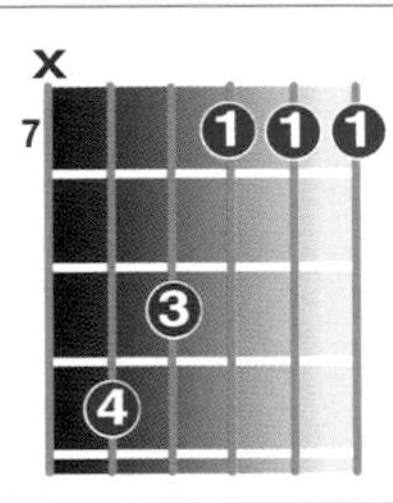

Gmaj7 G Major 7th
1st (G), 3rd (B), 5th (D), 7th (F♯)

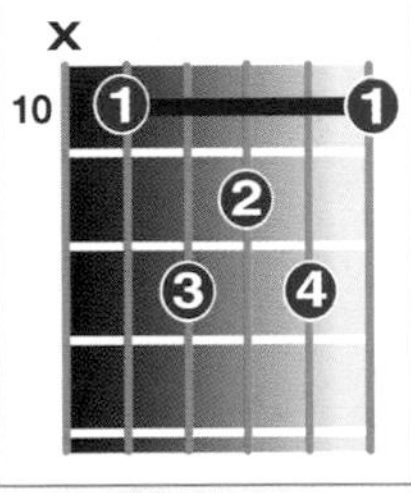

Gmaj7 G Major 7th
1st (G), 3rd (B), 5th (D), 7th (F♯)

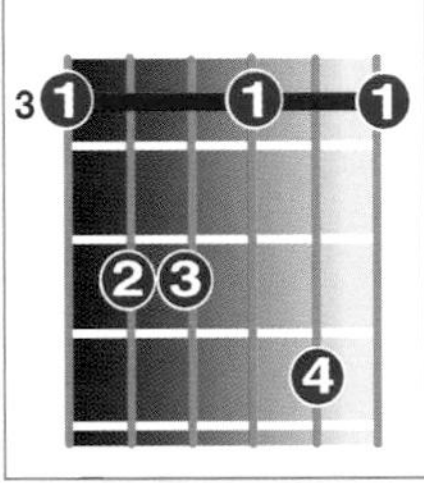

Gm7 G Minor 7th
1st (G), ♭3rd (B♭),
5th (D), ♭7th (F)

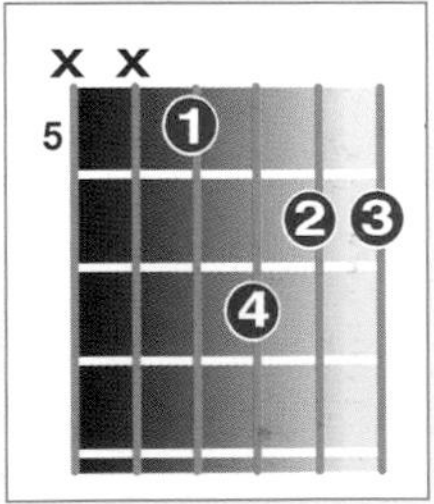

Gm7 G Minor 7th
1st (G), ♭3rd (B♭),
5th (D), ♭7th (F)

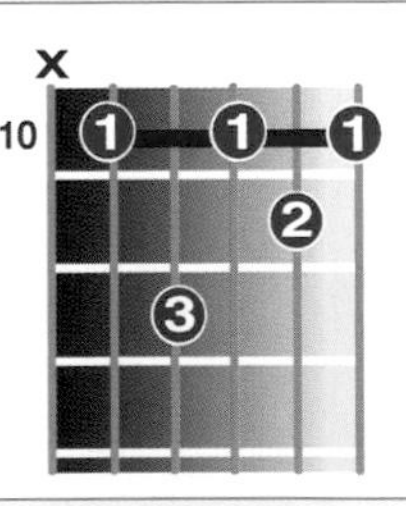

Gm7 G Minor 7th
1st (G), ♭3rd (B♭),
5th (D), ♭7th (F)

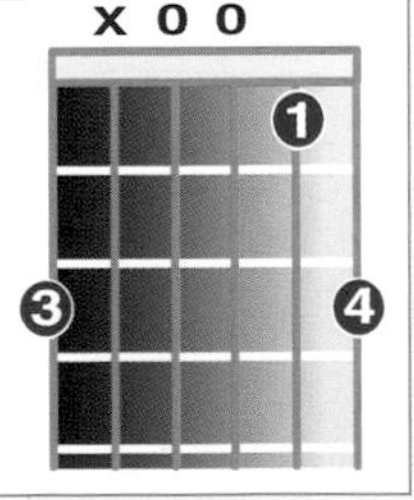

Gsus4 G Suspended 4th
1st (G), 4th (C), 5th (D)

Gsus4 G Suspended 4th
1st (G), 4th (C), 5th (D)

Complete Guitar Handbook

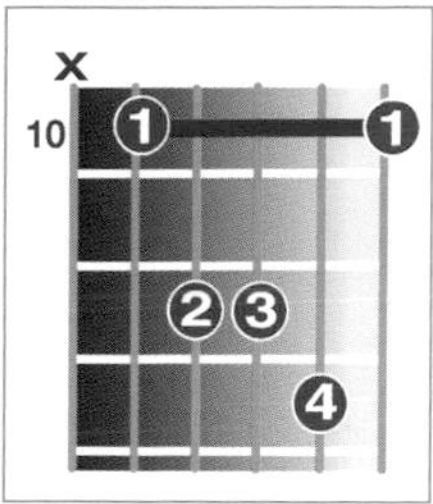

Gsus4 G Suspended 4th
1st (G), 4th (C), 5th (D)

G7sus4 G Dominant 7th sus4
1st (G), 4th (C), 5th (D), ♭7th (F)

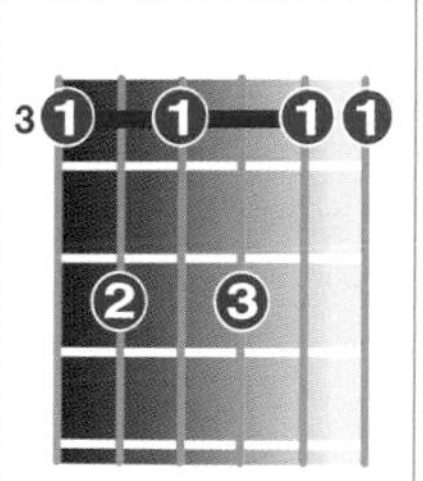

G7sus4 G Dominant 7th sus4
1st (G), 4th (C), 5th (D), ♭7th (F)

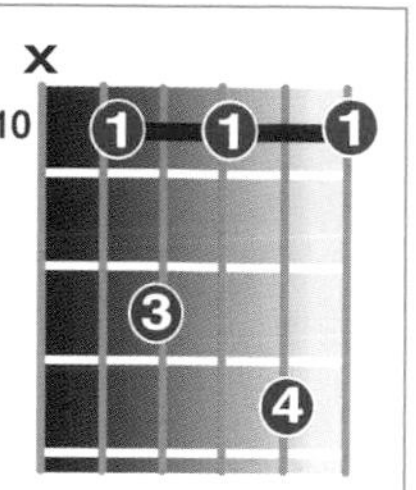

G7sus4 G Dominant 7th sus4
1st (G), 4th (C), 5th (D), ♭7th (F)

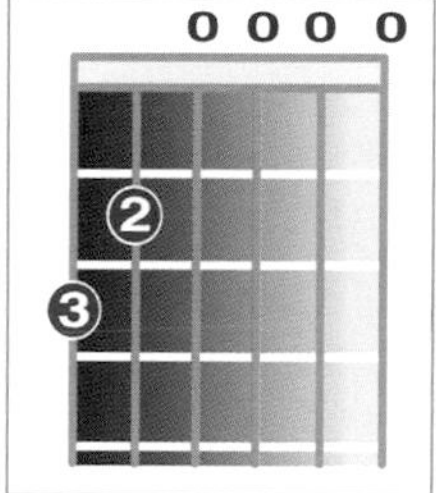

G6 G Major 6th
1st (G), 3rd (B), 5th (D), 6th (E)

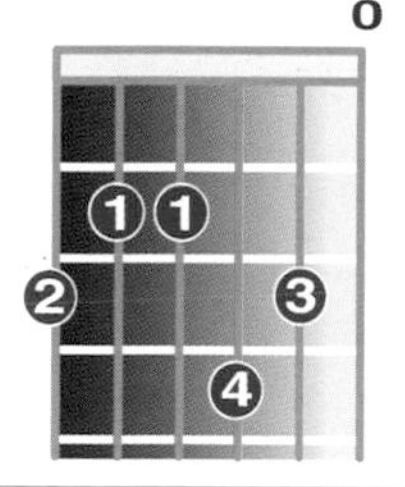

G6 G Major 6th
1st (G), 3rd (B), 5th (D), 6th (E)

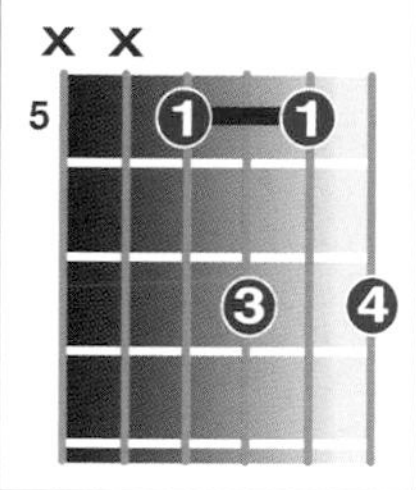

G6 G Major 6th
1st (G), 3rd (B), 5th (D), 6th (E)

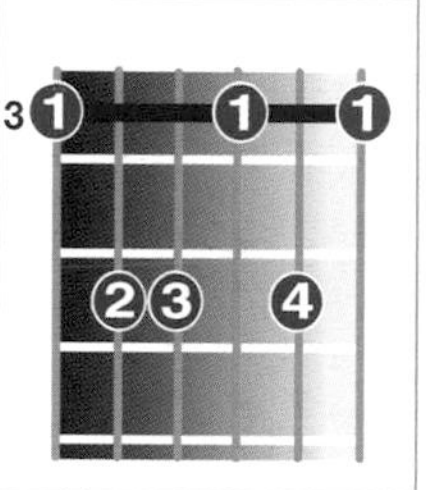

Gm6 G Minor 6th
1st (G), ♭3rd (B♭), 5th (D), 6th (E)

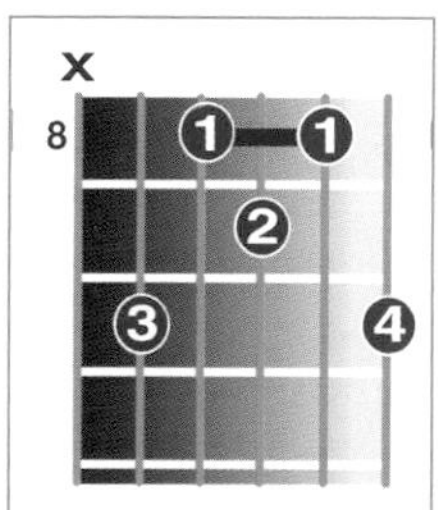

Gm6 G Minor 6th
1st (G), ♭3rd (B♭), 5th (D), 6th (E)

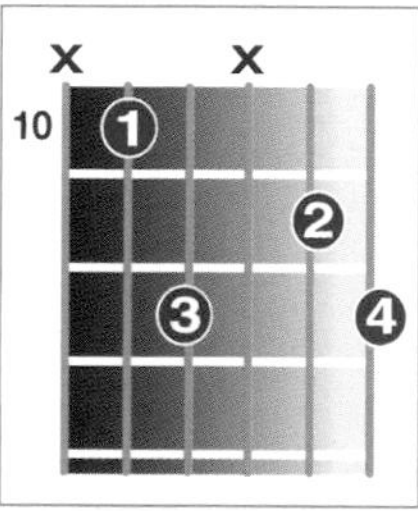

Gm6 G Minor 6th
1st (G), ♭3rd (B♭), 5th (D), 6th (E)

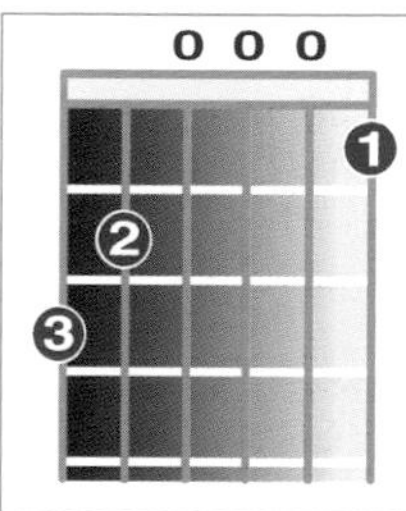

G7 G Dominant 7th
1st (G), 3rd (B), 5th (D), ♭7th (F)

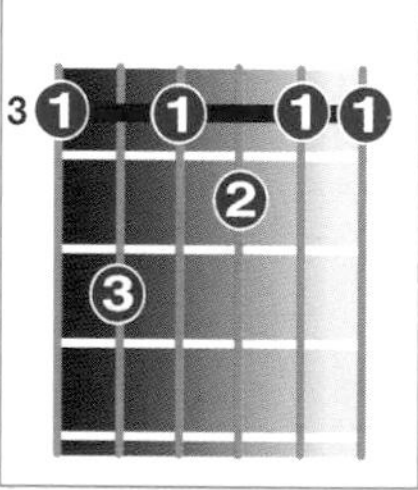

G7 G Dominant 7th
1st (G), 3rd (B), 5th (D), ♭7th (F)

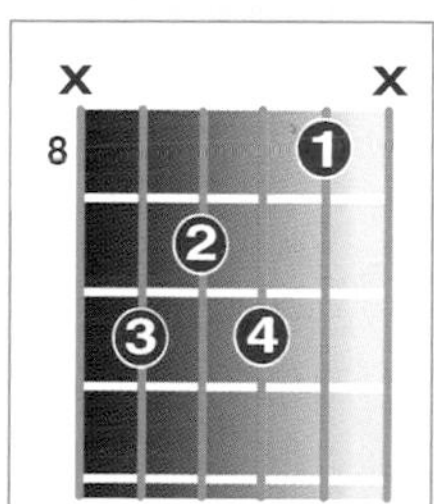

G7 G Dominant 7th
1st (G), 3rd (B), 5th (D), ♭7th (F)

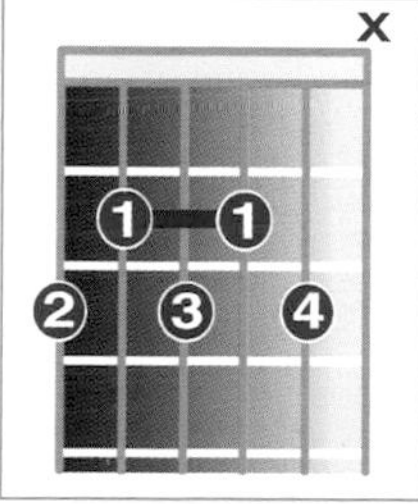

G9 G Dominant 9th
1st (G), 3rd (B), 5th (D), ♭7th (F), 9th (A)

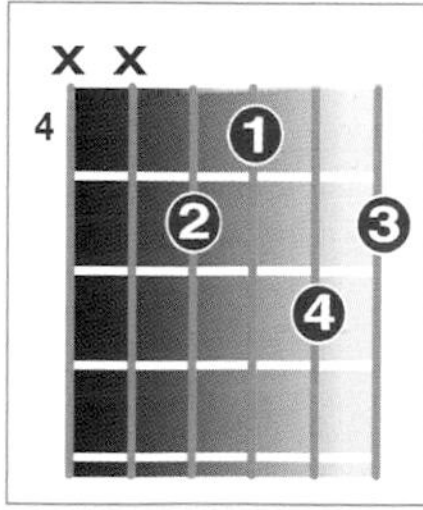

G9 G Dominant 9th
1st (G), 3rd (B), 5th (D), ♭7th (F), 9th (A)

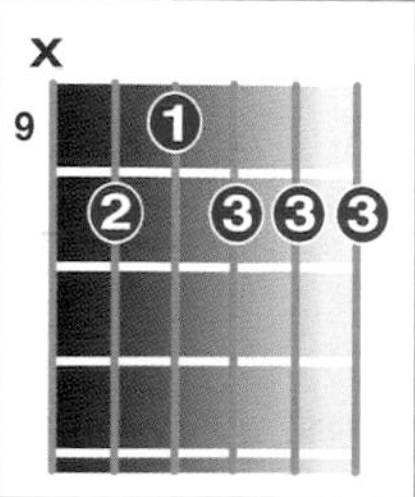

G9 G Dominant 9th
1st (G), 3rd (B), 5th (D), ♭7th (F), 9th (A)

Section Five: Chord Dictionary

G ADVANCED CHORDS

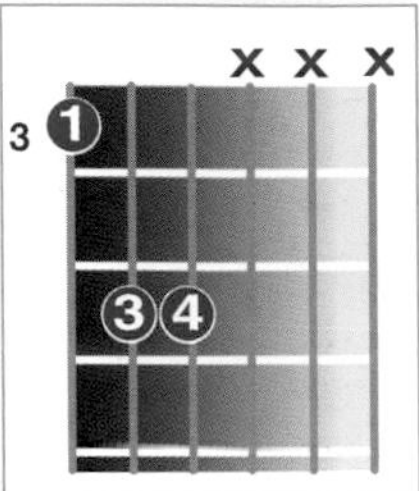

G5 **G 5th (power chord)**
1st (G), 5th (D)

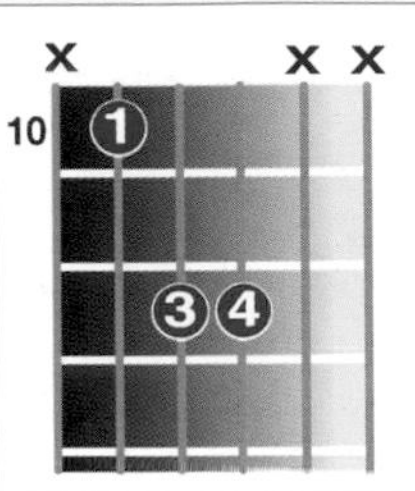

G5 **G 5th (power chord)**
1st (G), 5th (D)

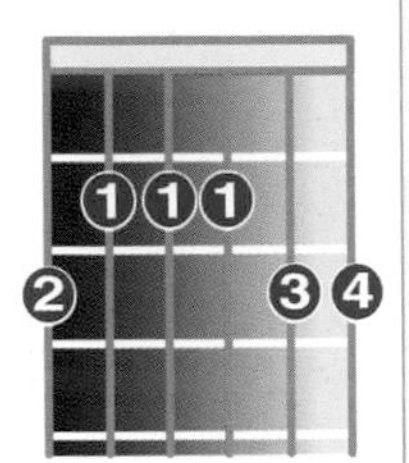

G 6/9 **G Major 6th add 9th**
1st (G), 3rd (B), 5th (D), 6th (E), 9th (A)

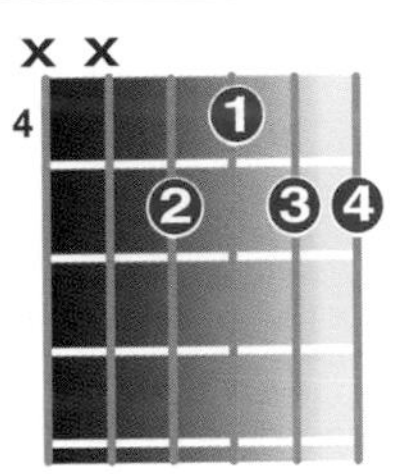

G 6/9 **G Major 6th add 9th**
1st (G), 3rd (B), 5th (D), 6th (E), 9th (A)

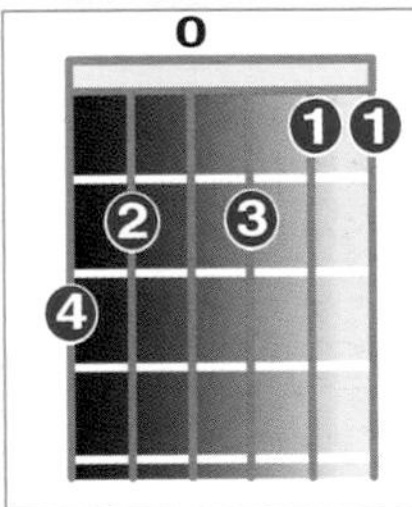

G11 **G Dominant 11th**
1st (G), 3rd (B), 5th (D), ♭7th (F), 9th (A), 11th (C)

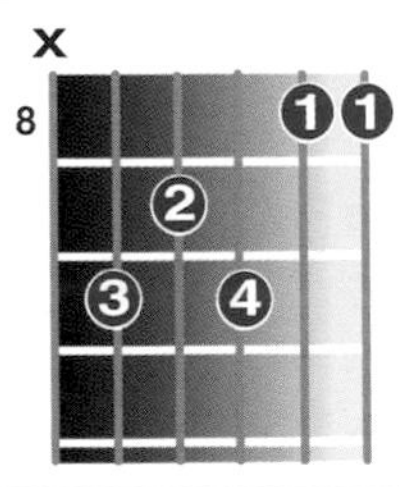

G11 **G Dominant 11th**
1st (G), 3rd (B), 5th (D), ♭7th (F), 9th (A), 11th (C)

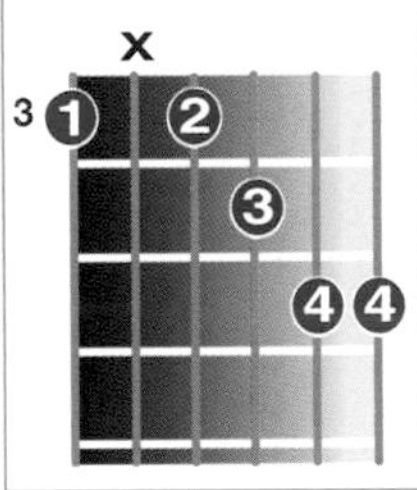

G13 **G Dominant 13th**
1st (G), 3rd (B), 5th (D), ♭7th (F), 9th (A), 13th (E)

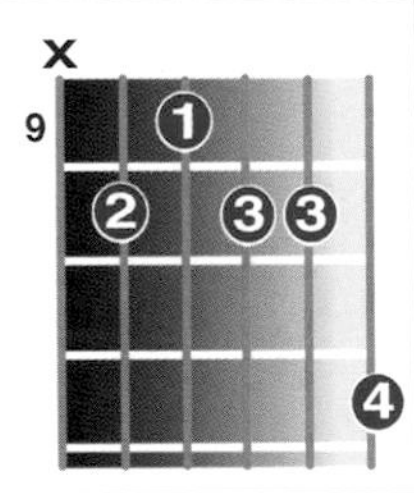

G13 **G Dominant 13th**
1st (G), 3rd (B), 5th (D), ♭7th (F), 9th (A), 13th (E)

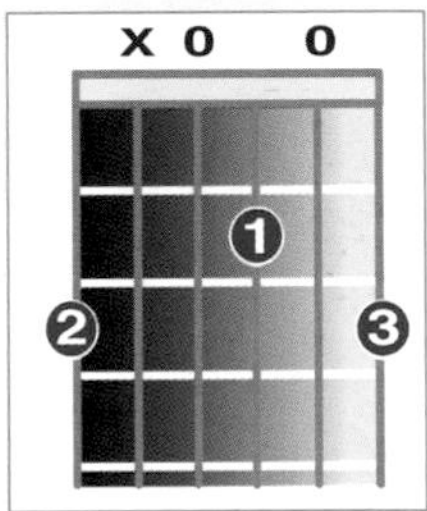

Gadd9 **G Major add 9th**
1st (G), 3rd (B), 5th (D), 9th (A)

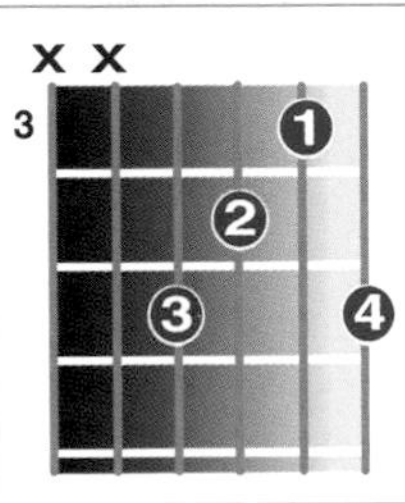

Gadd9 **G Major add 9th**
1st (G), 3rd (B), 5th (D), 9th (A)

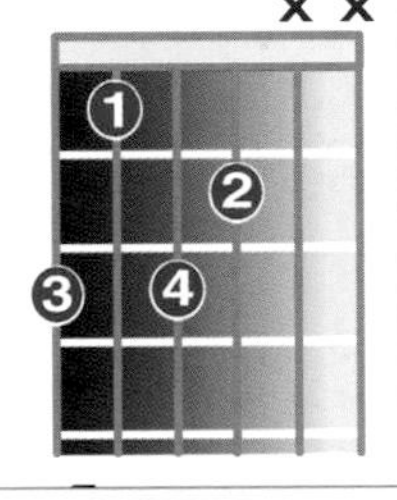

Gm9 **G Minor 9th**
1st (G), ♭3rd (B♭), 5th (D), ♭7th (F), 9th (A)

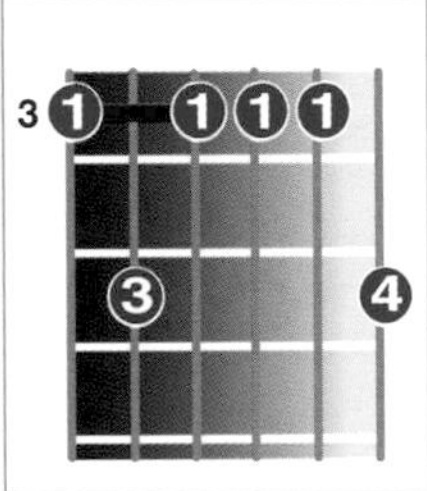

Gm9 **G Minor 9th**
1st (G), ♭3rd (B♭), 5th (D), ♭7th (F), 9th (A)

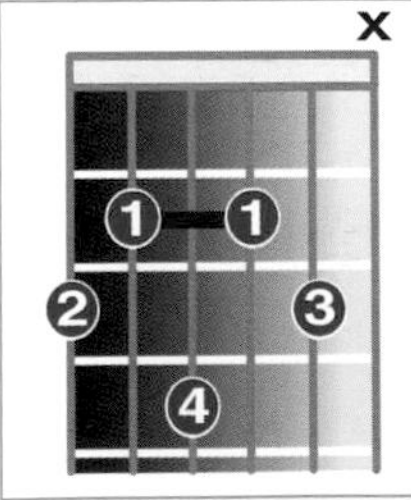

Gmaj9 **G Major 9th**
1st (G), 3rd (B), 5th (D), 7th (F♯), 9th (A)

Gmaj9 **G Major 9th**
1st (G), 3rd (B), 5th (D), 7th (F♯), 9th (A)

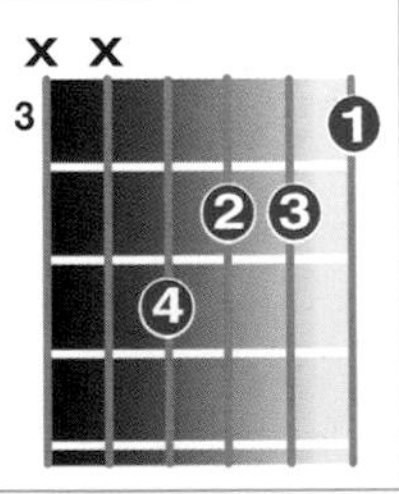

G+ **G Augmented**
1st (G), 3rd (B), ♯5th (D♯)

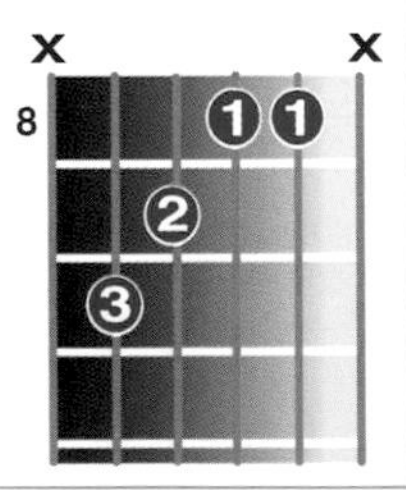

G+ **G Augmented**
1st (G), 3rd (B), ♯5th (D♯)

Complete Guitar Handbook

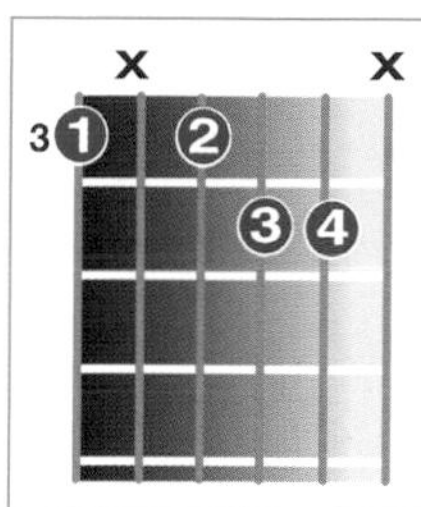

G7♯5 G Dominant 7th ♯5
1st (G), 3rd (B), ♯5th (D♯), ♭7th (F)

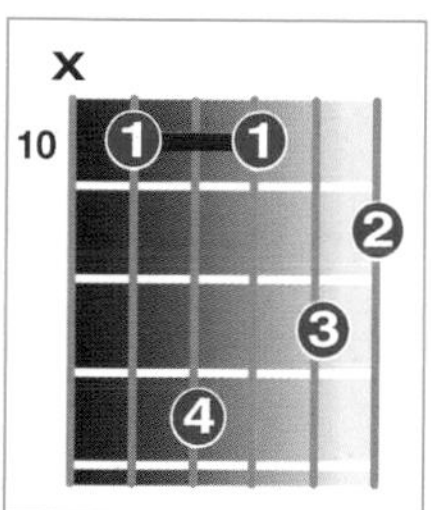

G7♯5 G Dominant 7th ♯5
1st (G), 3rd (B), ♯5th (D♯), ♭7th (F)

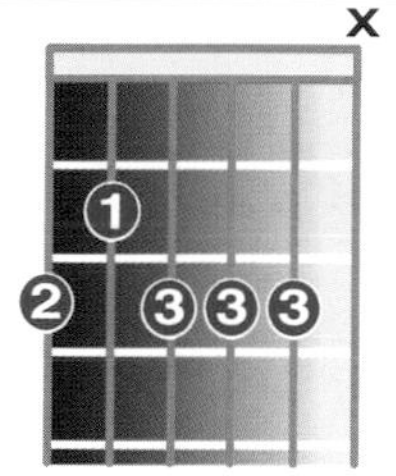

G7♯9 G Dominant 7th ♯9
1st (G), 3rd (B), 5th (D), ♭7th (F), ♯9th (A♯)

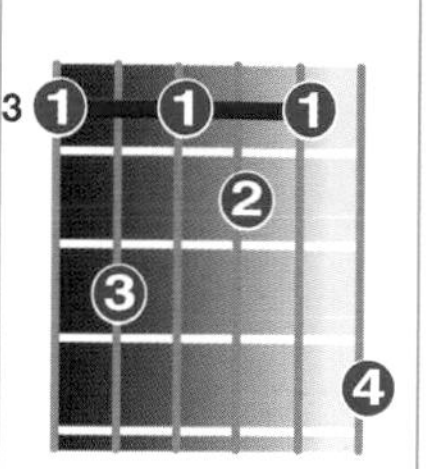

G7♯9 G Dominant 7th ♯9
1st (G), 3rd (B), 5th (D), ♭7th (F), ♯9th (A♯)

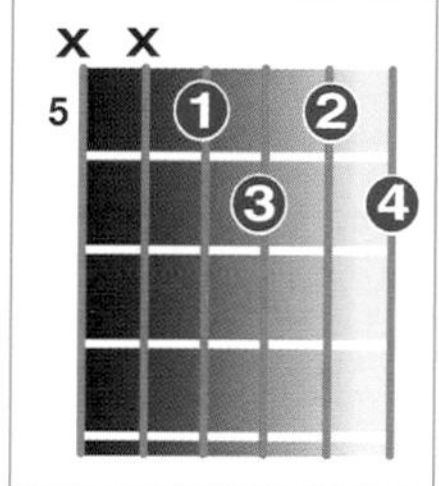

Go7 G Diminished 7th
1st (G), ♭3rd (B♭), ♭5th (D♭), ♭♭7th (F♭)

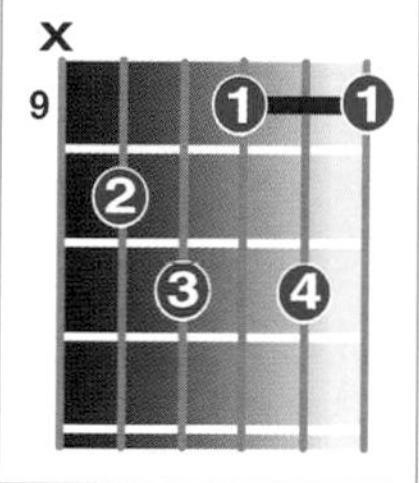

Go7 G Diminished 7th
1st (G), ♭3rd (B♭), ♭5th (D♭), ♭♭7th (F♭)

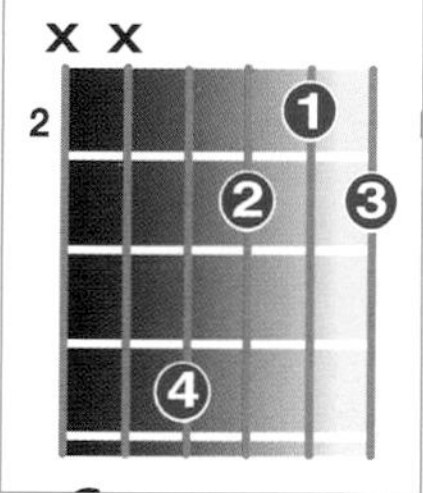

Go G Diminished triad
1st (G), ♭3rd (B♭), ♭5th (D♭)

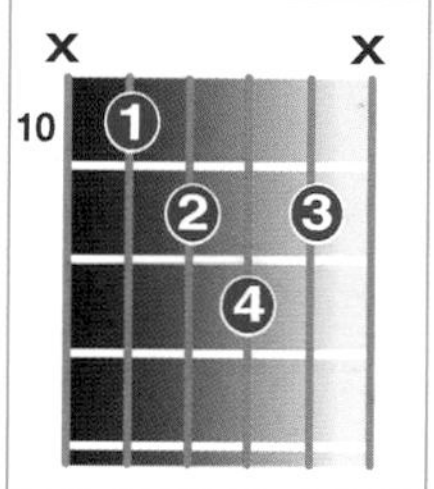

Go G Diminished triad
1st (G), ♭3rd (B♭), ♭5th (D♭)

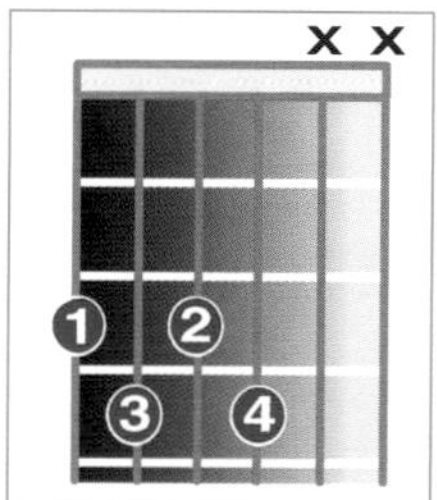

G7♭5 G Dominant 7th ♭5
1st (G), 3rd (B), ♭5th (D♭), ♭7th (F)

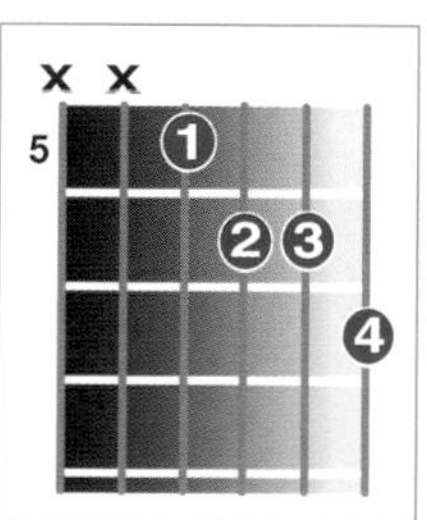

G7♭5 G Dominant 7th ♭5
1st (G), 3rd (B), ♭5th (D♭), ♭7th (F)

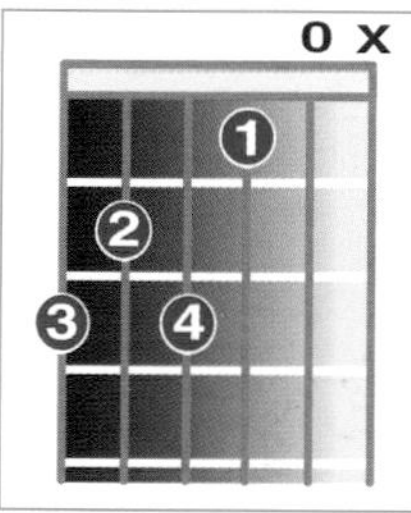

G7♭9 G Dominant 7th ♭9
1st (G), 3rd (B), 5th (D), ♭7th (F), ♭9th (A♭)

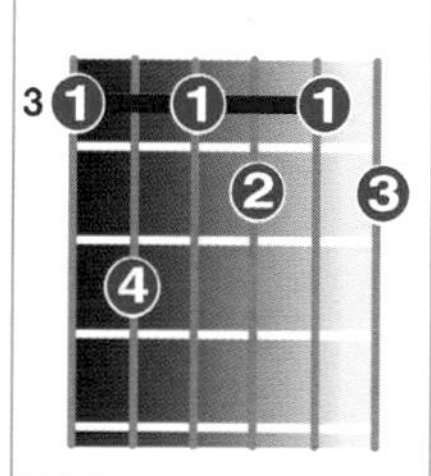

G7♭9 G Dominant 7th ♭9
1st (G), 3rd (B), 5th (D), ♭7th (F), ♭9th (A♭)

G9♭5 G Dominant 9th ♭5th
1st (G), 3rd (B), ♭5th (D♭), ♭7th (F), 9th (A)

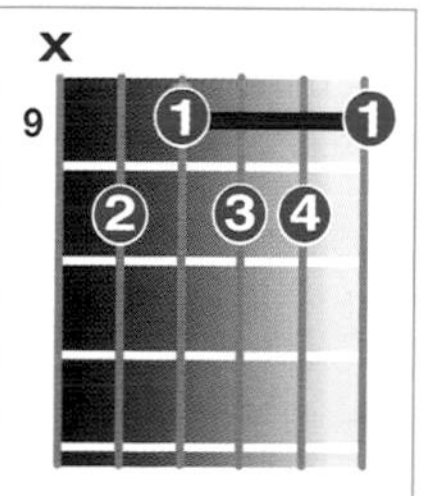

G9♭5 G Dominant 9th ♭5th
1st (G), 3rd (B), ♭5th (D♭), ♭7th (F), 9th (A)

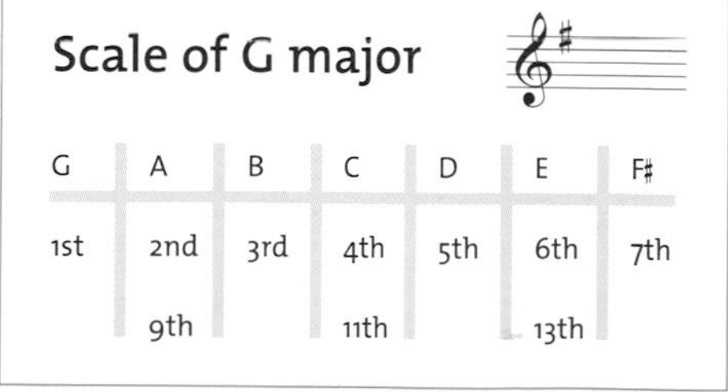

Scale of G major

G	A	B	C	D	E	F♯
1st	2nd	3rd	4th	5th	6th	7th
	9th		11th		13th	

Section Five: Chord Dictionary

A♭/G♯ MAIN CHORDS

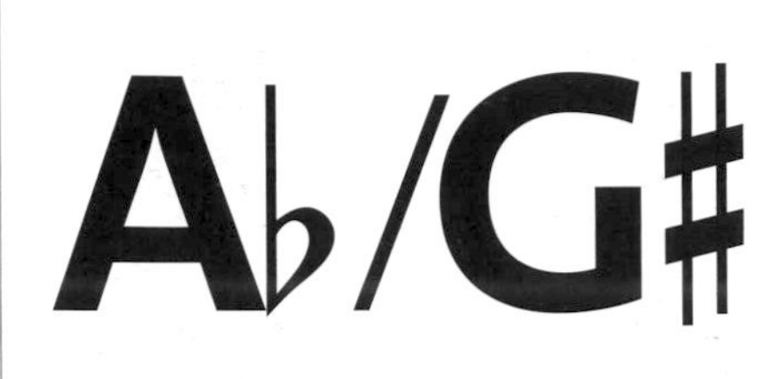

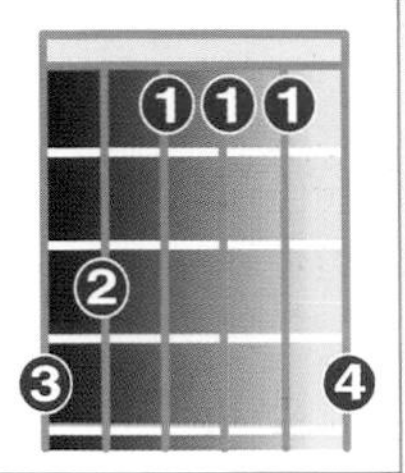

A♭ A♭ Major
1st (A♭), 3rd (C), 5th (E♭)

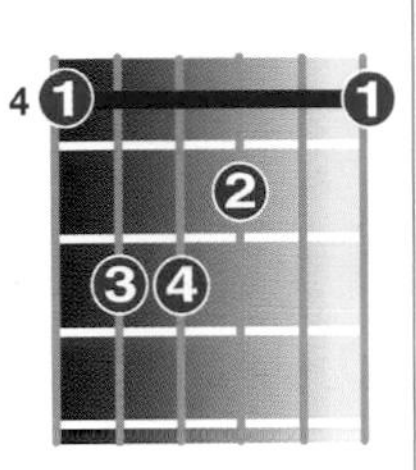

A♭ A♭ Major
1st (A♭), 3rd (C), 5th (E♭)

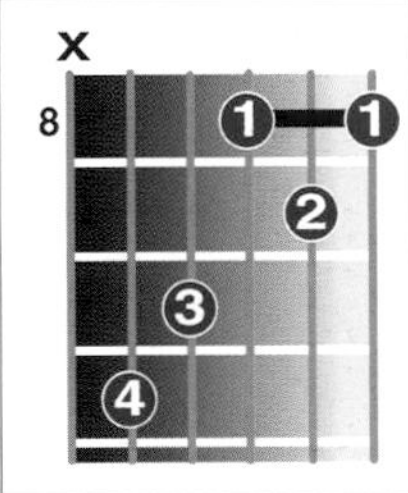

A♭ A♭ Major
1st (A♭), 3rd (C), 5th (E♭)

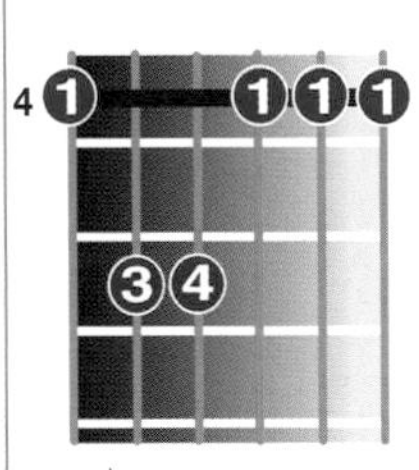

A♭m A♭ Minor
1st (A♭), ♭3rd (C♭), 5th (E♭)

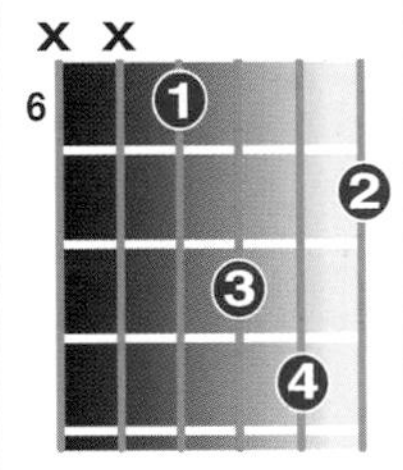

A♭m A♭ Minor
1st (A♭), ♭3rd (C♭), 5th (E♭)

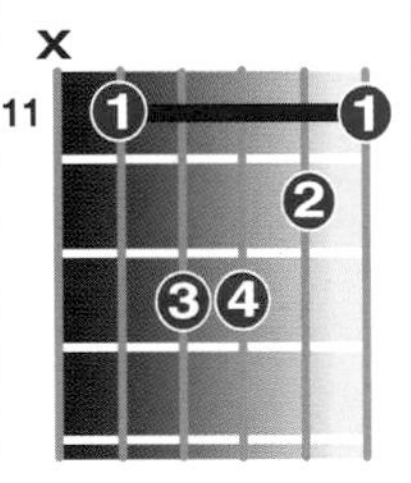

A♭m A♭ Minor
1st (A♭), ♭3rd (C♭), 5th (E♭)

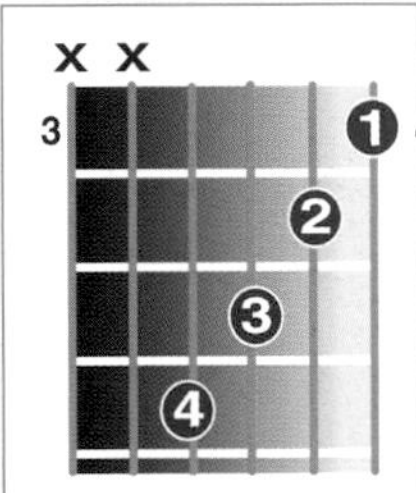

A♭maj7 A♭ Major 7th
1st (A♭), 3rd (C),
5th (E♭), 7th (G)

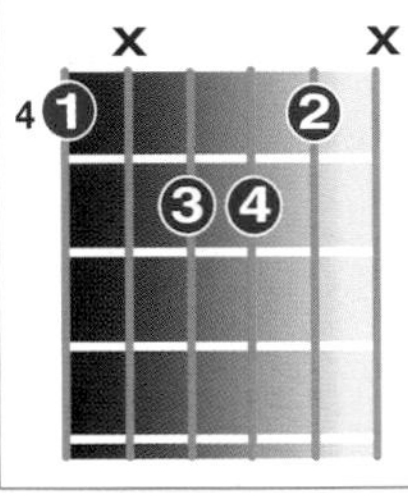

A♭maj7 A♭ Major 7th
1st (A♭), 3rd (C),
5th (E♭), 7th (G)

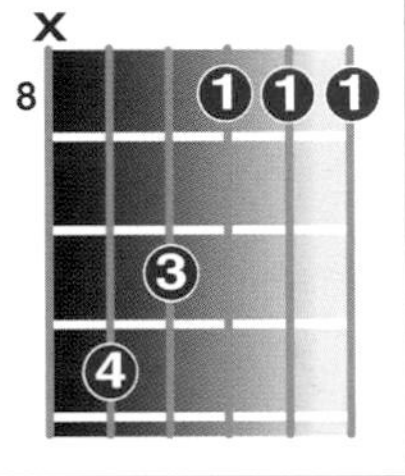

A♭maj7 A♭ Major 7th
1st (A♭), 3rd (C),
5th (E♭), 7th (G)

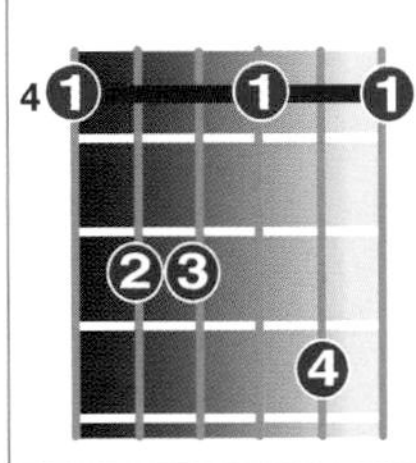

A♭m7 A♭ Minor 7th
1st (A♭), ♭3rd (C♭),
5th (E♭), ♭7th (G♭)

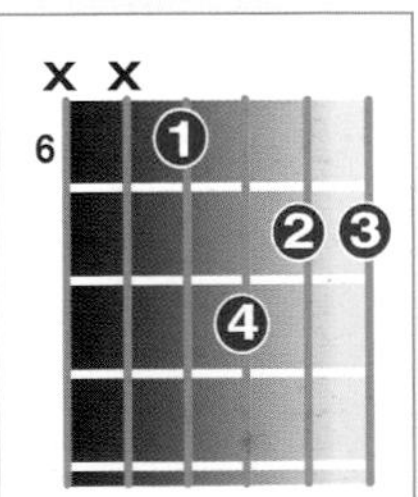

A♭m7 A♭ Minor 7th
1st (A♭), ♭3rd (C♭),
5th (E♭), ♭7th (G♭)

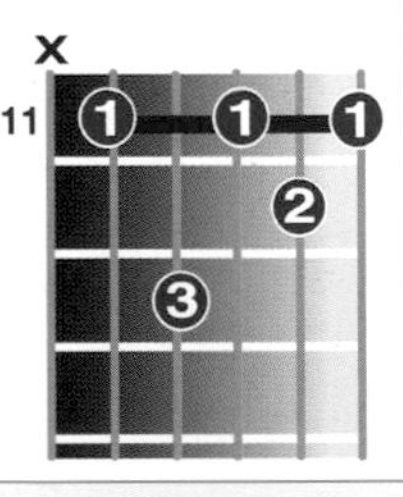

A♭m7 A♭ Minor 7th
1st (A♭), ♭3rd (C♭),
5th (E♭), ♭7th (G♭)

A♭sus4 A♭ Suspended 4th
1st (A♭), 4th (D♭), 5th (E♭)

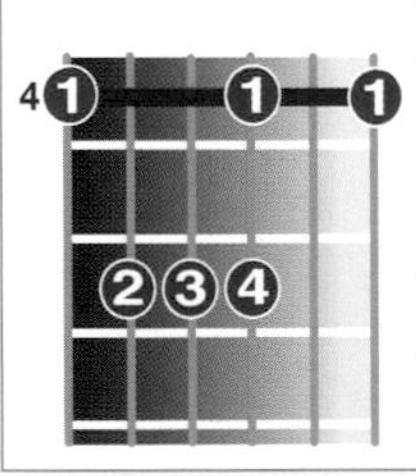

A♭sus4 A♭ Suspended 4th
1st (A♭), 4th (D♭), 5th (E♭)

Complete Guitar Handbook

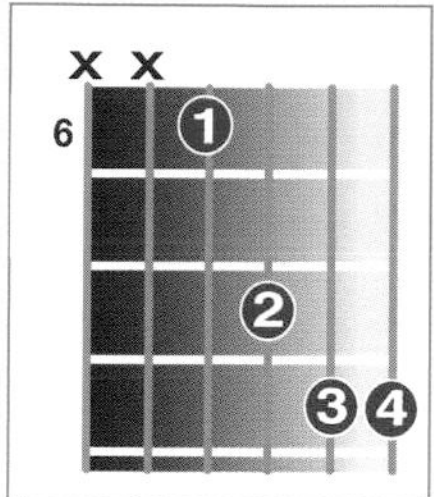

A♭sus4 A♭ Suspended 4th
1st (A♭), 4th (D♭), 5th (E♭)

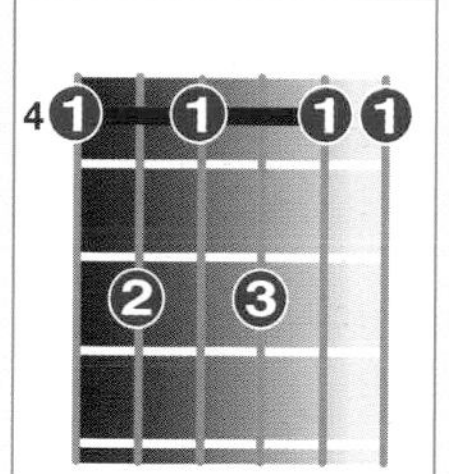

A♭7sus4 A♭ Dominant 7th sus4
1st (A♭), 4th (D♭), 5th (E♭), ♭7th (G♭)

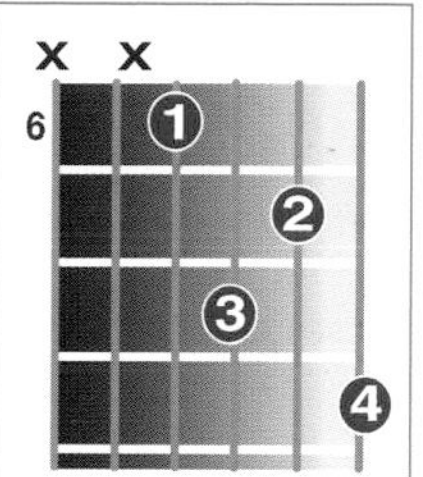

A♭7sus4 A♭ Dominant 7th sus4
1st (A♭), 4th (D♭), 5th (E♭), ♭7th (G♭)

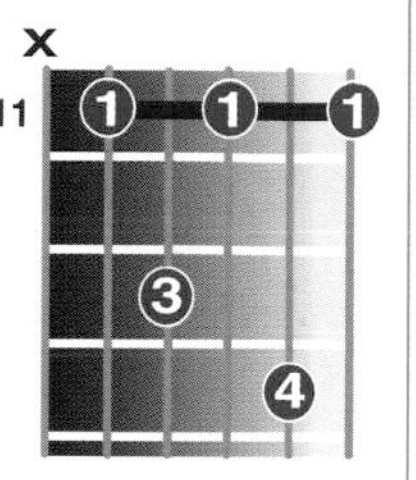

A♭7sus4 A♭ Dominant 7th sus4
1st (A♭), 4th (D♭), 5th (E♭), ♭7th (G♭)

A♭6 A♭ Major 6th
1st (A♭), 3rd (C), 5th (E♭), 6th (F)

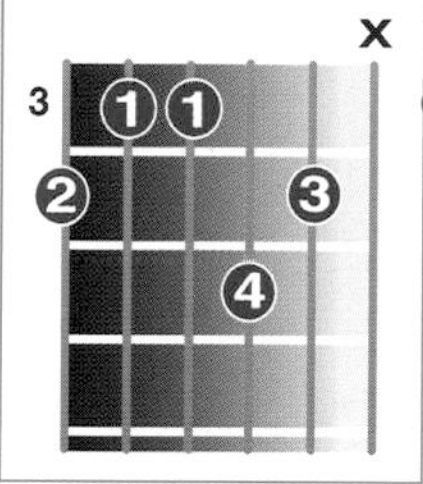

A♭6 A♭ Major 6th
1st (A♭), 3rd (C), 5th (E♭), 6th (F)

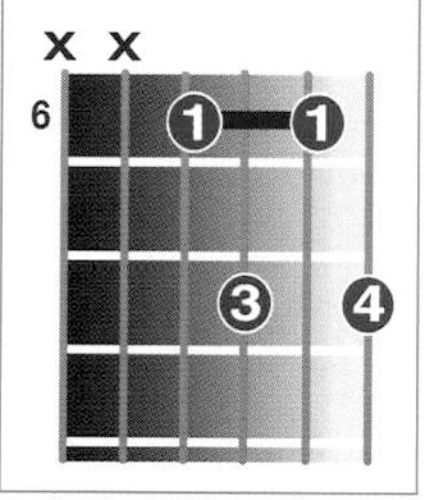

A♭6 A♭ Major 6th
1st (A♭), 3rd (C), 5th (E♭), 6th (F)

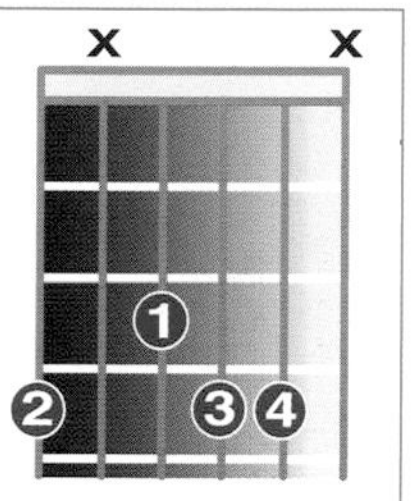

A♭m6 A♭ Minor 6th
1st (A♭), ♭3rd (C♭), 5th (E♭), 6th (F)

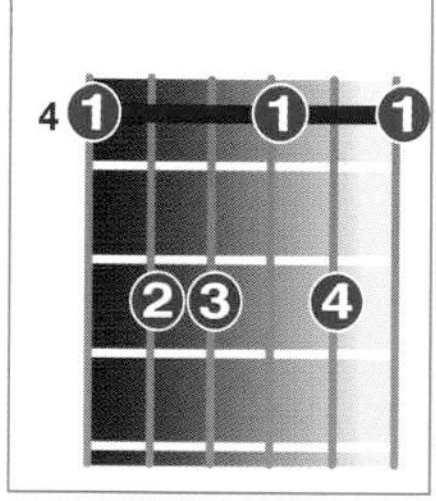

A♭m6 A♭ Minor 6th
1st (A♭), ♭3rd (C♭), 5th (E♭), 6th (F)

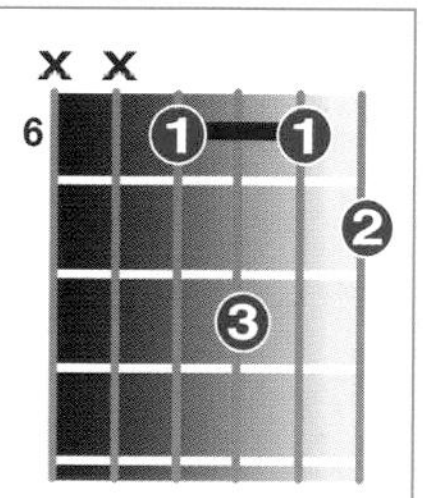

A♭m6 A♭ Minor 6th
1st (A♭), ♭3rd (C♭), 5th (E♭), 6th (F)

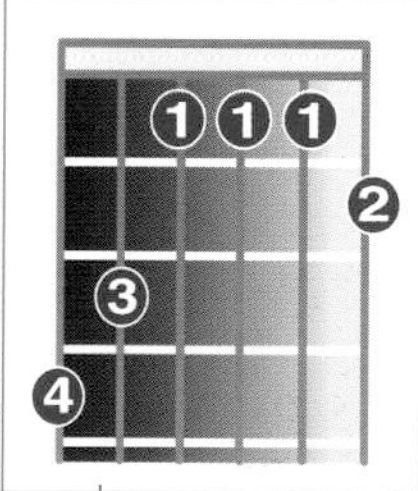

A♭7 A♭ Dominant 7th
1st (A♭), 3rd (C), 5th (E♭), ♭7th (G♭)

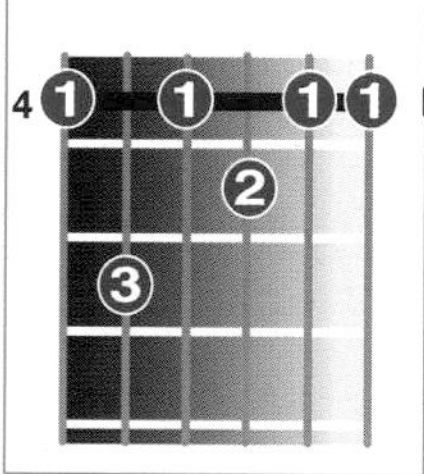

A♭7 A♭ Dominant 7th
1st (A♭), 3rd (C), 5th (E♭), ♭7th (G♭)

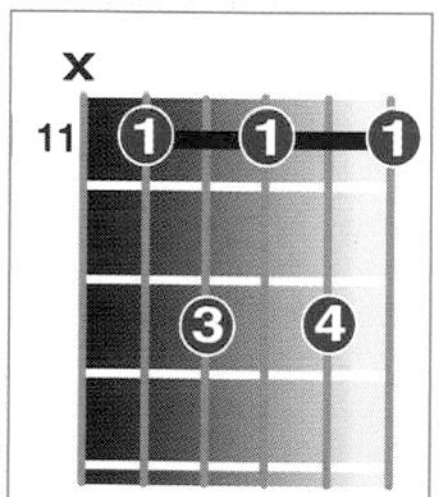

A♭7 A♭ Dominant 7th
1st (A♭), 3rd (C), 5th (E♭), ♭7th (G♭)

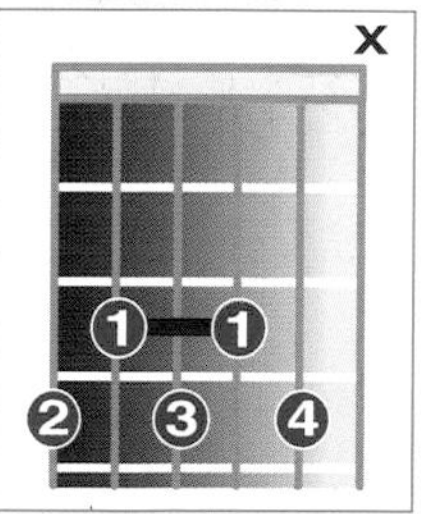

A♭9 A♭ Dominant 9th
1st (A♭), 3rd (C), 5th (E♭),
♭7th (G♭), 9th (B♭)

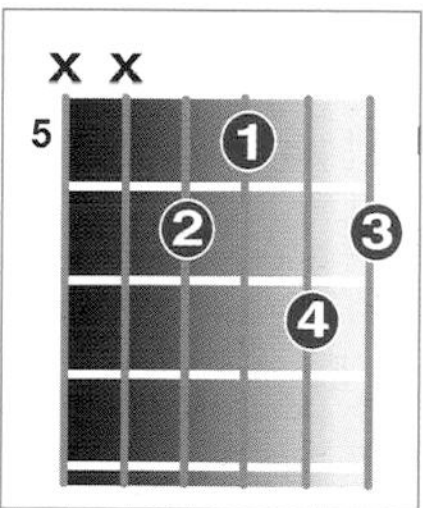

A♭9 A♭ Dominant 9th
1st (A♭), 3rd (C), 5th (E♭),
♭7th (G♭), 9th (B♭)

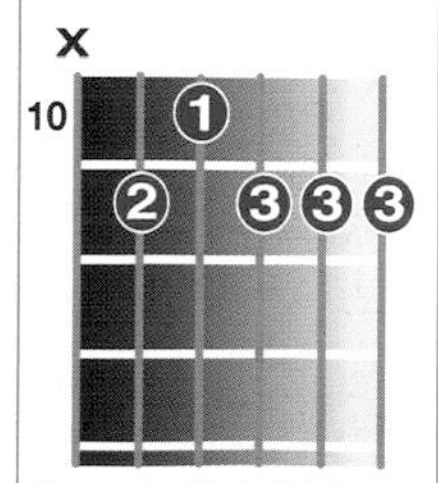

A♭9 A♭ Dominant 9th
1st (A♭), 3rd (C), 5th (E♭),
♭7th (G♭), 9th (B♭)

Section Five: Chord Dictionary

A♭/G♯ ADVANCED CHORDS

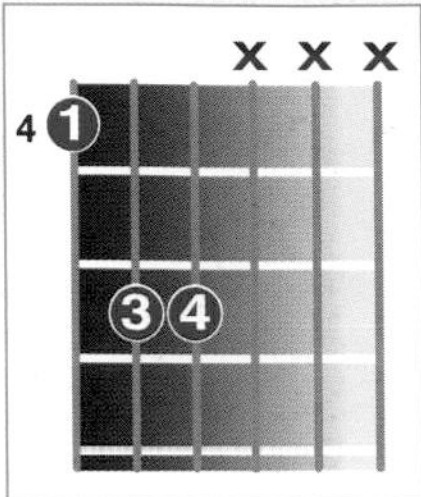

A♭5 A♭ 5th (power chord)
1st (A♭), 5th (E♭)

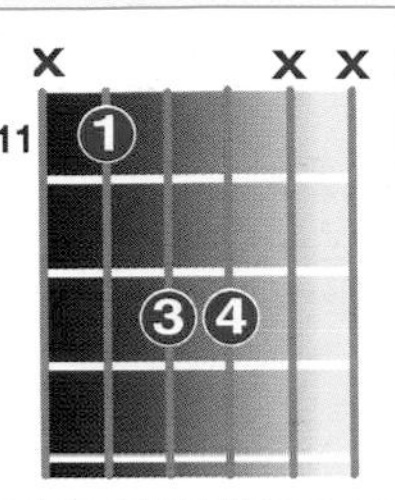

A♭5 A♭ 5th (power chord)
1st (A♭), 5th (E♭)

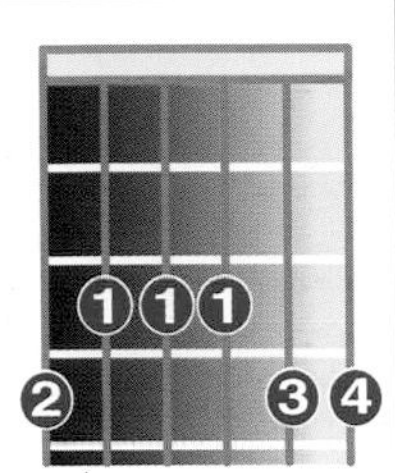

A♭6/9 A♭ Major 6th add 9th
1st (A♭), 3rd (C), 5th (E♭), 6th (F), 9th (B♭)

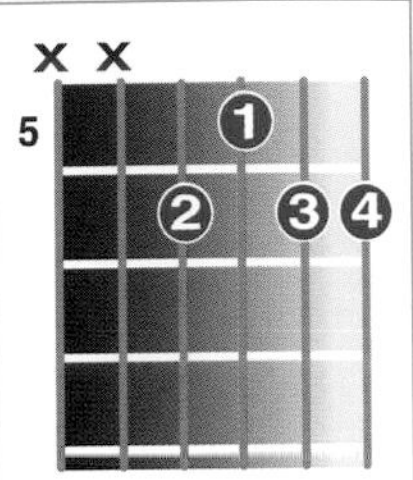

A♭ 6/9 A♭ Major 6th add 9th
1st (A♭), 3rd (C), 5th (E♭), 6th (F), 9th (B♭)

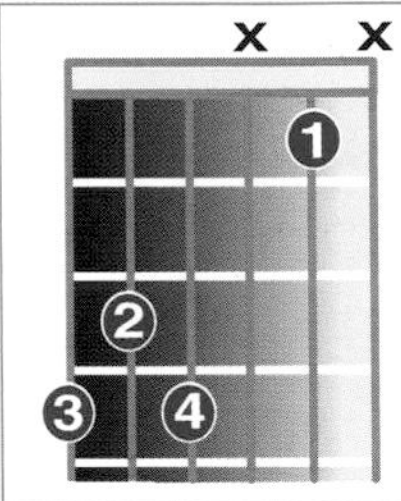

A♭11 A♭ Dominant 11th
1st (A♭), 3rd (C), 5th (E♭), ♭7th (G♭), 9th (B♭), 11th (D♭)

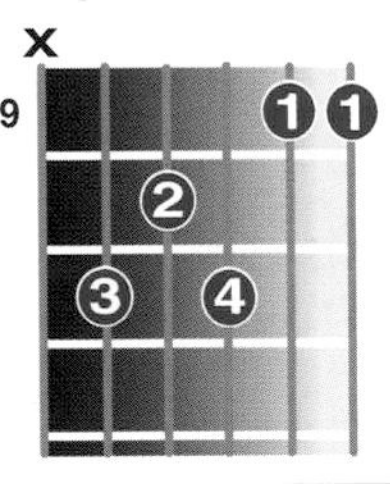

A♭11 A♭ Dominant 11th
1st (A♭), 3rd (C), 5th (E♭), ♭7th (G♭), 9th (B♭), 11th (D♭)

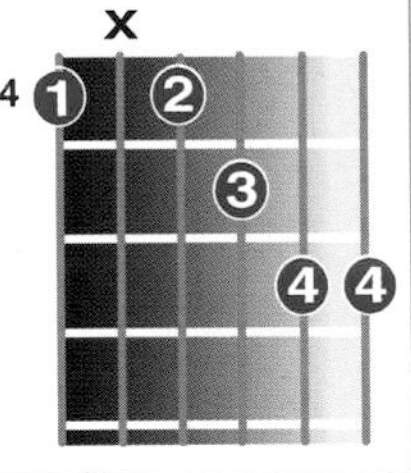

A♭13 A♭ Dominant 13th
1st (A♭), 3rd (C), 5th (E♭), ♭7th (G♭), 9th (B♭), 13th (F)

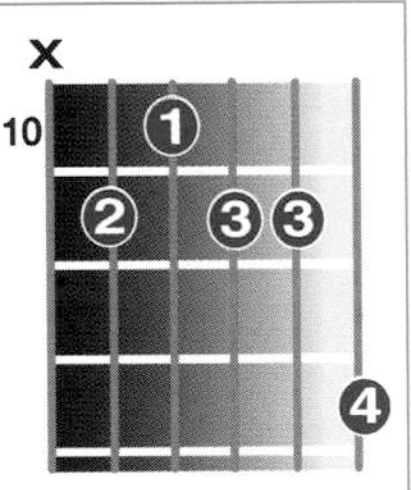

A♭13 A♭ Dominant 13th
1st (A♭), 3rd (C), 5th (E♭), ♭7th (G♭), 9th (B♭), 13th (F)

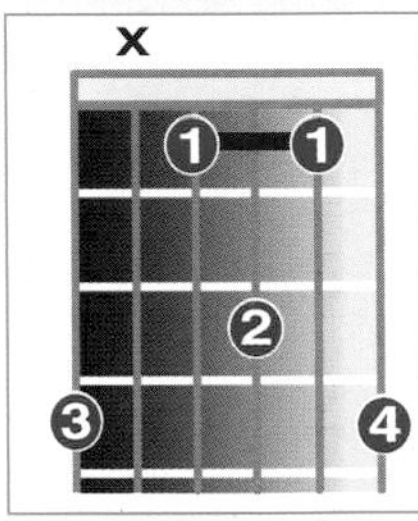

A♭add9 A♭ Major add 9th
1st (A♭), 3rd (C), 5th (E♭), 9th (B♭)

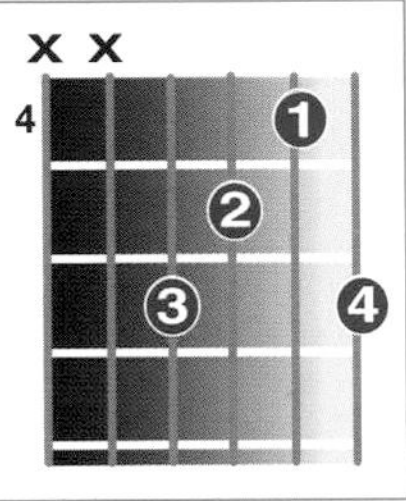

A♭add9 A♭ Major add 9th
1st (A♭), 3rd (C), 5th (E♭), 9th (B♭)

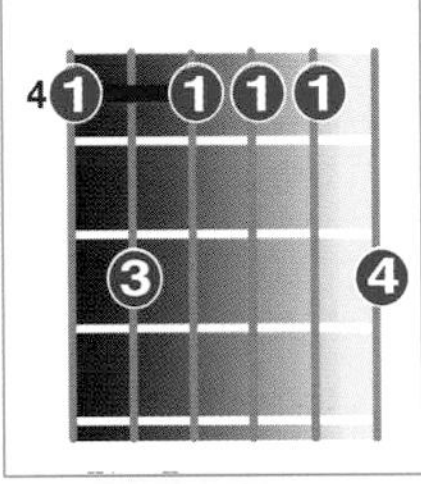

A♭m9 A♭ Minor 9th
1st (A♭), ♭3rd (C♭), 5th (E♭), ♭7th (G♭), 9th (B♭)

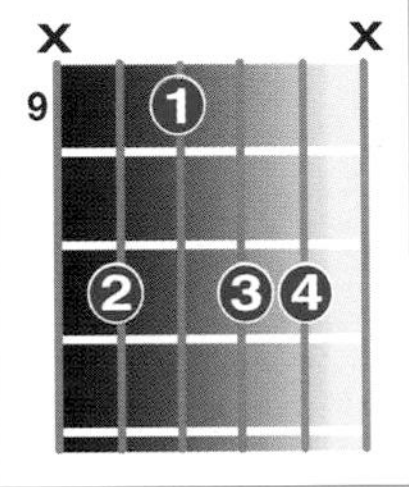

A♭m9 A♭ Minor 9th
1st (A♭), ♭3rd (C♭), 5th (E♭), ♭7th (G♭), 9th (B♭)

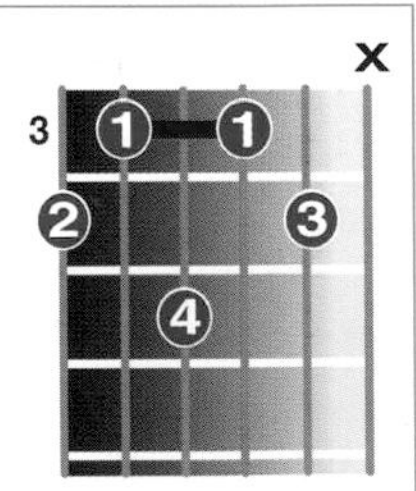

A♭maj9 A♭ Major 9th
1st (A♭), 3rd (C), 5th (E♭), 7th (G), 9th (B♭)

A♭maj9 A♭ Major 9th
1st (A♭), 3rd (C), 5th (E♭), 7th (G), 9th (B♭)

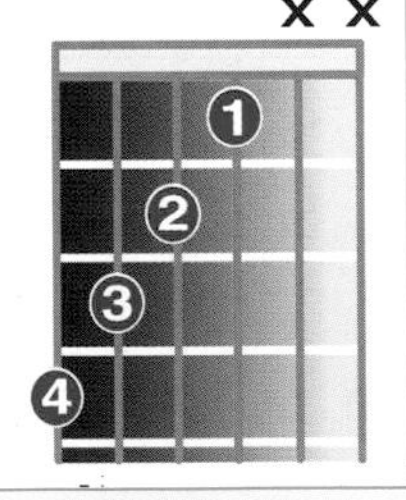

A♭+ A♭ Augmented
1st (A♭), 3rd (C), ♯5th (E)

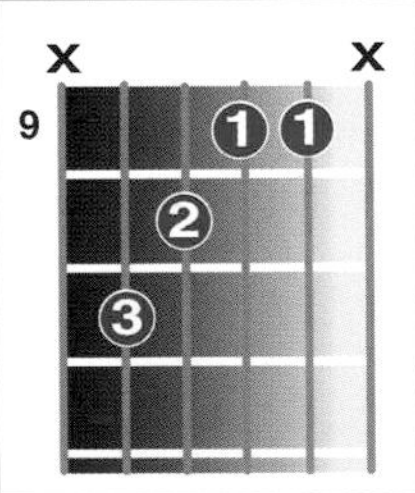

A♭+ A♭ Augmented
1st (A♭), 3rd (C), ♯5th (E)

Complete Guitar Handbook

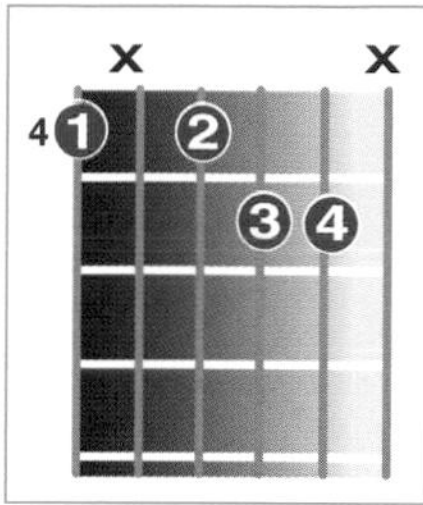

A♭7♯5 A♭ Dominant 7th ♯5
1st (A♭), 3rd (C), ♯5th (E), ♭7th (G♭)

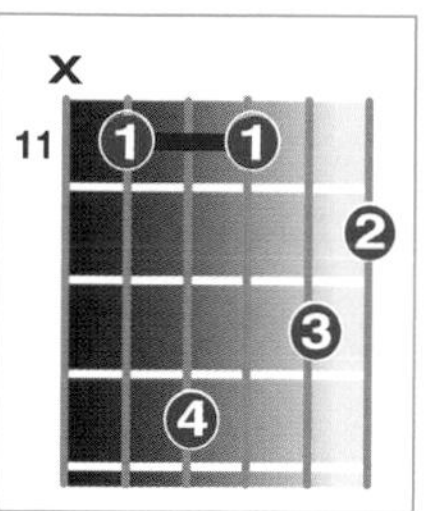

A♭7♯5 A♭ Dominant 7th ♯5
1st (A♭), 3rd (C), ♯5th (E), ♭7th (G♭)

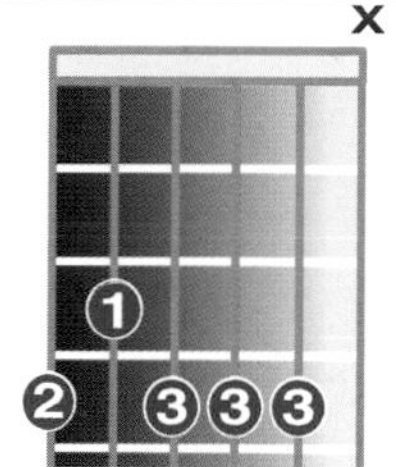

A♭7♯9 A♭ Dominant 7th ♯9
1st (A♭), 3rd (C), 5th (E♭), ♭7th (G♭), ♯9th (B)

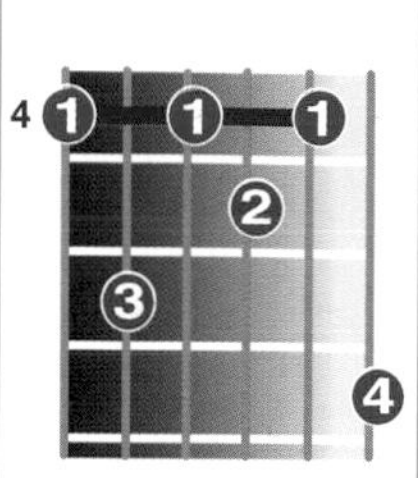

A♭7♯9 A♭ Dominant 7th ♯9
1st (A♭), 3rd (C), 5th (E♭), ♭7th (G♭), ♯9th (B)

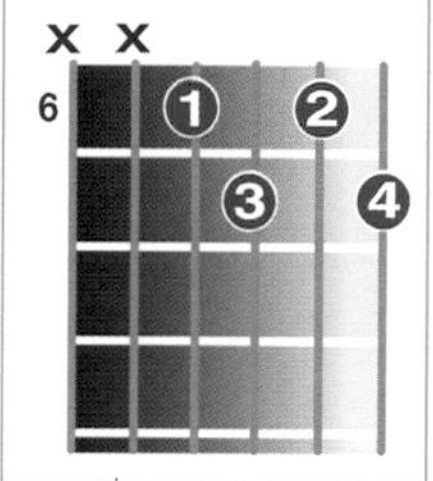

A♭o7 A♭ Diminished 7th
1st (A♭), ♭3rd (C♭), ♭5th (E♭♭), ♭♭7th (G♭♭)

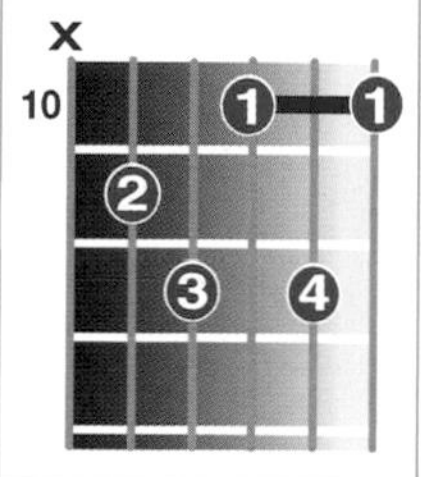

A♭o7 A♭ Diminished 7th
1st (A♭), ♭3rd (C♭), ♭5th (E♭♭), ♭♭7th (G♭♭)

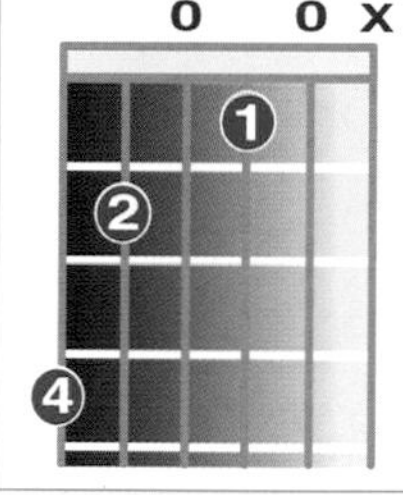

A♭o A♭ Diminished triad
1st (A♭), ♭3rd (C♭), ♭5th (E♭♭)

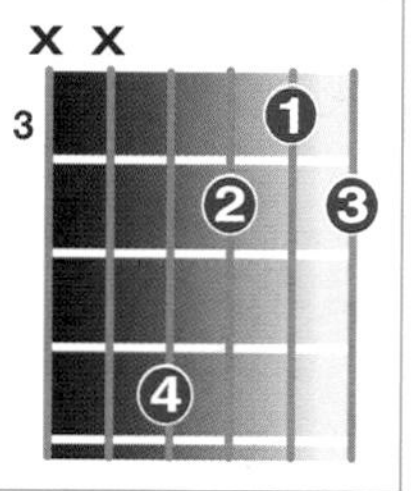

A♭o A♭ Diminished triad
1st (A♭), ♭3rd (C♭), ♭5th (E♭♭)

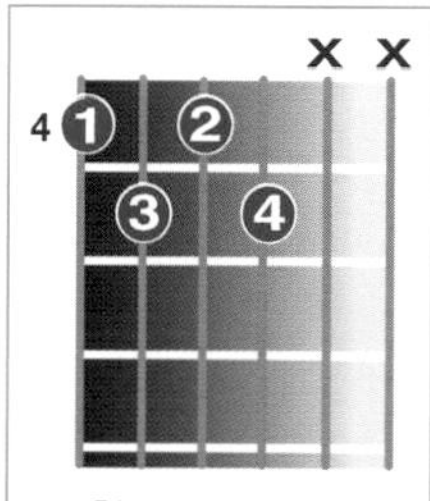

A♭7♭5 A♭ Dominant 7th ♭5
1st (A♭), 3rd (C), ♭5th (E♭♭), ♭7th (G♭)

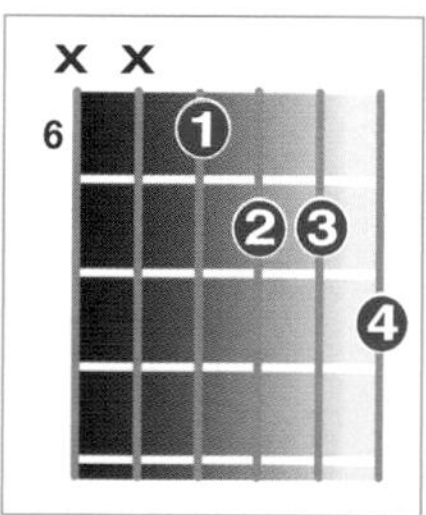

A♭7♭5 A♭ Dominant 7th ♭5
1st (A♭), 3rd (C), ♭5th (E♭♭), ♭7th (G♭)

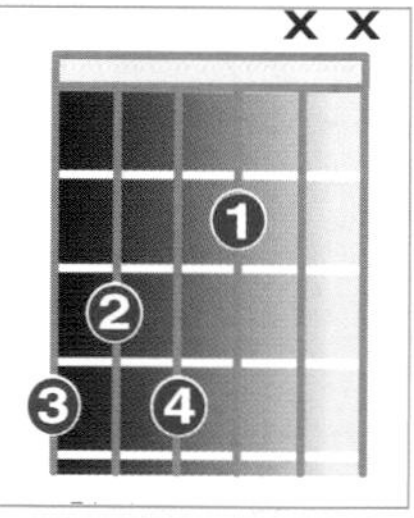

A♭7♭9 A♭ Dominant 7th ♭9
1st (A♭), 3rd (C), 5th (E♭), ♭7th (G♭), ♭9th (B♭♭)

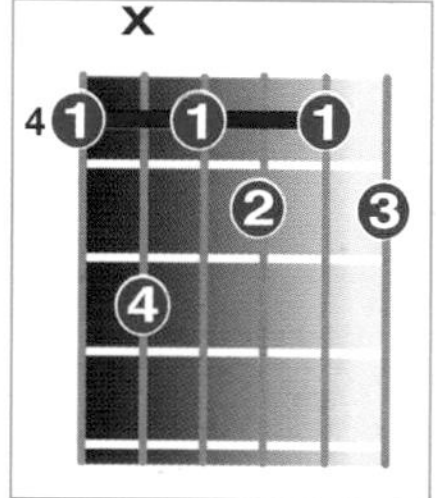

A♭7♭9 A♭ Dominant 7th ♭9
1st (A♭), 3rd (C), 5th (E♭), ♭7th (G♭), ♭9th (B♭♭)

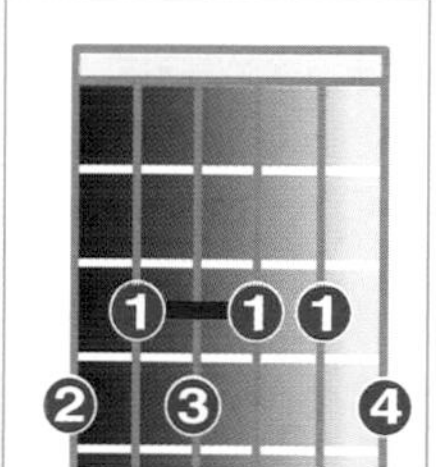

A♭9♭5 A♭ Dominant 9th ♭5th
1st (A♭), 3rd (C), ♭5th (E♭♭), ♭7th (G♭), 9th (B♭)

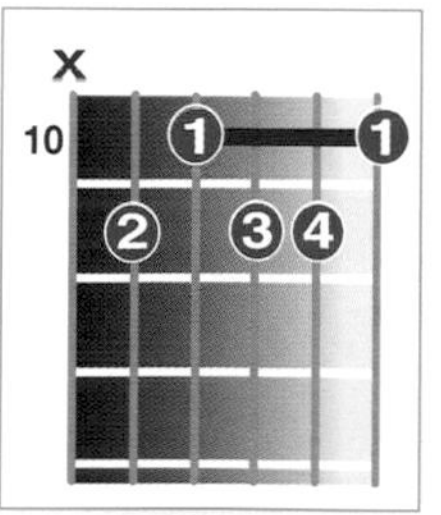

A♭9♭5 A♭ Dominant 9th ♭5th
1st (A♭), 3rd (C), ♭5th (E♭♭), ♭7th (G♭), 9th (B♭)

Scale of A♭/G♯ major

A♭	B♭	C	D♭	E♭	F	G
1st	2nd	3rd	4th	5th	6th	7th
	9th		11th		13th	

Section Five: Chord Dictionary

GLOSSARY

Action

The 'action' of a guitar refers to the height of the strings from the fingerboard and determines how much pressure you have to put on the strings in order to play them. Most guitarists prefer a low action set-up where the strings are set as close to the neck as possible to facilitate easy playing without causing fret buzz.

Active electronics

Active electronics is a battery powered circuitry that boosts a guitar signal to make it easier to drive an amplifier into distortion. It can also be used to change the tone of the guitar.

Archtop

An archtop guitar is an instrument with an arched (curved) top and back. Such guitars, carved from solid pieces of wood, became hugely popular during the 1920s because they were louder than the previously-used classical guitars. They are now used by jazz players.

Arpeggio

An arpeggio is the sounding of the notes of a chord in succession rather than all simultaneously. These can be played individually while holding a chord down or by picking out the notes separately on the fingerboard, just as you would when playing a scale.

Barre chord

A barre chord is a chord where one of a guitarist's fretting fingers (usually the first finger) is held down across many or all of the strings in addition to other fingers holding down separate notes. Barre chords can be used in all of the twelve different keys simply by moving them up or down the fingerboard.

Bend

One of the most common lead guitar techniques is string bending, where a player plays a note on a string and pushes it up towards the next string while still holding the note down. You can bend one, two or even three strings at the same time.

Bottleneck

A technique where a player moves a glass or metal bar up and down the guitar neck while playing to produce sliding pitches. Famous bottleneck players include Robert Johnson, Muddy Waters, Eric Clapton and Ry Cooder.

Box-shape

Most guitarists normally learn scales as box-shapes which show the finger

positions for notes in a particular region of the fingerboard. The pentatonic scale, for example, can be played using five box shapes that cover the whole guitar neck.

Bridge
This part of the guitar, along with the saddle, transmits energy from the string vibrations to the body of a guitar. It also spreads the mechanical tension of the strings. There are two main types of bridge: a fixed bridge is glued to the top of the soundboard with the strings anchored to it; and a floating bridge is held in place only by the tension in the strings that pass over it.

Classical guitar
The classical guitar is a large acoustic guitar with a wide neck over which metal-wound silk bass strings and gut treble strings are usually strung. It was the first type of guitar to feature struts – pieces of wood attached to the inside of the body to improve volume and tonal response – and, to this day, is always played fingerstyle.

Comping
'Comping' is a jazz term for accompanying. It usually means playing rhythm chords while a vocalist is singing or a lead performer is playing a solo.

Crown
The crown is the top of a fret on the guitar fingerboard. Crowns vary in width and curvature, and these differences influence the tone of a vibrating string: a thin crown tends to give a crisp treble edge to a string's tone while a thicker one produces a more mellow sound that would appeal to a jazz player.

Cutaway
This is a rounded area cut out of a guitar's body next to the neck so that a player can comfortably reach further up the neck. Guitars such as Gibson Les Pauls and Fender Telecasters have cutaways underneath the neck, while others including the Gibson SG, Gibson 335, Fender Stratocaster and numerous Paul Reed Smith models have cutaways above and below the neck.

Dot marker
Most guitars have these markers along the neck to help players navigate the fingerboard. They are usually behind the 3rd, 5th, 7th, 9th, 12th, 15th, 17th, 19th and 21st frets of the fingerboard. Other common markers are blocks (commonly found on Gibson and Ibanez guitars) and 'shark-tooths' (used on rock guitar models such as the Jackson Soloist). These markers are usually made out of abalone or plastic.

Complete Guitar Handbook

Double-stop

A two-note chord, melody or phrase.

Electro-acoustic

An electro-acoustic guitar is an acoustic or semi-acoustic guitar fitted with a 'piezo-electric' transducer (usually under the bridge saddle) and an on-board pre-amplifier. When plugged into a suitable amp, this produces a crisp acoustic sound with plenty of sustain and little feedback.

EQ

EQ is short for equalisation, a term describing the sound spectrum or parts of the sound spectrum of an audio signal. All audible sounds are pitched somewhere between 20Hz (the lowest) and 20KHz (the highest). An equaliser is a tone control that uses capacitors or other devices to cut or boost frequencies within this range.

F-hole

F-holes are ornamental sound holes found on a number of acoustic and electric guitars.

Fingerstyle

While most rock and pop guitarists play their instruments with a plectrum, all classical and flamenco guitar players articulate their notes with the separate fingers and thumb of their right hand (or left hand if they're left-handed). These players use their thumb to play the bass notes, usually with downstrokes on the bottom three strings, and their first, second and third fingers to play the other strings.

Flamenco

A popular folk music style from Andalucia in southern Spain.

Flatpicking

Flatpicking is a style where all notes, scalar and chordal, are articulated with a plectrum.

Complete Guitar Handbook

Footswitch
A footswitch is a device which allows you to change guitar sounds during a live performance without having to stop playing.

Fret
Frets are metal strips placed across the radius of a guitar's fingerboard to mark out notes a semitone apart. They make it easy for a guitarist to find precise notes in scales and chords. Frets come in all shapes and sizes: some are narrow while others are wide; and some are flat at the top while others are rounded.

Glissando
When a guitarist plays a glissando, he or she is sliding up or down the guitar neck in such a way that every note under the left hand finger is articulated. This is different from a basic slide where the only notes that can be clearly heard are the first and last notes played by the left hand finger.

Guitar, 12-string
These guitars have 12 strings arranged into pairs (courses) so that a 6-string player can easily handle them. Six of the strings are tuned identically to those on a 6-string instrument, while the other six are tuned as follows; the lowest four are usually tuned an octave above the conventional E, A, D and G strings, while the other two are tuned the same as the conventional B and E strings.

Guitar, 7-string
The seven string guitar is like a standard six string instrument with an additional low string, usually tuned down to a low A. It was first used by jazzers such as George Van Eps and has since been used by Nu Metal artists Korn and Limp Bizkit.

Hammer-on
A hammer-on is a technique where you play a note behind a fret on the fingerboard and then hammer one of your other fingers down behind another fret higher up on the same string. It is one of the most common lead guitar techniques used by blues, rock, jazz and even classical players.

Headstock
The headstock is a wooden structure attached to the end of a guitar's neck that the machine heads or tuning pegs are mounted on. It is also usually the part of the guitar that carries the manufacturer's name and logo plus any other significant details of the guitar model.

Complete Guitar Handbook

Humbucking pickups
Humbucking pickups have two coils instead of just one. These coils are wired in such a way that any electrical hum produced by one is cancelled out by the other. The result is a 'fatter' sound with less background noise. Humbuckers were originally launched by Gibson in 1955 and soon became a standard feature on their Les Paul, Explorer, Flying V, Firebird and SG guitars.

Intonation
The intonation of a guitar is correct when the notes behind every fret of the fingerboard all have the right pitch when the guitar is in tune. To check the intonation of your guitar, tune it up accurately and then listen to each note on each string. If any notes on any string are out of tune, you should be able to make intonation adjustments on the bridge screw that controls the vibrating length of that string.

Lick
A lick is a small musical motif such as a phrase or riff that can be incorporated into a lead guitar solo. All good solo players have a vocabulary of licks which they use in their lead lines.

Luthier
A luthier is a guitar maker. Originally the term was only used to describe lute and classical guitar makers but now it is generally considered to apply to builders of all kinds of guitars and fretted instruments.

Nut
The nut is a structure at the headstock end of the fingerboard that the strings pass over before they reach the machine heads or pegs. The strings lean on the nut and all string vibrations occur between here and the guitar's bridge.

Palm-muting
You can mute a guitar's strings by placing your right hand lightly across them. This is very useful if you're playing at high volume and don't want the strings to ring out unnecessarily. It can also be used to add more colour and texture to a rhythm or solo.

Pickup selector
A switch which allows a guitar player to choose between different pickups.

Pre-amp
Many amplifiers and DI boxes contain a pre-amplifier, a device that can be used to generate extra signal gain. Such devices are often used when acoustic instruments are amplified and when electric players need a bit more edge in their tone.

Complete Guitar Handbook

Pre-bend

A pre-bend is when you bend a note before you actually play it. In this situation you play the string from the top of the bend and then pull it back into its original position.

Pull-off

In many ways, a pull-off can be seen as the reverse of a hammer-on. In this case, a note is played and then the finger playing that note is pulled off the string to sound a lower note that is either an open string or one fretted by another finger.

Rake

A rake is an interesting effect a guitarist can produce by rubbing one of their fingers or hands along one or several of the guitar strings. A harsher raking effect can be created by performing it with a hard object such as a plectrum.

Rasgueado

Rasgueado (also spelt Rascuedo) is an instantly recognisable flamenco technique where the fingers of the right hand (or left hand if the player is left-handed) individually strum across the strings in rapid succession.

Riff

A riff is a short series of chords or notes that can be repeated to form a catchy sequence. Some riffs are so effective that they more or less take up a whole song!

Saddle

The saddle is the place on a guitar's bridge for supporting the strings. The distance between it and the nut determines the scale length (length of vibrating open string) of a guitar.

Scratchplate

A scratchplate is a plastic plate that is fixed to the lower front part of a guitar's body (underneath the soundhole on an acoustic steel-string instrument) to protect the body from wear and tear caused by the player's plectrums or finger picks.

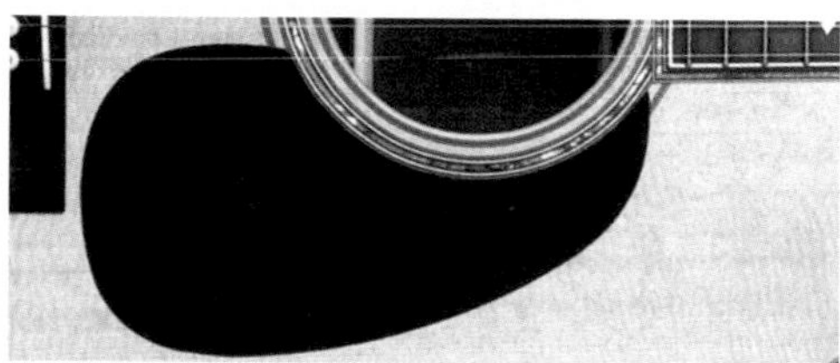

Semi-solid

During the late 1950s, Gibson introduced a range of semi-acoustic guitars that didn't suffer from the feedback problems that traditional 'electric-acoustic' models produced. These guitars, including the ES-355, ES-345, and the now famous ES-335, had thin hollow bodies with f-holes to let the sound out, a design which increased sustain and greatly reduced feedback.

Semitone

The smallest interval between two notes on a fretted guitar is called a semitone (S). Notes on either side of a fret are separated by a semitone. An interval of two semitones is called a tone (T).

Slide

This effect is produced when you play one note on the guitar and, while still holding the note down, slide up or down the guitar neck to another note. In a true slide, the only two notes you can hear clearly are the first and last notes, at the beginning and end of the slide, whereas a glissando is a sliding effect that is played in such a way that every note under the finger is articulated.

Solid-body

A solid-body guitar is a guitar with a body that has no cavities other than those used for inserting pickups and other electrical components. Solid-body electric guitar prototypes were developed during the 1920s and 1930s when amplified acoustic guitars gave musicians too much feedback.

Soundhole

The soundhole is the hole in the front of the guitar body through which sound projects from the soundchamber. Most acoustic guitar soundholes are round, although some are oval (as on early Gibson acoustics), D-shaped (as on Maccaferri guitars), or violin-like f-holes (as on the Gibson ES350).

Sweep-picking

Sweep picking is an advanced technique where a guitarist plays notes across the neck with economic pick movements. In some ways it is similar to the way a violinist will sustain a note with the bow by bowing in both directions at a consistent speed. This technique can be used to facilitate execution of ultra-fast arpeggios.

Sympathetic strings

Sitars and some specialist lutes and guitars have sympathetic strings which are not played but sound 'in sympathy' with strings that are. The sympathetic strings are tuned to particular notes and when those notes are played on the instrument, the corresponding strings start to vibrate and thus 'sing in sympathy'.

Thumbpick

Thumbpicks are often used by fingerstyle players who want to play the guitar forcefully without risk of damaging their thumbnails. A thumbpick fits over the end of the thumb with the pick protruding to strike the strings.

Complete Guitar Handbook

Time signature
A time signature is a sign placed after the clef at the beginning of a piece of music to indicate its meter.

Tremolando
Tremolando is a classical and flamenco guitar technique in which the first, second and third fingers of the right hand (or left hand for a left-handed player) play a continuous, repeating pattern on one note.

Tremolo arm
A tremolo arm (a.k.a. a 'whammy bar') is a mechanical arm attached to the bridge of an electric guitar that can alter the pitch of the strings; as the arm is depressed, the pitch of a note played drops, and when the arm is let go, the altered pitch returns back to normal.

Triad
Triads are basic three note chords that are also the building blocks of most other chords. There are four basic triads: a major triad is the first, third and fifth notes of the diatonic major scale (C, E and G in the key of C); a minor triad is the first third and fifth notes of the natural minor scale (C, E flat and G in the key of C); an augmented triad is a major triad with a sharpened fifth note (C, E and G# in the key of C); and a diminished triad is a minor triad with a flattened fifth note (C, E flat and G flat in the key of C).

Truss rod
The truss rod is a metal bar used for reinforcing and adjusting a steel-strung guitar's neck. It can be adjusted to keep the neck straight if the tension in it changes when different gauge strings are used.

Vibrato
Vibrato is a left hand (or right hand if you're left-handed) technique where a played note is moved rapidly to produce a fluctuation in pitch that gives more richness to the tone. Vibrato can be applied vertically (across the neck) or horizontally (along the neck). Vibrato is used extensively in classical guitar music, and in blues, jazz and rock guitar solos.

Violining
Violining is an effect where you use a guitar's volume control (or a volume pedal) to fade notes or chords in from nothing to get a nice, smooth effect. Rock legends such as Gary Moore, Jimmy Page and Mark Knopfler have used violining to much effect.

Complete Guitar Handbook

FURTHER READING

Amelar, C., *The Guitar F/X Cook Book*, Hal Leonard, 1997

Bacon, T., *History of the American Guitar*, Backbeat UK, 2001

Bacon T. & Day P., *The Fender Book: A Complete History of Fender Electric Guitars* (2nd edn.), Backbeat UK, 1999

Bennett, J. (ed.), *Guitar Facts*, Flame Tree Publishing, 2002

Brosnac, D., *Guitar Electronics for Musicians*, Music Sales Ltd, 1983

Carter, W., *Gibson Guitars 100 Years of an American Icon*, General Publishing Group, 1994

Chappell, J., *Scales and Modes*, Cherry Lane Music, 1994

Chappell, J. & Verheyen, C., *Rock Guitar for Dummies*, Hungry Minds Inc, 2001

Denyer, R., *The Guitar Handbook*, Alfred A. Knopf, 1992

Douse, C., *Really Easy Riffs*, Wise Publications, 2003

Duchossoir, A. R., *Gibson Electrics: The Classic Years*, Hal Leonard, 1981

Fliegler, R., *AMPS!: The Other Half of Rock 'n' Roll*, Hal Leonard, 1993

Goodrick, M., *The Advancing Guitarist*, Music Sales Ltd., 1987

Gruhn. G., Carter, W., *Electric Guitars and Basses: A Photographic History*, Omnibus Press, 1994

Hall, J., *Exploring Jazz Guitar*, Hal Leonard, 1991

Hart, C., *Routes to Sight Reading*, Registry Publications, 2004

Iwanade, Y., *The Beauty of the 'Burst: Gibson Sunburst Les Pauls from 1958 to 1960*, Hal Leonard, 1999

Kamimoto, H., *Electric Guitar Setups*, Music Sales Ltd, 1996

Koch, G., *Rhythm Riffs*, Hal Leonard, 2003

Latarski, D., *First Chords*, Warner Bros., 1999

Macdonald, R. (ed.), *The Illustrated Home Recording Handbook*, Billboard Books, 2004

Menasché, E., *The Desktop Studio*, Hal Leonard, 2003

Philips, M. & Chappell, J., *Guitar for Dummies*, Hungry Minds Inc, 1998

Pinksterboer, H., *Rough Guide to Electric and Bass Guitar*, Rough Guides, 2000

Rooksby, R., *First Guitar Rhythm Patterns*, Wise Publications, 1998

Ross, M., *Getting Great Guitar Sounds*, Hal Leonard, 1998

Schmidt, P. W., *Acquired of the Angels: The Lives and Works of Master Guitar Makers John D'Angelico and James L. D'Aquisto*, Scarecrow Press, 1991

Skinner, T., *Electric Guitar Playing Grade 1*, Registry Publications, 2004

Skinner, T., *Improvising Lead Guitar*, Registry Publications, 2004

Sicard, A., *Instant Lead Guitar*, Mel Bay, 1993

Wheeler, T., *American Guitars: An Illustrated History*, HarperCollins Publishers, 1992

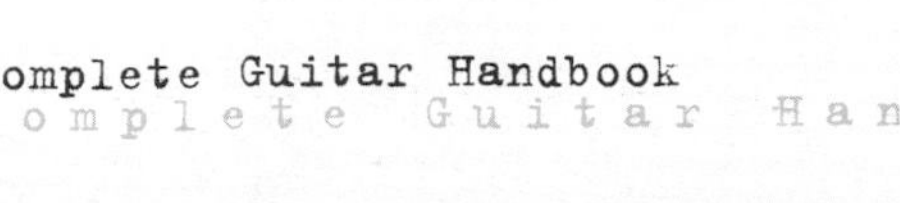

Complete Guitar Handbook

Wheeler, T., *The Stratocaster Chronicles: Celebrating 50 Years of the Fender Strat*, Hal Leonard, 2004

Wyatt, K., *Electric Guitar Basics*, Warner Bros., 1996

MAGAZINES

20th Century Guitar: www.tcguitar.com
Acoustic Guitar: www.acguitar.com
Bass Guitar Magazine: www.bassguitarmagazine.com
Classical Guitar Magazine: www.classicalguitarmagazine.com
Electronic Musician: www.emusician.com
Flatpicking Guitar Magazine: www.flatpick.com
Guitarist: www.guitarist.co.uk
GuitarOne: www.guitaronemag.com
Guitar Player: www.guitarplayer.com
Guitar Techniques: www.guitartechniques.com
Guitar Tutor
Guitar World: www.guitarworld.com
Total Guitar: www.totalguitar.co.uk
Vintage Guitar: www.Vintageguitar.com

DVD

Home Recording Magazine's 100 Recording Tips and Tricks, Cherry Lane Music, 2003

Learning Guitar for Dummies, Jon Chappell, 2001

WEBSITES

www.analogman.com: this is a site dedicated to analogue and vintage effects, including pedals.

www.BooksForGuitar.com: this site specializes in guitar education, with all titles being reviewed for quality before inclusion.

www.guitarists.net/: this site is for players of all ages, styles and abilities. Take part in a guitar-related discussion, look up some lessons and a lot more.

http://guitar.about.com/od/bluesjazzmetal more/: this site has links to resources that give advice on how to play in styles such as blues, funk and jazz.

www.guitar-player-resources.com/: a site giving advice to acoustic, electric and bass guitarists on everything from choosing a guitar, to guitar lessons and repairs.

www.guitartips.addr.com: this site is day-to-day resource for acoustic players, with tips and advice on care, preservation and maintenance of instruments, plus guitar chords.

www.harmony-central.com: this is a leading internet resource for musicians, with everything from news and product reviews, to classified ads and chat rooms.

www.musicfirebox.com: a lo-fi music information site.

www.projectguitar.com: this site includes tutorials, projects, links and further information to help you get the most out of playing solid-body electric guitar.

www.RegistryOfGuitarTutors.com: this site includes the only database of formally registered guitar tutors across the UK and overseas.

www.tonequest.com: The ToneQuest Report is a monthly newsletter published by and for guitarists.

Complete Guitar Handbook

CONTRIBUTOR BIOGRAPHIES

Michael Leonard (General Editor)
Michael Leonard began playing guitar at the age of 12, inspired by his elder brother's budget-priced but very fine Yamaha acoustic. He's worked in the music press since 1990, and has edited *The Guitar Magazine*, *Guitar Techniques* and – currently – Europe's longest-established musicians' magazine, *Guitarist*. As a freelance writer, he's contributed to *Q*, *Mojo*, *Blender* and many others. He lives with his wife and two children in Bath, England.

Albert Lee (Foreword)
Albert Lee is one of the world's most accomplished guitarists, as well as being a pianist, songwriter and singer. A Grammy award-winner in 2002, he has also been voted 'Best Country Guitar Picker' by *Guitar Player* magazine five times to date. He has toured and recorded both as a solo artist and with numerous bands including Country Fever and the Crickets, and most recently with Eric Clapton, Hogan's Heroes and Bill Wyman's Rhythm Kings. He has appeared and recorded with some of the music industry's greatest names, and in 2002 took part in 'Concert for George', a tribute to George Harrison. His latest album, *Heartbreak Hill*, was released in 2003.

Juan Martín (Foreword)
Juan Martín is a celebrated virtuoso of the flamenco guitar who has been voted as one of the top guitarists in the world by *Guitar Player* magazine. He resides in London but still has his home in Málaga, Andalucia where he learnt his art. He has recorded 18 albums and has toured the world giving solo concerts and appearing with his group. His DVDs and definitive flamenco method have taught hundreds of thousands the complex art of flamenco. The Spanish paper *El Mundo* said of him 'he has a terrifyingly good technique and an absolute dominance of the guitar, filling the concert hall with crystalline clarity.'

Rusty Cutchin (Consultant Editor; Recording)
Rusty Cutchin has been a musician, recording engineer, producer and journalist for over 25 years. His articles have appeared in *Cashbox, Billboard, Hits, Musician, Country Fever, International Musician* and *Recording World*. Songwriting and production work for Atlantic Records and Motown led him to a studio career during which he worked on recordings by artists including Mariah Carey and Yoko Ono, as well as on countless jazz, dance and hip-hop records. At the same he built a pro-quality home studio, before returning full-circle to journalism, becoming editor-in-chief of *Home Recording* and technical editor of *GuitarOne*. He is currently associate editor of *Electronic Musician*, the leading US magazine for the home-studio musician.

Cliff Douse (Musical Styles; The Great Guitarists; Glossary)
Cliff Douse is a music author, editor and composer based in the UK. His first book, *Scales & Modes for Guitar*, was published in 1990 with an endorsement from the legendary rock guitarist, Pete Townshend, and he has since written a number of other books and countless articles for some of the UK's foremost music and computer magazines. Cliff also recently edited *Guitar Techniques* magazine and the *Guitarist Icons* series for Future Publishing in England.

Complete Guitar Handbook

Adam Perlmutter (Guitar Gallery)
Adam Perlmutter has music degrees from the University of North Carolina at Greensboro and the New England Conservatory. He is a senior editor of *GuitarOne* magazine, and has authored several guitar instruction books and transcribed/arranged numerous folios.

Richard Riley (Maintenance and Customizing; Guitar Electrics)
Richard Riley is a guitar player and writer. He has recorded and performed with a wide range of artists and is a long-time contributor to many of the UK's leading music technology publications. As an artist and musician he is regularly seen in the mp3.com charts.

Michael Ross (Using Effects; Amplifiers)
Michael Ross is a freelance guitarist/producer/writer/editor living in New York. He is the author of *Getting Great Guitar Sounds* (Hal Leonard). He is the gear editor for *Guitar One* magazine, and a contributor to amazon.com, *What Guitar, No Depression*, puremusic.com and others. He would like to remind guitarists that it is 90% in the fingers.

Tony Skinner (Getting Started; Playing Rhythm Guitar; Playing Lead Guitar; Chords and Tunings; Essential Techniques)
Tony Skinner is widely respected as one of the UK's premier music educators. He is the director of the Registry of Guitar Tutors – the world's foremost organisation for guitar education. He is also the principal guitar examiner for London College of Music Exams and has compiled examination syllabi in electric, bass and classical guitar playing, as well as popular music theory, rock/pop band and popular music vocals. He has written and edited over 50 music-education books and is the editor of *Guitar Tutor* magazine and a columnist for *Total Guitar* magazine.

PICTURE CREDITS

Ampeg: 315, **Arbiter Group Plc**: Fender Musical Instruments Inc.: 112, 159, 190 (m), 209 (b), 241, 252, 272 (bl), 276, 303 (br), 318 (bl), 322, 347, **Boss**: 132, 135 (b), 137 (t), 139 (br), 140 (tr), 142 **Brian Moore Guitars Inc**: 349 (r), **C.F. Martin & Co., Inc., Nazareth, PA USA**: 274, **Rusty Cutchin**: 139 (t), 143 (t), 337, 343, 339, 341, 345, **DOD**: 129 (t), **Dorling Kindersley Ltd.**: 183 (t), 247, 253, 263, 270, 272 (br), 300 (t), 305, **Focusrite Audio Engineering Ltd**: 336, **Gruhn Guitars**: 175 (bl); Kelsey Vaughn: 250, **Ibanez**: 129 (b), **John Hornby Skewes & Co Ltd.**: 264, **Lark Street Music**: 249, 262, **Line 6**: 273 (b), 297 (br), **London Features International**: 126, 226, 243, 245, 294, 321, 342, **Marshall Amplification Plc**: 206 (br), 207, 313, 318 (t), 320, **Neutrik**: 331, **Osborne Creative Services**: 335 (b), **Parker Guitars**: 296 (bl), **Peavey**: 318 (br), **Planet Waves**: 304 (tr), **Redferns**: Richard E. Aaron: 191, 201 (t), 220; Jorgen Angel: 235; Glenn A. Baker Archives: 135 (t); Michael Ochs Archives: 33, 49, 124, 131, 136, 138, 156, 160, 165, 169, 177 (b), 208, 216, 230, 254, 324; Bob Baker: 210; Dick Barnatt: 96, 184; Paul Bergen: 134, 198 (m), 223; Chuck Boyd: 229; Carey Brandon: 234; Colin Burgess: 195; Steve Catlin: 190 (bl),198 (b), 244, 256, 257, 258, 261, 265; Fin Costello: 149, 185; Pete Cronin: 171, 201 (b); Geoff Dann: 242, 267; Grant Davis: 203 (b); DeltaHaze Corporation: 177 (tr), 222; Richard Ecclestone: 268, 325 (b), 344 (all); Max Jones Files: 192; Tabatha Fireman: 144; Patrick Ford: 41; Gems: 182; Suzie Gibbons: 325 (t); Steve Gillet: 175 (t); Harry Goodwin: 238; William Gottlieb: 231; Beth Gwinn: 122; Cary Hammond: 164; Mick Hutson: 64, 187, 203 (tr); K&K ULF Kruger OHG: 259; Robert Knight: 48, 121 (t), 215 (b), 236; Andrew Lepley: 193 (b), 197; Michel Linssen: 202; Robin Little: 10; Jon Lusk: 170 (t), 172, 173; Hayley Madden: 221; Gered Mankowitz: 200; Steve Morley: 137 (b); Leon Morris: 174; Bernd Muller: 309 (t); Opera News: 212; Odile Noel: 35 (t); PALM/RSCH: 152; Dave Peabody: 163, 255; Andrew Putler: 240; David Redfern: 29, 81, 153 (t), 158, 178, 194, 211 (t), 217, 233, 260, 308, 326; Lorne Resnick: 141, 239; Ebet Roberts: 34, 114, 123, 157, 186, 237, 246, 269, 333; John Rodgers: 128; Kerstin Rodgers: 145 (m); S & G Press Agency: 232; Donna Santisi: 65; Max Scheler: 140 (b); Jim Sharpe: 133 (t); Nicky J. Sims: 213 (t), 328; Jim Steele: 8; Peter Still: 227; Susan Stockwell: 251; Jon Super: 32, 145 (b); Peter Symes: 225; Gai Terrell: 161, 224; Richard Upper: 80, 214; Bob Willoughby: 228; Graham Wiltshire: 219; **Roland Corporation**: 35 (b), 199 (tr), 334, 348, **Sennheiser**: 327 (b), **Shure Incorporated**: 327 (tl), **Silent Source**: 330 (t), **S.I.N.**: David Corio: 167 (br), Eye and Eye/Jack Barron: 147, **Sound Technology Plc**: 206 (l), 323, **Stewart-Macdonald**: 303 (bl), **Sylvia Pitcher Photo Library**: Tony Mottram: 181, **TC Electronics**: 127 (b), **Tech 21**: 316 (t), **Topham Picturepoint**: 120, 218; Lipnitzki/Roger-Viollet: 150, **ArenaPAL**: 130, 148; Clive Barda: 213 (b); Sisi Burn: 154 (b); James Wilson: 141 (b), **The Image Works**: 332; John Maier, Jr.: 168; Dion Ogust: 329 (b), **Ken Vose**: 24, **Westside Distribution / Mesa/Boogie**: 314, **William Worsley**: 190 (br), 316 (b). **All other images courtesy of Foundry Arts**.

Complete Guitar Handbook

INDEX

Page references in italics indicate illustrations

Complete Guitar Handbook

Complete Guitar Handbook

Complete Guitar Handbook

Complete Guitar Handbook

Complete Guitar Handbook